DEDICATION

This diary is dedicated to those who work for, and towards the brotherhood of man, and to the soldiers, on both sides of the conflict, who died or were injured fighting for what they believed in (or were forced to believe in). To the journalists who were injured or killed covering the conflict. It is also dedicated to my wife Phyllis, and my three young children, Heather, Iona and Brian, whose love kept me going throughout my coverage and the compilation of this book. Finally, but not lastly, 'EYEWITNESS' was written for the people of Iraq.

ACKNOWLEDGEMENTS

I would like to thank the following people for their support and good will. Phyllis Galbraith; Sean O'Sullivan; Tod Robberson; Jim Rupert; Tish Durkin; photographer Simon Norfolk; the staff of the Al Fanar Towers; Kenji; Dana; Erich Collar; The Study School; Roslyn Elementary School; Snora; Julie; Keith Rigby; the Irna News Agency; Pvt. Nino Sanchez; United States Marine Corps; the US Army; the 101st Airborne; the F.I.F. in Mosul; the British Armed Forces; the country of Jordan; the staff of Americares aid agency; photographer Kevin Frayer; the Baghdad staff of CTV; Vendome Travel Montreal; Michele Noonan; Chantal Boulé; photographer Raffi Kirdi; the staff of the Kuwait Sheraton Hotel; Dr. Peter McLaine; the Montgomery family; the Galbraith family; Lindsay Galbraith; Andy Crozier; Charles Montgomery; Dom Pompeo; A.H. Campbell Gallery; Richard Hibbert; Ashley Sheltus; Michael Price; Robert Cote; Dominic Soulier; Isabelle Desaulniers; John Campbell; Copie Resolutions, Montreal; Don McKenzie of the Canadian Press; Frank Manley, copyeditor; David Gosselin, copyeditor; Normand Paquin of La Maison Du Livre; Cplc. Benoit Ladouceur; Reverend Roderick Withnell; Anthony De Palma; The Wilson's in Hamilton.

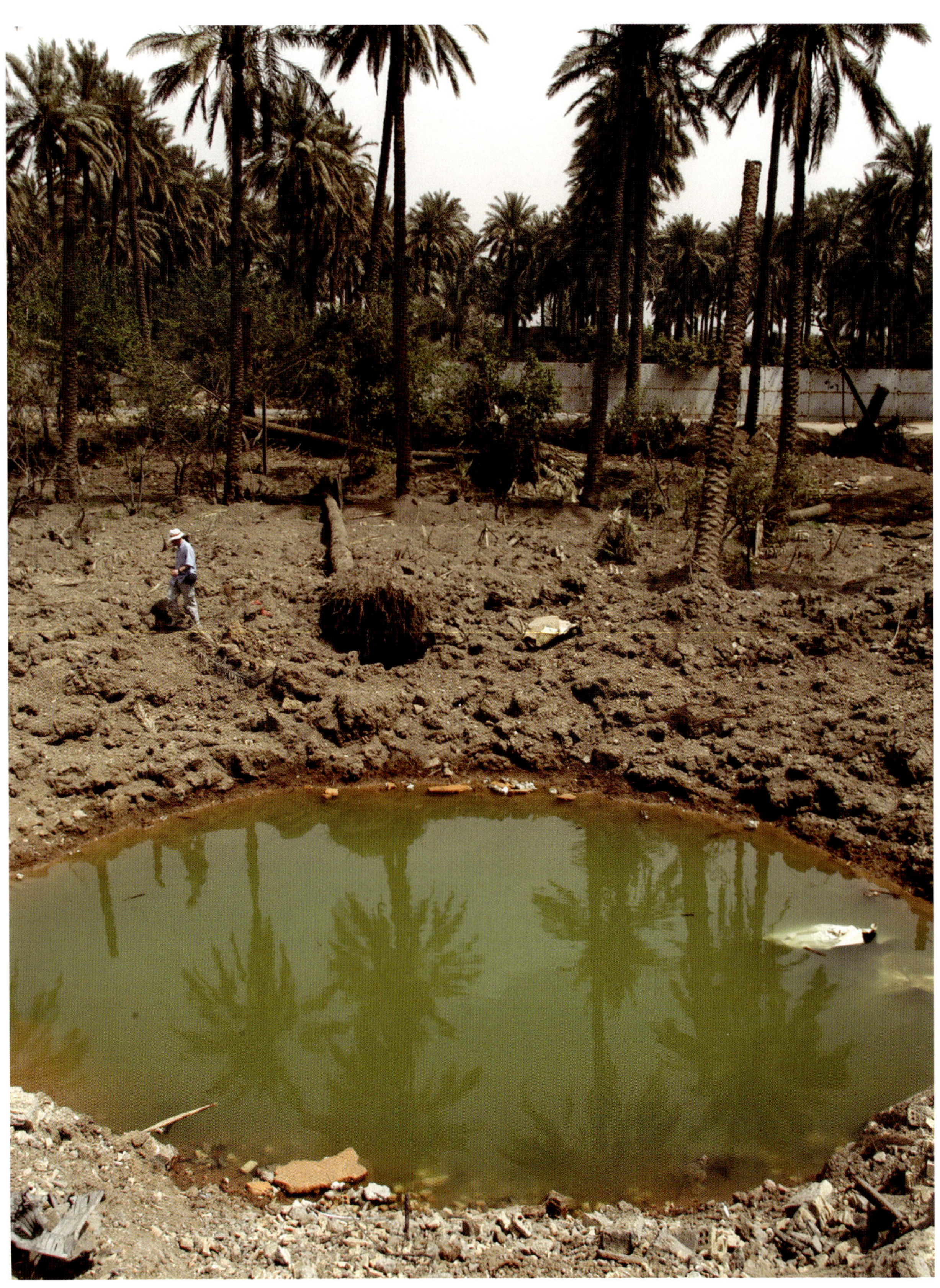

Bomb crater near the palm grove

INTRODUCTION

IRAQ - EYEWITNESS TO WAR: A PHOTOJOURNALIST'S DIARY is a day-by-day, personal eyewitness account of my 35-day sojourn in Iraq, Kuwait and Jordan, during Operation Iraqi Freedom. It begins with my arrival in Jordan on April 10th, 2003, and ends on May 14th, when I left Jordan for Montreal.

I went to Iraq to write a book about the war we don't often see – the war of survival on the streets and its effect on the population. During my daily coverage, I worked for the Dallas Morning News, The Houston Chronicle, The Associated Press, USA Today and Newsday, as a freelance photographer.

In 1991, I spent several weeks covering the Gulf War. At this time there were extensive restrictions placed on media coverage and much of the story was not really told. I believe that such stories should be told, and it was with this intention that I decided to go to Iraq in the spring of 2003.

Most of the coverage is centered in the capital city of Baghdad, where looting and anarchy ruled right up to the time I left. To get a pulse on how the whole nation was surviving the effects of war, I travelled from Kurdistan in the north, to Basra in the south. This gave me a better understanding of the Iraqi people, as the situation in Baghdad was unlike that in Kurdistan or the southern regions.

Many of the suppositions that are discussed in the diary have come true, with Baghdad evolving into a boiling pot of insurgency and daily horrors. To combat this, in November, 2003, American President George W. Bush introduced Operation Iron Hammer, a renewed assault on known insurgent hot spots and hideouts. As the hostilities spread throughout the country, so did Operation Iron Hammer. This culminated in Saddam Hussein's capture on December 13th, 2003, one of the prime objectives of the operation.

Regardless, the Americans were starting to lose the war of public opinion both at home and in Iraq, where they were being painted as an occupying force. More American soldiers were killed in post-war attacks, than during the war. President Bush, seeing the rise in anti-American feelings and attacks, set the deadline of the end of June, 2004 for handing over control of the country to an Iraqi coalition government. On May 29th, 2004, the Iraqi Governing Council named Iyad Allawi, a former opponent of Saddam Hussein, as Prime Minister to steer the country until proposed elections in January, 2005.

The root of my job as a journalist is to inform. I have tried to bring the reader a unique, unbiased perspective of the war, rather than the generic Shock and Awe campaign we all witnessed on television or read in the newspapers. I can only hope that this diary serves its purpose of giving the reader a fuller understanding of the situation in Iraq, by bringing you onto the streets of Baghdad, to see and smell the daily tragedies unfold.

*This diary is just that – a personal day-by-day account of my time in Iraq. **"Eyewitness"** is a record of my own observations and must be interpreted as such – it is a personal journey. It is my wish that Eyewitness To War be a balanced, non-partisan portrayal of the war from street level.*

Robert J. Galbraith
Montreal, August 30, 2004.

Day 1. Thursday, April 10th

(I arrive in Amman, Jordan from Paris; Ali the cabbie; getting settled; joy riders burn rubber; the Intercontinental Hotel; media circus; Jordanian press pass; organizing my gear; jetlag and anticipation; war just up the road)

I arrive in Amman, Jordan on a flight from Paris, France, at 7:30 p.m., Thursday, April 10th. My journey had begun about 12 hours earlier in Montreal, when I boarded a plane for Paris.

My wife Phyllis had already set me up at the downtown Lotus Hotel, over the Internet from Montreal. I take a taxi from the Amman International Airport. Ali, my taxi driver, tells me he can take me to a cheaper, cleaner hotel – the Rozana. I accept his suggestion.

Ali is a kind man, a former Amman police officer of 25 years, with the bite of a natural businessman. During our chit-chat on the way to Amman, about an hour's drive from the airport, he tells me he can set me up with his relative who can take me from Amman to Baghdad for $100 (all monies in U.S. currencies). I refuse his offer but thank him for the suggestion. I take Ali's phone number in case I need his relative's service.

He drops me off at the Rozana where I check in and set myself up. The hotel is rather nice, clean and cheap ($45), with a white marble entranceway and fresh-cut flowers. The staff is very friendly, but they think I am out of my mind for wanting to go to Iraq.

After unpacking my gear and spreading it out on the floor of my room (so as to better organize it for the upcoming journey), I go for a short walk to stretch my legs. I end up on a street corner ringed by shops and young people hanging out along the sidewalks. I stand drinking a Pepsi, watching teenage drivers joy-riding around a traffic island. The cars burn a thick, white cloud of rubber spinning around the circle. The smoke hangs like a fog over the crowd, as they whoop and holler at the thrill-seekers' antics. Car after car entertains the action-crazy onlookers. They are mostly in their late teens, hanging out and eating snacks from the neighboring restaurants. The police eventually appear and the crowd breaks up. No tickets are handed out, as it all broke up too fast to catch the culprits. This could have been a street corner anywhere in small-town USA on a Saturday night.

With the joyriding over, I take a taxi to the Intercontinental Hotel where the Jordanian Media Centre is located. It is a first-class hotel with a lavish exterior and interior, costing around $120 a night. The lobby is large and open, with a long reception and guest services desk along the inside entranceway. Another section is lined with boutiques and restaurants. I have to apply at the media centre for a press ID/exit visa, which will allow me to leave Jordan and cross into Iraq. On filling out an application, I am told it will be ready by noon tomorrow (Friday).

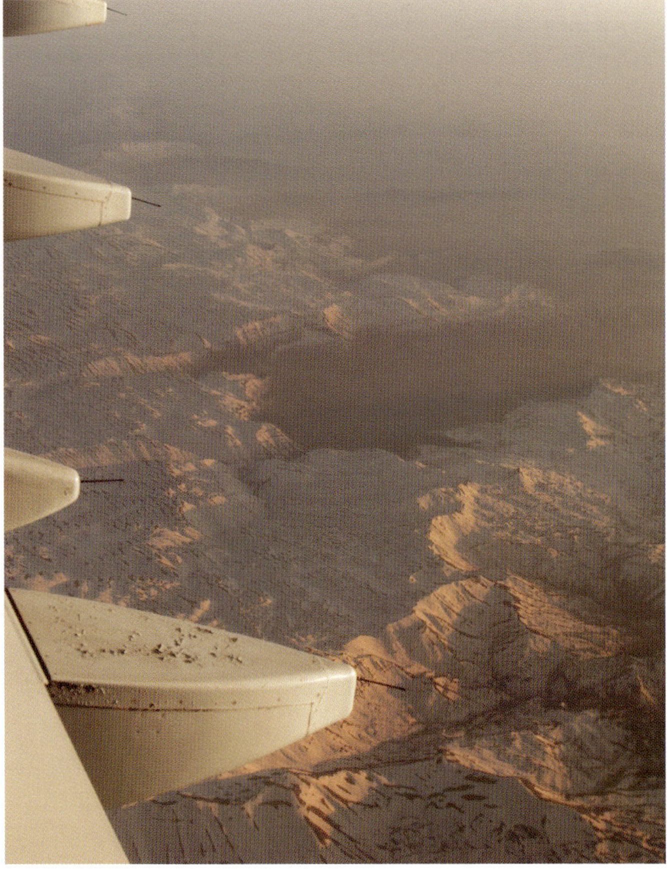

Flying over the Lebanese Mountains

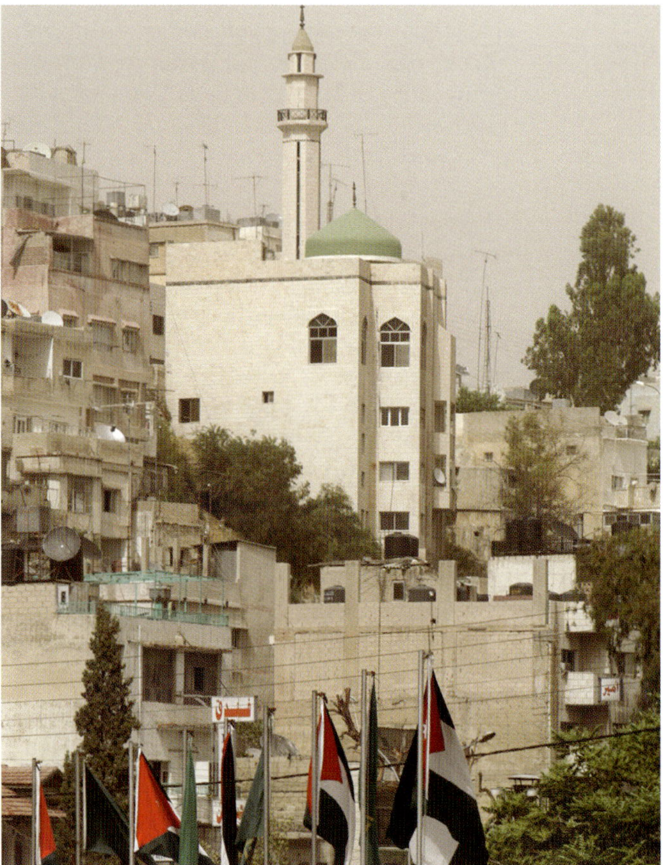

Modern Amman, Jordan

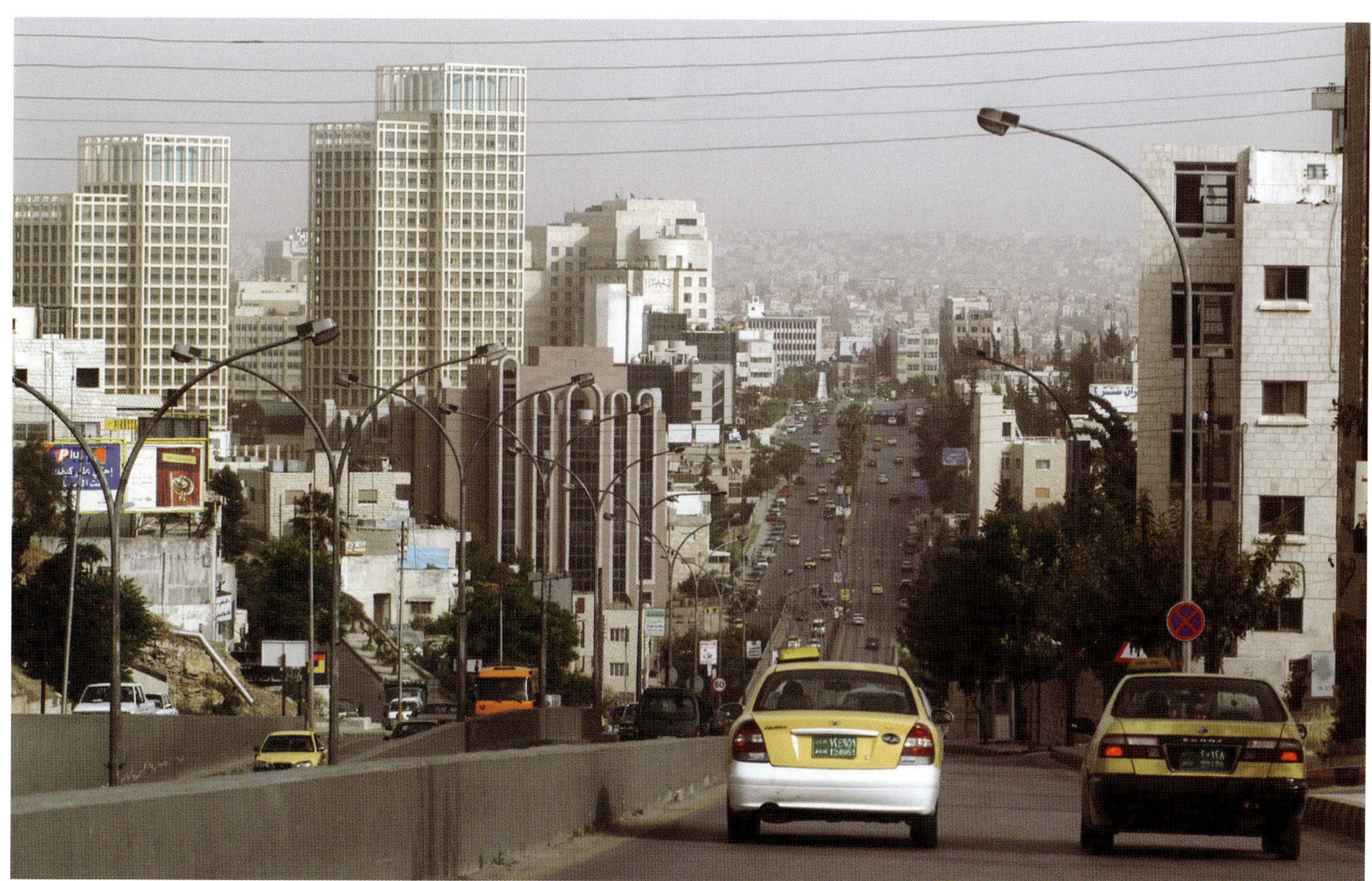

Downtown Amman, in beautiful Jordan

There are lots of media milling about, journalists from all parts of the world. They are all trying to get the latest information on press convoys going to Baghdad; they all want a way into Baghdad. A piano player in the café of the main lobby plays to an oblivious crowd of bustling journalists, lost in the talk of war and preparation. I sit watching the media circus, quiescent in one of the hotel's plush couches, drinking coffee and eating pistachio cookies. The sight of all the activity flicks a switch in my head and I start seriously thinking about my strategy to get to Baghdad.

I send a couple of e-mails home from the hotel press center then take a taxi back to the Rozana. Around midnight, I settle down to watch some TV, while organizing my gear into the basic essentials for war coverage. My strategy, once I cross into Iraq, is to be able to carry everything I own on my back, including camera gear, computer, clothing and some basic foods. I try to fall asleep, but am having difficulty due to jet lag and anticipation.

Day 2. Friday, April 11th

(Intercontinental Hotel; don't shoot journalists; taken out by friendly fire; journalist meeting at the Hyatt Hotel; organizing travel teams; meeting my travel companions; plans to leave for Baghdad that evening; journalists shot along the Amman-Baghdad highway; cars in good running order; Tish to take a chance crossing into Iraq without a visa; buying groceries; re-packing my bags; preparing to leave for Baghdad at 12:30 a.m.; champing at the bit)

Waking up after about three hours of sleep, I take a taxi to the Intercontinental Hotel. Outside in the parking lot, I photograph a color poster taped to the back window of a GMC Jimmy used to ferry journalists from Amman to Baghdad. It is a picture of a slain Al-Jazeera cameraman, Tareq Ayyoub, who was recently killed in Baghdad. The words "Don't Shoot Journalists" are emblazoned on it.

The vehicle also has three-foot-tall black lettering spelling "TV", taped onto the hood and each side of the vehicle. The lettering is large enough to be read from a great distance and is meant to protect the vehicle from being fired upon by friendly forces. But it also identifies the vehicle to hostiles, who may want to take revenge on a press vehicle. But there is a greater possibility of it being taken out by friendly fire.

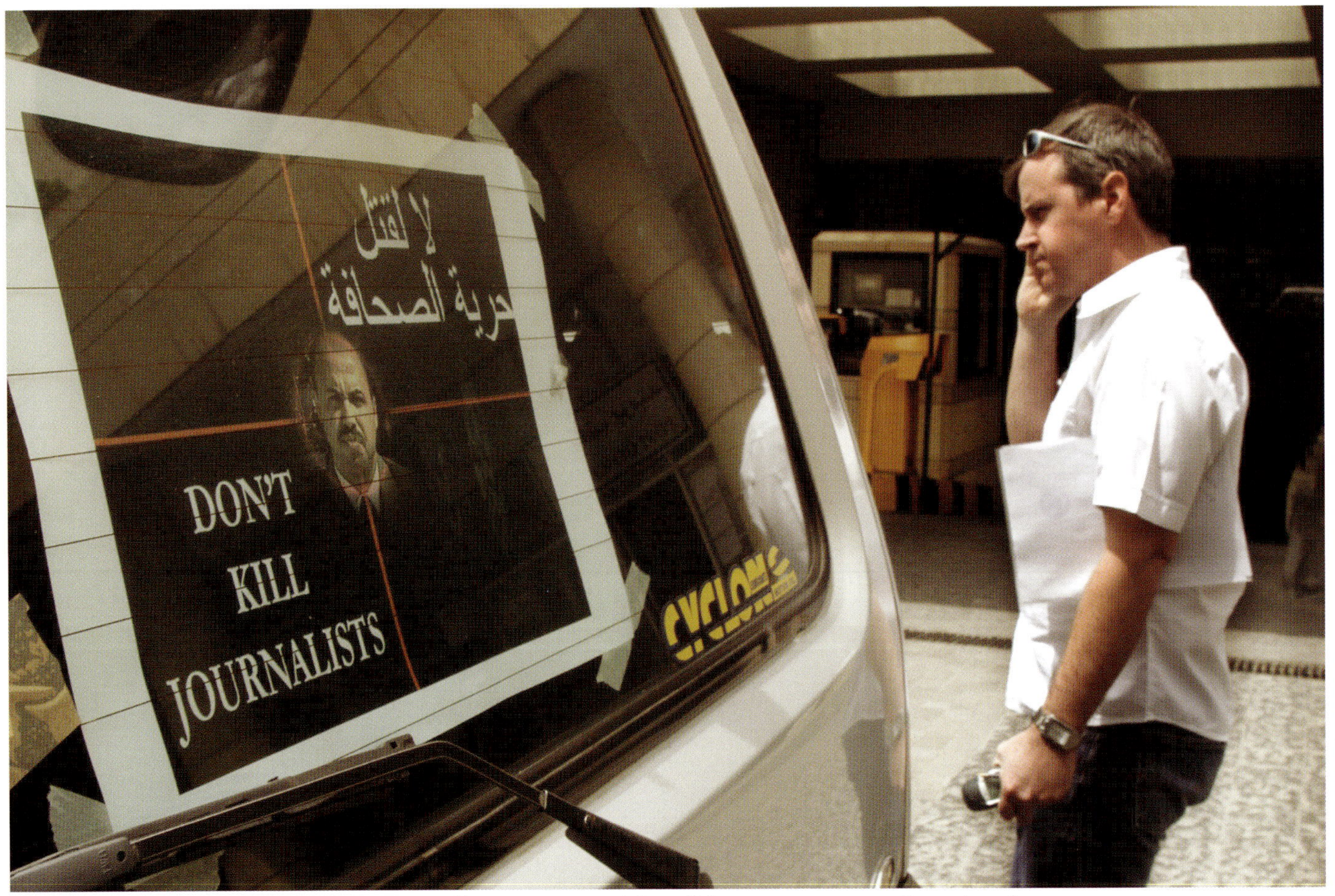

A journalist walks past a poster of slain Al Jazeera cameraman, Tareq Ayyoub

Inside the hotel, I hang out near the reception area, trying to find a ride or leads to a ride to Baghdad. There is lots of scuttlebutt, but not a lot of solid leads. Some journalists are willing to pay up to a thousand dollars to get to Baghdad. I am hoping to pay around $250.

At around 6:00 p.m., while I am having a coffee in the café piano lounge, two journalists approach and tell me about a meeting that has been called for that evening at the Hyatt Hotel. It is open to all interested journalists, to organize convoys of interested parties to Iraq and to discuss safety issues. Other issues, ranging from necessary preparations and equipment, would also be discussed.

About 15 journalists show up at the gathering, and we talk for about an hour. We decide to split up into two parties. One group will leave early tomorrow morning, the second the following day (Sunday). I choose to be a member of the first group. There was no time to lose – delays could result in lost money and opportunities. I have to get on the road a.s.a.p.

The group I am in includes American journalists Tod Robberson of the Dallas Morning News, James Rupert of Newsday, Tish Durkin of the New York Observer and Sean O'Sullivan, an independent filmmaker producing a film on humanitarian efforts during the war.

I feel I am in with a group of solid journalists. James Rupert speaks Arabic (which will come in very handy, to say the least), and is a solid reporter. Sean O'Sullivan has already been living in Baghdad for some time now, so he knows the layout of the city. Tod Robberson has covered the recent situation in Afghanistan and was until just recently, the South and Central American correspondent for his newspaper. I am the only one who covered Desert Storm in 1991, but my most valuable strength is my adaptability, and my street smarts. Tish gives the group balance, with the discipline of a feature writer and the unselfish ambition for honest journalism.

Our team is to leave Amman for Baghdad Saturday morning at 12:30 a.m. It will be a four-hour drive to the Jordan-Iraq border, where our two taxis will wait to form a convoy with other vehicles. At sunrise we will cross into Iraq. There are confirmed reports of journalists being shot, wounded and robbed along the Amman-Baghdad highway. Anyone who does not take adequate security measures can end up dead. It's that simple!

We had agreed that our cars, driven by Iraqi taxi drivers, should have a spare tire, extra gas, and be in good running order. The vehicles are in good shape with friendly drivers, one of whom speaks English. Most importantly it is agreed that neither vehicle lose sight of the other during the drive across the desert and, if one car has to stop, then both cars stop.

Tish doesn't have her exit visa. It was to be processed that day (Saturday) at noon, which is when we plan to be on the highway and half way to Baghdad. She realizes she may not be allowed across the border without it, but is willing to take the chance. We tell her it is her decision, and we would be willing to help smooth the way if we can. I like this young lady's attitude, she is very smart and shows no fear.

With the plans for the voyage finalized, I take a taxi back to the Rozana to get packed. I make a short stop at a grocery store, stocking up on canned goods and other supplies. I am careful of the weight of the items and their nutritional value. Nuts, canned tuna, chocolate bars, dried fruit, water and powdered juice go into my shopping bag. Back at the Rozana, I trim my travel pack to the bone, taking only what I absolutely need for the journey.

I leave a backpack of extra gear with the front desk clerk, telling him I will pick it up on my return from Baghdad. With my gear packed and slung on my back, I head to the Hyatt Hotel for the rendezvous with my travel companions.

We meet in the lobby, then I order a club sandwich from the hotel café, while we go over the final details of the trip. After our snack, we start loading the vehicles under the muted lights of the hotel's canopy. The team is upbeat and champing at the bit to get under way as it closes in on midnight.

Day 3. Saturday, April 12th

(Leaving Amman, Jordan for Baghdad, Iraq; "she's having my baby"; Tish allowed through army checkpoint; unusual talents; our last good meal; passports stamped; I agitate American Special Forces; flexing his muscle; bus bombed; conflicting accounts; Happy Travel bus company; Australian soldiers; desert oasis; gunfire from the roadside near Al Fallujah; destroyed war machinery; open sewers; anarchy and destruction; looting frenzy; Americans block overpass; a burning city; looters carrying weapons; last line of defense; the smell of war; Iraq in an overwhelming situation; Smart Bombs used in Baghdad; checking in at the Al Fanar Towers; shootout at the Al Fanar Towers; should I lose my head; ducking from tree to tree; no power or hot water; the generator; canned supper; gunfire in the darkness; the bogeyman)

At 12:30 a.m., with all the gear secured and accounted for, we climb into our vehicles. The two cars start driving through the night-lit streets of Amman towards Baghdad, 600 miles east. We pass through the destitute northeast side of the city, where the buildings are in disrepair and lined by dirty side streets. This is very different from the squeaky-clean central region.

Heading out of the suburbs and into the inky-black desert, we drive past an oil refinery pumping out noxious-smelling gasses. This is a familiar smell to me, being raised in the steel-producing town of Hamilton, Ontario. Small clusters of homes and outposts pass by the window like fleeting ghosts as we head deeper into the desert's cool darkness, towards the Iraqi border.

About an hour east of Amman, we are directed to stop at a small checkpoint manned by the Jordanian Army. The checkpoint consists of a couple of large green army tents strung-up along the desert highway. As expected, the guards

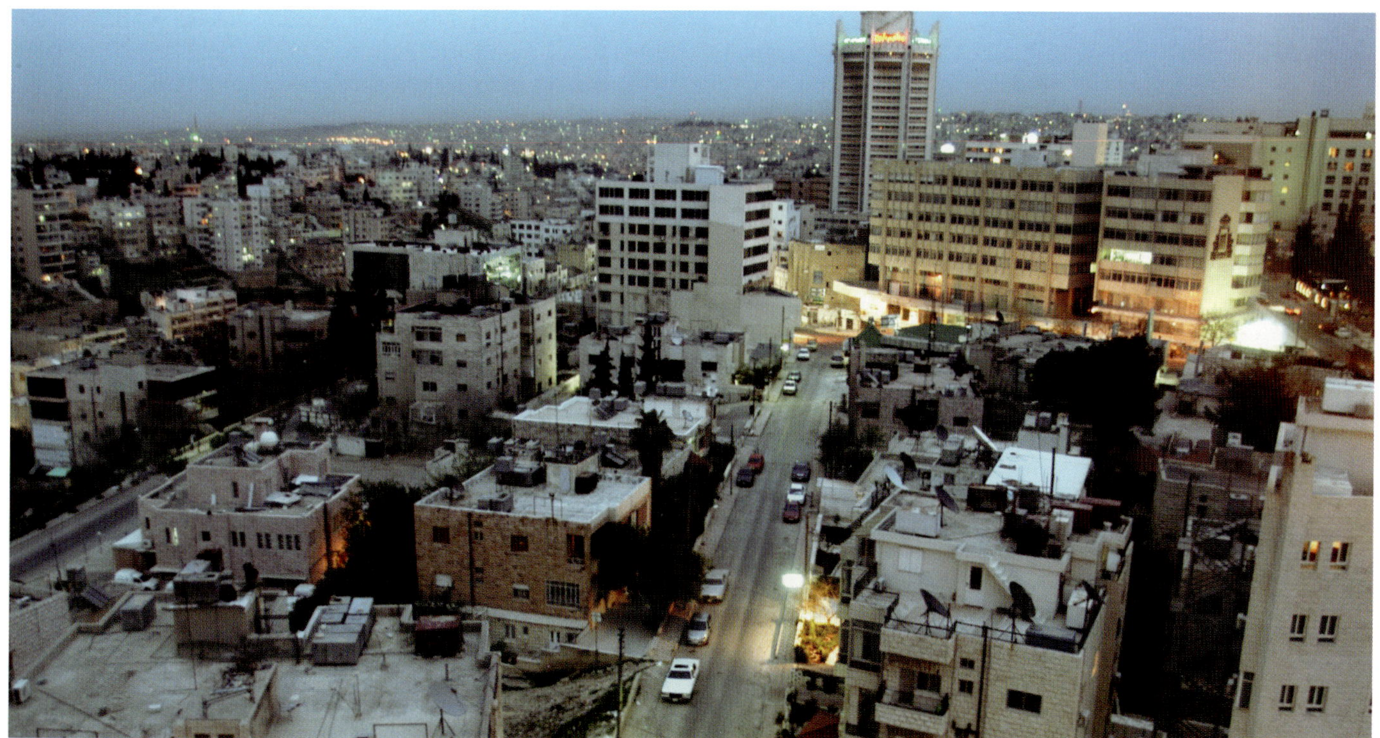

Amman at night

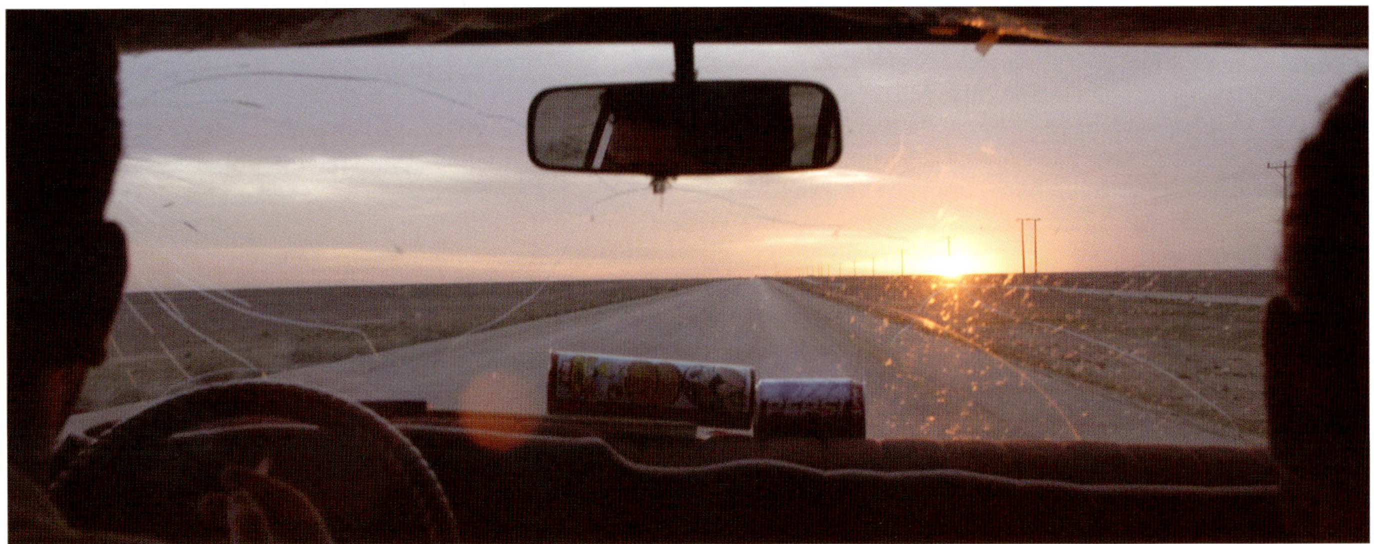

The sun rises as we approach the Iraqi border

give Tish a hard time because she does not have her exit visa. Ten minutes into the discussion I tell the guards that she is part of our team, and for her own security we can't leave her behind. "She would be a lone woman, by herself, in a foreign country! We are her only friends!" I tell them. I try to distract the guards from the issue at hand by breaking into discussions about hockey and fishing, letting them know that we are not a security risk by putting a warm face on us.

When things take a turn for the worse, I start to gently hug Tish, as though I am her boyfriend. In a somber voice, I tell the guards that she is carrying my baby and that if she has to turn back, we all will. This performance is all a big show – improv theatre! But it works, and after a brief discussion between the guards, they tell us to board our vehicles and hurry on to the border.

Tish is very lucky not to get turned back and she thanks us for our camaraderie. As we drive away we laugh and joke about our first misadventure and success at the checkpoint. Tish thinks the baby line was a classic.

A short way down the road we stop for gas and a snack in the small village of Ruwaysha, an hour from the Iraqi border. The diner is very brightly lit, with large chunks of meat hanging from hooks in the butcher section. Old men sit drinking tea (called *chai* in Iraq) and eating kabobs and rice, with fresh-baked flatbread. We pay our bill and continue on. Just before sun-up, 5 a.m., we reach the Jordan-Iraq border.

The border crossing is hopping with activity as the numerous press vehicles and cargo trucks wait to enter Iraq, their occupants getting their paperwork organized. Waiting in line at the border immigration office we all get our passports stamped without any problems, after paying the $20 fee. It takes about two hours to be processed, but the bustle of the transients is entertaining. We sip hot tea and eat melted cheese and pita sandwiches while waiting for each other's turn in line. This would be one of the last of the good meals, or snacks, that I would eat in a long while.

Just before crossing the border, the other members of the group put on their bulletproof jackets and helmets. I don't have any of this gear, and for a brief moment I feel vulnerable. But this is no time for second thoughts about security; I will be all right.

As we pass into Iraq I take a photo from the car window of a U.S. Army Humvee positioned on the border, which turns out to be a vehicle of the American Special Forces. A soldier standing beside the Humvee shouts over at our taxi,

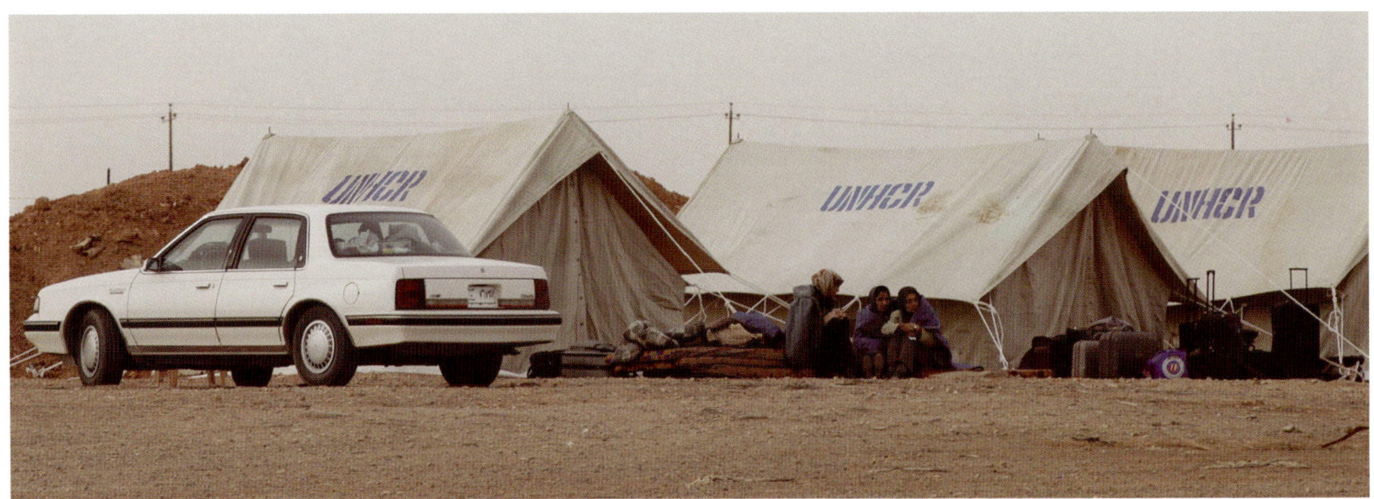

Refugees on the Jordanian-Iraqi border

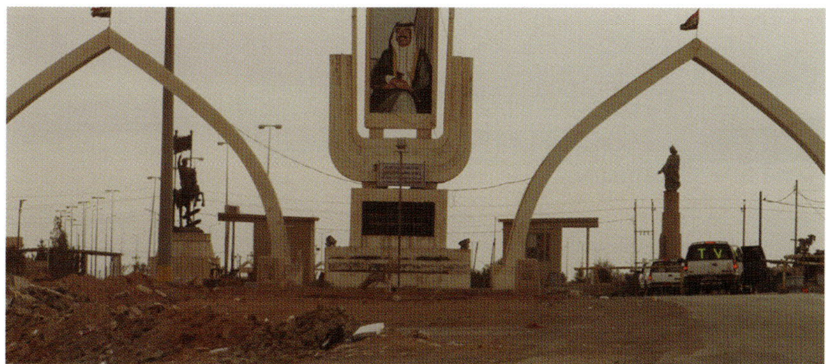

A smiling Saddam at the Iraqi border crossing

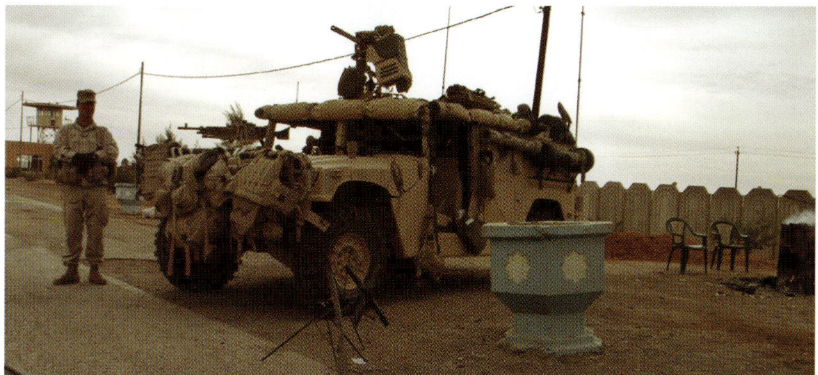

American Special Forces at Iraqi border

warning us not to take any pics of his team. I ask permission to take a pic only of his equipment-burdened Humvee. He agrees, as long as he is not in the photo. Just across the Iraqi side of the border, I take another pic of a different Humvee parked along the road. Suddenly a soldier appears from the side of the Humvee and jumps in front of the car, banging his fist on top of the hood. Holding his rifle he points his finger in my face, telling me that I had been ordered not to take pictures. He is quite agitated, so I apologize and promise it will not happen again.

I think he is being over-dramatic, and feel like asking him if he needs a laxative. He had obviously just talked on the radio with the first soldier that I photographed, and now he is really teed-off. I fear he is going to drag me out of the car and smash my camera, but I guess he had gotten his point across, and tells us to move on quickly. Tod tells me that the guy was just trying to flex his muscle in front of the journalists, whom we believed he probably hated with a passion. Tod asks me how I would feel if I were a soldier stuck at some boring hole-in-the-wall border crossing while a war was being waged just up the road. The border area is not heavily guarded, just a couple of Humvees and some Jordanian border cops. There is not much here.

We drive into Iraq and gas the vehicles up beside a road sign that reads "510 kilometers to Baghdad." We are in a convoy of 30 cars, which we hooked up with at the border for safety. The road from here to Baghdad is a blistering strip of asphalt, cutting through the sea of desert sand.

It is a nice, sunny, hot day to drive, with high cirrus clouds above. Marsh hawks fly over the sands and sparse clumps of vegetation, tilting from side to side (as is their habit), looking for small mammals or bugs to catch. There are rugged plant species, many with thorns or heavily perfumed, growing sporadically in the sand.

Buff-colored sandstone outcroppings and bluffs, formed by wind and erosion, rise above the desert flatness. In isolated areas of desert I see large herds of 200 or more goats and sheep being herded by shepherds. We fly down the highway at 90 miles an hour, nodding off to sleep for 15 minutes here and there, but not wanting to miss any-thing of the journey. I have only slept about five hours in the last three days and feel a little burned-out and almost nauseous. Before long, the convoy breaks up and moves off at its own pace. Now it is just our two cars driving alone across the ocean of burning sand.

Near the town of ar-Rutbah (300 miles west of Baghdad and 100 miles southeast of the Syrian border), we stop alongside a highway bridge to photograph a bus that had been bombed by the coalition forces. The bomb, or bombs, had ripped a huge 20-foot gaping hole in the middle of the highway bridge, through which you can see the dry riverbed some 30 feet below. The structure's cement and steel supports are twisted and broken, leaving just one makeshift lane to squeeze over the bridge. The bus is largely intact, except for all the blown-out windows and the charred insides. It had not been hit directly, but was blasted by the nearby explosions. Large rocks (used like makeshift jacks) have been jammed under the vehicle's axles by looters. When the air is let out of the tires, the vehicle frame is suspended on the rocks, allowing the thieves to remove the tires and rims.

One of our drivers tells us the Americans targeted the bus (during the bombing campaign in Baghdad) because it had originated in Syria and was apparently carrying supporters of Saddam's regime. He says the

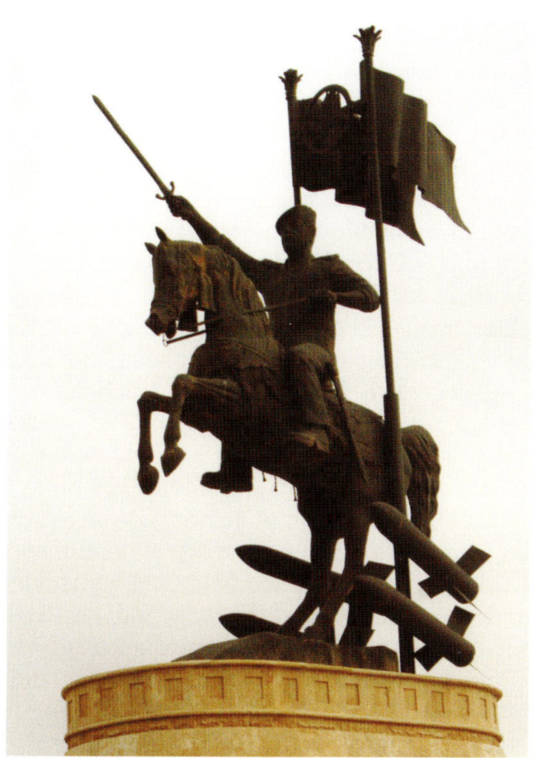

Saddam rides a stallion flanked by missiles

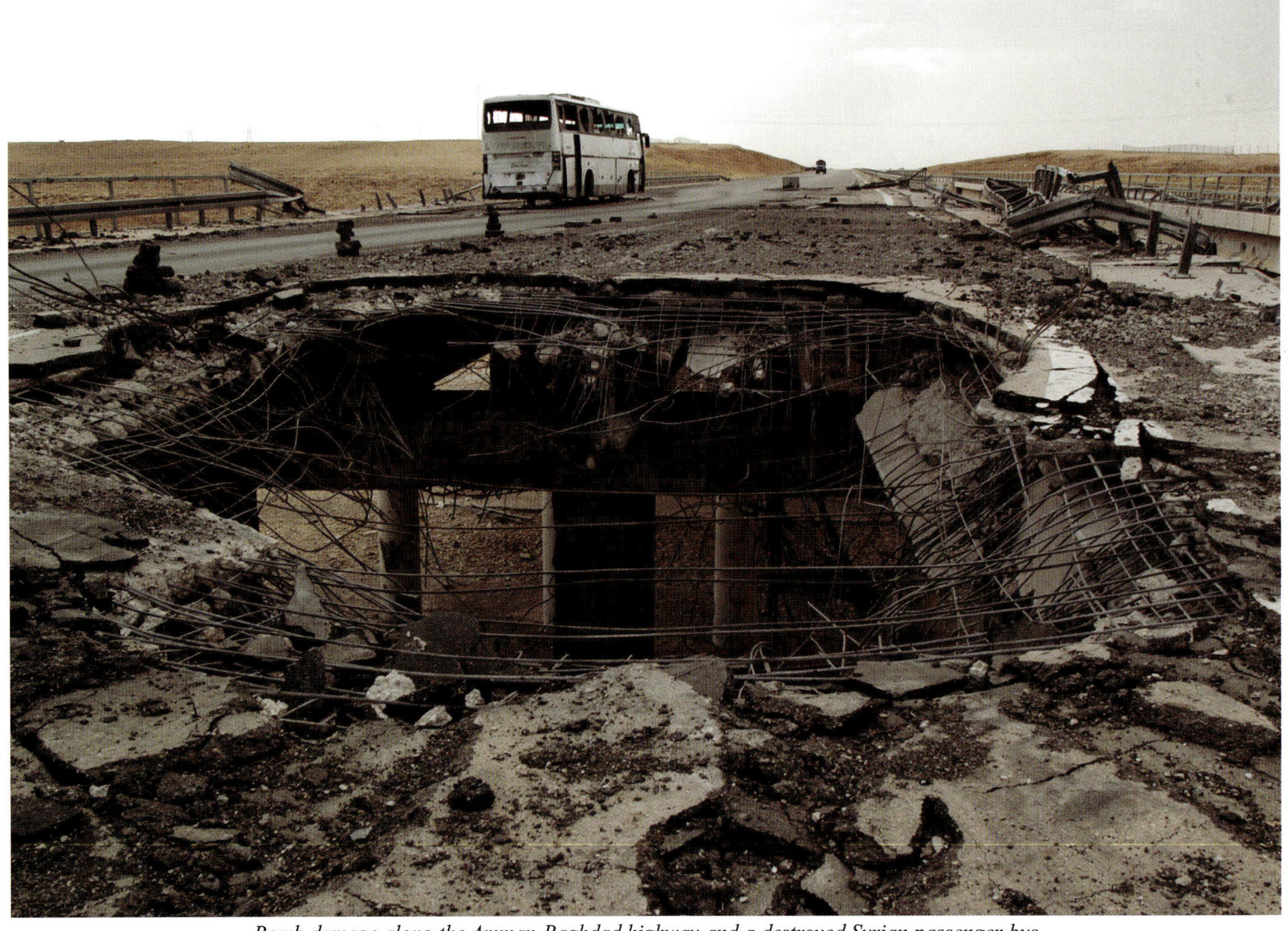

Bomb damage along the Amman-Baghdad highway and a destroyed Syrian passenger bus

passengers may have been intending to unbalance the country by looting and instigating disorder, after joining up with the Republican Guard in Baghdad.

According to another account of the bombing, it was carrying 37 cross-border workers returning to Syria. They had stopped on the overpass for a break when the bombs hit them. The Syrian Government claimed five workers had died in the blast. I wonder if they even knew what hit them – I doubt it. The name of the bus company was Happy Travel.

We continue driving, hour after hour, over the black asphalt strip of stone and tar. Less than two hours from the outskirts of Baghdad, we are waved through a small checkpoint manned by Australian coalition soldiers. They are unlike any other soldiers I have seen; tall, full-bearded and well tanned. They remind me of the Beach Boys, only bigger and leaner. Beside the checkpoint rests their amphibious, six-wheel all-terrain vehicles, loaded on the top and sides with various ammunition boxes and personal gear. Their vehicles look similar to those smaller models used by hunting and fishing outfitters in Canada. We wave at the Australians, and they return the courtesy.

There are dust devils, 15 to 30 feet high, swirling around the open desert. It is a spooky surreal sort of sight, and I think about being lost out there in the sea of scorching sand. It was almost a year ago that I was above the Arctic Circle, dressed in seal, caribou and dog skins, photographing a story for one of my clients. At that time, the temperature in the Arctic was – 45 degrees F. Now, here I am in another situation, with the temperature hovering around 100 degrees F. This is what I love about being a journalist, I am able to visit and see and feel the extremes of weather, and cultures. Death is never far from the journalist covering war, but the thrill of discovery and a hunger for the story outpaces it, usually.

It is near the city of Al Fallujah (30 miles west of Baghdad) that the landscape starts changing into a pastoral oasis, with palms and legumes growing in the increasingly marshy and cultivated land. It is obvious to me that we are near, or on, a major floodplain, possibly of the Euphrates River. There are groups of mud-brick homes along the roads and fields. Children run up from the fields and wave at us as we pass. Birds (many species of dove, herons and insectivores), flutter and scavenge amongst the reeds and marsh plants that line the ditches and gullies separating the fields. It is amazing to see the desert transform from sand to greenery. But these green zones are not continuous – they are broken up by expanses of sand and dryness, where the road veers away from the river or where irrigation is too labor intensive.

We start to hear sporadic gunfire coming from the surrounding area, and hope that it is civilians firing their AK-47s and handguns in victory celebrations over the downfall of Saddam. The team keeps a low profile in the cars, and starts putting on their flak jackets and Kevlar helmets, which they had taken off earlier because of the heat. I sink low in the car seat, sandwiched between Tod and our travel packs, with my shoulders tucked down to my knees. I don't want to take a stray bullet, especially without any bulletproof gear on. We keep hunkered down until we pass the main brunt of the gunfire, but we can hear rifles and pistols going off from a number of directions as we continue our drive. We just hope that no one takes a pot-shot at us.

Highway overpasses are shattered by aerial or tank bombardment. Armaments and wreckage from destroyed APCs (armored personal carriers), trucks, tanks, and cars are becoming increasingly visible along the highway the closer we get to Baghdad. Cinder-block bunkers built on the overpasses by Saddam's forces are broken and abandoned. A destroyed Iraqi tank sits under a grove of palm trees. Young boys play soldier in the charred remains of an APC lying at the side of the road. Approximately one-third of the military vehicles look untouched by the destruction of war, perhaps abandoned by the retreating Iraqi soldiers. To the northeast I see a huge plume of black smoke, staining the sky for miles. I suspect it is from burning oil, but it reminds me more of a massive tire fire.

On the bluffs lining the edge of the highway, I see a masked man dressed in bright red running shoes, a white cotton jacket and jet-black pants. He has an AK-47 assault rifle slung across his shoulders. He may be a well-dressed terrorist, or part of a local militia guarding his community from assault. Had we been a threat, he could have emptied his clip into our cars, then disappeared into the expanse of sand dunes. We are all very vulnerable to stray bullets or outright ambush, and, as a result, our senses are peaked to the max.

We can barely make out the skyline of Baghdad, through a black and hazy shroud of smoke which covers the entire city and its suburbs. Plumes of thick black smoke billow from burning warehouses, factories and private buildings. Iraqi tanks and support vehicles lie pulverized at the side of the highway, their blackened remains grossly twisted and contorted from the explosive power of the bombs that hit them. Entering the western Baghdad suburbs, the flow of traffic increases and becomes a solid chain of vehicles driving in and out of Baghdad.

An American tank is blocking a partially destroyed overpass we are supposed to travel over, while a burning truck lies on its side at the bottom of the overpass. The Americans may have just taken this vehicle out. Because of this blockade, we have to make a detour through a small neighborhood where open sewers flow down the alleyways. I climb onto the roof of the taxi to photograph the train of people, some with bundles on their heads, walking across the dusty, littered expanses of burning outer Baghdad. I wonder if some of the articles these people are carrying are from looted buildings.

The western suburbs of Baghdad look like something out of *Dante's Inferno*, a city set ablaze in a looting frenzy. The highway quickly becomes two lanes of trucks full of pilfered goods, and a small number of families trying to escape the city in their heavily laden pickups and cars. At the sides of the road lie the cast-off stripped and broken vehicles, some of which had carried so much booty that they broke down from overloading. A forklift is being dragged along on

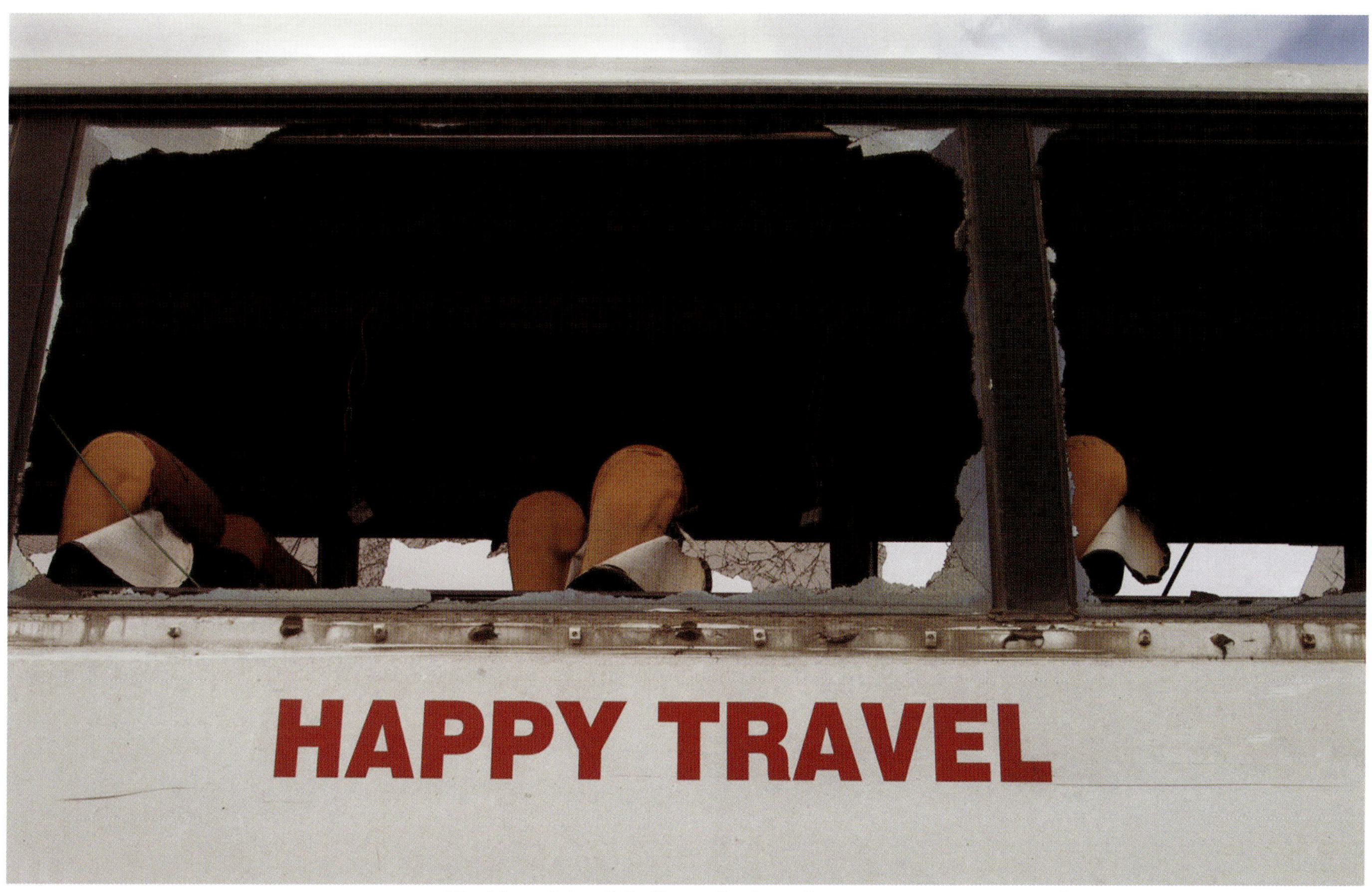

The blast claimed the lives of at least five occupants

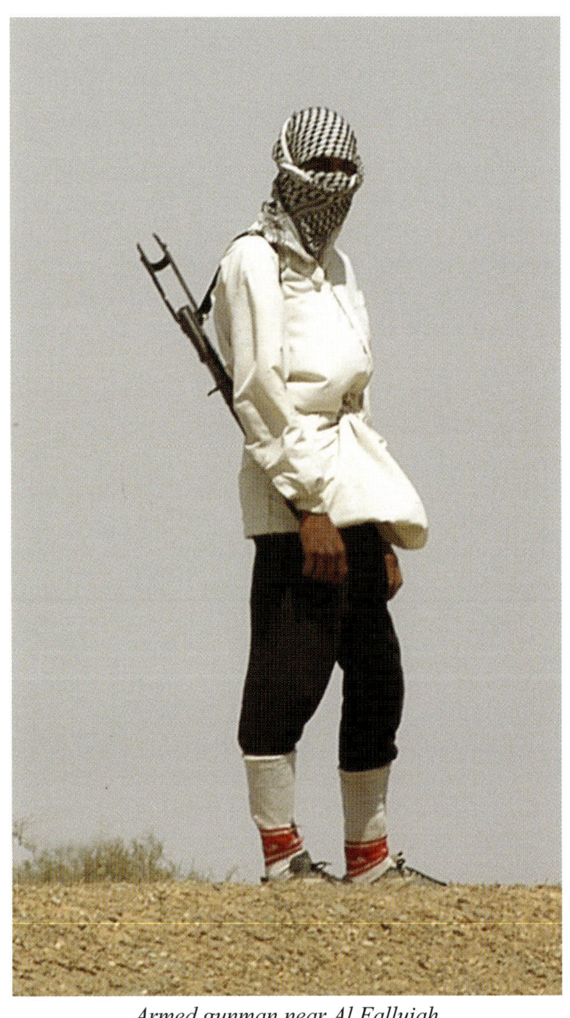

Armed gunman near Al Fallujah

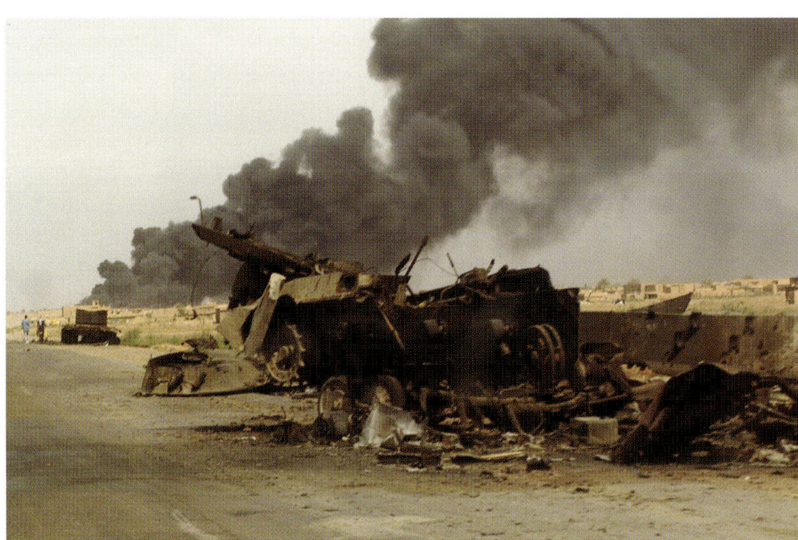

Iraqi military wreckage

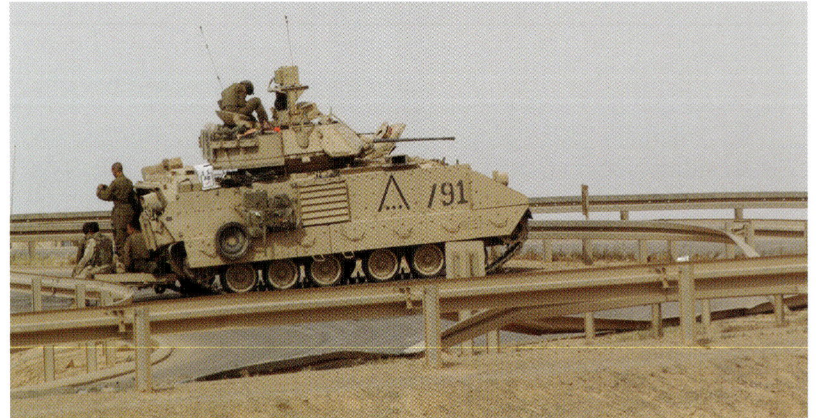

American soldiers guard overpass

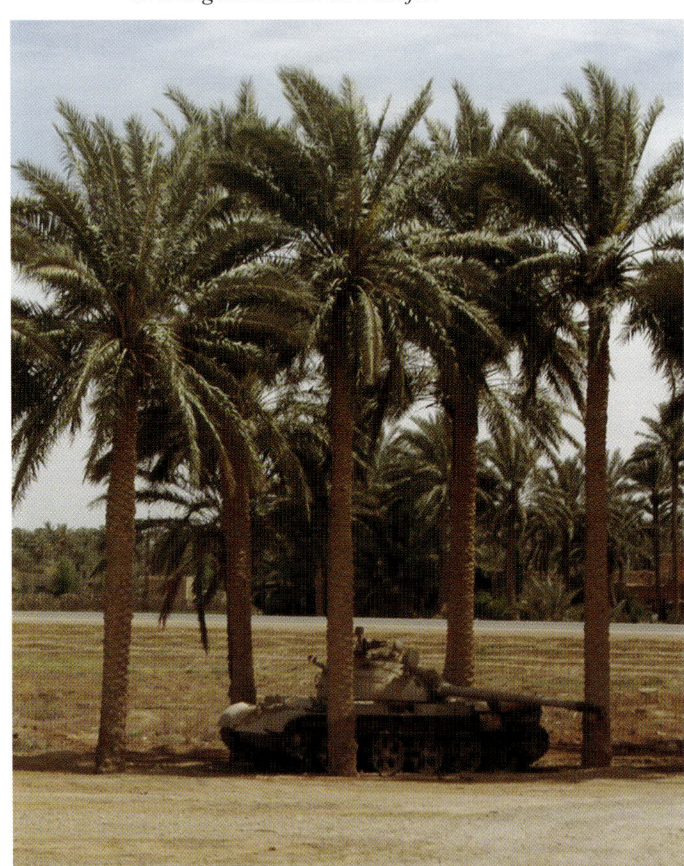

Destroyed Iraqi tank concealed in a palm grove

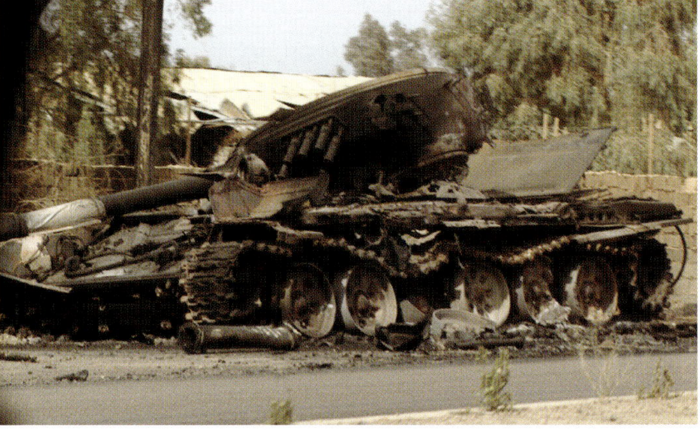

Burned and exploded Iraqi tank

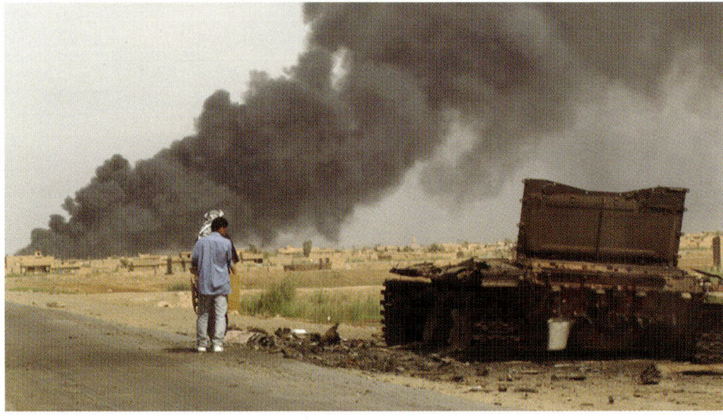

Onlookers survey carnage

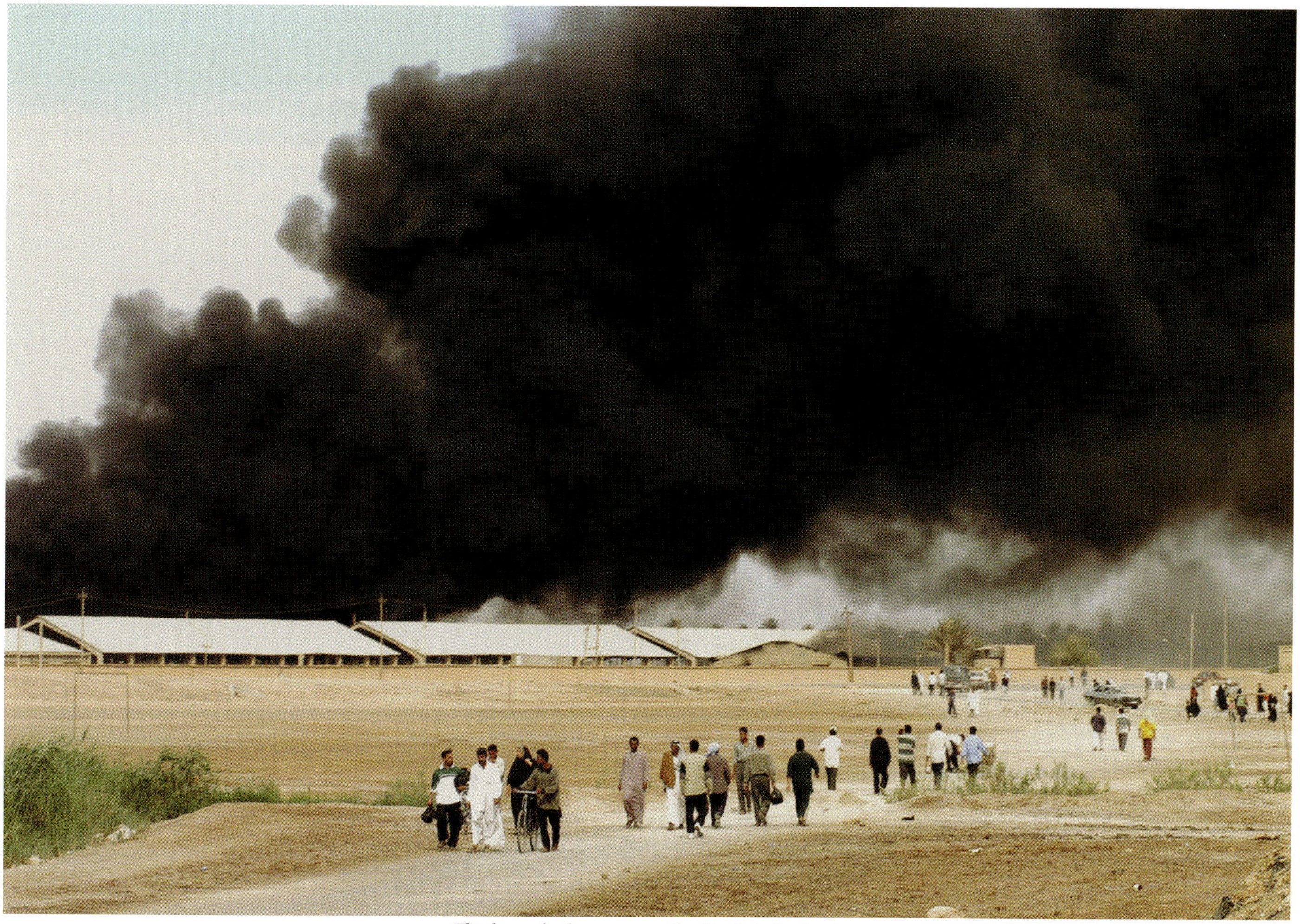

Thick smoke looms over the Baghdad suburbs

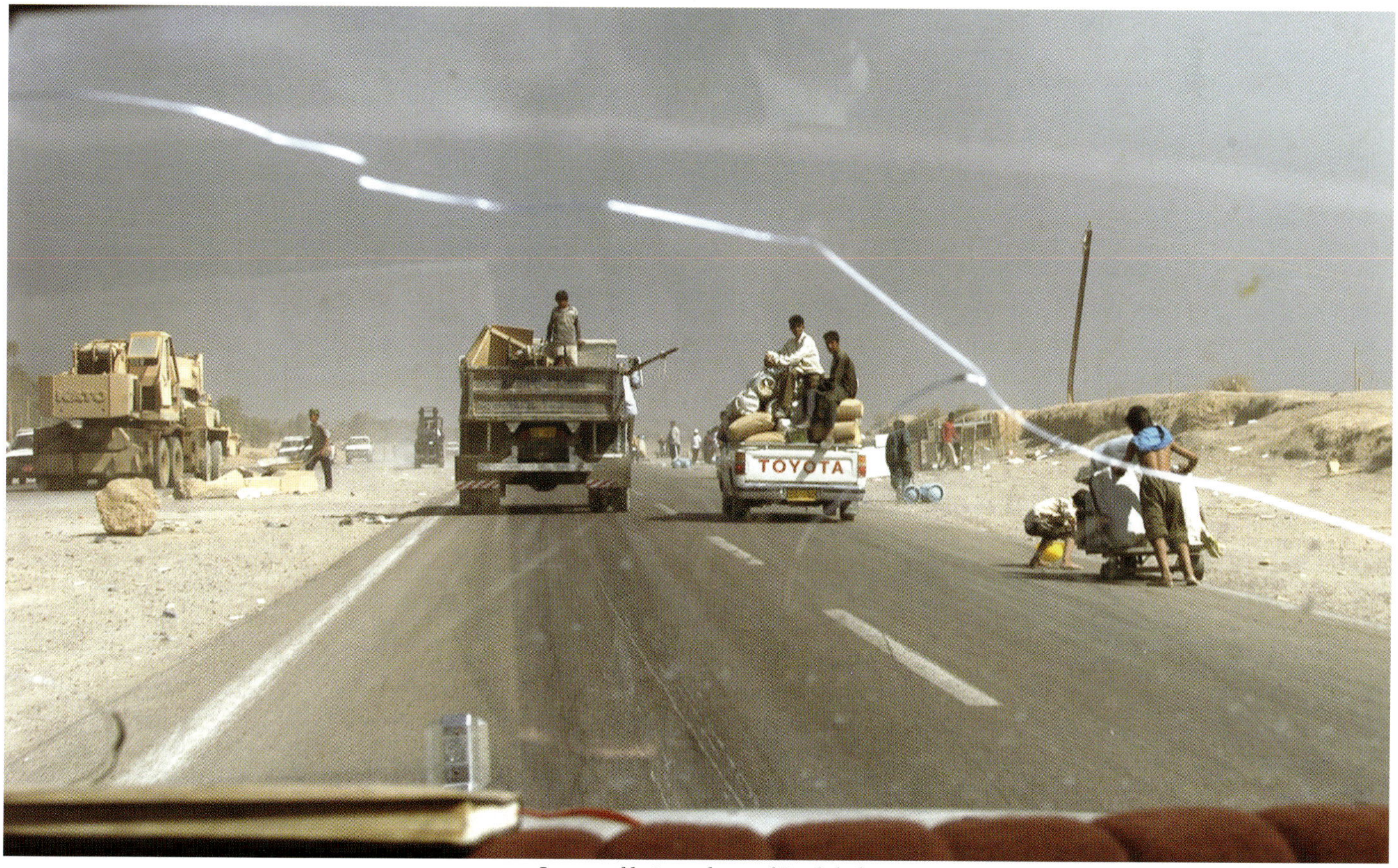

Looters file in and out of Baghdad

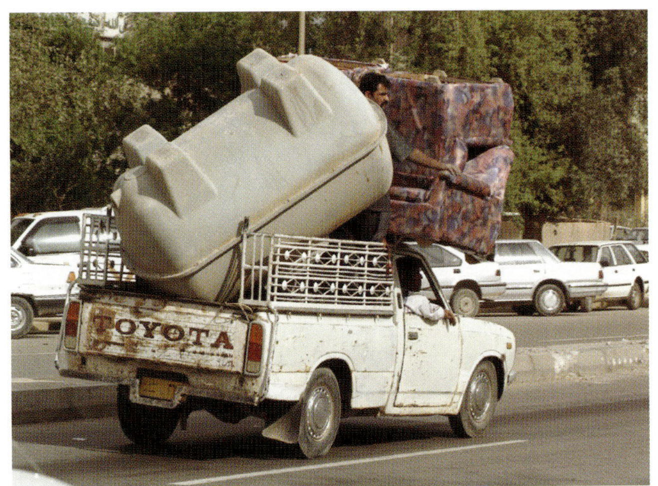

Truck-full of looted goods

its rims by a truck, showering the roadside with sparks. Looters carry 20-foot lengths of cast-iron piping, used in sewer and water systems. Donkey carts carrying luxurious chairs and stolen air conditioners, navigate the busy road. Everyone is looting or carrying looted goods. Others are going through the spilled remains of APCs and other vehicles dotting the fields and roadside. Baghdad is a festival of anarchy.

I observe two cement fallout bunkers along the roadside, with a small graveyard dug beside them. The bunkers look destroyed. Most of the dozen or more graves appear to have been freshly dug. Perhaps these are the graves of people who succumbed to the killer bombing raids.

I start to notice that more and more of the looters are brandishing AKs and handguns. I use great caution in taking my pictures. It wouldn't take much for one of them to open fire on us, but they seem happy to see us Westerners and wave at us. The looters are of all ages, from shoeless children, to teenagers, to old men and women.

The amount of thievery and devastation is inconceivable, and I find myself running out of superlatives to describe the scenes. Inside our car it is as hot as a blast furnace; it must be over 100 degrees F. We drive past a large amount of concentrated military carnage. Destroyed and abandoned military vehicles of all sorts litter the area, creating a huge landscape of burned vehicles and destruction. Some look as though they had tried to hide from aerial bombardment, by parking their war machines behind houses and under palm groves.

Tod tells me this band of war machinery, which surrounds Baghdad, was Saddam's last line of defense to protect the city. The smell of war is everywhere. It's a unique, though stimulating smell of burned rubber, diesel fuel, wood smoke, garbage and overheated engines. Baghdad central (just five miles away), resembles a large, out-of-control barbecue. Smoke is rising everywhere.

Smiling and laughing looters sit on top of their booty-filled trucks, looking like Humpty Dumpty, with AK-47s gripped in their hands. There are quite a few tank pits (trenches dug into the sand to partially conceal the tank and make it less of a silhouette to attackers) lining the side of the road, but most of the tanks appear to have moved on. Tractor-trailers, used to carry the tanks, are abandoned along the shoulders. Looters work the roadside, stripping the trailers of wheels, batteries and engine parts.

A large painted stone mural of Saddam holding a shotgun stands marred by a chisel and splattered with paint. Another has been pitted by automatic gunfire. Tractors towing large power generators, stolen from nearby factories, crawl along the highway.

Most of the tanks, troop carriers, trucks and APCs, are painted with the buff, yellow-brown camouflage paint that is used in desert settings. Others are more ingeniously disguised with mottled shades of greens and browns. But the fancy paint jobs didn't help hide the machines and men from the modern technology the Americans possess; as a result they all lie smashed and burning. Their ordnance and other weaponry are strewn about their smoldering remains, along with the cast-off clothing and personal items of the soldiers who were either killed, captured, or had deserted their posts. Turbaned old men and young children are stripping the machines. Perhaps it is a grandfather-grandson team?

We pass one truck towing two other trucks with blown tires, hooked together by a long chain. A double-decker bus is being robbed of its wheels and rims while stranded and trashed along the roadside.

I see what looks like an Apache helicopter flying two miles to the east of the highway. Soon I see three more helicopters. They fly low, about 100 feet above the ground, cutting through the black smoke, while

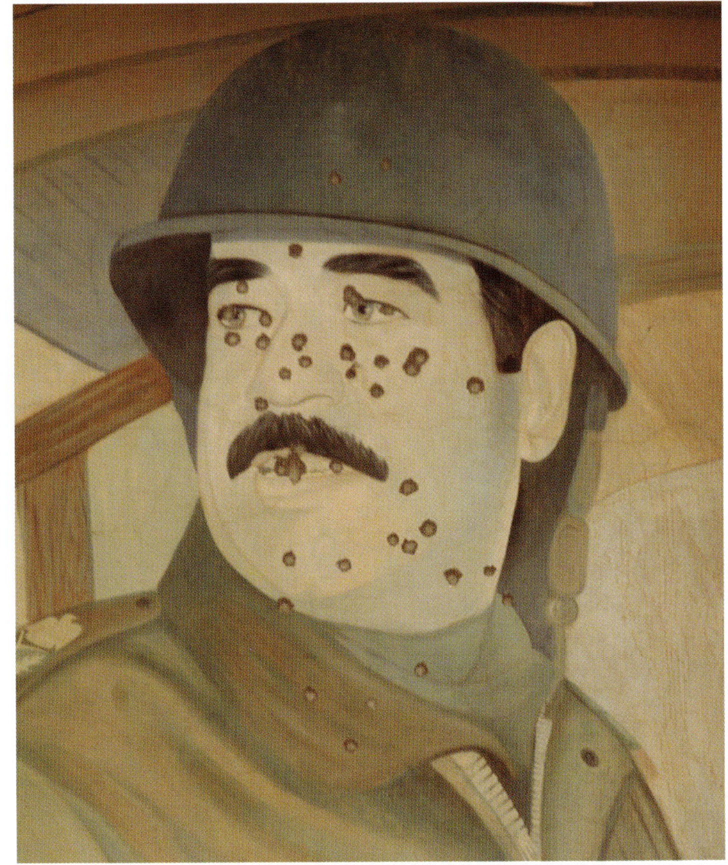

Bullet-ridden mural of Saddam

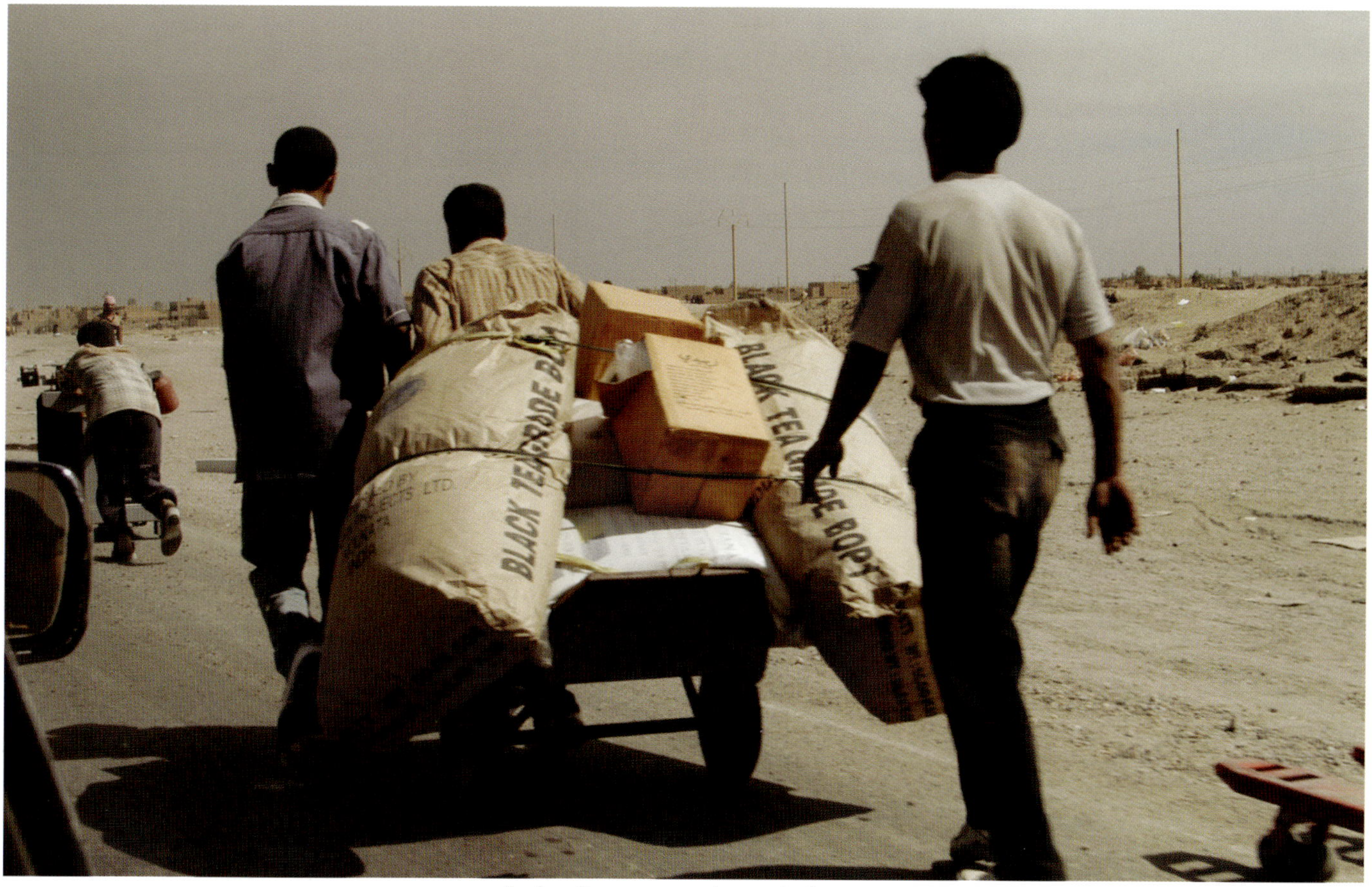

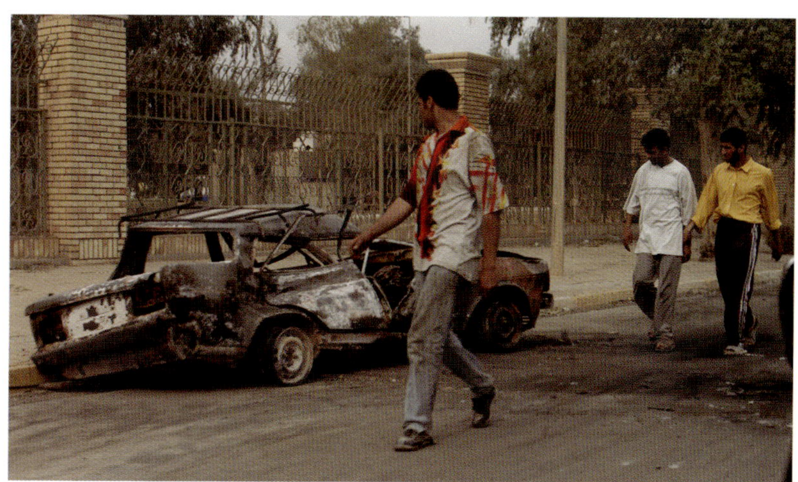

Sacks of tea are carted away by looters

below hysteria and anarchy reign. The helicopters look like marsh hawks on the hunt, their noses titled downward, looking for targets.

Propane tanks, bathtubs, generators, anything you can get your hands on, are all stolen and loaded onto vehicles. People walking along the roadside are waving at us and cheering. They show no fear of reprisal from their lawlessness. It is as though taking what is not yours is a normal everyday thing to do. To looters and non-looters alike, it is an atmosphere of immense joy and revenge.

We pass two U.S. tanks driving away from Baghdad. They seem out of place amongst the overloaded trucks, donkey carts and thievery, but I am happy to see them in the neighborhood. The sight of the soldiers puts us a little more at ease, knowing that there is help nearby if we really need it. This is especially important to our morale, since everyone but us, seems to be armed.

Small convoys of Humvees drive past, manned by Marines, with their weapons pointing out of the vehicle windows. We pass through a U.S. checkpoint, but they are apparently looking for those most wanted members of Saddam's military and administration. They are letting everyone go through, waving the looters, and us, past without stopping.

I am seeing a lot of Saddam murals and posters, some twenty feet high, on stone walls and across the sides of buildings. Most of them have been gouged, defaced, shot up, broken apart and set on fire. Judging from the number of these murals, and they are everywhere, the Iraqi people either loved or were forced to love Saddam with a deep passion. The defacing of the murals and looting probably exposes their true feelings about this man and his politics. The madness and destruction indicates to me, that these people are taking revenge on their former leader and his government. But in actual fact, they are stealing from each other. While the ministries and any government buildings are the first to be looted, no business, be it a mechanics shop or a hardware store, is exempt from the looting.

Pulverized civilian vehicle

We are witnessing the looting of a country, and these small "ma and pa" type businesses are the backbone of the common folk. It will take a lot to bring Iraq back from this type of anarchy. I also believe that we may be seeing the beginning of the end for Iraq. The situation is overwhelming, and the few soldiers that we see are only able to protect themselves and their fellow soldiers, if that. They have neither time nor manpower to quell this tidal wave of looting and burning. The situation is terrible.

Anti-aircraft guns poke out from their concealment, hidden in clumps of trees along the median strips of the highway. Soldiers' bunkers dot the roadside, dug into the sand and covered with palm fronds, corrugated steel sheeting and meshing. Outside the bunkers, people are looking at and picking up shoulder-fired RPGs (rocket propelled grenades) and mortars that lie strewn about with helmets, clothing and every sort of weaponry. With these types of arms lying about, it wouldn't take much effort for a couple of people to gather up a major arsenal of weapons. There is obviously nowhere near enough manpower to control the looters, just judging from this drive into the city.

Reaching the city, we pass a building housing one of the Ministry of Communications' transmission stations. It has been completely destroyed by Smart Bombs (self-guiding weapons intended to maximize

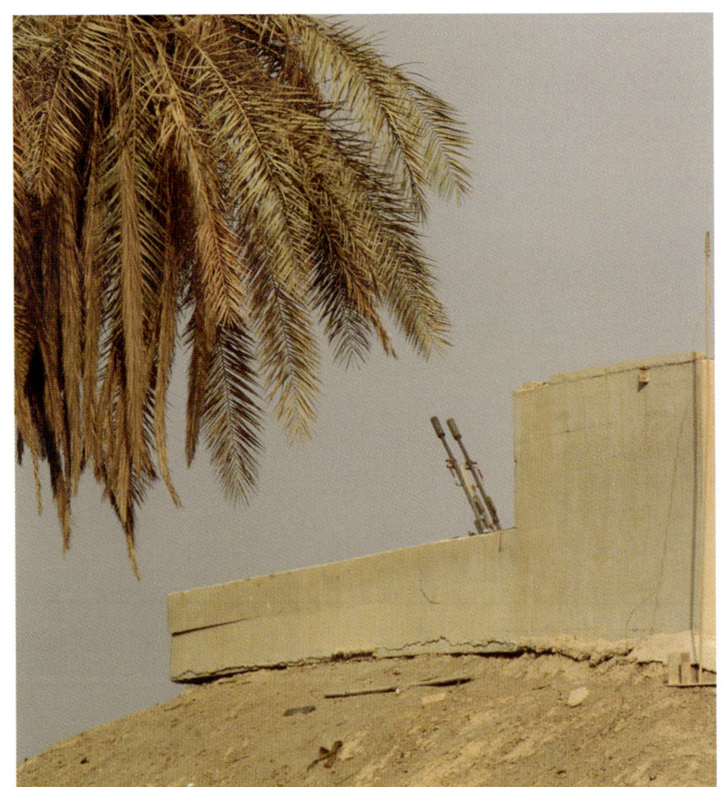

Anti-aircraft guns poke out from under a palm tree

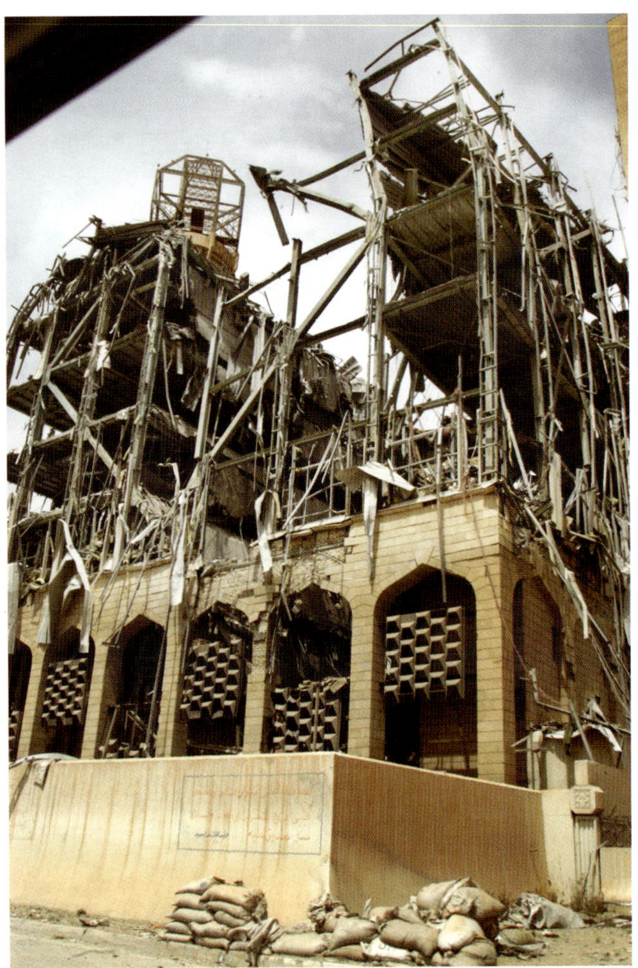

Precision bombing of communications building by Smart Bombs

damage to the target while minimizing collateral damage. They make use of computer guidance systems. These bombs cause the targeted buildings to collapse onto themselves and burn, as opposed to the conventional bombing practice of blowing the building to bits. They seem to be the bomb of choice, as it leaves little damage outside of the building. It is meant to be controlled, contained bombing, perfect for a city where you don't want to obliterate the entire metropolis. This type of bomb struck many of the ministry and government buildings, including Saddam's palaces. But they can also, and do, go astray and kill civilians).

The communications center looks like a huge deformed skeleton of twisted steel and hanging concrete. A pickup truck drives past us carrying a large water-holding tank and a couple of luxurious 17th century French-style chairs. These items were probably stolen from a ministry building or, more likely, one of Saddam's palaces.

Entire apartment buildings and office towers are burning, while crowds rush in and out of the decimated structures carrying furniture and everything else that can be found in a building. The scene looks like something out of the H.G. Wells' novel *The War of the Worlds*. It is unbelievable but real, and it is happening all around me. I feel very fortunate, as a journalist, to be witnessing all of this mayhem.

We arrive in downtown Baghdad around 6 p.m., where the looting and burning continues unabated. We park outside the Palestine Hotel, which, along with the Baghdad Sheraton, take up the entire city block up to the eastern shoreline of the Tigris River. Sean asks a soldier how we get access to the Al Fanar Towers (situated next to the Palestine and Sheraton Hotel complex). We drive around the block and are given access at a Marine checkpoint, just outside the eight-storey Al Fanar

Towers. Our drivers park the cars in front of the Al Fanar.

Sean has already been living at the Fanar for a month or so. (When I met him in Amman, he was there to pick up some supplies for his documentary and take care of some other business). We start unpacking our bags from the vehicles and bringing them up to Sean's room on the third floor, and to another we had rented on the second floor. We didn't want more than three persons to a room; it would make it uncomfortably close. For the first few days I decide to shack-up with Jim and Tod on the second floor. I will sleep on the floor the first night and we will rotate from there, on a day-by-day basis. The rooms have two single beds in them. Tish and Sean will room together.

The rooms are nice and hospitable, and before we know it we are unpacked and settling in. Each room has a small balcony, which looks south along the Tigris River. We store all our water we bought in Jordan, about 20 litres each, on the balcony. No shops are open; it would be suicide to open any!

Just as we finish unpacking (about 6:30 p.m.), automatic gunfire is heard just outside the Al Fanar front doors. I grab my digital camera, with 20-35mm zoom lens attached, and fanny pack (which contains my 80-200mm zoom lens, 1.4 converter, flash, spare batteries and memory flash cards), and head downstairs. People are standing in the hotel lobby ducking away from the windows, while watching the goings-

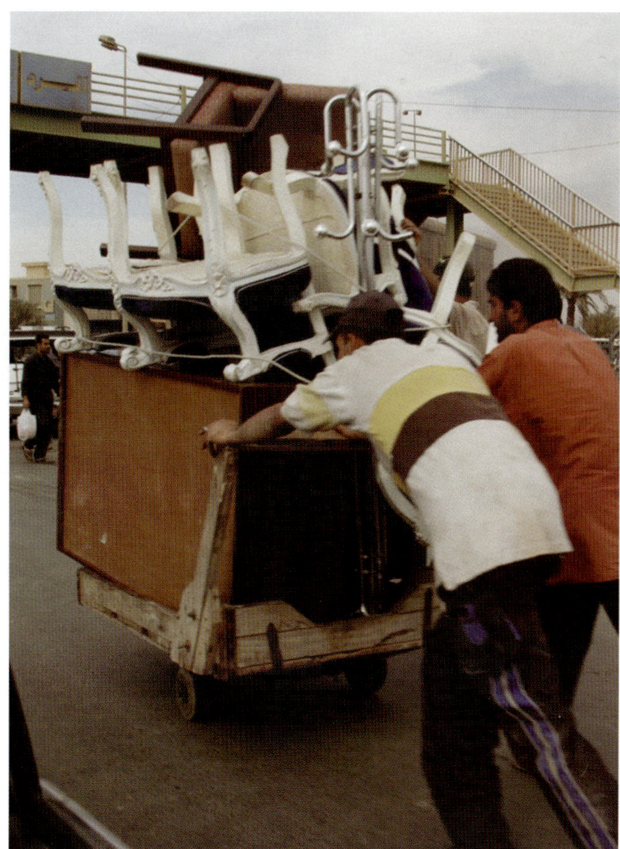

Looters cart away luxurious furnishings

on outside. I take a deep breath and, crouching low, dart out the hotel door to the building next door. Ducking around the side of the building and up the back stairs, I meet Eric, a photographer from the Detroit Free Press. He motions me to the second-floor patio, where we look out onto the street.

Amidst the close-range gunfire we see Marines running out from their two huge amphibious assault vehicles. They run towards the riverfront, ducking behind trees and cement walls, with their rifles grasped in their hands. The gunfire seems to be coming from all directions, as I raise my head above the stuccoed wall of the patio to have a look. It can just as easily be my head that will be blown off as the enemies.' But I put this fear behind me, knowing that I cannot do my job if I don't chase the bullets!

The machine gunner on one of the vehicles fires his 50-calibre weapon in the direction of the Tigris River. It is a huge, scary noise. He squeezes the trigger in five-second bursts; thumpa-thumpa-thumpa-thumpa. I gather my thoughts while ducking behind the stucco wall. Determined to follow the soldiers, I head downstairs and start running across the street in the direction of the heaviest fire. Ducking from tree to tree, I thread my way across the open expanse which separates the Tigris from the buildings lining the riverfront road (Abu Nawwas St.). About 30 feet from the shoreline I see a group of 20 Marines hunkered-down behind a flood-retaining wall that borders the muddy Tigris. Their weapons are all at the

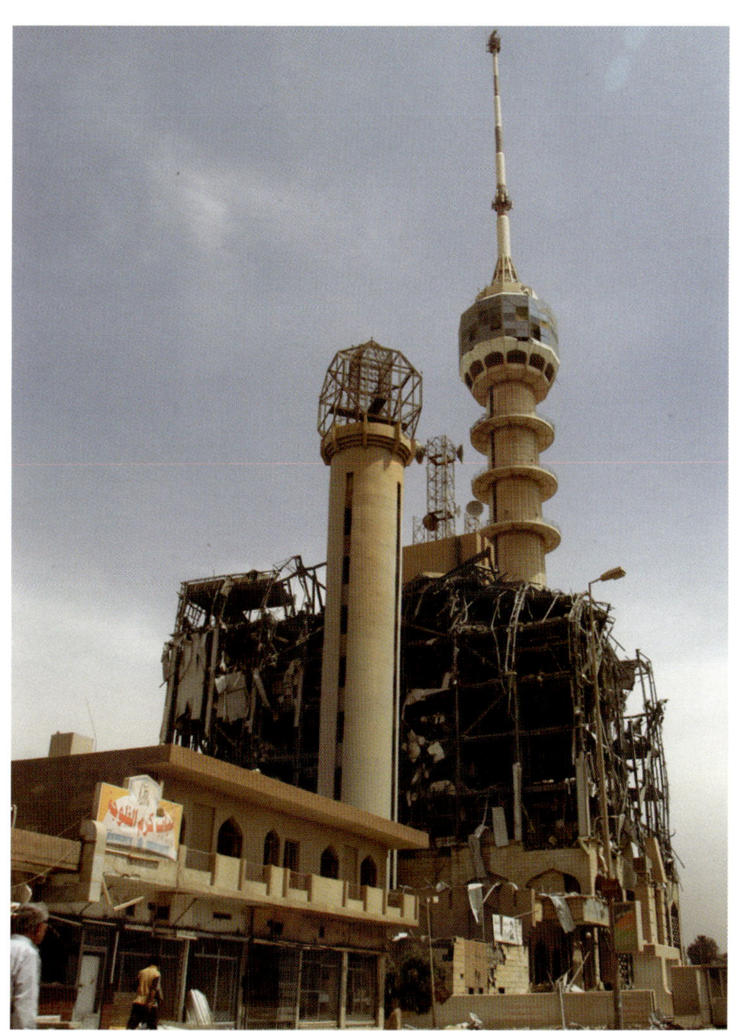

Destroyed communications building

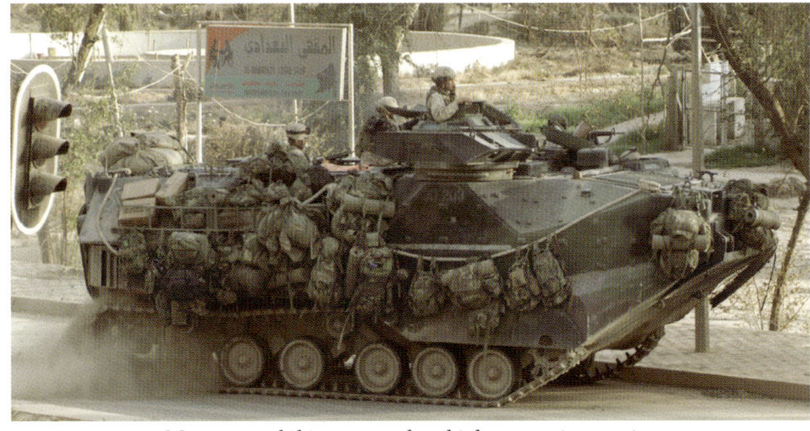

Marine amphibious assault vehicle moves into action

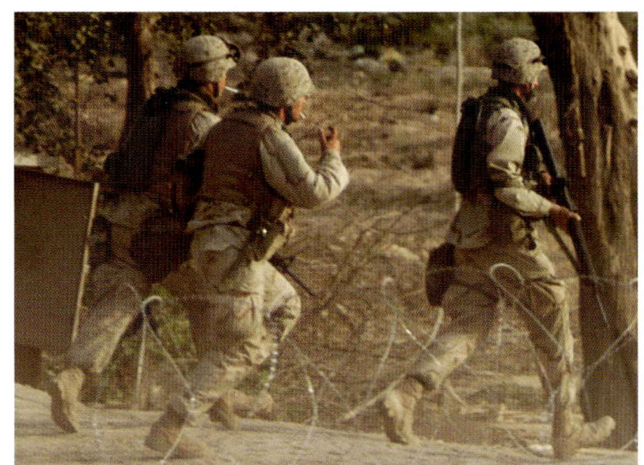

Running to the sound of gunfire

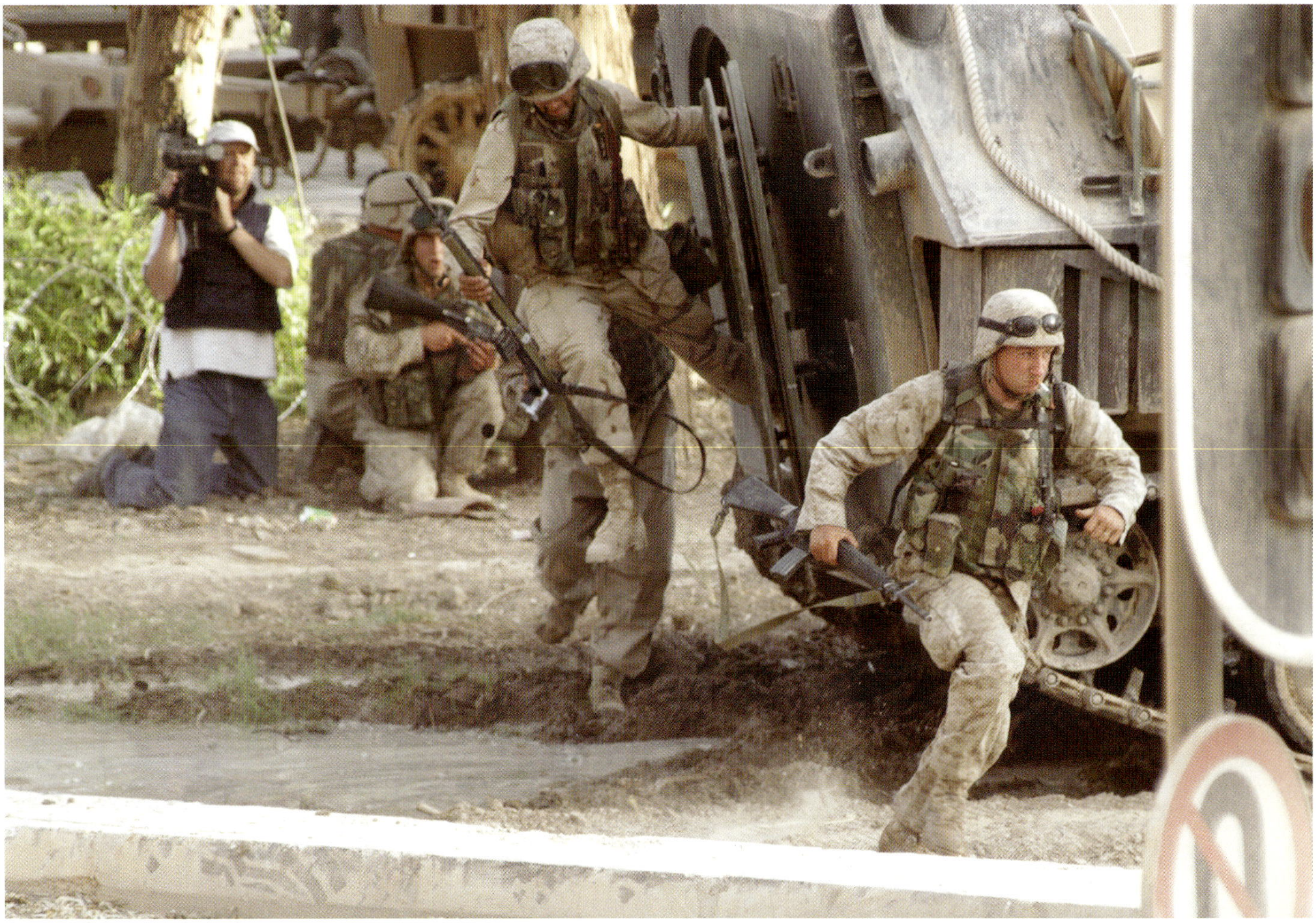

Marines exit their amphibious assault vehicle

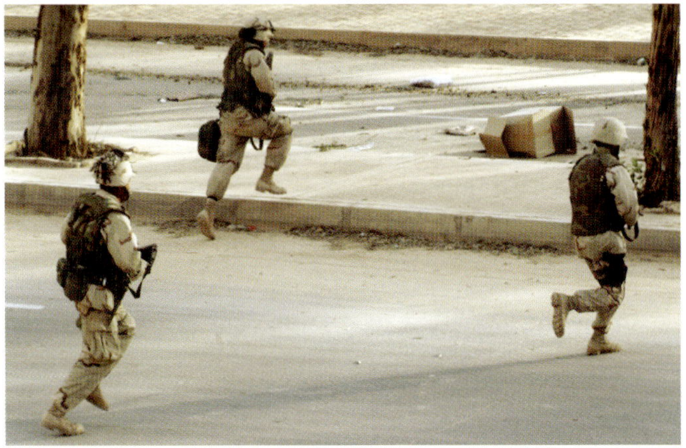

Marines run towards the Tigris River shoreline

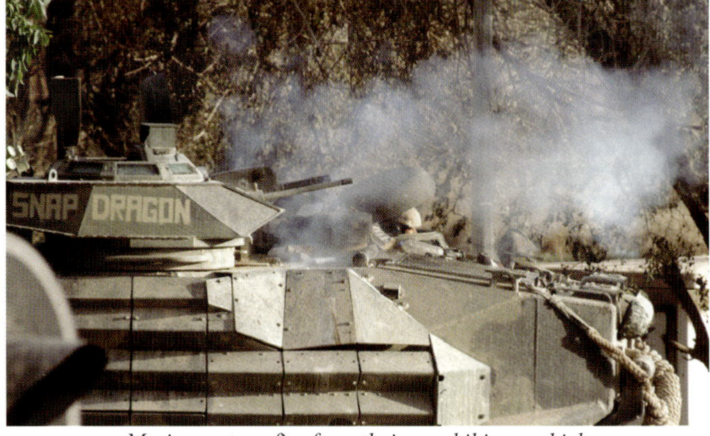

Marines return fire from their amphibious vehicle

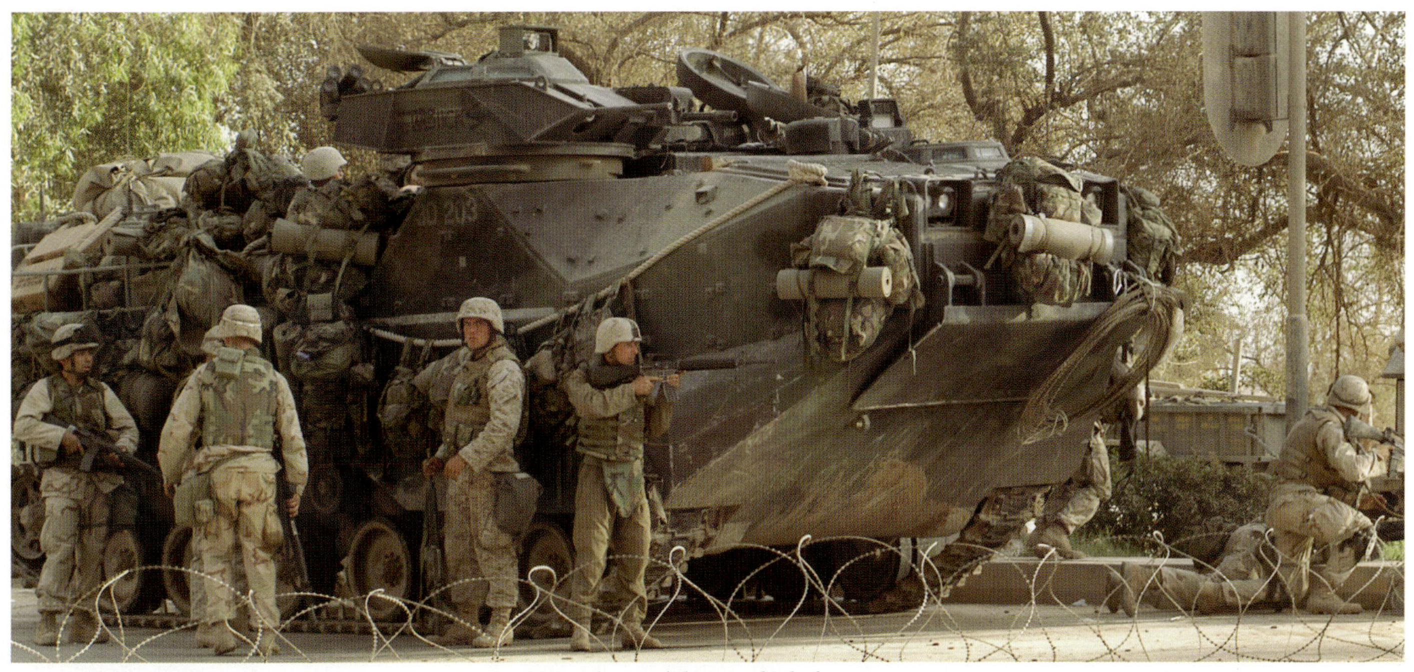

Using the amphibious vehicle for cover

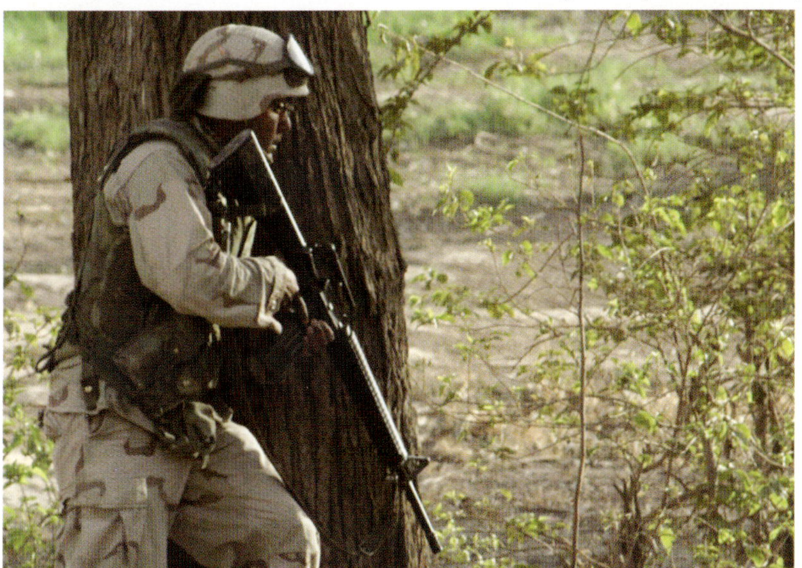

Using a tree as cover from enemy fire

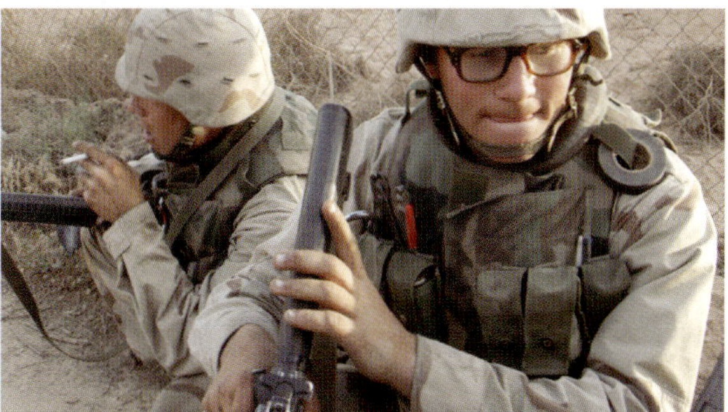

Resting after the firefight

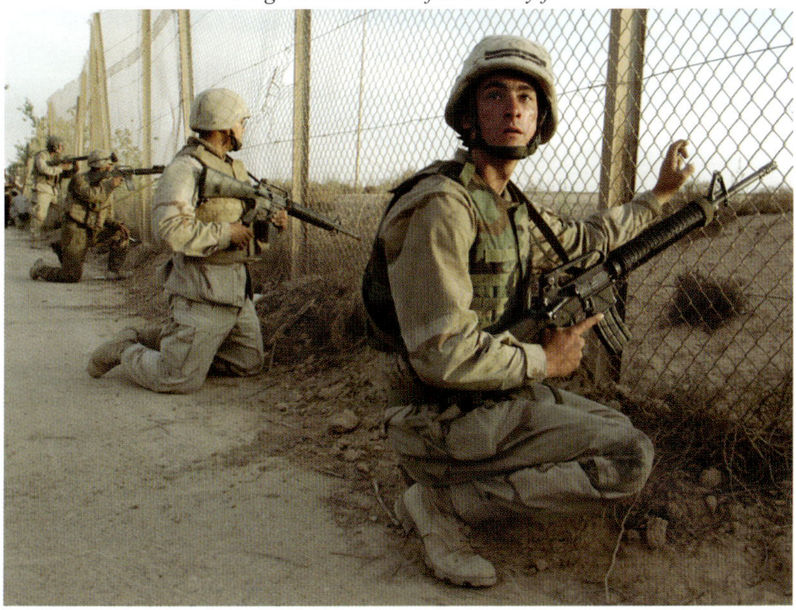

Marines fan out along the riverfront watching for the enemy

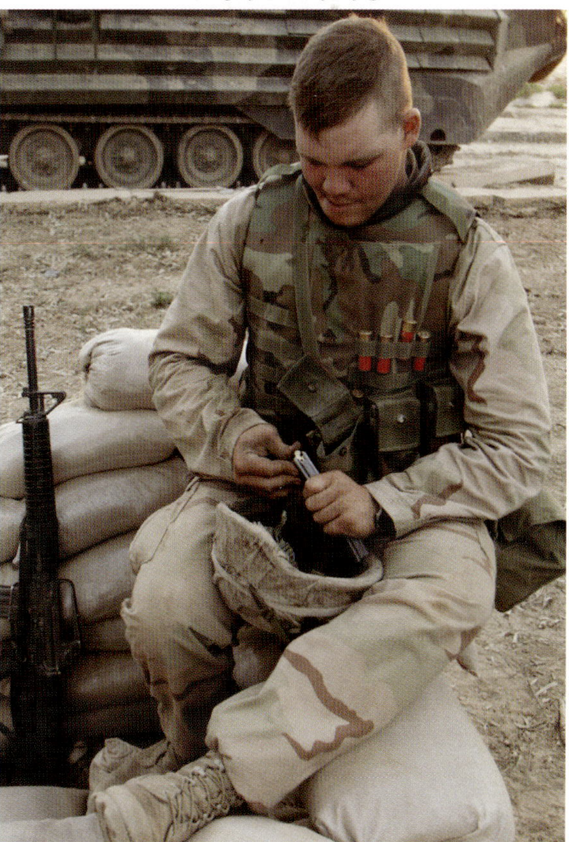

Reloading bullets into an emptied clip

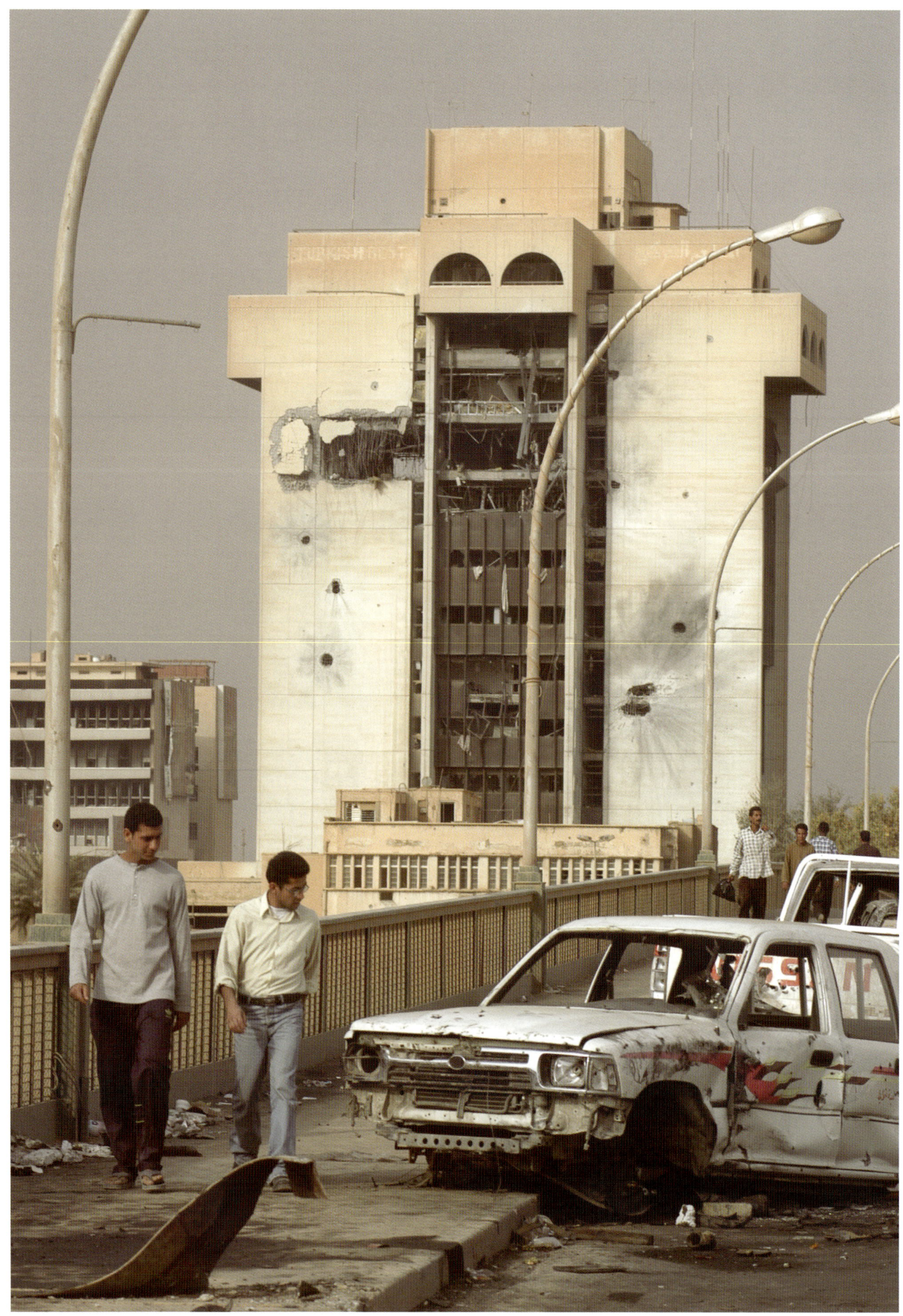

Destruction in central Baghdad

ready position, as I continue snapping photos. The main brunt of the attack seems to be coming from across the river, where Saddam's huge Republican Palace complex is located. The rifle and machine-gun fire soon dies down, and I sit having a cigarette with the soldiers, trying to figure out just where the enemy is. There are many reeds and rushes growing along the shorelines, great places to hide and fire upon the Americans. The firefight lasts about fifteen minutes, and shortly after, I head back to the Fanar to find my buddies.

I go upstairs to meet the gang, and we discuss getting some food downstairs in the Fanar dining room. However, we find that all the food has been eaten, so we order a pot of coffee and eat some of the dried foods we brought from Amman. We have a pleasant dinner of canned fish, nuts, flatbread and candy bars. The regular staple in the dining room (rice, broiled chicken, flatbread and bean soup), runs out quickly, and we learn that you have to order before 6 p.m.

The city power grid has been inoperable since the start of hostilities, so the only electrical power comes from generators. The Fanar has an industrial-sized oil-fired generator hooked up outside the hotel. It seems to run sporadically, and is unreliable at best. But even the little amount of time that it does operate is a real blessing. It fuels the reception lights, elevator, the lobby television, a few other lights and the kitchen. There is enough power left over so that the guests can plug into a power bar and run their computers or charge batteries. Every three hours the fuel tank runs empty and the power is lost. If you do not regularly save the work on your computer, you could lose your file. Candles and flashlights light the darkness when the power goes out.

We are in bed by 1 a.m., but not ready for sleep, staying up late, chatting and laughing animatedly about our long day and the strategy for tomorrow. We decide to hold off on any coverage plans till morning, when we can get a fresh pulse on the situation in Baghdad. Outside our windows we hear gunfire resounding from different areas of the city, filling the night sky with the sounds and streaks of tracer bullets. It would be insanity to wander anywhere away from your hotel once darkness has fallen – the bogeyman definitely lurks out there!

Day 4. Sunday, April 13th

(Ballet school destroyed; trench network; love letters to Saddam; ballet school used to store ammunition and weapons; Red Crescent Society burns; Sean rescues medical supplies; vigilantes round up looters; thieves beaten by vigilantes; head into a cement wall; our taxi driver is a thug; looters rob a mosque; returned booty; looter's hand chopped off; Baghdad police officer; "the looters are from other countries"; Italian woman calls the Marines baby killers; I move to Sean and Tish's room; a love of our jobs)

The next morning we awaken to our first full day in Baghdad. In the Fanar dining room (over a light breakfast of jam, flatbread and bottomless thick coffee), we discuss what we will try to cover today. Tod and Jim had heard from a lady in the hotel about the looting of a Ballet School. The lady, who had just visited there, said it was disgusting to see the destruction at this school for young girls. We feel it is a bit of a pansy story, especially since Baghdad is under siege, but we decide that it would be a good starting point for today's coverage and we will run into more breaking news.

We head off in two cars, driving over a bridge spanning the Tigris River. The city is being torn apart by looting and numerous black fires burning out of control. Many of these fires are in collapsed buildings, which were hit by bunker-busting, or other so-called Smart Bombs.

Driving through the city we see banks being openly looted with no resistance. Looters run in and out, while thick black smoke spews from the barred and broken windows. Smashed store windows expose near-empty interiors, with just the broken dregs of the stock "smashed and useless."

Arriving at the ballet school, we find it to be a small group of cement bungalows connected together in an "H" shape. The front lawn has two large trenches dug into it (four feet across by five feet deep and 14 feet long) covered with sheet metal and a sprinkling of dirt for camouflage. The trench entranceways, covered by a dirty green tarp, lead down into the dank covered chamber where the soldiers slept. Sleeping bags, uniforms, helmets and weapons lie about the perimeter of the trenches. It looks as though the occupants left in a hurry, leaving their military uniforms behind. I grab an Iraqi helmet made of bullet resisting Kevlar from outside a bunker and throw it in the taxi. I will keep it with me in case we are shot at or assaulted by mortars.

The school has been badly plundered. All the office equipment has been stolen, including typewriters and staplers. The linoleum floors are covered with pages of kids' drawings, and all sorts of papers and broken furniture. The students had made colorful little drawings and messages, which were still tacked to the walls, expressing their love and devotion to Saddam; little love letters and drawings written to "Their Saddam." Some of them depict a flower-garlanded Saddam, smiling and wearing his black sunglasses, or clutching a shotgun. By the style of the drawings, it seems the children who attended this school were between seven and 12 years of age.

I find another larger trench network in the backyard of the school. I wonder whether the school was operating while the soldiers lived in the trenches. Or in other words, did the soldiers use the school and children as shields from attack? All indications confirm to me that the school was used as an armory and base by the Iraqi Army, at the same time as the

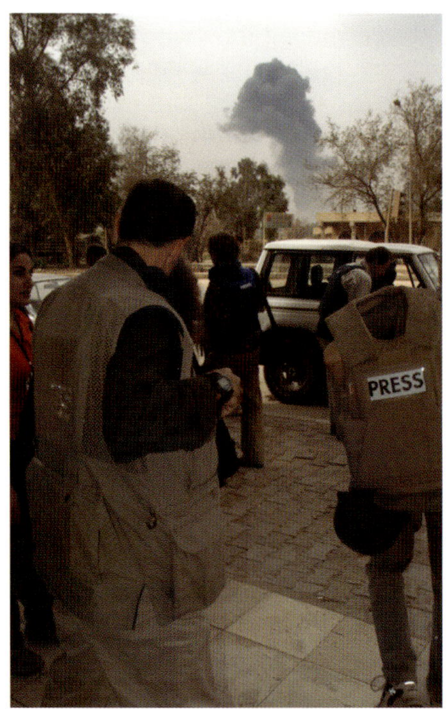
Leaving the Al Fanar Towers in the morning

children were attending the school. To Westerners, using children as human shields is a horrendous, cowardly practice, but to the Iraq Army, this might have just been a practical way to stave off attack. The children would be sacrificed for Saddam's dream if need be, under the guise of a cultural dissimilarity between East and West.

We leave the school and, after a short drive down the road, we stop at the International Red Crescent Society Headquarters (the Muslim equivalent to the Red Cross Society). It is located just across the street from the gutted and burning Saddam International Trade Fair complex. Getting out of the cars, Tod and Jim start talking with one of the society officials to see how they are making out. I see smoke rising from one of the rear buildings and go round to take a look. Society staff are running in and out of the burning facility, grabbing boxes of medical supplies. Other staff are trying to control the fire with extinguishers, but they soon run out of retardant.

Sean jumps into the melee and starts rescuing supplies from the ill-fated building. With the stifling weather and the heat of the fire, Sean looks like he is ready to pass out from heat exhaustion. With his face turning pinkish-purple, I grab him and advise him to take a break or he will get heat exhaustion. Gulping from our water bottles we make our way back to the front of the headquarters, as the fire overtakes the building.

The team starts interviewing an official about the fire, when I notice a man brandishing an AK-47 in the middle of the road, just 100 feet from us. We dash away from the interview and over towards the gunman, who is stopping vehicles and forcibly pulling people out of their cars and trucks. He is a burly man with a black moustache, dressed in a blue dress shirt and black pants. Had he been in Montreal, this man would have been carrying a briefcase and heading for the office – here in Baghdad, he carries a machine gun.

We rush onto the road and see three other armed men stopping traffic; one is carrying a handgun, the other two, AK-47s. The gunmen stand in the middle of the busy two-lane roadway, stopping vehicles they suspect are being driven by looters. Some of the vehicles are brimming with office furniture, sacks of rice, tea and every other type of booty. The gunmen block the cars or trucks by pointing their weapons at them, then motioning the vehicle to stop. Opening the vehicles' doors, they drag the suspects from their seats. Throwing them up against the car, the gunmen forcefully interrogate the passengers about the origin of the articles. If the gunmen feel the suspects are being less than truthful, they hit them repeatedly across the face with hollow, ringing slaps. This technique of intimidation (which could be considered barbaric and illegal in Canada) seems to be the method that works here in Iraq. After a few slaps the suspects are spilling their guts about where they got the spoils of war.

One of the Red Crescent officials tells me that the gunmen are vigilantes who have had enough of the mayhem, and decided to take the law into their own hands. This all started when the looters ransacked and burned the neighboring Health Ministry warehouse where vital medical supplies were stored. One of the vigilantes is a former Iraqi police officer; the other two are Red Crescent volunteers. They tell us they felt as though something had to be done to stop the wave of destruction and thievery, and this is their course of action.

It is a dangerous scene of guns, violence and panic, as gunmen pull people from their cars, while other vehicles whiz by the commotion, not wanting to be pulled over and checked. Some of the vehicles have children in them, which the

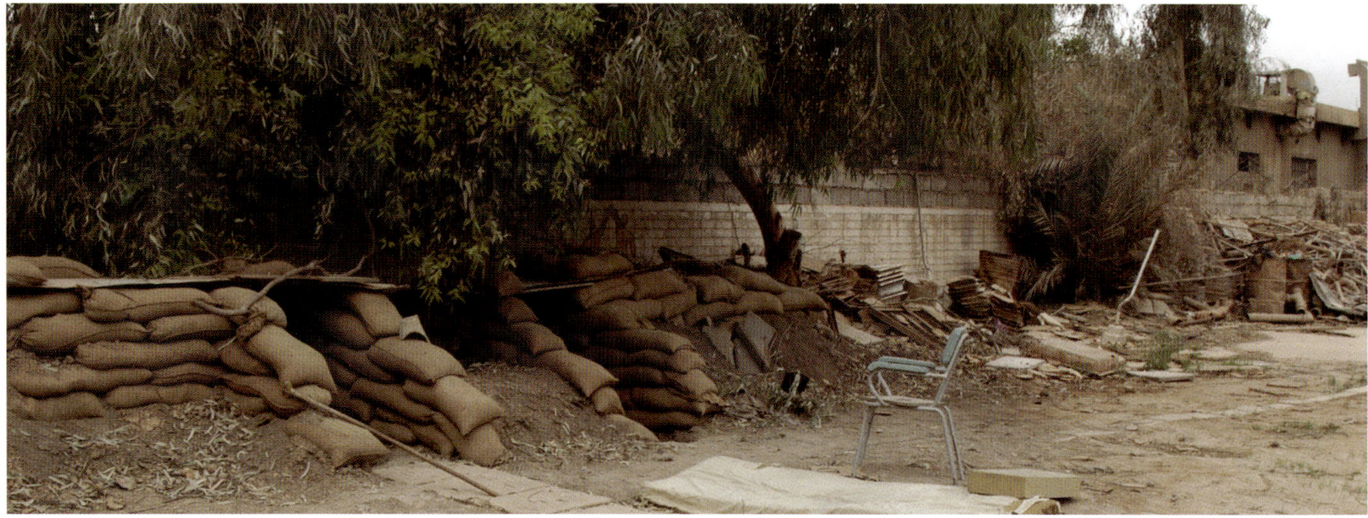
Iraqi soldiers' trenches inside the grounds of the Iraqi Ballet School

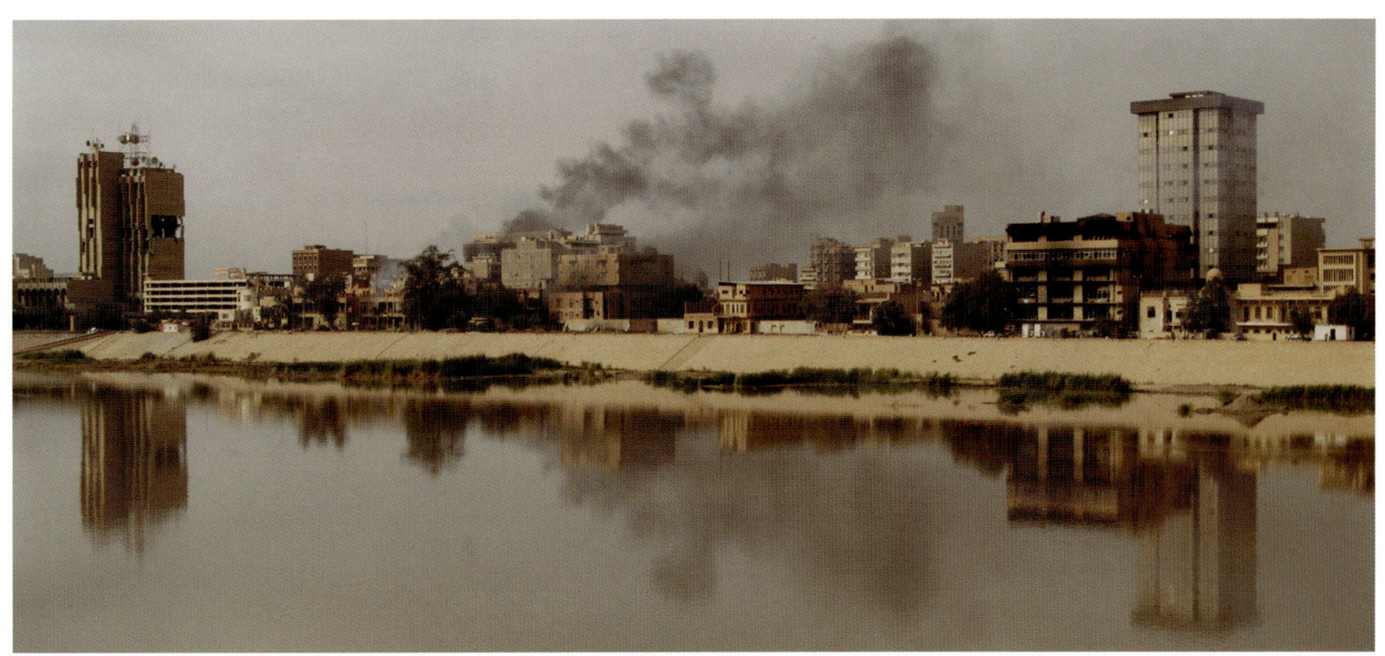

View looking north-east along the Tigris River

gunmen let pass. I start to think that if they pull over a car with guns in it, we could have a hell of a firefight between the vigilantes and thieves. I watch the goings on very carefully, keeping my eye peeled for any unusual circumstance that might trap me in the crossfire of a gun battle. All my senses are red-lining, my camera firing on autopilot, I can see behind my head.

The vigilantes appear to be picking out cars containing young and middle-aged men. On discovery of a vehicle with suspected stolen property, the vigilantes force the car to the side of the road. The suspects are manhandled into an open garage of the Red Crescent Society. Here other vigilantes (some with machine guns) bind the suspects' hands in heavy electrical wire and push them down in a corner of the garage where they are interrogated further, with slaps across the face and a fresh roughing-up. One suspect gives his interrogator a hard time and is thrown headfirst into the cement garage wall. He collapses unconscious from the impact and lies sprawled on the dirt floor – but no one bats an eye. All around us the action is hot and heavy!

One of four vigilantes, with a thick wooden bat in one hand, stands over the 12 captured looters. He evilly eyes the bound thieves, just waiting for an opportunity to use the club. I then realize that this guy is our taxi driver, one of the two drivers who chauffeured us here from the Fanar. This driver, a Turk living in Baghdad, has become caught up in the violence and taken it upon himself to stop the looters.

I am not happy about his involvement; we hired him as a taxi driver. From this point on we would make sure that any drivers followed our directions to a "T". Any misjudgment by an indecisive or tactless taxi driver could cost us our lives. We decide not to hire this man again.

Back on the street, one of the gunmen sees a looter carrying a sack full of goods. He shouts at the man (about 100 feet away from us) to drop his sack. Not getting a response, the vigilante fires a blast from his AK-47. As the bullets burst in the dirt all around him, the elderly man freezes, and then drops his sack. Stepping quickly, he disappears into the collapsed destruction of the Fair Grounds. He is one lucky thief!

There is no quarter given. If you do not do exactly what you are told, you will get your head punched in,

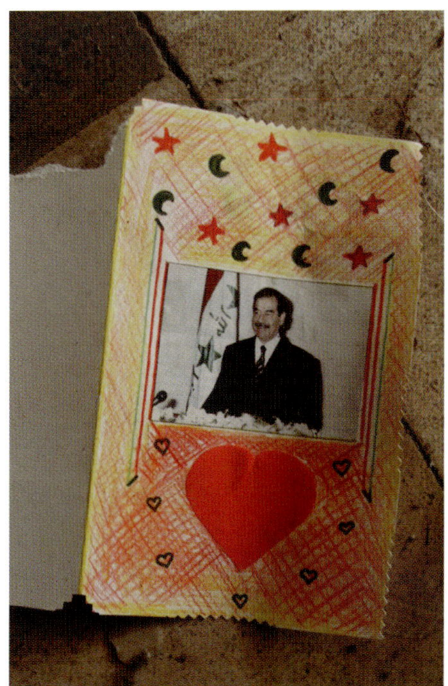

Little love letters to Saddam

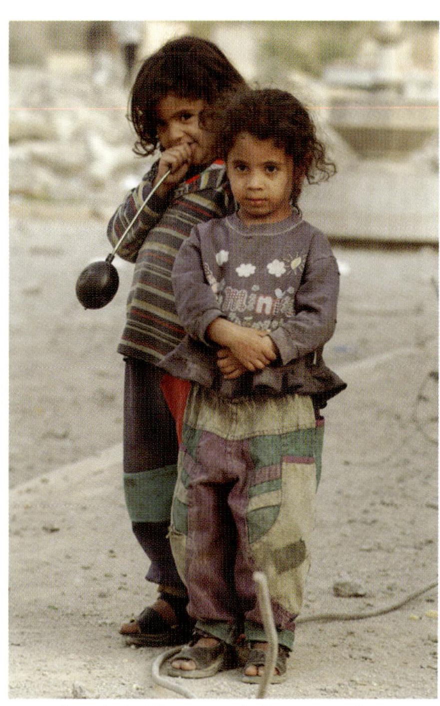

Local children watch the journalists

21

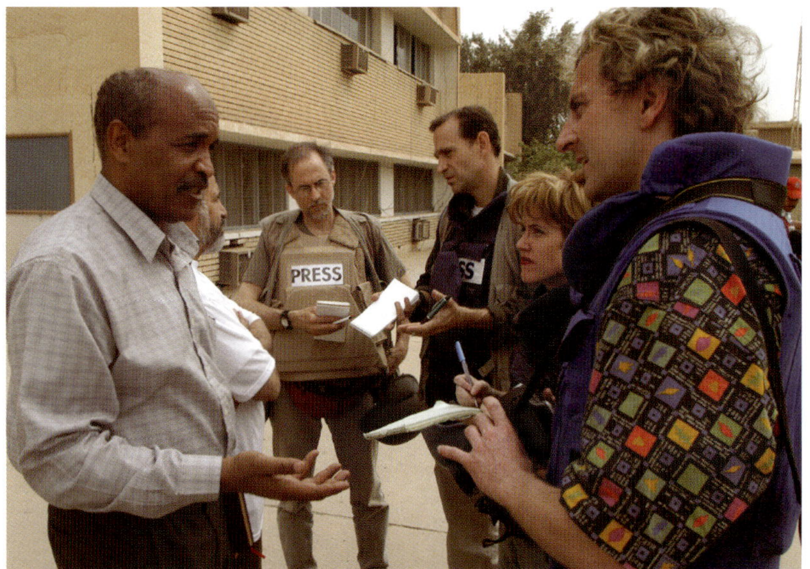

A Red Crescent Society official (left), is interviewed by Jim, Tod, Tish and Sean

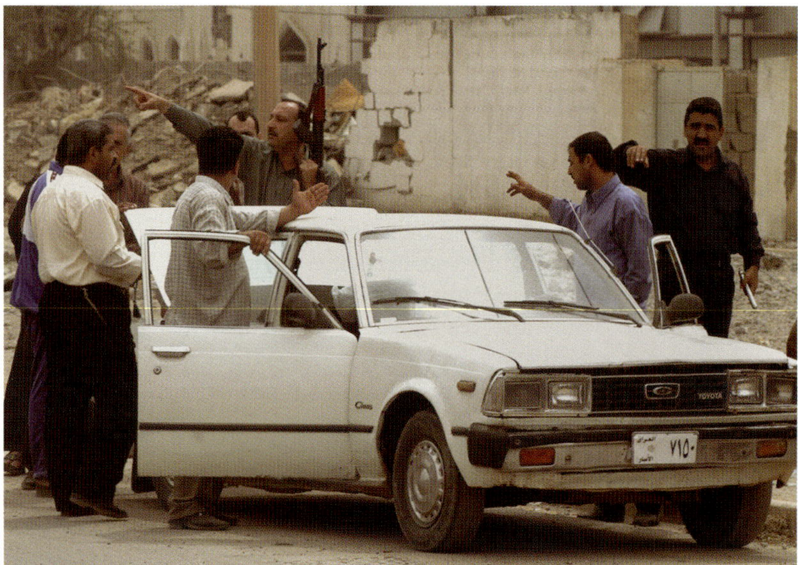

Vigilantes check a car and its occupants

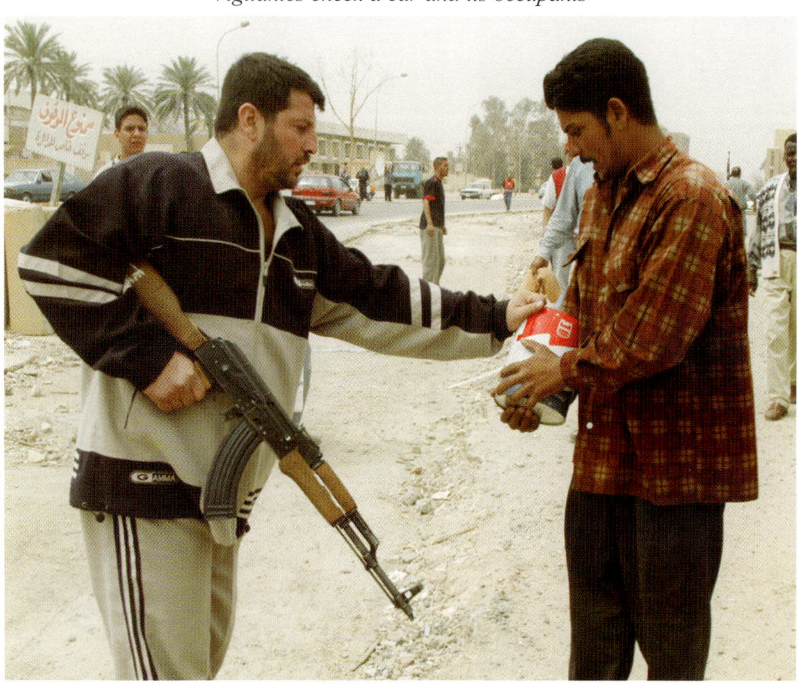

Man carrying a can of tomatoes is checked by gunman

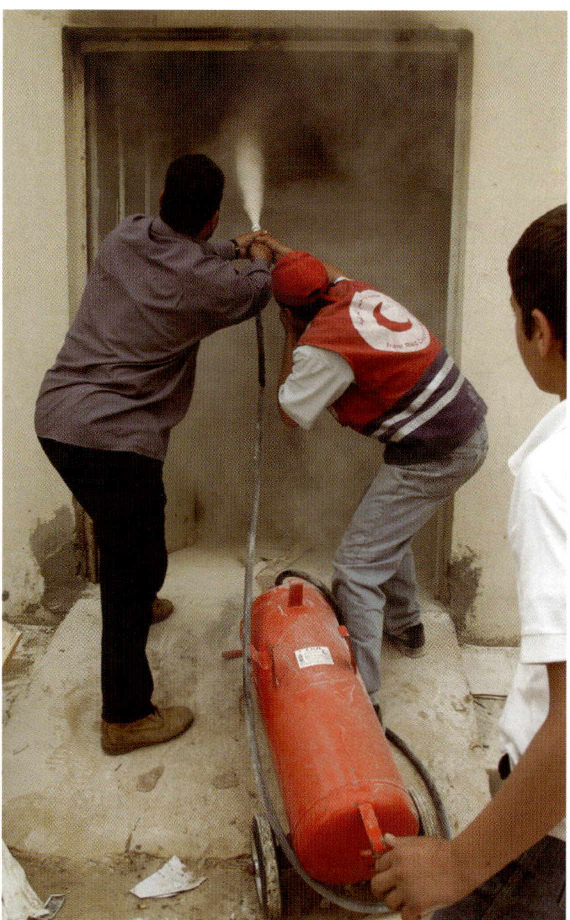

Red Crescent Society staff fight a fire in their building

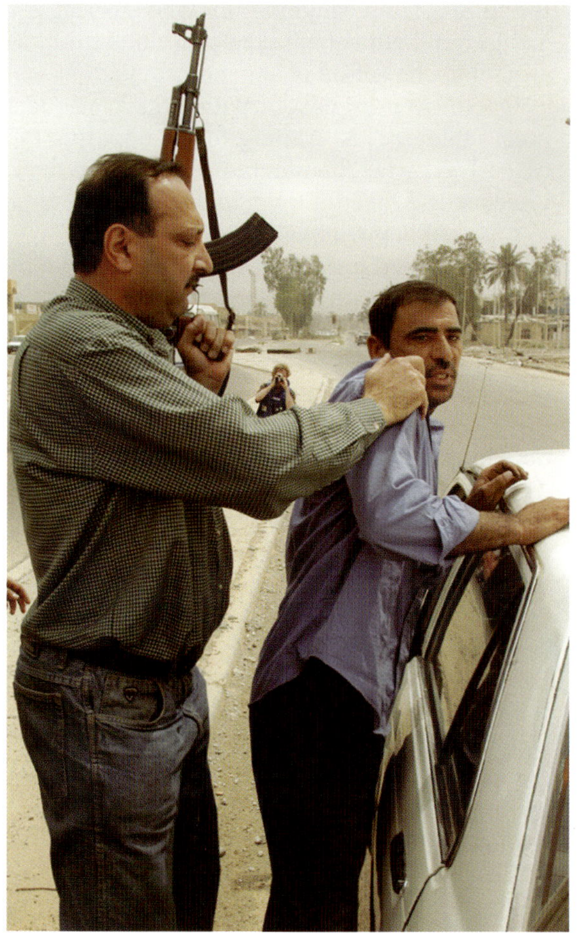

Vigilante holds a suspected looter

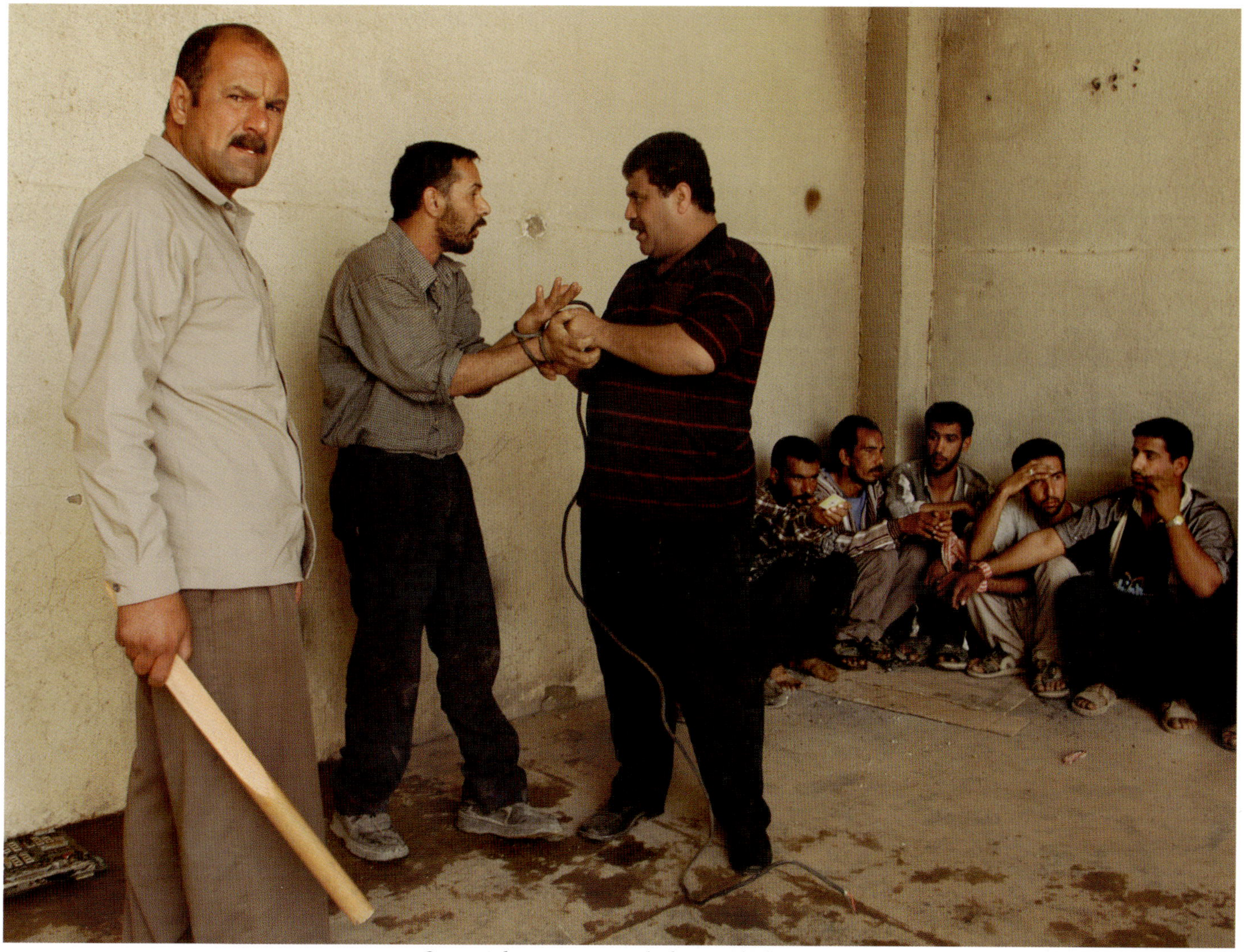

Our taxi driver casts a wicked eye at the looters

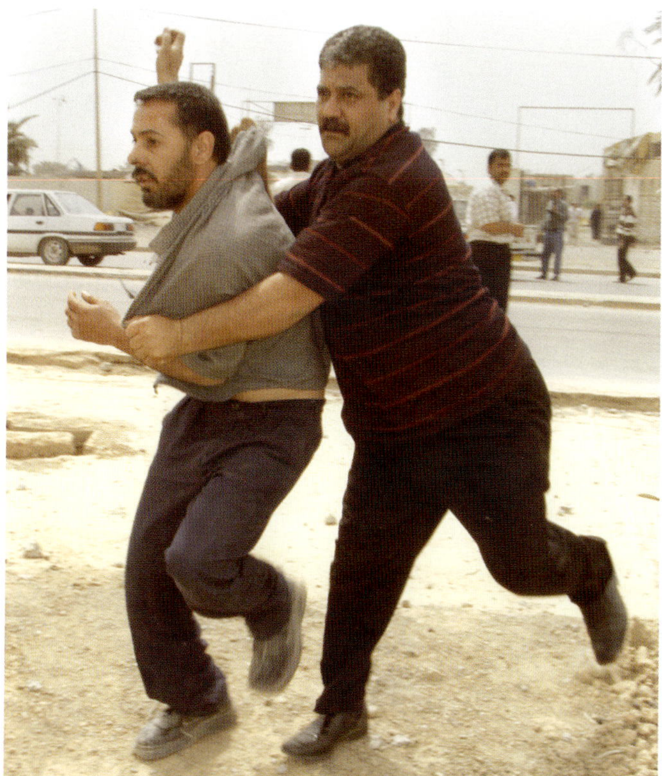

Manhandling a suspected looter

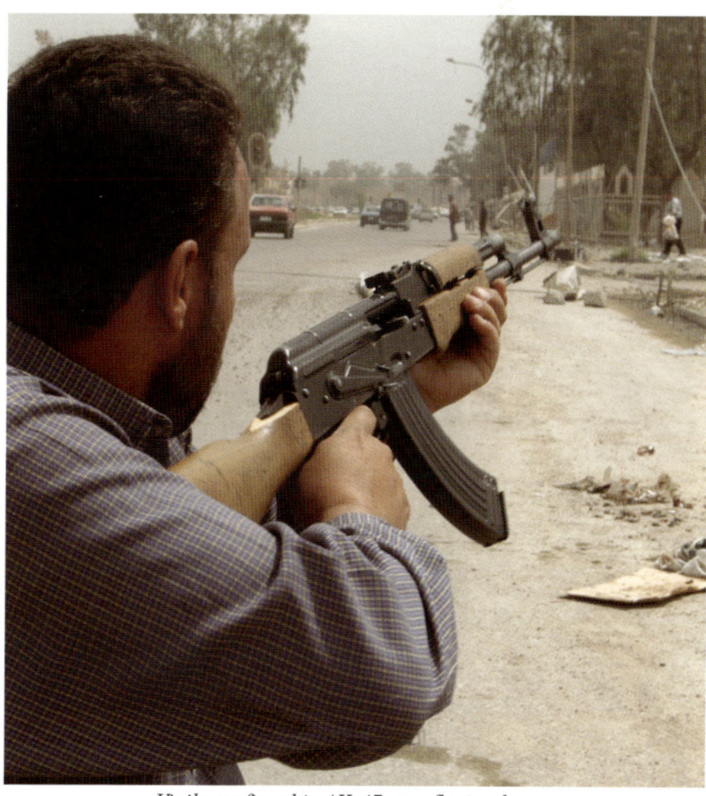

Vigilante fires his AK-47 at a fleeing looter

batted in, or shot. It is a bloodbath waiting to happen, a civil war pitting vigilantes against looters. I wonder if this sort of clash could spread to other parts of the city.

So far it has been a great morning for photos and words. Action like this is what I am looking for, and it cannot get much better. War is a very dangerous and life-threatening affair, but the adrenaline rush of placing your life on the line is very stimulating. It feeds my hunger to cover more breaking news.

We decide to leave the Red Crescent Society and visit the pillaged Omar al Mukhtar mosque in the upscale Yarmuk suburb of Baghdad. We heard rumors of a looter who had his hand cut off for looting a mosque in Al Hillah. Worshippers who were guarding the holy building caught the man and chopped off his right hand. They wanted to send a message of warning to other looters. Iraq's top Muslim cleric had issued a *fatwa*, a religious declaration, condemning the looting as contrary to God's law.

Tod was told that as of yesterday, the day after the hand was cut off, a large pile of stolen material had been returned and left outside the Mukhtar mosque by those who feared reprisals from worshippers. Word had spread about the incident, through the voices of the worshippers and clerics. As a result, other mosques were finding stolen articles returned and stacked up outside the buildings. Some of the articles outside the al Mukhtar mosque included cars, a safe, sacks of tea, office furnishings, bedroom furnishings and tools. Two large trucks were stacked with other stolen and returned goods. It appears that the threat of losing your hand, and spiritual exile, is enough to make some of the culprits return their booty.

While we are outside the mosque interviewing head cleric, Sheik Abdurrazak Abdulkarim, a uniformed policeman walks over and introduces himself, then kisses the hand of the cleric. The presence of the policeman pleasantly shocks us; it is the first time we have seen anyone wearing a uniform, apart from the coalition troops. He tells us he came to the mosque to show residents that some sort of order had returned to the neighborhood. The cop wants to let people know that normality can and will return. He tells us he has not worked since the bombing started, and is willing to work for as long as necessary, without pay, to get his city back in order. This man, with a 9-mm pistol strapped in its holster, is a hopeful symbol to me, much like the vigilantes at the Crescent Society.

Yarmuk is a well-kept, upper-middle-class neighborhood, with tidy properties and neatly dressed children. A couple of young boys hang around on their bikes, asking us to take their photo and inquiring where we are from. Logs, crates and other debris barricade the street intersections. The residents keep an eye on the roadblocks, and are ready to fight to defend their community. Some residents stop to tell us that gunfire is heard every night after sundown, and it has become very dangerous to venture outside their homes after dark. There are also rumors that armed thugs are breaking into and robbing people's homes. Because of this, the community is organizing to keep them out.

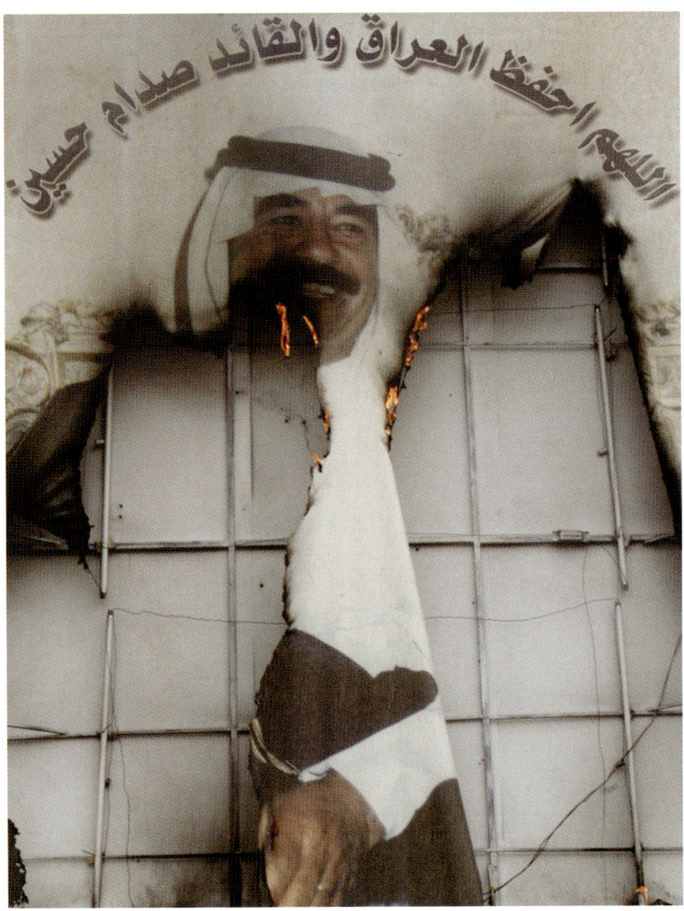

Burning portrait of Saddam

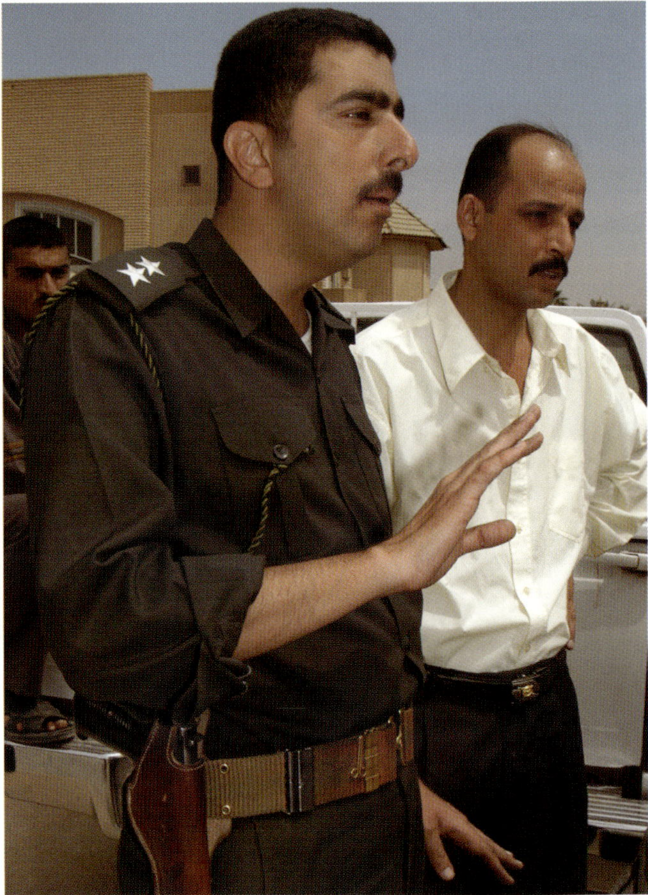

Armed Baghdad police officer keeps the peace in Yarmuk

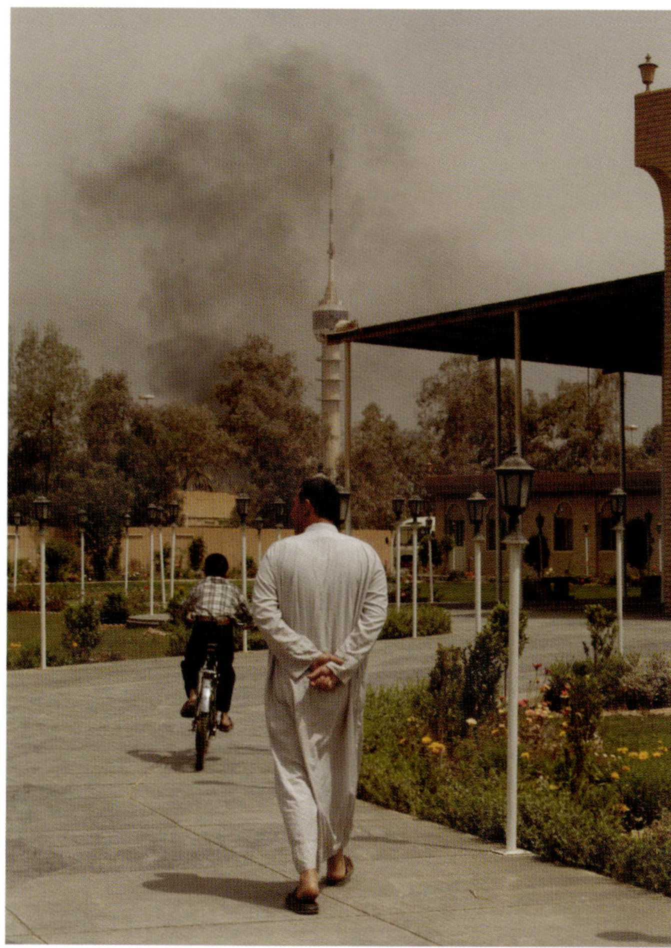

War is not far off, even within the sanctuary of the al Mukhtar mosque

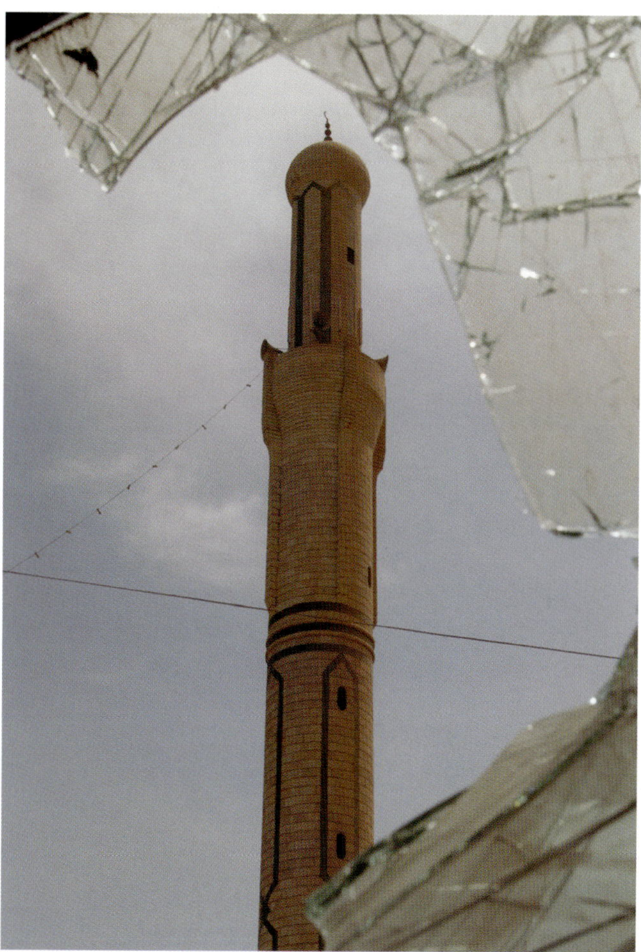

A shattered car window frames the al Mukhtar mosque tower

One of the mosque helpers, a young man of about 24, comes over and comments that, "The looters are made up of just one percent of Iraqis. The rest of the looting is being organized from outside the country." Continuing, he states that, "The looters came with the U.S. Forces. The Americans let the looters in. Bush should get us relief, medical aid! We need help from all the world." I ask him what they do when they catch looters. "When we catch thieves, we hit and beat them," he says. "These looters are from the Republican Guard, the Baath Party, the ministries, and outside the country!"

During the 20 minute drive back to the hotel, through the remnants of one of the world's greatest cities, I lie back in the taxi seat recalling a fantastically thrilling day. I feel as though I am in journalistic heaven, surrounded by the hell of reality. I wonder how I can be so happy, while being surrounded by this misery. Am I a sadist or a complete idiot? But these concerns all end as a warm stream of satisfaction flows from the tip of my toes to the last hair on my head.

Arriving back at the hotel I take a walk over to the Palestine Hotel where I see a woman, with a heavy Italian accent, shouting insults at and calling the Marines baby killers! Later in the evening, the same woman comes up to me in the Fanar dining room, as I finish my supper, and asks if I am finished with my plate. I answer yes, and she takes it over to her table and finishes off the rice left on it. She tells me she is a writer with the NGO agency 'Voices in the Wilderness.'

I move into Sean and Tish's room, leaving Tod and Jim more room to do their daily reporting. This is a better set-up, as the three of us, all freelancers, are able to talk about our coverage and what to do the following day without interrupting the two staff writers. It is also the site of much black humor, where we keep ourselves entertained with each other's memoirs. We have become close friends and share a love of our jobs.

Day 5. Monday, April 14th

(Tod, Tish, Sean, Jim and I visit Saddam City; pools of human waste; fetid mounds of garbage; city of the poor; shoeless children; Marines and Iraqi Police launch dual patrols in Baghdad; new police uniforms; organizing the joint patrols; clashing with suspected looters; guilty until proven innocent; banks being robbed; the Central Bank of Baghdad; looter shot dead by Marine; the smell of urine and burning paper; crowd endorses shooting of looter; civilians chant "USA – George Bush"; tears of joy; the "ghost" gun; telling them what they want to hear; looter dealt a dead man's hand; photos to Associated Press; a great day)

After breakfast Sean, Tish, Jim, Tod and I drive to Saddam City (unofficially renamed Sadr City after the fall of Baghdad, it will be referred to as Saddam City in the diary), a 15 minute drive north-east of central Baghdad. It is a city populated by 2 million Shi'a Muslims. Jim and Tod had been invited to meet a former Iraqi Army officer who had been tortured during Saddam's regime. Driving into Saddam City, the place reminds me of Gaza City in Israel, only worse. Rundown mud and cinder-block buildings melt into each other, separated only by laneways with open troughs of raw sewage. The air has a musky, mouldy smell to it, fed by burning trash and the dust kicked up by a multitude of feet and

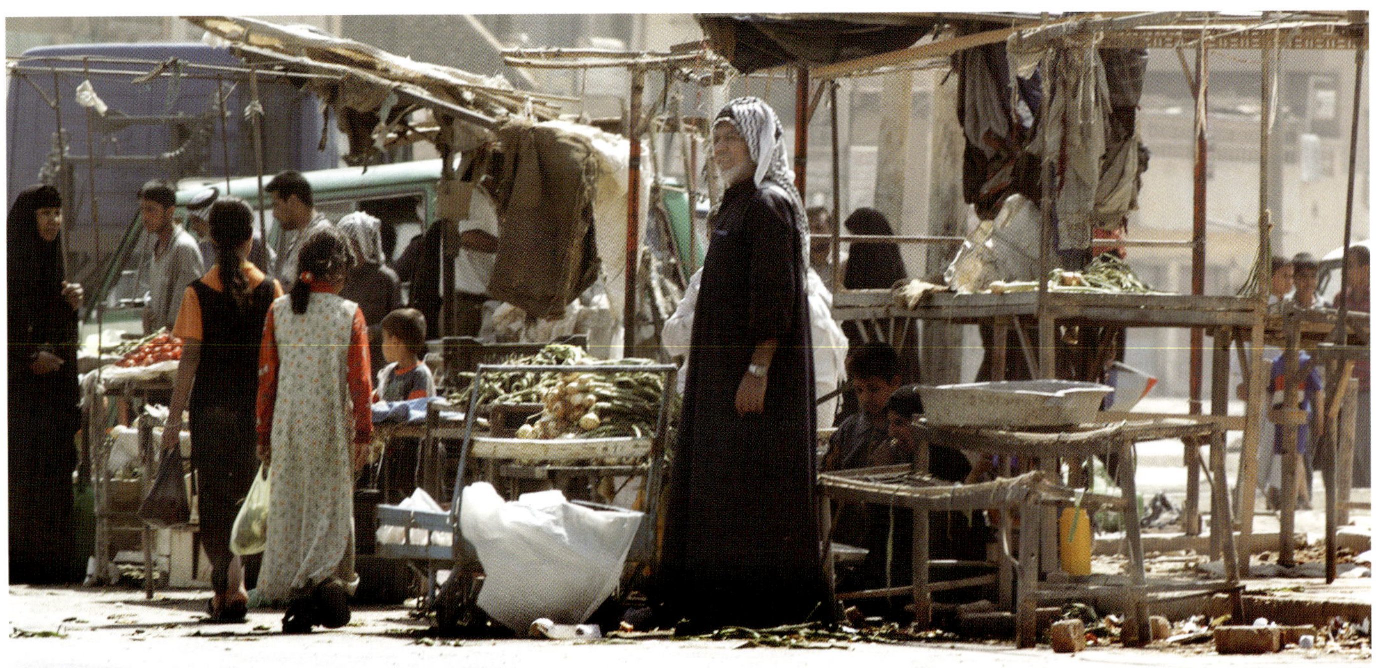

A vegetable stand in Saddam City offers little produce to those who can afford it

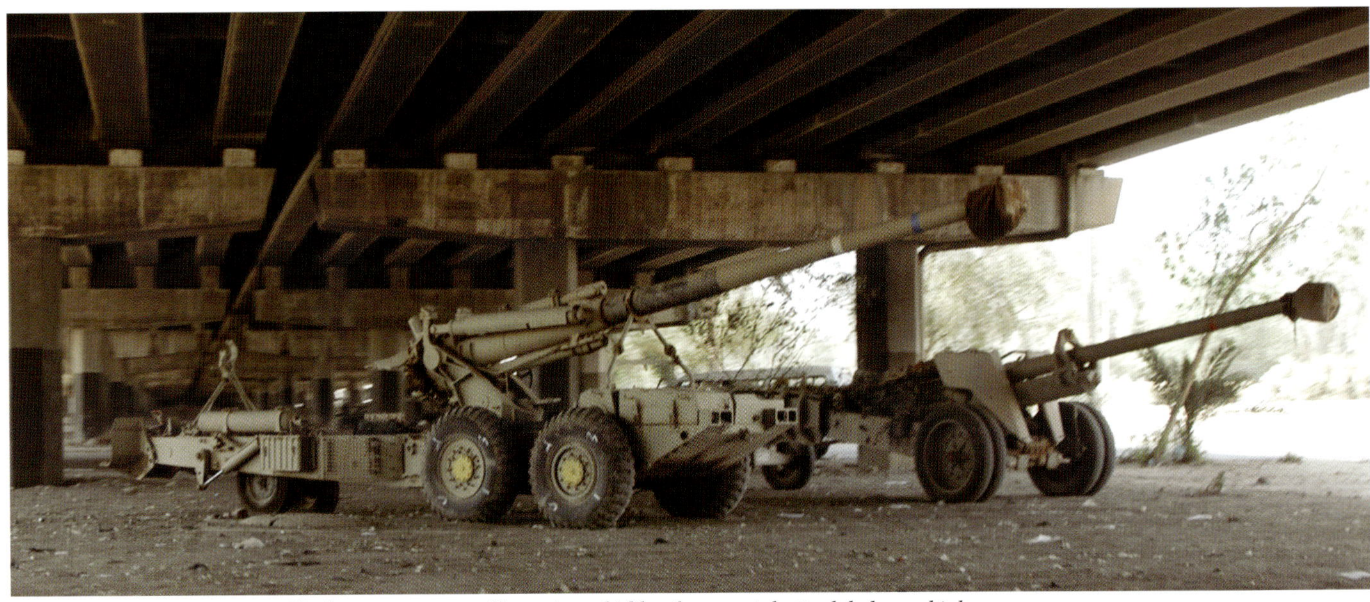

We drive past two artillery pieces hidden from aerial attack below a highway overpass

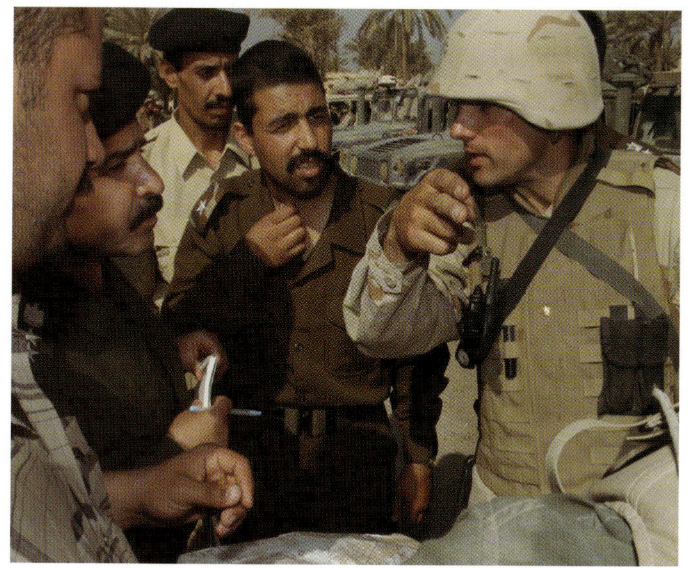

Iraqi police and Marines discuss the patrol routes

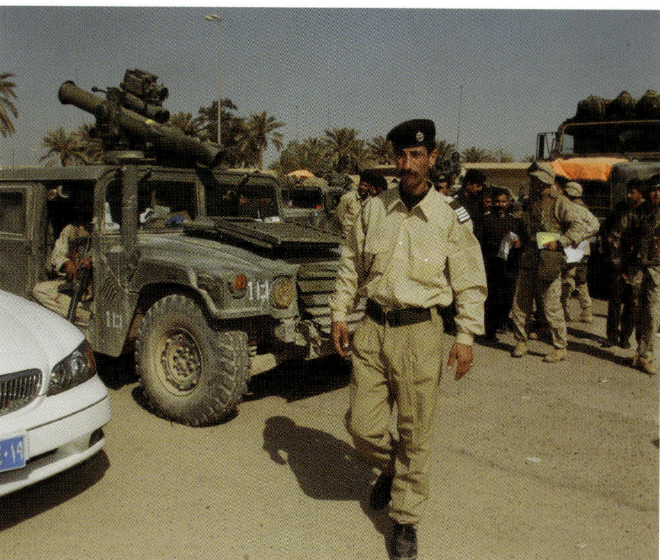

An Iraqi policeman wears his new uniform

exhaust spewing cars. Sheep and goats stand tied on top of fetid mounds of rotting garbage, forage for edible tidbits. This is the city of the poor. Shoeless children chase each other through the muck and open pools of sewage.

On each side of the main road running into Saddam City, I see three masked men with AK-47s in their hands. They are standing on some oil drums with religious slogans hanging above them. They are dressed completely in black, including a black hood, with a green bandanna wrapped around the head. They do not notice us in our taxi, but I notice them, and we pass by quickly without incident. Had they seen us, it might have been different. They were a group of well-organized, scary-looking individuals, rather than a local citizens' vigilante force. They are trying to control who enters the city.

We stay at the officer's home for an hour or more then head back to the Fanar. Although Tod and Jim got some good notes from the officer, there were no visuals for me to photograph. So it was a bit of a wasted morning, but it was refreshing to meet with the locals, especially the children. Away from the main road running through Saddam City, there are some simple but well-maintained properties, compared to the squalor of the status quo.

On Sunday evening we heard rumors that the Marines would team up and go on patrols with former members and new recruits of the new Baghdad Police Force. We didn't know if this was going to happen or not, as there is so much misinformation being passed about. There is no real updated local news, except for hearsay, so we have to screen fact from fiction. Following a false lead would be a waste of time and could put us in a dangerous situation. The combined patrols is just one of the many stories we heard being thrown around.

Thinking we would check this lead out, at about 1 p.m., Tish, Sean, Tod, Jim and I hire a taxi and drive to the building housing the former Baghdad Police Academy, where the Marines were to meet the police. This is the first step in implementing a new and credible police force, which had disbanded after the bombing of Baghdad had started. They will eventually be responsible for policing Baghdad, or so it is hoped. This will allow the Marines to continue to place all their effort into the war at hand, rather than being relegated to the duties of a police force. It is hoped that the initial presence of the Marines on the police patrols will give the new Iraqi force credibility and visible support.

There are no other journalists at the Academy. It looks as though we have an exclusive on the start of the patrols. After showing our press passes to Marine sentries, we are allowed onto the parade square of the Academy. We are asked to speak with Marine Major Petrucci, assistant operations officer of the Regimental Combat Team 7. He is the go-between for the Marines and police.

The parade square is a hive of activity as a hundred police officers walk in and out of the academy building, clutching plastic packages with brand-new police uniforms. New cops tuck in their crisp shirts while talking with veteran colleagues. Others don their new green police jackets and gather in small groups, getting their patrol instructions from their officers. Some are dressed and waiting in cherry-topped police cruisers. Police and Marine officers pore over maps of Baghdad, pointing out their routes and going over last-minute details. Meanwhile, a dozen Humvees and personnel wait for instructions, watching all the hustle from the middle of the parade square.

The five of us meander over to the officers meeting over the maps. I introduce myself and my colleagues then ask Major Petrucci about the possibility of going out on a Humvee to photograph the new joint operation. Surprisingly, the major tells me he will try his best to get us teamed up with a patrol, but he can't guarantee all three of us will get to go out. We are told to be patient, and that he will speak with the drivers to see if they would mind us going with them. Jim and Tod will follow in the taxi, and cover the public's reaction to the dual force as it patrols.

Petrucci tells me he is happy to see some media at the launch of the patrols, as it is important to show this type of dual cooperation being implemented.

We are milling about watching and photographing the activity when Petrucci walks over to us and tells Tish she has a ride in a Humvee. He escorts her to one of the vehicles and introduces her to its four-man crew. Tish beams with excitement as she hops in, ready to go on her first patrol; it is 2:30 p.m.

I jokingly ask Petrucci if the crew that Tish is teamed with is his favorite crew. Catching on, he laughs then winks at me. Some of the Marines have not been this close to a woman in months. I feel so happy to see her happy! The boys lucked-out too, they would have the company of an energetic, intelligent, and pretty journalist.

Moments later Sean is set up in another Humvee. I stand alone thinking I might get left behind, as the parade square empties fast. Finally Petrucci comes over and tells me I'm in luck, "We found you a Humvee." I am directed over to my crew, the Chicano Humvee. All four crewmembers are Spanish-speaking Americans. During the patrol they mostly speak English, with a smattering of Spanish. They are in their late teens and early twenties, and represent the changing face of America; Hispanic Americans from all corners of the country. It isn't a white man's army anymore – but a rainbow army.

Once again, it is a burning hot day, and the plastic water bottles roll under my feet as I sit in the back seat, encased in a shell of armor plate and bulletproof glass. We wait at the Academy gates for the green light to move out. We drive off with an escort of two police cars, sandwiched between a second rear Humvee.

The small convoy drives through the streets of Baghdad, the gunner sitting in his pulpit, hands clenching the handles of the 50-calibre machine gun. There is a driver and a navigator sitting up front with assault rifles cradled across their laps. Another Marine is seated across from me in the back seat.

We stop at the front door of the smoldering Commercial Bank of Baghdad. The Marines jump out and grab a looter leaving the bank. They frisk him and find nothing, but he tells them there are others inside the bank. I grab the gas mask from this mans face and follow a Marine into the smoking bank with the mask on my face and camera ready. We move slowly across the debris-cluttered first floor. We can't see more than a few feet ahead because of thick smoke and decide to head out. This is a good idea, as we know the looters have gas masks, which make them capable of ambushing us in the choking darkness.

Strewn about the street outside the bank lie identification cards, burned Iraqi money, broken safety deposit boxes, paperwork and strips of historic film showing Albert Einstein meeting world leaders (around the time of the Second World War). It is all under our feet and across the roadway, probably discarded from someone's safety deposit box, now empty on the curb. I consider keeping some of the film, but decide not to. One of the Marines throws a four-foot strip of the rare film into the back of our vehicle.

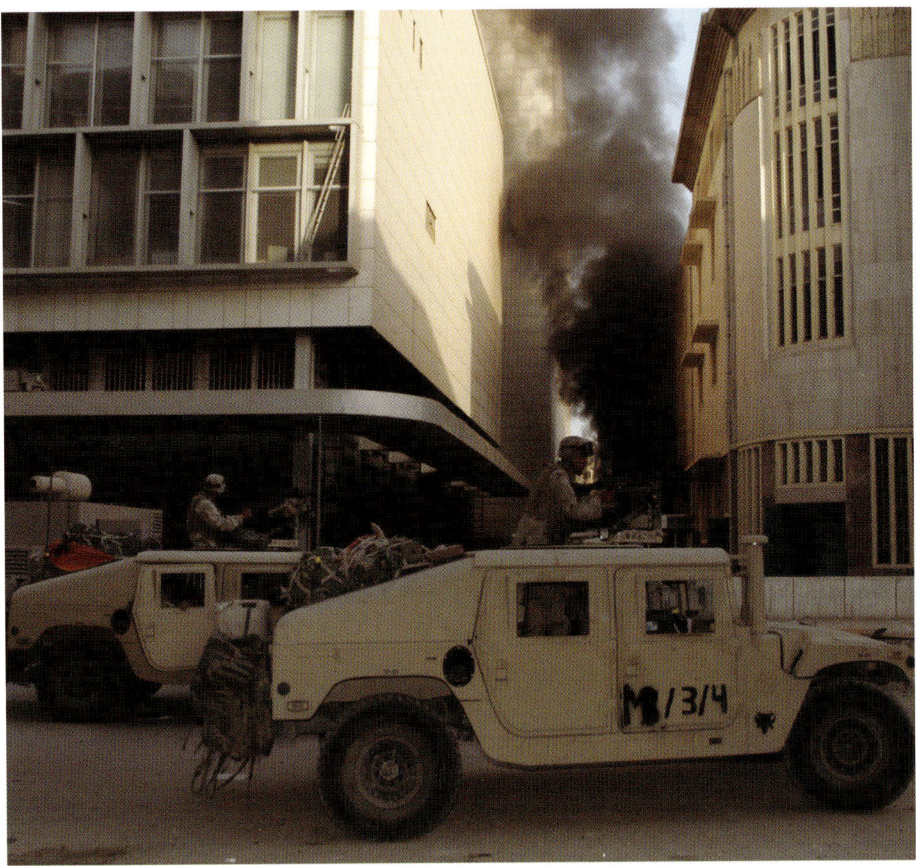

Humvees patrol Baghdad streets to a backdrop of burning buildings

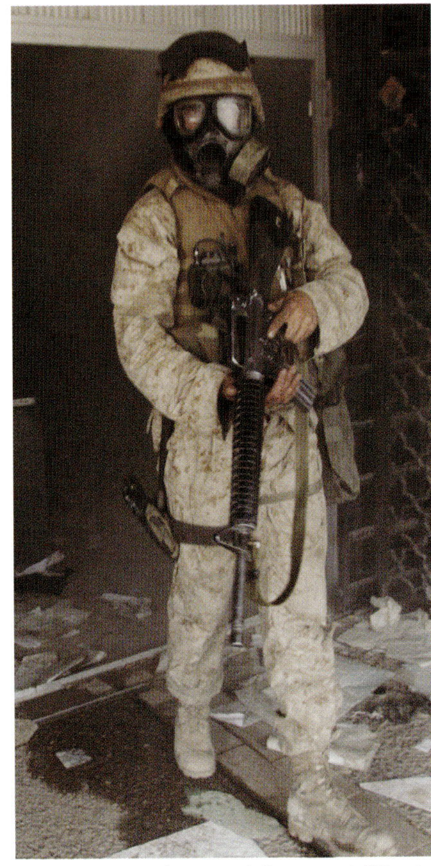

Marine exits the gutted Commercial Bank

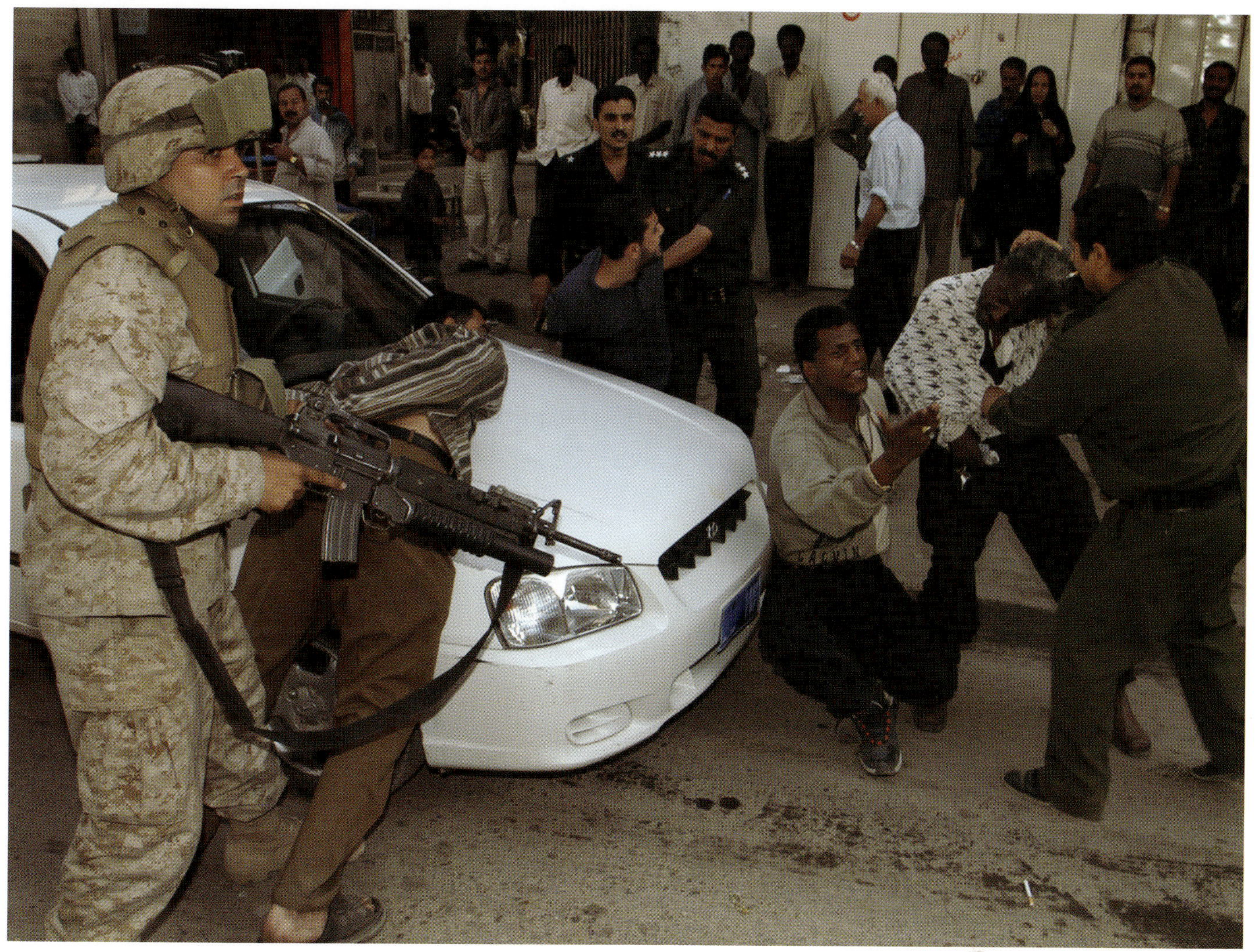

Iraqi police manhandle suspected looters as a Marine pins one suspect to the hood of the police car

Continuing on, we drive off the main road and into a heavily populated area with narrow streets, lined with shops selling their meagre supplies of nuts, bottled sodas, cigarettes and strips of fly-covered goat meat. Many of the shop owners are just going through the motions of keeping their businesses open, to stay busy and keep their minds off their miseries.

I see the lead Humvee pull over onto the sidewalk and three of its crew (the driver remains at the wheel), jump out and dash over to assist the three police, who are out of their cars trying to contain four suspects (the two police cars had moved ahead of us while manoeuvring the streets). My crew jumps out with their weapons pointing in the direction of the large crowd that is gathering. The crowd is just curious, and want to see what the soldiers are doing in their neighborhood. I jump out and stand beside one of the Marines, who is keeping a close eye on the crowd and the rooftops.

The cops are grabbing the four middle-aged men and physically dragging them toward the squad car, while throwing punches and threatening to pistol-whip them. The suspects raise their hands in submission while pleading with the cops. They throw them up against the cruiser, continuing to slap them, while at the same time shouting questions at them.

One of the Marines grabs a suspect and throws him across the hood of a squad car where he pins him. The police corral the suspects into a tight circle of pleading, fearful men, their arms raised with open hands, begging not to be beaten. Moments later, the police are slapping the suspects on the back of the head, telling them they are free to go. The four men disappear into the crowd as we jump back into the vehicles. I don't know what the four were suspected of doing; the Marines were not sure either. But I guess the message was being sent out by the police to the public – we're back! And we have the Americans behind us!

This type of aggression seems to be the policing technique that works best here. In this country you are guilty until proven innocent. In Iraq, aggression is met with even greater aggression. This was how Saddam ran the country. He understood the way things work here – the bigger the gun, the more power you claim.

Our patrol leader instructs the crews to return to base to get heavier weaponry, after he overhears some civilians make threatening comments to his men while they were out of the Humvees handling the four suspects. Close to my truck I hear a civilian threatening a Marine, "We will be ready for you when you come back," says the elderly white-gowned man. The Marine, furious at the threats, climbs into the vehicle while mumbling under his breath to the crew, "I'm going to get me one of them bastards!" We drive out of the area, looking for more trouble.

Soon we are patrolling along the banks of the Tigris River, when the lead police car abruptly stops. The officers jump out and start running like impalas, with 9-mm pistols in their hands. They chase after some suspects, disappearing around a corner as the Marines and I jump out to pursue the police. We lose sight of them but soon find them a short distance from where we stopped. The cops are holding a suspect, slapping him across the back of the head while frisking him for cash or stolen weapons. The cops pull a fistful of Iraqi dinar from his jeans. The man pleads with the police that the money is his and it is all he has. The Marines stand near the cops with their weapons pointing outwards towards the buildings and alleyways, ready for reprisal. The police reconsider, seemingly convinced that this man had done nothing wrong and let him go.

We walk along the riverfront where the police grab a couple of men sitting on the riverbank who are drunk on white gin. A couple of slaps and a thorough frisking and these drunks are released, but not before the cops break their bottle of gin. We walk along eyeing the rooftops and alleyways lining the shore, wary of a possible sniper attack from overhanging buildings. Turning away from the riverbank and into

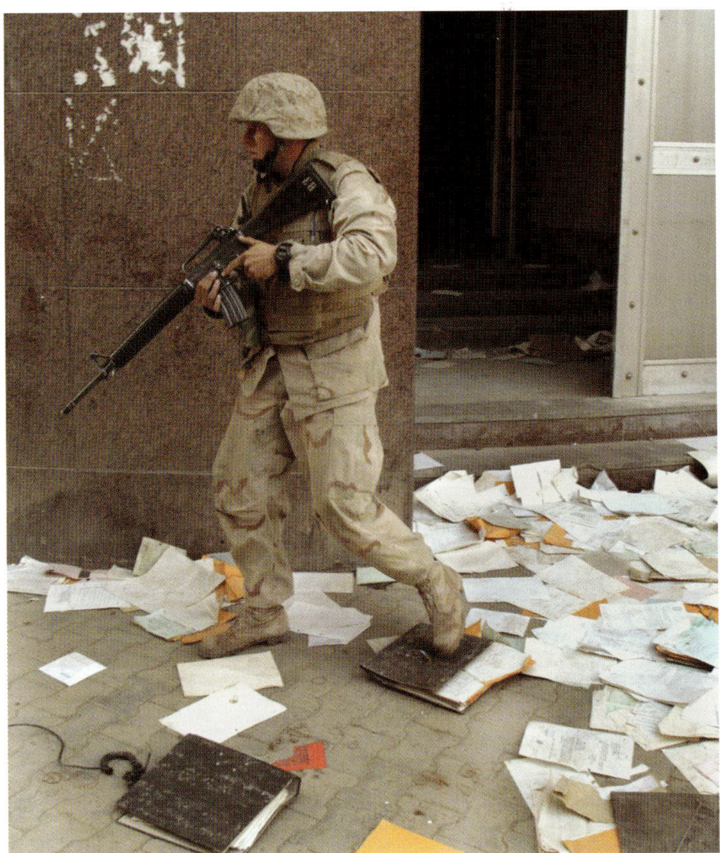

Marine checking bank for looters

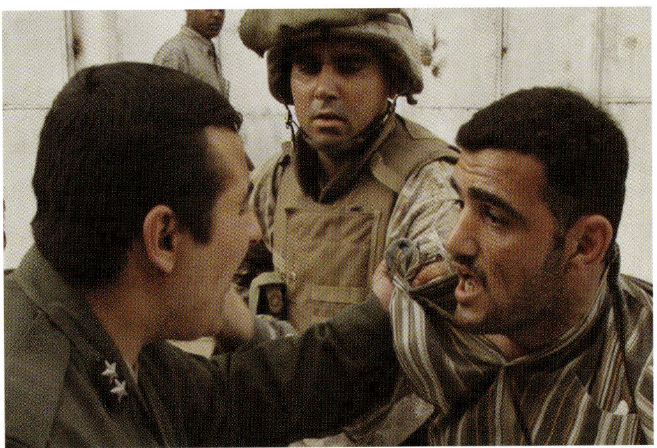

In Iraq, you are guilty until proven innocent

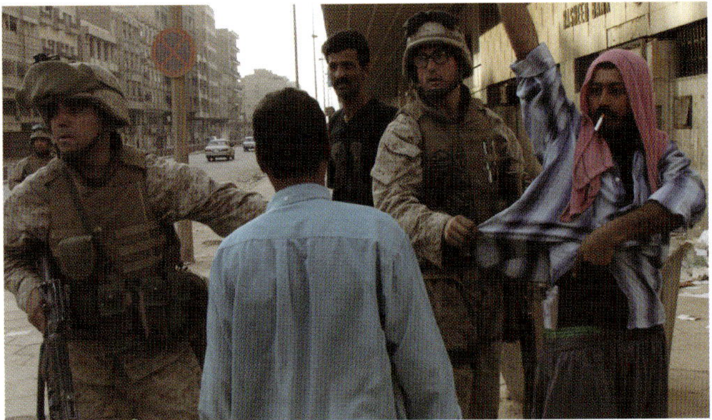

Catching a looter at the Rasheed Bank

an alleyway surrounded by shabby buildings and piles of rotting garbage, the police and Marines start talking with an elderly man in a black Arabic gown.

He tells the Marines that the same looter he saw yesterday robbing the Central Bank of Baghdad, has returned to loot the bank again. His face is painted in disgust as he tells us that most people in the neighborhood believe this man has stolen nearly one million dollars in U.S. and Iraqi currency from this institution. This is not inconceivable – everything is wide open – banks and every other institution. All you need are big balls and you can get rich fast. I am sure that paupers became millionaires overnight from emptying banks.

We drive off looking for the Central Bank, but before we reach it, we stop at the Rasheed Bank. A Marine jumps out of the Humvee and runs over to a man leaving the bank. The Marine holds him until one of the policemen comes over and starts frisking him. The looter has a bundle of Iraqi dinar in one hand, which he hands to the police. The cop slaps the man and a heated argument breaks out. He slaps him again after finding another cash bundle tucked into his shirt. After making sure that the man is not holding any more cash, the cop belts him across the face one last time and tells him to get out of the area. The man staggers off into one of the alleyways as the Marines toss the two bundles of dinar into the back of the Humvee, and we move on. The value of both these bundles of cash would be about $30, or around two to three months' wages to the average Iraqi. So there is a fortune to be made by looting, if you don't get ripped-off by another looter.

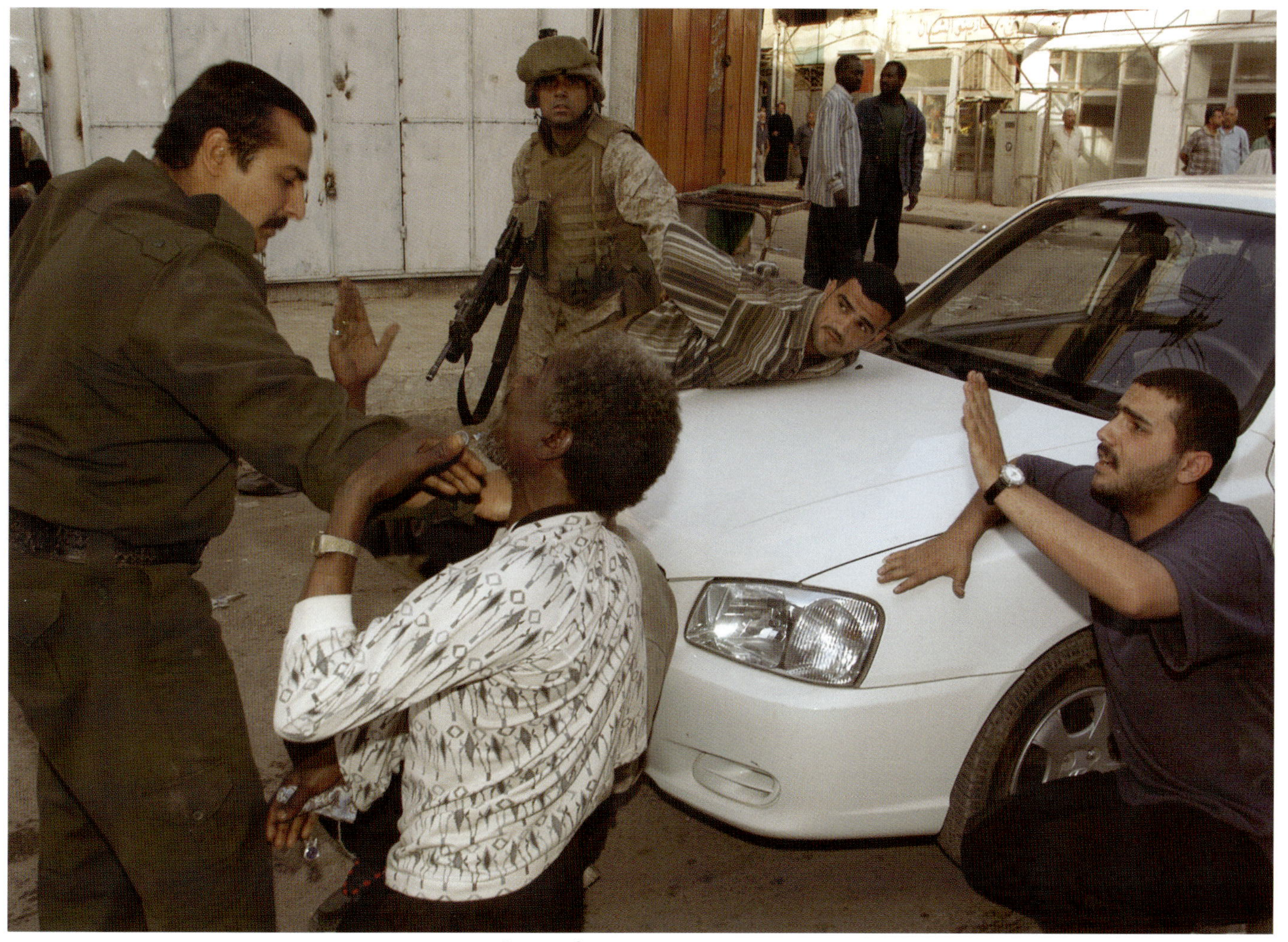

Iraqi police interrogate suspects

The sun is just starting to set as we see our target meters ahead – the Central Bank of Baghdad, Iraq's largest bank. There are people running in and out of the front entranceway of the bank and disappearing into a nearby alleyway. The police are the first to jump from their vehicles. They sprint towards the bank like crazed lunatics, their pistols flailing in their hands. They disappear chasing the looters down the alley flanking the bank, where I can hear the crack of small-arms fire.

As we climb out of our Humvee, a Marine loses his patience with the police tactics and starts cursing them for being so maverick. "These fools are not only risking their own lives, they're risking ours. We are supposed to be working as a team." The cops are acting like Superman, showing no fear while running toward the gunfire.

Seconds later a cop reappears from the alley, telling us the obvious, "Some of the looters are armed!" I follow tight behind the lead Marine, using him as a shield, or blocker, should some gunfire come our way.

We are just 50 feet away when we see a group of eight looters running out of the bank's front door, heading for the alleyway. The looters, suddenly seeing us approaching, are startled, and bolt back and forth in front of the bank like horses spooked by a fire, looking for somewhere to escape. The lead Marine, who I am following, drops into a squat position on one knee, points his weapon (an M249 Light Machine Gun) at the looters and shouts at them to stop and lie down on the ground or he will open fire; but they continue running. The Marine snaps his weapon tight into his shoulder and fires a short, three-second blast from it. The bullets burst like a chain of firecrackers, a foot above the panicked looters' heads. The hollow sound of the echoing gunfire rebounds along the darkening, surreal Baghdad street. The robbers duck low, trying to avoid their death, but one of the bullets ricochets downwards, burying itself in the head of one of the looters. He drops like a rock, his face crashing into the cement sidewalk, his arms involuntarily jerking and his fingers twitching at his sides. Seconds later, the looter lies dead, facedown in a spreading pool of dark, oozing blood.

I hurry over with the lead Marine, sticking to his side like a shadow (though avoiding touching him). He nudges the body of the dead looter with the muzzle-end of his weapon. The looter is stone-cold dead; his life has become as germane as the piles of stinking garbage that line the cavernous streets. He is a well-dressed, large man, and by all appearances, looks as though he could have worked at this bank in more stable times.

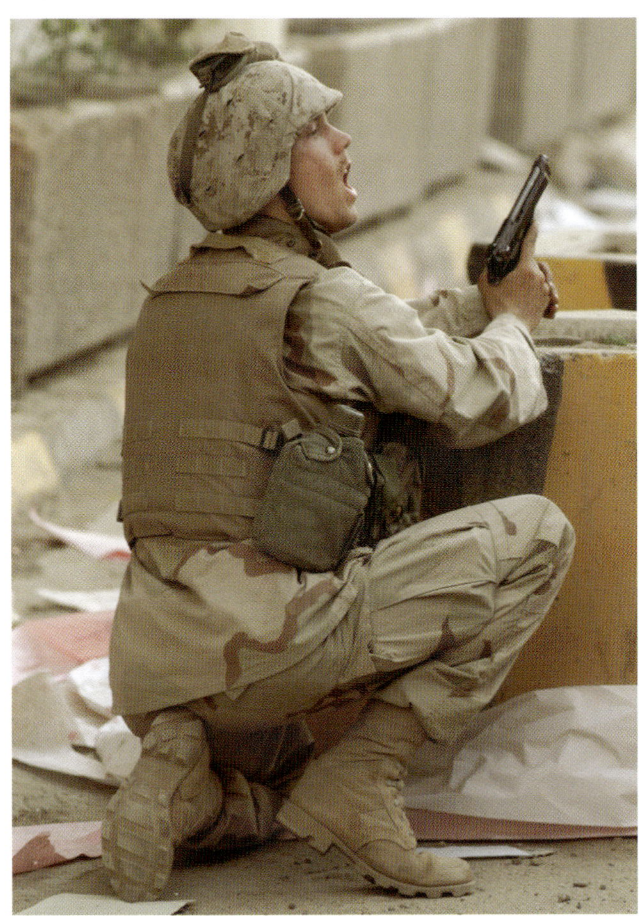

Marine covers his comrades during a street patrol

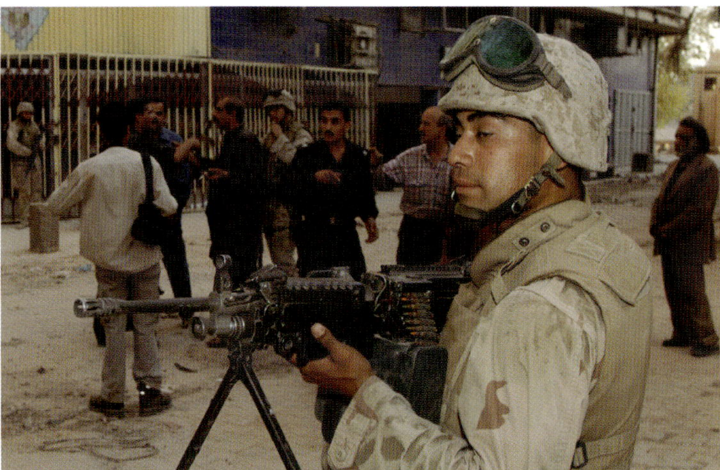

Marines and police check neighborhood near the Central Bank of Baghdad

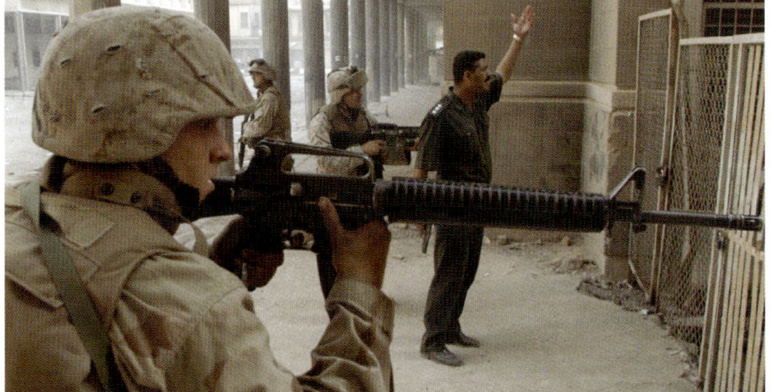

The patrol plays a game of cat-and-mouse with the looters

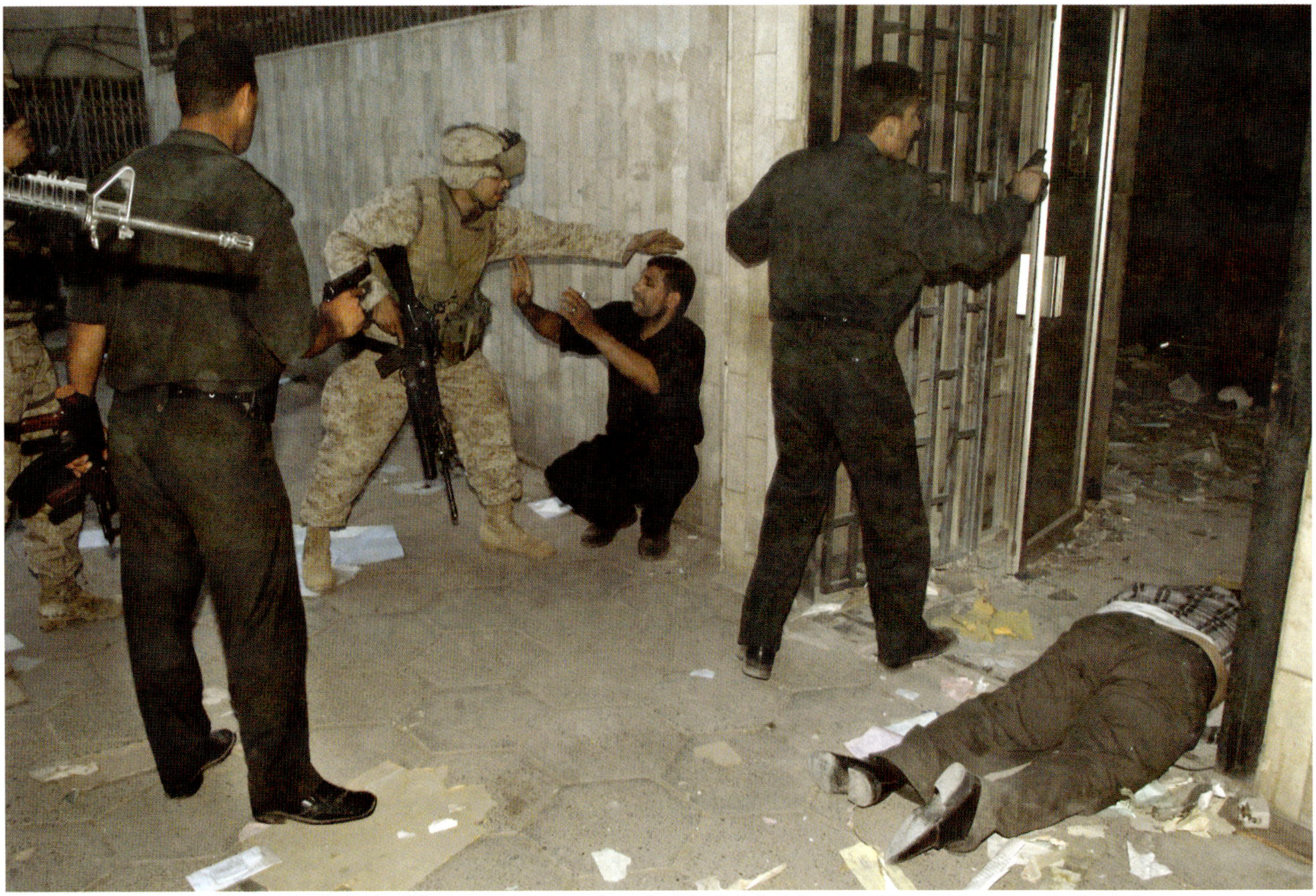

A panicked looter pleads for his life outside the Central Bank of Baghdad while a dead looter lies across the bank doorway

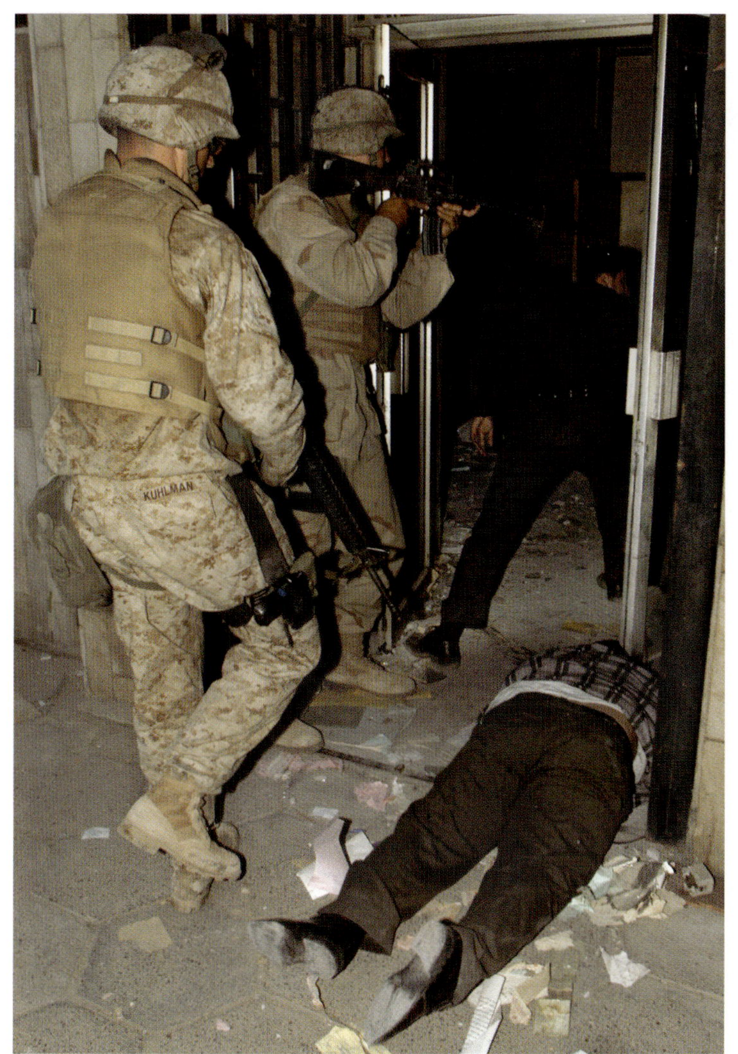

Marines and police search the Central Bank for looters

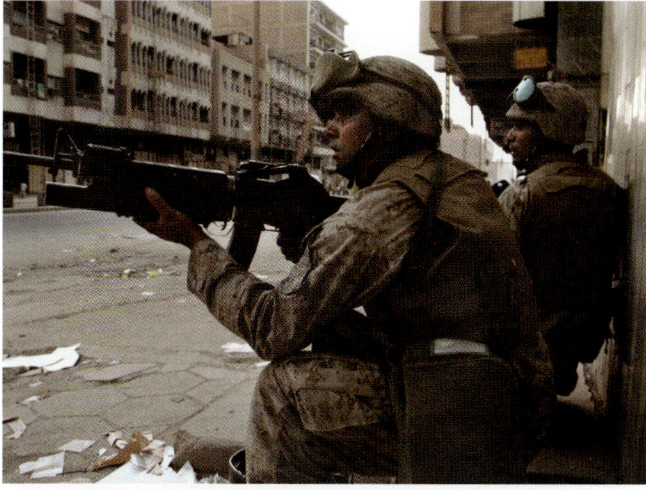

Marines cover the entranceway of the Central Bank

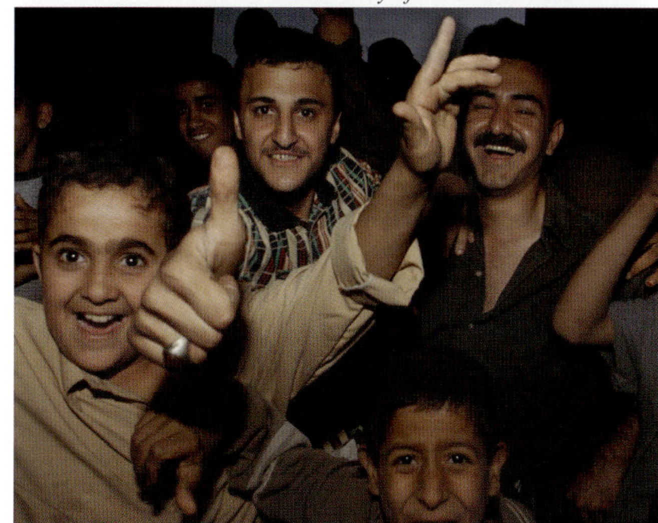

Iraqis celebrate the killing of a looter

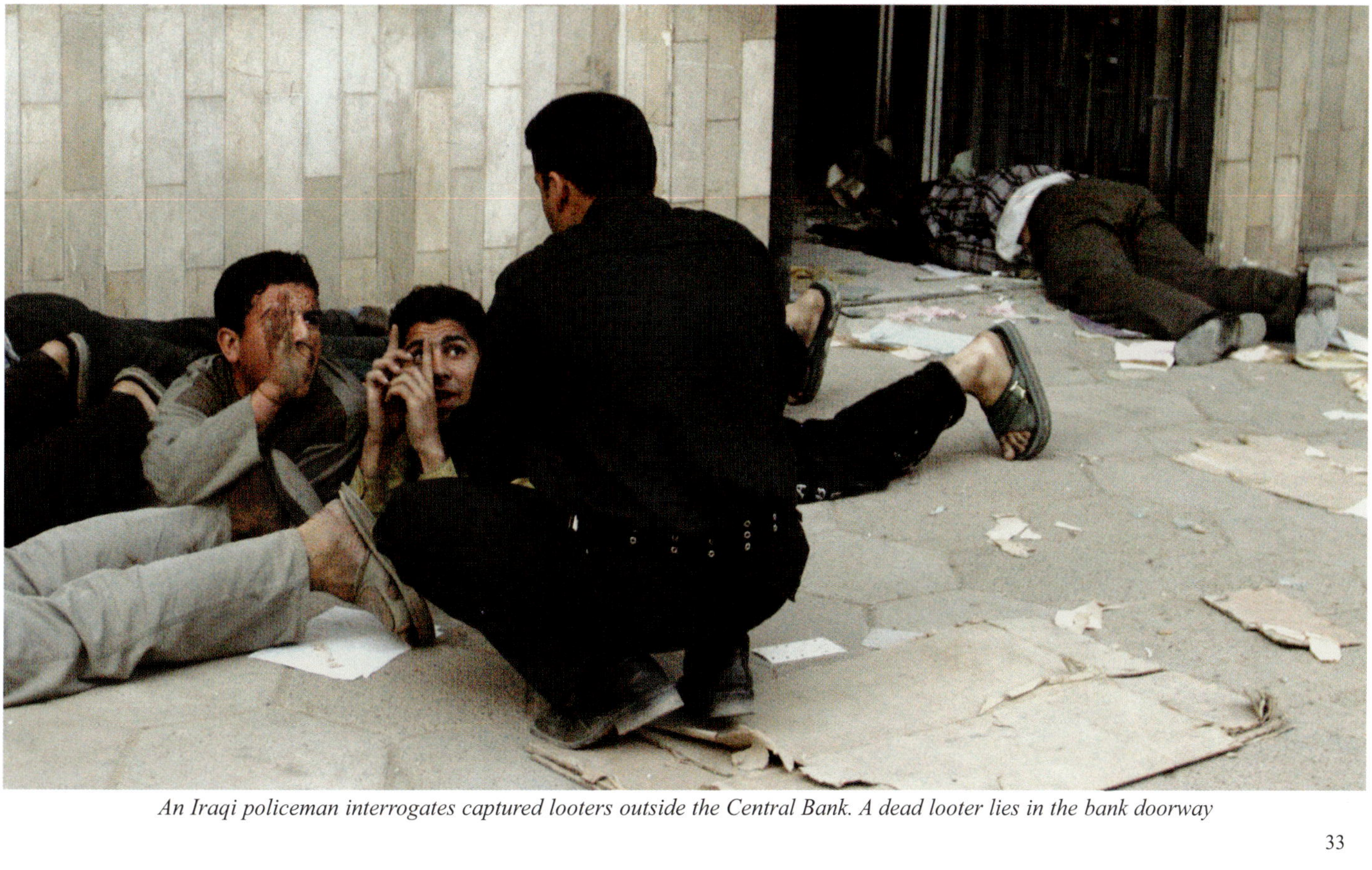

An Iraqi policeman interrogates captured looters outside the Central Bank. A dead looter lies in the bank doorway

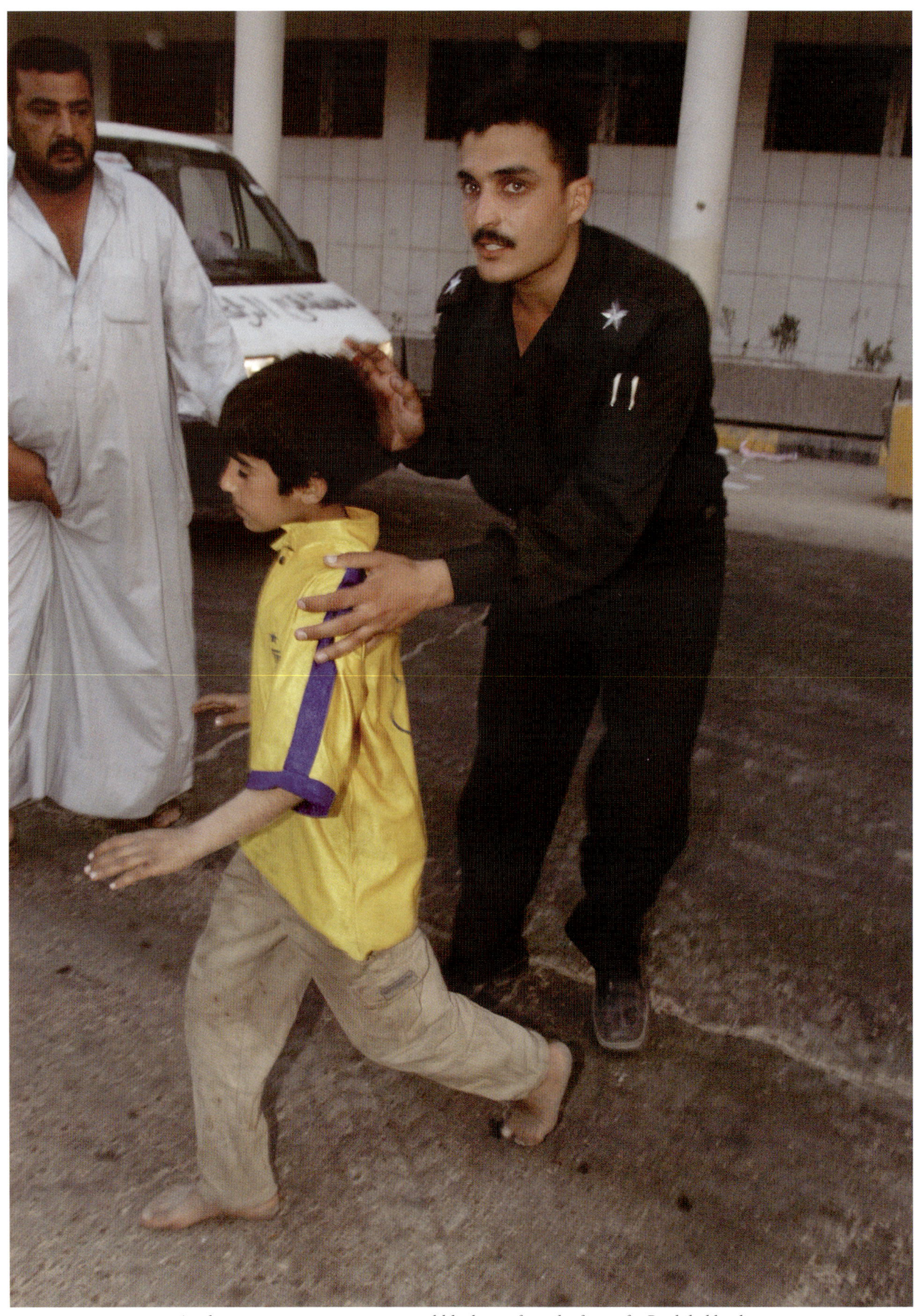

A policeman turns away a young would-be looter from the front of a Baghdad bank

One of the cops shouts for the Marines to come to the side alleyway, saying he spotted a looter carrying an AK-47. The Marines, four of whom are now in front of the bank, start running toward the alleyway when I hear muffled voices and commotion coming from inside the bank entranceway. I shout to the Marines in a hushed voice. "Marine," then motioning to my ear and pointing to the bank doors I say, "there are more inside!"

Two Marines immediately return with two cops. All four, with weapons at the ready, step over the corpse (being careful not to get any blood on the soles of their boots), and walk into the darkened, smoke-choked bank. Seconds later they reappear from the smoke escorting six looters. The startled robbers have their hands raised in the air, pleading for their lives, as they step over the body of their dead colleague. The look on their faces is of primeval fear, as they glance down at the body.

Once outside the bank they are pushed to the ground, and the Marines return to the alley to search for weapons. The police start to interrogate the thieves, who are all flat on their bellies, crying hysterically with hands raised, and tears of fear rolling down their smoke-blackened faces. A couple of the captives are so fearful that they piss their pants, and the smell of fresh urine and burning paper hangs suspended in the thick twighlight air. It is a brutal scene. One cop is threatening to pistol-whip one of the captured looters, who has became completely hysterical and cannot stop crying and pleading for his life. A Marine comes over and pushing his rifle muzzle into the thief's cheek, tells him to "Shut up or die!" This is going on while gunshots are heard coming from the alleyway. The looters are frisked and roughed-up by the police, then told to get lost. They all run off into the darkness, some with their pants stained, but all lucky to be alive. There are no operating prisons or jails in Baghdad that could hold the thousands of looters, so they have to be freed (very probably to loot again).

With the situation under relative control, I walk over to the Marine who shot the looter. He is crouching down in the ready position covering the alleyway. I put my hand on his shoulder and say to him in a comforting tone, "Good job soldier, good job!" He looks up, and nods. Soon after, the other Marines go over and comfort the soldier, who appears to be in a momentary daze or shock.

The word is given to return to the Humvees, and we hustle cautiously and at the ready, back across the street to the vehicles. By this time, darkness has fully set in, and a large crowd of civilians has gathered around the Humvees and police cars. Getting closer to the vehicles, I judge that we are about to be attacked by the mob as they squeeze closer to the vehicles and us. We jump into the Humvees, the Marines pointing their weapons out toward the crowd, who now surround the vehicles. "This is going to get really ugly," I say to myself. But to our astonishment, the throng breaks into simultaneous applause, while chanting, "USA – George Bush – USA – George Bush!"

The crowd surges even closer, offering their outstretched hands in thanks to the Marines, police and myself. Their outpouring of gratitude is extremely moving and spontaneous. Shaking the crowd's grasping hands with one hand, I take photos through the window with the camera grasped in the other.

We drive off into the falling darkness, with the crowd still chanting, "George Bush – USA – George Bush – USA." It is a stunning surprise to me that these people are cheering, while the looter lies dead across the street. But they, like most Iraqis, just want what we have – to be able to control the destiny of their own lives. They don't want these thieves sucking the life out of their country's financial institutions, or any other business. These are the real voices of Iraq, though they are not heard through the anarchy, power grabbing and lawlessness that dominates this drowning nation.

As we drive off, one of the Marines asks another if he saw the looter with the AK-47 running from the bank, just before the shooting started. He replies, "Yeah, I saw the son-of-a-bitch with the AK." Another voice from the darkness of the back seat also replies, "Yeah. I saw it too." The driver turns to me and asks if I saw the AK. "Oh yeah, I saw it," I tell him.

But there was no AK in the looter's hands. I was up close and right behind the lead man who fired at the looters; I can still see it all as plainly as if it happened this morning. I am willing to give the Marines the benefit of the doubt because at the time it was getting dark and there was a lot happening, especially when the shots were fired. But regardless, I did not see the AK-47, and I have damn-good eyes.

The death was an accident; I saw the bullet flash down into the looter's head. Perhaps the Marine felt he may be disciplined for shooting an unarmed man, therefore the "ghost" gun scenario clears everyone from fault.

Fifteen minutes later we rendezvous with Major Petrucci, who is just finishing loading confiscated currency into the safe of a closed restaurant. This cash is from all the patrols that day, and a guard team is posted to guard the safe. Petrucci pulls me aside to ask my opinion of what happened during the shooting. I tell him what he wants to hear: "The Marine acted professionally, with his colleagues' and the police patrol's safety in mind." I reiterate that "This Marine, may have saved my life and quite possibly other lives by responding as quickly as he did." I give the Major the story he wanted to hear – with a cherry on top. I don't want to see this soldier disciplined for accidentally shooting the thieving bloodsucker. The looter took the gamble of robbing a bank – and ended up being dealt a dead man's hand.

With the patrol over, I return to the Fanar to meet the crew over dinner. We talk animatedly about the highlights of our patrols and the Humvee crews. Everyone had a great experience, and some exclusive material. Tish is writing a humorous piece in the New York Observer about her Humvee crew getting lost. Jim and Tod got their story of citizens' response to the patrols. Sean shot some great film of his patrol. It was a memorable day.

Later in the evening, I wait in the Fanar to transmit two pics of the bank shooting to North America, but the guy who has been letting me send photos on his satellite dish is too busy to give me time on his system. In a panic, I head over to the Palestine and ask if anyone can transmit my two best photos, or if anyone wants to buy them. It is nearly 11 p.m. and I am in a major rush to get the material aired. Finally I end up at the office of Associated Press. I ask to speak with the photo boss and tell him about my photos. He loads them into the computer, saying he likes them and will take both, for $50 each. Realizing that it is late and that I want the pics to go on the newswire, I agree, and the photos are sent to New York. It is a paltry amount to be paid for the news value of the two photos, considering that they might have cost me my life. But I know where not to bring my photos next time. He pays me in cash and I leave for the Fanar – it's nearly 1:00 a.m. What a day!

Day 6. Tuesday, April 15th

(City is a journalist's dream; team leaves on day trip to Tikrit; the Black Hole; destruction at the North Gate; irrigation ditches; the stench of decomposing human flesh; body parts in pickup truck; latex gloves; weapons market in Samarra; ten-year-old arms dealer; lawless hell pit; start a private war; Saddam's holy mural; palace compound looks like a huge prison; visiting Saddam's palace compound; soldiers hung-over from violence of battle; Tikrit the ghost town; meeting Canadian photographer Kevin Frayer; red sandstorm; Tang and candy bars)

At around 9:00 a.m., the four other team members and I sit in the Fanar dining room going over the possible news stories of the day, or situations that we feel will become news. The dining room is full of journalists and NGO people going over their plans. There are numerous leads and hypotheses. In fact, there is enough happening all around us that we do not need to watch news broadcasts to know what needs to be covered. I personally do not monitor the news broadcasts. If you can't go out and find your own news, you shouldn't be here. The city is a journalist's dream.

We decide to go for a drive to Tikrit, the birthplace and hometown of Saddam, a two-hour drive north of the city. The town had just fallen to the American Forces yesterday.

About twenty minutes north of the Fanar, in the middle of a residential neighborhood in Ad Gahreb, we drive past a huge black crater and the twisted and pulverized remains of two or three Iraqi transport trucks and what could have been a tank. The vehicles, parked right alongside a row of duplexes, were bombed by the Americans because they were being used to store munitions. All the homes near the site have been hit heavily by the afterblast, and are missing entire walls and roofs. Even the palm trees are burned and blackened, like burnt wooden match sticks. A group of white-gowned men sit in the middle of the blast site drinking chai. The starkness of the white on black, is a scene I will not soon forget and would have made an absolutely incredible photo, had we time to stop. It is a site of horrible destruction where upwards

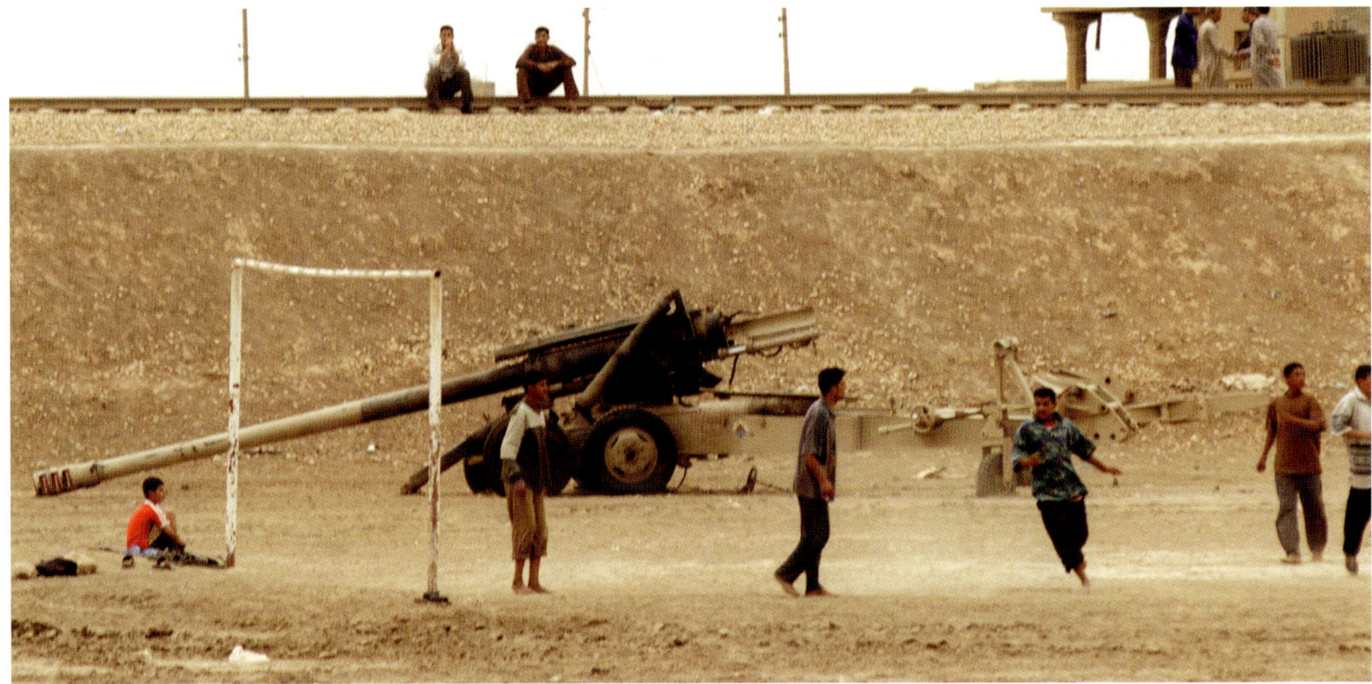

Teenagers share the soccer field with an artillery piece near Ad Dawar

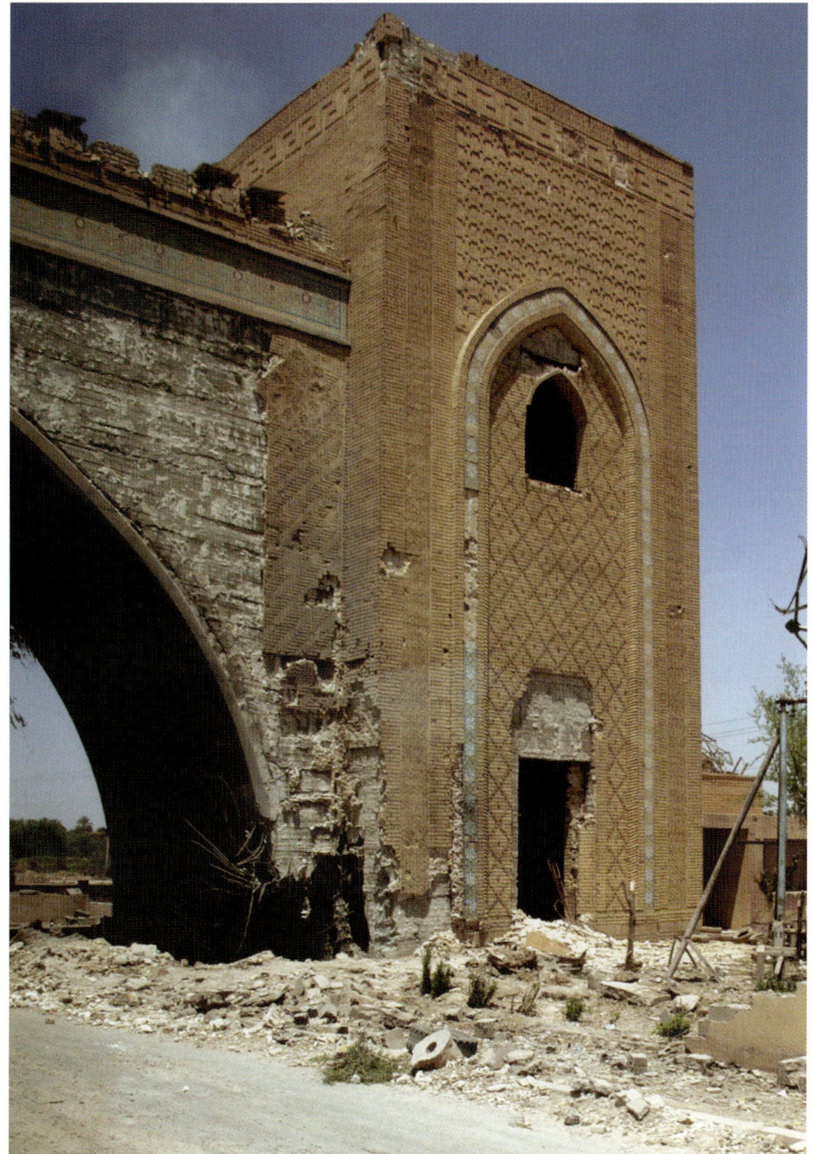

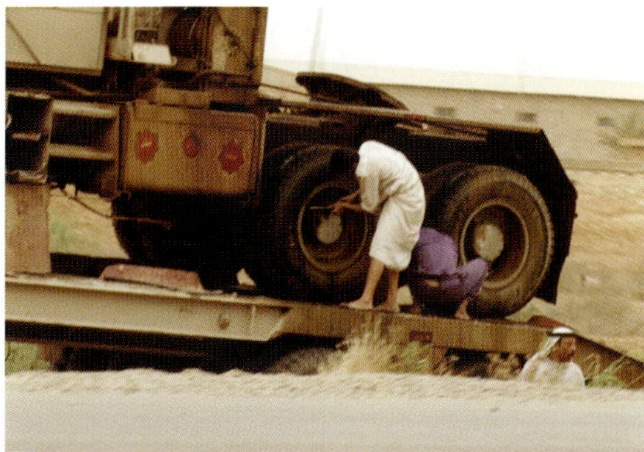

Looters strip a truck on the highway to Tikrit

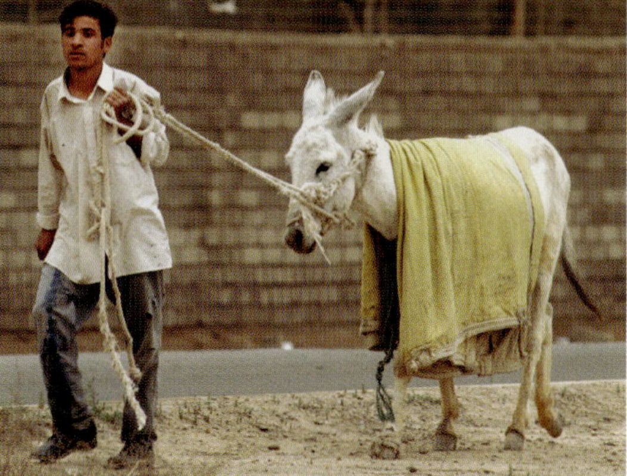

A boy leads a donkey near Tikrit

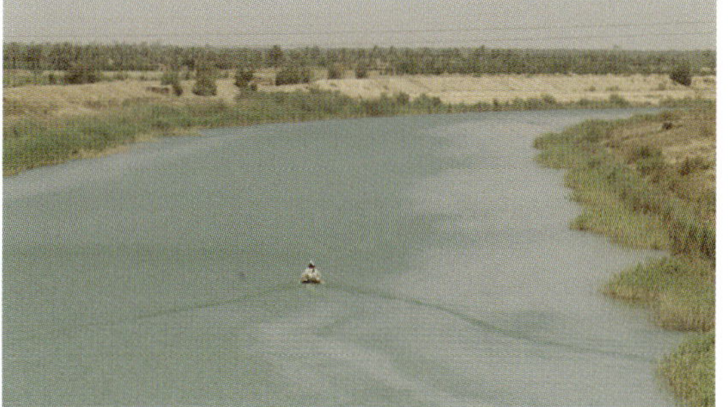

The Tigris River north of Baghdad

Baghdad's North Gate damaged by fighting

of twenty residents were killed. I will have to come back at some point and grab some pics. I nickname it the Black Hole.

Once out of town we drive through the North Gate (45 minutes from the Fanar), the last line of defense for Saddam's Baghdad. A massive amount of military hardware lies destroyed or abandoned by the sides of the road and in the outlying fields. Multiple rocket-launching vehicles, artillery pieces, tanks, APCs, and a host of various support trucks and tankers, lie smashed and useless. Scavengers are going through the vehicles looking for articles to sell or keep for themselves. It is an ugly site of untold horrors and I get the shivers just imagining what must have happened here.

The area north of Baghdad comprises farmlands and clusters of farm buildings, with patches of isolated greenery lining the irrigation canals along the edge of the highway. Most of the irrigated fields lie withering and parched in the relentlessly burning sun. A mangy dog pauses long enough to look up at us, then continues biting into the carcass of a dead cow, lying bloated and eviscerated in a roadside field.

Tanks and APCs lie overturned and smoldering in the deep irrigation ditches, barely visible due to the high-growing reeds that line them. The stench of decomposing human flesh coming from the ruined vehicles is overpowering and horrendous. We cover our mouths with our handkerchiefs, trying to avoid breathing in the sickening reek.

As our cab drives onward, I catch a glimpse of an unsettling scene in the back of a Toyota pickup at the side of the road. In the truck bed lie a human hand, arms, legs, torsos and other body parts. Near the edge of the rushes, white-gowned men wearing facemasks and latex gloves spread open the reeds, looking for destroyed vehicles holding human remains. I am the only one in the cars to see this, but due to the road being only a dirt two-lane highway and packed with traffic, we can't stop to photograph the recovery scene. I am also in a bit of shock from seeing the grisly scene, and it takes me 30 seconds to snap out of it. The flashback will remain in my head for a long time.

Somewhere on the road to Tikrit, about an hour out of Baghdad, we take a wrong turn and end up on a dusty road with heavy traffic. Refugees packed into overloaded trucks are coming from the north, heading south towards Baghdad.

Many people are walking with bundles on their backs. A heavy talcum-powder-like dust bursts up from the passing cars and trucks, covering the road in a brown foggy haze and coating everything inside the car. I keep my camera covered with a cloth or bandanna, as the dust finds its way into every crack and crevice.

We enter into the tiny adobe mud-brick village of Samarra, packed with traffic, shoppers and vendors. People have set up shop right along the main village street and are selling everything from green beans to portable RPG launchers. AK-47s lie on the ground, stacked like firewood and ready for sale. Grenades, bayonets, pistols, sniper rifles and military clothing lie in heaps, with vendors hawking them to the passers-by. Most of the weaponry looks richly colored and brand new, like the sniper rifles that are propped up for viewing in their bright wooden packing boxes

A young boy of about 10 walks through the bustling market with two bayonets crossed and tucked into his belt. An RPG is slung over each of his shoulders. He is an infant weapons dealer! Potential buyers are test firing the new AKs and other weapons, shooting them into the air of the crowded market. What a scene; it's the Wild Wild West!

We get stuck in a small traffic jam at a "T" in the dusty road of the village. I start feeling claustrophobic and exposed,

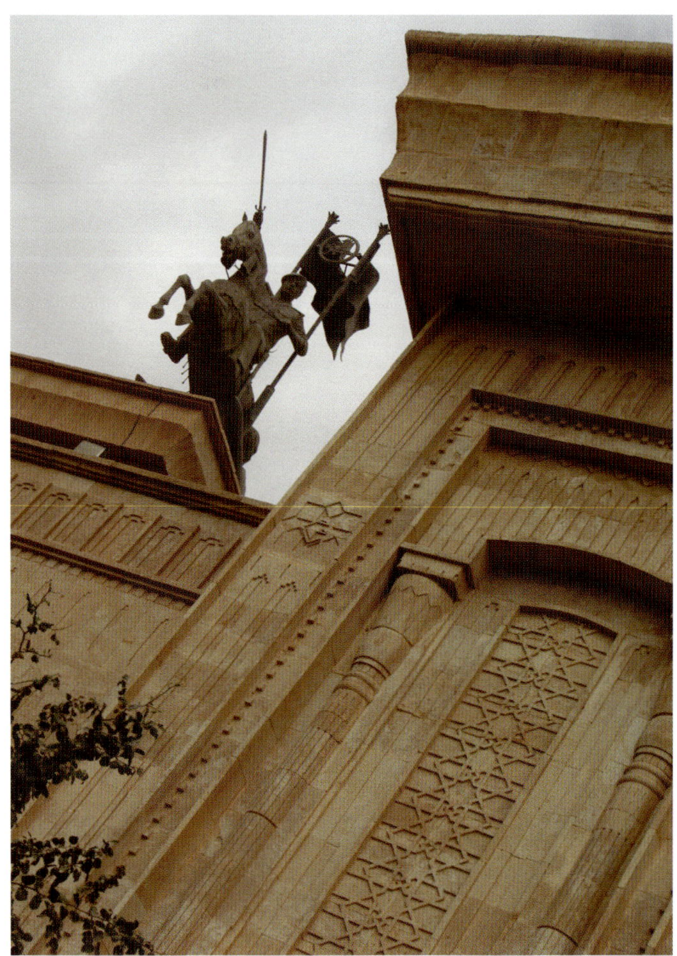

Architectural details of the Tikrit palace stonework

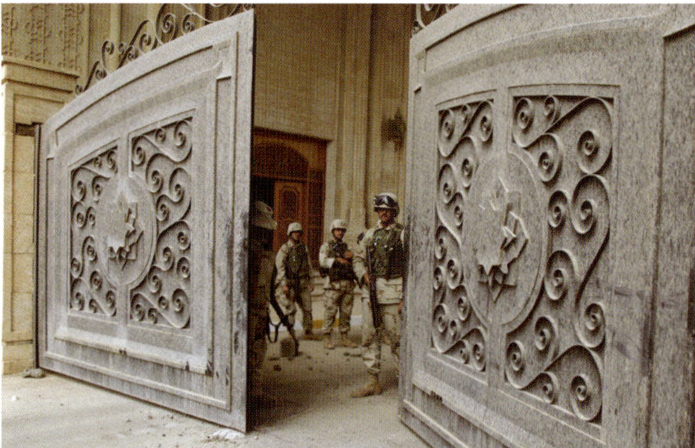

Huge iron gates at the Tikrit palace complex

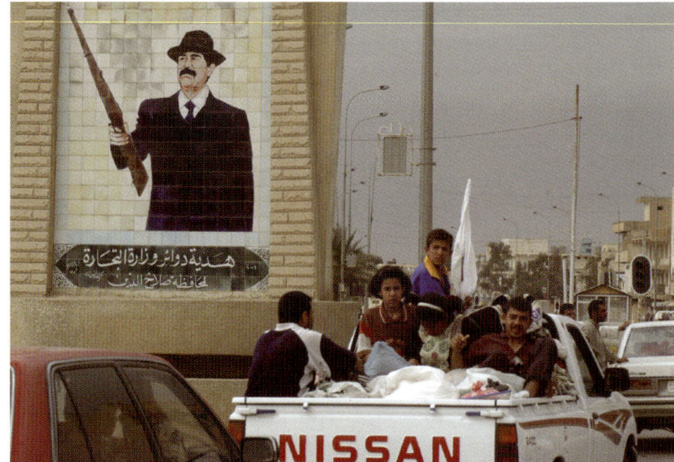

Undamaged murals of Saddam are common near Tikrit

with guns going off on both sides of us and the closeness of the civilians. I start thinking; what if some young kid, like the one carrying the RPGs, sees us Westerners in the car and decides to take us out with one of his rockets? Maybe the boy's father wishes death upon the evil ones from the West. Perhaps this would be enough for the kid to shoot at us, thinking that his father would feel he was a hero, or a martyr. It is too much of a very real possibility in this dusty, lawless hell pit.

Finally, after a couple of very tense minutes (but it feels like hours), we get out of the gun-happy congestion and continue north out of the village. It does not take long to see where all the weapons are coming from. We pass two large military warehouse complexes just off the roadway. They look like weapons armories. Local people are walking and driving into the warehouses, exiting with donkey carts, trucks and cars full of rifles and other military supplies. There are enough boxes and cases of weapons to start a private war, or at least take over a neighboring town. It is all up for grabs, and entire families of fathers, wives and children are looting the warehouses in a continual procession.

I can't believe this is happening. There are American troops using this same road; why aren't they securing these warehouses? These weapons could return some day to haunt them.

We keep driving north and soon realize that it is taking us much longer to get to Tikrit than it should. We cross the Tigris River, flooding out across the farmland. Fishermen cast nets from dugout canoes, then draw them back. Yesterday,

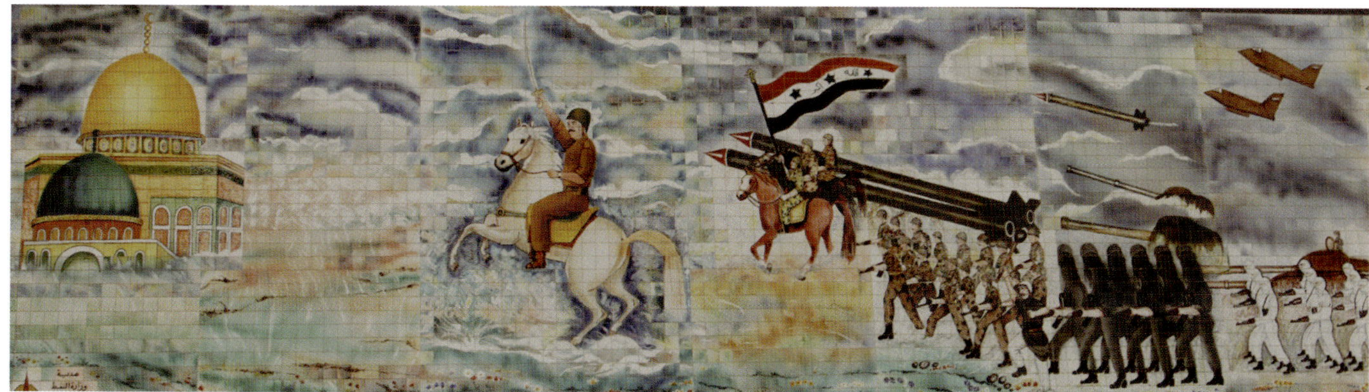

Saddam leads his armies to glory in a mosaic on a highway overpass

in Baghdad, I saw a donkey cart with a large 30-pound carp lying in the back. The fisherman told me it was caught that morning in the Tigris. I wish I could go fishing.

As we near Tikrit, we start seeing more and more murals of Saddam in the median of the roadway or beside the entranceways of warehouses and manufacturing buildings. Graffiti on a stone wall reads, "Down USA" But someone has altered the graffiti so it now reads "Go Downtown USA". We pass under a highway overpass displaying a commemorative mosaic of Saddam. It shows a dreamy, cartoon-like sequence of images of Saddam in a general's uniform, riding a white stallion with a sword in his raised hand. To his rear, his armies march as in victory, with Scud missiles flying overhead. White-and black-hooded *Mujahideen*, clenching rifles in their hands, march onward with the regular uniformed troops. It is Saddam's vision of a *jihad* against the west.

Some of the roadside Saddam murals we pass are intact, unlike those in Baghdad, which were all destroyed or vandalized. This gives us a glimpse into the lingering reality that Saddam still has many supporters here in his hometown, otherwise the murals would have all been defaced. He had gained his power and success through his close friendships and support from this town.

We are nearing the outskirts of his huge palace compound and can see black smoke rising a mile off in the distance where the town of Tikrit is situated. There is a well-kept road to the right of the highway leading to his palace compound. The entranceway is a massive stone structure with huge black iron gates adorned with ornamental ironwork. It is guarded by American soldiers. Above the gates, is an archway of warm beige sandstone, complete with a large ornate dome embossed in gold leaf and the finest stonework. Flanking each side of the gates, a larger-than-life bronze statue of a stallion-riding Saddam, with sword in hand, stands on top of towering sandstone columns. A cluster of miniature bronze missiles points outwards at his feet, ready to sweep him off to victory. This is the same statue that I saw at the Jordan-Iraq border on April 12th. A 12 foot-high wall surrounds the entire palace grounds, with glassed-in guard towers strategically positioned every hundred meters. From the outside, it looks like a huge prison complex rather than a palace home.

After showing our press passes to the Marine sentries, we are allowed through the gates and onto the palace grounds. The two palaces are visible a half mile further down the rose-fringed roadway. Jim informs us that we only have an hour to spend in Tikrit, as he has an early deadline for his story. He hadn't expected it to take us three-and-a-half hours to get here, as we took the wrong turn on the road south of Samarra. While Tod, Jim and Tish interview soldiers at the gates, Sean and I hustle towards the palace complex due to the increasing time constraints.

Leading up to the first palace, American soldiers rest along the flowered roadside. Some soldiers are sleeping on lawn chairs or cots; others hang their laundry on ropes tied between the fancy French-style street lamps that line the roadway.

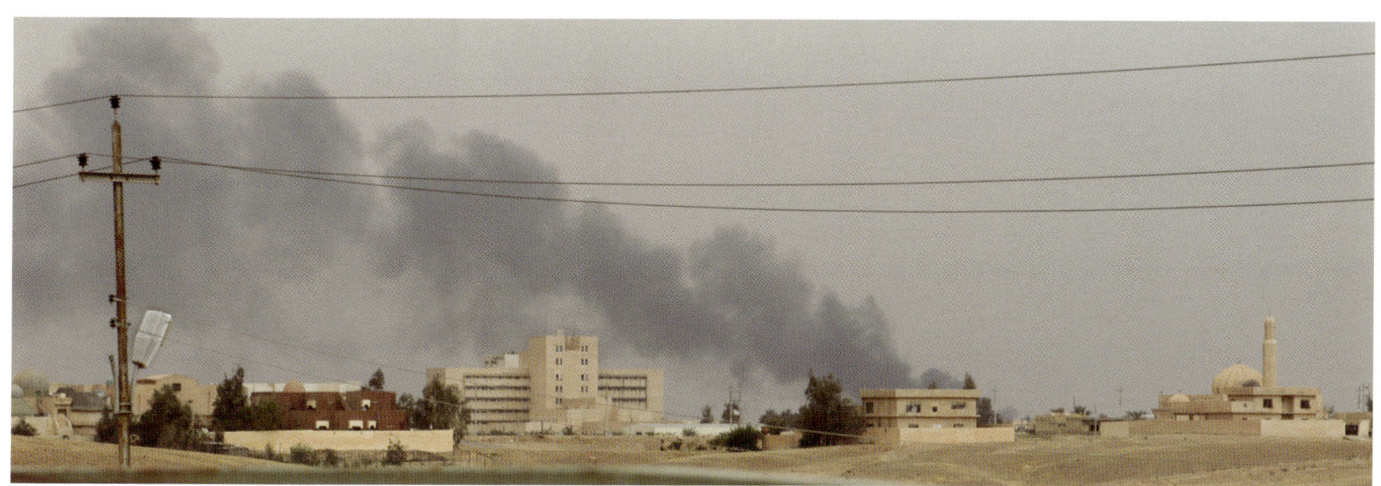

Smoke rises from a Tikrit suburb

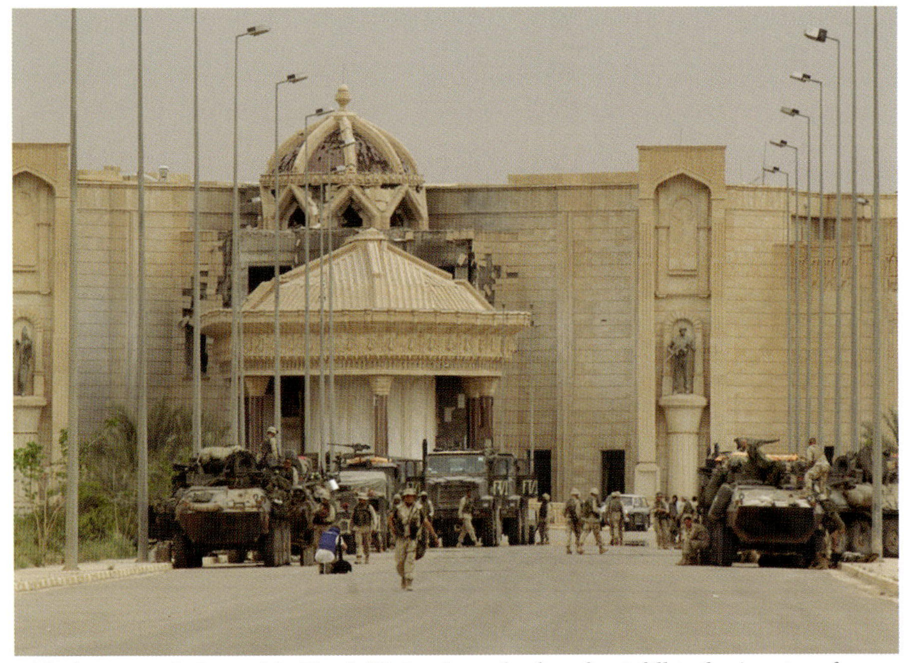

Marines camp in front of Saddam's Tikrit palace, the day after it fell to the American forces

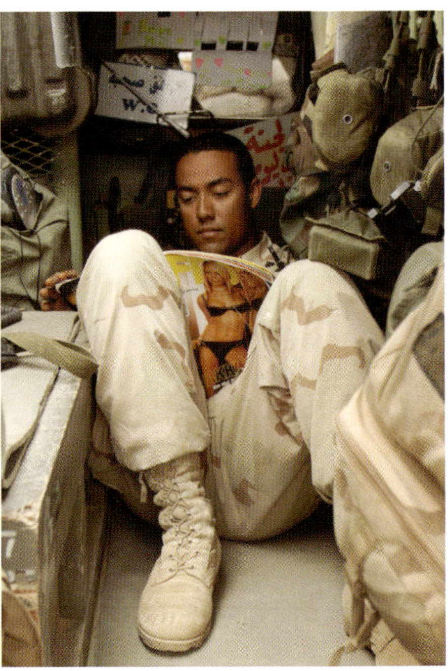

A Marine reads during some downtime

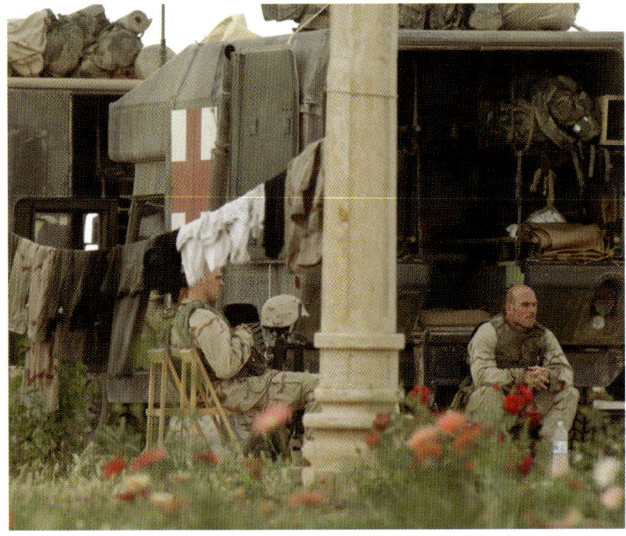

Medical staff dry their laundry and relax after the battle for Tikrit

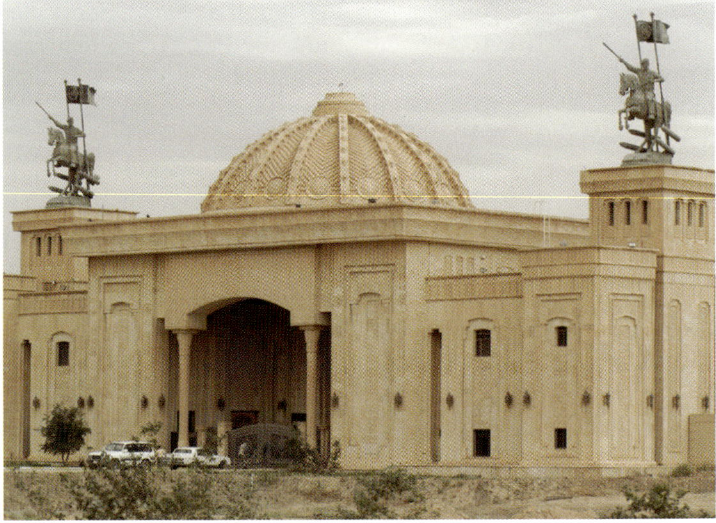

The entranceway to Saddam's Tikrit palace compound

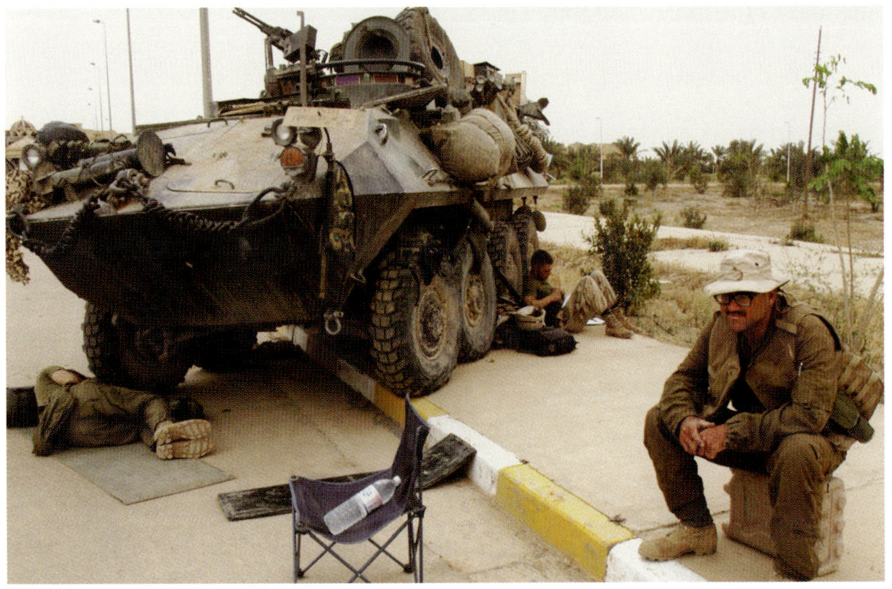

The day after the battle for Tikrit

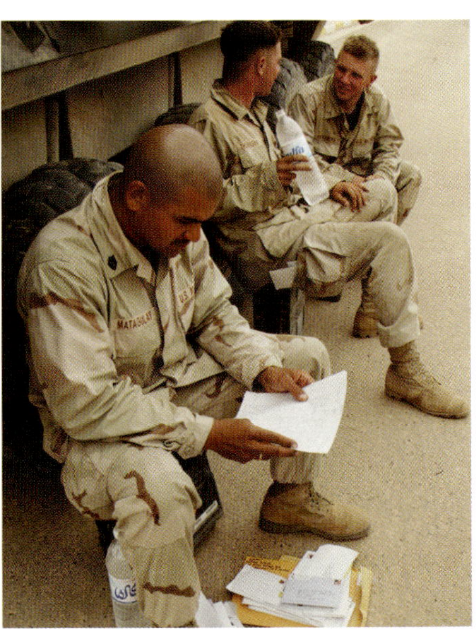

Reading the mail from home

Some lean against their war machines, or sit on ammunition boxes reading mail from home. Another group chats beside a Humvee while playing cards. I pass by an open APC and see a soldier lying in the vehicle reading a porn magazine. All about him rests the clutter of personal packs and boxes of ammunition. There are brightly colored drawings pinned up inside the troop carrier, drawn by school children back home, thanking the soldiers for protecting their freedom and the USA

There are 30 or more vehicles and over 100 soldiers along this stretch of road. It is hard to say accurately just how many soldiers and how much equipment there is, as they are spread about the entire compound (which also hosts a network of smaller buildings for use by relations, employees and guests). All the soldiers look as though they are burned-out from a rough night partying, or a couple of sleepless nights. But I know why they are exhausted; they had just fought to take this town and palace yesterday. Having survived that, they were left to battle with their exhaustion. They don't talk much, nor do they seem to want to. Their bodies are here, though their minds are in a far-off place. It is evident on their faces and in their body language: they are hung-over from the violence of battle.

As I approach the first palace it doesn't look as impressive as some of the others I have seen in Baghdad, but we are restricted to only certain parts of the grounds, and are not allowed to visit the main palace as it has been rendered too dangerous to visit due to the bombs that hit it. The sentries won't let us into the smaller of the two palaces, nor do we have time to go through the protocol of gaining access through the chain of command. A large front wall and dome of the palace entrance has been destroyed by missile fire. From the glimpses that I can see, the inside of the building looks devastated by a Smart Bomb, while the outside is largely intact. The doorway is extremely opulent, richly decorated on the outside with intricate stone carvings and abalone shell inlay enhancing the richness of the thick wooden doors.

Because of the lack of time, we decide to head along the highway to Tikrit, a couple more clicks up the road. We can hear bombs exploding and see Apache Attack helicopters quartering in the direction of the nearby town of Oujah. They are wrapping up the remnants of resistance.

Soldiers are guarding a checkpoint on the main road into Tikrit. Their job is to keep the looting to a minimum by controlling the roadways in and out of town, and from what I can observe, there is very little evidence of burning or looting; in fact, the place is a ghost town. There are very few civilians milling about, and no obvious signs of heavy bomb damage. I take pics of the town, showing the soldiers guarding the roadways and behind their hastily built trenches. There isn't a hell of a lot to shoot, but I need these generic pics regardless.

While walking and shooting the town, I am very surprised and delighted to see my Toronto-based friend, Kevin Frayer (photographer for the Canadian Press), on assignment for the Associated Press. It is great to see Kevin, and we embrace in a tight hug, then go our separate ways. War heightens the bond between men – be it enemy or friend.

With time running out, we start driving back to Baghdad.

About an hour south of Tikrit we are caught in a sandstorm and rain shower. The sandstorm rises like a sandy blanket, a cloudbank of swirling, terra-cotta-colored sand and dust. It twists like a wall of madness, and in seconds we are engulfed by the whirling phenomenon. Blotting out the sun, it turns the whole sky into a sandy dream.

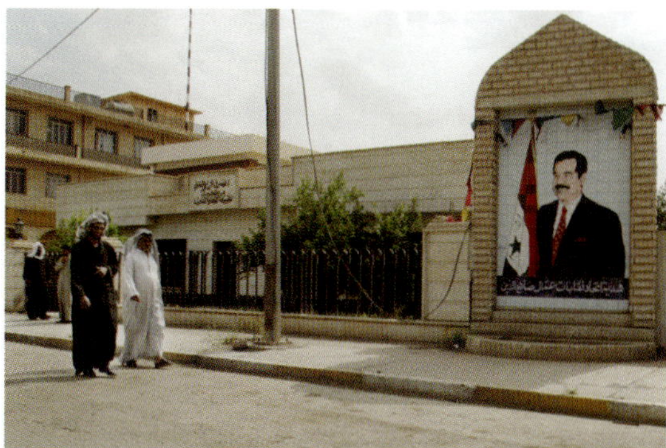

Tikrit has been spared the destruction of war and looting

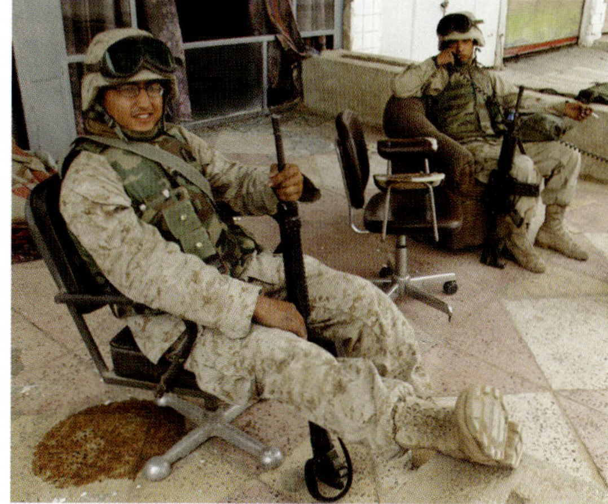

Taking a break from sentry duty

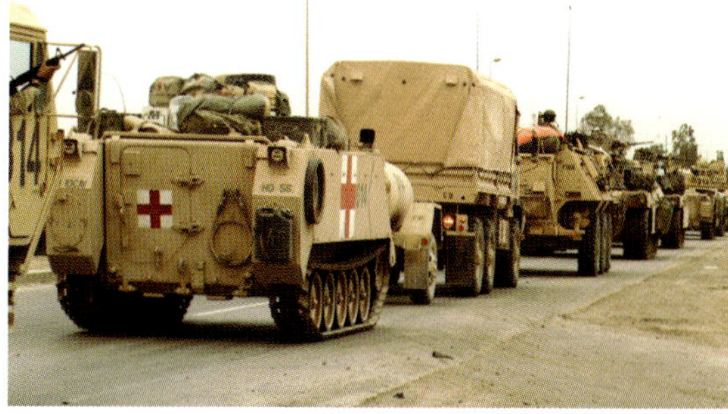

A convoy of military vehicles moves north

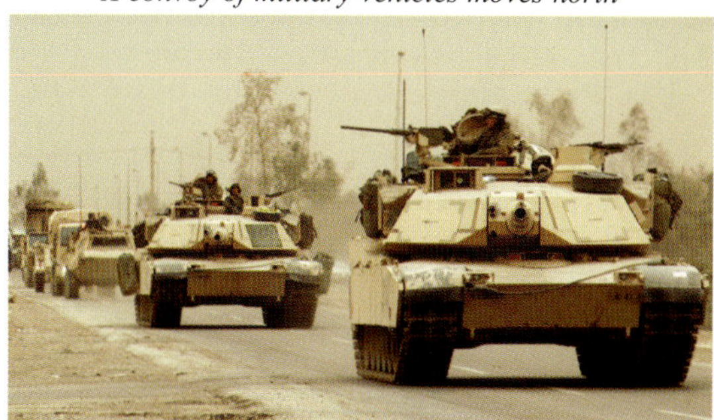

Tanks move north to Tikrit

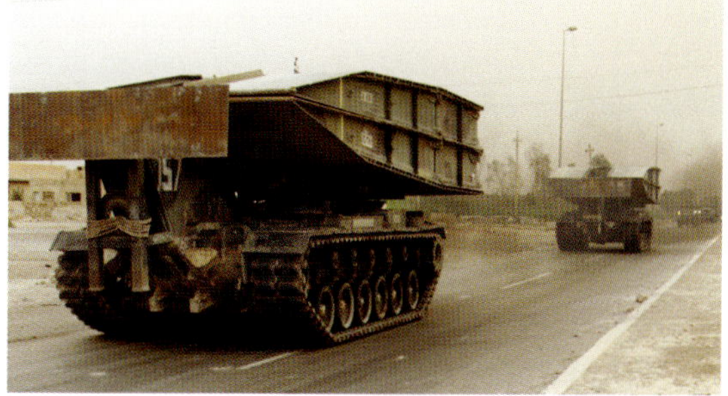

Automated bridge extenders move north

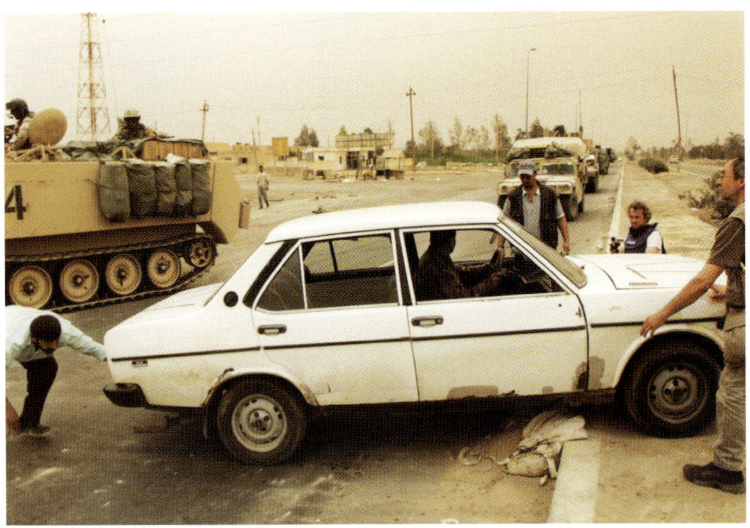

Our taxi gets stuck on road median while trying to avoid a military convoy

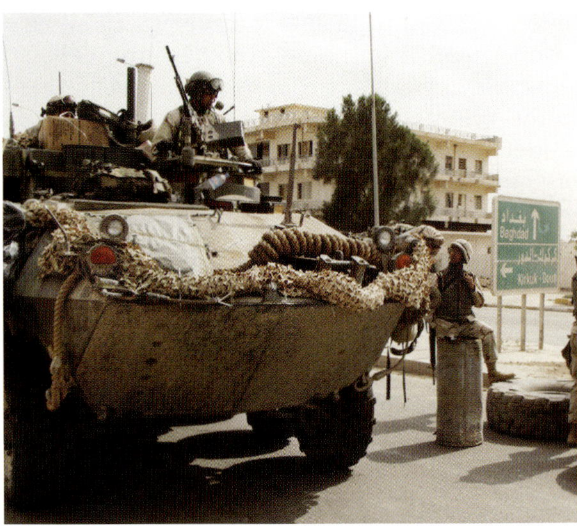

Soldiers keep looters from entering and destroying Tikrit

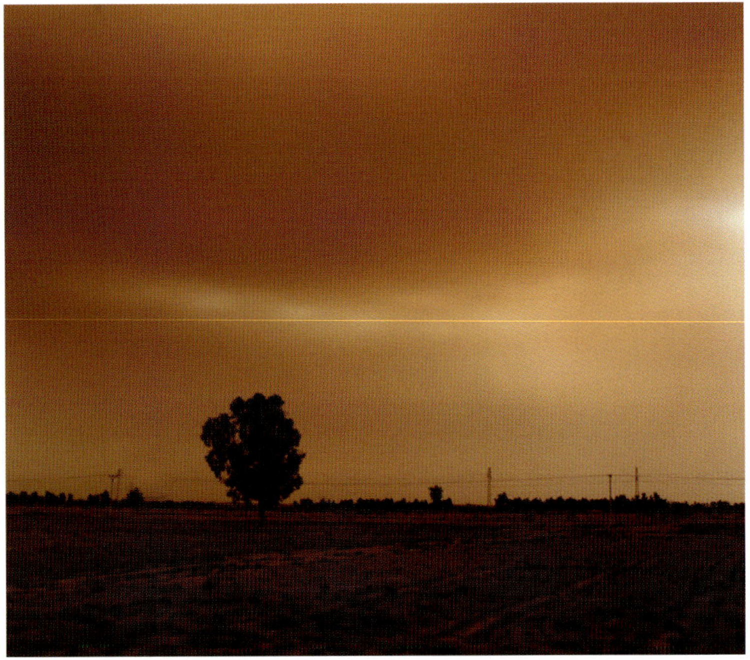

A red sandstorm moves across the desert near Samarra

A rain shower starts to fall, only it isn't rain, it is red muck. The gummy mud coats the car and streaks the windows. After the five-minute tempest passes, we pull over to the side of the road to clean the windows. It is great to see the storm, then the rain, but I would not want to be caught outside while one was raging. It would be too easy to lose your way in the swirling sand, only to be baked in the overpowering desert heat that follows.

Shortly after the storm, we stop at an army checkpoint. At the same time a large convoy of military equipment plies its way north, taking over both lanes of the highway as it passes. One of the sentry troops complains to me that he can't get any chewing snuff. He is ecstatic when I hand him my tin of Copenhagen (snuff). He offers me a package of cigarettes in return and we both shake hands.

We make it back to our hotel after another gruelling mission. There is some hot water available, so I have a reviving shower, then go downstairs for the staple dinner of broiled chicken, bean soup and rice. After supper, Sean, Tish and I lounge in our room drinking Tang and munching on candy bars. We discuss strategy till 1:00 a.m.

Day 7. Wednesday, April 16th

(Marines attend to injured Iraqi looters; girl presents Marine with flowers; Al Kadamiyya Prison; horrible rumors of drowned prisoners; flooded jail cells; vulnerable to misinformation; instigator fires up crowd; I speak with soldiers about the prisoners; I speak to the crowd; an American god or a Muslim god; peace be with you; tears of joy wet my cheeks; the crowd breaks up; Sean and I visit the Iraqi Museum of Civilization; speaking with museum staff; an AK-47 in his lap; museum looted while American soldiers guard the Ministry of Oil; I meet Nino the Marine; the battle for Al Kut; pink mist-vaporized blood; kept coming to their deaths; Iraqis show close compassion to troops; small trickle of foodstuffs)

In the morning, the team meets in the Fanar dining room for coffee. The crew decides to look into the religious gatherings planned for the upcoming Christian holiday of Easter, which takes place over the weekend. This is of no interest to me, so I decide to look into the rumored underground prisons where Saddam was supposed to have held hundreds if not thousands of prisoners. It is also speculated the cells had been flooded while the prisoners were in them. I felt that if these prisons did exist, and I could get some pics of the prisoners being greeted by their families, they would be great material. But up until now, the underground prisons were just folklore.

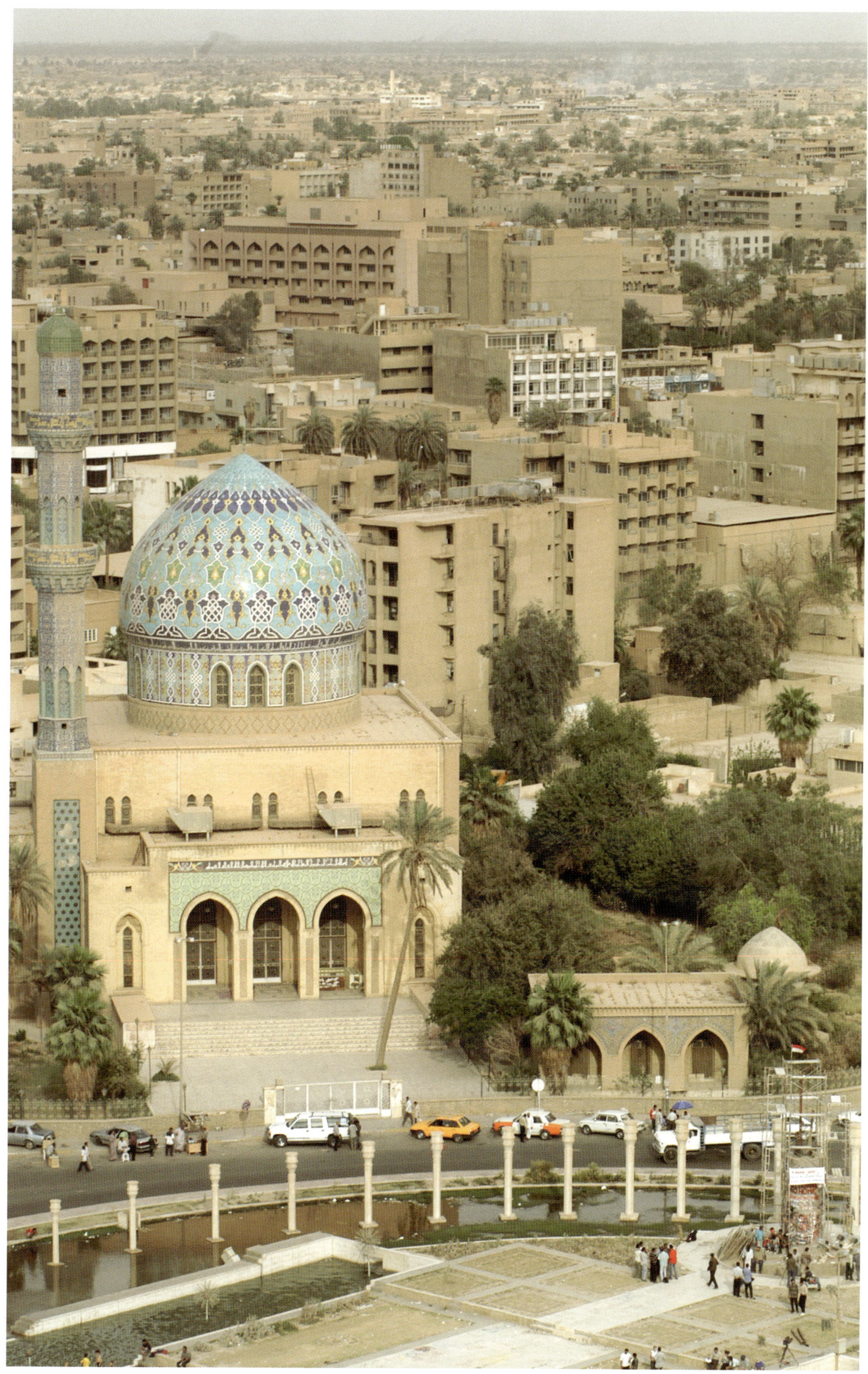

View of Baghdad looking east, with Firdos Square and the Shahid mosque in the foreground

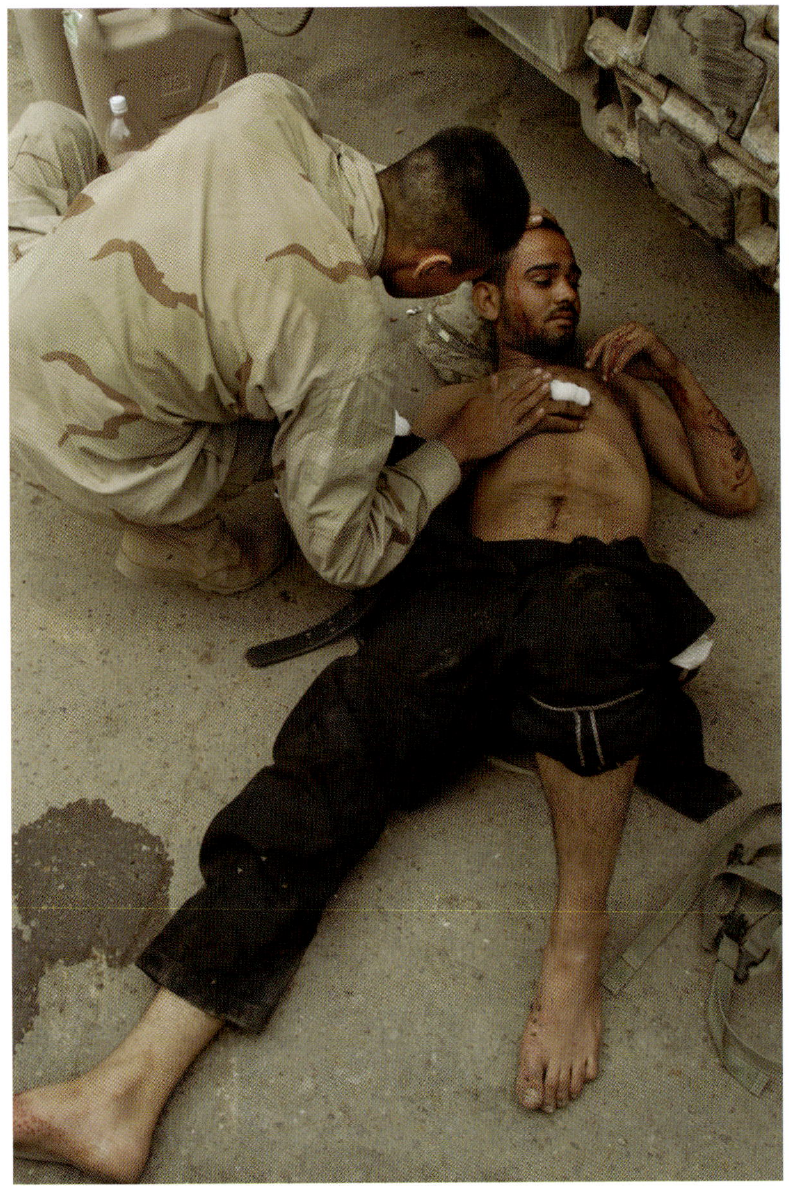

Marine medical staff attend to a looter injured by a store owner

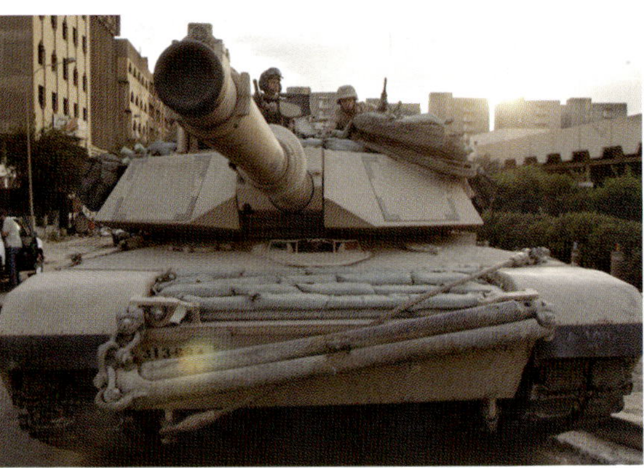

American tank outside the Al Fanar

I decide to walk up to the main road, about a block away, to flag a taxi to the Al Kadamiyya Prison, also known as the 5th Department Prison by the coalition forces. I had also heard over the past couple of days about another supposed underground prison in Halal City.

Just before catching a cab, I photograph a Marine Medical Officer treating two looters who had been beaten by a storeowner. Laid out beside an amphibious assault vehicle, their wounds are largely scrapes and scratches in need of some first aid.

Shortly after this, I see a young Iraqi girl of about five years old, presenting a Marine with a bunch of flowers. Her father had brought her to the Palestine complex to present the gift. It makes a nice pic.

When I arrive at the site, which actually is an underground prison, the Americans guarding the place won't let anyone into it. About a hundred grieving and impatient Iraqis wait outside the walls; some had been returning here for a few days. They are grasping for any information on the state of the prisoners, and some claim that the Americans had found prisoners but are not letting them go free. Others are spreading the hateful rumor that the Americans were letting them drown, as it was believed that Saddam had flooded the underground compound.

Rumors are rampant throughout the distraught crowd, and a man is firing them up with false accusations. None of what he is stating makes any sense to me. The lack of solid information leaves the crowd spreading all sorts of misinformation. This is a major problem in Baghdad – no mode of information distribution, such as newspapers, radio or TV, is available to provide the people with updates on how the war is advancing or on relief efforts. People are vulnerable to misinformation and it is easily spread, especially if tinged with some sort of horror. The setting is a time bomb of anger and the longer I stay the crazier the scene is becoming.

I take it upon myself to try and quieten down the crowd. Through an interpreter, I ask the crowd what the Americans would hope to gain by letting the prisoners die, especially with all these witnesses. "They are working with Saddam or Saddam's old guard for their favors and disclosures," say some in the crowd.

Seeing that these helpless people need to know what is really happening, I walk over to the gates of the prison and matter-of-factly speak with a soldier from Tennessee. I tell him about the growing anger in the crowd and that it is becoming explosive. He is very open to what I am asking. A second soldier comes over and stands by his side, listening to what I am saying. The two sentries, thankful that I am trying to calm the crowd, start to tell me about the status of the prison.

They tell me that they have just finished pumping out the water, which they believe had been flooded into the underground holding cells on Saddam's request. One soldier informs me that two days earlier, an Iraqi civilian had directed the coalition forces to the prison. This man supposed that some of his family were down there, either dead or dying. He was part of the crowd asking for answers two days ago, when news first leaked about the alleged underground prison.

"It was believed that 600 prisoners were trapped and rotting below," said one of the soldiers. "The man returned this morning and we actually took him into the now dry compound, to show him that we found only cells, and not one drowned or dead prisoner. We gave him a tour of the prison and he went away contented, after telling the crowd what he had seen, but now a new batch of victims' families have appeared. Every day a new group of faces shows up," he says. "It's difficult for them, but we can't keep up with informing everyone or every group like this. There are no prisoners or bodies; just empty jail cells and some shackles."

I ask if it would be all right for me to tell the crowd what he had told me. He agrees, saying, "If it would help relieve their stress and the hate piling up against us, then go right ahead." He ends by saying in a hushed voice, "I want to let you know as a soldier, that if I thought that I was involved in any sort of crime to allow someone to drown or die in this manner, I would resign from the forces and go public. I couldn't and wouldn't serve in an army which would commit such acts, and that's a fact!" He concludes, "I wouldn't be able to live with myself."

I go back into the crowd, which immediately surrounds me, asking questions from every direction. Some are crying hysterically but most are hanging on for the words that I have to relate.

I tell them (through an English speaking Iraqi in the crowd) that I would believe these ordinary American soldiers even if it were my own child, or member of my family that was allegedly held in this prison. "Why," I ask, "would they want to lie to you? What would they have to gain from this tragedy? Wouldn't they rather set the prisoners free, in front of media like myself?" I continue to tell them that the soldiers are just grunts from everywhere USA. "These soldiers have families too." I tell them that I live in Canada, along the U.S. – Canada border, and that many Americans are my best friends and good neighbors and I would stake the reputation of my country on what these soldiers said. "Please try to understand what I am saying as a voice from Canada. These soldiers are men as you and I are men; please respect that and understand that we are all men under one god and that no god would wish these sorts of atrocities on his people, be it an American god or an Islamic god. Peace be with you and I pray that some day soon your lost family members will walk across your doormat to take their place in your world."

Continuing on, I address the crowd concerning their fear for the future of their country's existence. I use the analogy of a woman having a baby to describe the pain Iraq is going through. "Iraq is

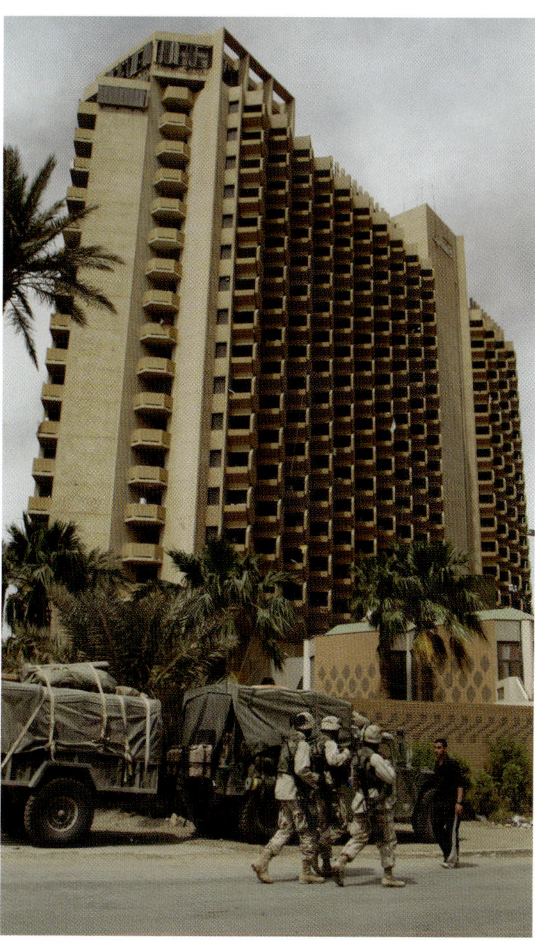
Soldiers patrol under the towering Palestine Hotel

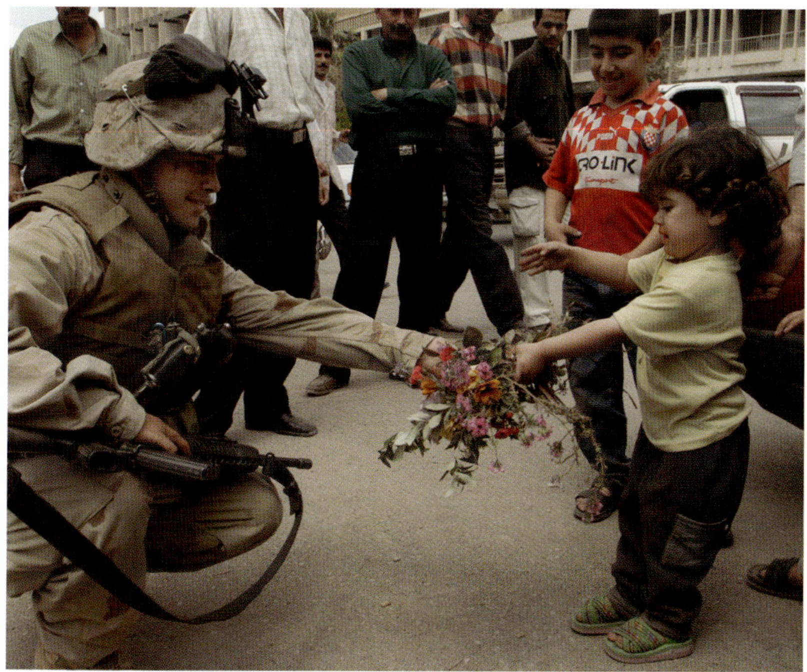
A young Iraqi girl offers a Marine a bunch of flowers

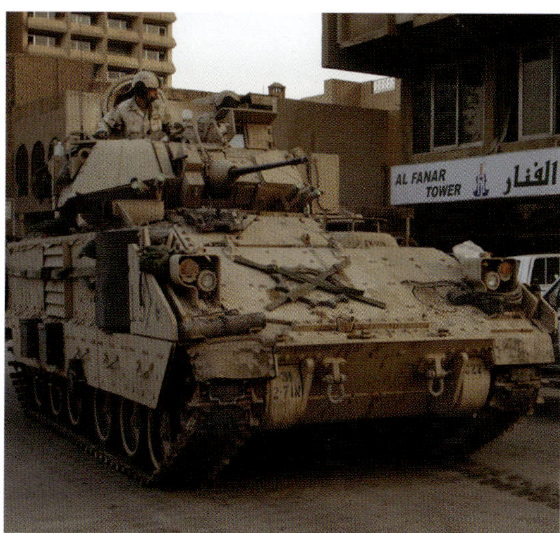

Marines patrol past the Al Fanar Towers

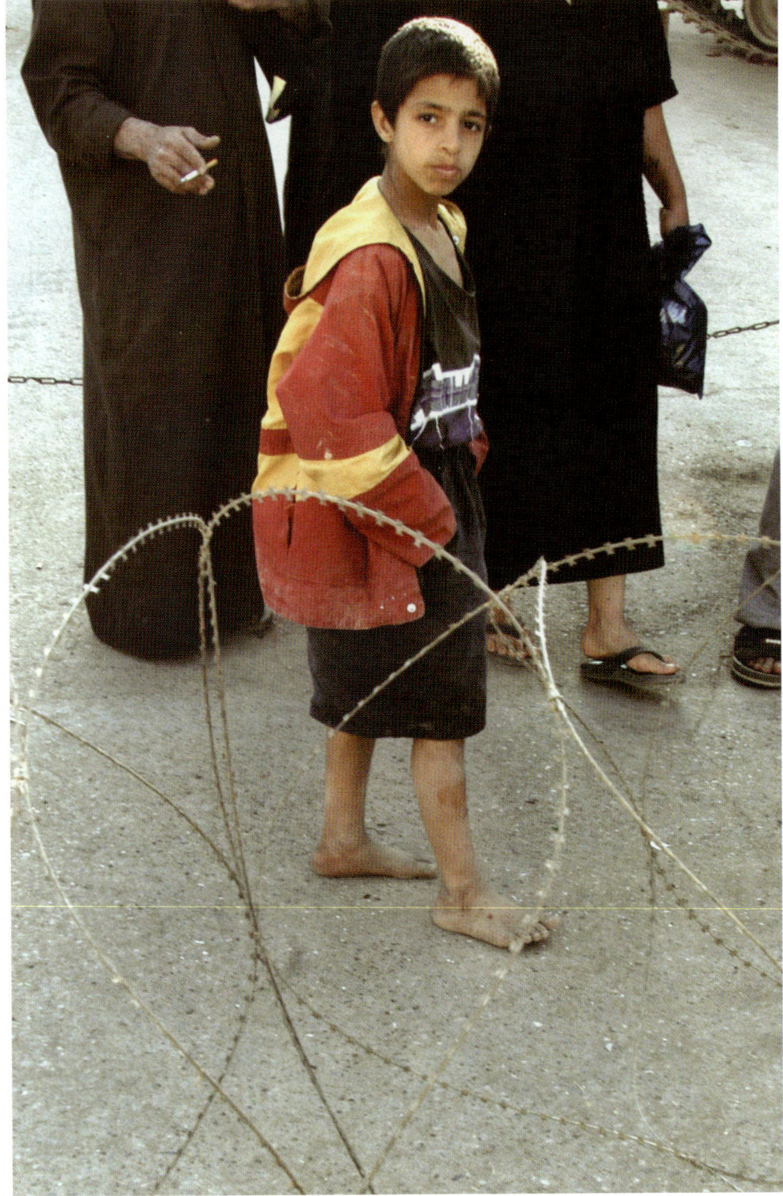

A young barefoot street orphan looks for handouts

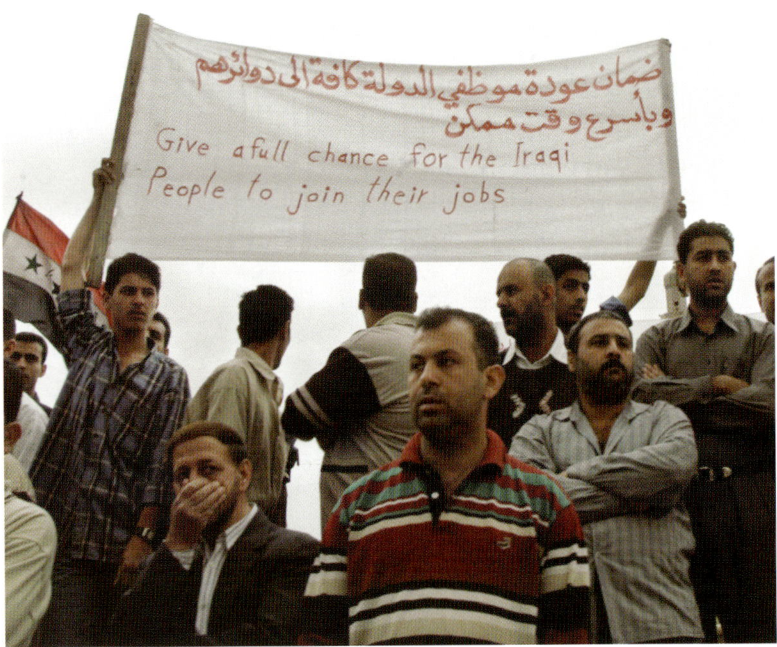

Unemployed Iraqis protest for job opportunities in front of the Palestine Hotel

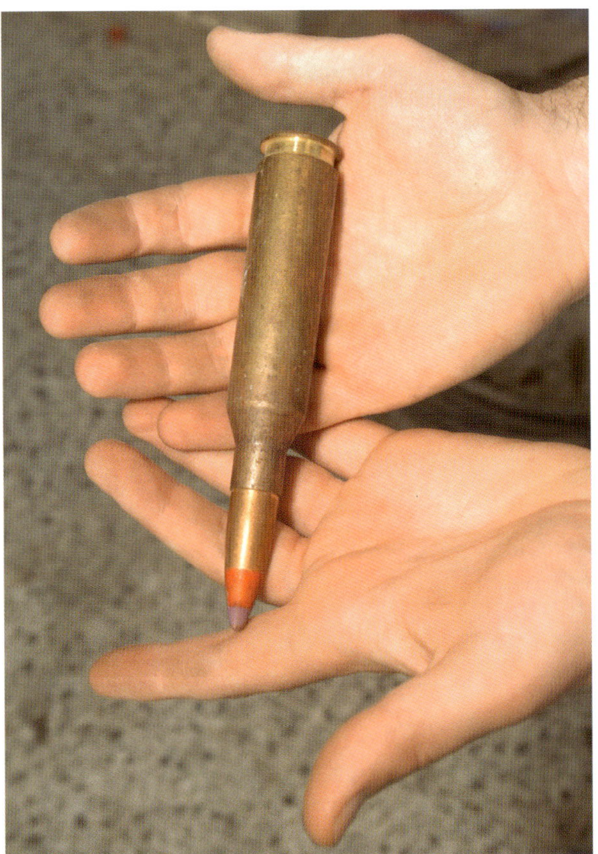

A 23 mm armor-piercing round

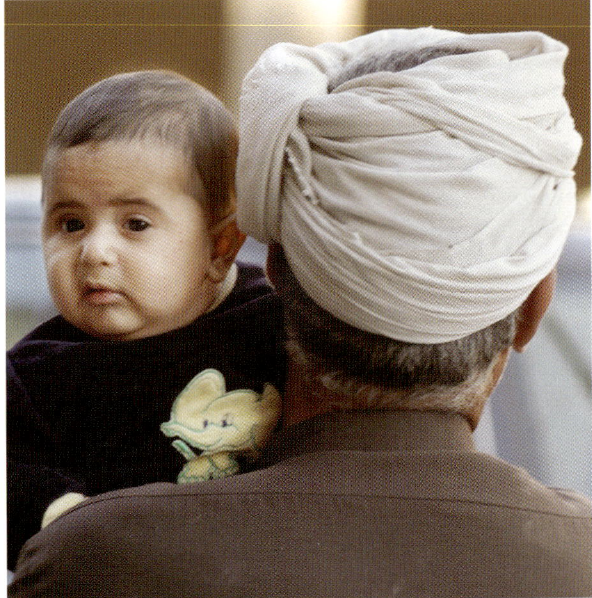

A youngster watches the photographer

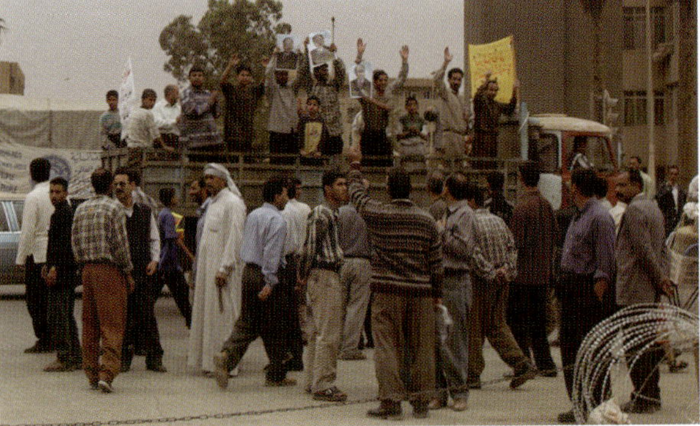

For the first time in a generation, Iraqis can demonstrate

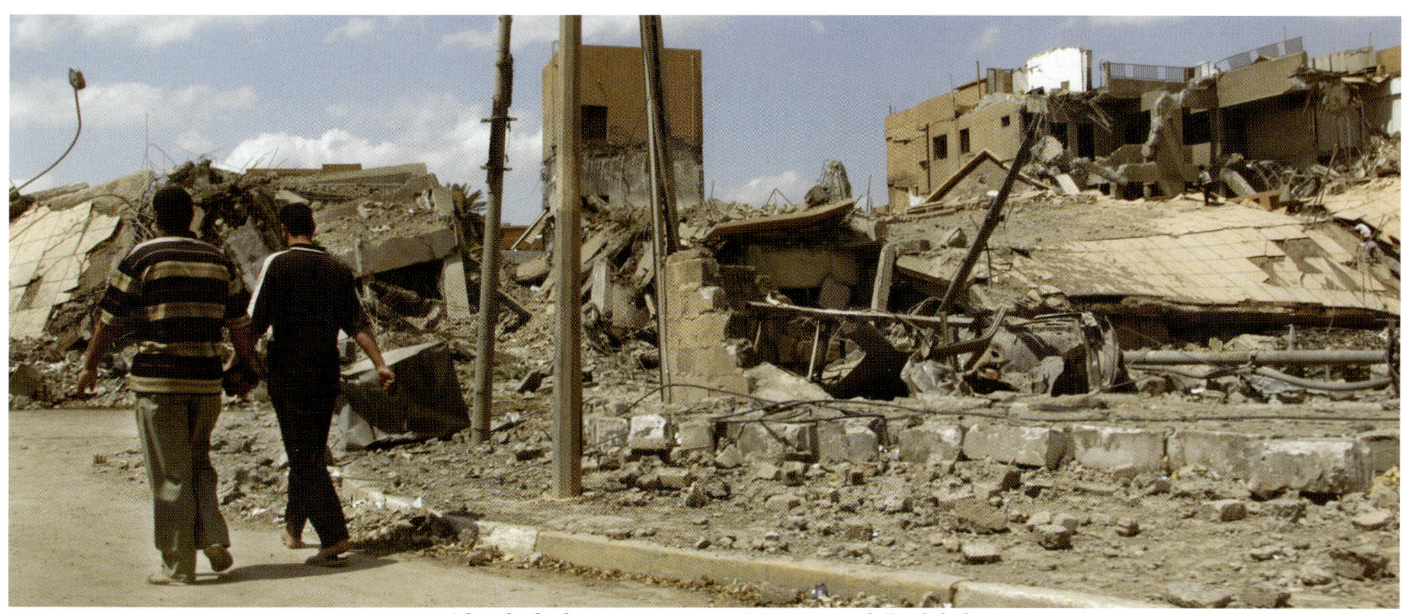

A bombed telecommunications center in north Baghdad

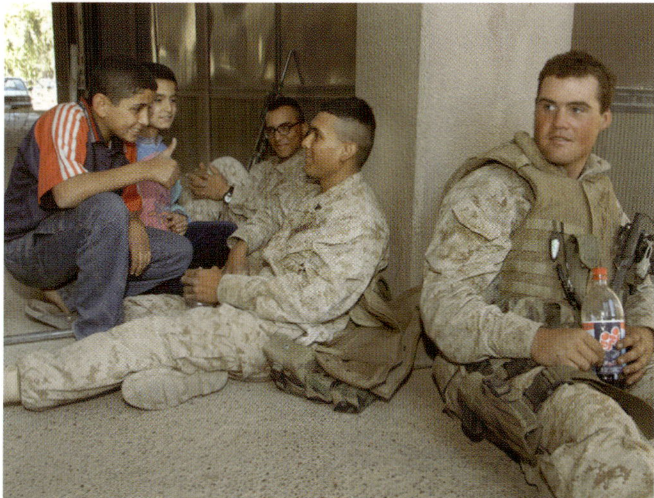

Local boys chat with Marines and share some laughs

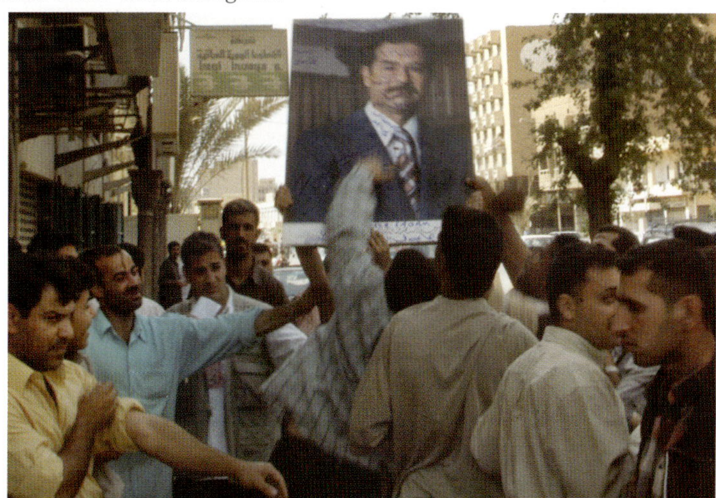

Iraqis vent their frustration

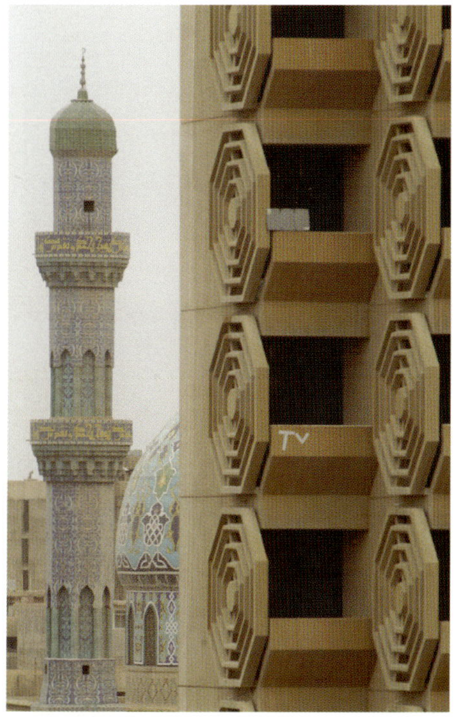

A melding of old and new architectural styles

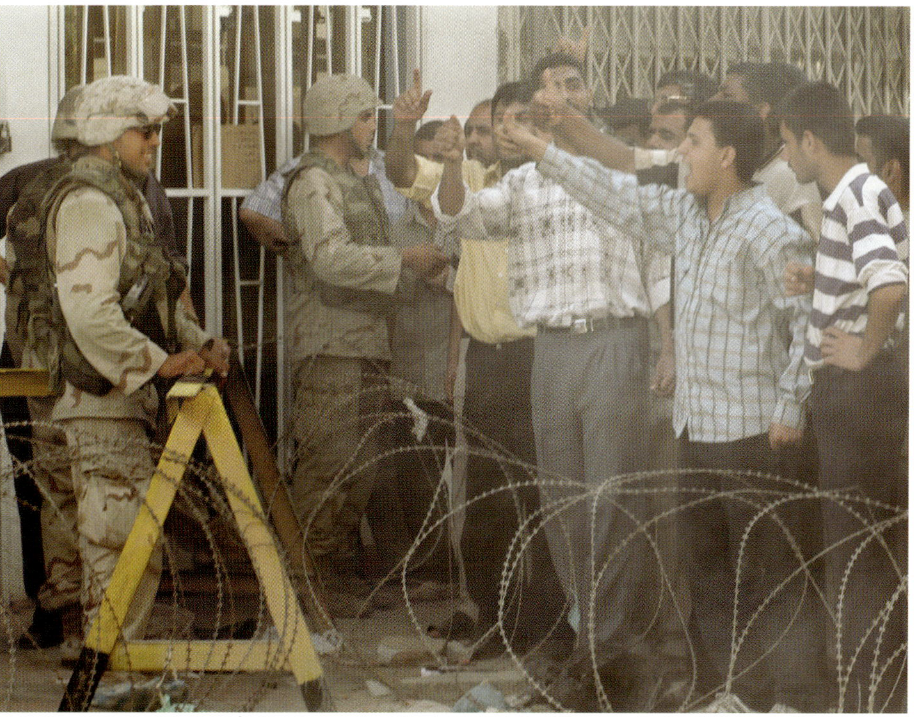

Another demonstration over the lack of jobs in Baghdad

being re-born – and is going through the agonizing contractions of birth." While glancing into the eyes of the black-gowned women in the crowd I speak on. "You know the pain of childbirth, there is no escaping or hiding from it!" The women nod their head in acknowledgement. "Mother Iraq is giving birth to a new progressive nation," I tell them. "And with birth there is pain. But the pain is soon forgotten when the swaddling infant is embraced in your arms. You look at the child as a new beginning, the birth of hope!" The crowds eyes are riveted to me – I choose my words carefully. "Please try to be a bit more patient and understand that the baby will arrive soon, and the pain you are going through now – is the price of freedom, which gives all men and women the right to decide the road they take in life. My heart and thoughts are with you, we are all brothers, are we not!"

My newfound diplomacy eases the now contemplative crowd. All at once they break out in beaming smiles as the mass of humanity grabs at me to kiss my cheeks and hands, with tears streaming down their faces. Old men with stubbly beards, kids, and mothers – they all want to shake my hands and kiss me. My cheeks are wet with their tears as they tell me. "Thank-you Canada, thank-you mister!"

It is truly a moving situation, and I have put their fears to rest, at least for today. Never before have I felt so indulgent – and vulnerable to the concerns of my fellow man. I have never stood in front of a crowd and spoken the way I just did. I don't know where it came from. I am starting to find out that war is a great educator, and I am one of its students.

I drive back to the hotel to see my friends and break the news regarding the supposed drowning of prisoners. I had

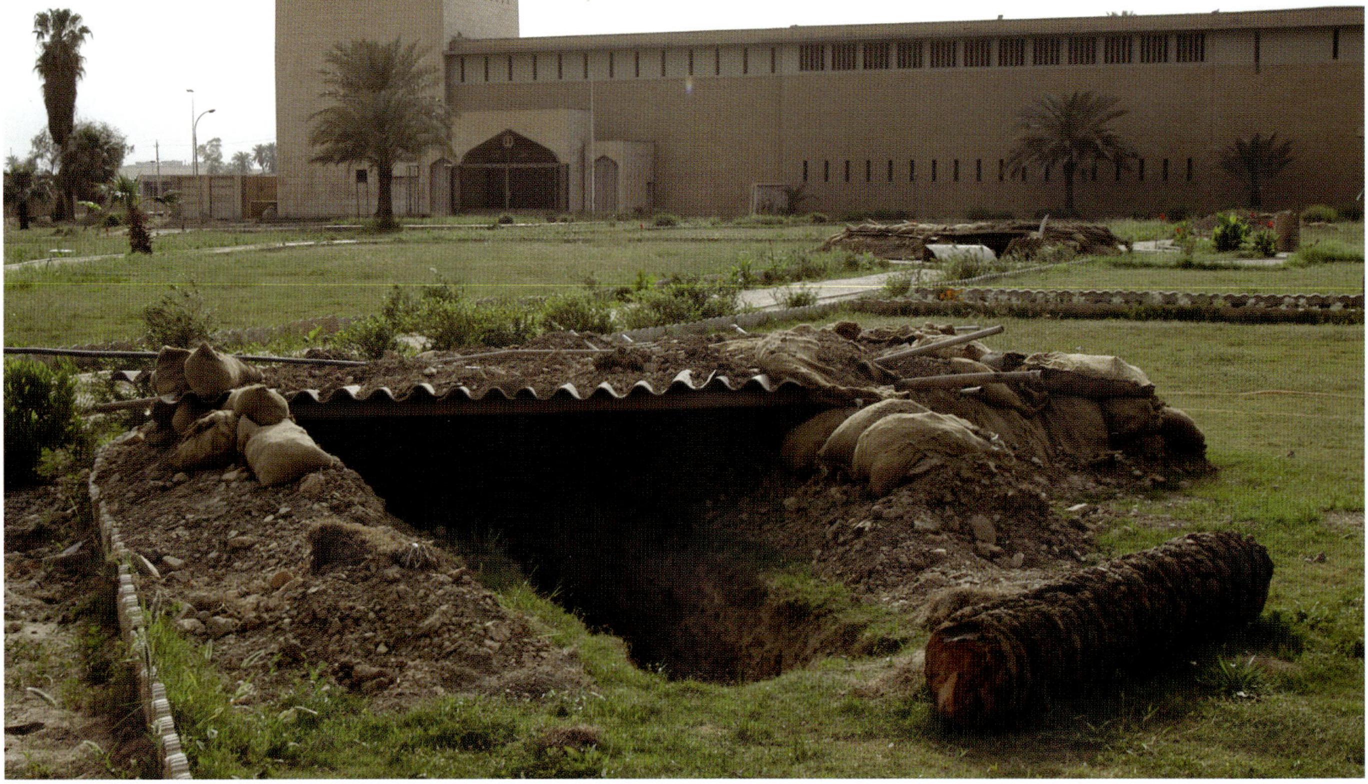

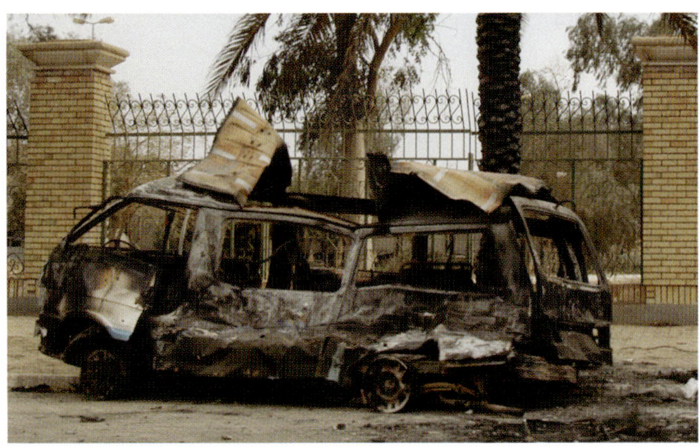

A trench dug into the lawn of the Iraqi National Museum

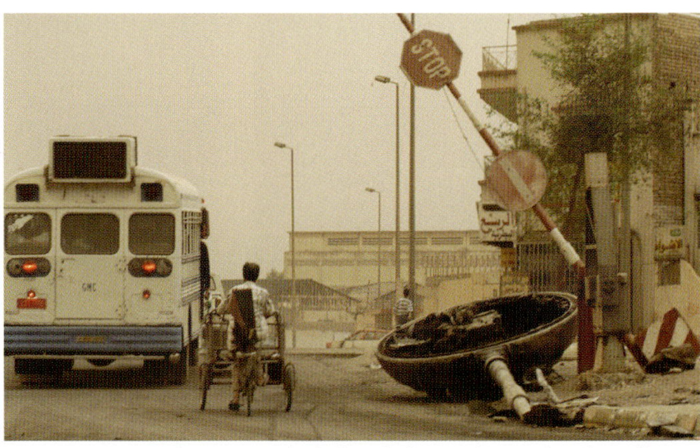

More roadside destruction littering the streets of Baghdad

A gun turret from an exploded tank shares the road with traffic

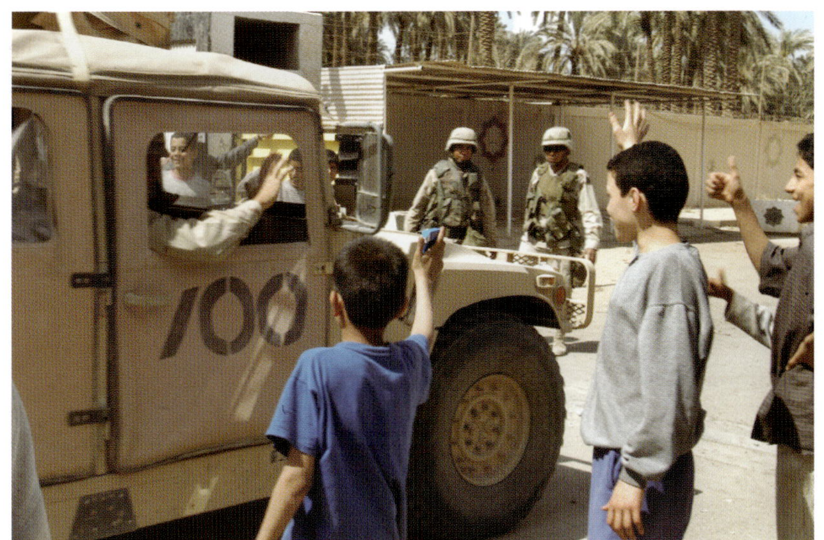

Young boys wave at soldiers driving into Al Kadamiyya Prison

spent a good part of the day at the prison, and the satisfaction of seeing the crowd calmed down made my day a complete success, plus it gave me a little downtime.

It is getting late, and with a little daylight remaining; Sean and I decide to take a cab to the Museum of Civilization, a 15 minute drive from the Al Fanar. Yesterday I had heard rumors that the museum had been looted, but up until now we had been covering mostly human tragedies.

Arriving outside the museum, we go over to the main entrance but it is locked. A large blackened hole, about the size of a garbage-can lid, has been blasted into the stonework above the doors. It is the result of a shell explosion, fired by a tank.

We walk over to the side entranceway, where we see a small group of men mingling near the doorway. One of the four men is a curator, another is sitting on a plastic chair toying with an AK, and the other two lean against the wall smoking cigarettes, looking like they are at a funeral. Introducing ourselves to the curator, I offer my sympathies for the loss of the museum's treasures. I tell him it is a loss to the entire world and not just Iraq, then ask him why someone would want to loot historic artifacts. Where would they sell these items and to whom? Weren't the looters mostly interested in televisions, furniture, money and other easily resalable items? Why steal 4000-year-old clay urns and oil lamps?

Obviously distressed, he picks up where I left off: "What would a looter want with a 3000-year-old urn or mosaic? What would a looter do with a 4000-year-old statue?" Like a grieving father he continues. "What would a looter want with these items, is he going to go to the souk and sell them?" he insisted.

He tells us what he believed was the real reason behind the museum being looted. "It was organized, this looting was organized from the outside." He describes the events leading up to the museum being looted. "Just before the outbreak of the war, we noticed men with pens and notepads walking around the museum exhibits, marking down select items," he said. "As soon as the hostilities broke out – I believe they had already set in motion a plan to loot the museum. It would have taken a little advance organization from the black-market dealers, but without anyone protecting the museum, it would have been a simple operation to fill the orders placed by the collectors."

He voices his frustration with the American Forces, whom he holds responsible for not protecting the museum. "Before the war started we were promised by the American Intelligence that the museum was a top priority for protection. Now look, almost a week after the bombing stopped and where is our protective American Force?" he asks angrily. "I'll tell you where they are – they are down the road guarding the building housing the Ministry of Oil and its oil transactions and paperwork. They were protecting a building full of paperwork while the world's history was carried away on a looter's back – this is just unbelievable!" He throws his arms up in disgust and frustration.

We ask if we can go inside the museum and take some photos, but he prefers that we return the following morning. On the way back to the hotel I could not help but compare the ransacking of the Iraqi Museum of Civilization to the burning of the great library in Alexandria (which contained the writings of Aristotle). I also believe that the now-impoverished museum will turn into a huge story over the next few days.

Later that evening I met with some Marines who came to the Fanar for supper. Sean and I sit at their table, speaking with Nino, a young Hispanic. Nino told me that before 9/11, he was a peace-loving man, involved in humanitarian issues, such as the treatment of Native Americans. But 9/11 had changed that, and now he fought against terrorism. He was the first person in his family, in five generations, to complete college. We have much in common and become close friends in a very short time.

Nino is poet, and keeps a diary of poems he has written while in Iraq. He reads me a poem he had written after he fought in the battle for Al Kut, which he called Pink Mist. It was a moving piece of word art, describing how he felt as he emptied his clip into line after line of

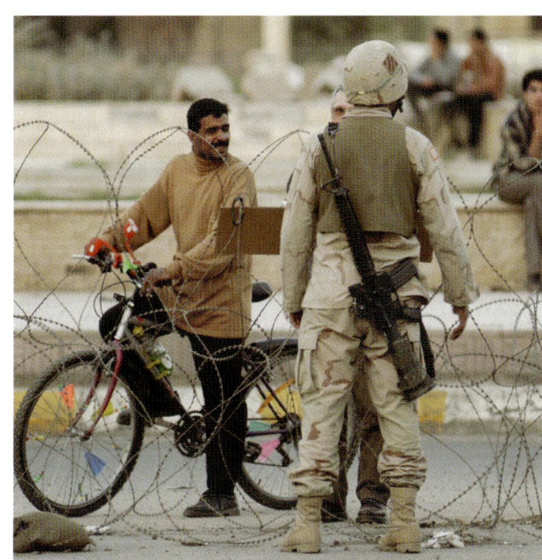

Bicyclist talks to a soldier through a barbed-wire fence

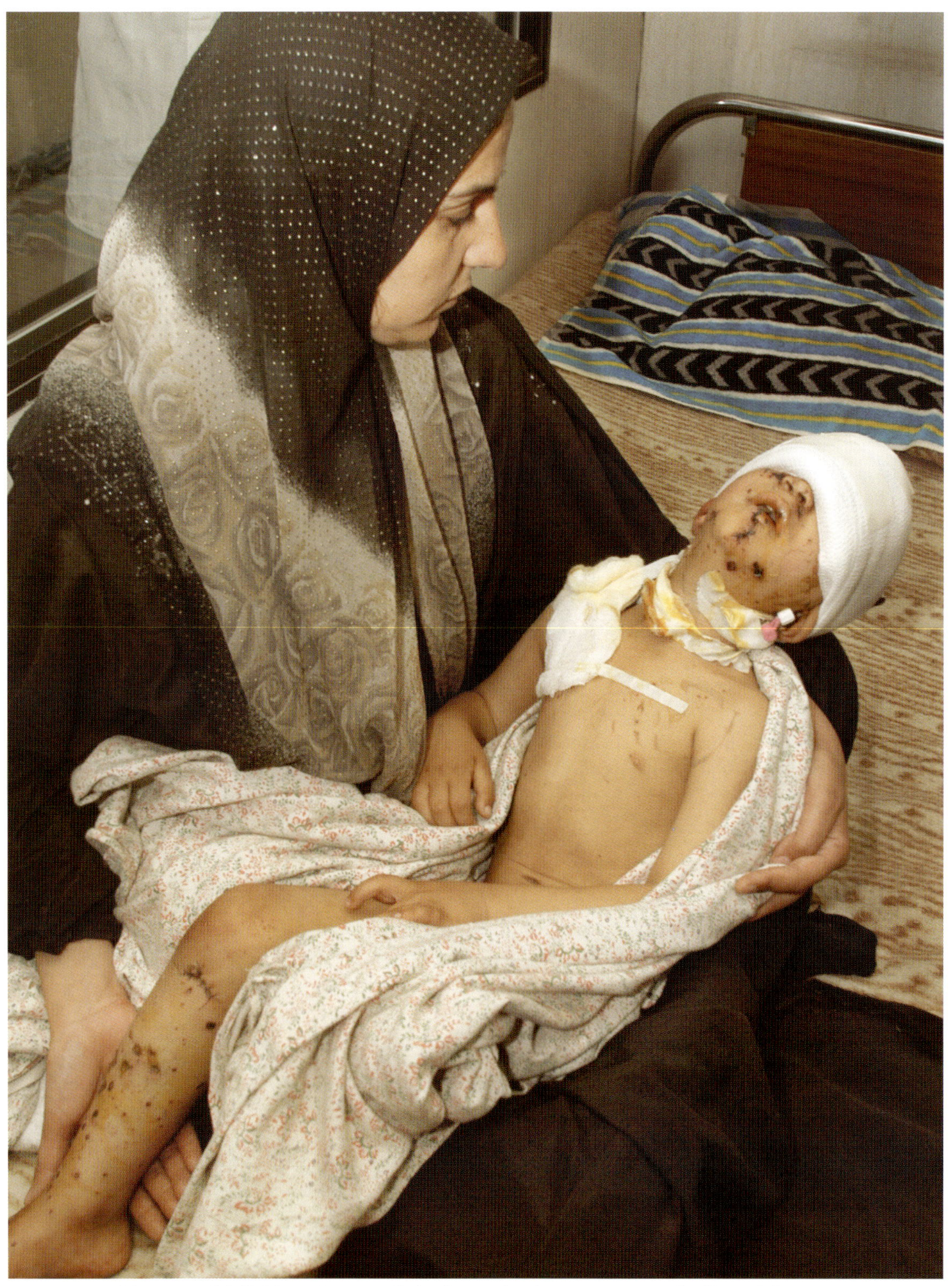

Five-year-old Ali Mustapha is cradled in his mother's arms, a victim of collateral damage

advancing Iraqi youth soldiers. They were Saddam's teenage warriors, and as the Marines advanced upon their positions, the boy soldiers came streaming over a hilltop with outdated rifles and handguns. By the time the gunfire died down, all that was left was a pink mist – hanging like a fog above the battlefield. The 50-calibre machine gun and rifle fire pulverized the advancing Iraqi troops, blowing them apart and turning them into a pink mist of vaporized blood and flesh. "They just wouldn't stop," said Nino. "Line after line of them. They should have laid down their weapons, but they just kept coming to their deaths."

Nino tells me he and his two buddies, also sitting at the table, have not had a shower in over a month. I ask Sean and Tish if they would let these soldiers take a shower in our room. They agree, and I leave the room key where Nino can find it. They will take their shower tomorrow.

Nino describes how average Iraqis are showing an outpouring of compassion towards the troops and showering them in gifts. Some of Nino's fellow Marines say that they will never have to buy cigarettes or candies again, since they have been given so many by the Iraqi public. Most of the Marines speak about the average Iraqi with admiration and concern. But I wondered how long this love affair will last – as every day the situation is getting worse for the Iraqi people. Bakeries and vegetable vendors are slowly starting to open their shops and a small trickle of foodstuffs are becoming available, to those who could find and afford them. The reality is that most Iraqis don't have a penny in their pockets to buy any food. So the suffering will continue.

Day 8. Thursday, April 17th

(Doctors are part-time gravediggers; visiting Kadamiyya Hospital; Haider the translator; collateral damage victims overwhelming the hospital; five-year-old Ali Mustapha Ghaleb; description of a cluster bomb; misery in the hospital room; bomblet explodes in boy's face; tank crews hand out treats to children; "it's Saddam's fault"; young girl killed by a cluster bomb; "maybe you will even lose your life"; visiting the home of a cluster bomb victim; pulverized flesh; live ordnance litters area beside a soccer field; tombstone waiting for you; drunks toy with live mortars; a gaggle of children; live bomb stuck in ground; a fresh collection of nightmares; Nino's gifts; Voices in the Wilderness writer set straight; never judge a book by its cover)

Earlier this morning, Tod and Jim had heard from Haider, our translator, that doctors at a local hospital had become part-time gravediggers. Apparently, they are burying the hospital dead in the back lot of the hospital grounds. The dead are mostly civilian casualties, those who had shown up at the hospital for treatment of their wounds, but succumbed to them. The doctors have to dispose of the bodies by burying them, before they pile up and become a health problem. Why waste electricity to run a morgue, when it is needed more to save lives?

Sean and Tish are still covering the Easter story, so Jim, Tod and I leave the Fanar early in the morning, heading for Kadamiyya Hospital in the Al Mustansiriyah area of Baghdad.

Just after arriving, Jim and Tod stand outside the hospital entrance interviewing two doctors that Haider had just introduced us to. Haider is the king of the translators, the best of the best! Not only does he speak educated English and Arabic, but he knows people in all sorts of important positions and trades, like some of the doctors at this hospital. Our driver Adel, is a polite, quiet spoken man with a great knowledge of Baghdad. I am glad these men work for our team, they make our jobs easier and safer.

I overhear the doctors talking about victims of collateral damage, some of whom they had buried on the hospital grounds. Almost simultaneously, Jim, Tod and I ask if there are any collateral damage victims presently recovering in the hospital. The doctor tells us there are many such victims, and many children maimed by cluster bombs. The situation is overwhelming the hospital.

Just off to the other end of the entranceway, a car leaves the hospital driveway with a rough wooden casket on its roof, covered by a black shroud with religious writings on it. These people are picking up the corpse of a family member. They will bury their own dead, at their chosen location.

We ask one of the doctors for permission to see and talk with the collateral damage victims. He says it will not be a problem, and leads us through the busy hospital hallways, up the stairs, and into a large recovery room with six beds. One bed contains an adult man who was wounded in the side by shrapnel. Another bed holds an elderly woman who has a non-war-related injury. Two others hold young children, the victims of two different cluster-bomb accidents, two beds are empty.

In the nearest bed sits a middle-aged woman in a black gown. She is sobbing and clinging to the bandaged and partially clad body of her young wounded son. It brings to mind the marble statue of Michelangelo's La Pieta, which depicts Mary cradling a dying Jesus in her lap. The boy's name is Ali Mustapha Ghaleb; he is five years old. Ali was maimed Monday while playing with one of the unexploded bomblets from a cluster bomb, near his home in Baghdad.

His doctor, Dr. Ausama Saadi, tells us that Ali is blind for life, and because of a lack of electricity, he is unable to use a CT scan to diagnose the damage caused by the deep wounds in Ali's head.

Cluster-bombs are used to kill ground movements of troops and destroy mechanized equipment. They are a horrendous weapon when used in residential areas. But the restrictions and laws against their usage are lost in a fog of international politics and open breaches.

A typical cluster bomb holds 130 bomblets. Most are cylindrically shaped and hollow like a bell, and about the size of a small can. Painted green or yellow, they are filled with hundreds of small pill-sized pieces of metal. The cluster bomb has a timer on it, which is pre-set to allow the main bomb casing to open just above the ground or higher, spilling out its load of small bombs. The bomblets spring out in a horizontal web-like pattern then explode simultaneously, showering an area the size of a soccer field with the deadly white-hot, armor-piercing shards. The timer is set to go off at a height where the bomber wants the bomb to do the most damage. This type of bomb spills out a blanket of death on the battlefield and is mostly used to kill ground troops, destroy missile sites and other military hardware. "They are not supposed to be used in civilian areas, but we had to use them in an urban environment because that is where Saddam put those weapons," said an official with U.S. Central Command.

At least 20 percent of the bomblets misfire. Scattered on the ground, the little bombs remain live but deadly. Anyone who picks one up, or kicks at one, is likely to set it off and be killed or injured.

Young Ali is sobbing and writhing in pain with what looks like deep cigarette burns all over his limp body. His head is particularly pocked by the unsightly, open black wounds. A large white bandage covers the top half of his little head, including both eyes. Entrance wounds heavily puncture his legs. It appears, by the pattern of wounds, that Ali was in a squat-

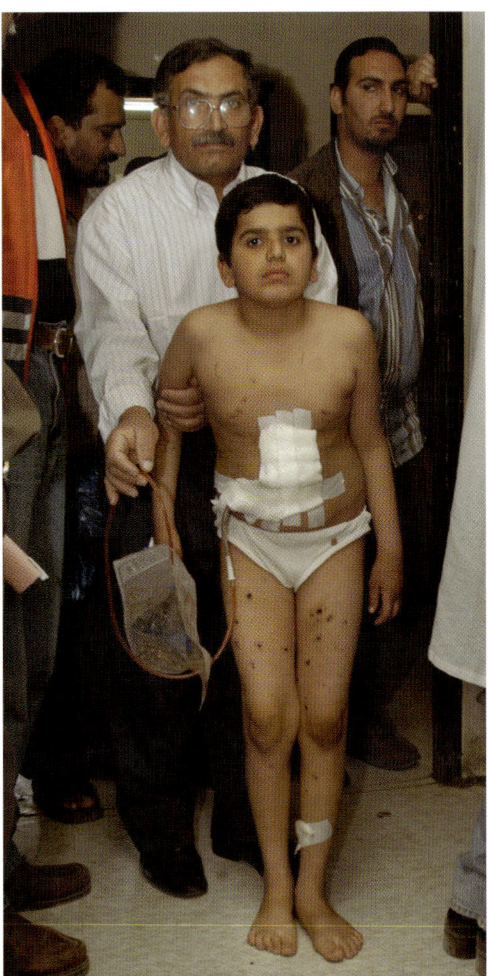

Another room, another cluster bomb victim

ting position when the bomb exploded in his face.

Ali is six years younger than my little son, Brian (who is back in Montreal with my wife Phyllis and his sisters – 13-year-old Iona, and 16-year-old Heather). I fight to control my emotions, which are tearing me apart inside. Ali and his mother are a hideous sight of misery and pain.

As his tearful mother rocks her crying little boy back and forth, Tod and Jim start interviewing her about what happened. The boy's father, Mustapha Ghaleb, who stands somber beside his wife and son, nods his approval for me to continue photographing the gut-wrenching scene. Ali looks like a limp, dying fish draped across his mother's arms. Both are wells of despair, and after taking a dozen photos, I start to think about my children, and have to leave the room to get back my composure and suck down a cigarette.

It is extremely difficult, but I am determined to stay strong, and not get too overwhelmed by the emotion of the situation. This is much easier said than done.

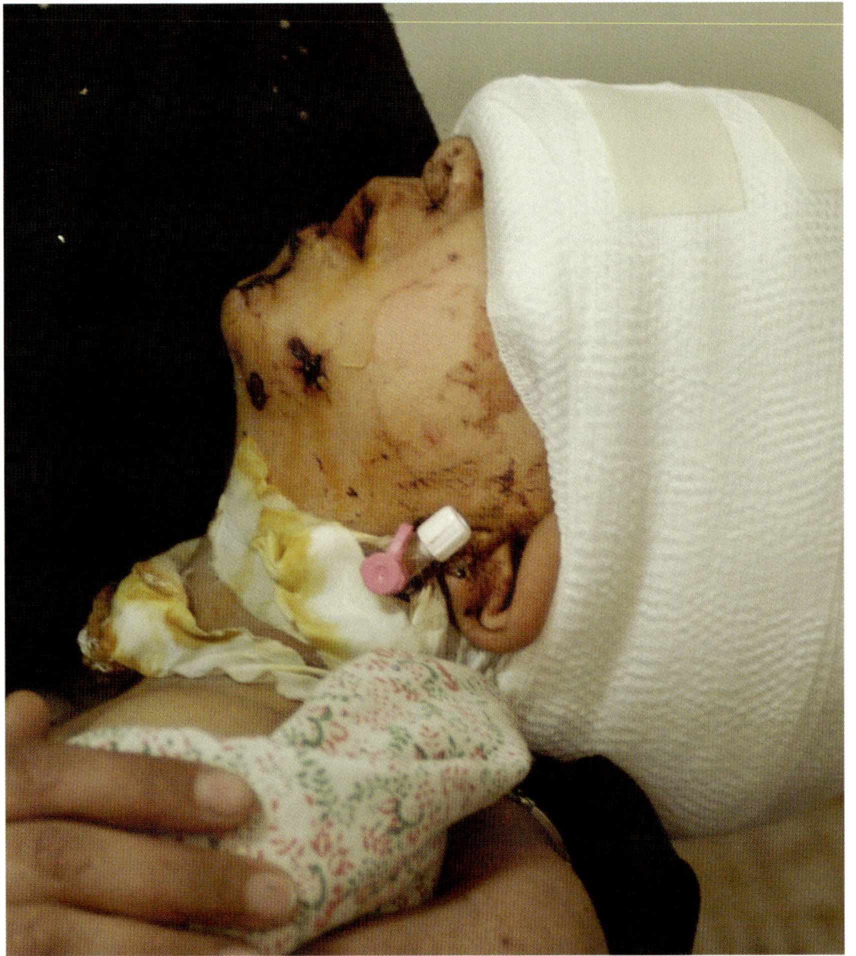

Deep cigarette-like burns scar Ali Mustapha from the top of his head to the tip of his toes

Having my smoke on a hospital balcony, I look down onto Al Hill Street, a main roadway, and see three American tanks flanking the hospital. The crews are sitting on top of their machines handing out candy and food to a swarm of at least 70 children. I see the soldiers smiling and laughing, while making sure each kid receives a treat. It is a happy scene of kids and young troops, a typical scene between soldiers and children.

After my smoke, I take a deep breath and go back into the sick room. Ali is still moaning and groaning, as though imprisoned in an inescapable nightmare. His mother, Muna Hassan, keeps dabbing her eyes with a hanky, while describing what happened to her son on Monday.

"Ali was out playing with some friends when he picked up the bomb lying on the ground. He thought it was a toy of some sort. Then the bomb went off in his face." Tod is trying to fight back the tears I can see welling in his eyes, but continues. "Who do you blame for your son's present condition; who do you feel is responsible for Ali being maimed?" The father speaks up immediately: "It's all the fault of Saddam Hussein," he says forcefully – and shockingly to us. Tod does not want him to be courteous towards us and not speak the truth, just because we are Westerners. We have to know the absolute truth about whom he feels was responsible.

Both Ali's mother and father speak in unison. "It was the fault of Saddam Hussein! If Saddam hadn't set the stage forcing the hand of the Americans to come here, then this wouldn't have happened! We blame Saddam Hussein!" reiterates the father. Three stunned journalists

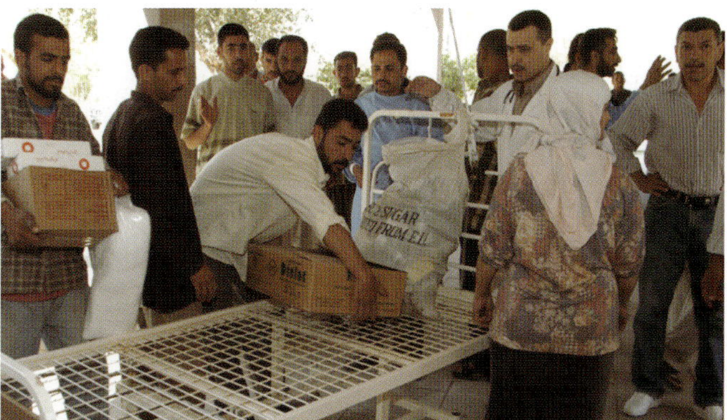
There are even fewer medical supplies at this hospital in Medical City

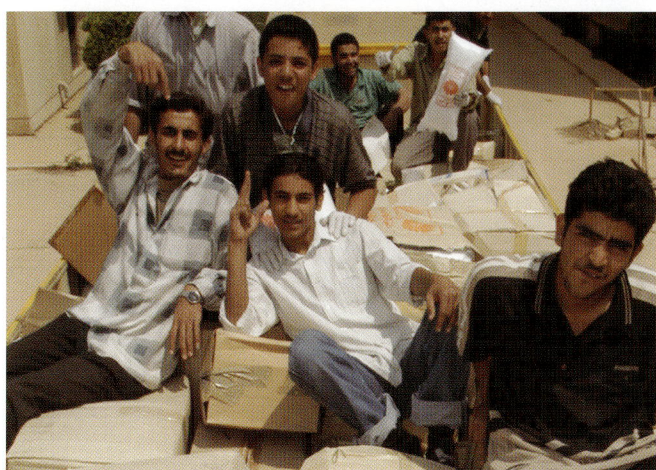
Volunteers ready to unpack medical supplies at Kadamiyya Hospital

stand frozen in disbelief at the parents' statements. We, or at least I, expected them to blame the Americans!

Leaving Ali's mother, as she covers the little boy in a blanket, we chat with a boy of 11 who is occupying a nearby bed. Like Ali (though not to the same terrible extent), this boy's body is peppered with the same cluster-bomb wounds. Most of his wounds are on the legs. He had also been playing with a cluster bomb when it exploded. His condition is stable enough that he can walk with assistance. He can also speak and see. Ali can't do either; he just lies in his mother's arms – crying and moaning.

We leave this room and visit another, just across the hall. A mother and her teenage son and daughter each occupy a bed in this room. All three were wounded by cluster bombs. The mother tells us that her 17-year-old son, Saif brought the bomblet home from the west Baghdad suburb of Farusiyyah, not realizing it was a bomb. The youngest daughter, seven-month-old Rawand Muhammad, found the bomblet in the living room and started to play with it when it exploded. The young girl died instantly, her body torn to pieces. Three other family members were also injured. When neighbors rushed over to bring the wounded to the hospital, four other bomblets were found in Saif's car. Saif threw the bombs out of the window of the moving vehicle but they exploded, blasting them with more shrapnel and blowing out three tires.

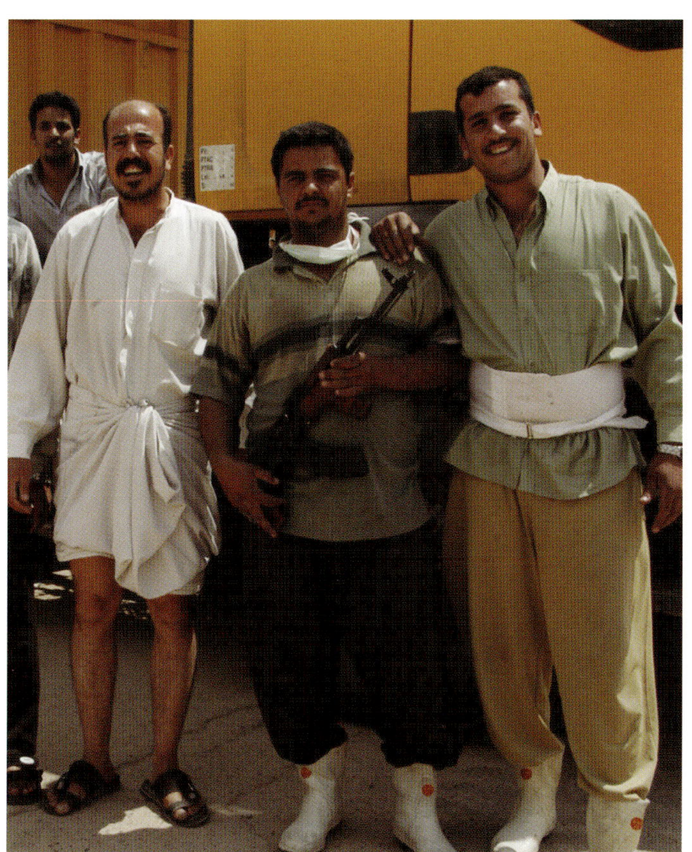
Kurdish truck crew carries an AK-47 to repel bandits

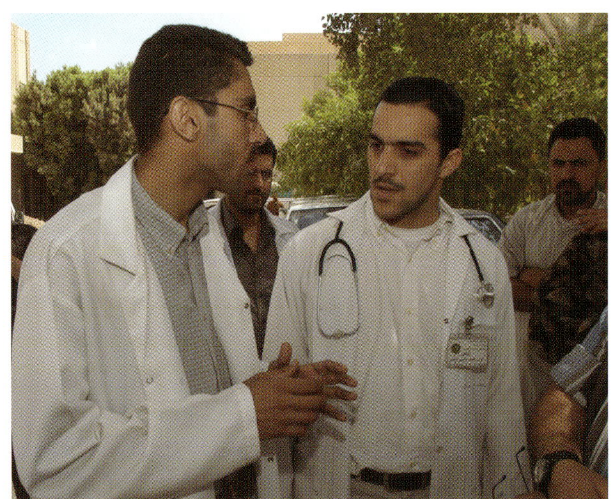

Doctors Saadi (left) and Fawaz discuss Ali's case

It is a different room, a different condemnation. "It's the Americans," say the son and mother. "They brought this upon us. Now I will never see my daughter again," says the crying mother. She tells us her husband was not at home when the bomb exploded, and we can go visit him to see where her daughter was killed. We all agree, and she gives us the directions then asks, "If you find any remains of my daughter, please collect them for me, no matter how small; I need something to bury."

Having had enough of the grief, I leave Tod and Jim to take more notes, and retreat to the hospital entranceway. An AK-47 is propped-up against the sliding glass doors. A hospital worker tells me the AK is in place to protect the hospital from looters and bandits. Guns are everywhere, a big part of wartime life in Baghdad, and seeing the AK-47 leaning on the glass is as mundane here as a snow shovel leaning against a doorway in Canada, or New England.

In the hospital parking area I see an 18-wheeler transport truck packed to the brim with medical supplies. The truck has just arrived, and the eight-man crew is starting to unpack its cargo. Amongst other things, these boxes hold gauze padding, IV units and bedding. I photograph the crew (some of whom are from Kurdistan and dress in bloomer pants, with the legs tied at the bottom and a sash around their waists) posing outside the truck; one of them holds an AK. They tell me they have to carry the weapon to ward off any attacks from thieves (other trucks have been attacked and their drivers killed). One of the Kurdish crew tells me, "If you don't carry guns, then you won't have a truck for very long. Maybe you will even lose your life."

I see Tod and Jim standing outside the entranceway, and walk over to meet them. They tell me we are going to visit the home where the young girl was killed, in hopes of meeting the father, Muhammad Suleiman.

We arrive at the three-storey mud-brick house in the densely populated district of Hurriyah. The laneways are well kept and some local residents are out cleaning their properties. The father of the dead girl welcomes us at the front door and leads us up to the second-floor living room.

On the walls of the small room hang a calendar, some religious posters and a map of Palestine. Plastic flowers, ornamental porcelain figurines and a copy of the Koran sit on top of two end tables flanking the couch. A large woven plastic rug, decorated with red peacocks, covers the floor and a deck of playing cards is scattered across it. There is a 10-inch hole in the ceiling. On the floor immediately below, the rug has a two-square-foot piece missing from it, where the bomb was dropped and exploded. Its tattered edges are blackened and coated with blood. The brunt of the impact gouged a four-inch hole into the cement floor.

Grape-sized pit marks from the shrapnel pock the walls and ceiling. These are splattered with congealed blood and small pea-sized pieces of hard, blackened human tissue. Streaks of dried blood are etched into the walls. The lacy white curtains covering the broken window glass are speckled with burn holes and pulverized flesh.

Two cousins and a doctor friend of the family join us in the house. The father points to the large pie-sized blast hole in the carpet covering the middle of the floor. He walks over and reaches down, lifting up the ragged and blackened carpet. Under it is a large pool of dried blood. It is not a pretty sight – another shock to my already shocking day.

Burned into the couch I find a piece of worked metal about an inch-and-half long by a quarter inch thick in the shape of a long pear, or elongated bottle. It is part of the shrapnel from the bomblet. It may be a key to identifying the type of cluster bomb it came from. (There are many different types of cluster bombs, for different types of targets).

The father offers to take us to a destroyed Iraqi Army warehouse about 1000 feet from his home. He tells us that a cluster bomb was dropped beside it, probably to kill the Iraqi soldiers and arms stored inside. We walk a good block before arriving at a large building, flanked by two soccer fields full of young adults playing the world's most popular sport.

Spent and live 50-calibre bullets are everywhere. They are lying on the sidewalk and on the soccer pitch. Walking around to the side of the warehouse we see the main point of impact. A good third of the warehouse and a number of trucks outside (probably used to store and transport arms) have been pulverized by at least one cluster bomb. All kinds of live armaments are strewn about, including mortars of various types, and boxes that look like large sardine tins, containing rounds of 50-calibre

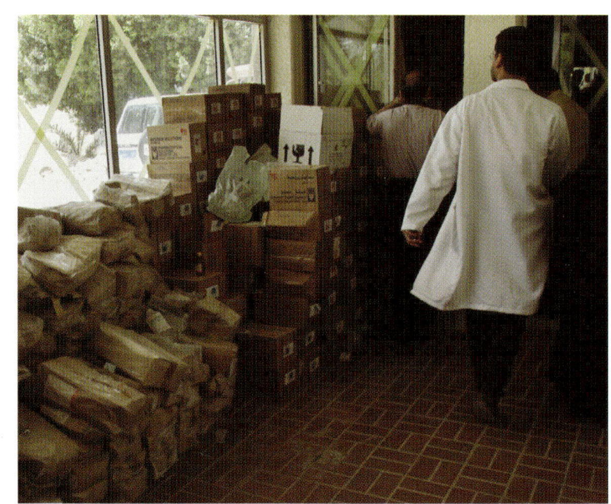

Emergency supplies line the hospital lobby

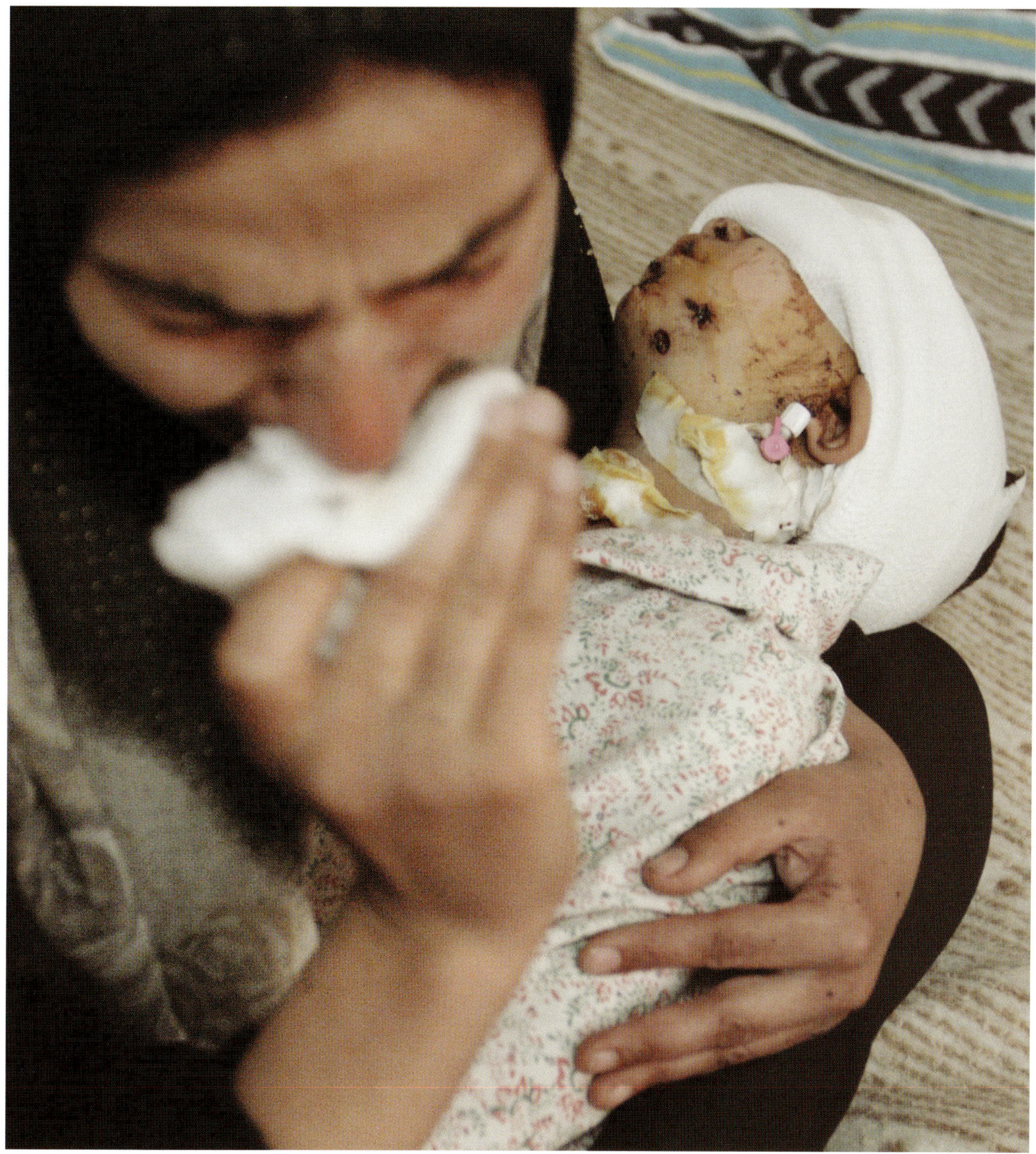

Five-year-old Ali Mustapha Ghaleb is blinded for life. Shrapnel wounds cover his face and head

ammunition. Many of these cases are burst open and burned. The whole area is awash in wreckage and unexploded ammunition. But I can't see any rifles or machine guns. The locals probably took these easily portable weapons for themselves. I don't see any cluster bomb duds.

We have to step very daintily, at times on our tiptoes, manoeuvring through the debris-strewn mess. This is a situation where if you drop your camera or your water bottle, you could trigger an explosion. All you don't need to do is step on a mortar, or half-buried grenade. There is a string of loosely connected slit trenches dug around the warehouse perimeter. These are full of mortars, ammunition, flares, clothing and personal objects like a pocket Koran.

A group of six children has latched onto us, following us around the bomb site. It is too dangerous to keep our eyes on these kids (who we have been repeatedly telling not to follow us or touch any weapons), while watching out for ourselves. I worry they might step on a bomb and kill themselves, and us with them. Finally, we are so annoyed with them that we ask the dead girl's father to implore them, in Arabic, to leave. They keep their distance after that. But things only get crazier.

Two inebriated men, drinking from a large bottle of white rum on the warehouse office steps, stagger over to see what we are up to. They are incoherent and feeling no pain. When about 50 feet away, they start showing off, picking up live mortars and pretending to pull the firing pins. This is getting scary; they are staggering and almost falling over with the

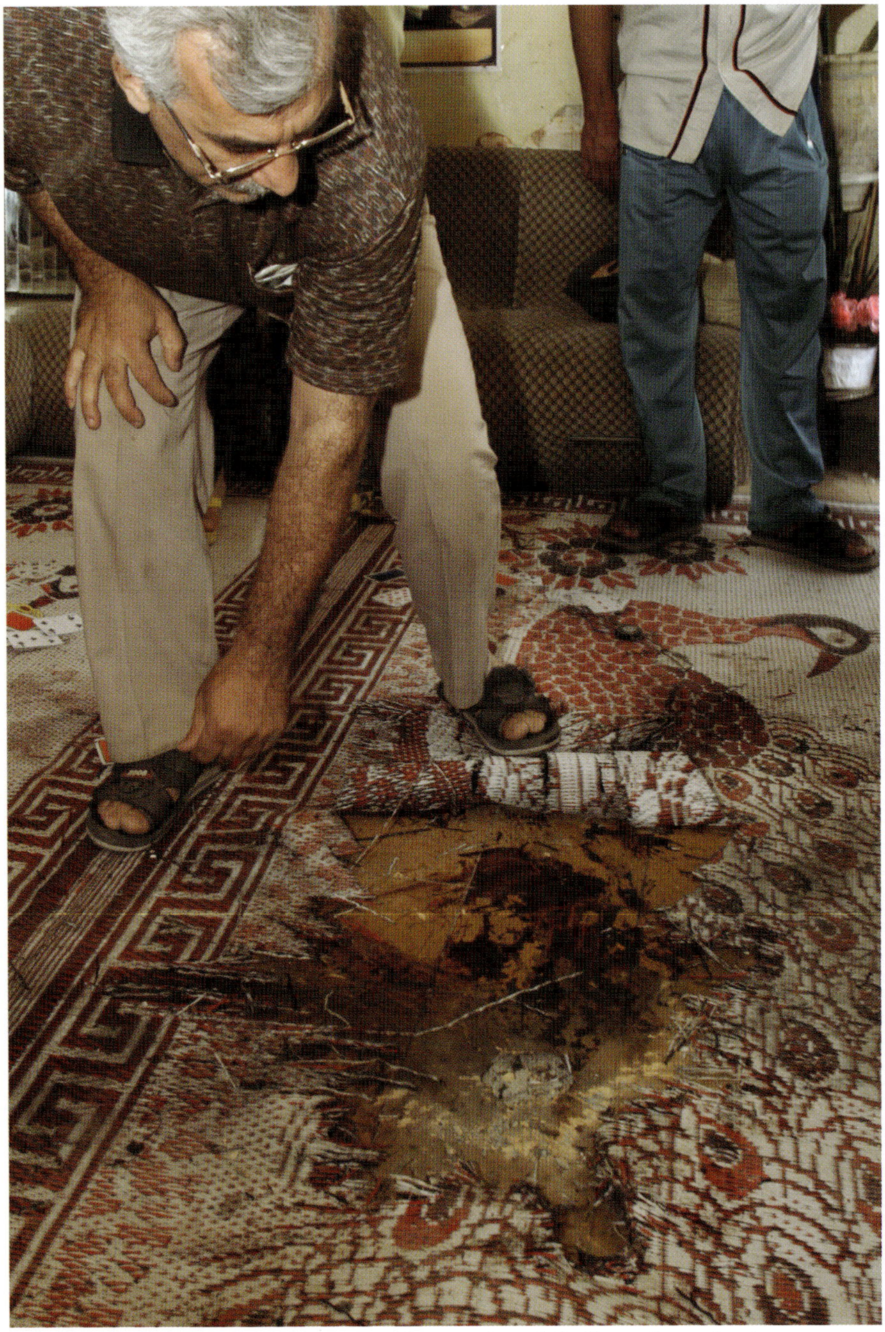

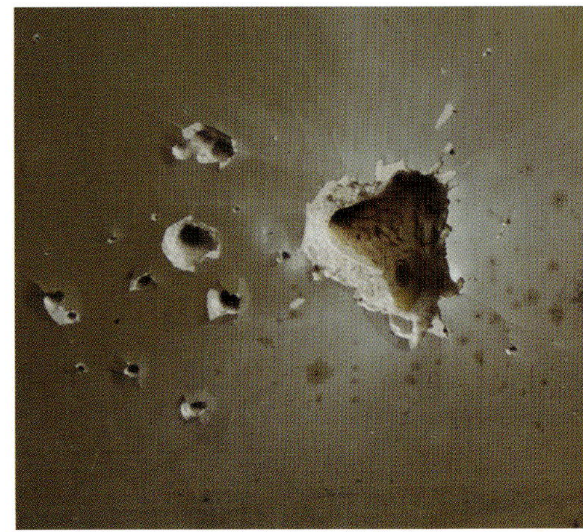

Shrapnel holes blown into the ceiling

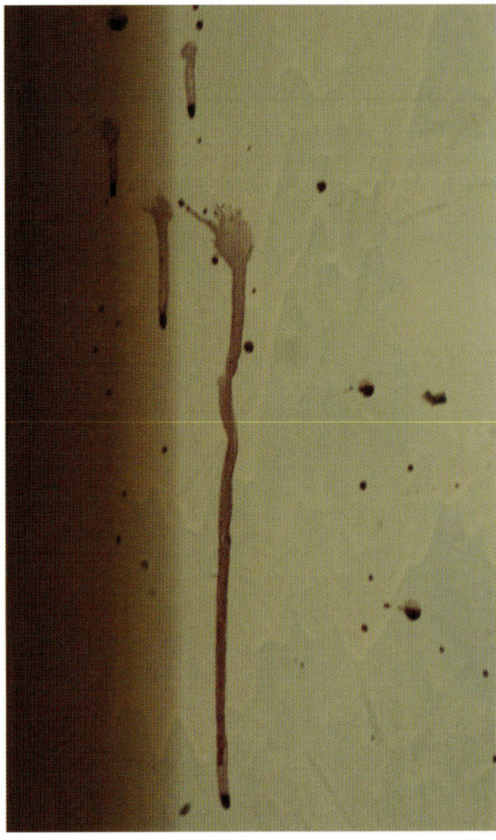

Dried blood and flesh fragments streak the walls

The home where 7-month-old Rawand was killed by a cluster bomb

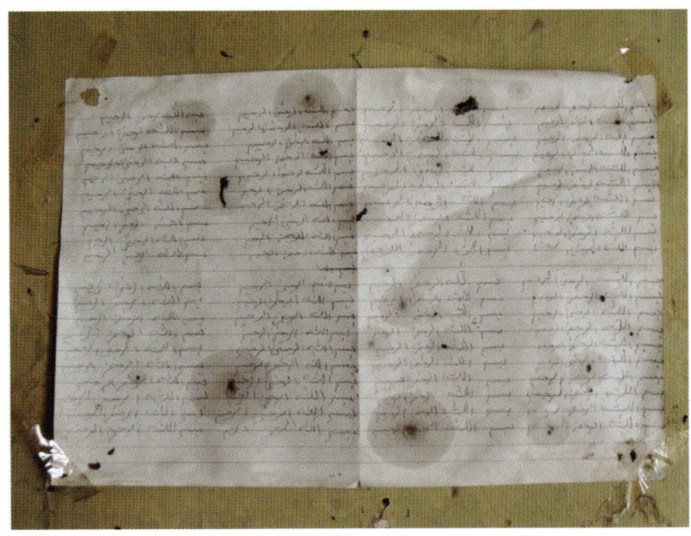

A letter on the wall is stained with flesh

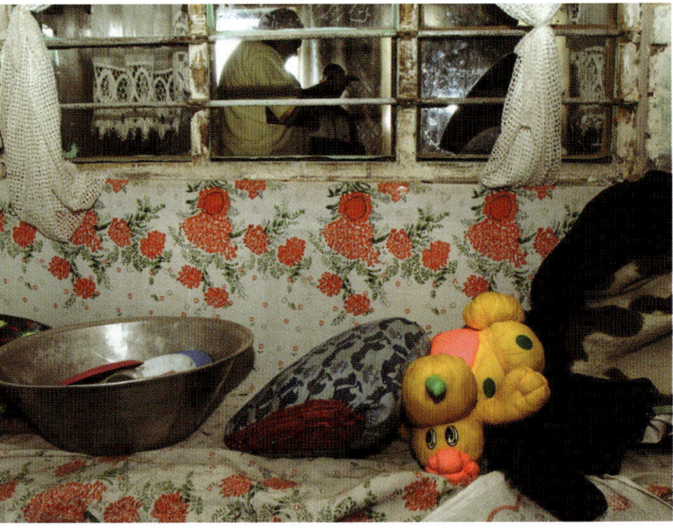

Though young Rawand is dead, her toys are strewn about the home

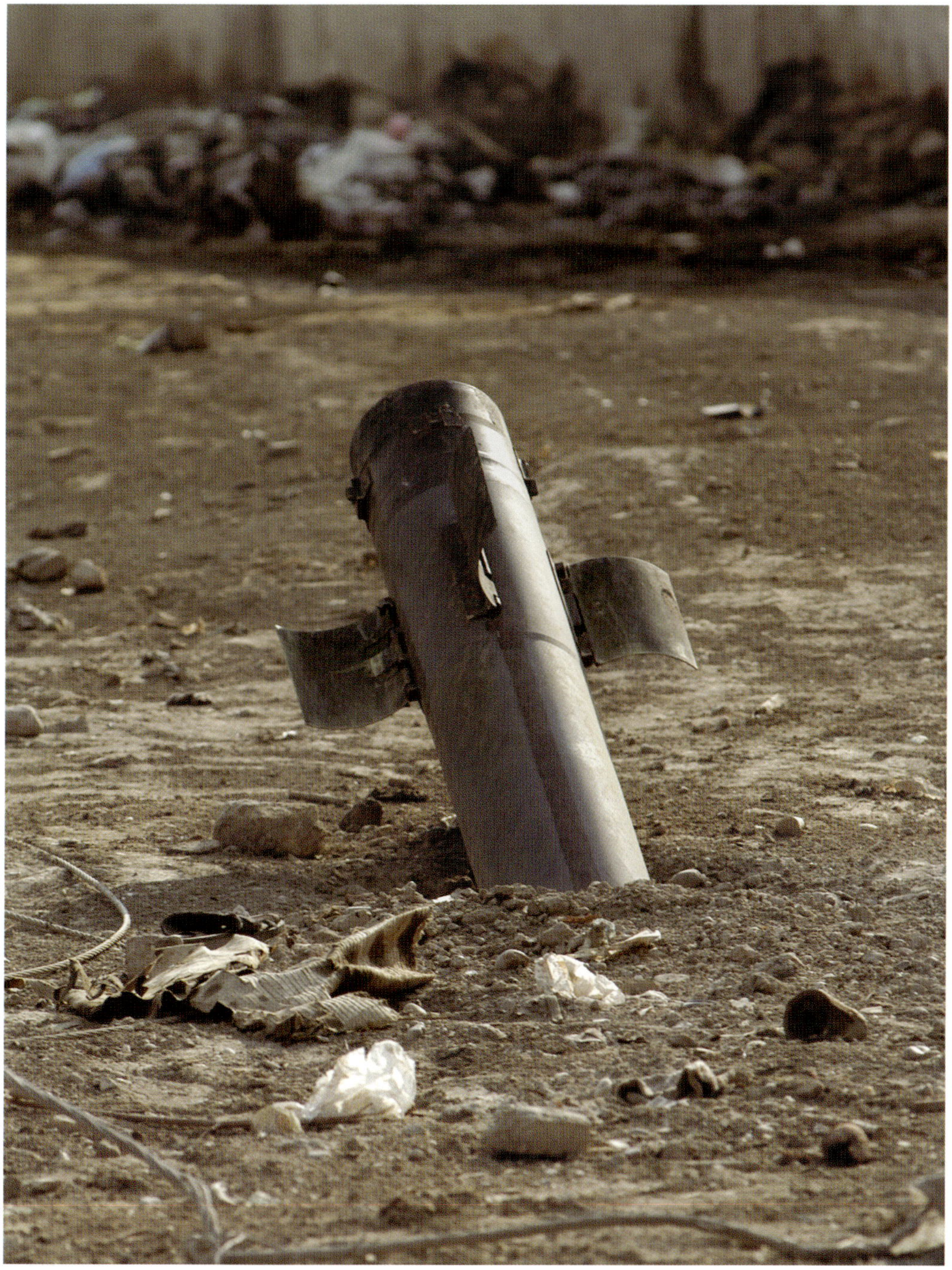

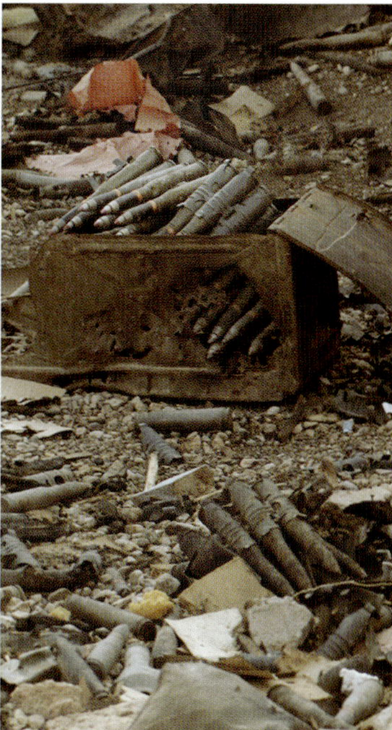

Fifty-calibre rounds near soccer field

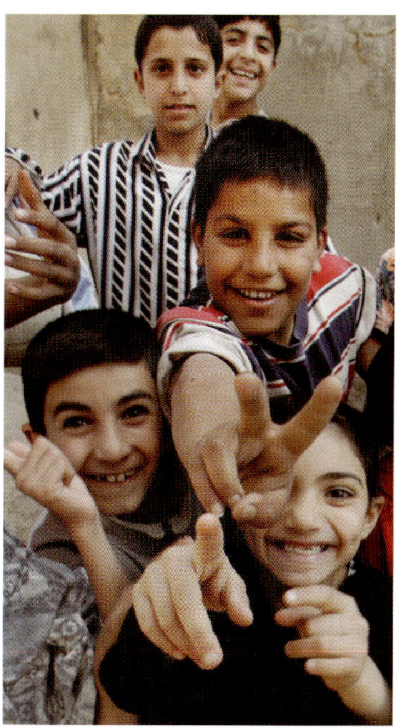

Children from the Hurriyah district

Live bomb stuck in the ground near the Hurriyah district

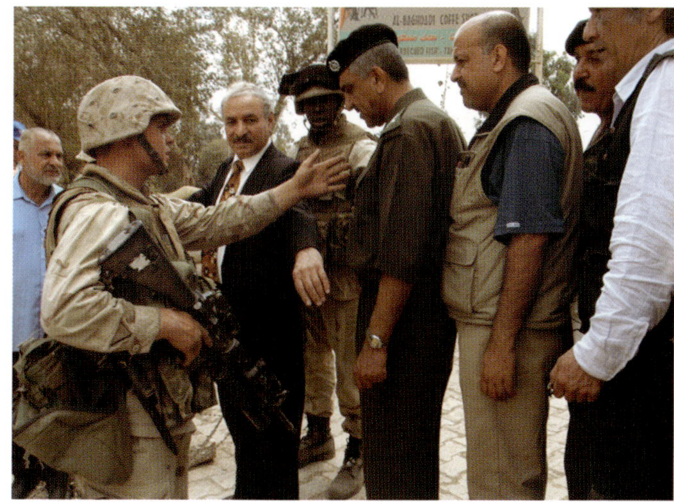

Marines check all for concealed weapons outside the Palestine Hotel

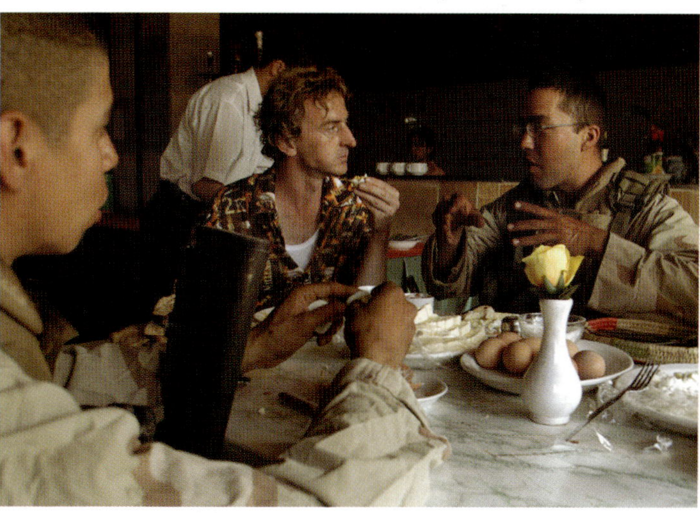

Sean and the Marines in the Al Fanar dining room

bombs in their hands. Seeing this, I immediately shout over to Tod and Jim. "The drunks are messing around with the mortars and pretending to pull the pins! Let's get the hell out of here before someone blows us up!" I do not have to repeat myself. We all dart out of the area, leaving the drunks and the usual entourage of kids and gawkers standing in the field full of live bombs.

We are not going to take any unnecessary risks with our lives – just to be polite or accommodating. I had just been to the hospital and witnessed the horrors that exploding ordnance can bring, I am not going to take any chances. I had promised my family that I would come home alive, and I am going to live up to that.

Iraqi kids (like most other children) always want to follow the journalists. I guess these kids have not seen many Westerners and the fact that we dress differently and carry a camera makes us an attraction, rather like a circus. Downtown, where it is more destitute, street orphans and the other homeless and abandoned souls constantly beg for food and money. The kids here don't ask us for anything, except to take their pictures. They have cleaner hygiene and are less shabbily dressed. At times, we journalists feel like the Pied Piper, with a gaggle of children constantly shadowing us.

Here is another Iraqi military installation in a heavily populated area, beside a soccer field, bombed by American planes. While driving away from the warehouse we see a large unexploded bomb, six feet long and two feet thick, stuck into the hard-packed earth beside an intersection lined with shops. Embedded at a 45-degree angle, a third of it is buried nose-first into the ground, the rest of the body and tailfins sticking above. It looks like a giant sausage, just 400 feet from the warehouse and soccer fields. I wonder if this bomb was meant for the warehouse, but had strayed off-course. We decide not to go near it, staying about 50 feet away. Just the vibration from us approaching could be enough to set it off, so I use a 200mm zoom lens to photograph it. It would have been dropped from an American bomber. The Iraqi Air Force, not wanting to commit suicide by fighting the massive American air machine, did not even get off the ground at the start of the war.

We head back to the hotel with a fresh collection of nightmares from our daily reaping of news. Entering my room at the Fanar, I find an Iraqi bayonet and Iraqi flag draped across my bed. A letter lying on the flag is from Nino, thanking us for letting him and his friends use the shower. It's a fine, unexpected gift and the letter says they are from the battle at Al Kut, in south-eastern Iraq.

I am downloading my photos onto the laptop, in the lobby of the Fanar. A small group of journalists and NGOs is gathered around looking at my photos of Ali Mustapha. They are gasping at the sight of the images, asking where I took them and what had happened to the boy. The Italian woman, who works for Voices in the Wilderness, is looking over my shoulder at the photos, with her hand covering her mouth in disbelief. Suddenly she becomes all friendly to me and starts complimenting me on my work. I take this opportunity to straighten her out a little. I tell her that when she first saw me and found out I was a journalist she personally attacked me as an American sympathizer, without knowing who

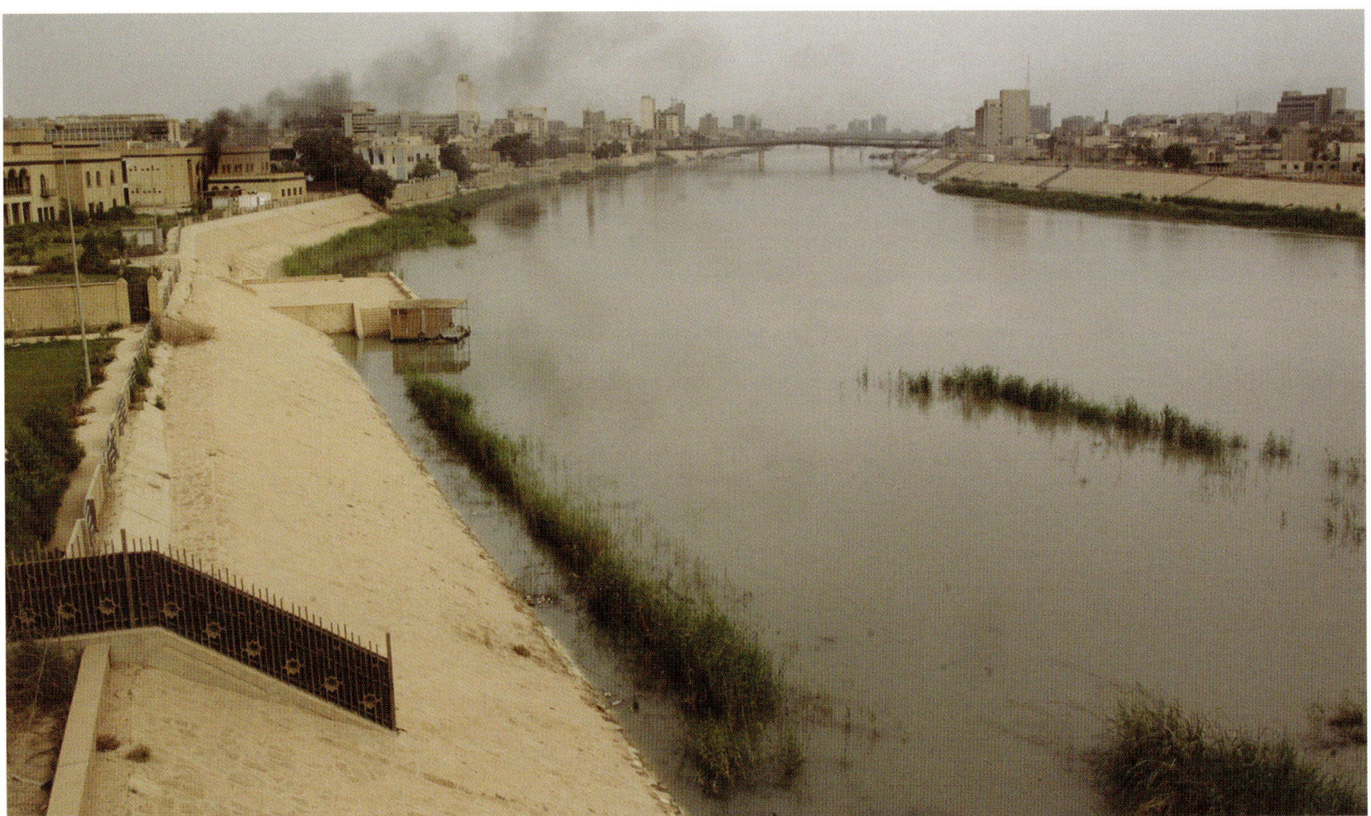

Tigris River looking south

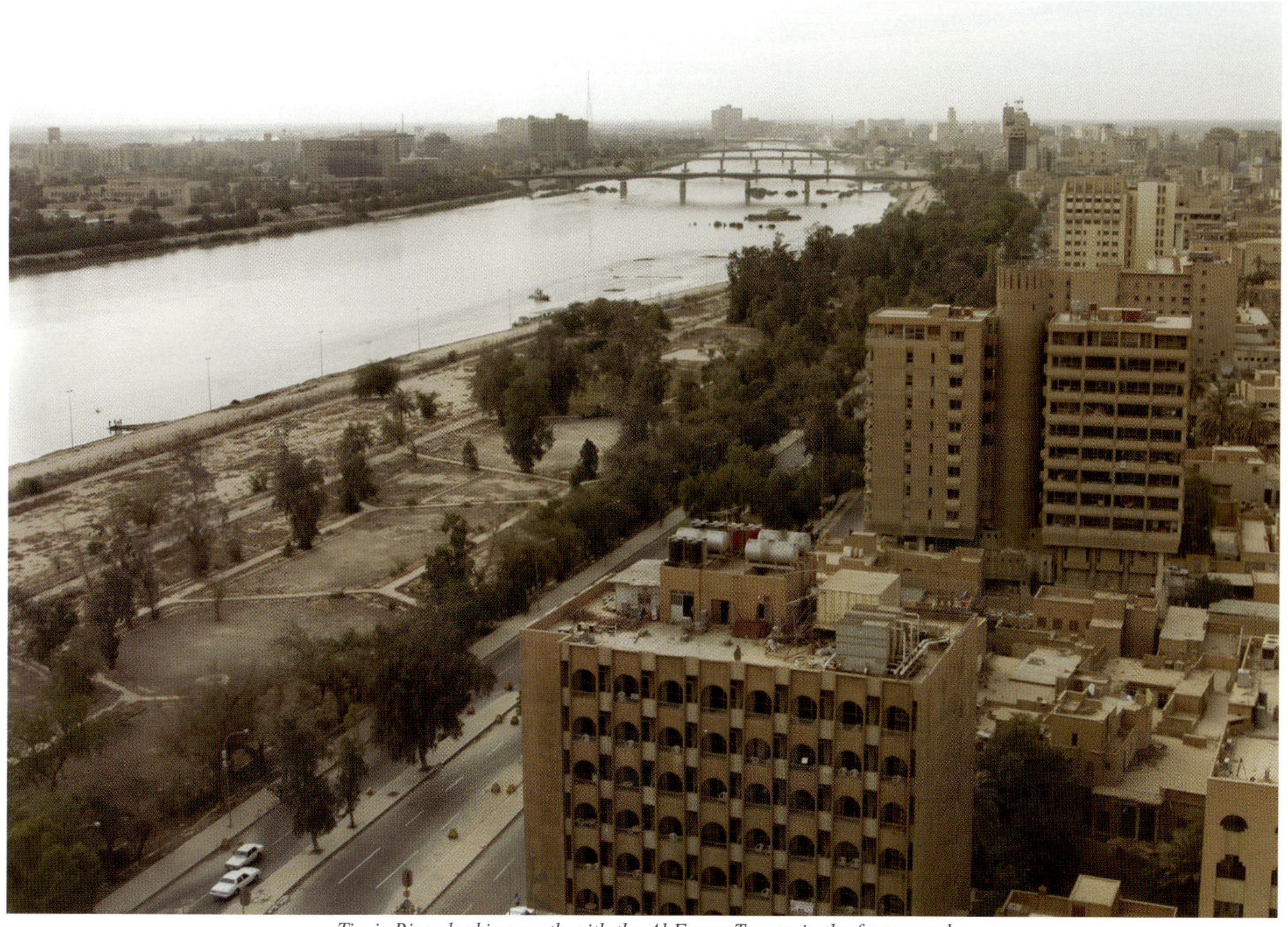

Tigris River looking north with the Al Fanar Towers in the foreground

I was. I let her know that three of our team covered this story and that between us, readers in the United States and around the world will read about these instances of collateral damage and how they occur. The other journalists and NGO people looking at my laptop were also going to cover the story because of our work. So I just leave her with a little food for thought – never judge a book by its cover!

Day 9. Friday, April 18th

(Food is scarce as shops slowly start to open; bottled water and tainted water; illness from drinking tainted water; contaminated vegetables; meeting photographer Simon Norfolk; looking for the Black Hole; tour of the looted Ministry of War; burned military documentation; chemical warfare retardant kits; bombed bunker; looters rob mosque; he's not Jesus; ground-to-air missiles; shop owners clear debris; destruction in the palm grove; depleted uranium weapons; lost both legs below the knees; John Otis of the Houston Chronicle; Free Prisoners Committee; the search for missing family; pink placards; there is no God in Baghdad; Saddam's executioner; description of a Meals-Ready-To-Eat (MRE) ration pack; Karbala tomorrow; Nino leaves Baghdad; journalist Patrick Graham in looter raid; a bigger, more deadly weapon; the dangers of using a satellite phone at night; bedside chats; a picture of my family; the wild dogs of Baghdad; a melody of rifle and machine-gun fire)

There is still no electricity in Baghdad, except for generators. Some shops are slowly starting to open, and if you can find one you can buy bottled water, sodas, candies, and some canned goods. There are some vegetables for sale, onions, garlic, and fava beans, but these look past their peak and inedible, at least to me. Some meat is available but it is suspect, because there is no refrigeration.

Walking past a shop window, I see a leg of goat hanging on a hook. The meat looks black, because it has so many flies covering it. There is no way I will eat anything but my daily supper at the Fanar dining room. The chicken is well broiled, the rice is boiled and the soup is boiled, so all bacteria are killed. This meal is my only means of sustenance, besides candy, tea and bottled water. One blessing is that you eat less in this heat.

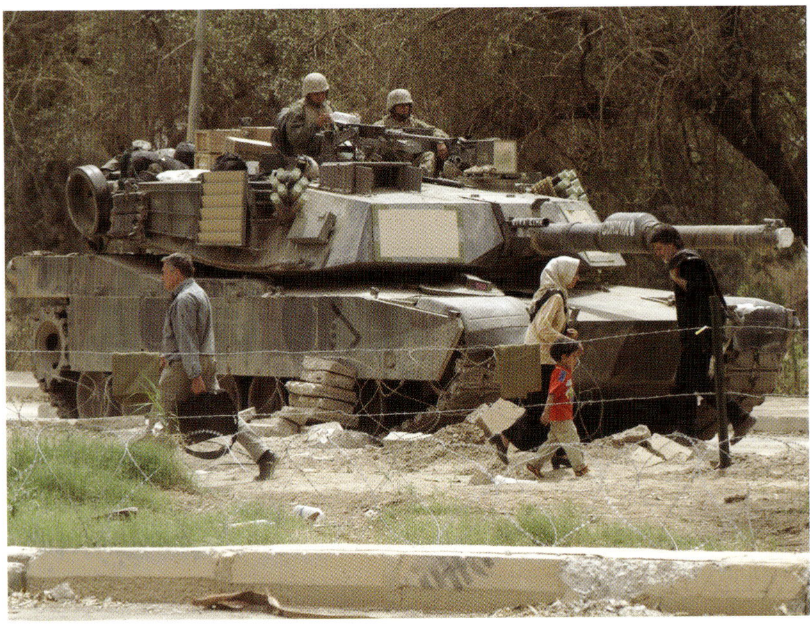

Journalists and residents walk past a checkpoint in front of the Al Fanar

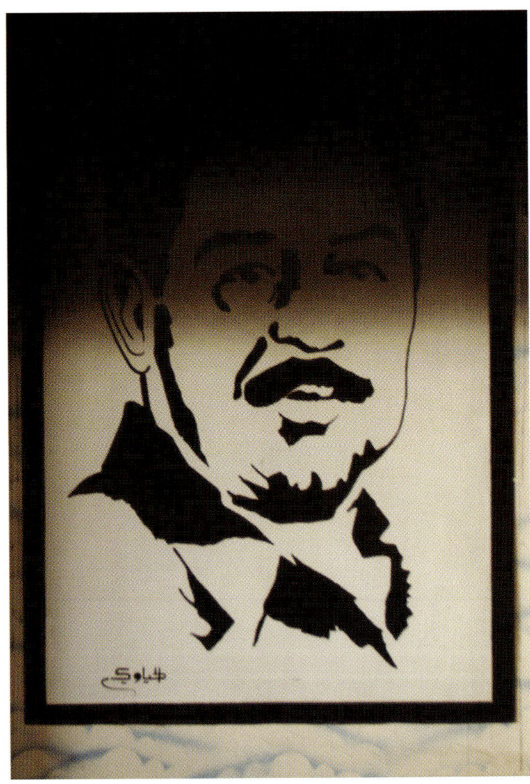

Smoke-blackened portrait of Saddam in War Ministry

Water is much more important than food, and I am drinking at least five litres a day. The basic rule of survival here is that you procure your own water and try to have a constant supply of it. I also mark my initials on my plastic water bottles so I don't drink someone else's. This helps ensure that I don't drink water that might be contaminated.

Early this morning, Sean came down with a terrible case of diarrhea and exhaustion (that I named "Saddam's Revenge") from drinking some water offered him yesterday by a well-meaning civilian. Now he lies incapacitated in his bed.

But the sickness is not restricted to journalists. I notice that some of the Marines are walking about looking like the living dead. A good third of the force is down with diarrhea and fever. I ask one of the Marines if he knows how they all became sick. He tells me that many had eaten shish kabobs, which contained a lettuce and parsley garnish. I tell him that the raw vegetables are the most likely source of their illness.

The city water supply comes from the Tigris River, which is contaminated with rotting corpses, sewage, chemicals, and all sorts of weaponry. The river water is sprayed onto the farmers' vegetable crops, which end up on the kabobs. You have to be either insane, new to the city, or extremely naive, to take any chance with the water or food here.

I have some in-depth knowledge of water treatment and water-borne maladies, from covering stories on tainted water in my home province of Quebec. In Southern Quebec, the population's health is continually threatened because of pollution from agricultural runoff (pig manure, cattle manure, fertilizers and pesticides). So even though I am a world away from Quebec, there is a little bit of home in Baghdad.

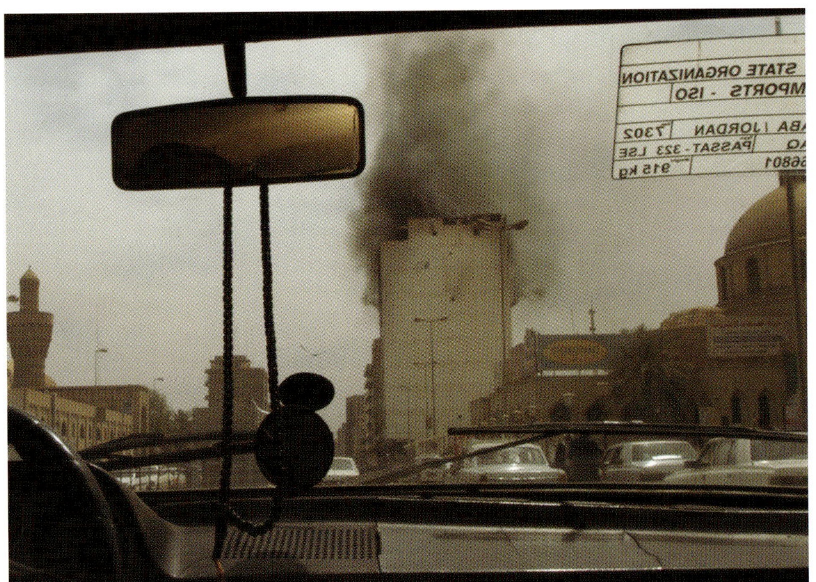

Driving through downtown Baghdad

I am losing weight at an alarming rate, just under a pound a day. But I know my limits of starvation, thirst and exhaustion, and walk a fine line between them. (I continually force myself to binge on water, drinking much more than my body feels is necessary). It takes strong discipline to control the body and mind. My job is to stay healthy and cover the material needed for my book.

Since I've been in Baghdad, the only fruit I have eaten is a couple of oranges I bought yesterday at a fruit stand. Even eating an orange has its pitfalls. After peeling the orange, I wash my hands before touching or eating the flesh. It is possible to transfer bacteria from the rind onto your hands, then onto the flesh, and finally into your mouth.

Even counting money can make you sick. By wetting your thumb to separate the bills, bacteria from the paper (which has gone through many hands), can get into your mouth. You have to be very conscientious about cleaning your hands before they touch your mouth.

Around 10 a.m., I am having a coffee in the Fanar with Simon Norfolk, a freelance photographer working on assignment for the New York Times Magazine. An art photographer, rather than a news photographer, Simon works with a large-format camera and tripod. He is staying at the Fanar, and I had met him on Wednesday, when he first arrived from England. He is an opinionated, though soft-spoken man in his 30s, who religiously wears a wide-brimmed floppy hat, which protects his shaven head from the relentless fire in the sky. He looks rather out of place with that hat, camera and tripod, but he fits in well with our small team of friends.

Living in Britain, he arrived in Baghdad to show his readers the horror of war from his anti-war perspective. He does not have much love for the American Forces, and is outspoken about it, but not to the point of being a loose cannon. I really like the guy. He has a good humanitarian heart.

With the rest of the team covering the Easter story, Simon and I decide to go looking for the bomb-damaged site I nicknamed the Black Hole (on April 15th).

While driving towards the Black Hole, we pass the complex housing the Ministry of War. It is smoldering, while at the same time being looted. We decide to stop and take a look.

Walking through the main wrought-iron gates, we see looters going in and out of the buildings. Two looters are hanging around by the gates, and they smile and nod, greeting us as we walk into the compound. There are a half a dozen well-kept, yellow brick buildings, with well-manicured gardens of roses and sunflowers. Entering the main building, adorned with a large, partially burned mural of Saddam, we meet a couple of looters trying to unscrew the doors from an office entranceway. We smile and wave at them. They return the courtesy, then get back to work as we explore further. Nearly all the rooms or offices have been burned or heavily vandalized. The offices, which days ago held stacks of military records and other documentation, have been completely gutted by fire, leaving behind a smoldering heap of grey ashes and heat-twisted cabinets.

The main hallway has a larger-than-life portrait of Saddam painted on it. Smoke from the fires has blackened the top half of the painting and hallway, so we can't make out the top part of his face and head. Another room, untouched by fire, is littered with hundreds of books about military hardware and books written by Saddam. His face looks up at me from the covers of some of these books. Crates and crates of chemical-retarding kits, for treatment of mustard gas poisoning, have been broken open and spilled about the floor of two rooms. On the floor of another office lies a broken and looted safe. A portrait of Saddam, his face gouged by a knife, hangs on the wall.

One section of the building was used as living quarters for the soldiers who guarded the facility. Here one room is full of cots and burned uniforms. In a room next door, ammunition, ranging from 50-calibre machine gun rounds to mortars, lies scattered about the floor. Most of

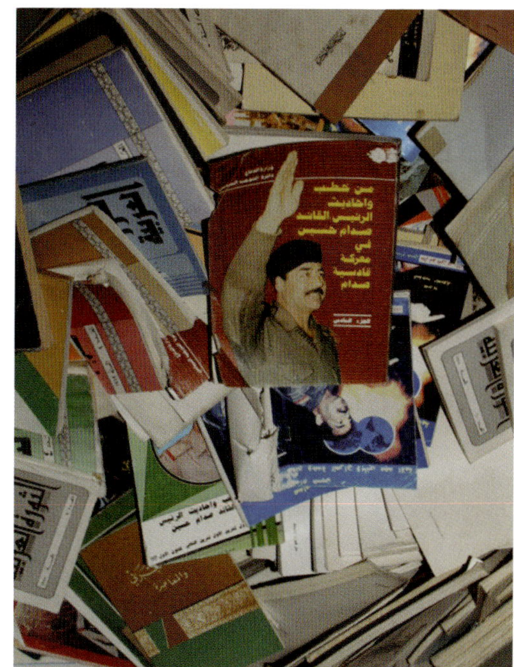

Books written by Saddam scattered on Ministry floor

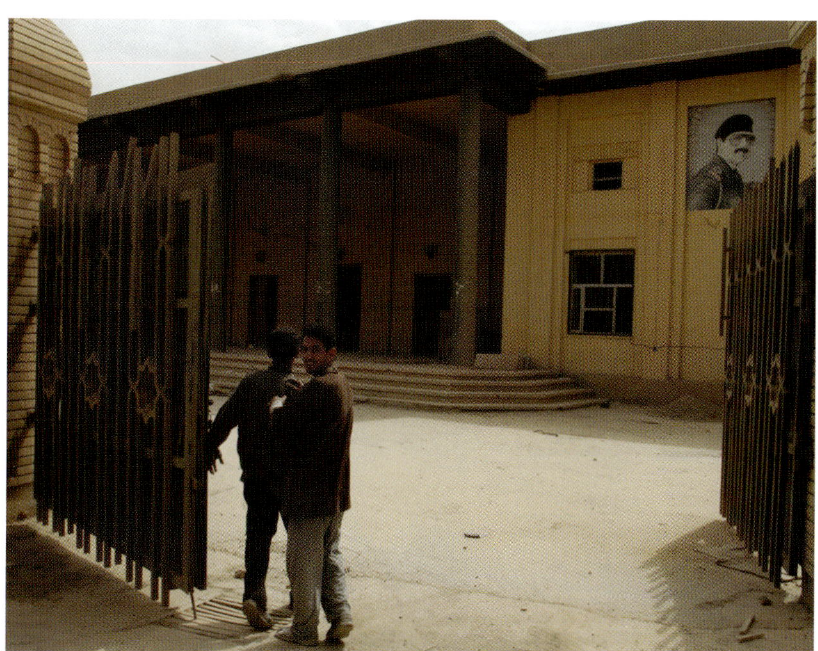

Looters greet us at the main gates of the War Ministry

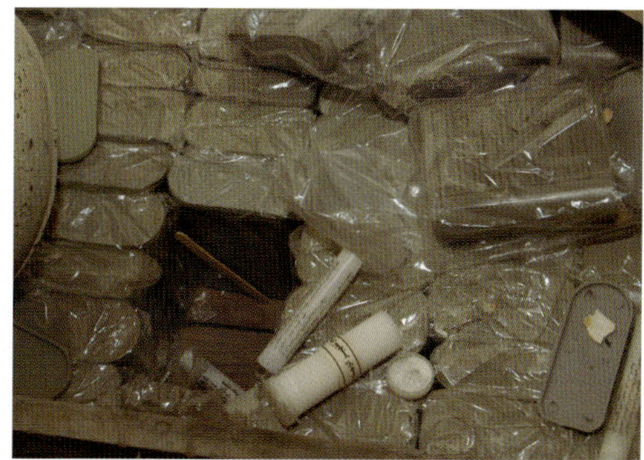

Crates of poison gas retardant kits fill Ministry room

the ammunition looks as though it has been stolen, judging by the number of empty wooden cases strewn among the spilled live munitions. I enter a mess hall where 40 soldiers would sit on cement benches and eat off long concrete tables covered with plastic tablecloths decorated with flowers. We find what we thought was a washroom, but it is really a jail, with 10 iron-gated cells. The cells are about the size of a public washroom stall, with a hole in one corner, which served as a toilet.

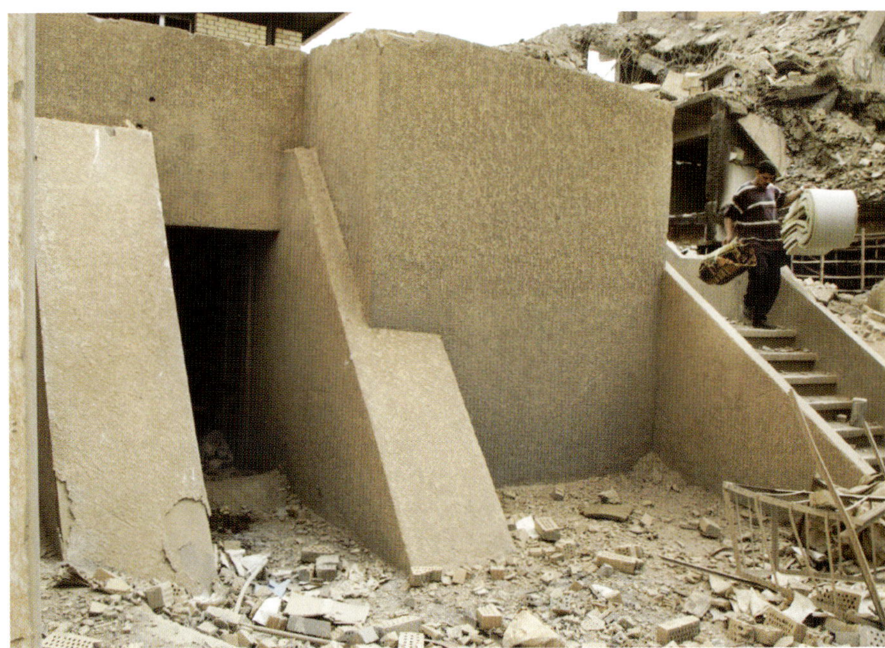
Looter carries booty past a bunker hit by a bunker-busting bomb

We leave this building and outside find the remains of a heavily bombed underground bunker. Its heavy iron door has been blasted off its hinges from the force of the explosion, which looks like the work of a bunker-buster bomb. The stairs leading down into its belly are cluttered and blocked by debris and sections of the caved-in bunker. "No-one would have left there alive," I say to Simon. A solitary looter, carrying a bunch of foam bedrolls, walks past us smiling, and nods his head at us, as if to say, "Hi, how are you?" Even in wartime, there is room for courtesy. We all have our jobs to do – looters loot, photographers take pictures – and as long as we stay out of each other's way, we all succeed on our own terms.

Continuing on our little tour, we see a more ornate building of Arabic style, which may have been the officers' quarters. Looters, including some young boys and their father, are busily removing and carrying wooden doors and unscrewing light fixtures from the outside patios of the building, and loading them onto a donkey cart. Others are carrying off iron bed cots. I try to take a picture of a looter unscrewing light fixtures, but he turns to me and waves me away saying, "No pictures mister!" I rest my camera around my neck and walk on a little. There is enough to shoot without upsetting the looters. I start taking pictures of one man carrying a door on his back. He also tells me not to take his photo, but I had already shot a couple of fast

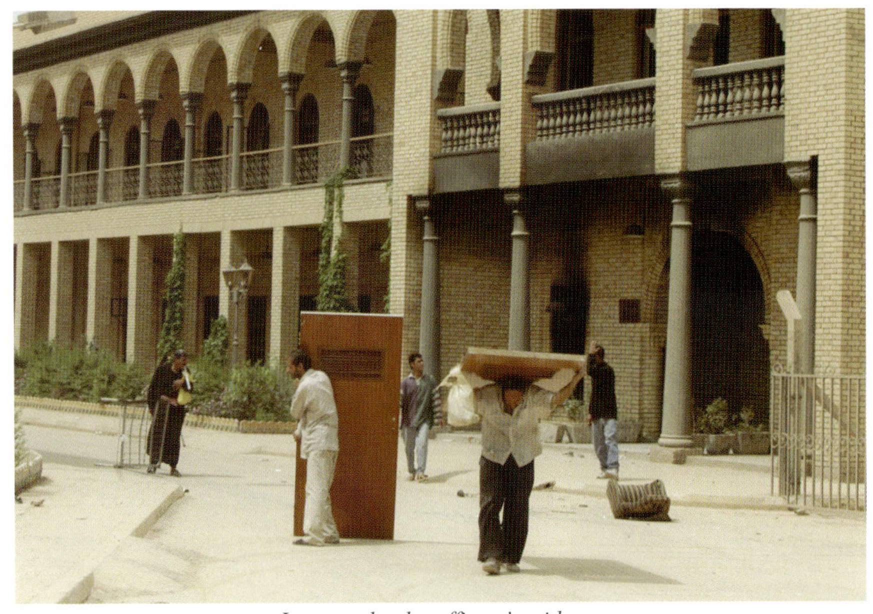
Looters plunder officers' residence

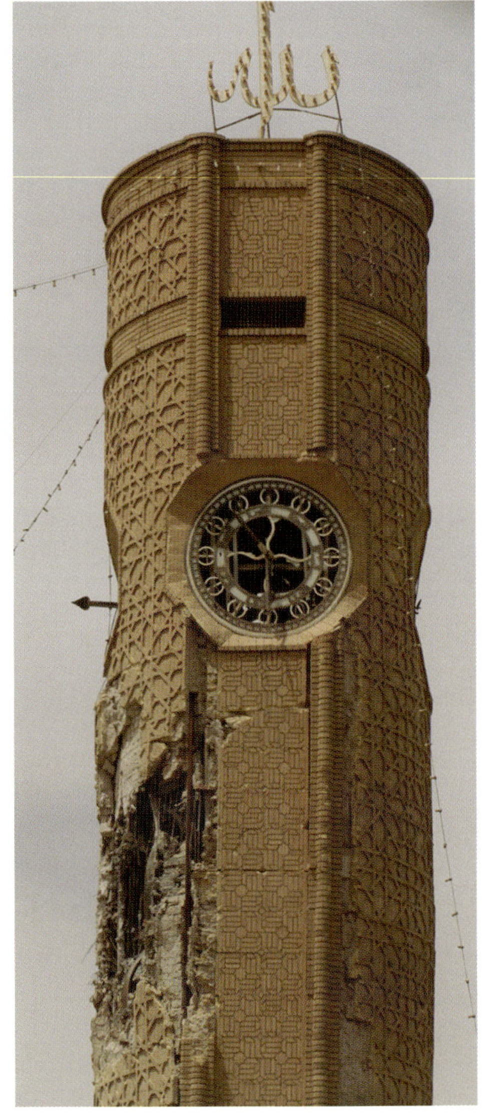
Bomb-damaged tower of Al Khulafa Mosque

frames before he saw me. He looks like Jesus carrying the cross, only it is a stolen door, and he's not Jesus.

Walking on, we find a beautiful small mosque, decorated in the typical Arabian style with blue, white and yellow-glazed mosaics covering its dome and entranceways. We peer inside and see that it has been vandalized and looted to the bone. Nothing remains except a smashed-up gold and crystal chandelier, still hanging precariously from the ceiling. Dangling wires stick out from the walls, where the looters stole the light fixtures. Even the electrical receptacles have been unscrewed from the walls.

I find it hard to comprehend why looters would rob from a mosque, but I had seen it at the mosque in Yarmuk. I wonder just how righteous some of the Iraqi people are, to loot their own mosques. Are they doing it to feed their greed, or is it because of dire necessity, a need to feed a starving family. A good portion of the mosques I have seen in Baghdad, with the exception of the Al Shahib mosque (across the street from the Palestine), have been intentionally hit by tank rounds or used for rifle target practice. I personally doubt that the Americans were responsible for much of this damage. It would have been a real public relations catastrophe if American soldiers were observed shooting at a mosque. They have enough enemies; they don't need any more. More likely, the damage to the mosques is part of the running blood-feud between Sunni and Shi'a Muslims.

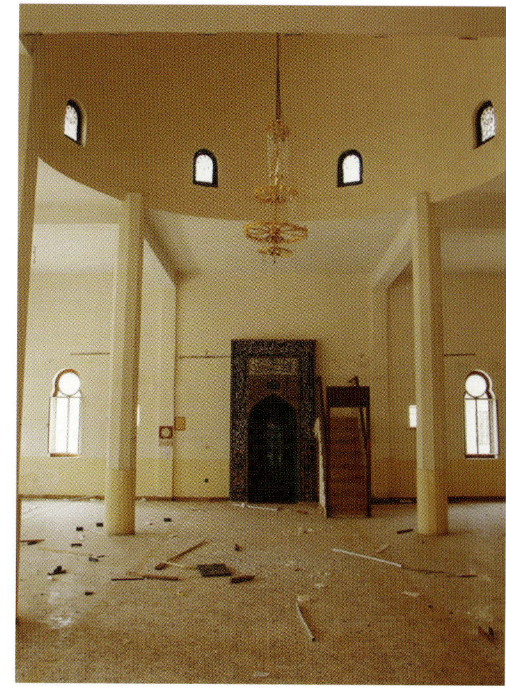
Looted mosque at the Ministry of War

Leaving the ransacked War Ministry, we keep driving in the general direction of the Black Hole. We have no schedule, we are news shopping – in a manner of speaking. Taking a road along the shore of the Tigris River, we see two 25-foot surface-to-air missiles lying on a truck launcher. One of the missiles has its nose cone separated and sits on top of the truck's cab roof, like a beige dunce cap. Stopping the car we go over to the army checkpoint, 200 feet from the missiles.

The soldiers are not guarding missiles, which have been disarmed, but are guarding the entranceway to Saddam's Al Adamia Palace, which the missiles were meant to protect, I assume. We ask the soldiers if we can visit the palace and take pictures, but they refuse, saying we will have to go through the chain of command. That would take half a day, so we ask to photograph the missiles and truck, which they agree to.

A skinny, brown dog lies sleeping under the rear end of the missile-launching truck, avoiding the mid-day sun. At our approach, it gets up and wanders a short distance off, as I take a picture of the two sentries near the missiles. The ground here is a fine talcum-like soil I had seen elsewhere in the city and the desert. It puffs up like a thick fog whenever your boots move through it. Getting back into the car I notice the powder has coated my pant legs, all the way up to the knees.

We stop and take some pictures of storekeepers cleaning up the broken glass and rubble from inside and outside their shops. Life is slowly coming back to the streets, starting with the shops being repaired and opened. Whether they have a product to sell is another matter, but going through the motions keeps the owners occupied, or so they tell me.

Heading on, the cab drives past a large grove of date palms covering four or more acres, carpeted with farmers' fields.

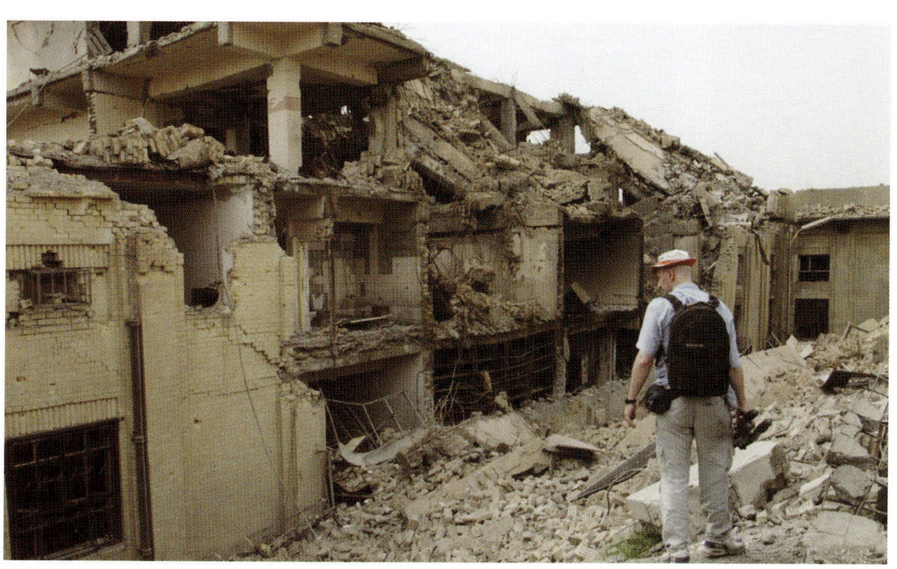
The destroyed Ministry of War

There is the mangled wreckage of an Iraqi tank sitting half on the sidewalk, half on the road. We get out for a look as the stream of regular traffic flows on, oblivious, or just inured to such carnage. It had been struck by a direct hit, and the resulting explosion made the tank look like black Swiss cheese. Burned and burst tank shells lie contorted and fragmented amongst the 50-calibre machine gun rounds and burned metal lying outside the tank. Inside the tank's burned shell, all that remains is a layer of grey powder and some exploded tank rounds. The heat had been so intense that shiny globs of melted aluminum from the control and launch panels stick to the armor-plated floor like melted wax from a candle.

Interspersed amongst the palm trees we notice at least 20 destroyed tanks and APCs. All but a handful have been spared from destruction. Simon and I walk through the palms, being careful where we step, in case the area is mined. Following the well-worn pathways through the fields, I stop to photograph the wreckage as Simon walks ahead. Some of the tanks look as though they had exploded from the inside out, and others destroyed from the outside in. Fifteen minutes later I walk over to see how Simon is doing. He tells me that I should be careful not to touch the vehicles, especially those that look like they exploded from the inside. He warns me that they were probably hit by depleted uranium shells, and most likely have remnants of the uranium dust on and inside them. This dust, if touched or inhaled, can cause all sorts of medical problems, including a variety of cancers and birth defects. I wished I had known this before I had climbed onto them and touched parts of the exploded weaponry.

Simon is a photo veteran of Afghanistan, and had seen this sort of weaponry before. He explains how the uranium bombs function. The shell strikes the vehicle, penetrating through the outside armor and into the cabin, leaving a small entrance hole. Once inside, the shell explodes, turning the tank into a cauldron of intense white heat that incinerates everything inside. Milliseconds later the heat sets off the tank's own rounds, which are stored in the cabin. The resulting massive explosion blows the tank apart at the seams. The extreme heat burns the tank's metal shell to a rusty-red tint.

A tank hit by a conventional shell would have a large, one-foot wide gaping hole in it, with the ragged edges pointing inwards, and less evidence of an intense heat flash.

We meet a few farmers walking across their unplanted fields amidst the wreckage. They go about their work, tilling the land into furrows with hoes. I wonder if the uranium dust could find its way into the soil (washed off by rain), then be absorbed by the crops, contaminating whoever eats the produce.

Hundreds of live mortar rounds and machine gun rounds are spilled from the back of tanks and APCs that were not hit and destroyed. I take a badge from a beret I see lying outside one of these vehicles. Simon collects some molten globs of aluminum and burned and crushed 50 cal. shells. He is taking these objects back to the hotel to be photographed as part of a still-life photo feature on war.

Walking a little further into the grove, we find a large destroyed, cement and cinder-block building, the former home of the head of the Iraqi Parliament. It is completely flattened by what must have been a huge bomb, and it is difficult to make out just what it must have looked like before being struck. A huge bomb crater, at least 30 feet across and filled with over 10 feet of water, lies open beside the flattened home. It is the largest bomb crater I have ever seen.

We jump back into our taxi and head a little further down the dirt road that flanks the grove. We drive past a small American military installation where six handcuffed prisoners sit outside its walls, encircled by a fence of barbed wire and guarded by two soldiers. Stopping a short distance ahead, we get out to look at a truck with a big blue tarp covering it. Sticking out of the tarp are the creamy white heads of four anti-aircraft missiles, each about 12 feet long. Another truck with a single missile is parked on the other side of the dirt road. A third truck, with a large satellite dish mounted on it, was the control center for the missiles.

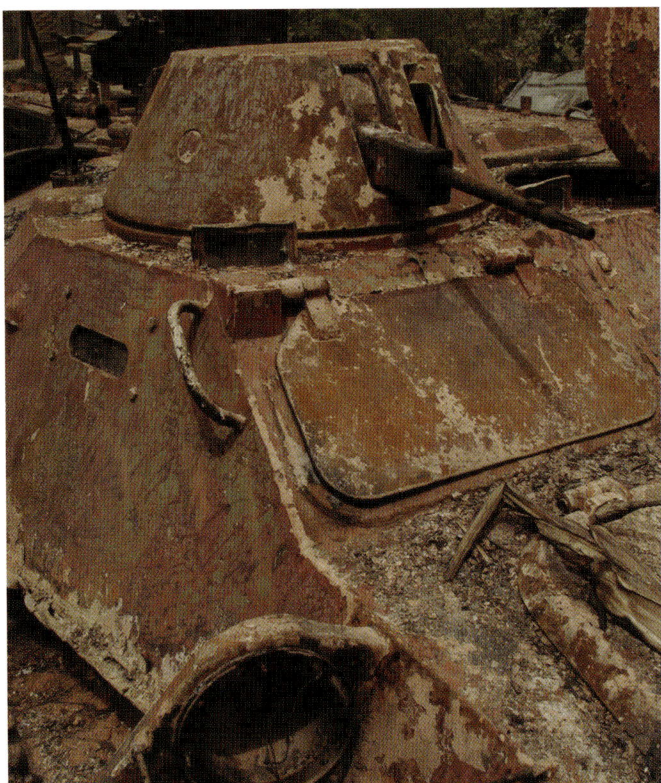

Light armor personal carrier burned red by a depleted uranium shell

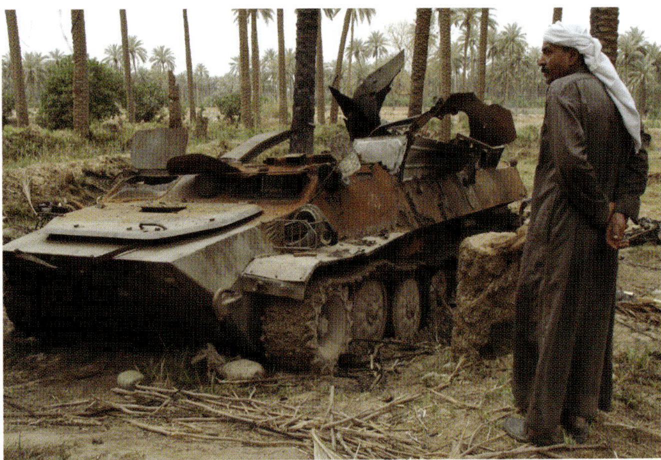

Palm grove farmer surveys the damage to his fields

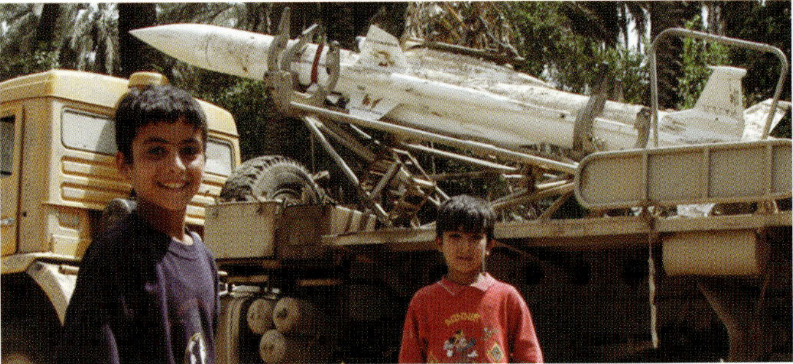

Young boys play pretend soldier with live anti-aircraft missiles as props

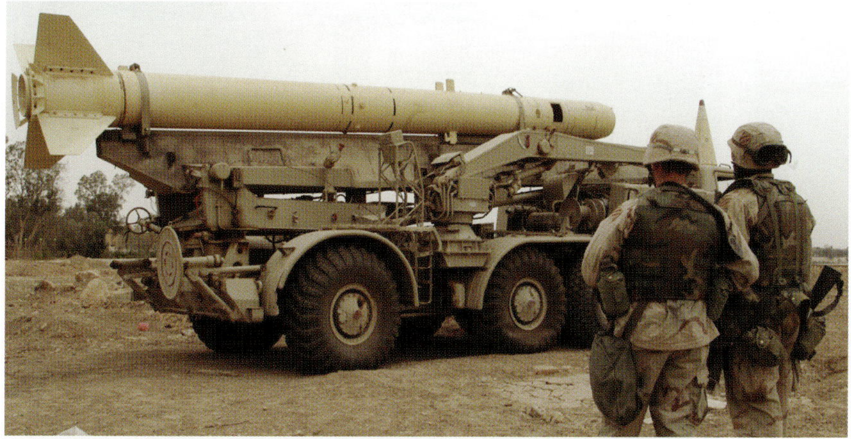

Surface-to-air missile and launcher at Al Adamia Palace

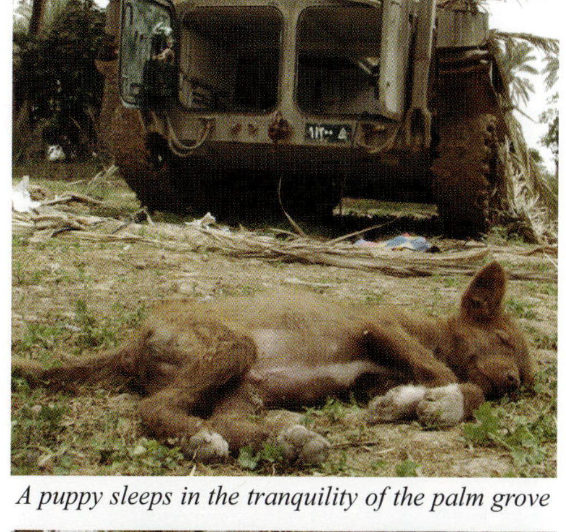

A puppy sleeps in the tranquility of the palm grove

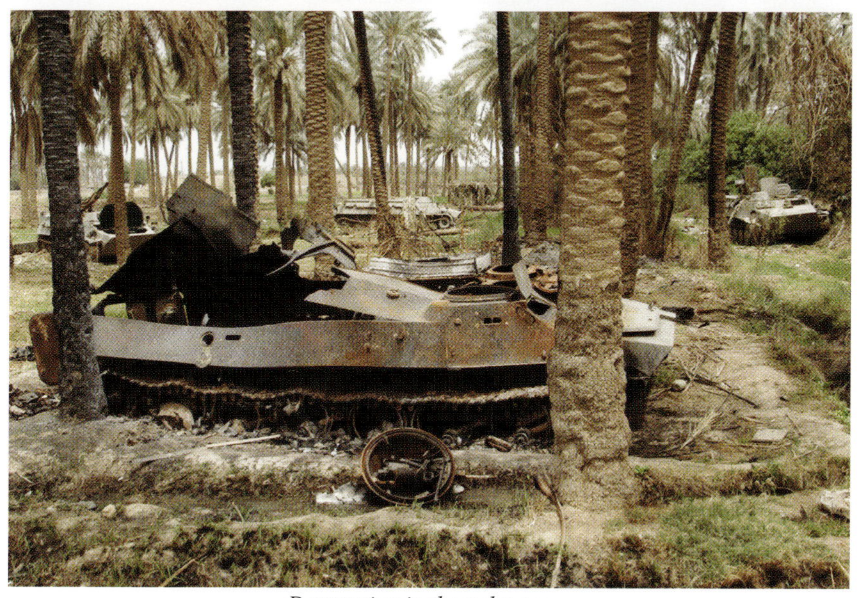

Destruction in the palm grove

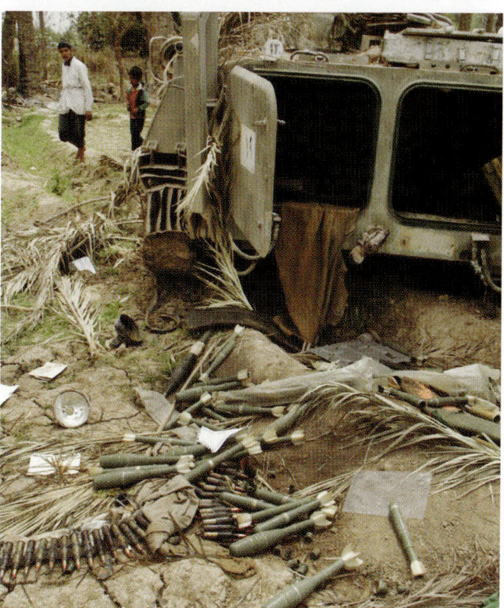

Bombs and large calibre rounds spilled from an APC

Across the road from the missiles is the entranceway to a large brick palace-home. We walk onto the property and up the laneway to see that bombs had hit the building. Half of it is blown away. It is a large well-maintained property, lined with flowering trees and rose gardens. Undoubtedly a very rich man owned this property. Two young boys are snooping around the shattered mansion but don't have the look of looters. A local man comes over with his young daughter and tells us the property used to be his farm, but a member of Saddam's family had kicked him off and taken over the property, expanding it and installing the gardens and large home. The man smiles when I ask him if he is upset that it had been bombed.

He asks if we would like to meet his brother, who recently had both his lower legs blown off after stepping on a live mortar bomb in the palm grove. We agree, and are taken on a short walk to a small group of clean mud-brick buildings, separated by a small laneway. He leads us into the home and introduces us to his brother, a man of about 45 years of age, lying on a sponge bed mat on the floor. He is wearing a typical Arabian-style gown, which he pulls up at the waist, exposing his shocking predicament. Both his legs are missing below the knees, clean white dressings cover his two matching stumps.

The man's children crowd into the room with other family members. They bend down at his side and hold his hand. He does not seem to be in any pain, and chats while hauling away on a cigarette. This man has a supportive family and a nice clean, though not luxurious, home in which to recover from his injuries. We wish him and his family the best, and walk outside to find our cab.

It is getting late and we decide to save the Black Hole for another day, so we drive back to the Fanar, after a busy and successful afternoon. At the hotel I refresh myself with tea and some chocolate-covered coconut candy bars (my favorites).

An hour before sundown, John Otis, a reporter with the *Houston Chronicle*, comes over to speak with me. I had met John, a third-floor guest, yesterday in the lobby of the hotel. He is a nice guy, quiet but smart, and like the rest of us, looking for exclusive feature material. He asks me if I would go for a drive across the Tigris, to the home of one of Saddam's former bodyguards and executioners, to take photos to accompany an article he is writing. This opulent palace-home, located just down the road from Saddam's huge Republican Palace, was looted and had been taken over by a group of people calling themselves The Committee to Free Prisoners.

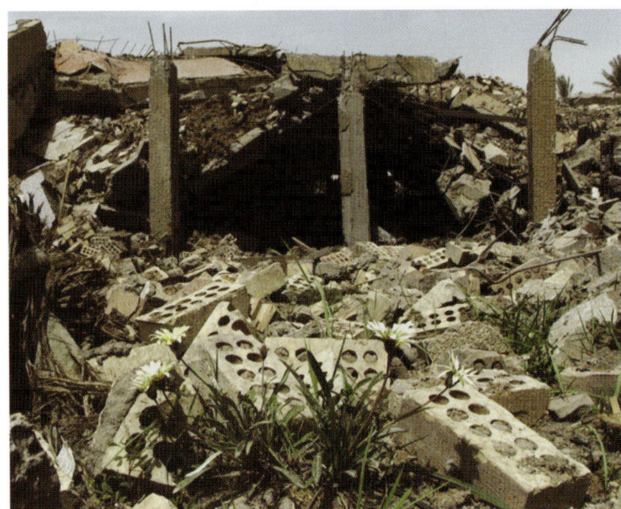

Home of parliamentarian struck by bunker-busting bomb

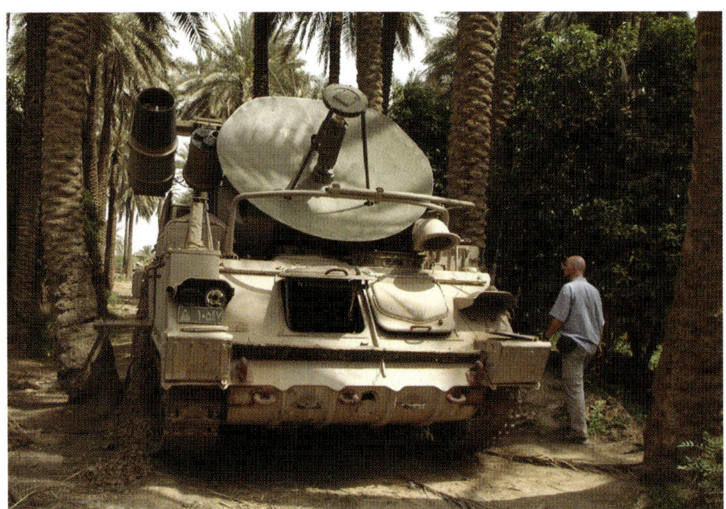

Missile guidance system for anti-aircraft missiles

John explains that during the looting of the home, large volumes of records had been found. These were the official documents listing the executions and imprisonment of thousands of Iraqis during Saddam's reign.

Arriving at the home, the volunteer group has taken over the house and are compiling the documents and writing the names of the victims on pink Bristol-board sheets, which are pinned to the outside walls of the building. Over 100 people are gathered outside the building, scrolling down the lists, trying to find the name of their missing family member or members. Most of these people have no idea whether their loved ones are dead or alive; some had been missing for over 20 years. Inside, the volunteers continue to pore over the original leather-bound books, adding new names onto the pink placards.

There is a throng of people pushing and surging forward, trying to get close enough to read the lists of names. It is a heartbreaking scene of helplessness, indescribable grief and frustration. People are crying and asking me to help them find their relatives. Old ladies beg me for information, as young boys and girls cry on their mother's shoulders. Baghdad has become a city of endless grief and hunger.

I step aside from the mass of misery and, looking out over the muddy Tigris River (which skirts the roadside), I plead for inner strength, to help pull me through this new nightmare unfolding in front of my eyes. It is at times like this, I think to myself, when all men need a god to lean on. But deep down inside I know that no god will help me, or these poor desperate people. There is no god in Baghdad, only the quick and the dead thrive here.

But the misery continues, regardless of my prayers, as fingers, like numerous bony pencils, scroll down through the lists of the dead. A man pinning up a new list is engulfed by the desperate crowd.

Inside the building, the Free Prisoners people have cleaned up the place fairly well, but they could not cover all the signs of looting and damage. The rooms are large and freshly painted, with white and black marble floors. A large gold

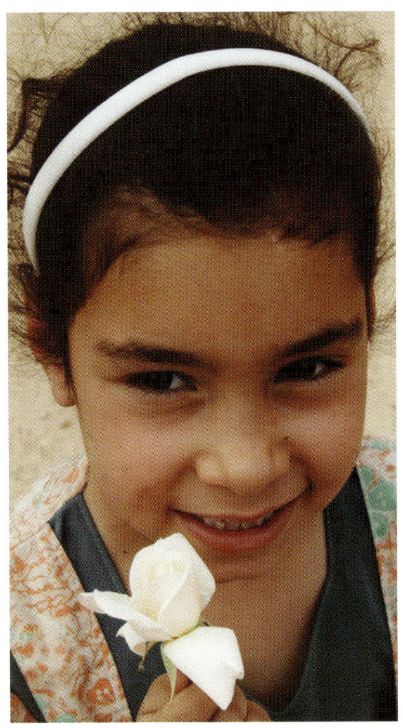

Young girl and rose

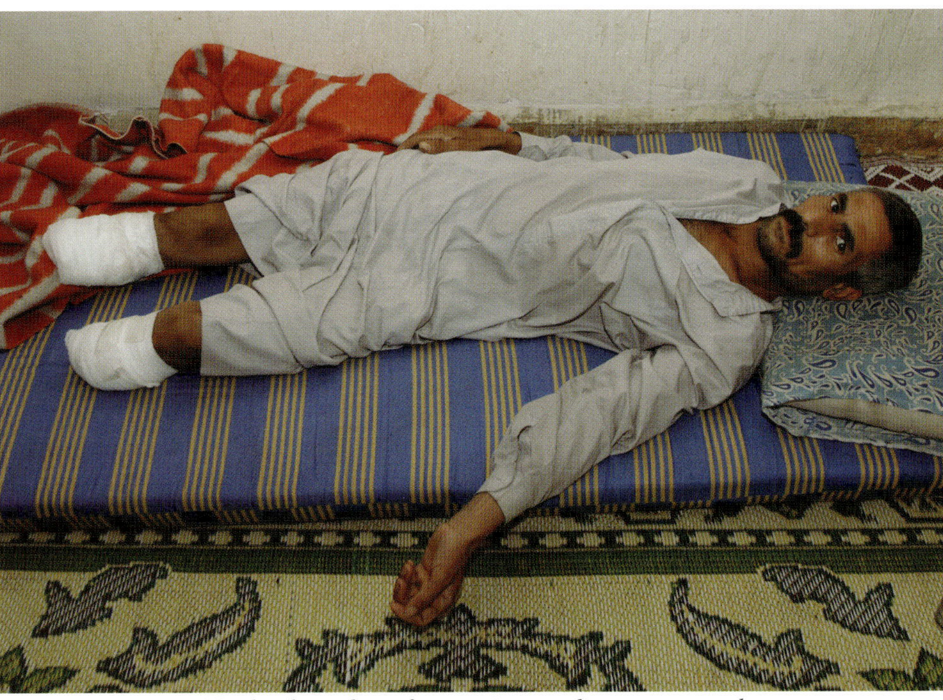

Man lost lower legs after stepping on a live mortar round

and crystal chandelier hangs intact from the foyer ceiling. A magnificent spiral staircase leads to the upstairs rooms and bathrooms, where gold-plated doorknobs and bathroom fixtures still remain, perhaps overlooked by the looters. Most of the windows are broken and all the furnishings stolen. Its design is the same as many of Saddam's residences, but on a much smaller scale. Two large, central air conditioning units on the roof, recently cooled the brow of Saddam's Executioner, while he sipped his sweet tea.

Having all the photos I need, I drive back to the Fanar and transmit them to the *Chronicle,* using a friend's satellite (powered by the hotel generator).

I meet John in the Fanar lobby. After describing what I photographed at the Committee to Free Prisoners, he asks me to go with him tomorrow to photograph the pilgrimage to the Shiite holy city of Karbala (an hour-and-a-half drive south of Baghdad), where millions of faithful are expected to gather. I accept the assignment, it sounds like a good road trip.

Because it is getting late and I missed my dinner, I finish off the remains of an MRE that Nino had earlier given to Tish. (MRE or Meals-Ready-To-Eat is a modern version of the ration pack. It contains individual food portions in vacuum packed pouches, along with all the fixings like jam, peanut butter, crackers, chocolate, dried milkshake, Tabasco sauce, toilet paper, candies and matches etc. One of these food pacs can feed me for at least two days).

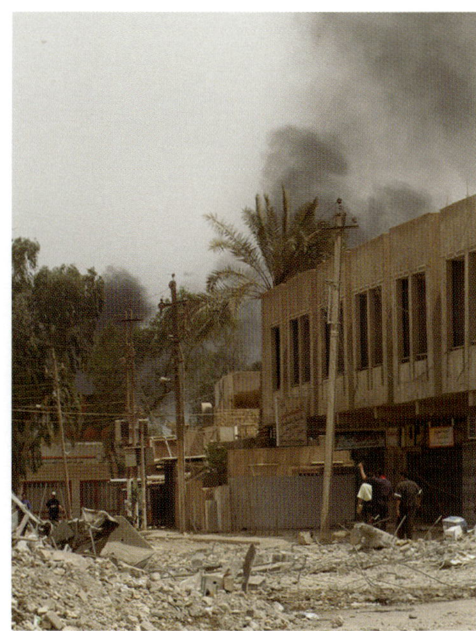
Driving back to the Fanar

Nino drops by the hotel to tell us his unit will be pulling out in the morning and that the regular Army is taking over from the Marines. "The Army isn't as disciplined and professional as the Marine Corps," says Nino. He also states that, "To a Marine, Army stands for 'Ain't Really Marines Yet!' It is sad to hear that my Marine friend will be leaving. We hug and promise to keep in contact, and he returns to his platoon. I will always remember this soldier, who to me represented the real face and heart of the American soldier.

Earlier in the week, Tish had introduced me to Patrick Graham, a freelance reporter from Toronto. I am sitting and talking with him, while having a coffee in the Fanar dining room, and he tells me about a life-threatening situation he had been in two days ago.

He was having a candle-lit dinner at the home of an Iraqi family (that he was writing a feature about), when two thieves burst through the front door and started blasting away with handguns. Patrick ducked under some furniture to avoid the gunfire, while his host grabbed his AK-47 and started firing blasts in the direction of the attackers. Seeing the bigger, more deadly weapon, the thieves turned heel and ran, disappearing into the darkness of an alleyway.

Patrick tells me that the attack was all over in a few seconds. No one was injured, but it showed me that the looters, now arming themselves, were becoming even more dangerous by attacking family residences. I expect this sort of thievery might start happening more frequently, as the looters' main targets – government ministries, banks and shops – are emptied of their valuables. Until electrical power can be restored to the city, the armed looters will take advantage of the darkness to commit their beastly acts.

I go outside the hotel and into the darkness of the street to make a rare phone call to my wife Phyllis, on Tish's Thyria satellite phone. To work, the phone has to be pointing south, in the direction of the satellite. Most of the time it does not work inside the hotel, and sometimes it does not even work outside, even on a clear night. It is a temperamental device, but it is the only way we have of communicating with the outside world.

The problem with using it at night (which was when my family was at home and awake), is that when it is operating, its bright green LCD screen illuminates your face. (There are no street lights, the city is blacked out). This makes you a target to any creep skulking in the darkness, and when gunfire goes off in

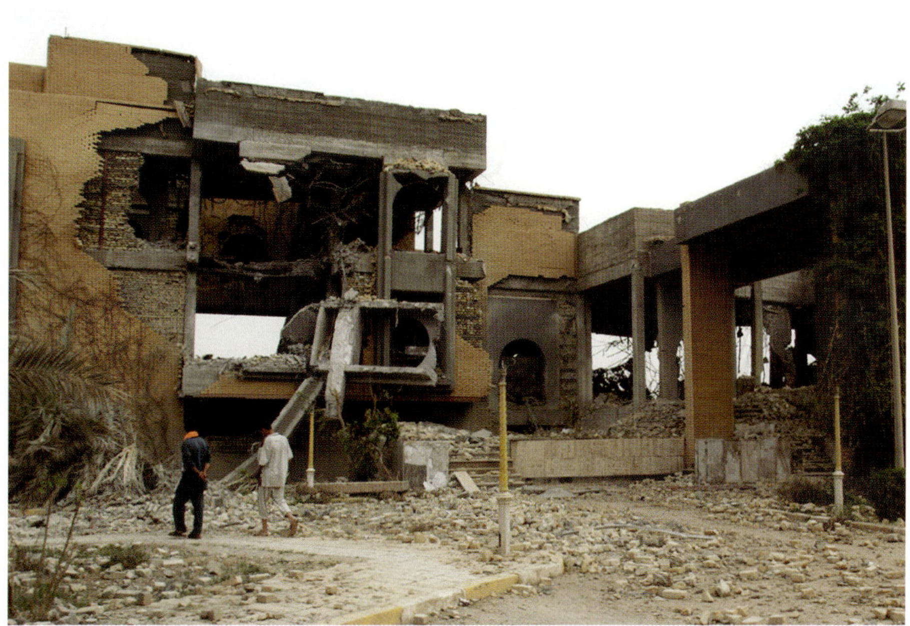
Bombed luxury residence near the palm grove

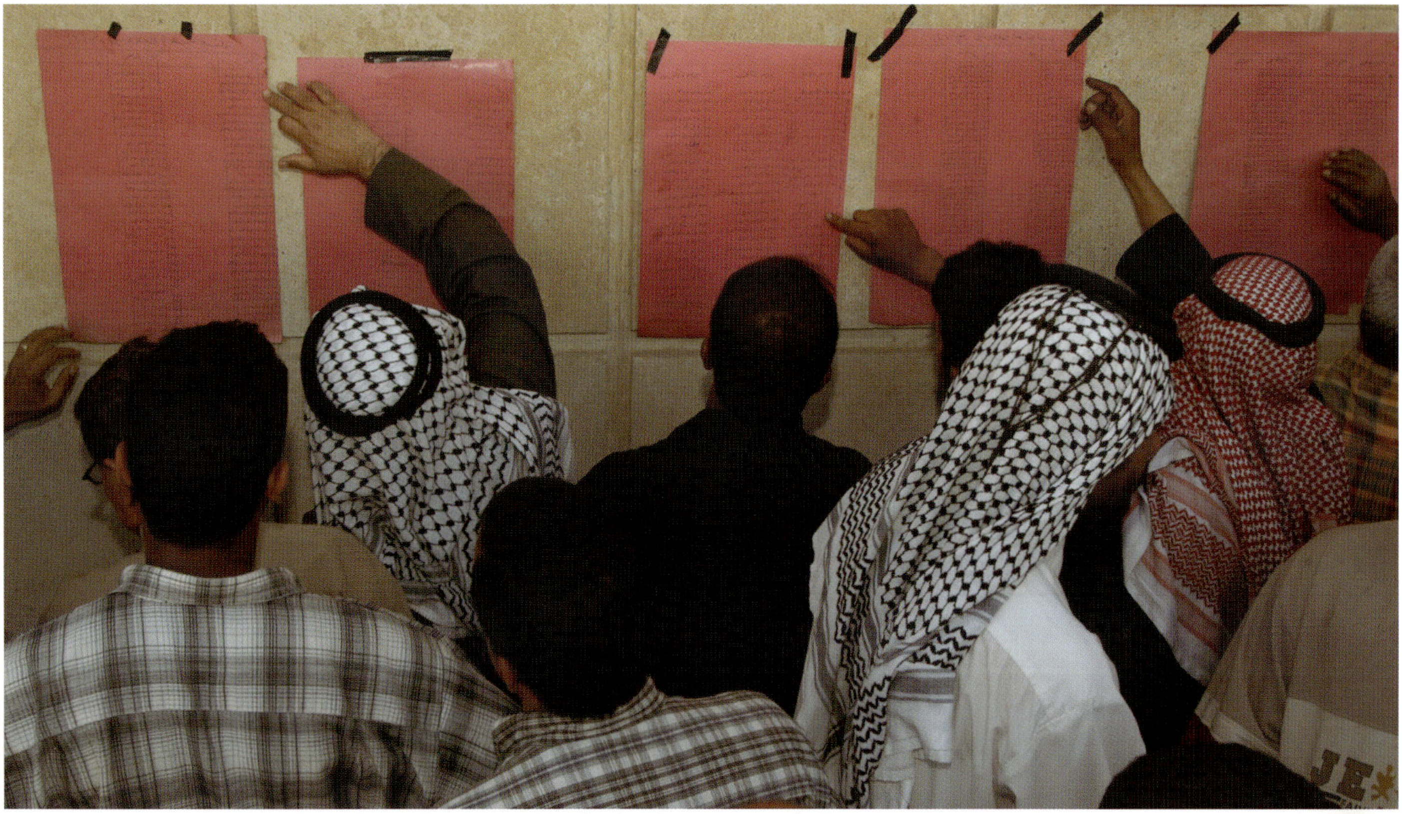

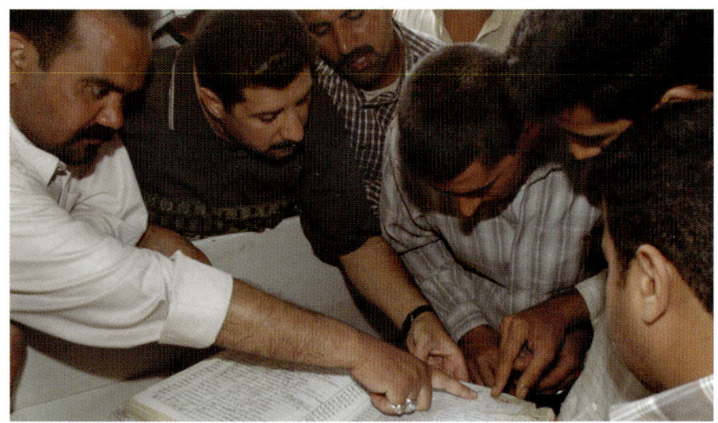

Charts listing the names of the dead and missing outside the Committee to Free Prisoners

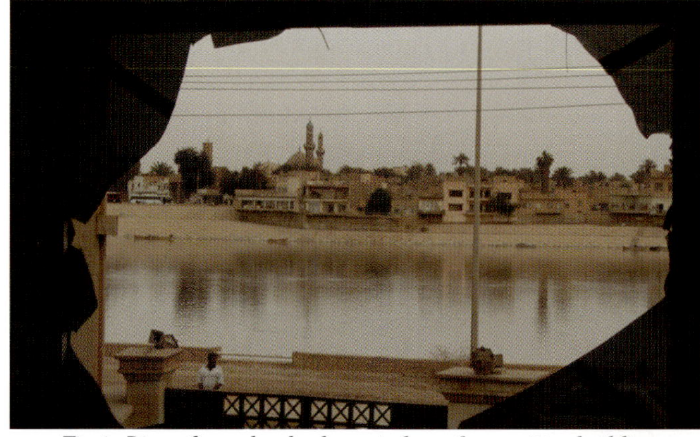

Searching for names of missing family members

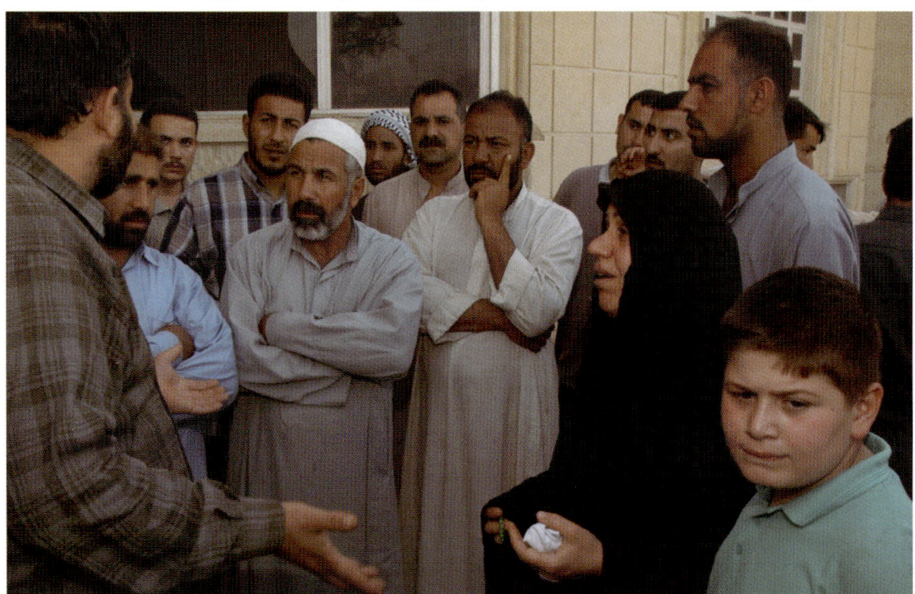

Tigris River through a broken window of committee building

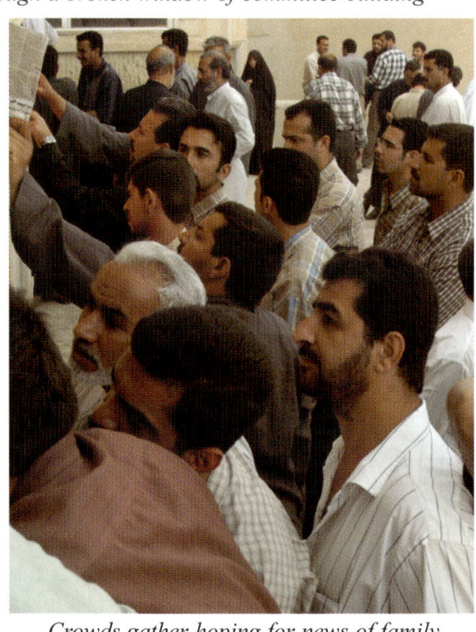

The faces of disappointment. Many will never see their missing family members again

Crowds gather hoping for news of family

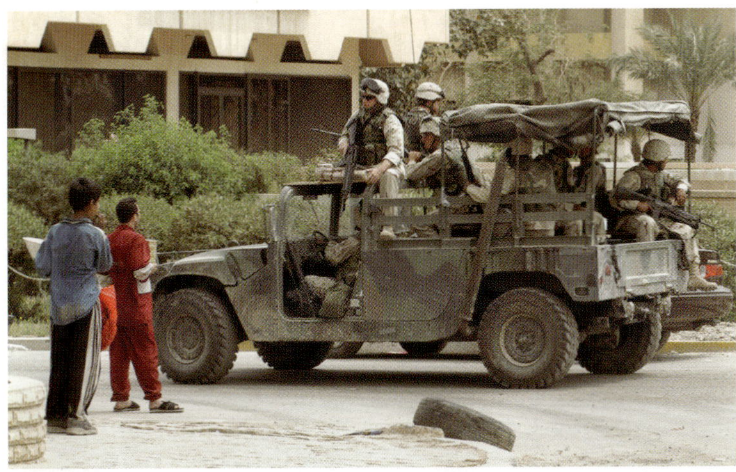

Soldiers patrol in front of the Fanar

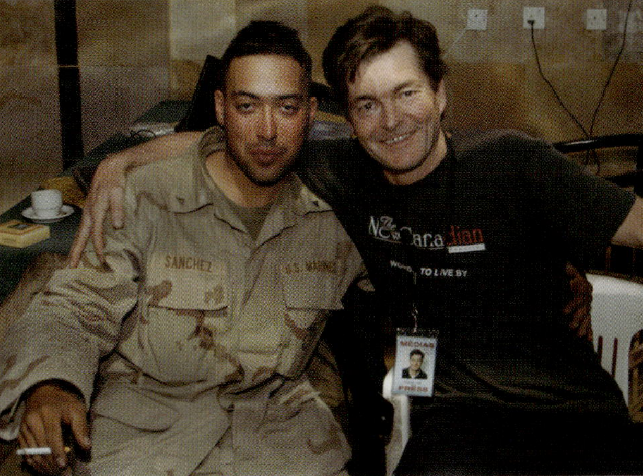

Marine Nino Sanchez and author at the Fanar

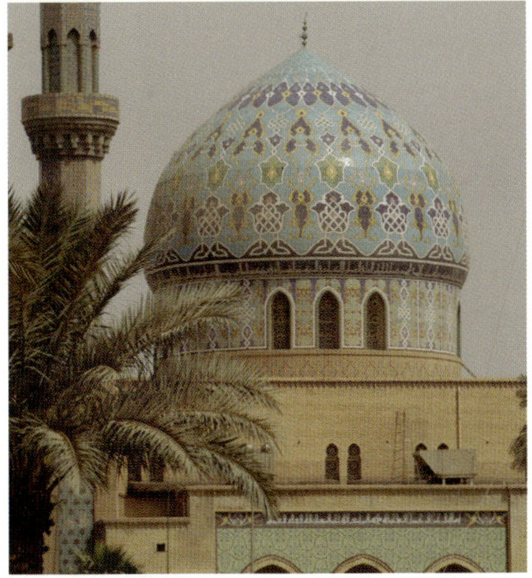

The magnificent dome of the Shahid Mosque

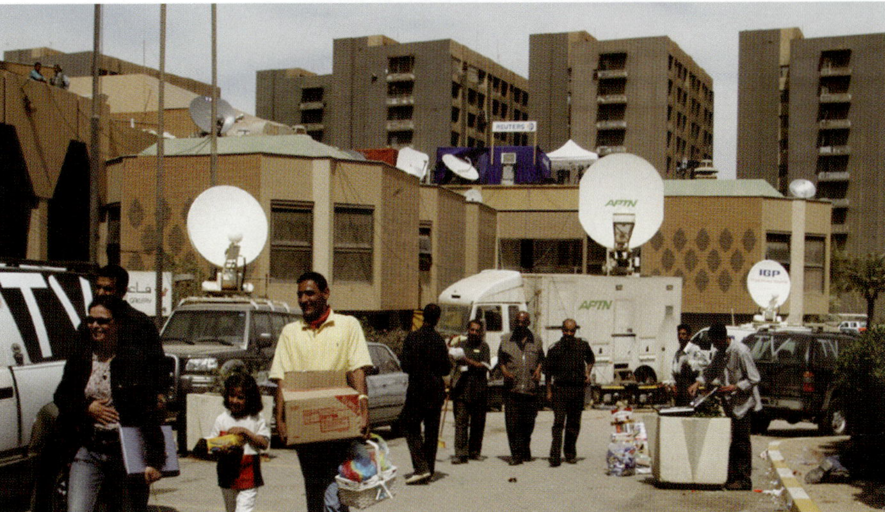

Media satellite dishes spring up like flowers in front of the Palestine Hotel

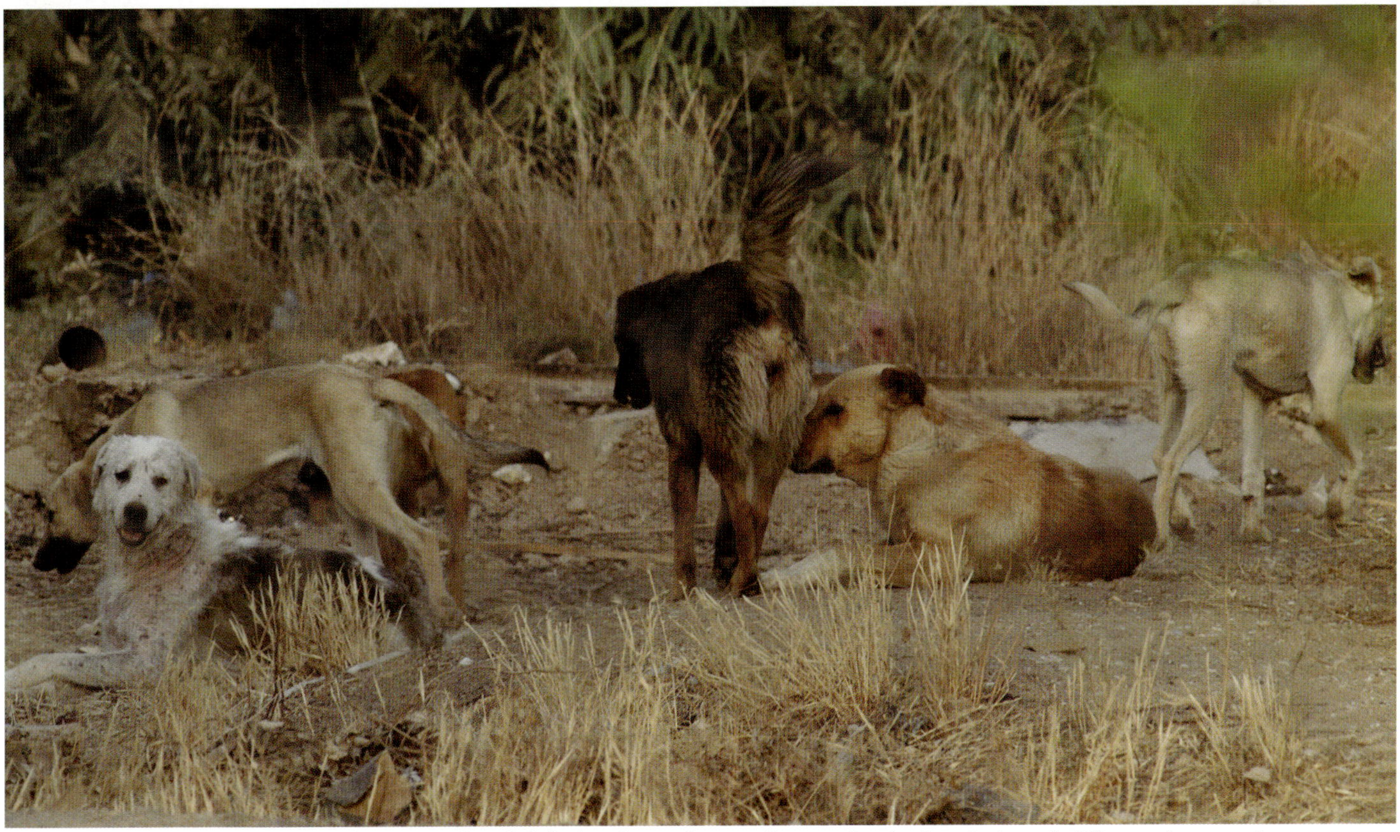

Wild dogs and thieves rule the streets of Baghdad after the sun has set. To many Iraqis, there isn't much difference between the two

your vicinity (as it regularly does), it scares the living hell out of you. Sometimes you cannot tell if they are firing at you, or if the gunshots are coming from a block away, as the phone has to be held tight to the ear to hear the person at the other end. This confounds your hearing, hampering your ability to determine where the shots are coming from.

Tod has a satellite panel, which he and Jim use to send their stories and e-mail back to the States. But they are usually on deadline when I want to send a message home, and I feel as though I am imposing.

Most evenings, Sean, Tish and I stay awake chatting till 1:30 in the morning, discussing our day and the way events are unfolding. The talk ranges from Sean's upcoming trip to France, where he will be an usher at the Cannes Film Festival, to my involvement with the peregrine falcon reintroduction effort during the mid-1980s. We puff on cigarettes and gobble down candy bars during our bedside chats. These are the best of times, and without the support of my four friends ("our news platoon"), life and work would be much more difficult and dangerous.

Just before going to sleep, I am downloading some images when I stumble upon a picture of my family, taken the afternoon I left Montreal. I weep at the sight, and hide my head under my blanket so that Sean and Tish cannot hear me. I am surprised to see the photo on my laptop, and thought I had removed all my family pics from it. I only have so much time to do my job – my emotions must be held at bay.

The wild dogs of Baghdad, sometimes in packs of around 10 animals, howl us their lullaby outside the hotel, as they do every night. Earlier in the day, when the dogs usually wander the streets in packs of two or three, I saw a group of eight dogs, eagerly chasing a boy of about seven years old down the street. The boy ducked into a nearby building and the dogs moved off. They were hunting the boy, and might have torn him to pieces had they got the chance. I drift off to sleep to the nightly melody of rifle and machine-gun fire, leaving the wild dogs and thieves to run the streets.

Day 10. Saturday, April 19th

(The Marines move out; security risk heightened; satellite transmitters; warm water; the generator helps the journalists; charging our laptops; our friend the flashlight; staking out a power bar; elevators from hell; the Clam Shell; the road to Karbala with John Otis; green and black flags; mass of humanity on pilgrimage to Karbala; badly burned man; Al Hussein mosque; treated very warmly in Karbala; the Shi'a Muslims are a well organized political force; transmission problems; sniper shoots at me as I leave Palestine Hotel; babbling like an idiot; close call; I spend the night on Palestine Hotel couch)

I get up at 5:30 a.m., having been awakened by the sound of tanks rumbling down the street and soldiers shouting orders. I go out onto the patio and see the Marines packing up their equipment in the early dawn, readying to move out of the area. They roll up the barbed wire fencing from their roadblocks and hang it on the side of their amphibious vehicles, along with their packs, cases of ammunition and other equipment. In less than an hour, the Marines and their checkpoints are gone, except for those directly outside by the Palestine, where the majority of the journalists and some of the army and civil command are lodged.

There is no electrical power in the city, unless the establishment you are staying in has a generator. The Fanar is one of the fortunate ones. It has an industrial-sized diesel generator and fuel tanks alongside the hotel. The noise from it is relentless, but you get used to it after the first four or five days. Before the war, the city power facility was fuelled by oil, but now it is inoperable. Electricity is available to Fanar guests in the lobby for charging laptops and batteries. The generator is a blessing and allows us to continue our work. Without the generator, we would be living and working in the Dark Ages.

The hotel lobby is well lit, but there is no electricity in the rooms, where we rely on our flashlights. The flashlight is your best friend, whether in the field, or when the generator cuts out, and you are stuck manoeuvring the tricky hotel stairwells in pitch-blackness.

When walking around at night (there is a dawn-to-dusk curfew, but I didn't even know about it, nor has it been an obstacle to me), we carry a flashlight to illuminate when approaching military blockades or checkpoints, so that the soldiers know it is friendlies who approach. If you have it turned on all the time, it makes you as a target. We tried using a kerosene lamp in our room for lighting, but the smell is disagreeable (it makes us feel a little queasy). We do not use candles often, as they are sensitive and less portable.

The generator runs for about four hours on a tank of fuel. When transferring to a secondary tank, the power is cut off for between five and ten minutes, while the hook-up is being done. We learn this routine fairly quickly, and save our computer data frequently, in case of a power crash and possible loss of material. There are many journalists and NGOs trying to get the use of the two power bars available. Sometimes you must stake out a slot, to make sure you are the next in line to charge your equipment.

The 18 storey Palestine and Sheraton also have a generator for lighting and the elevators. But power to the elevators is sporadic, and you do not want to go through the inconvenience of being trapped in one when the power crashes. When this happens, and it is frequent, the guests have to use the stairwell to get to their rooms. It can be very inconvenient and exhausting, especially if your room is on the upper floors and you have to carry a laptop and cameras. This is one of the reasons we stay at the Fanar; it is only eight stories high and less of a target. The Fanar elevators also work infrequently, but I prefer the stairs; they are healthier and easier. One of the hottest commodities for sale on the streets of Baghdad is a portable generator, looted ones of course. If you have one of these units, you have power to run various electrical appliances, including television and radio. It can also light your home and keep thieves and fear at bay.

There is still no clean, drinkable water available from the taps, though there has been running water (contaminated as it may be), flowing from the faucets since the time I arrived in Baghdad. We have occasional warm water for taking a shower or washing up. Being able to take a shower is very important in this heat, as it cools and relaxes the body muscles and keeps a person sanitary and less vulnerable to parasitic pests or infection.

Since there is no phone system, the only method of communicating with the outside world is by satellite phone or a satellite transmitter, such as the B-GAN Satellite Transmitter (also referred to as a 'Clam Shell'). It is the number-one choice for sending and receiving e-mail, if you are lucky enough to have one.

At 8:30 a.m. I meet John Otis in the hotel dining room for some coffee. (Cream is just a dream here, perhaps that is why so much chai is drunk; it does not need cream). We discuss our drive to Karbala and what we can expect there. It is the first time (since the Baath Party took power in 1968 and started arresting marchers) that Shi'a Muslims are allowed to hold their holy pilgrimage. More than a million worshippers, from all over Iraq and some neighboring countries, are expected to converge on the small holy city of 750,000. Some journalists are speculating that upwards of five million faithful could gather. To the Shiites, the march to Kabala is a celebration of not only their religion, but the shedding of the chains of suppression by Saddam and the Baath Party. They are being reborn after more than 30 years.

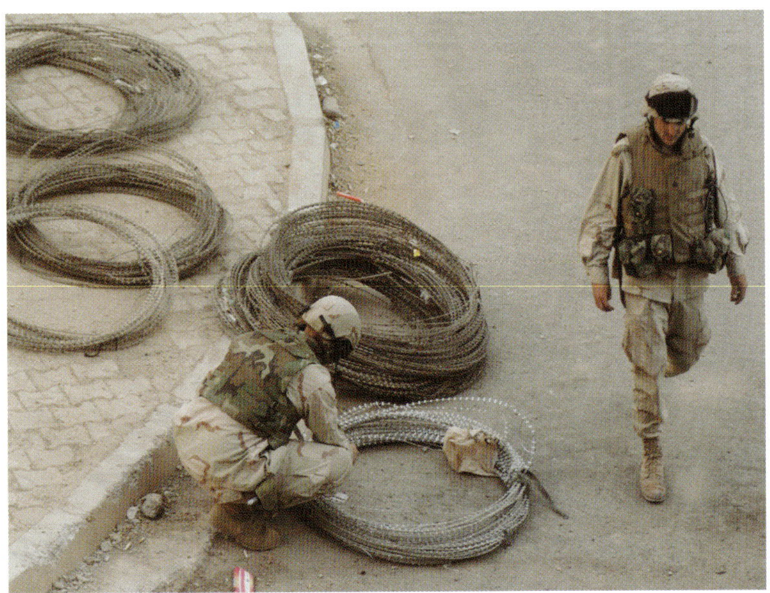

Bundles of razor-wire are prepared for loading

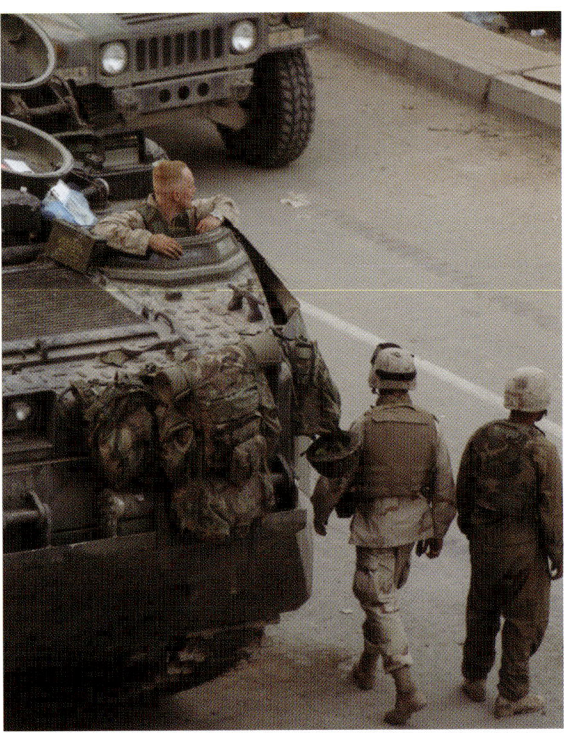

Waiting for the word to go

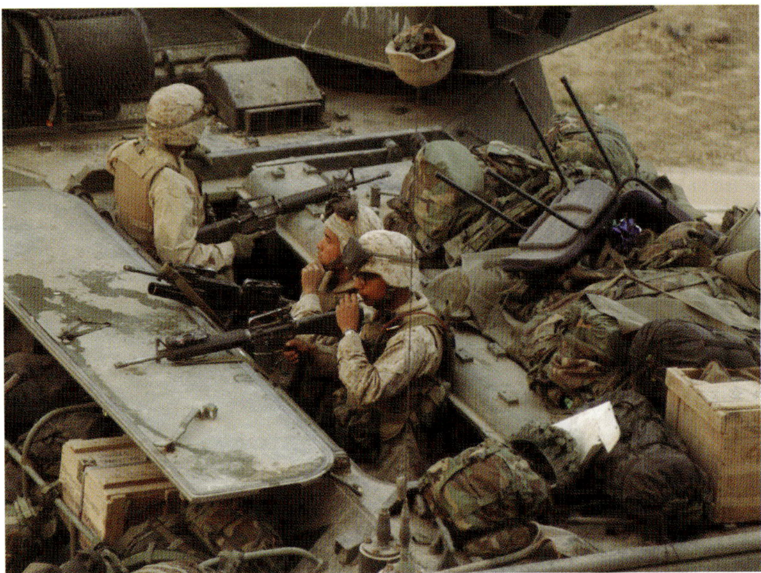

The departure of the Marines lowers the level of security around the Fanar

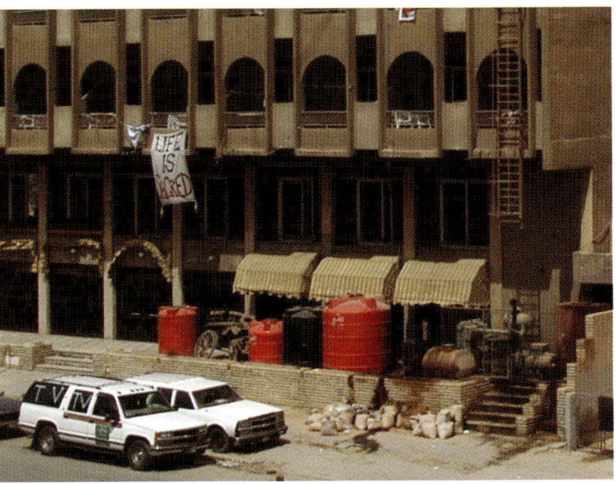

Diesel generator and fuel tanks outside the Al Fanar

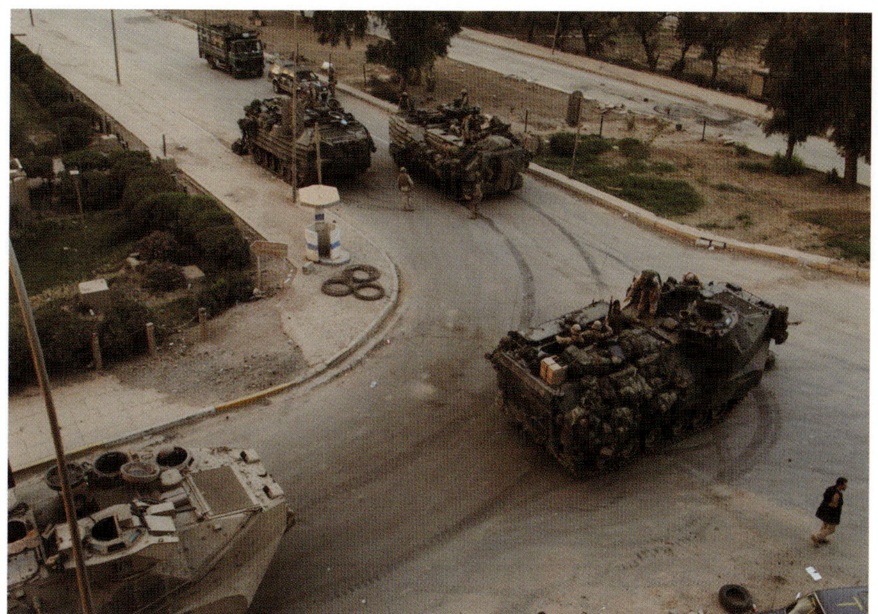

The Marines move out of the area of the Palestine Hotel in their amphibious assault vehicles

The pilgrimage and worship lasts the weekend, culminating on Tuesday, the most sacred day of the event. John wants to get a jump on the story before the roads become too congested with pilgrims and traffic as the holy day approaches. John is a very quiet journalist, who uses experience and knowledge to get his material. He does not come off as aggressive or pushy, even though he is well over six feet tall. His soft eyes, calm voice and warm smile make him a great person to work with.

As soon as we leave Baghdad and merge onto the main southwest highway to Karbala, we see pilgrims marching and chanting. The highway threads across the desert, and the pilgrims are spread out along the highway shoulder, mostly in small groups of about five to twenty, marching south in a long endless chain. They carry religious banners and large green and black flags. The green flags represent a better future, the black ones remind them of their past suffering. They march as crusaders, a continuous chain of people drunk with religious immersion and spirit. The procession is made up of old men, adults, teenagers, children and a sprinkling of women.

As we make our way further south, the chain of humanity becomes larger and thicker, ten shoulders across in places, spilling over the shoulder and onto the blacktop of the highway. A halo of beige dust engulfs the endless human ribbon, stirred up by thousands of marching feet. Roadside kiosks, set up by the locals, provide free water, first aid and snacks to pilgrims. In medical tents, sponsored and manned by the Red Crescent Society, their blisters and exhaustion are attended to. The Red Crescent Society is a well organized and extremely capable group of people. I tip my hat to their dedicated staff and volunteers.

It is a weekend of giving and rejoicing, like one huge, happy family. Some of the devoted have been walking for days to get to the mosque; some are in wheelchairs. A grotesquely crippled man, with deformed arms and legs, is crawling along the highway on hands and knees, like a crab. This is his display of piety to his god, but I wonder how, being so low to the asphalt and dirt, he can stand the heat from the sun and the oven-like temperature. No man should suffer so; his strength in his belief makes him a giant amongst regular mortals. I admire this man's conviction, and will always remember him as a most pitiful sight, though glowing with admiration and dedication to his god and his people.

This is the best-organized event I have seen since my arrival in this country. No wonder Saddam had stopped this pilgrimage. If these people can organize and take care of themselves like this, then perhaps they can organize and govern a country. Saddam, a Sunni Muslim, knew the potential of the Shi'a Muslims.

When we stop at the side of the road to interview the pilgrims, they are friendly and accommodating. Everyone, it seems, wants to get his opinion across to us. We have to tear ourselves away to continue on, or become the ear to every worshipper bound for Karbala. But they are now free to openly glorify their god and convictions, without fear of retribution from the Baath Party thugs. To the Shi'a Muslims, it must be like a blind man being able to see light for the first time. There is a magical feeling of rebirth amongst the worshippers, you can see it in their eyes as they embrace your hand or hug you.

We stop at a small village where a bottleneck of people and traffic clog the streets. In this festive atmosphere, shop owners wave at us and say, "Hello mister!" Others offer us delicious hot tea in the usual small, decorated glasses, a third of the glass filled with sugar. A small silver-tinted spoon is used to stir the sweet, addictive concoction. I have to turn down offers of bread and vegetables (I don't like to eat when I am working, it slows me down).

The narrow main street is a sea of people, as wave after wave of pilgrims, beating their chests in unison and chanting to Allah, move through the streets like soldiers on a victory parade. The energy that engulfs the mass of worshippers, carrying all along, is hypnotizing, and stimulating.

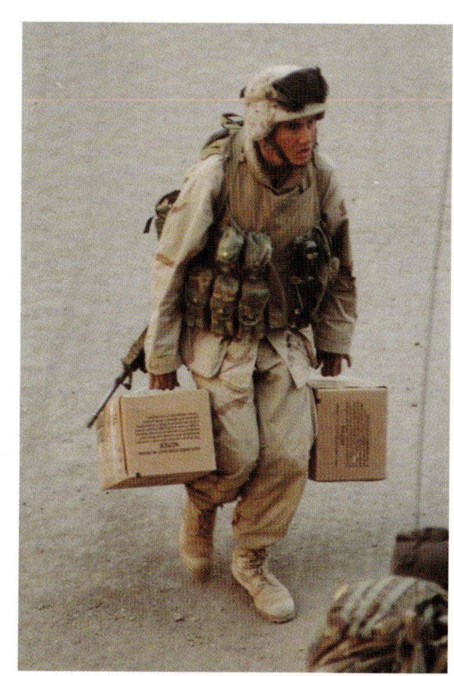

A Marine carries a load of equipment

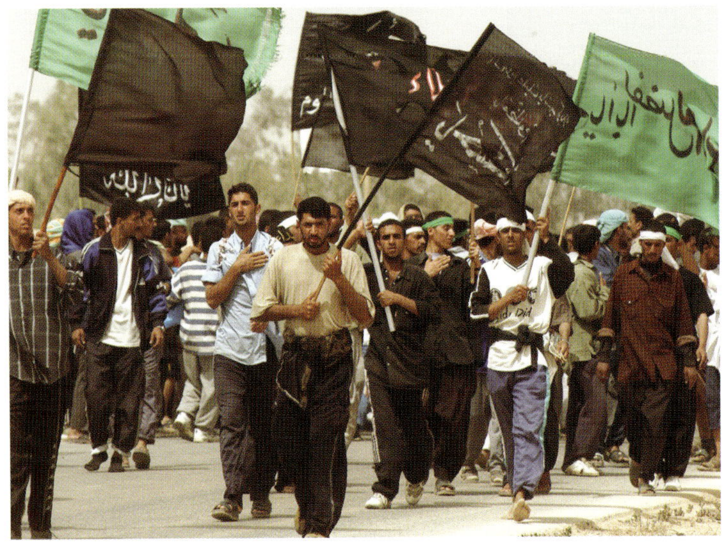

Shi'a pilgrims march to the holy city of Karbala

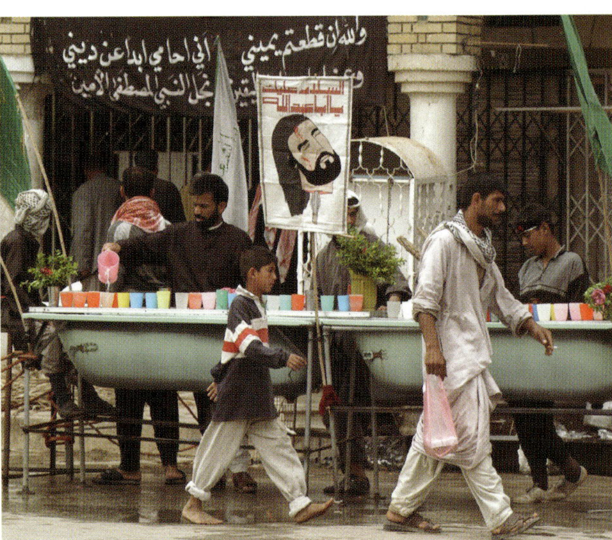

Kiosks offer refreshments and aid to pilgrims

Flags and banners are flying, held up by men wearing bandannas with religious inscriptions scrawled across them. Suddenly, as though awakening from a dream, John grabs me out of the swell and tells me it is time to go.

Jumping in the car, we make our way out of the village and continue driving alongside the growing throng. Dozens of weary pilgrims splash and soothe themselves in a branch of the Euphrates River, next to the road. Hearing and seeing the splash of water in such a dry, hot place is refreshing. John and I have our bottles of water, and drink from them religiously.

We drive through a small village and see an overturned pick-up truck. A hysterical, crying man runs from the vehicle with a six-year-old-girl draped across his outstretched arms. Her head is bloodied and she looks in pretty bad shape. I turn away as a mob of panicking bystanders reaches into the passenger cab for other occupants. We keep moving, knowing there is really nothing we can do. It is an ugly fragment of suffering in a sea of religious vehemence and joy.

The caravan of people veer off from the highway and follow a shortcut along a railway track. The detour is about three miles long, then it joins up again with the highway. A pick-up truck full of chicken crates drives past us, with a badly burned man sitting in the outside cargo area. All he is wearing is a white loincloth. The skin on his back has peeled into large, page-sized sheets of hanging skin. His face is disfigured and burned. The legs show rolled-up and crumpled skin at the ankles, where the skin has pulled down. His skin has melted.

The road to Karbala shows almost no signs of war. There is just a handful of bombed vehicles on the highway and a few overpasses have been struck by bombs. But there is not a lot of infrastructure or armaments to destroy.

We drive right into Karbala and park our car a five-minute walk away from the Al Hussein mosque, one of the Shi'a Muslims' most holy sites. The town is surprisingly small, with the mosque being the centre of attraction. We walk through the narrow but clean side streets where fruit, candy and cigarette vendors sell their wares. I buy two very tasty bananas, which I gobble down with great pleasure. Some of the fruit vendors are selling fresh lettuce, tomatoes and other vegetables. This is the first time I have seen this variety of vegetables in Iraq. It seems almost normal here, as though it has always been this way, compared with the hopeless situation in Baghdad.

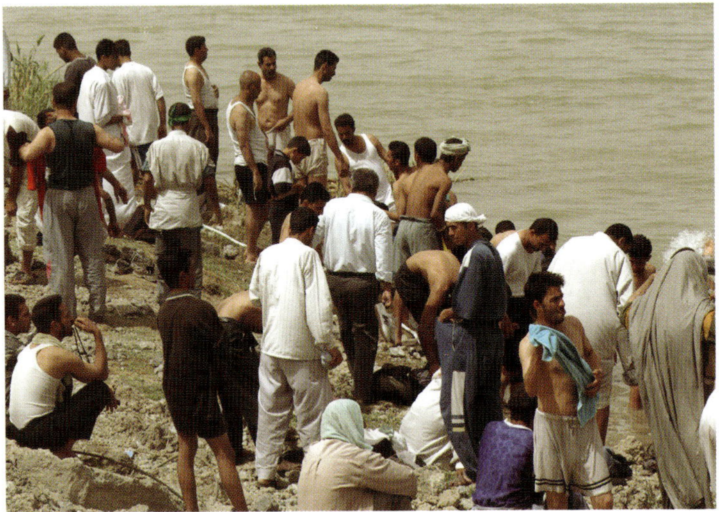

Weary faithful pause from their march to bathe in the Euphrates River

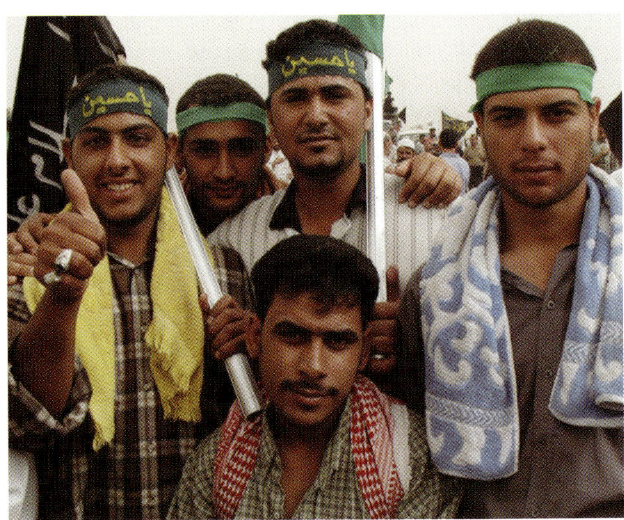

The journey to Karbala is a festive, though devoutly religious event

We walk into a magnificent square, the size of four football fields. Situated in front of us, at the head of the square, is the stunning Al Hussein mosque. Its 25-foot-high outside walls are covered in mosaics made of stunning blue, white and gold tiles. These walls enclose the inner compound (restricted to all but the devout), where two towering golden domes rise like twin suns out of the mosque compound. It is 'eye candy' to this photographer, a kaleidoscope of color and culture. The arrangements of the different tones of blue mosaics pleasantly startle the eye.

At the main doorway of the mosque, John talks with a security man, dressed in a maroon-colored turban, about meeting the head cleric of the mosque. The man disappears into the interior of the mosque, and then returns minutes later with the cleric, dressed in a black gown with starched white shirt and white turban. By his side are two other maroon-turbaned security men. John starts interviewing him while I wait for the opportunity to ask the religious leader for permission to photograph in the square and outside the mosque. After the interview I ask the cleric if it is safe and not insulting to the worshippers to photograph the gathering. He responds, "Don't fear – go ahead. It's not a problem!"

I am not too in tune to Muslim tradition and culture. In some Muslim countries, taking a person's photograph can be a dangerous undertaking and an insult to the person, particularly women Muslims. A journalist, in a situation like this, should be sensitive to the cultural differences and not just stick a camera or notepad in someone's face without thinking about common courtesy and a respect of a person's right of refusal. Though sometimes the rules must be bent slightly.

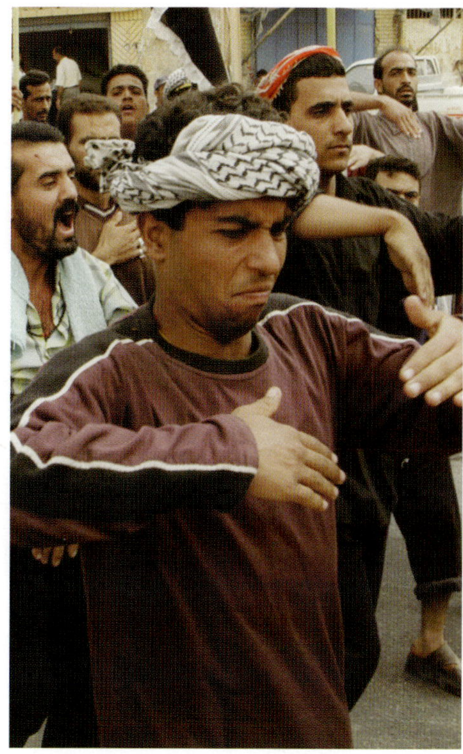

Worshippers in a trance-like holy state

Just prior to this, a parade of golden-helmeted-horsemen, with colorful yellow plumes and spectacular crimson gowns passed down a nearby road. I rush over with John, but it is too late, they have already disappeared. It would have made for a stunning photograph.

We walk through the crowd, where vendors sell popcorn, ice cream, soft drinks, prayer stones, native crafts and fried sweet pastries. John starts to interview people randomly, while I snap away. Another cleric comes up to us, while we are interviewing and taking pictures, and asks us to stop asking questions of the worshippers and taking photos.

This is just what we had asked the first cleric to prevent from happening. John tells him that we spoke to the head cleric who had said it would be fine to do our jobs, if there is no obvious objection from the crowd. He leaves us alone to go about our affairs, but it left a bitter taste. Are the clerics such control freaks that they feel the worshippers cannot speak for themselves? This situation for the cleric wasn't a safety issue, but a 'control the information issue.' Do the Shi'a people have to be policed like sheep by the clerics? Can no man speak for himself without some fanatic editing his words? The majority of Iraqis want to be able to speak their mind without fear of reprisal from a religious or totalitarian leader.

Everyone is a control freak in Iraq, no matter what side you may be on. In my opinion, this kind of power grabbing could lead to civil war and the eventual break-up of Iraq. Everyone wants to be the shepherd; no one wants to be the sheep.

Making our way down to the other end of the square, we see a similar, smaller walled mosque, with only

This man, sitting in the back of a poultry truck, has been burned so badly his skin has melted

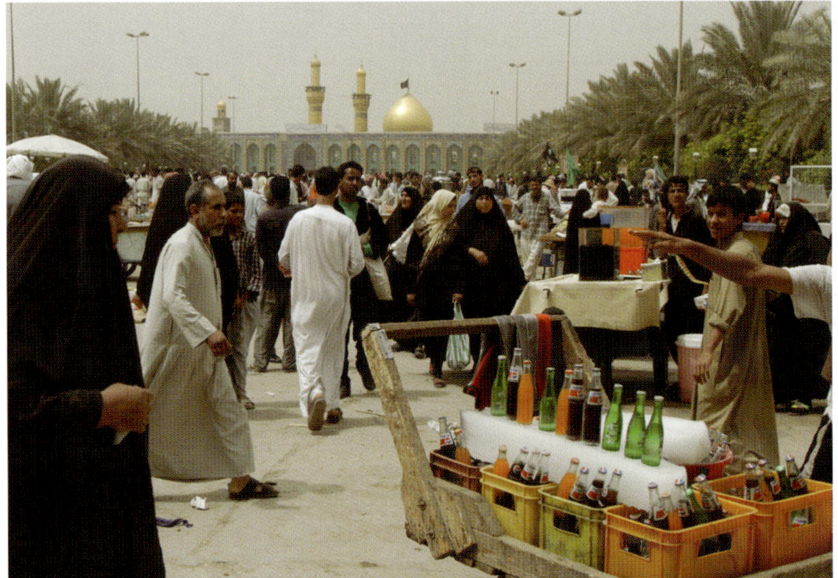

Al Hussein mosque in Karbala overlooks a busy square where vendors sell iced drinks

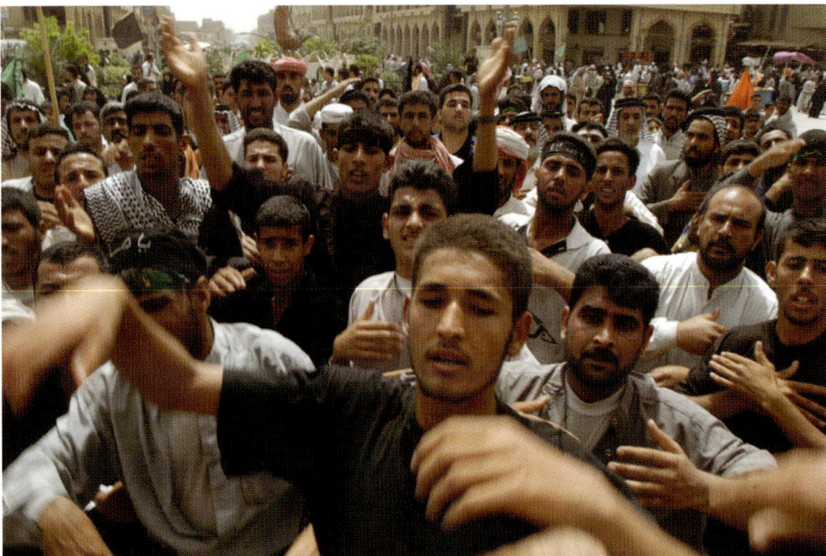

A wave of entranced worshippers surge forward toward the Al Hussein mosque

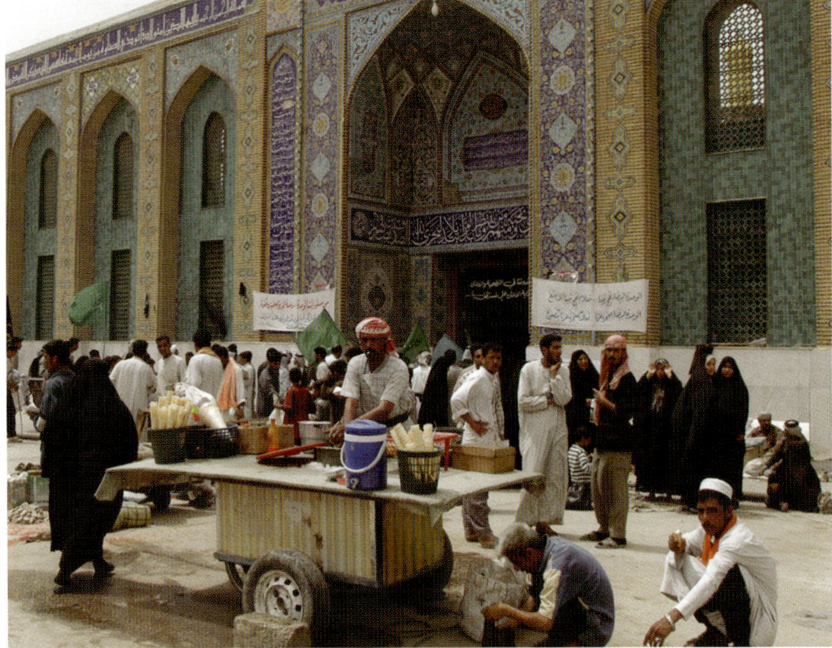

For the first time since 1968 the Shi'a can hold a pilgrimage to Karbala

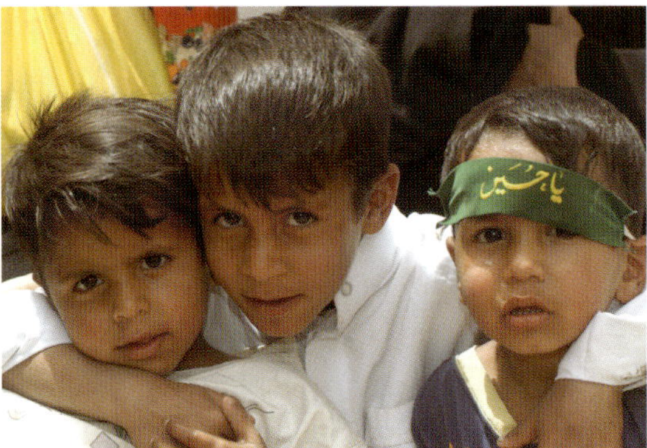

Young pilgrims

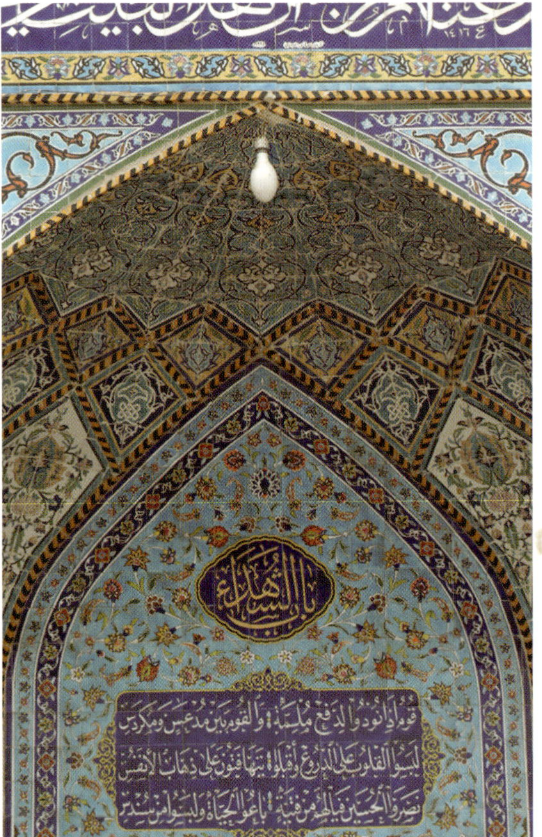

Magnificent mosaic and glaze details of archway

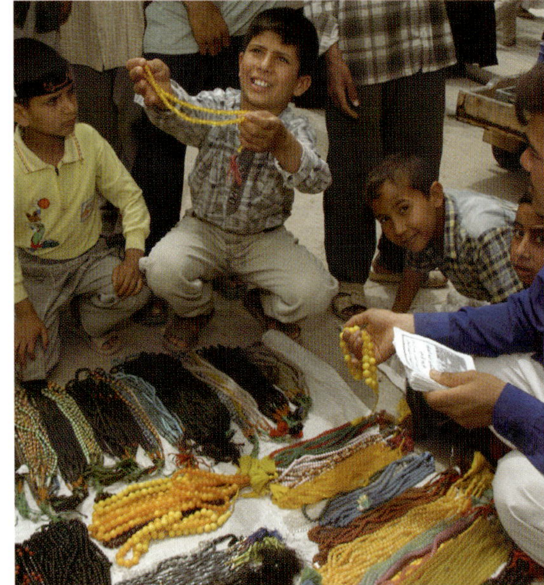

These boys are a ray of sunshine for Iraq's future

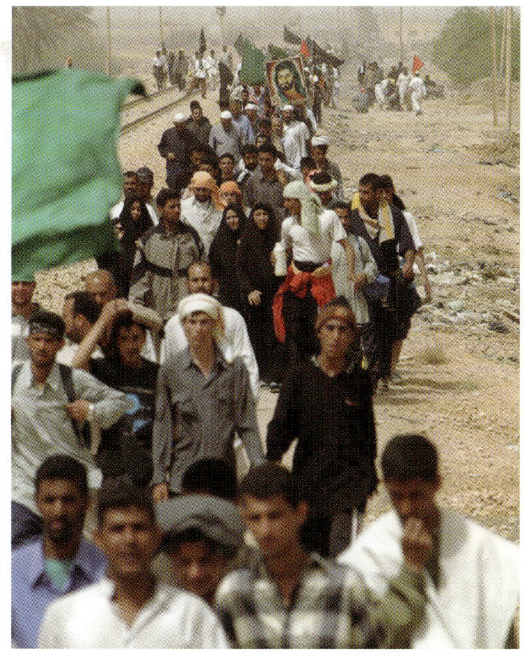

A chain of people detour along railway tracks

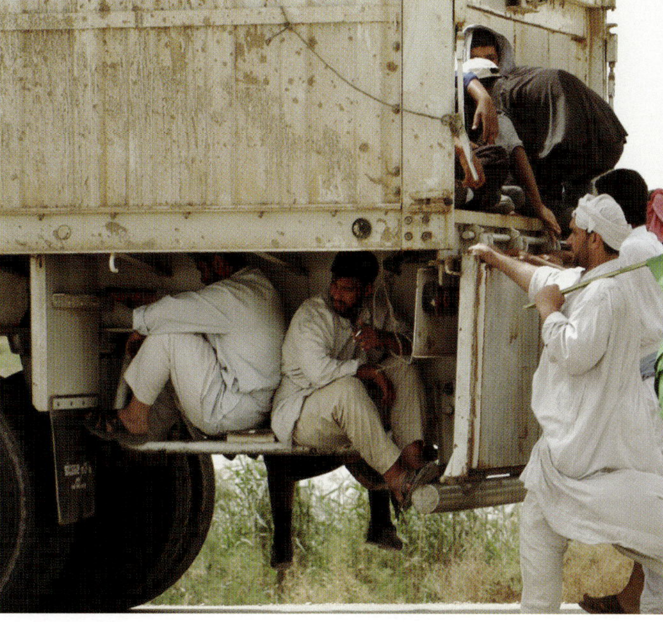

Marchers hitch a ride on a truck

one golden dome. It is not as large as the first but is comparable in its beauty. John interviews while I take pics of the mosque's architecture and the people in the square. Vendors are offering me gifts of ice cream, nuts and tea. They ask me where am I from. When I tell them Canada, they smile and offer their hands to shake. Everyone here loves Canada, because many Iraqis fled there after Saddam rose to power. So there are many family links between Iraq and Canada. But, at the same time, they ask why we are not helping Iraq now with food and medicine, when they need it more than at any other time.

I walk about the bustling crowd (which I estimate to be half a million people) waiting for John to finish so we can move on, when a black-cloaked woman asks me to sit for a tea with her family. They sit upon a small pile of mats outside the walls of the mosque, selling hot tea from a large stainless steel tankard. I sit down and offer my Marlboro cigarettes to the smiling and giggling family group, who watch me with curiosity. They have never met a Westerner. I hope I set a good example. My cigarettes are lit and passed around, and we all drink tea and smoke while trying to converse using sign language and facial expressions. It is really nice to be enjoying these friendly people's company. I feel right at home, like neighbors, though our cultures and homes are worlds apart. It is a warm interlude of friendship and understanding.

John waves me over, and we walk back towards the head of the square where we are caught in a large crowd of people pushing and shoving to get through the congested gates of the main mosque. It is a moving human mass, and raising my camera above my head to take some photos, I lose my footing and am swept up in the human wave. With claustrophobia fast closing in on me, someone grabs my arm and pulls me aside from the pulsing throng. It's John again. He tells me it is time to make our way back to the car. I grab a bunch of bananas on the way.

We are desperate to get back to Baghdad because John has to meet his deadline. So we leave friendly Karbala, this time going against the human chain, which continues marching and pouring into the city. We stop at the roadside a few times on the way back, so I can take some photos of the human river.

During one stop by the railway track detour, I slip while crossing a small wooden bridge. My leg drops down through the ties, scraping the skin from my shin. My camera smacks hard onto one of the ties, cracking the hot shoe on the flash. The rim of my 200 zoom also cracks, but I push the cracked pieces together again. Luckily the camera is fine. My leg and forearm hurt like hell, but I am still in action. Breaking my digital camera would place me in a bad situation as I only have a film camera for back up, and a small handful of film. (Once you've gone digital – you'll never want to use film cameras again).

I take pics of pilgrims resting and refreshing themselves inside a large public tent made of colorful towels, mats and blankets. The heat and the dust are relentless, but the worshippers, like waves of spawning salmon, keep marching onward to Karbala, drawn to their Mecca. By Tuesday, 3.5 million pilgrims will reach Karbala.

Driving back through Baghdad I reflect on how the visit to Karbala was an incredibly visual and spiritual experience. To see this mass of humanity, dedicated and happily marching as one large family, was a very warm distraction from the misery of Baghdad. Never before have I seen anything like it. I wonder if these people will be the ones to eventually pull this country together, towards an acceptable form of democracy.

When we arrive back at the Fanar, I try to find my Swedish friend who was helping me transmit my photos overseas, but I cannot find him. Finally he shows up, but tells me he has too much work to do and cannot transmit my photos for me. It is now past midnight and I am concerned about getting the images to Houston for the morning's paper. I head to the

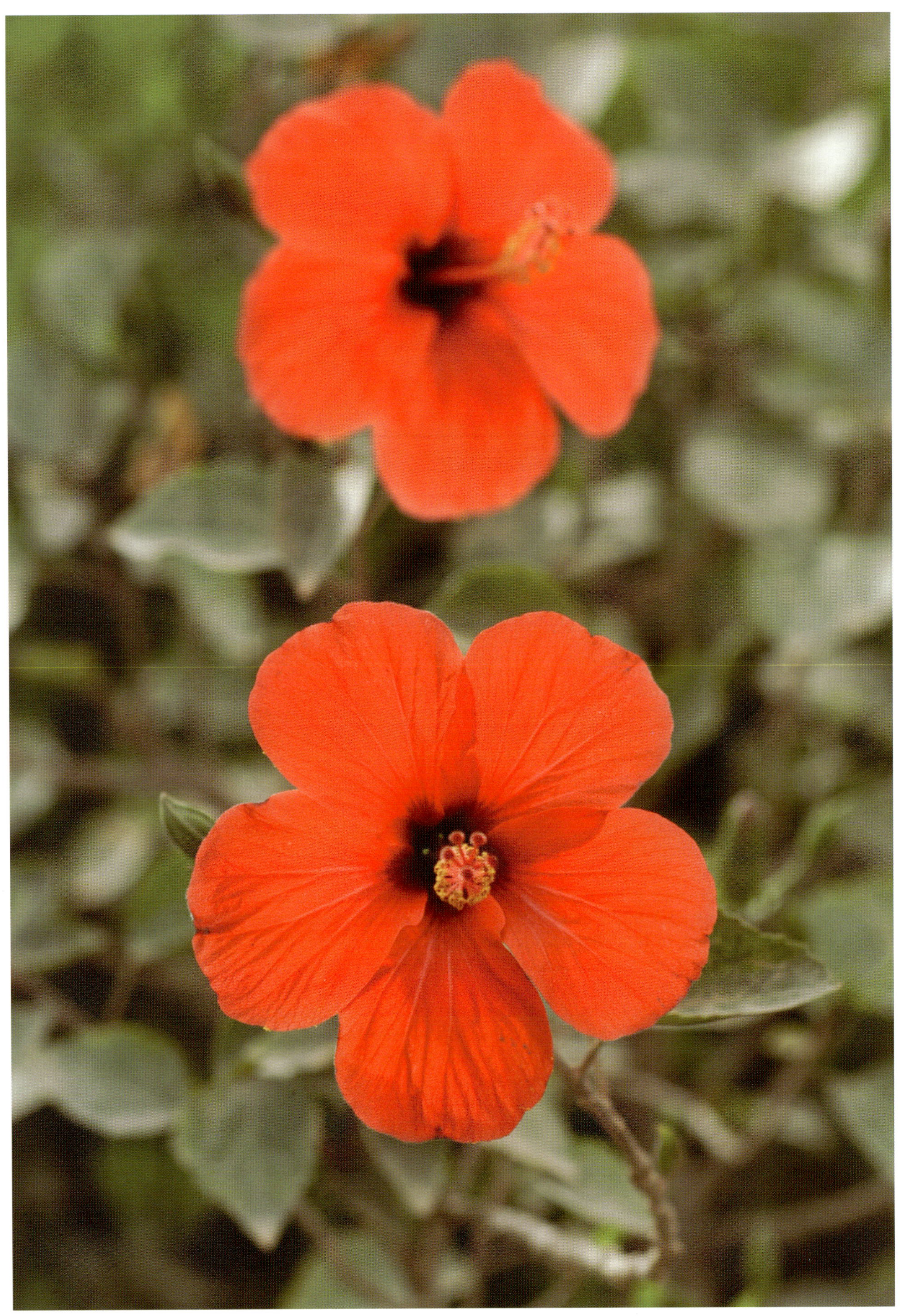

Hibiscus are found in most Iraqi gardens and public areas. The Iraqi people love flowers

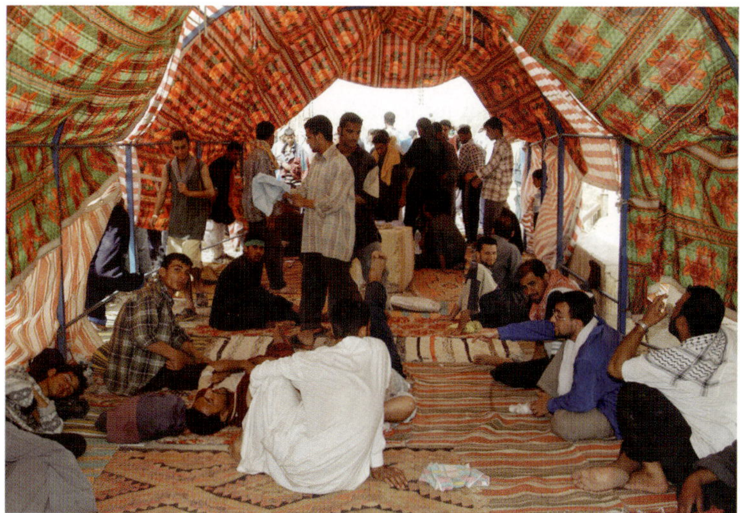

A tent of colored blankets offers a place of rest on the road to Karbala

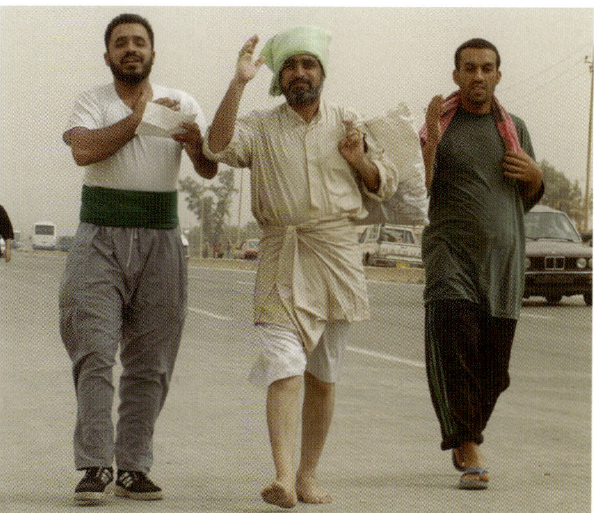

Pilgrims chant and wave welcome

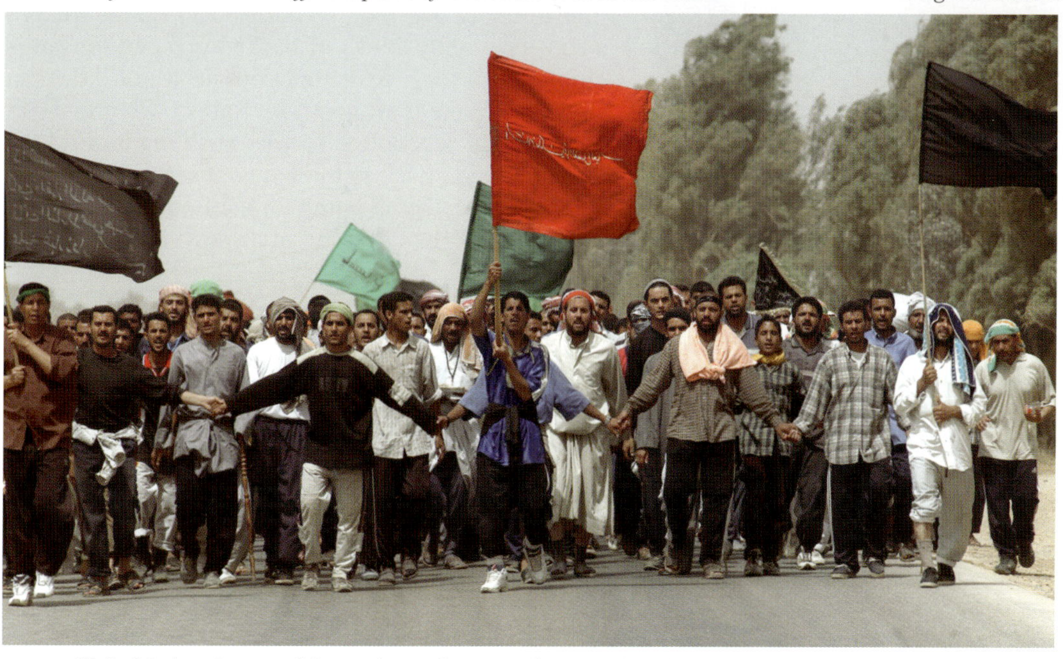

Shi'a Muslim devout celebrate their religion as they march to the Al Hussein mosque in Karbala

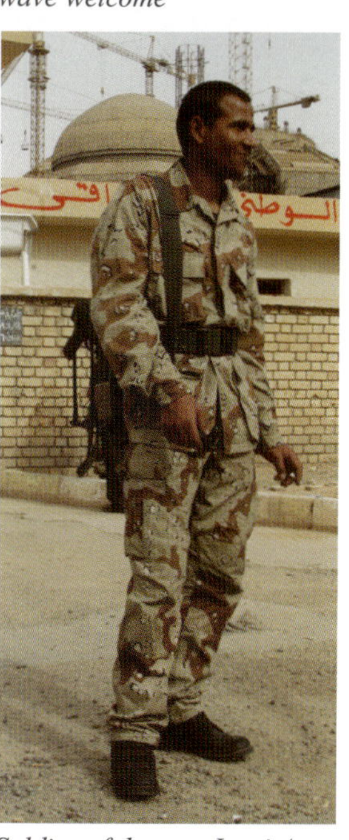

Soldier of the new Iraqi Army

Palestine to try to find a way of transmitting my pics. I search frantically for someone to help me transmit. Finally, at around 3:30 a.m., a technician with CNN lets me send them by their satellite link. I am terribly stressed-out at this point, but relieved to get the pics overseas. The photos would appear the following day on the front page of the *Houston Chronicle*.

This is the kind of situation you can find yourself in if you don't own your own B-GAN transmitter, or some similar type of technology. The B-GAN is the missing link to profit and ease of mind that I do not own. Had I possessed one, it could have made me a lot of money, at least enough to recoup the cost of it, without all the stress I am going through. The next time I travel to an area without the *Internet*, I will make sure I have the necessary tools to do my job and not be left behind the eight ball. The B-GAN system, like most other necessary electronic equipment, is only available outside war-torn Iraq. If you possess the best and latest equipment, your chance of survival definitely increases.

Photo-journalism is a dangerous and difficult way to make a living. You work hard all day long in the relentless heat, then work half the night organizing and transmitting. Then, getting up early the next morning, you start all over again. It is the kind of pace that can physically and mentally exhaust a person and leave them open to illness and danger.

By 4:30 a.m., I am finished and ready to leave the Palestine for the Fanar. I walk through the hotel front doors chatting with a CNN translator who is going to another area of the hotel complex. Just as we are ten feet outside from the main entranceway of the hotel, bursts from an automatic weapon are striking all around us. The bullets, from an AK-47, ricochet off the road and through the trees above our heads. In a knee-jerk reaction, I turn back and ducking low, hustle back into the Palestine lobby. "Boy, that was close," I say to the interpreter, who is shaking and laughing like a babbling idiot, a typical response from someone who has just cheated death. We both cheated death, and do we know it. This is just what I mean when I say your chances of survival increase if you have the best equipment. If I had my own trans-

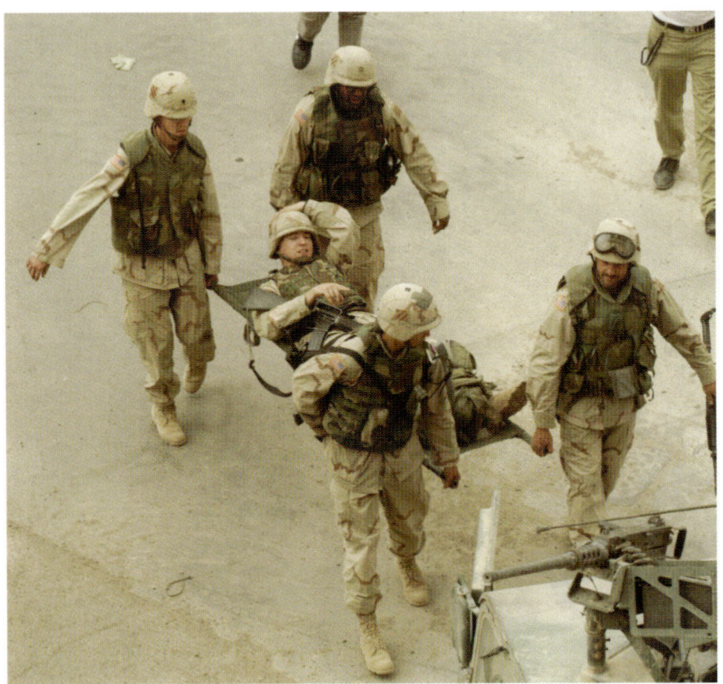
An injured soldier is carried from the Palestine complex by his comrades

mitter, I would not have needed to go out and expose myself at night.

A soldier approaches us in the lobby and nonchalantly warns us to not leave the hotel until the sun rises, at the risk of our lives. It doesn't take much more to convince me, and I thank the soldier. I try to get some sleep on a couch in the lobby, but most of the couches are occupied by people who cannot get accommodations and are being allowed to sleep on the furniture. Some of these people are drivers who have to get up at sunrise to ferry their media clients to whatever story they are covering. It is either sleep here at the Palestine, or risk my life in the 30 seconds it takes to dash across the complex and street to the Fanar.

I lie exhausted and numb, trying to get comfortable on an undersized couch, with my laptop case pinned under one foot, so no one can rip me off as I sleep. The lobby stinks of backed-up sewage, and is chilly. It is a long, irritable two-hour wait till the sun rises, but I take it all in stride. I muse war and death have no real schedule – so why push my luck?

I finally get back to the Fanar at around 6:30 a.m. and head up to my room where Tish and Sean are sound asleep. I grab my place, this evening on the floor, and fall into a deep sleep. This will be my first good sleep since leaving Montreal, and I am happy to be in a warm room with my snoring friends. Small comforts mean so much.

Day 11. Sunday, April 20th

(Sleep till noon; I buy Cuban cigars from a street vendor; cheap booze; injured soldier carried on stretcher; some down time; visiting the Baghdad Zoo; I hire a young bodyguard for $5; the zoo is destitute; meeting the lion keepers of Baghdad; animals are stressed; live prey for the lions of Baghdad; looters and lions; tour of the zoo in an APC)

I wake at noon, feeling like a new man from my long undisturbed sleep. I take a shower then head downstairs for coffee. Outside the hotel a man asks me if I want to buy any Cohiba – Cuban cigars. He is selling them for three dollars each. I buy his seven remaining cigars, with the intent of eventually trading them for other articles such as food. All sorts of booze are available from the transient street vendors, from Pinch Scotch to Gilbey's Gin, at $10 for a 26-ounce bottle.

The cigars and booze are part of the looted booty from one of Saddam's palaces, or so the vendor tells me.

While putting the cigars away in my hotel room, I see an injured soldier being carried on a stretcher to an APC. He has a foot injury, but he is smiling as his soldier friends carry him to the vehicle. He might have stepped on something sharp or badly sprained his ankle.

I walk about the neighborhood taking feature photos of soldiers and civilians. It is a down day, and after last night's shooting and close call with death, I need one. It is time to raise my head above the water a little and take it easy for a day, to re-group my mind and body. I buy some water and some sweeties from a nearby shop, and bring them back to my room.

At around 5 p.m. I decide to take a drive to the Zawra Park and Zoo (the Baghdad Zoo). I heard that the animals are being killed and eaten by the looters. Arriving at the zoo's front gates, I start walking around the expansive complex. I am soon followed by a group of five teenage looters. I stop to chat with them, being still close enough to the gate and safety of the main road. I would be a sitting

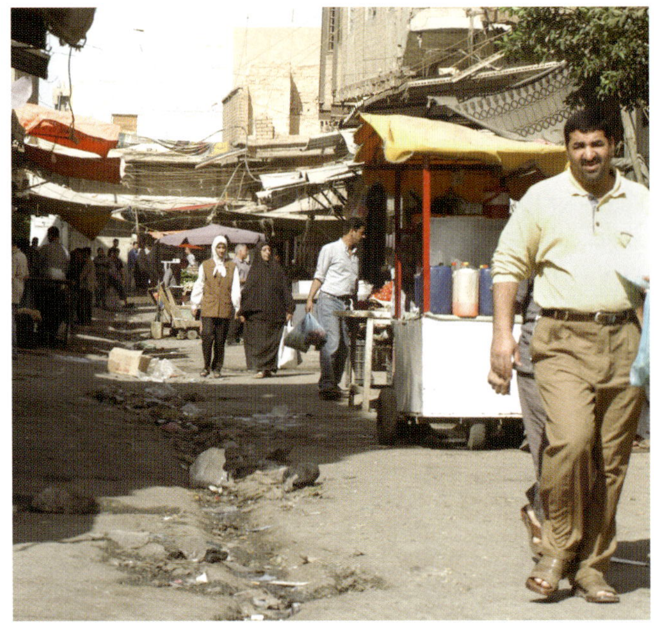
Market in downtown Baghdad

duck for the looters, so I decide upon another strategy to protect myself while touring the zoo. I decide to try buying them off.

I ask the oldest and largest looter if he would escort me around the facility for $5. He nods his approval and, leaving his friends behind, we start walking quickly, looking for the lion cages. But the place is huge and apparently empty of any animals or people. We walk for over an hour, passing all the empty animal pens before finding the lion enclosure. As we approach, a voice calls out in English for us to stop and identify ourselves. I identify myself as a journalist, looking for the lions and those responsible for their upkeep. The man, an American soldier, calls for us to come forward. I raise my camera in extended hands above my head and ask my escort to do the same with his hands. This is no time to be shot by accident in the failing light (not that anytime is a good time).

The soldier is one of three who have been posted to guard the three lions, two tigers and two bears that are the last remaining live residents of the zoo. (But the principle reason for guarding the zoo grounds is not really for the safety of the animals, but more to prevent mortar attacks from being launched from the zoo grounds, against the

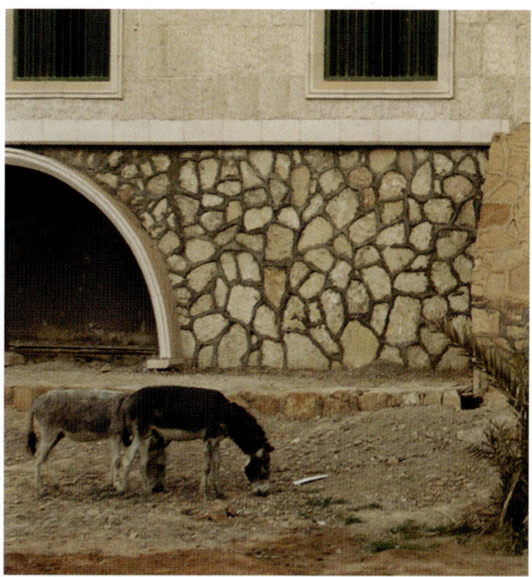
Live donkeys await their fate inside the lions' den

Ar Rasheed Hotel, where the American Forces Command Headquarters are located, directly across the street from the zoo). All the other animals have been eaten, stolen, shot or released. The soldiers tell me that their concern is that a looter might let the carnivores loose, possibly threatening lives and causing panic. For a brief moment I have a vision of lions attacking the looters.

One of the soldiers is from the Bronx. He tells me he used to visit the lions at the Bronx Zoo as a child, and has a close affection for lions. He is proud to be guarding the noble beasts (for three days now). They tell me they feed them by tying a live donkey to a rope inside the fenced lions' den. The lions, which are kept in their cages, are then let out into the enclosure, where they attack and eat the helpless animal. It is brutal and savage, but it

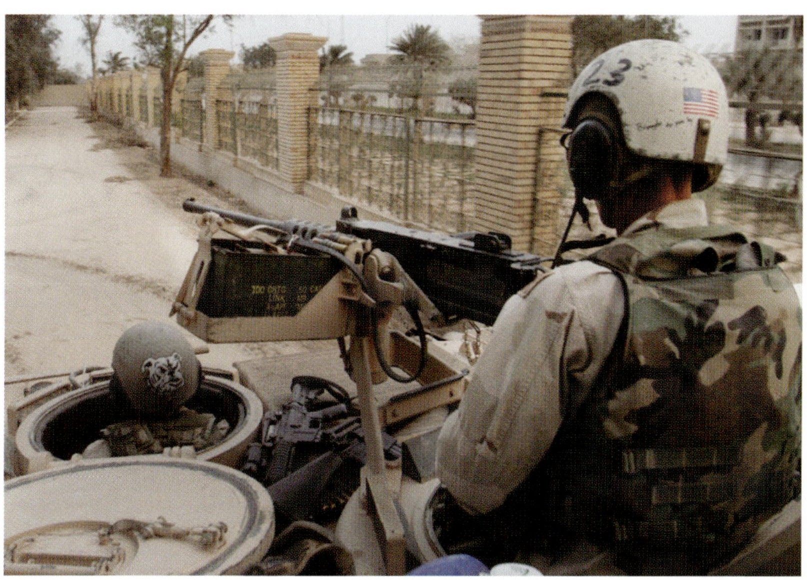
Exiting the Baghdad Zoo with an army escort

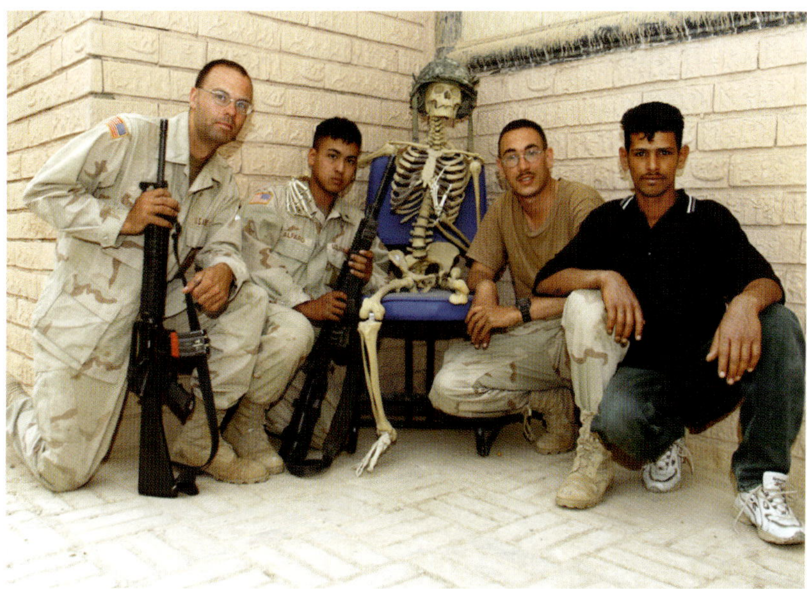
The lion keepers of Baghdad, skeleton mascot and my hired bodyguard (right).

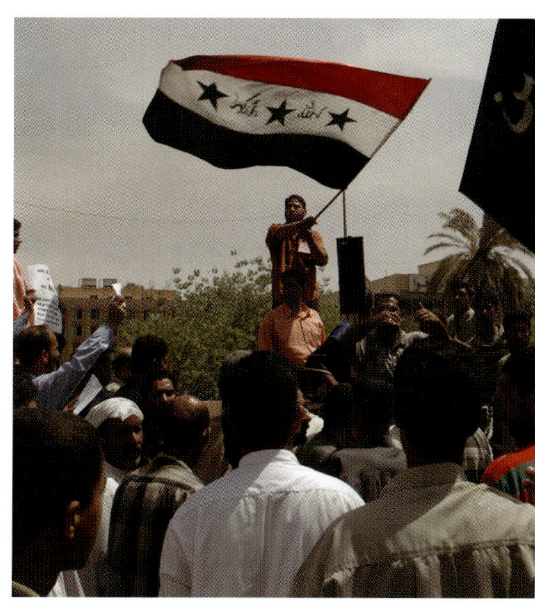
Demonstrations occur daily in front of the Palestine

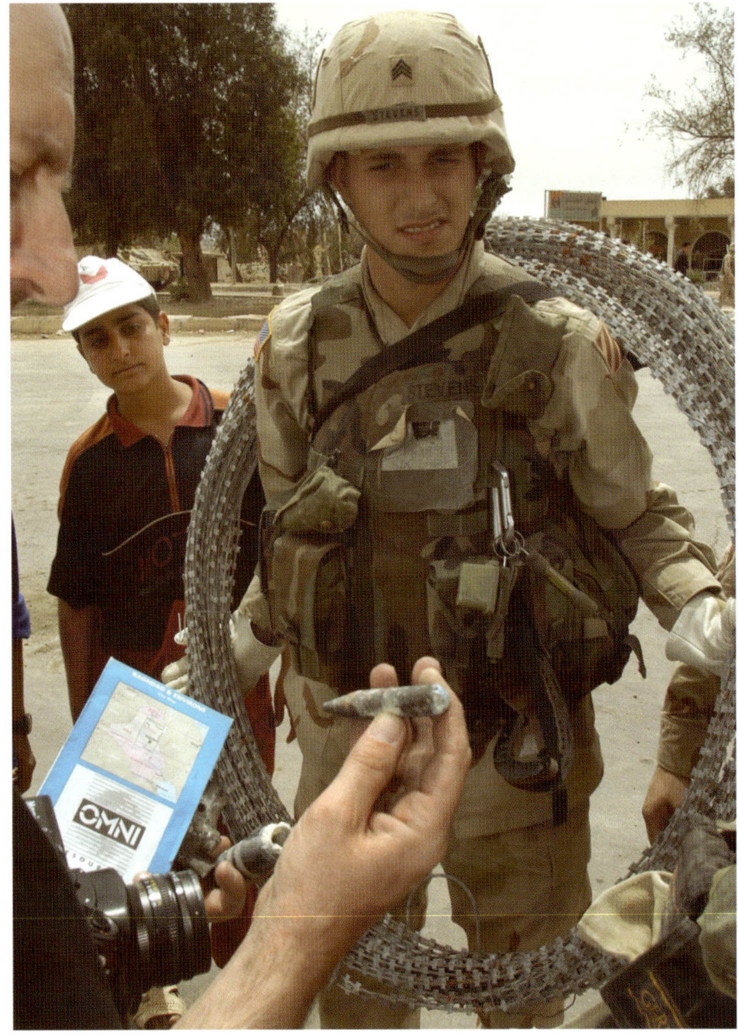
Examining a depleted uranium bullet

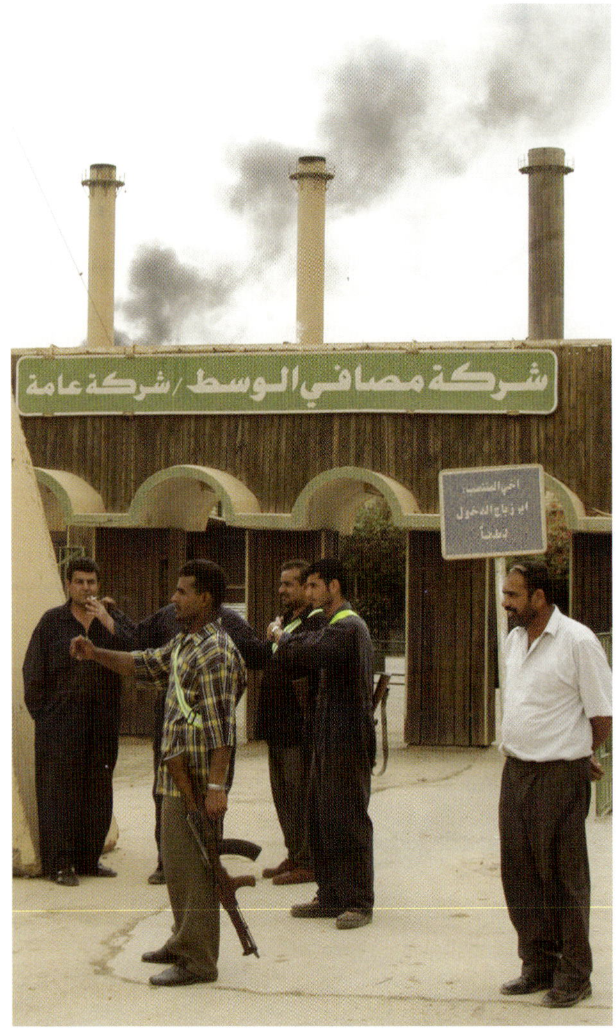
Armed guards at the gates of the Ad Dawrah Oil Refinery

stimulates the beasts to eat. The soldiers tell me that even the lions and tigers have been affected by the war and are stressed from the bombing and the activity of the looters. Prior to the soldiers' arrival, the animals had been without food or water for three days, and the felines wouldn't leave the security of their pens. I catch a glimpse of the lions of Baghdad, hiding in the shade under an overhang of the pen facility.

It is starting to get dark, so we begin walking back towards where I think the main gates are located. There is no way I want to be stranded in this no-mans-land, especially after dark; it would be suicide. After a half hour, I realize I am lost in the massive compound. I see one of the lion keepers patrolling the grounds in his APC, so I flag him over, asking for directions out of the zoo. He starts describing the route, then offers, "Hell, why don't you both hop aboard and I'll drive you over?"

We drive through the maze of pens and featureless expanse, while sitting beside the gunner on top of the clattering APC. My teenage bodyguard is thrilled riding on this war machine. He beams and chuckles as the APC clambers over the zoo grounds. It is too noisy to talk.

We reach the gate and thank the soldier for his courtesy. The teenager runs over to a waiting car and his friends. They all see him arrive on top the APC and want to know what it was like. I slip him the five-dollar note as he animatedly describes our visit to his buddies. We shake hands and he hugs me tight as I flag a taxi to the Fanar. Back at the hotel I eat supper with Sean and Tish, then take it easy the rest of the evening.

Day 12. Monday, April 21st

(Depleted uranium bullets; visiting the Ad Dawrah Oil Refinery; a great sign for Iraq; over two-thousand Shi'a Muslims protest in front of the Palestine; the confinement of religious leader Mohammed al-Fartussi; lending a soldier $10; payroll problems)

Before breakfast, I am having a smoke outside the Fanar when Simon comes over and starts to talk with a soldier I am with. Simon shows the soldier two spent rounds of 50-calibre, depleted uranium bullets. He had found them when we visited the palm grove on April 18th. The soldier, who is surprised at the heavy weight of the bullets (compared to conventional rounds), had never seen one and warns us to be careful handling them.

After a light breakfast, Sean, Tish and I decide to go for a drive to the Ad Dawrah Oil Refinery, south of Baghdad. For the past two days we have seen a huge smoke stack spewing fire and black smoke in the south sector of Baghdad. This indicated to me that the refinery was at least partially operating and oil was being refined. This is a great sign for Baghdad, as it means oil production is getting underway, providing people with jobs and an injection of much needed cash for the country. The opening of the refinery is a good business story.

We approach the gates of the refinery and stop at the gatehouse, where we talk to some employees and guards. They tell us we cannot visit the refinery yet, and to contact the coalition headquarters in Baghdad if we want permission for access. Watching 18-wheeler tanker trucks full of refined petroleum products leave the refinery, we thank them, and then jump back into the car and head back towards Baghdad.

Cruising around, we look for news or any feature ideas. We stop beside two small shops where we stock up on supplies of candy, fruit, water, soda pop, nuts, cookies and jam. This is the first time we have stocked up on food since we arrived in Baghdad. We have been buying water wherever we can find it, but finding these two stores with a pretty good selection of snack food is a blessing. A short time after, we stop to photograph a mass of children swarming around a stopped Humvee patrol of four vehicles. A throng of excited children, wanting to have their photos taken, surrounds Sean. He takes it all in stride, with big smiles while snapping photos. He looks so happy and at home surrounded by the children. I grab a couple of pics then we head off again.

Arriving back at the hotel I bump into John Otis, who asks if I have any recent pics of Iraqis demonstrating. I tell him I already have some pics from previous small demos but will keep an eye open for anything new. His feature is due later in the week so there is no great rush.

I decide to get some air and stretch my legs. Walking over to the Palestine I see a huge demonstration happening in front of the hotel. Two-to-three-thousand Shi'a Muslim demonstrators are amassed, chanting, waving flags and holding portraits of their religious leaders and martyrs. It is the largest demo I have seen in Baghdad, and very timely for John's photo request. The demo is spread out across the main street (Al Khulafa St.) fronting the Palestine Hotel.

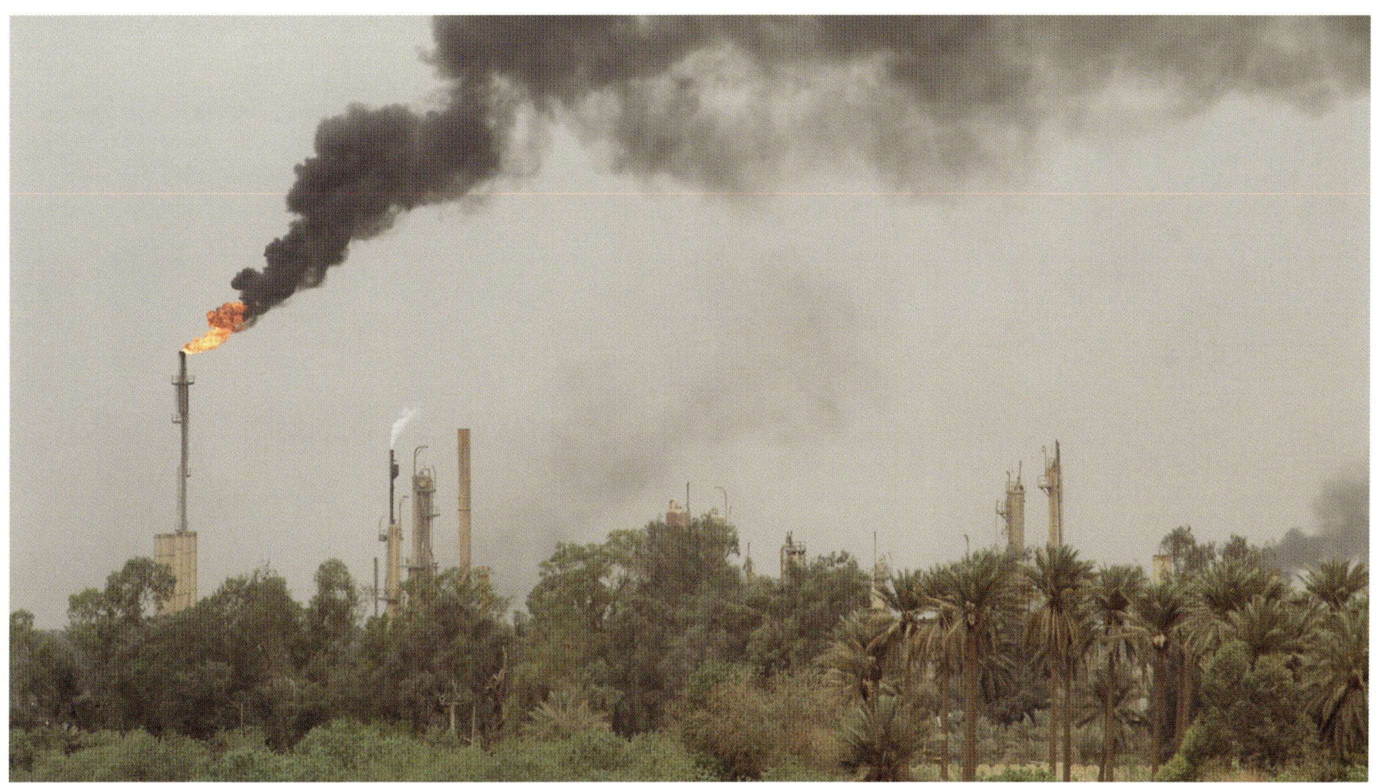

Thick black smoke pours from a smokestack of the Ad Dawrah Oil Refinery. Oil is the backbone of the Iraqi economy

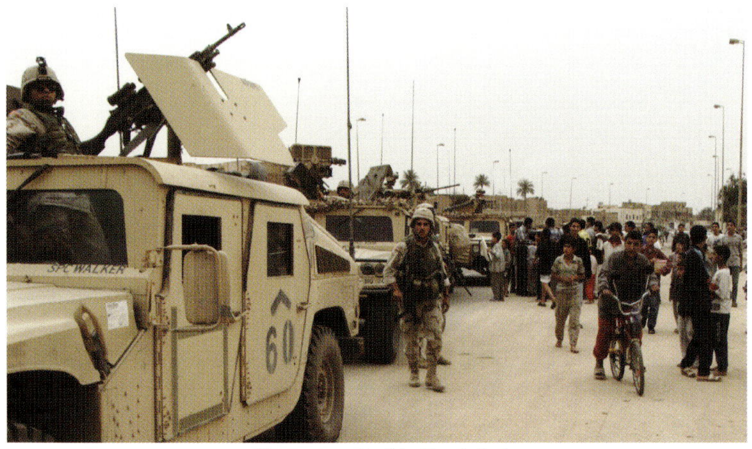

Humvee patrol in Baghdad

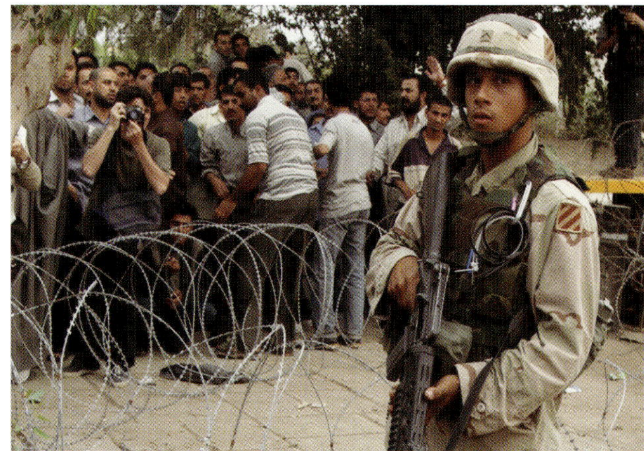

Soldier keeps alert during Shi'a demonstration

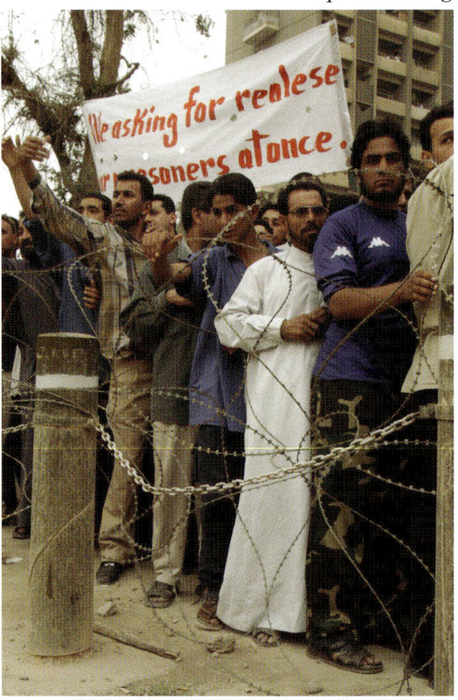

Shiites ask for release of cleric al-Fartussi

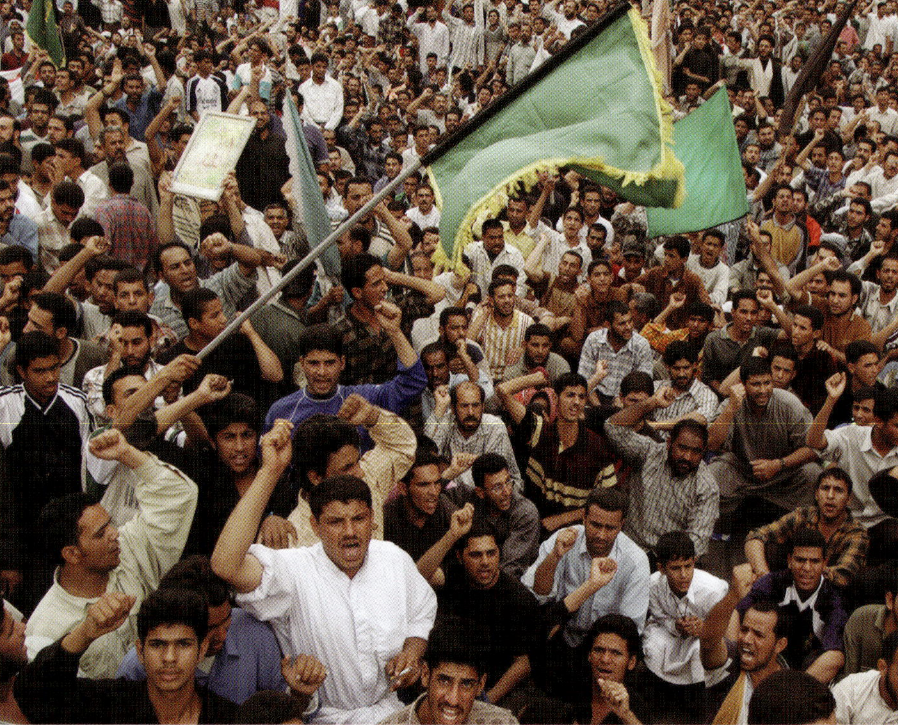

Shi'a Muslims demand that the Americans release their religious leader, Mohammed al-Fartussi

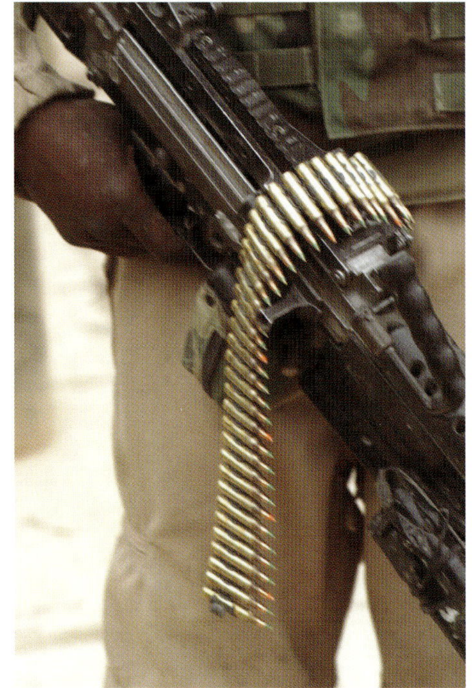

The biggest gun rules in Iraq

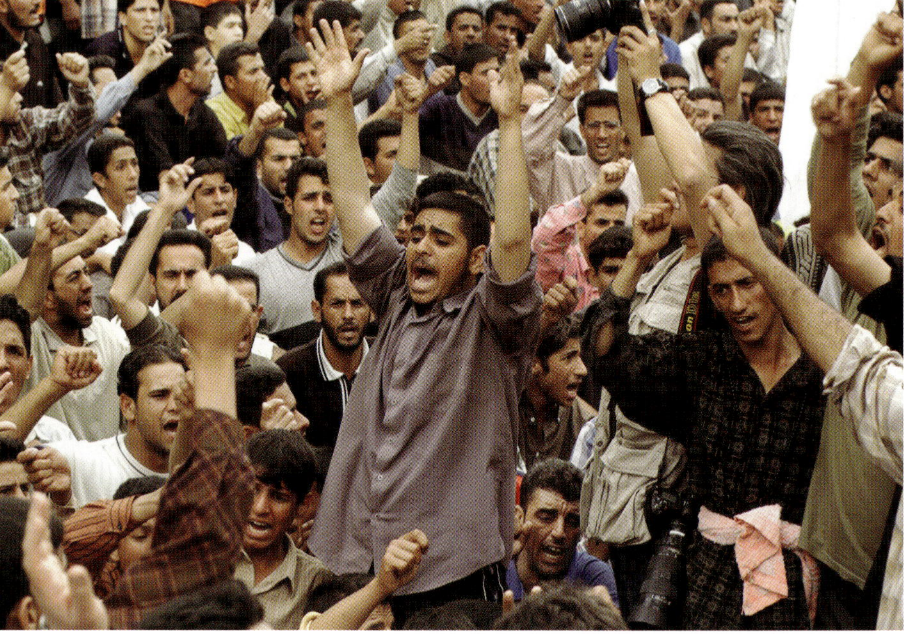

Shi'a Muslims make up 65%, of the Iraqi population. They want their voices heard

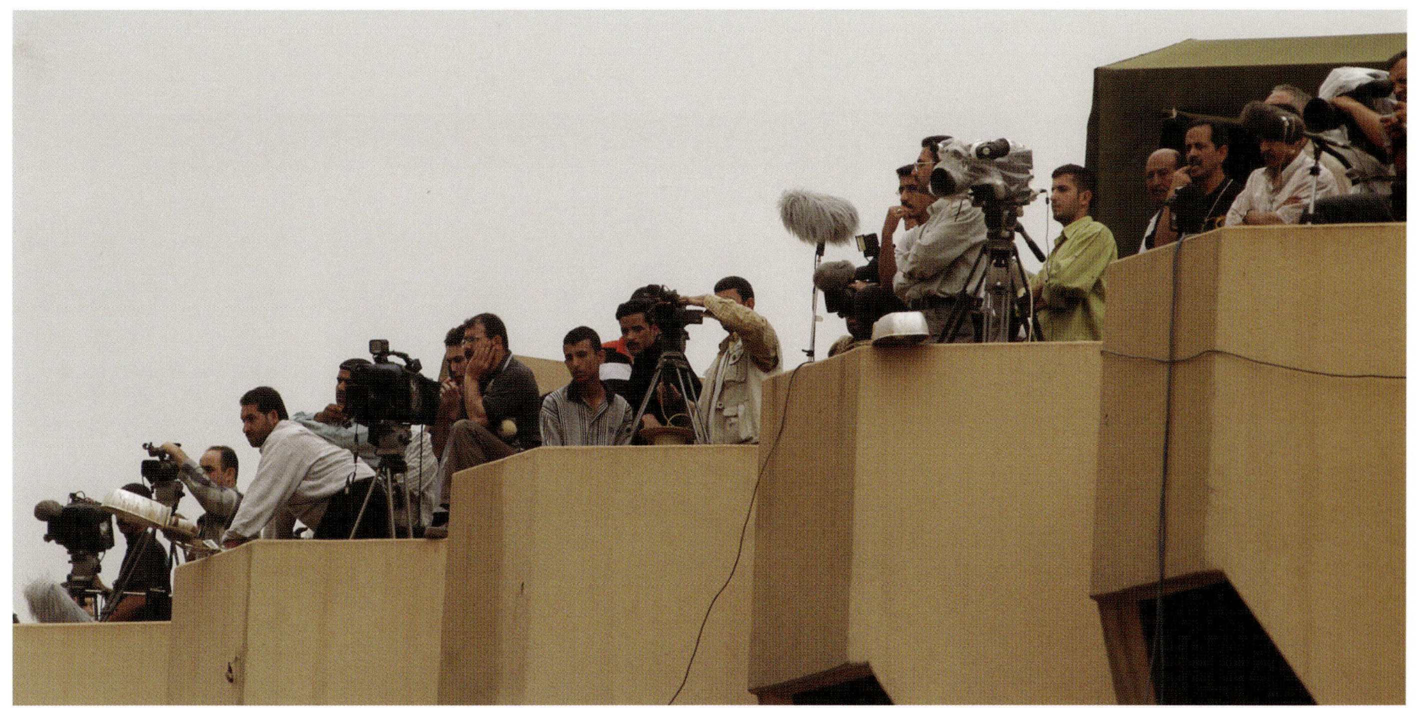

Television media cover the Shi'a demonstration from the second floor patio of the Palestine Hotel

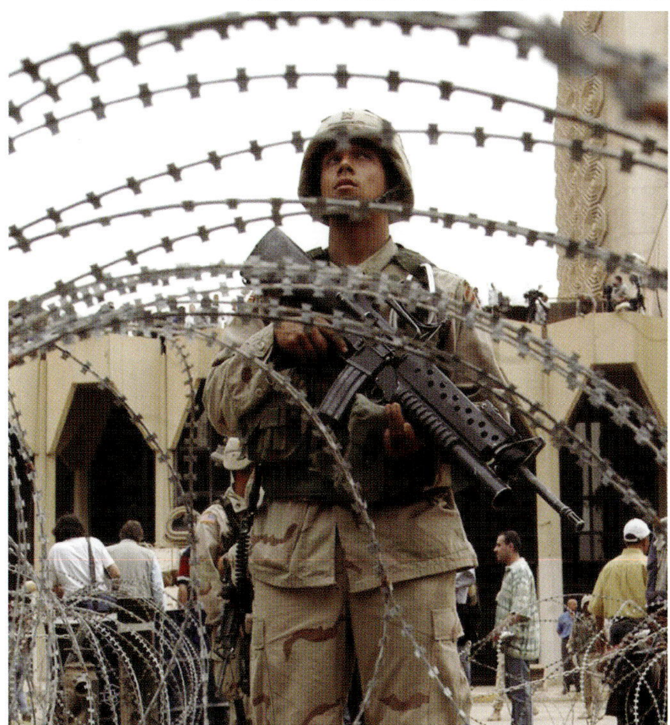

A soldier keeps a sharp lookout for danger during the demo

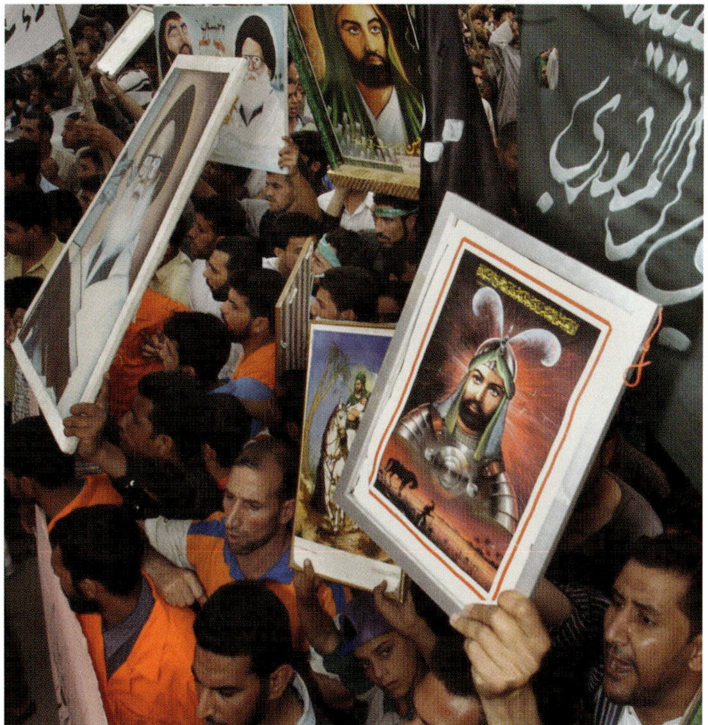

The Shi'a are a highly religious people

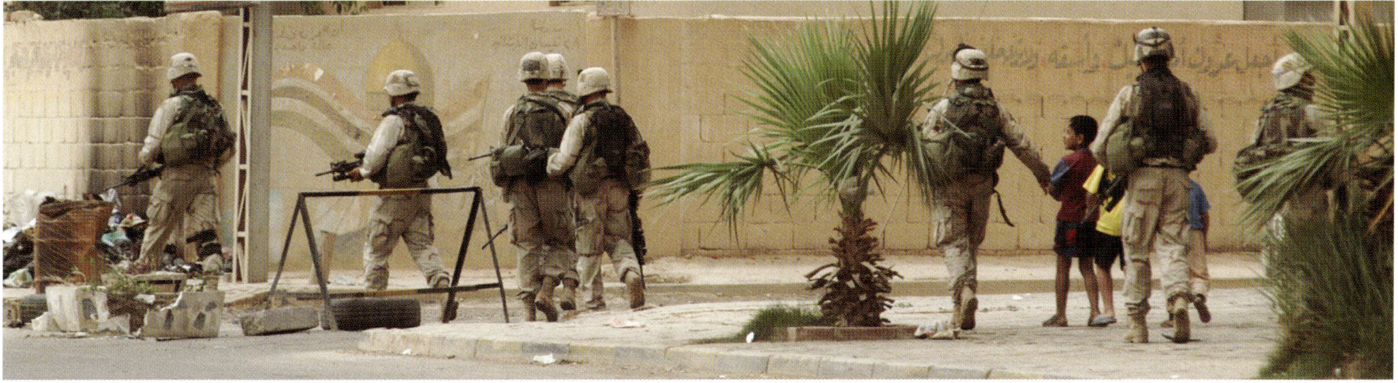

Soldiers patrol the side streets and alleyways of downtown Baghdad. Children follow the soldiers, asking for handouts or marching alongside them

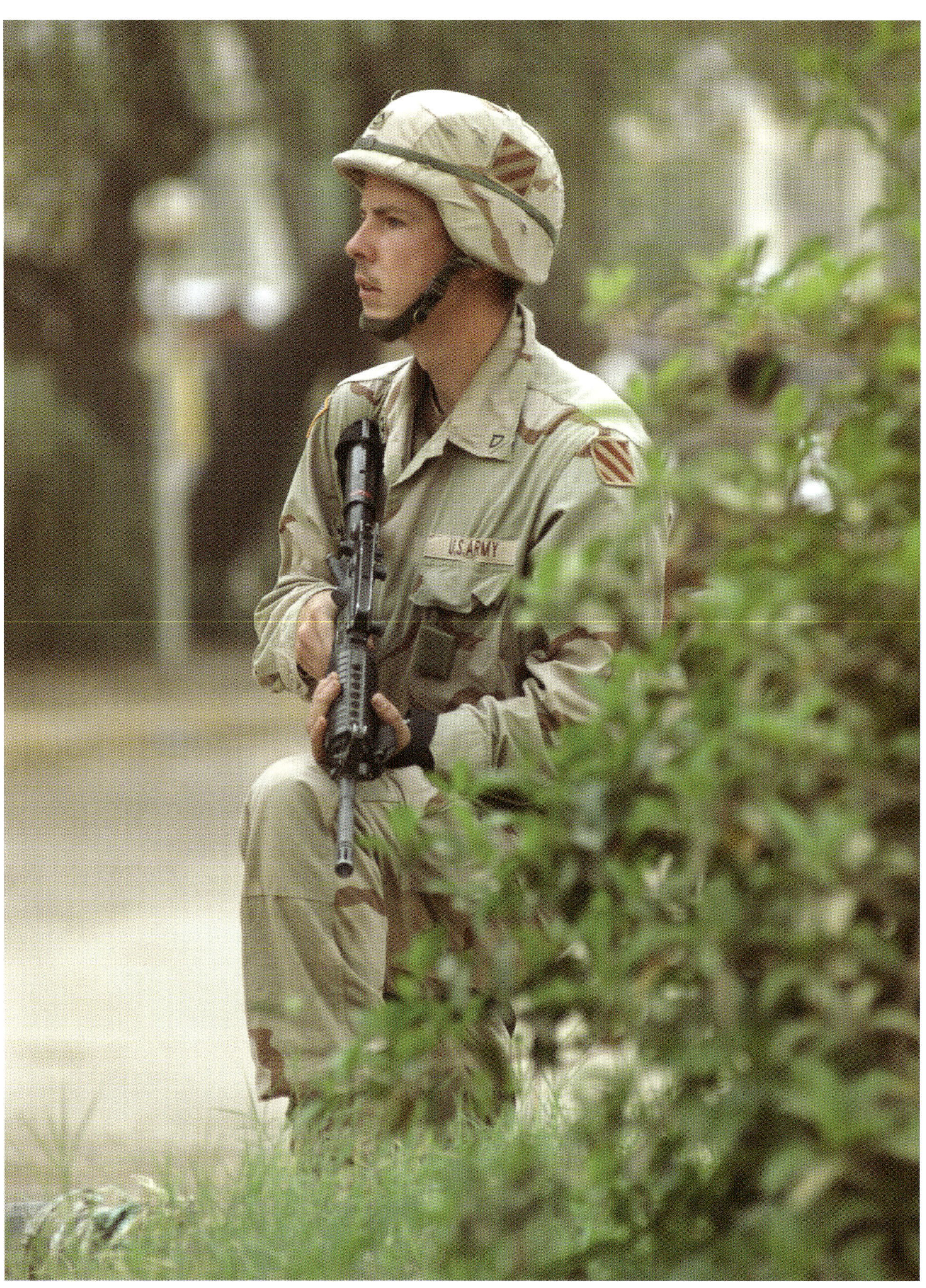

The imprisonment of Shiite religious leader Mohammed al-Fartussi has led to a rise in anti-American feelings

The protest was called after the confinement and interrogation by the Americans of leading Shiite religious leader, Mohammed al-Fartussi. Al-Fartussi is perhaps the most influential man in Iraq, because of his position within the majority Shiite population. In actual fact, at this point, no decision on Iraq's future can realistically be considered without the green light from Fartussi.

Climbing up onto the roof of a Red Crescent van, I start shooting the demonstrators, who by now have reached a trance-like state. They chant, flail their arms and beat their chests in religious fervor. A Shi'a cleric leads the chanting and choreographs the demonstrators through a loudspeaker at the front of the crowd. I grab some great shots before the other media, who had seen me on the van roof, come down to street level and start climbing up beside me. (They had had their cameras set up on the second-floor balcony of the Palestine Hotel). As the roof of the van starts to crush in from the weight of the journalists, a Red Crescent worker tells us to get down.

I find my way to the barbwire security fence encircling the Palestine, guarded by the army. Showing my press pass I am allowed into a secure area, where I take a deep draught from my water bottle and try to get my breath back. I love shooting stuff like demonstrations, and this one was one of the best because of the color and the powerful expressions on the faces.

I walk around to the side of the hotel where I start chatting with a soldier named Paul. He is stationed at one of the four checkpoints guarding the short roadway separating the Palestine and Sheraton. I ask how he and his colleagues are making out; he tells me he is broke and does not even have enough coinage to buy a soda. Continuing, he comments on how the paymaster has been unable to pay the soldiers because all the banks have been robbed, so they are waiting for cash to arrive from overseas to pay the men. Paul is a friendly guy, like the majority of the soldiers, and I take an instant liking to the young man. Reaching into my pocket I pull out a ten-dollar bill and hand it to him. He is shocked at my offering, and guarantees that he will get it back to me any way he can, even if he has to mail it to me back home. He takes my address, just in case we don't see each other again. It gives me a great feeling to help this guy out.

Day 13. Tuesday, April 22nd

(Covering political parties in Baghdad; city power grid in partial operation; thick black smoke; residents tear down a billboard of Saddam in Al Jamea; traffic police; upper-class Mansour; the Iraqi Democratic Party (IDP); family of children live in abandoned warehouse; chestnut brown eyes; she is my hero; visit to the slums of Saddam City – alias Sadr City; guns for sale at roadside market; firing into the air; Tomcat Jet Fighter checks gunfire; a Palestinian resident supports the American position on Iraq; Iraqi Olympic headquarters burns; visiting the Iraq Communist Party headquarters; male-female segregation; hamburgers from heaven boost morale; over 30 new political parties; party headquarters of the Iraqi National Congress (INC); AK-47 leaning on doorway; firefight at the INC; a good day to die; blinding sun; I try to keep my head; taping the firefight; "A little hot on the roof?"; returning to the hamburger stand with Tish and Sean; culinary bliss; grocery store has many foodstuffs; hydro grid back on in isolated locations; out for supper at the al-Ghutra restaurant with Tish, Tod, and Sean; avoiding fresh vegetables; my friends become culinary guinea pigs)

Over breakfast, John Otis asks me if I can work for him today, to which I agree. He wants me to accompany him and shoot pics for a feature story on upstart political parties in Baghdad. The pics and story are scheduled to run in this coming *Sunday Houston Chronicle*.

We drive south towards Al Jamea where we stop to photograph the four large smoke stacks of the Baghdad Power Facility. One of the stacks is churning out thick black smoke (the generators are oil fired), showing that at least part of it is up and running. This could be a sign that electrical power could soon be flowing in the city. As with the petroleum refinery, spewing smokestacks are a good sign of progress being made in the industrial sector.

We stop a little further along in the ritzy sector of Al Jamea where we see a group of civilians trying to pull down a large aluminum billboard of Saddam's face. The ten men wrestle with the mural until it falls to the ground, kicking up a cloud of brown dust. The gang hops onto the fallen aluminum sign, jumping up and down on Saddam's face. We give them the thumbs up, to which they raise a cheer, and then drive on. This is a well-kept area of rich homes that look like mini palaces, complete with ornamental gardens and hedges. John tells me this part of town is where some of Saddam's relatives lived.

A group of five policemen, wearing white shirts and caps and green pants, stand on a busy street corner beside their white police motorcycles. This may be the first time I have seen police dressed in this manner and I wonder if they are city traffic police.

We drive to the outskirts of Mansour where we stop outside a burned and looted brick building. This one-storey building is the new home of the Iraqi Democratic Party (IDP), and a former office of Saddam's Baath Party. There are about twelve party supporters sweeping up rubble from inside and outside the burned building. All its windows are broken and the interior is gutted and blackened by fire. One man is spray-painting the party initials, IDP, on the outside walls of the office in large red lettering. John interviews them as I walk around to the side of the building.

I meet a family group of six children, aged 4-13 years. Their parents disappeared during the bombing and are considered dead or missing. The children are now living in a small abandoned warehouse beside the new IDP office. They are shy at first, but after I offer them some lollipops they warm up to me and smile and chuckle as children do. I feel horribly empty, knowing what it must be like to survive this war, as this little family is trying to do. The 13-year-old is the older sister of the family; she fulfills the role of father, mother, big sister and provider. Her country might be Iraq, but her little world clings to her hands and shirtsleeves with a runny nose. She makes sure the kids thank me for the candy while corralling them together like baby chicks. She is my war hero; she deserves the medals; she embodies the spirit of survival with dignity in an undignified world. I pass a $20 bill into the palm of her hand. Her chestnut brown eyes meet mine, and we smile together; then I turn away, looking for more misery to show my continent. I feel like crying – my heart is broken again. I feel like dying, though I have never been more alive.

We leave the fledgling IDP, letting them get their house in order, and head northeast to Saddam City. Arriving in the impoverished town, rotting and burning garbage is piled wherever there is an open space to dump it. The smell and sight of it along the roads, beside the open-air markets and in the alleyways, is overwhelming. Young shoeless children search through the waste for metal or anything they can recycle and sell. There are no green pastures in Saddam City, just fields of despair, smoldering trash and the finality of hereditary poverty.

There is an open-air market on the large median separating inbound traffic from outbound. Driving past the market we see people firing AKs and handguns into the air. Vendors are selling the weapons and the prospective buyers are trying them out, firing them off to make sure they work. With the sporadic gunfire going off just 40 feet from the car, I glance up to see a U.S. Tomcat Fighter jet slowly passing over the market at a very low altitude, looking for the source of the gunfire. I think for a moment that the plane might bomb the market, killing the gun dealers and us, but it revs its engines picking up speed, then flies out of sight. I decide to look into the gun sales situation tomorrow when I have more time.

We stop at a mosque where the head cleric tells John he does not have the authority to comment on politics or the war. John is a little upset by the man's paranoia and refusal to speak, so we drive on and stop along a road lined with well maintained homes, well back from the filth of the main road splitting the town. John interviews a homeowner who has a good grasp of American history, referring to the bravery of George Washington and the intelligence of Thomas Jefferson. He tells John that he supports the American invasion, saying that it is necessary for the people of Iraq to see Saddam ousted before the rebuilding can start. He is a retired office furniture salesman, originally from Palestine, and well educated.

We bid him farewell then head back downtown, passing the burning headquarters of the Iraqi Olympic Committee, with the Olympic symbols freshly painted on its outside walls. It must have been looted recently as I have seen quite a few people wearing Iraqi Olympic Team sweat suits in the downtown area.

We stop at the office of the Iraqi Communist Party, ten minutes south of the Palestine. The place is bustling with party

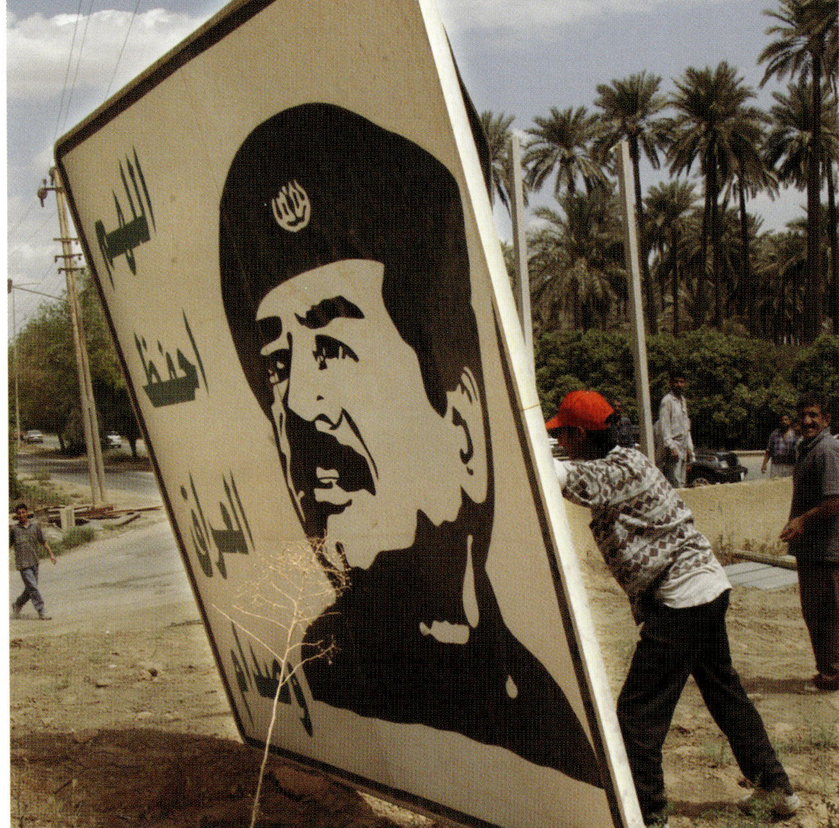

As far as these people are concerned, Saddam is a bad memory that has to be erased

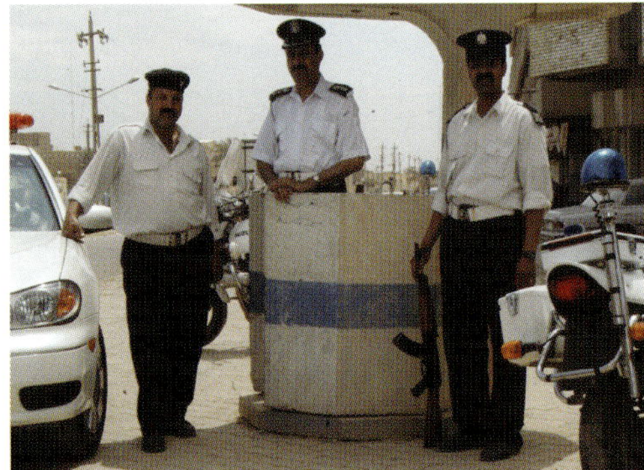

Baghdad police are on the streets again

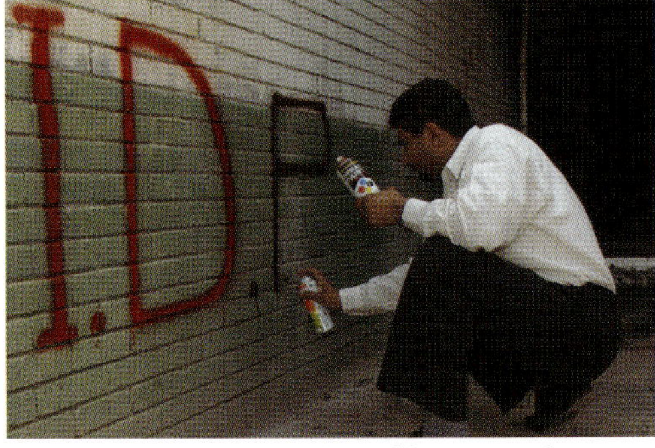

Iraqi Democratic Assembly sets up shop

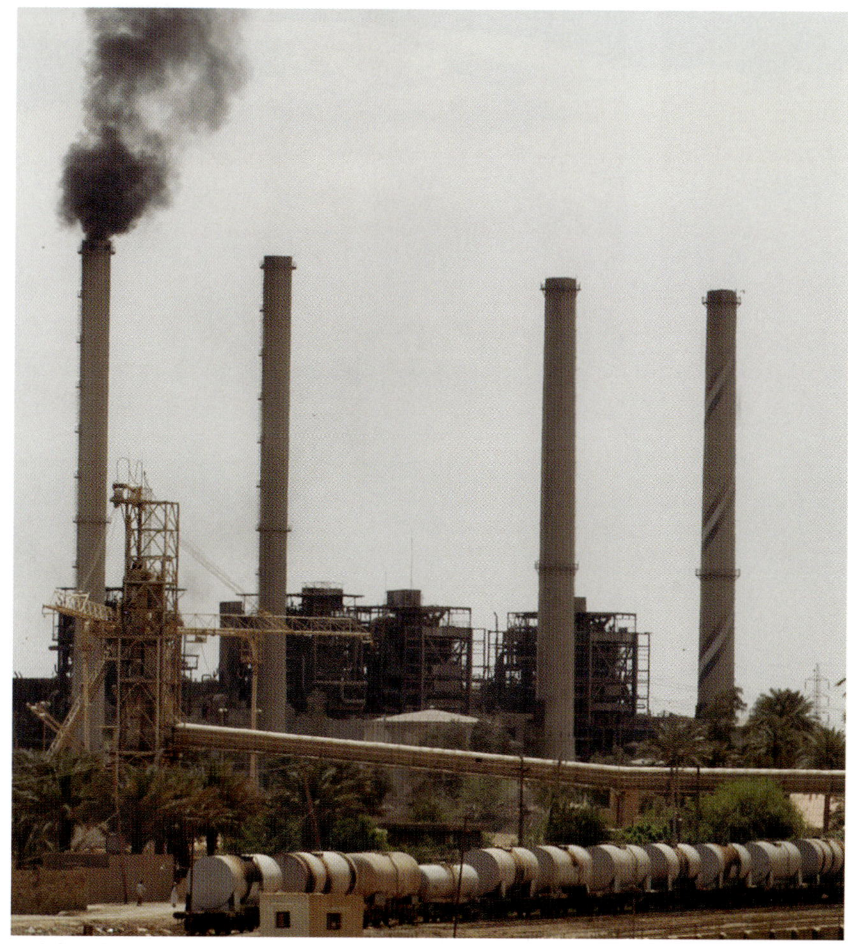

Oil is shipped in tanker trains to fuel the Baghdad Power Facility in south Baghdad

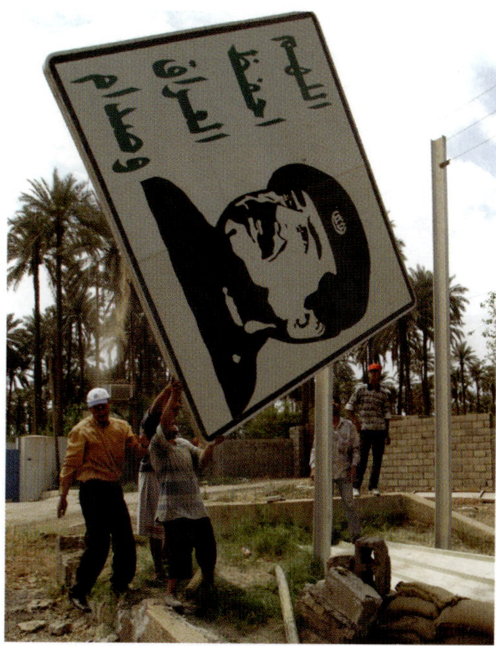

A portrait of Saddam is dismantled in Al Jamea

supporters organizing leaflets and brochures describing their party policies and handing them out to visitors. I photograph supporters folding party leaflets at the front desk. A small metal statue of Vladimir Lenin sits on the desk, serving as a paperweight.

Confident that we have the pictures and information we need from here, we head off to a nearby take-out restaurant that has recently re-opened in the chic Al Karradah district. It is well known for its delicious hamburgers and fries, which you order from a sliding window. A second sliding window has a sign hanging in it; it reads 'WOMEN.' This is the window that women are supposed to order from, separate from the men.

There isn't a dining room, tables or chairs; you are meant to eat in your car or along the roadside curb. My burger is handed to me wrapped in a sheet of waxed paper. It consists of a large, well-done, handmade patty, sandwiched in a Kaiser-style bun and lightly spread with a brown, HP type of sauce. It is incredibly delicious! My taste buds have awakened from their hibernation. I order another. This is the first great tasting food I have eaten since Montreal. The burger lifts my spirits and I feel just great.

Apparently, there are over 30 new political parties forming in this country where the people have been under the dictatorship of one political party for over 30 years. Most Iraqis have never voted before; now they have to choose to support a political party that they may never have heard of. The situation for the voter will be overwhelming. Who do you vote for? It is too much, too fast, for the populace of Iraq.

Making matters even more confusing, is how the voters are expected to find out about the parties and their agendas. There are no newspapers or media broadcasts to inform them of their choices. This blueprint to democracy all looks good back home in America, where people wrongly believe Iraq's push towards democracy is moving ahead. But in reality, the right to choose a political party is all a 'dog and pony show,' or wishful thinking. The establishment of new political parties at first appears like a good idea, but it is overwhelming to these impoverished and worn people, for whom every day is a lesson in survival. The American administrators are expecting too much, too soon.

Buzzing on our burgers, we head off to the luxurious Hunt Club in Mansour, now the new headquarters of the London-based Iraqi National Congress (INC). This is one of the many former exiled political parties, which have begun setting up office in Baghdad, now that Saddam is gone. The building is a very large Mediterranean-style mansion with an expansive flower garden and yard. Walking through the iron gated wall

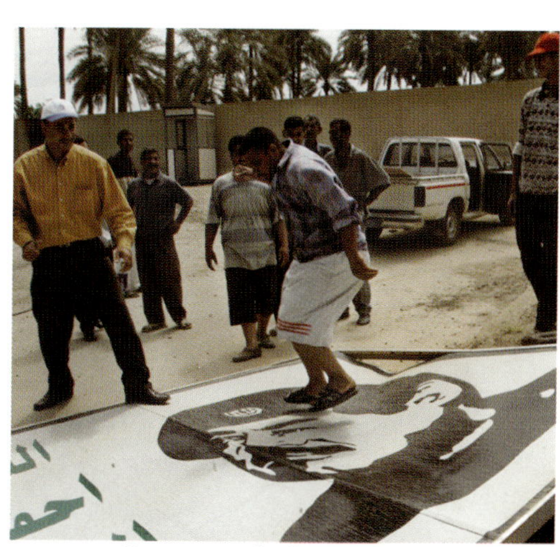

Dancing on the face of Saddam

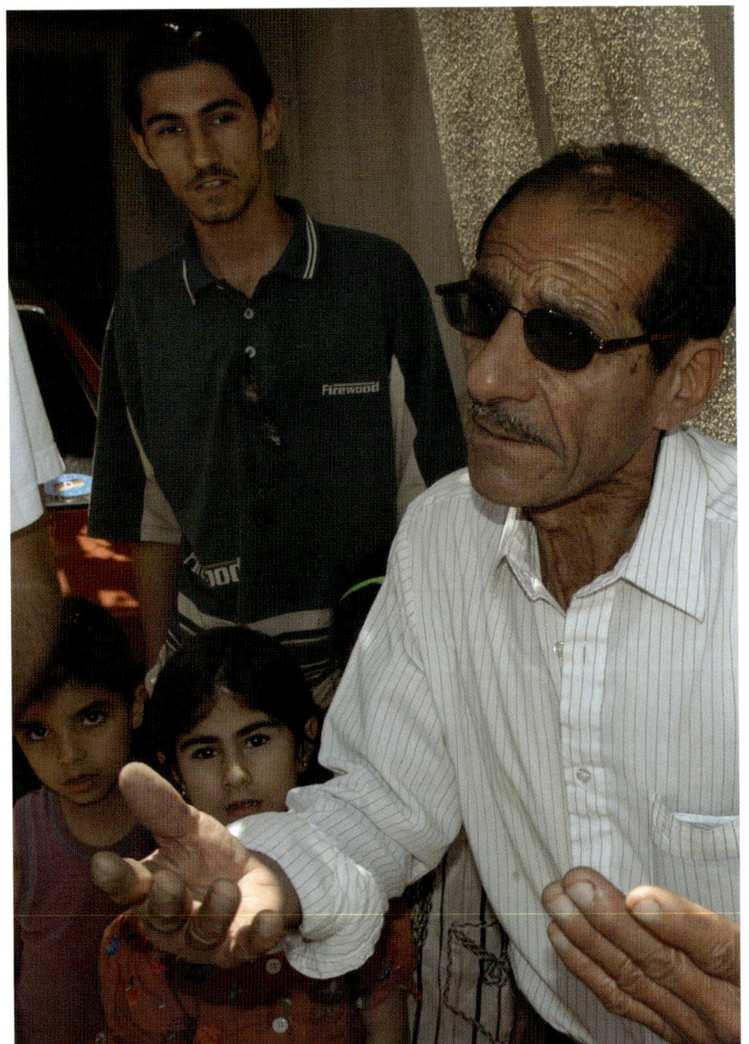

This family from Saddam City is better off than many. The children are clean

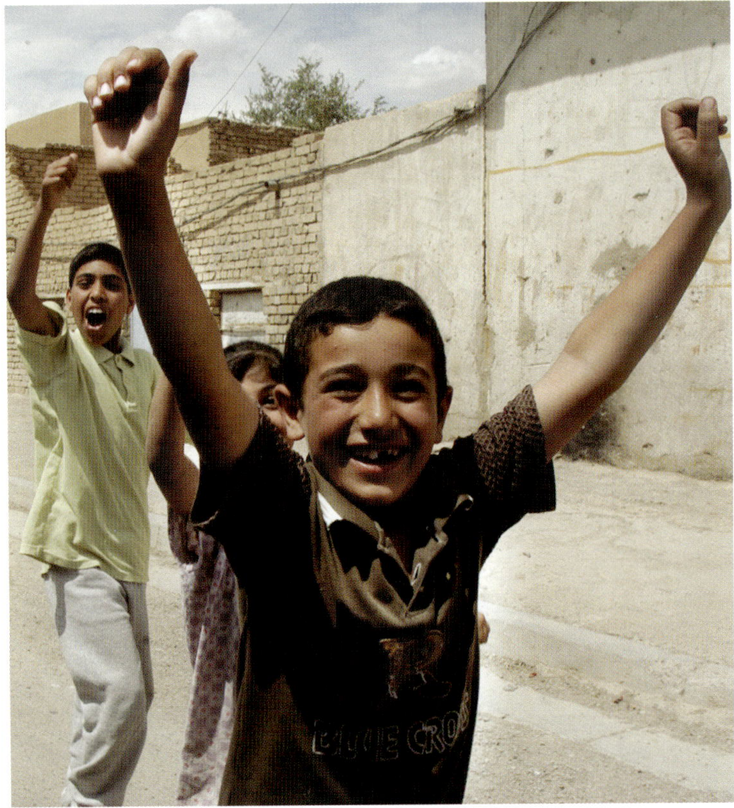

Local children, in a clean section of Saddam City, chase alongside our taxi

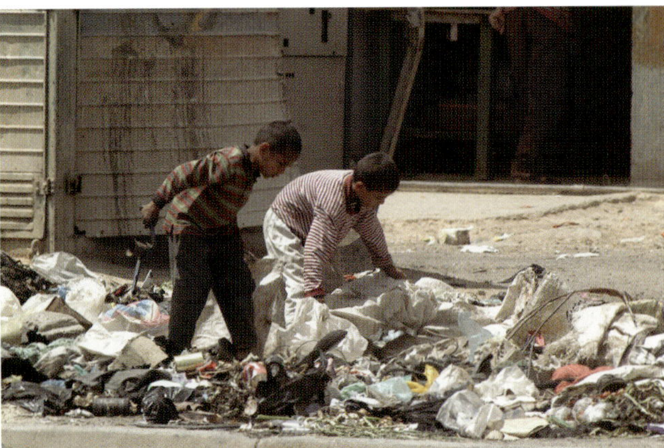

Children scrounge through garbage in Saddam City

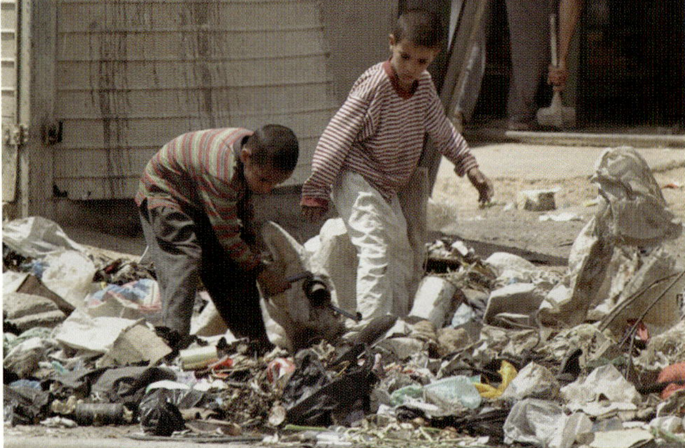

Anything recyclable is collected

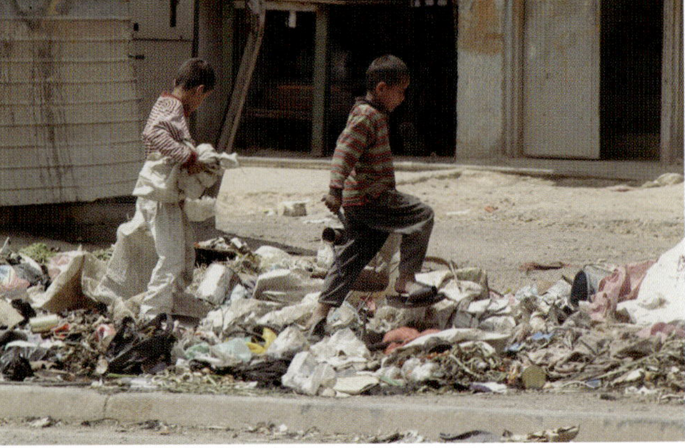

Moving on to another pile

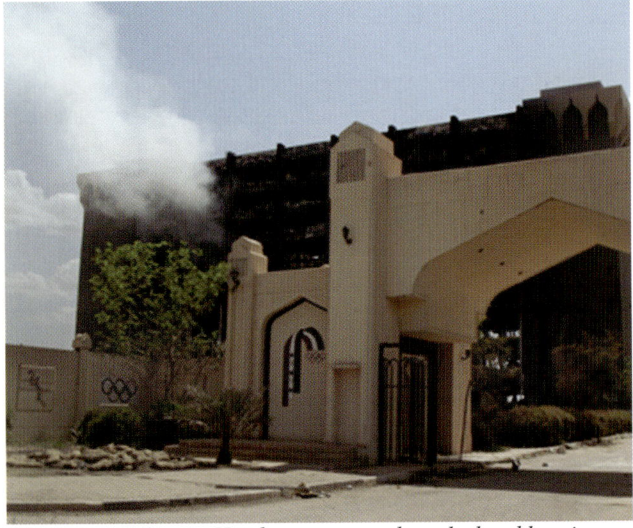

The Iraq Olympic Headquarters stands sacked and burning

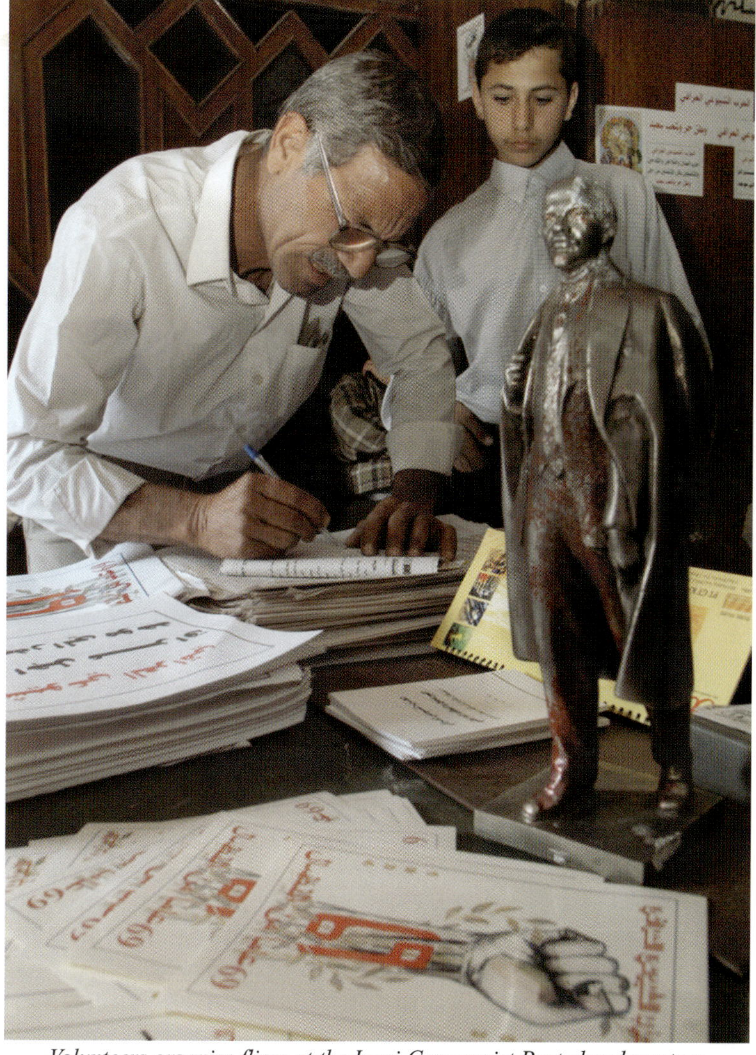

Volunteers organize fliers at the Iraqi Communist Party headquarters

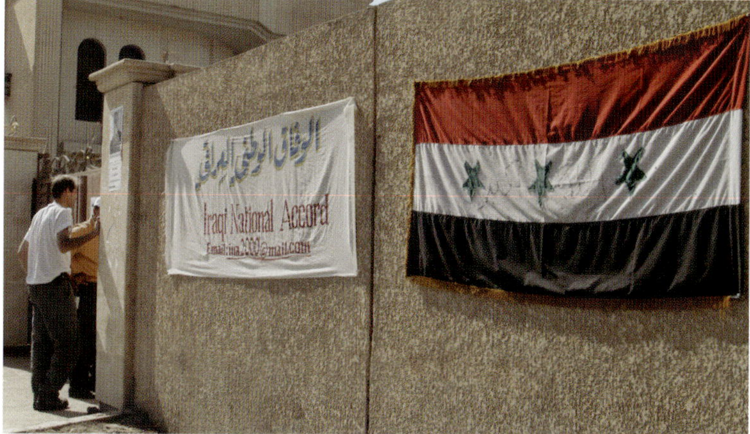

The luxurious Hunt Club, now the base of the Iraqi National Congress

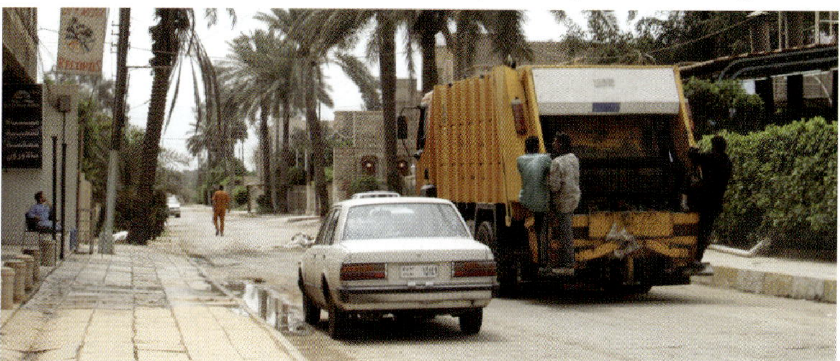

While garbage buries Saddam City, Al Karradah has garbage pick-up

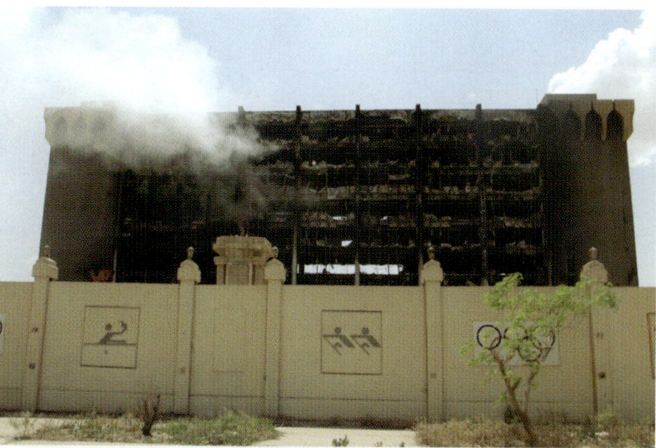

The Iraqi Olympic Headquarters is just a burned-out shell

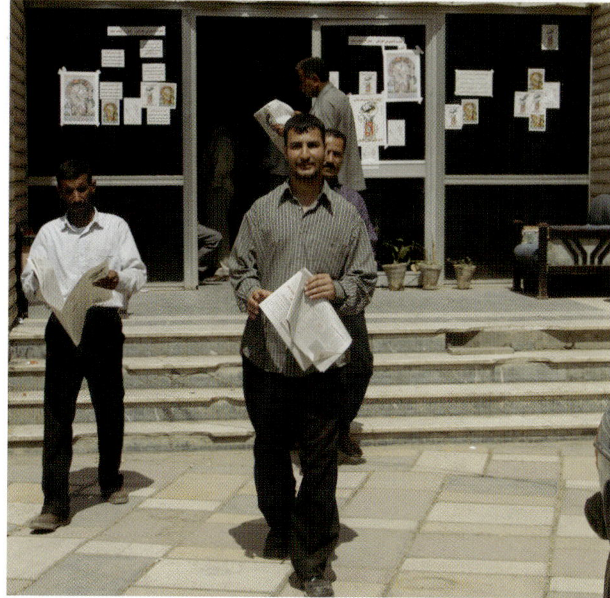

The Communist Party attracts the curious

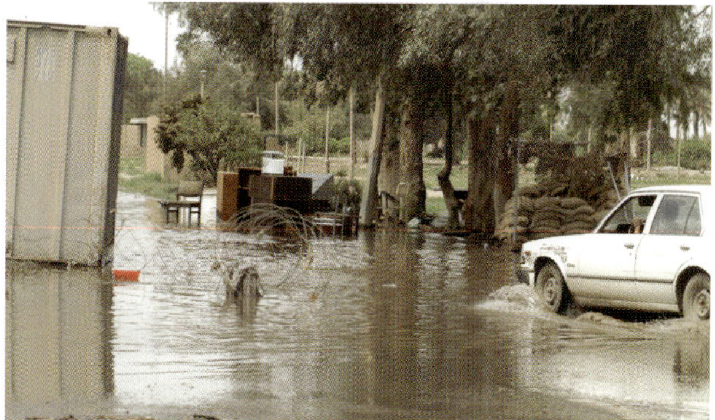

Broken water main floods army checkpoint near Mansour

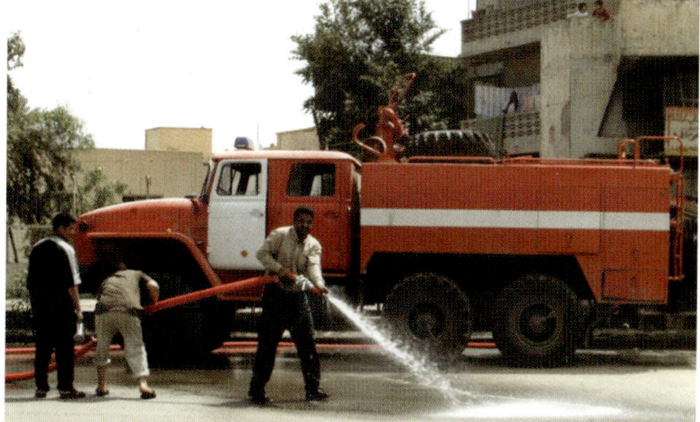

Volunteers hose-down the streets of Al Karradah

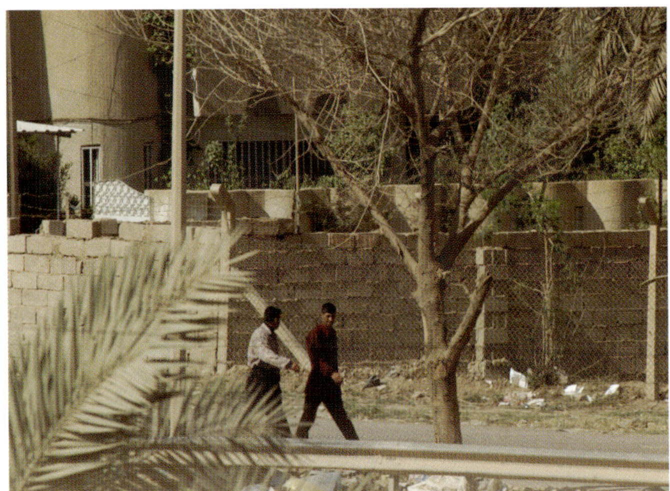

Pedestrians walk in the crossfire during shootout near the INC

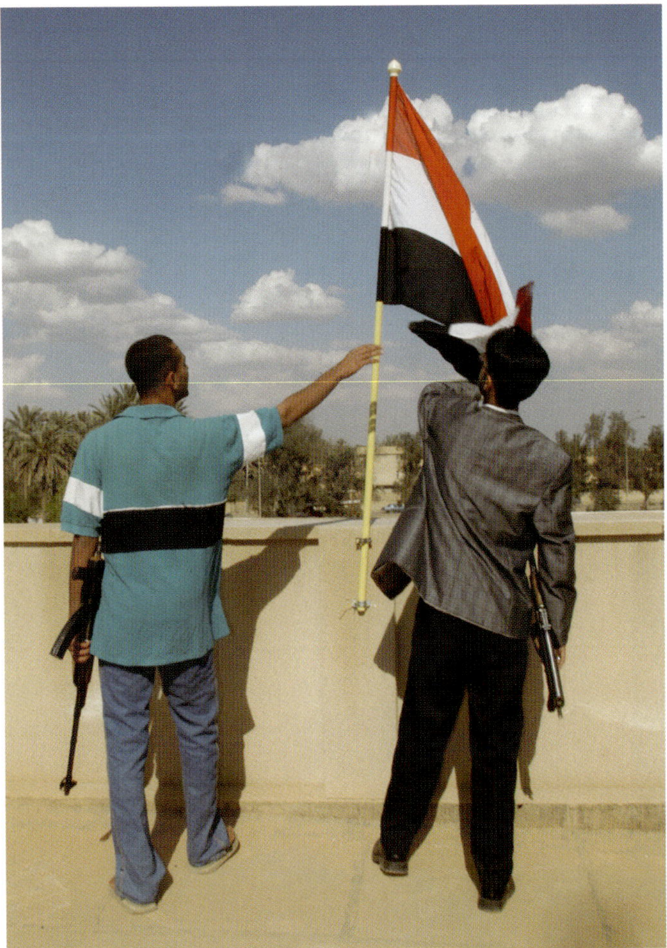

Security officials unfurl Iraqi flag on roof of the INC

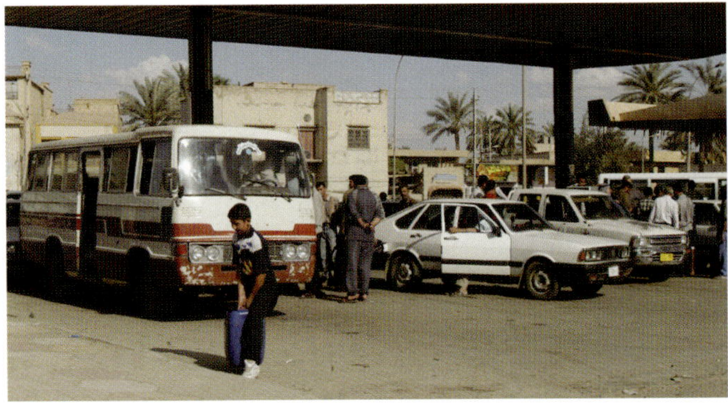

People line up for gas, or Benzyne as it is called in Iraq

that surrounds the property, I notice an AK-47 leaning against the lavish mahogany front doorway. Inside the richly decorated building, it is furnished with fine leather couches, golden light fixtures and a beautifully woven Persian rug.

John starts interviewing one of the party supporters as I walk around, looking at the interior of the spacious place. Minutes into the interview, I hear gunfire erupting outside. It doesn't sound like we are being attacked, but the shooting is going on all around the building or very close by. "It looks like we showed up just in time for the party," I whisper to John. I ask a security member, one of two guards who greeted us at the front entranceway, to take me to the roof of the three-storey building so I can try to photograph the gunfight, or at least see what is going on. I have to have a look at it, even if it means me leaving this property. My stomach starts to turn, as it always does at times like this.

It is a blazing hot, intense hazy day. The sun is almost blinding me, making it difficult to see clearly through squinting eyes. I take off my red ball cap, as it could make me a target, and peer over the edge of the chest-high stucco wall that surrounds the roof and now protects me from incoming fire. The gunfire is coming from two or three different locations within a 300 feet circumference of the building, but I cannot locate any of the shooters because the surrounding area is covered by large homes and expansive treed gardens where gunmen can hide. There are also tree-lined alleyways and laneways threading throughout the neighborhood.

Most of the gunfire is from small arms fire and AK-47s, and then the distinct thump of 50-calibre gun erupts. I turn on my tape recorder and place it on top of the stucco wall, taping the sound of the fight. Sneaking around the roof in a low crouch and keeping my head below the firing line, I stop, then stick my head over the wall to try to pinpoint the location of a shooter. I keep my head in a vulnerable position for only 10 seconds at a time or less, before lowering it and moving a few feet to the left or right, then raising it again. This method of bullet evasion makes me a harder target to pinpoint then hit, should one of the shooters decide to take a crack at me. Still, I cannot locate who is shooting at whom, and from exactly where. Feeling like a duck in a penny arcade, I pull my head below the wall and take a breather as the gunfire intensifies.

I raise my head again, but my eyes feel like fried eggs from the glaring sun. It is blinding me, and I have a difficult time squinting through the glare looking for the shooters. It is as good a day to die as any, I say to myself. I keep bobbing and weaving when the two security guards come crouching towards me with AKs in their hands. They tell me that John is looking for me and to come downstairs. I ask them who is doing the shooting. They tell me they believe that an American Special Forces detail are trying to clear out a party of armed Saddam supporters, but the guards don't know any more details. I head downstairs to greet John. When I see him he asks me, "a little hot on the roof?" We smile and then head out of the building as the gunfire continues behind us. But it's just another day in Baghdad. During the crossfire, bicyclists pedaled down the street as though on a Sunday afternoon outing. It is as though gunfights are a normal part of everyday life, or a slight ripple in it, here in Baghdad. We drive back to the Fanar.

In the late afternoon I drag Sean, Tish and Tod out to the burger stand. At first we get lost trying to find the place, as it is getting dark, but eventually we do. Sitting on the sidewalk eating our burgers, my three friends are transformed into a state of culinary bliss. They cannot believe how delicious the burgers are. They keep exuding orgasmic grunts and moans of satisfaction. They agree with me – nothing beats these burgers! This meal has been the eating highlight of our tour so far, boosting our spirits and energy. Who would ever believe that hamburgers could give such a boost to our morale? But they do.

Next door to the burger joint is a grocery store with many foodstuffs that we haven't yet seen available in Baghdad. Canned vegetables, eggs, cooking oil, noodle soups, canned fish, fruit juice, honey, corned beef and bags of chocolates and toffees sit upon the half-empty shelves. It takes me a little while to clue into the fact that there is electrical power on at the store, and not from a generator. The fridges are operating; the fluorescent lights are on! This is the first time we have seen the city power grid up and running. This is a great step forward towards normalcy in Baghdad! According to the store manager, the power was turned on this morning, but only in small areas of the city. That smoking smoke stack that I photographed this morning was a prelude to the power being turned on. Life in Baghdad is slowly, very slowly, starting to become more livable, but only in isolated oases like the burger stand and grocery store.

Getting back to the hotel, I go for a walk to the Palestine and take some feature photos and chill a bit before the sun sets. Returning to the Fanar I see Sean, Tod and Tish. They ask if I want to go to a nearby restaurant for supper, to which I agree.

It is a brightly lit place called the al-Ghutra restaurant. It is bustling with waiters and diners and is very clean and comfortable. The waiter brings me endless glasses of chai. The sugar buzz is uplifting. The service is great and the food is delicious, but I only eat the broiled kabobs, pickles and fresh, hot flatbread. Even though the place is clean, I decide to pass on the fresh vegetables, but my friends gobble them up. Because of my vegetable paranoia, I decide to wait to see if they survive the vegetables, and if they do, I will return over the next few days and eat the greenery along with the kabobs. My friends and colleagues have become my culinary guinea pigs. They must think I am nuts, but could you imagine if we all fell ill? I cannot take any chance of getting sick; it could kill my book project. I am financing this journey with my own funds, so I just can't take the chance.

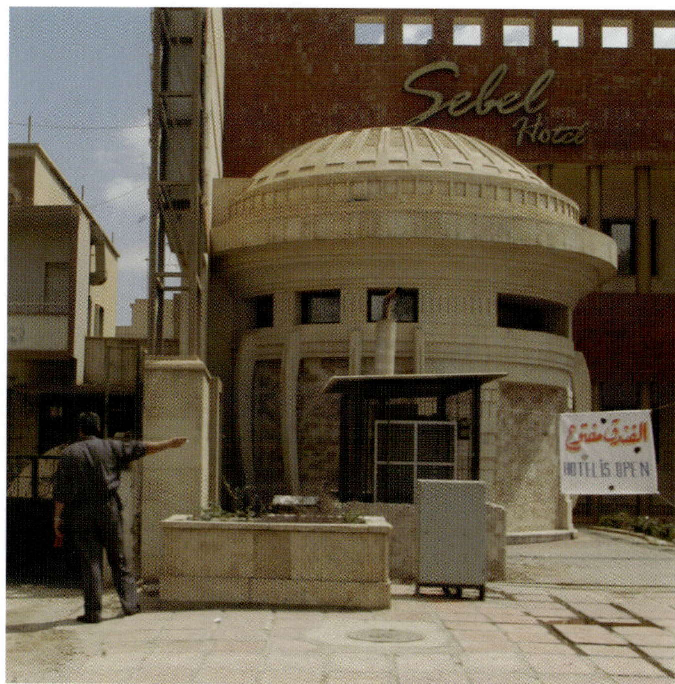
This restaurant in Al Karradah is open with the return of electricity

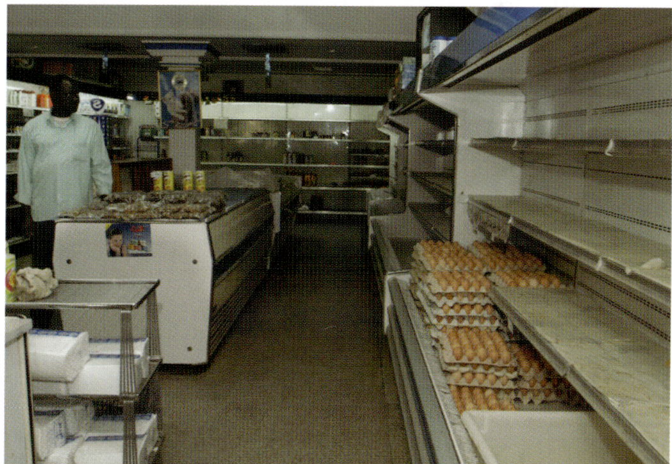
The city power is on in Al Karradah, bringing it out of the Dark Ages

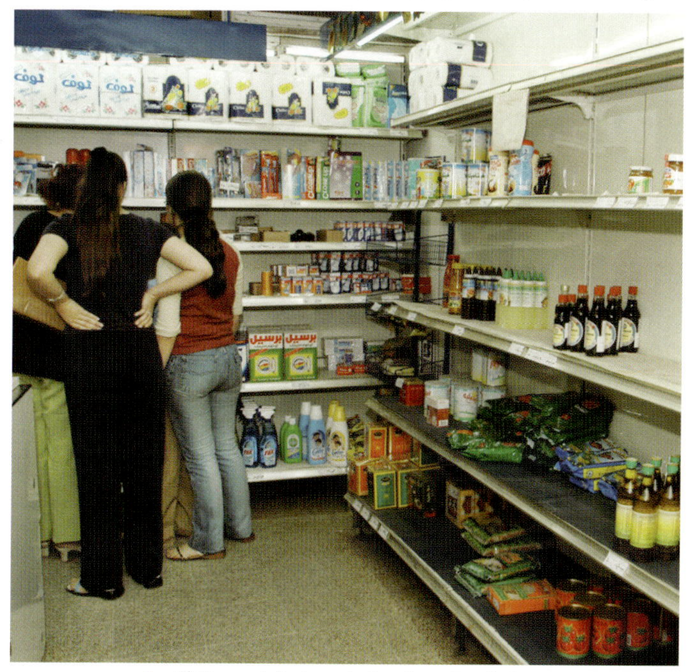
In Al Karradah there is food on the shelves

Later that evening we lie in our beds, or floor, discussing our day over some dried figs and chocolate bars. The chat is all about the burgers and the gunfight. I am sure Sean, Tish and Tod are more appreciative of my role in the team, as I brought them to the burgers (but John is the real hero). So my status went up a notch with my great friends. The burgers were a touchstone with our life back home. We go to bed happy, stuffed and in good spirits.

Day 14. Wednesday, April 23rd

(Trading cigars for MREs; golden booty; a strange journalist; Saddam's private train; visiting the little-damaged Baghdad Railway Station; cleaning up the train station; Baghdad government Internet office sacked and burned; Internet spooks; agents of paranoia; reporter tells of guns for sale in Saddam City; visiting Saddam City; bogus driver's licenses and license plates for sale; like organized gypsies; "Why are you here?" Sean pick-pocketed by angry crowd; we come close to being mobbed; the dummy wallet; a very scary moment; Scandinavian journalists accosted and their lives threatened by gun dealers; an ugly incident; Iraqi National Library looted and burned; national book treasures turn to dust; a flock of ibis and prowling bee-eaters; out for supper with Tod, Tish and Sean; I eat fresh veggies for the first time in two weeks; knife-carrying man shadows us from restaurant to hotel; a better man; lacking sustenance; ready to pick up a gun; an air of rebellion; SARS epidemic knocks Iraqi war from front pages of Canadian newspapers; horrendous nightmare; the bloodied face of Baghdad)

I eat a light breakfast then go for a walk with my seven Cohiba cigars, in their original box, tucked under my arm. I walk over to the first soldier I see and ask if he would be interested in trading some MRE food packages for some cigars, Cohibas! He asks me if I am kidding, then seeing them as I open the box, his eyes bug out. He asks me how many MREs I want; I tell him one per cigar. He replies, "You got a deal my friend!" I trade him six Cohibas, saving one for myself. He leans into the back of his APC and grabs a large box filled with rations. "How's eight MREs sound?" he asks. Not only does he give me the MREs, but he offers a choice of menus. "What do you want, Swiss Steak, Noodles and Beef Filipino, Pork Chops in Gravy, Chili and Crackers, Beef Stew, Chicken Fillets?" He is as happy as I am as we shake hands to seal the deal. I proudly carry the golden booty up to our room and store them in a corner under a blanket. They will be kept aside until we go to Kurdistan, a trip we have been talking about for the past few days. My bartering skills

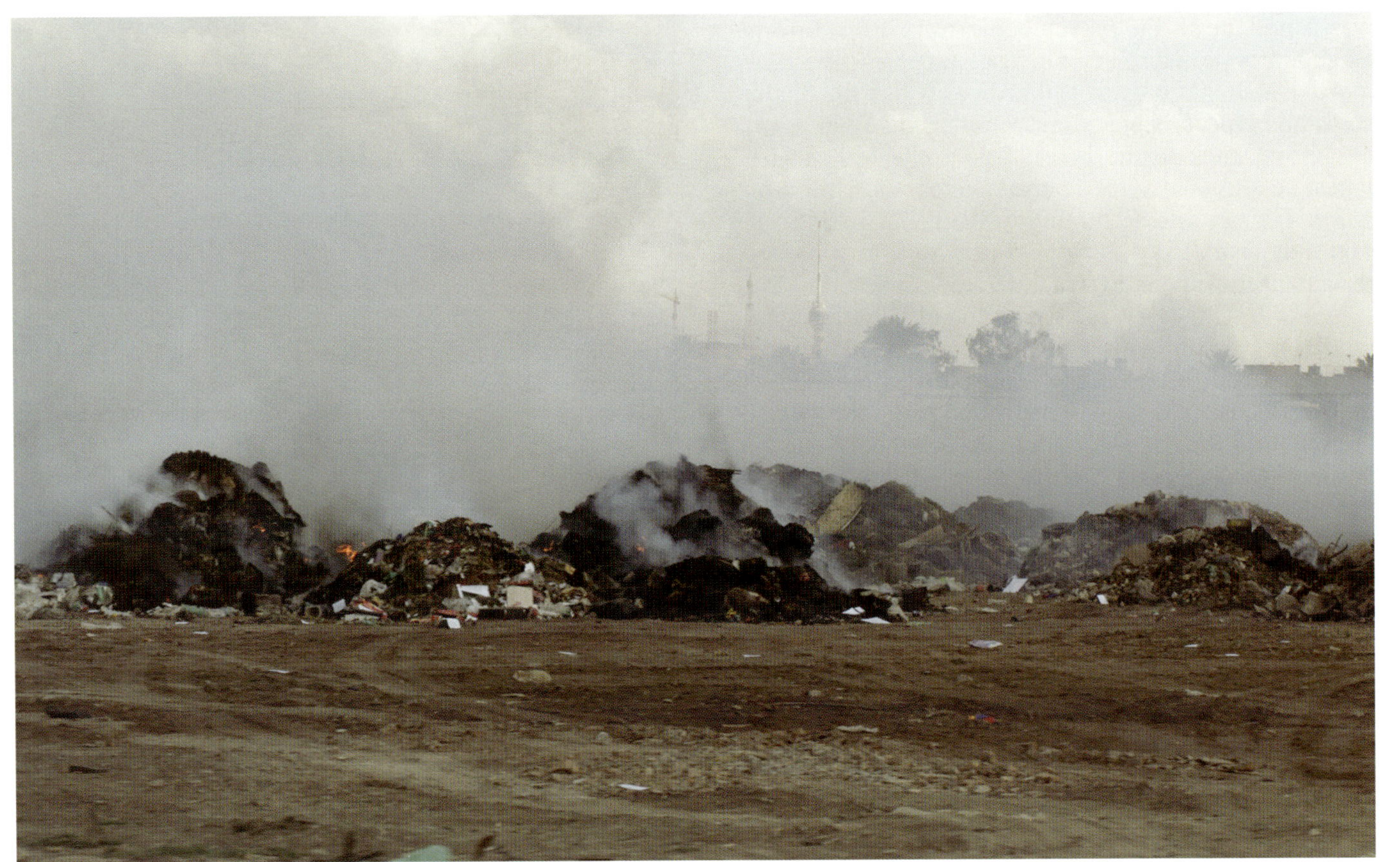

Garbage from Al Karradah is piled and burned in a vacant lot in the outskirts of the suburb

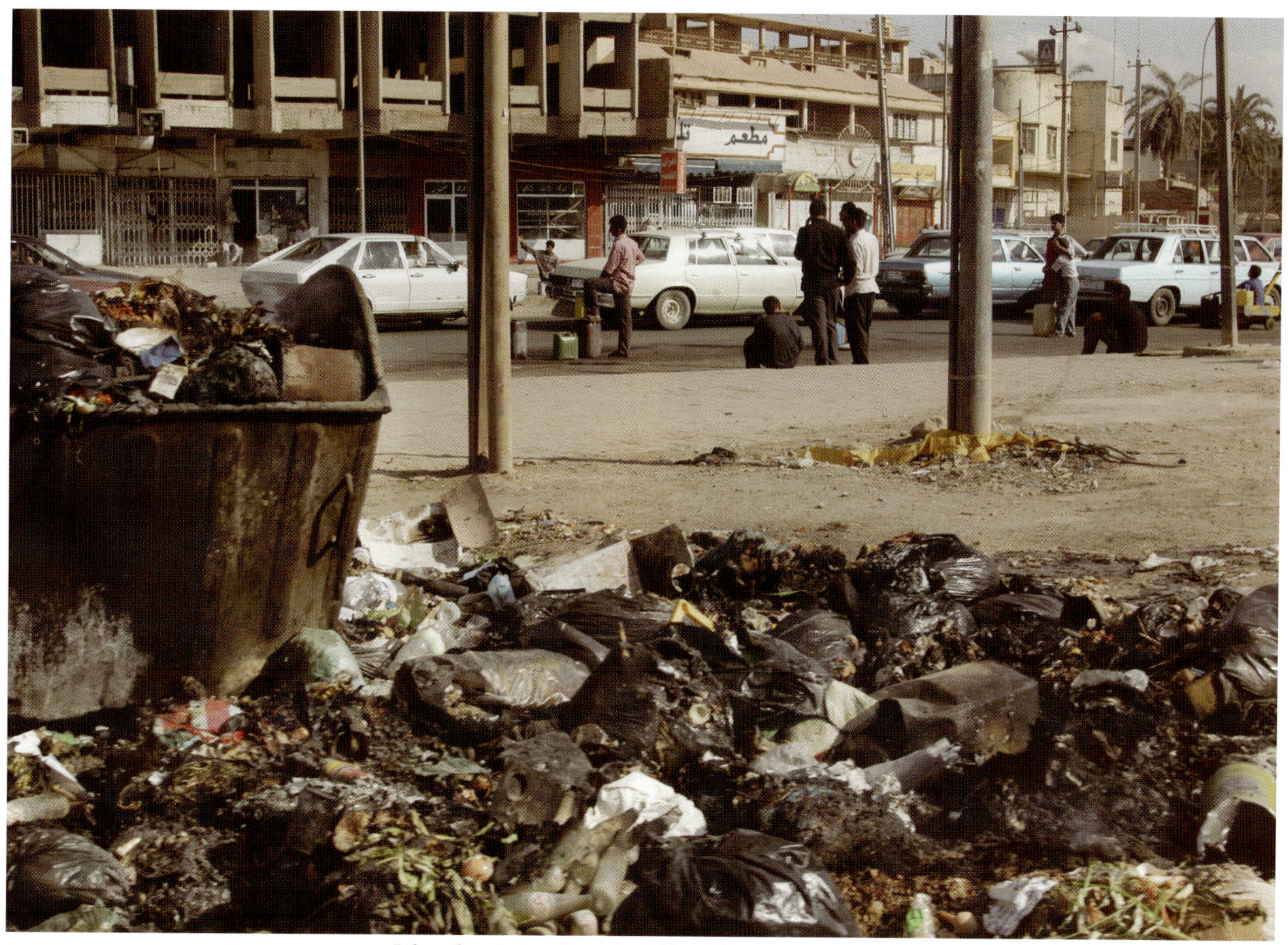

Piles of rotting garbage are a blight throughout Baghdad

paid off big this time! Later in the day I see the soldier hauling away on a Cohiba in the back of the APC. I ask him how it tastes; he replies, "Delicious!"

Shortly after this, a supposed Iraqi-born journalist comes up to me and asks who I work for, and how I feel about the war. Before long he is accusing me of not knowing what the Iraqi people feel, or want, and of being misinformed. He is one of the pseudo-journalists (activists who use the cover of press credentials to feed their Yankee-hating audience through some obscure web site or newsletter) from the Al Fanar, which seems to be the hotel of choice for this kind of nut. I do not even know who this guy works for, but I know he is not a real journalist, just from his mode of questioning. He is trying to demean me, while drilling me with his point of view, which is basically that all Westerners should go home, and that the Americans are murderers. Fanatics like this are dangerous as they discredit honest, hard-working journalists and cloud the truth.

Around 11 a.m., Sean and I go to the Baghdad Central Train Station (near the zoo), to look for the rumored personal train of Saddam. This luxurious train allegedly carried Saddam throughout Iraq, but was used more often between Tikrit and Baghdad. Arriving at the station, it is in the process of being cleared of debris, after being looted and partially gutted by fire. People with brooms and dust mops are cleaning out the refuse and trying to get the station up and running. Former employees are arriving, cleaning their offices and arranging them into a workable condition.

Rail officials inform us that the rail infrastructure is largely undamaged, and that the trains could be running in three days. We cannot find any info on the Saddam Train, although a number of employees confirm that it does exist. We walk about the station, looking at the clean-up operation, which is going ahead with great ambition. Luckily, the station is in much better shape than most of the other government-operated buildings. But it is largely constructed of marble and sandstone, which doesn't burn, unlike some of the more modern government buildings.

Outside the train station, next to the parking area, we see a group of a dozen men burning piles of computer paper and broken furniture in a large fire. Sean and I go over for a chat and find out that they are former employees of Saddam's Information Ministry. Their job, up until the bombs started falling, was to monitor all incoming and outgoing *Internet* messages and other electronic information for treasonous or anti-government communications. The ministry personnel tell us that thieves had looted the computers and files, and that they are trying to prepare their offices for the day when the *Internet* and other communications return, whenever that may be. These guys are well-dressed and

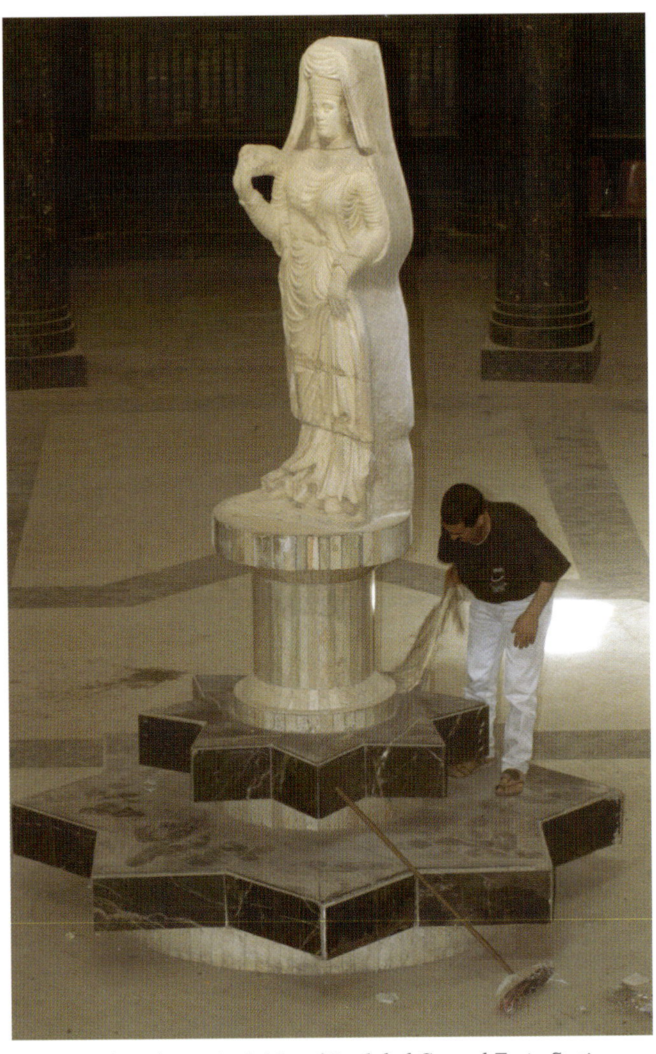

A worker cleans the lobby of Baghdad Central Train Station

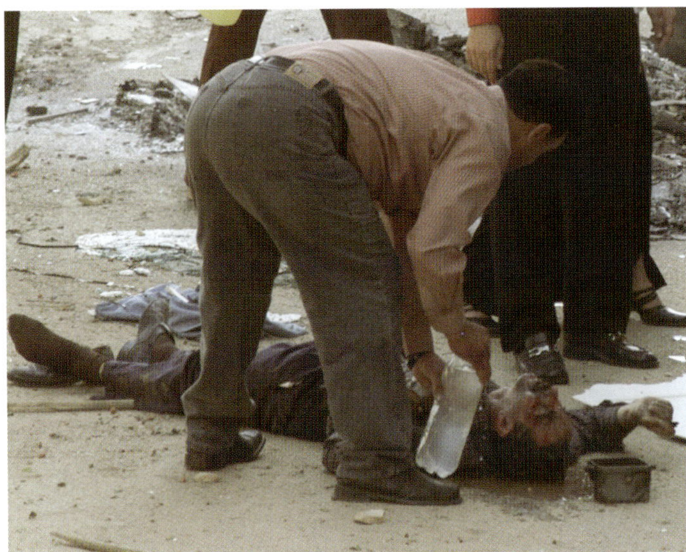

This badly-beaten man lies unconscious outside Central Station

well-educated professional computer experts. But for now they are reduced to cleaning out their offices and burning the rubble.

Sean tells that these computer experts were Saddam's computer police. They were agents of the paranoia that Saddam held over the country. Before the war, they would have been very much feared – and therefore powerful. Now they hold brooms in their hands, instead of people's lives.

We leave the train station and head back to the Fanar where we consider going to Saddam City to cover the black-market gun trade. Earlier this morning, we had heard from Ken Lee, a freelance writer with the New York Daily News, that the black market gun trade was flourishing in the markets at Saddam City (which John and I witnessed yesterday), and that it is a good feature story. Sean and I grab our water and camera gear and head for Saddam City.

Reaching the slums of Saddam City we see vendors selling everything from very tired looking vegetables to bogus driver's licenses and guns. Storefronts are largely closed because of a lack of supplies. Most business is conducted along the roadside and on the trash-covered parkway. Small groups of people stand along the median, holding out brand new stolen license plates in their outstretched hands. The plates are for sale, with no need for paper work or government involvement. Thousands of vehicles have been looted from the government ministries and private residences. So being able to purchase new plates, without paperwork, made your car safe from possible confiscation by the infant, though

largely unorganized, Baghdad Police Force. Further along the road, other vendors hold out blank driver's licenses to prospective buyers. You can probably find a looted vehicle for sale, if you went into the crowd and started asking around. Markets are probably the best way to sell looted property, as no sane police officer would go near them without a heavily armed backup team. We hear the blasts of close gunfire, but we can't pinpoint exactly where it is coming from. It is a spooky atmosphere.

We step out of the car and walk slowly into the crowd of vendors on the parkway. Our cameras are tucked under our arms and at our sides, so they do not attract attention. But regardless of our caution, it doesn't take long before a crowd of children and adults are surrounding us to see why we are at the market.

One grubby-faced man asks us, in broken English, what we are here to photograph and write about? We tell

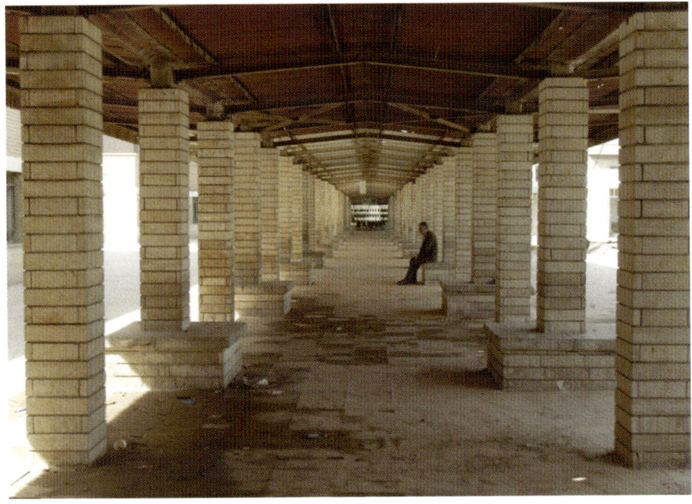

According to officials, the train station could re-open soon

him we want to photograph the activity of the market and show the unsanitary conditions the residents of Saddam City are living under. In an angry voice, he tells us that yesterday some journalists did a news piece that showed guns being sold openly in the market, and that the exposure was bad for the vendors. He said they feared reprisals by the Americans who are now aware of the gun dealing because of the journalists (as though shooting AKs into the air has nothing to do with the increased surveillance). This does not look good on us.

Next he asks us why we do not do stories about the starving people living in squalor with no food for their children? I tell him that yesterday I was in Saddam City covering a political story that will mention the condition of this city and the state of the people who live in it.

In the span of a few minutes over 50 people are squeezing in on us to hear what we are talking about. I start feeling a bit claustrophobic and very vulnerable. It is not a happy gang. One wrong word or move by Sean or me and we could be torn to pieces by the mob. I glance down and see that my camera jacket pocket is open. Reaching down to button it, I feel a hand against my hand, inside the pocket. The mob is squeezed so tight against us that I couldn't tell the crowd was trying to pick our pockets.

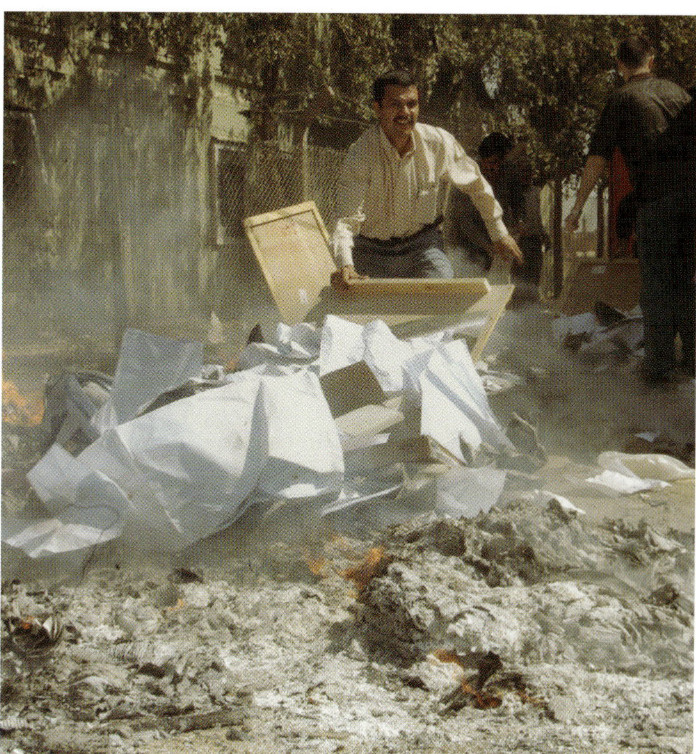

Former Ministry of Information staff burn debris from looted office

I fasten my pocket then lean over and whisper into Sean's ear, "Let's get out of here fast, someone just tried to pick my pockets." Sean reaches into one of his pockets. He looks back at me and says, "My wallet is gone." I tell him, "Let's get out of here," then reiterate, "calmly". At this point anything can happen; mob mentality can be a very scary thing.

Without letting the crowd know we are aware that they are trying to rob us, we slowly edge our way out of the crowd, all the while smiling and being gracious, and start walking in a direct line towards the car. This is a situation where you do not want to return to the car and find your driver is off buying vegetables or trying out an AK. Thankfully, he isn't, and we slip into the car and tell the driver to, "Get out of here quickly!" As we drive away he tells us that there was no way he was going to leave his car unattended, especially in Saddam City.

I realize that we had just escaped a very volatile situation and although I was extremely concerned for my life, especially after hearing that they knew about the news broadcasts, I tried to wear a face of calmness, so as not to startle anyone into attacking us. That place scares me, and I know that we are very fortunate to escape with our cameras and money, let alone our lives.

Sean tells me that he lost his sucker wallet, or so-called dummy wallet. (The sucker wallet is a tactic used by journalists to thwart a thief from stealing your real wallet and its important papers. Most of us wear a hidden money belt, to hold cash and papers. When covering politics and riots back home in Montreal, I always carry a dummy roll of film. This was in case I photographed someone doing something they weren't supposed to be doing, and they saw me and wanted the film. So I would use sleight-of-hand to exchange the hot roll for the blank roll, letting the person think he had the evidence; but in reality, the hot film was tucked quickly into my pants).

Sean is not as upset by what had happened as I am. But I am very concerned by these people's obvious hatred of Westerners (or perhaps it is hatred directed against journalists). This close call will go down as one of my

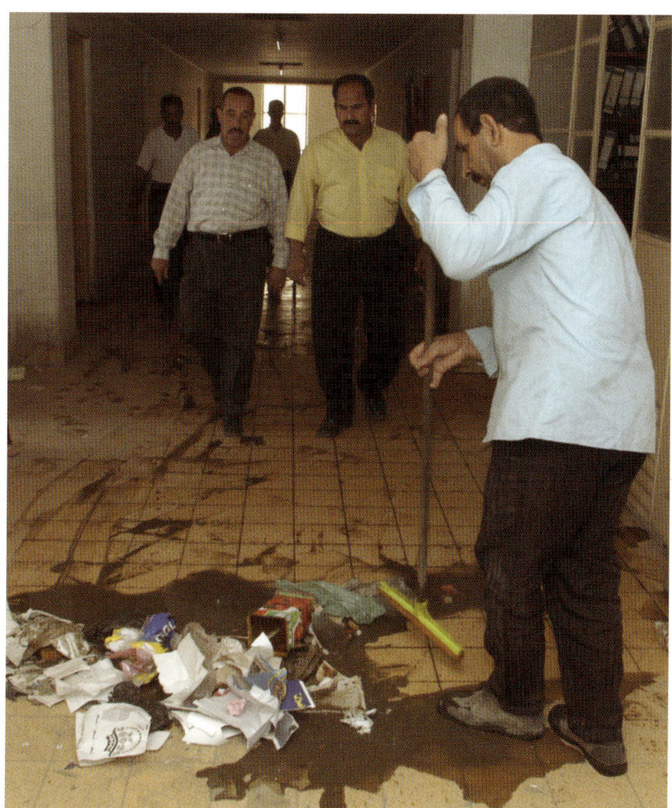

The train station was looted, but not gutted

scariest moments in Baghdad, especially considering the proliferation of guns and our helpless state. Perhaps, and most likely, if I lived in this slum with my family, and I had no work to provide food for them, I would do whatever it took to feed my family. It is easy to return to the safety of our little hotel and have a meal and working toilets; but put yourself in the shoes of the Shi'a and expatriate Palestinians who live in Saddam City – how far would you go to feed your children? How much misery could you take before your basic animal survival instincts kick in? Remember, we are all human beings, and regardless of being black, white, yellow or red skinned, we all get hungry.

About ten minutes from the Fanar we see the Iraqi National Library being looted and burned. The looters have piled mounds of books and furnishings on the front lawn of the building. They are trying to sell the items to passers by; others are carrying the books off to waiting vehicles. Many of the books look ancient and fragile. Some have golden bindings and lettering, and are probably very precious. I would imagine that many of these books will disintegrate to dust over the next few days, and simply blow away. What a sad sight. A short distance down the road stands the looted Iraqi Museum of Civilization.

Just after we return to the Fanar, two Scandinavian journalists return to the hotel looking very shaken up and in shock. They tell Sean and I that they had been out reporting on the gun black market in another part of Baghdad when they barely got away with their lives. The nervousness in their voices and their erratic movements showed they were still reeling from what had happened to them.

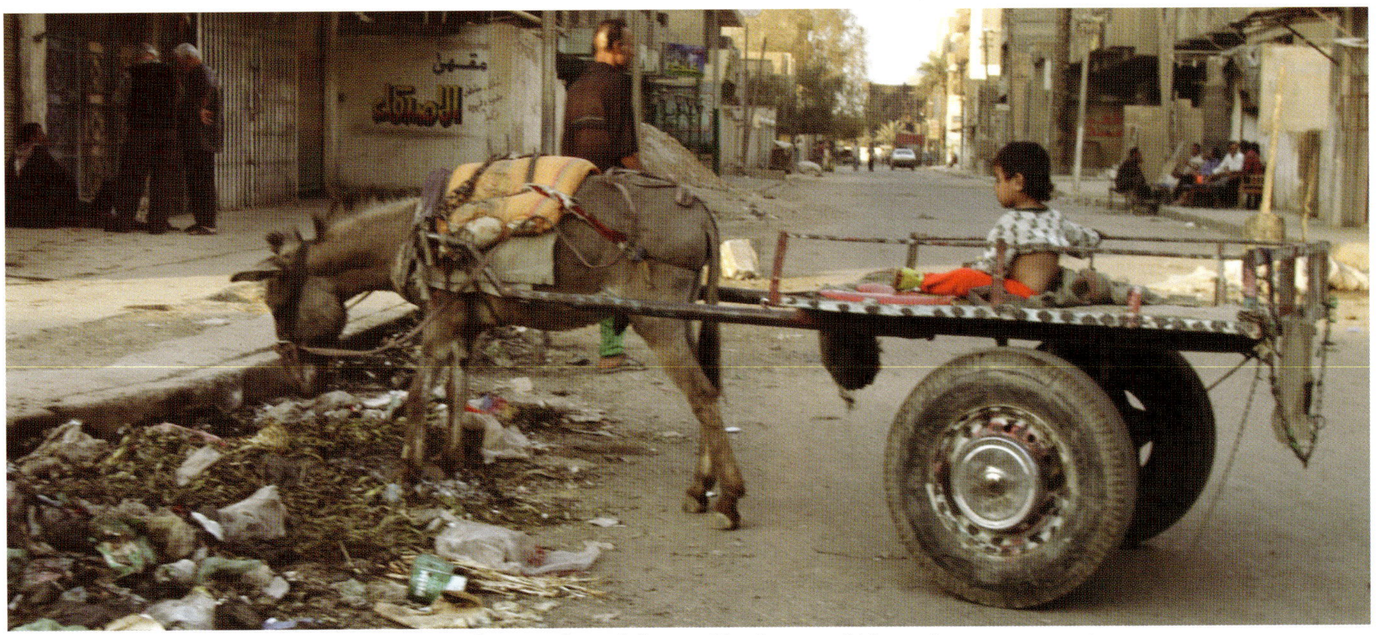

Donkey eats discarded vegetables from roadside trash

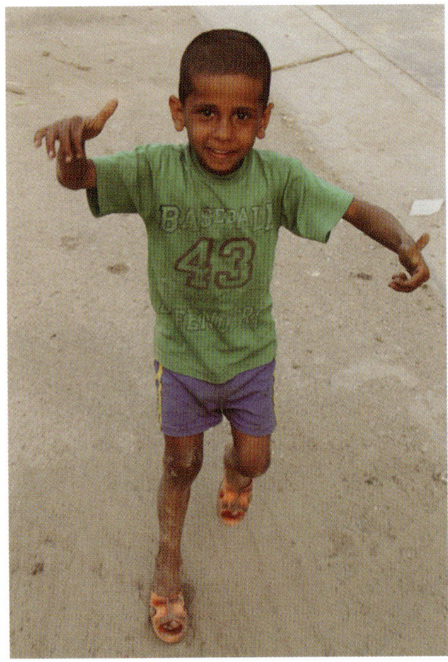

A little well-wisher follows our car

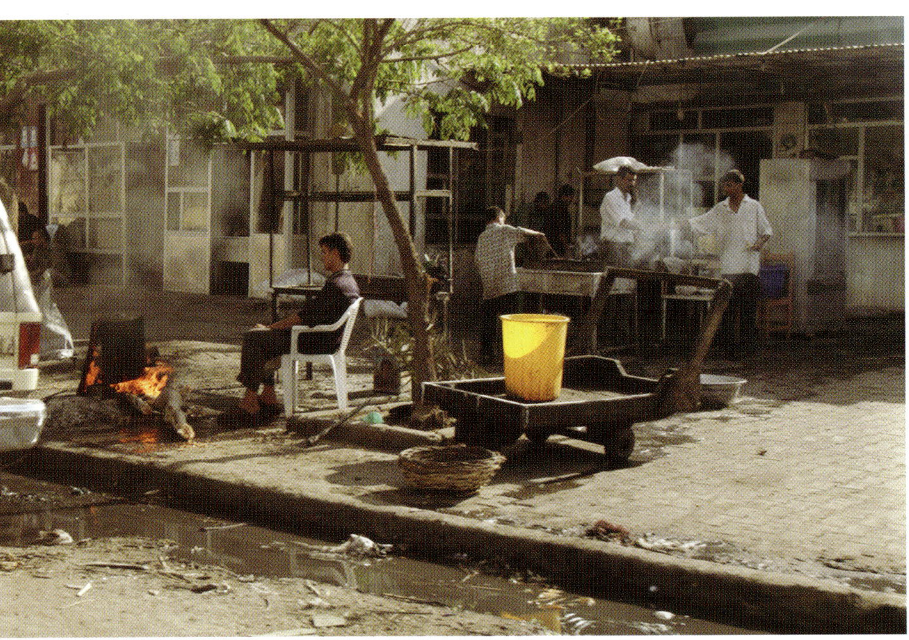

Iraqis want to get back to work but have few resources or money at their disposal

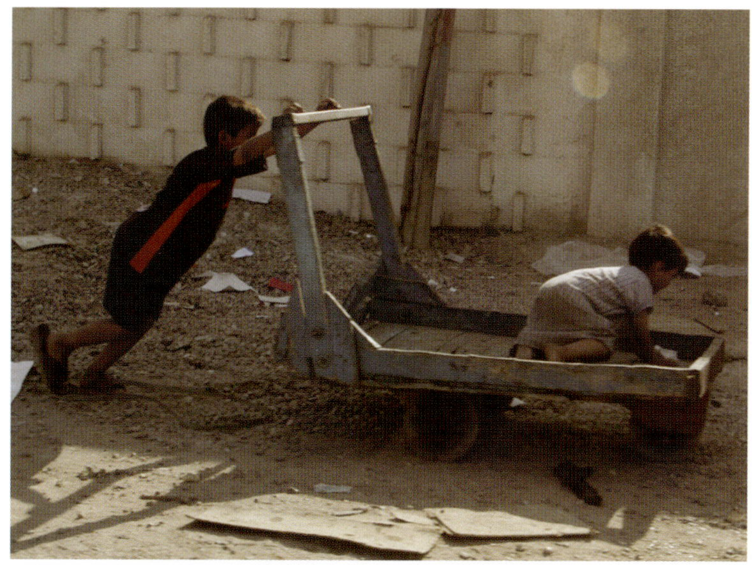
Children play with pushcart

Apparently, the two journalists were trying to interview and photograph gun dealers, when the dealers became agitated by their presence. A group of men brandishing AK-47s and bayonets, squeezed in tight around them. Those holding the knives held them in front of the journalists' faces, while those holding the AKs put their weapons up at the side of the journalists' heads and fired them into the air. With the gunshots ringing in their ears and fearing for their lives, the two journalists broke loose from the crowd and ran in the direction of their car, only to see the driver running for his life away from the car, as a gang of vengeful locals chased him down the road. The two journalists kept running away from the gunmen and luckily came across a military patrol, which picked them up and drove them out of the area.

They don't know what happened to the driver, who had all their money and some cameras in his car. It was a sobering experience for them, and for Sean and I. This, or worse, could have happened to us in Saddam City. Today was a valuable lesson in why you need a reliable driver and streetwise colleagues. Once again I realize that we freelance journalists have a difficult job with little gratitude or security. I write a note and post it in the Fanar lobby, advising other journalists of the problems we had covering the gun black market, and to use extreme caution if they decide to cover this story.

Just before sundown, I go for a walk along the river close to the Fanar. I want to get a look at some of the interesting bird life along the riverbank. Just before sunset the birds are very active, taking advantage of the cooling temperature to prey on bugs, small rodents and lizards. I photograph a flock of ibis (the sacred bird to the ancient Egyptians) flying along the Tigris, against the backdrop of an orange sunset. It is peaceful and sedate to be on the shoreline of the Tigris, near the nature and water, though it is dangerous and risky. The shrikes, bee-eaters and magpies are moving through the thorny shrubbery in small groups, looking for bugs. Wood doves peck at the sporadic vegetation, trying to find seeds or berries to satisfy their hunger. I am glad to see that the natural world keeps the same rhythm and balance as it always has, as this helps balance me. This is the same strip of land where the firefight took place the first day I arrived in Baghdad.

Tod, Sean, Tish and I decide to go out for supper. Grabbing a taxi, we head to the al-Ghutra restaurant, where we had supper last night. Once again, the food is terrific. We eat chicken and lamb kabobs with fresh warm flatbread. I also eat the garlicky-type dips and vegetable salads, (since no one got sick from the vegetables last night). The four meals, more like a buffet, total $17.

Leaving the restaurant, we decide to walk back to the hotel (a twenty minute walk), even though the streets are black and without lighting. I personally do not like the idea, but I decide to go along with my friends, our team. The fact that it could be dangerous is slightly stimulating.

Walking along the main road, I notice a suspicious man following thirty feet behind us and just off to the side. He follows along in the darkness, watching us while staying at the same distance from us, pausing when we pause. Realizing that we are in a perfect ambush zone, I keep my eyes glued to him, should he make an abrupt move. My friends keep walking, oblivious to the escort, as I fall back a little behind the group to keep a closer eye on him. I notice that he has a long bayonet knife clenched in his hand, held at his side. As long as he keeps his distance, I try not to spook him or unnecessarily alert my friends, who walk along chatting animatedly, unaware. This guy is looking for an easy target. But he has picked the wrong one, and after this afternoon's fracas in Saddam city, knife or no knife, I am ready to kill or injure if necessary to protect myself and my friends. Welcome to the jungle!

Finally we reach the lights and security of the Palestine without incident. I turn back and nod, then smirk at our

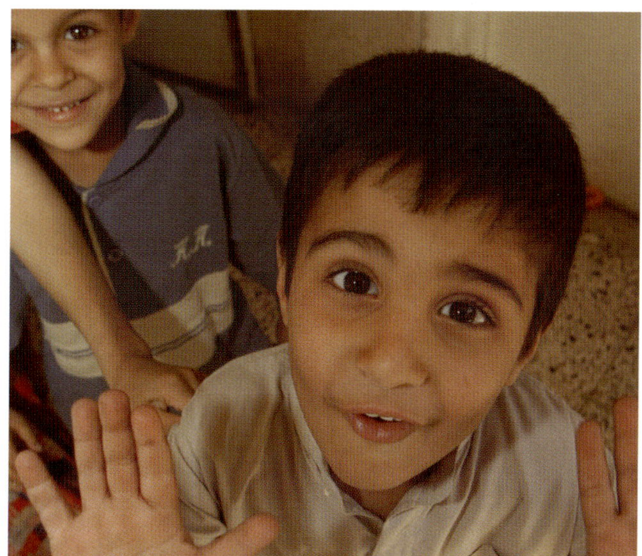
These young boys from Saddam City are well groomed

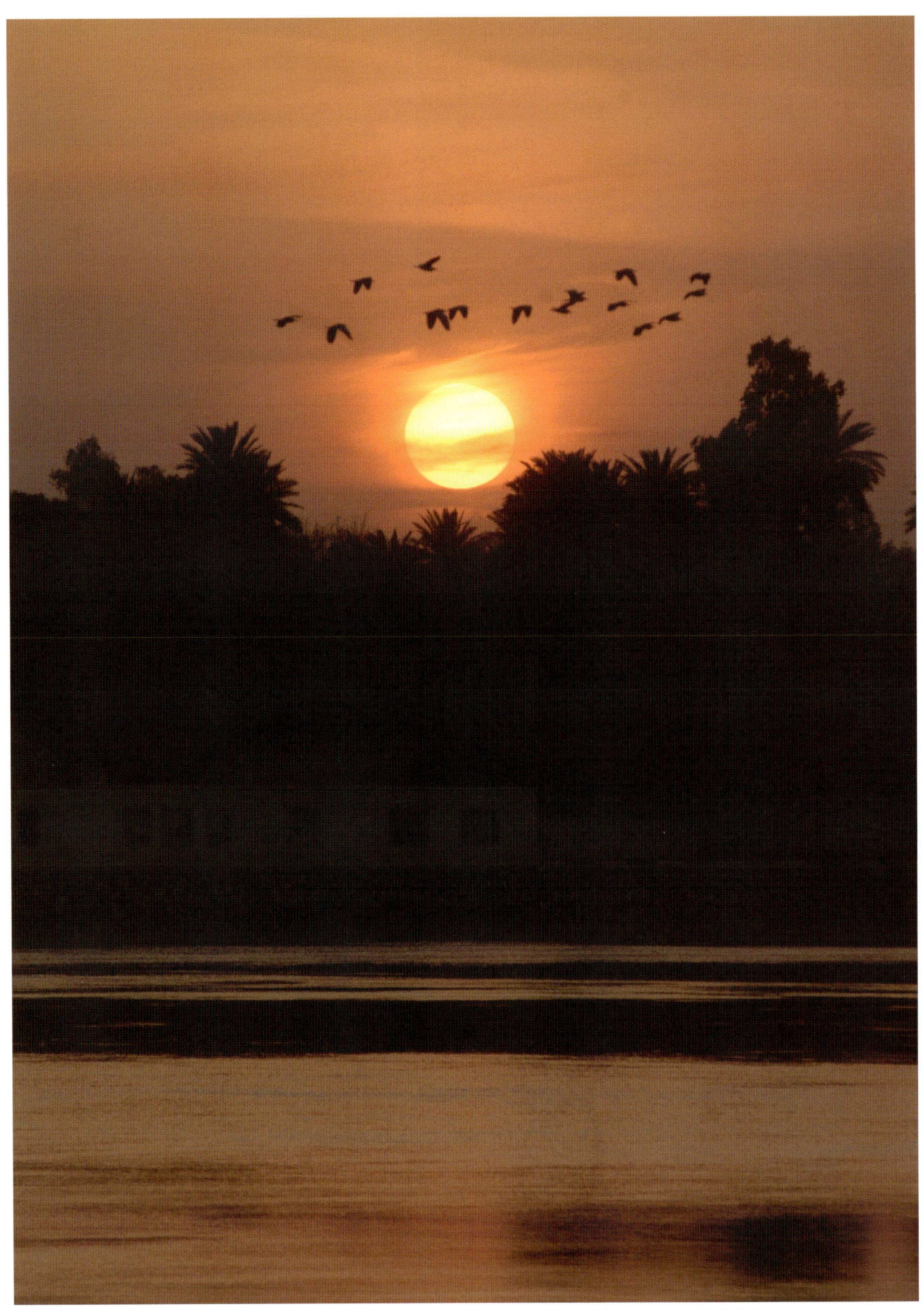

A flock of ibis fly along the western shore of the Tigris River as the sun sets in Baghdad

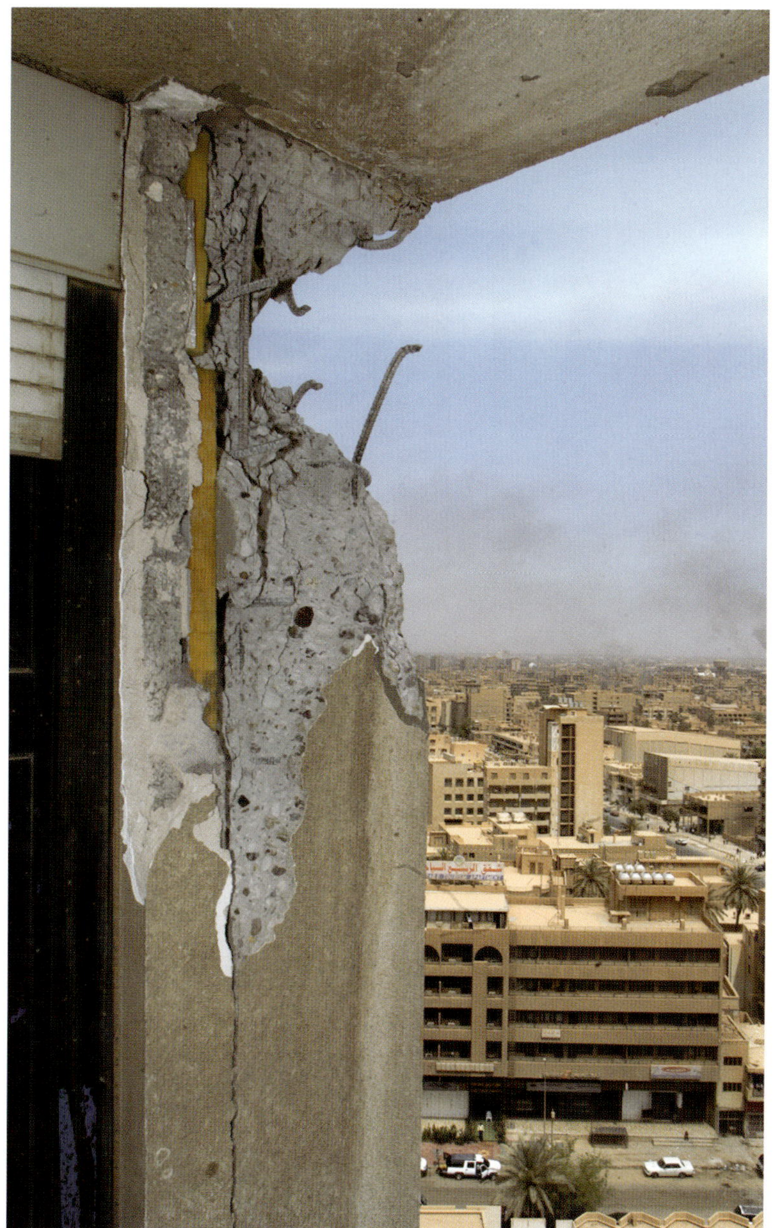

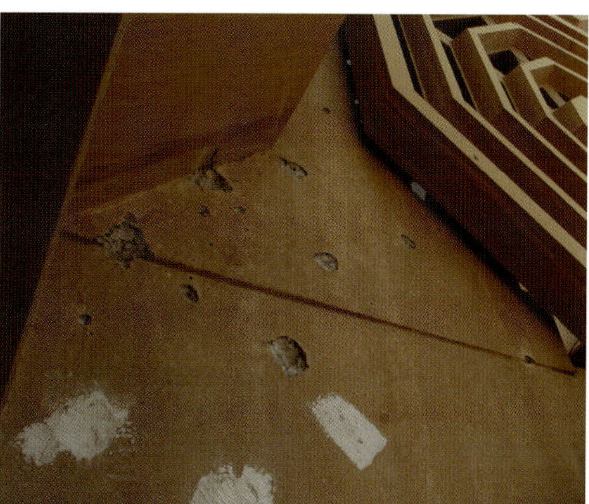

Shrapnel damage mars the 14th floor balcony of the Palestine

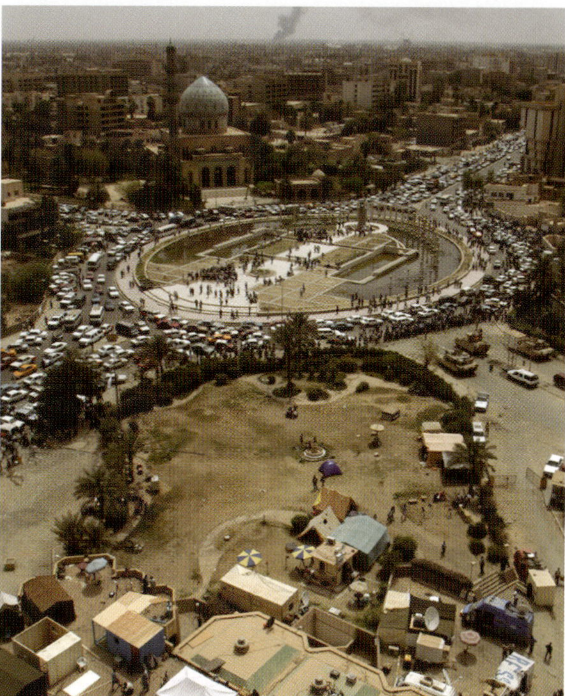

View of Baghdad looking south-east

A tank shell hit the Palestine Hotel's 14th floor, killing two journalists

escort as he disappears back into the cover of darkness. I just want to let him know that I had seen him and was not intimidated by him or his knife. My friends are surprised and didn't notice the stalker.

There is a good chance that he had some armed friends following even further back of us, waiting for an opportunity to rob us journalists. Anything and everything is possible in war-torn Baghdad where there is no law or order. This is not a place to be naive, overly aggressive, or too opinionated. Like the rhythm of the wildlife on the riverfront, balance is everything.

Tod was saying that if the people of Iraq don't receive any nutritional or medical aid soon, then journalists and soldiers could end up becoming targets. But this I had already figured out. Residents in Saddam City have been telling us that they are near starvation, and that if they don't receive food basics, they will either use their weapons to acquire food, or join a local terrorist group (who are offering food and support to new recruits). It is a dangerous situation for all concerned, but the residents have little choice; they have to feed their families. I feel it will only be a matter of a few weeks before Baghdad explodes into shootings and ambushes targeting Westerners, unless serious aid arrives to quench their hunger and heal their children. The city has a heavy air of rebellion hanging over it, and it is getting heavier as every day passes.

In a satellite phone call to my wife this evening, serenaded by the wild dogs, she tells me that the war has been pushed off the front pages in Canada and replaced by the SARS epidemic.

This evening I have a horrendous chilling nightmare. Amongst other ghastly visions I remember, Arabic dressed soldiers are shooting and killing my family in the old section of Quebec City, but I cannot help them. It is a horror-mare of horrendous proportions, and I take it as a warning to take a break or slow down from the bloodied face of Baghdad,

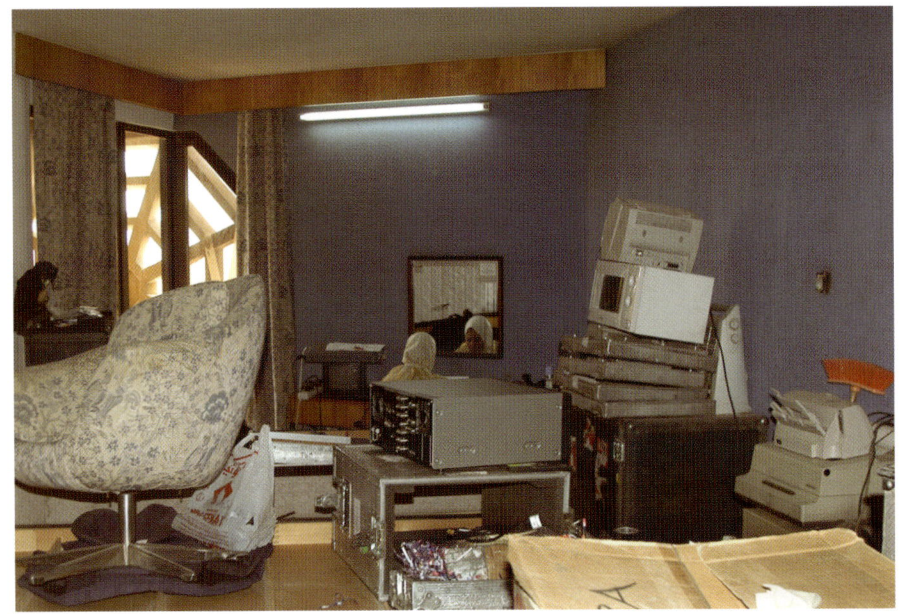

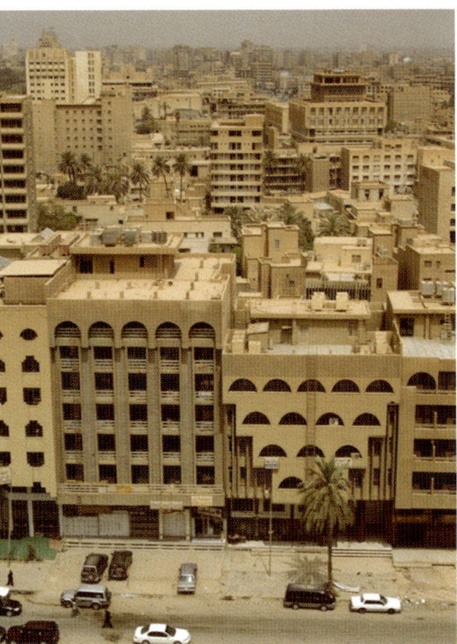

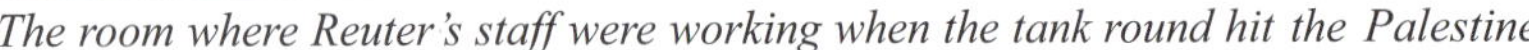

The room where Reuter's staff were working when the tank round hit the Palestine   _Baghdad looking east_

and the misery. I cannot take many nightmares like this without it affecting my daily work. Horror-mares cause you to become withdrawn from reality, and stymie your ability to reason clearly. These two negative forces can seriously endanger your life and those you work with. It is time to get out of Baghdad for a couple of days. My brain has warned me that I need a break.

Day 15. Thursday, April 24th

(Photographing the Reuter's death room at the Palestine; two journalists killed by tank shell; description of shell damage; media shanty-town at Palestine; gasoline generators line the Palestine patios; new courier service; I meet Italian NGO again; engineer turned cabbie; surface-to-air missile destroyed by cluster bomb; cluster bomb kills in Ad Dawrah; web of destruction; destroyed and damaged homes; blood splatters; Americans shell tank alongside a school; more collateral damage; pool of blood marks the site; description of cluster bomb shrapnel; war is hell; I forget my water; dehydrated and exhausted; the nap; another ghastly nightmare; Saddam's boots; out for supper with Tish, Todd, Sean, Simon and friend; making travel plans to Kuwait with NBC News crew; exhaustion can be deadly; I leave for Kuwait in the morning; my plans for Kuwait; in bed by 2 a.m.)

Up at 7 a.m., I look out from my balcony at a thick, hazy, still morning. These meteorological signs usually prelude a hot stifling day. After having a few cups of coffee, I take a walk over to the Palestine, trying to settle my nerves and lack of confidence generated from last night's nightmare. I carry my usual work tools – my camera, fanny pack and small backpack containing a 1.5 litre bottle of water.

The Palestine lobby is the usual busy scene of activity with soldiers, administrators and journalists going about their work. There are several hundred people living in the Palestine Hotel.

I decide to take the elevator to the 14th floor and see if I can get permission to photograph the bombed room where two journalists were killed by a shell fired by an American tank, on April 6th. The tank fired from the Al Jumhuryah Bridge, which spans the Tigris River just a mile north of the Palestine. Reuters television cameraman Taras Protsyuk, 35, and Spanish television cameraman Jose Couso, 37 were killed when the round blasted the balcony they were filming from. Three other journalists were wounded.

If you give the tank crew the benefit of the doubt, they must have thought the journalists (who were on the balcony filming the siege of Baghdad), were the enemy. Perhaps they thought the camera tripod with its long lens mounted on top, was a rocket launcher or mortar of some sort (but this is a real stretch of the imagination). The round hit the outside balcony killing one; another was killed inside the room. The resulting blast showered the room's occupants with shrapnel and chunks of concrete.

The top corner of the balcony has a large shark-sized bite out of it where the shell struck. Shrapnel marks of various sizes pepper the wall below it. The Reuter's crew, who let me in to take my pictures, are in the accompanying room smoking cigarettes and drinking Scotch. They are very somber, soft-spoken and obviously still shaken and numb. I talk with one photographer who tells me that your time could be up anywhere, at anytime. He says he was covering another news story in another part of Baghdad when his colleagues were killed. "It could have been me!" It must be hell for these journalists to keep on working with this kind of luggage hanging around their necks. Only time can heal the scars left by such a tragedy.

There is a hell of a lot more to this strike than meets the eye. I believe, and you can believe what you want, that this was a careless strike by the Americans, an accident of huge proportions. I have heard others say the strike was intentional, aimed at intimidating the non-embedded press and press in general. The American military would like to control the media and the message being distributed by them. The vice-grip restrictions on press coverage during the Gulf War were the proof of this, (when the media giants bowed to military restrictions on coverage). At this time, while our leading news organizations drank cappuccino and ate custard cakes in five-star hotels in Riyadh, a war raged just up the road. And who brought us the coverage; who filmed the action; who did the voice clips? – it was brought to your television screens and newspapers by the United States Armed Forces. Remember Schwartzkopf with his the pointer and video clips?

The world media, who must have thought – "gee, this is an easy way to cover a war, and cheap" – had been shammed by the Pentagon. The White House did not want another Vietnam showing up on American TV or in print. The conspiracy theorists would ask, "How do you prevent independent voices from covering the war, how do you plug these holes? You embed them with your own troops, and intimidate those who don't follow the rules or play the embedded game." But as I have mentioned, war is a confusing event and a breeding ground for conspiracy theories. The only absolute certainties of war are death and suffering.

I take some panoramic photos of the city from the death room side window, then, offering my condolences I leave. I catch the elevator to the second floor balcony, where most of the big name media broadcast. All the satellite dishes, support equipment and plywood shacks make the place look like a technological shantytown. Noisy gas generators line the main laneway from the hotel to the patio. They run around the clock, fuelling the cameras, lights and editing equipment. Some power from the hotel generators makes up the extra energy needs.

In the lobby of the hotel there is a small table being set up by a courier company. The person manning the table tells me he can have a package couriered back to Canada for $35 a half kilo. Besides sending a package with someone leaving

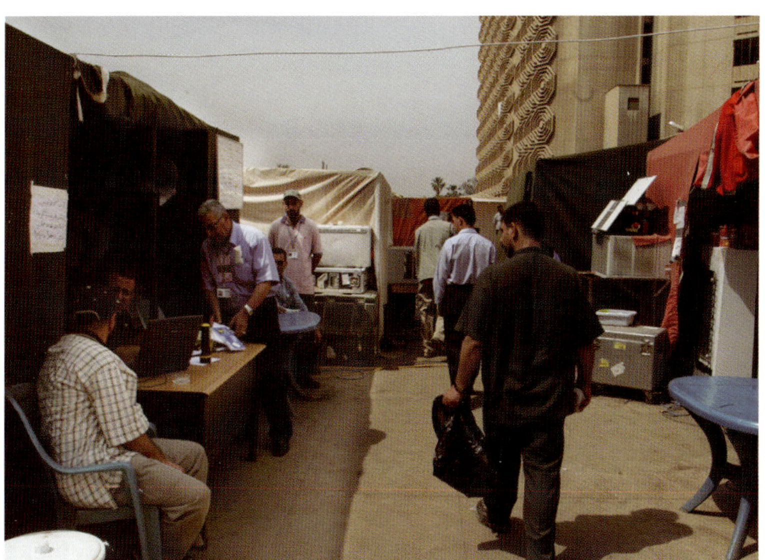

The international television media camp on the Palestine patio

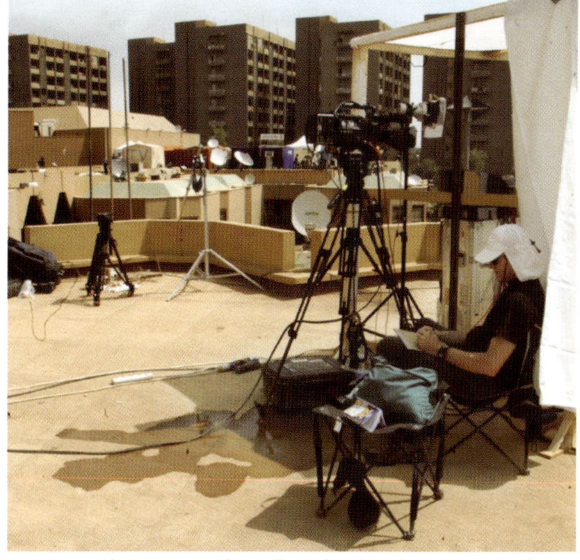

A journalist escapes from the relentless heat in a shadow

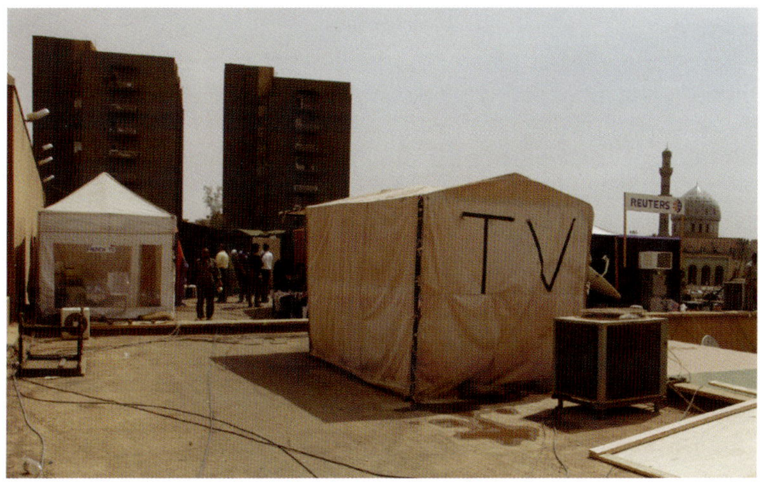

A television editing tent

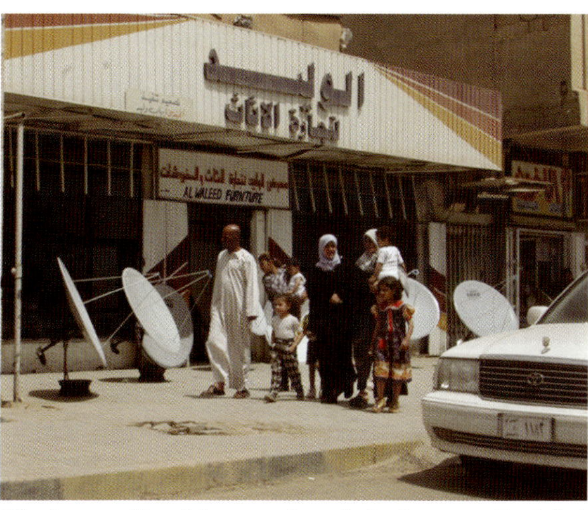

The first satellite dishes seen for sale in downtown Baghdad

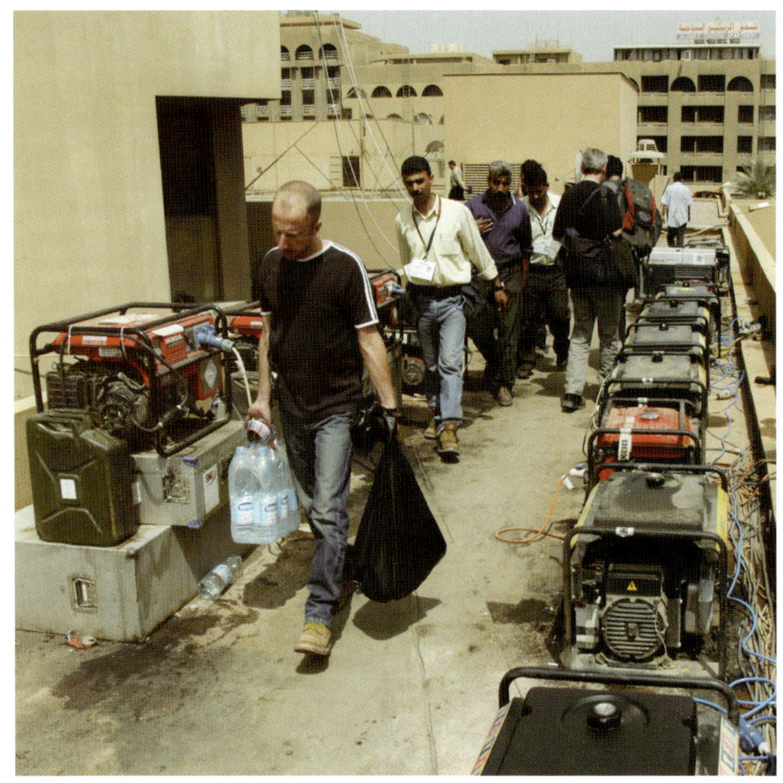

Lines of gas generators keep the electricity flowing

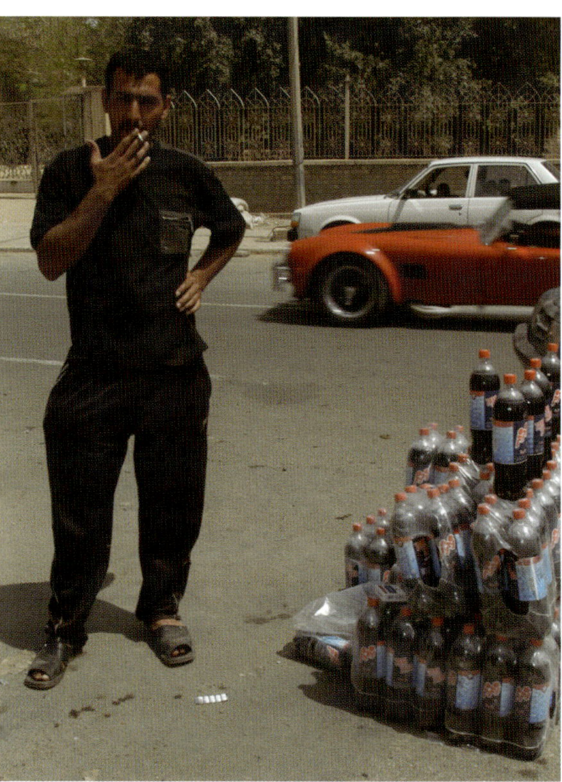

Soda vendor trying to make a living. Note the hotrod in back

the country by convoy, there is no other method of sending a package overseas or to Europe. It would be a good way of sending some photo CDs back to Montreal, or my flag from Nino.

I see the Italian 'Voices in the Wilderness' writer in the lobby of the Palestine. She sees me in the crowd and waves me over with a smile.

The Italian is sitting having a coffee with an elderly man of about 62, who she introduces to me. He tells me about an area in the south Baghdad suburb of Ad Dawrah, where a cluster bomb was dropped to destroy a surface-to-air missile. According to this man, seventeen civilians were killed as a result of the attack.

Near this site lay another, where an American attack on an abandoned tank allegedly killed 14 children while they played on the machine. The unemployed man offers to drive me to both blast sites for a small fee. I am a little reluctant to accept his offer, as it is so brutally hot out, and I do not want to go on a wild goose chase (especially since he is a friend of the Italian, and therefore probably not credible).

Agreeing to go along with him, I climb into his little Russian boxcar. On the way to the bomb site he tells me he is an electrical engineer who has no work and no source of income for himself and his wife. A very soft-spoken man, he is apologetic and embarrassed as he asks if I would mind paying a very small fee – any amount! Initially, he had gone to the hotel to look for work as a driver or interpreter, but with no luck

We reach Ad Dawrah and stop beside a row of well-kept houses fronting the Ad Dawrah Expressway. A six-foot long section of a surface-to-air missile lies destroyed on the street curb between the houses and highway. The tail section has been blown from the missile and sits in the island median that separates the east and west lanes. The traffic is too busy for me to cross and get a picture of the tail. Sections of the missile are missing, and were most likely pulverized by the blast. The large section lying on the curb resembles a large yellow water heater, and looks similar in size and color to other surface-to-air missiles I have photographed in other areas of Baghdad. This missile would have been fired from a launcher truck, but I can't see the truck anywhere.

I photograph a small section of the missile shell where the specifications of the missile are painted on. The lettering is all in English, with no indication of country or manufacture. It is indicated as being built in 1992, well after Desert Storm and after the sanctions were implemented. Perhaps it was built in the U.S., and then sold to an arms dealer in Europe, who then sold it to Saddam, without the Americans being aware of it.

The missile shows the telltale impact signs of a cluster bomb attack. A hole the size of a grapefruit has been blasted into the thick side of the missile. At the impact point, it is pitted with symmetrical pea-sized indents. These shrapnel marks spread out from the impact area in symmetrical bead-like patterns, similar to beads strung on a necklace. Leading from the hole is a three-foot long fracture, running along and splitting the missile's half-inch iron fuselage. It is cracked like a nut, from the impact of just one tennis-ball-sized bomblet.

The driver tells me that 17 residents were killed by the blast, and at least twice that number wounded.

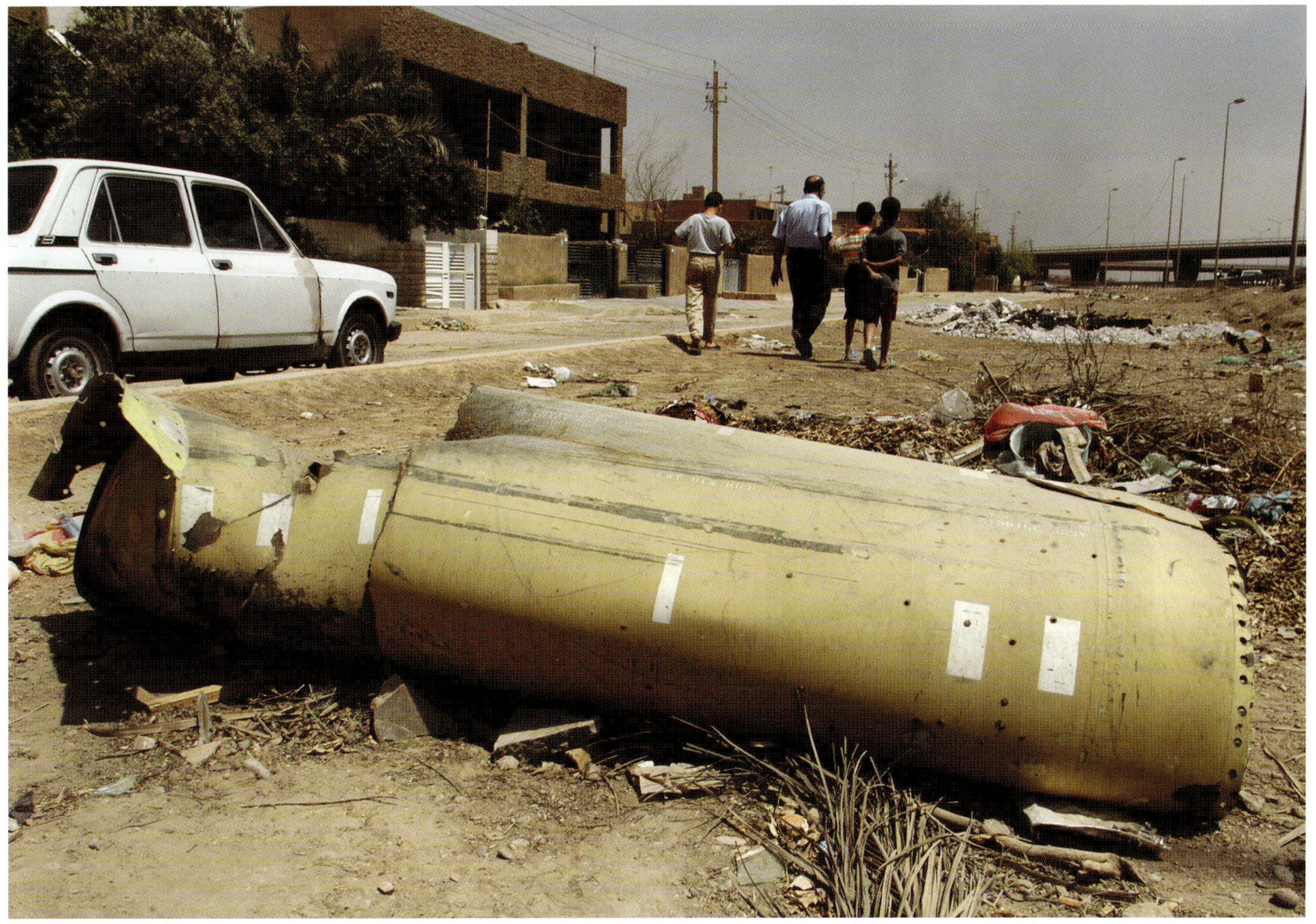

An Iraqi surface-to-air missile lies destroyed by a cluster bomb along the Ad Dawrah Expressway, flanking a residential area

There is a section of road where three separate holes, the size of a grapefruit, are gouged into the asphalt. This type of damage I have seen on other occasions on other roads (such as the Highway of Death outside Kuwait City in 1991) where the marks indicated cluster bomb impacts.

Grape-sized pockmarks scar the face of the buildings and the stuccoed walls in front of the homes. The closer to the missile, the greater the damage. One building has been badly damaged by fire, while many others have smashed windows and extensive exterior damage. The shrapnel hits are everywhere, spread over a residential area equal to two football fields.

A resident shows me her car, which had been parked outside her home near where the cluster bomb exploded. All its windows are shattered. The car body has been pierced by hundreds of small pea-sized holes. Luckily, no one was outside the family home at the time. A small group of clean dressed, smiling children follow the driver and I as we survey the damage.

A block away, at the neighborhood bakery shop, the baker invites me in to see the damage to his store. The shop windows are shattered by what looks like bullet holes; broken glass is everywhere. The walls inside and outside are pitted by shrapnel hits. In his hand, he shows me twenty pieces of metal he picked up from the floor of his shop. They look like tiny barrel-shaped beads, a quarter-inch tall. They are made of a high-strength metal alloy, each of which (there are hundreds per bomblet) would have been packed tightly together around an explosive core. The baker hands me a small bag full of fresh hot buns and says; "For you my friend." I open the bag and breathe in deeply. Then glancing up from the bag, I smile at the baker and respond; "Mmmm!"

On the sidewalk across the street from the bakery is a large pool of hardened and congealed blood. It marks the location where a passer-by was killed by the explosion. Anyone caught outside when the bomb was dropped (or to a lesser degree inside their homes), would have been unable to escape the spider web of death.

Jumping into the car we drive a short distance down the road, stopping beside a large vacant lot. Two-storey stuccoed homes and a kindergarten school surround the two-acre lot. It is used by the local children as a playground, and as a makeshift trash dump. Near one edge lies the contorted wreckage of what used to be an Iraqi tank. Perhaps only a third of the tank is visible. It was hit by an American air strike. What had not been pulverized has been blown apart and is resting more than 100 feet from the twisted hulk. The disemboweled engine was hurled across the street and rests against a resident's iron garden fence. The turret lies 150 feet from the point of impact, cushioned in a pile of garbage. Other large chunks of armor and mechanical parts are scattered over a large part of the vacant lot and surrounding streets.

A four-foot-deep crater has been gouged into the earth alongside the wreck. It must have been a massive explosion, judging from the complete and thorough destruction of the tank.

According to my driver, the Iraqi crew abandoned the tank during the bombing of Baghdad. The day that the bombing ended, a group of local residents contacted the American forces in their area and told them that the tank had been abandoned and not to bomb it, because it is in the middle of a residential area beside a school. Two days later the Americans bombed the tank. Local children had been using the abandoned tank as a playground, including the time when the bomb hit the tank. Fourteen children were killed instantly by the blast; more were wounded.

Parts of the exploding tank had struck and damaged neighboring homes, starting some small fires. The tracks had been blown off the tank and slammed into the wall of the children's school. A resident walks me across the street, 150 feet from where the tank lay, and shows me a cement and stucco wall that encircles a two-storey home. He points to an area of the wall where it looks like someone had thrown a tin of rust colored paint across it. He tells me it is the bloody imprint from a young child who was blasted into the wall by the force of the explosion, and died.

I try to comprehend why this tank was blown up after the locals had warned the officials that it was abandoned. It is hard to understand the reasoning behind it. Was it just a bad accident, a blunder of immense proportions, an act of stupidity, of miscommunication? War is not as orderly as cutting brownies in a baking pan; accidents and instances of painful irresponsibility occur. Perhaps I should categorize the shelling of the Palestine in the same folder as this tank or the cluster bomb just down the road. This is what happens in war; it always has and always will. We can make rules to kill by – but ghastly incidents will continue to happen. War is hell.

We leave the wreckage and bloody imprints and head back to the Fanar, I am exhausted and dehydrated. I forgot my water in the Palestine lobby earlier in the day, while talking to the Italian woman. Leaving my water behind was not a smart thing to do. As a result, I am exhausted to the point of collapsing, and badly dehydrated. I go upstairs and take a nap for a couple of hours, awakening later with a pounding head and backache. Even worse, I have another horrific nightmare, or napmare in this case, and am badly shaken and nauseated. For the next hour I lie in bed trying to regain my energy.

In the morning Sean had told me he heard that a photographer working for Getty Images (and staying at the Palestine), was travelling to Amman in the morning. I had mentioned to Sean earlier that I would like to go to Amman or Kuwait for a couple of days, to take a break from the war. With the recurring nightmares, headaches, loss of weight and memory fatigue, I know it is time to get out of Iraq for some chill time. This might prove a timely opportunity. I would also be able to get my camera cleaned and the flash repaired. Trying to shake off the cobwebs after my rest, I go for a walk to the Palestine to try track down the photographer.

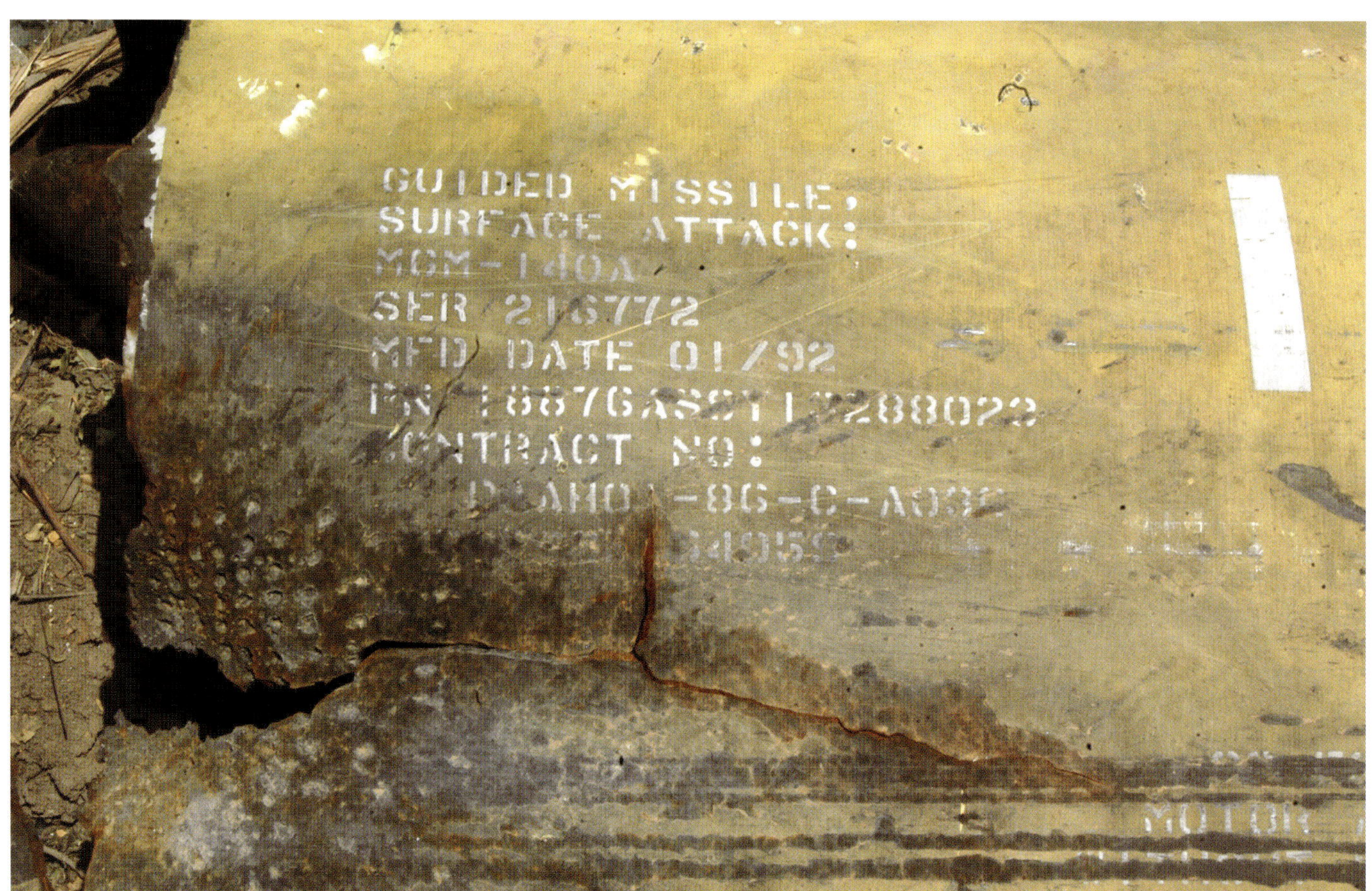

Tell tale damage of a cluster bomb. The indentations, spread out in a bead-like pattern, are characteristic of a bomblet impact

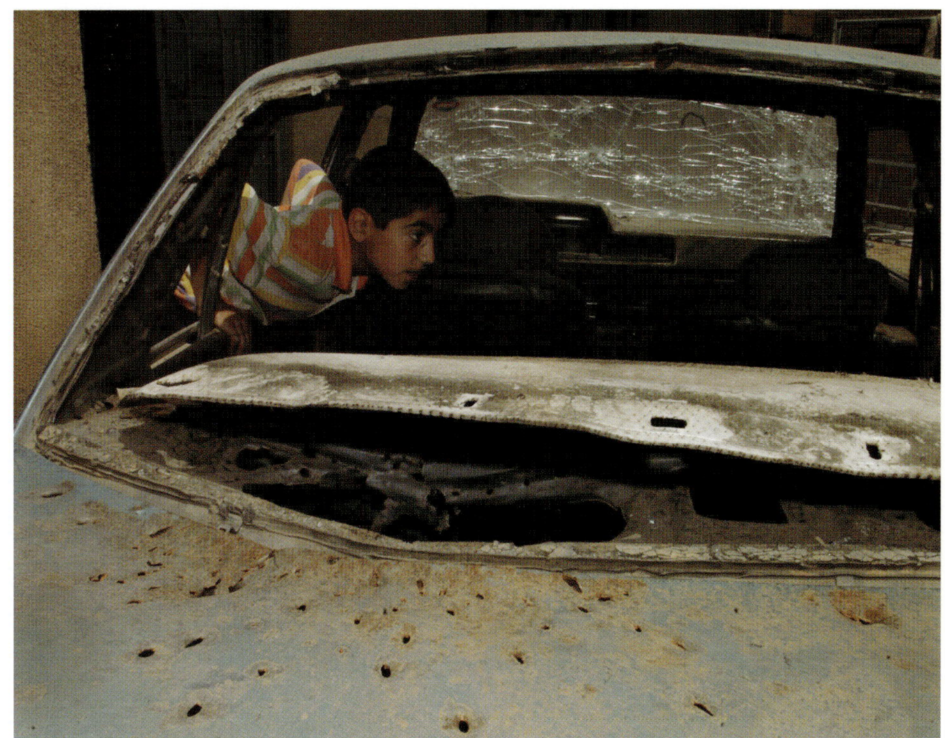

Shrapnel from a cluster bomb destroyed this car in Ad Dawrah

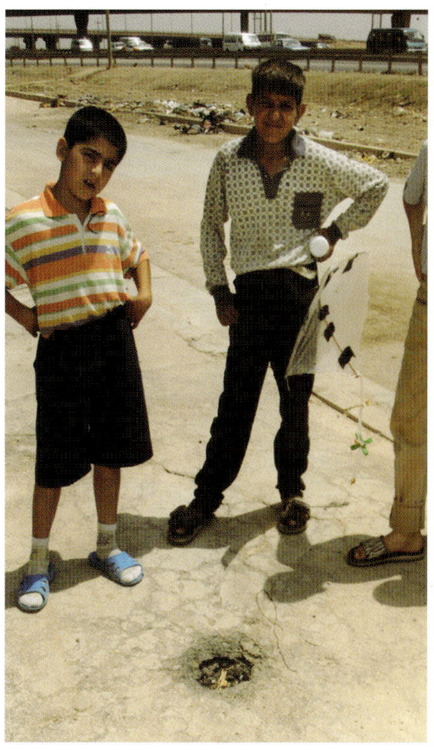

Hole in road caused by bomblet impact

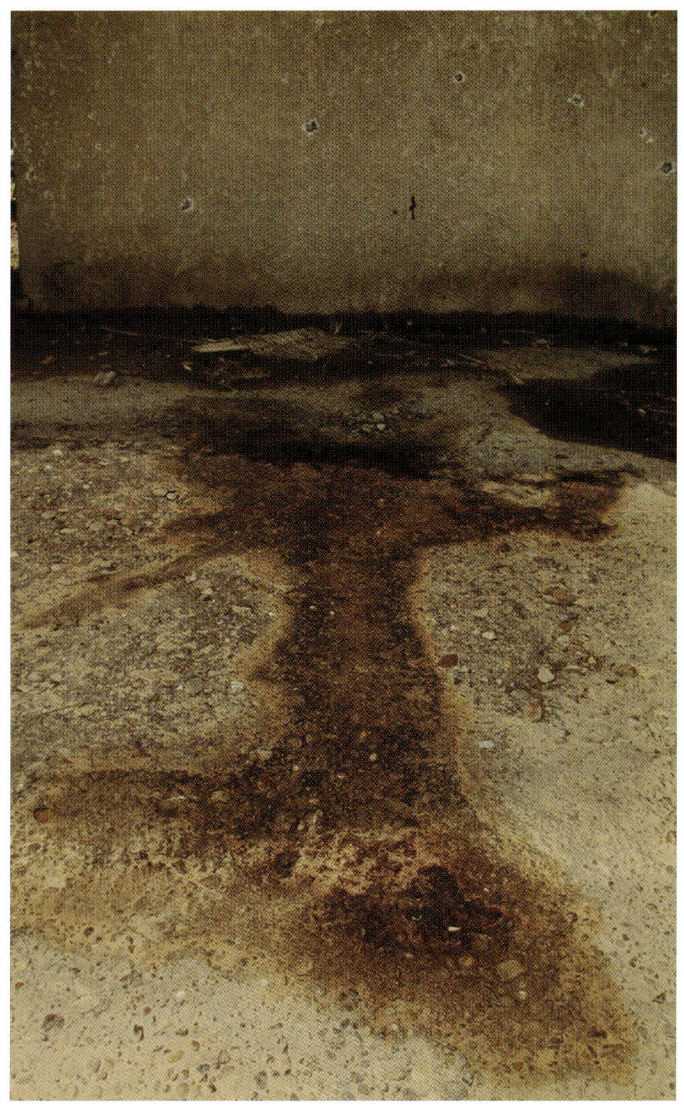

Dried blood from cluster bomb victim. Note shrapnel holes in wall

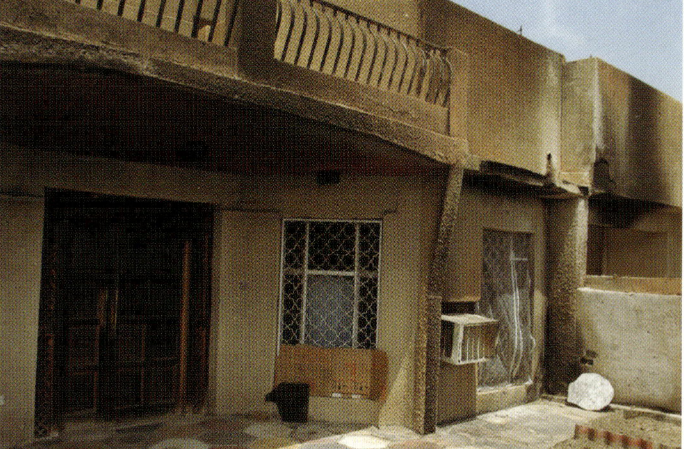

Homes burned and damaged by a cluster bomb

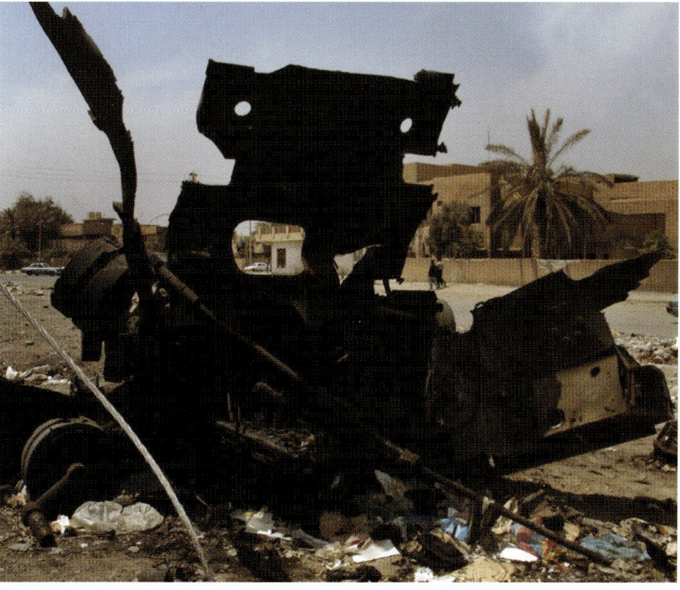

Pulverized Iraqi tank hit by American air strike

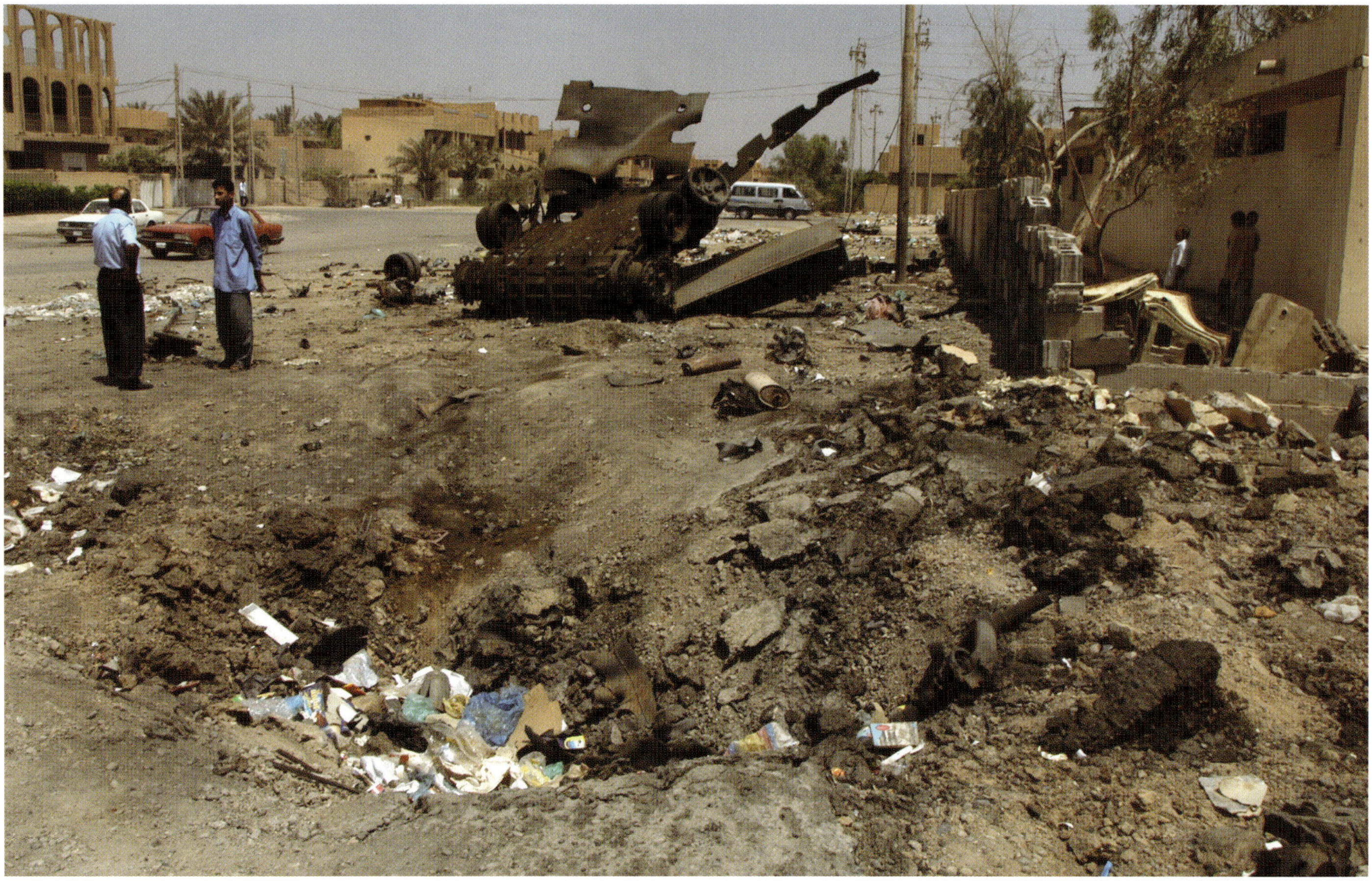

An American airstrike demolished this tank beside a kindergarten school in south Baghdad, leaving a gaping crater

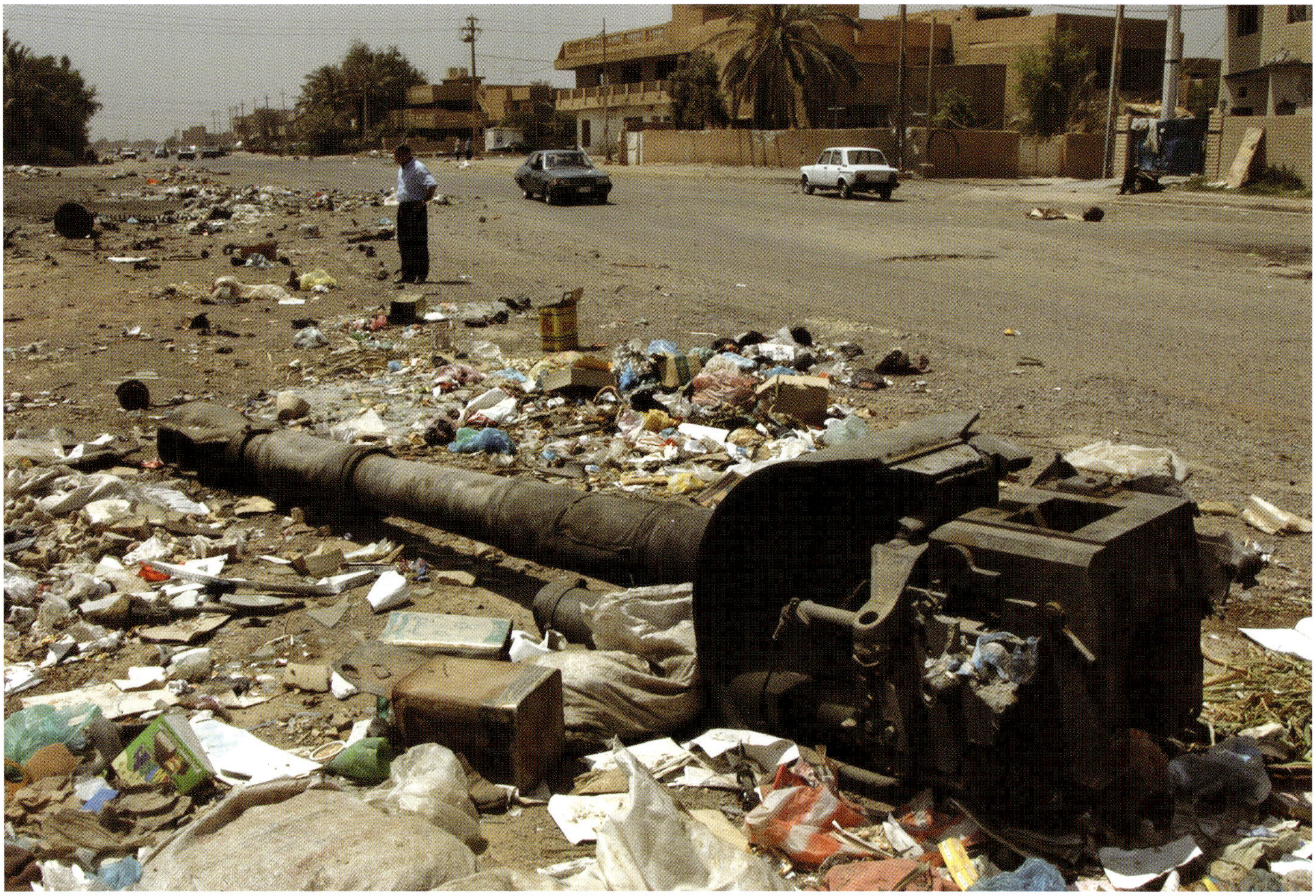

The tank turret was blasted 200 feet from the main body of the tank.

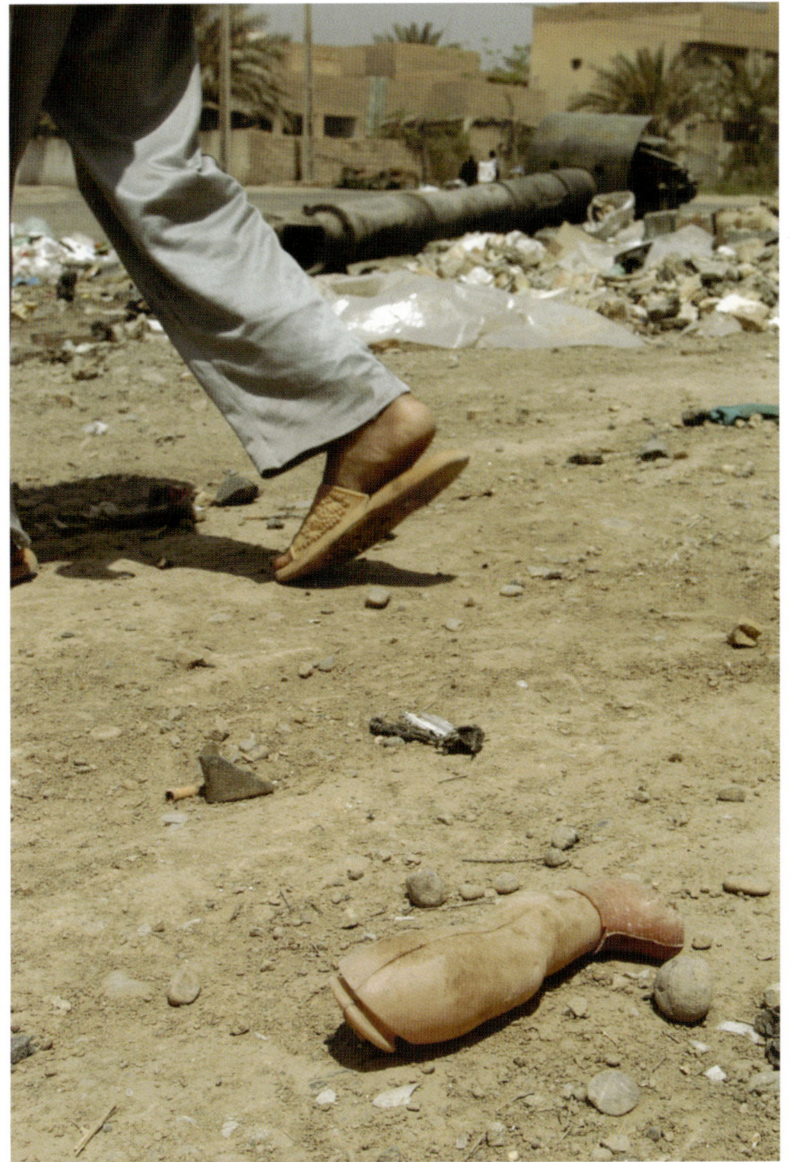
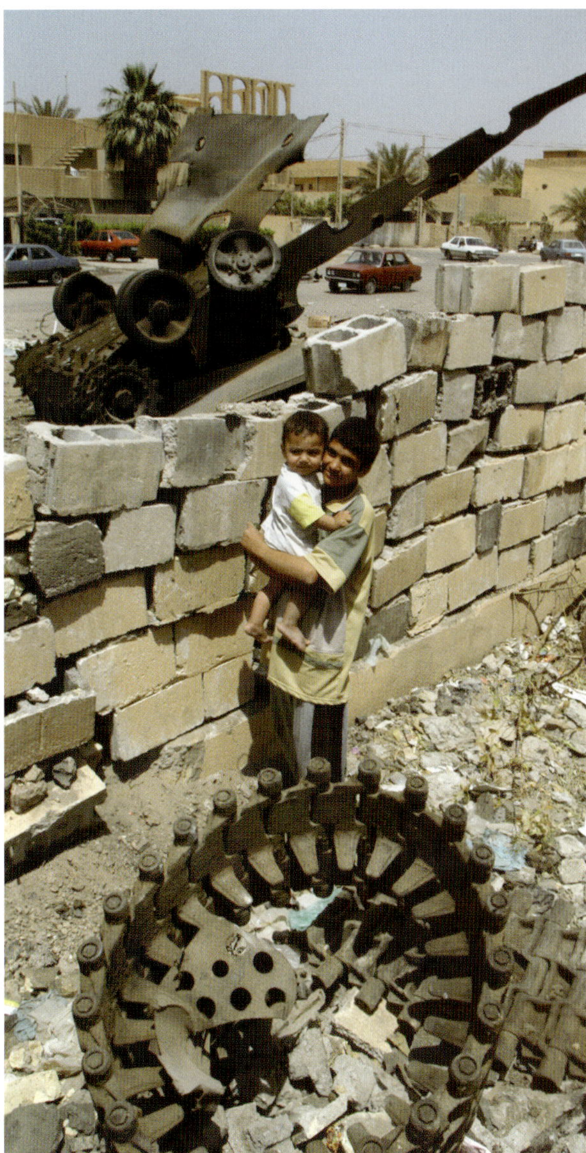

A doll's leg lies near where the tank was struck

The rebuilt wall separating the school from the open lot

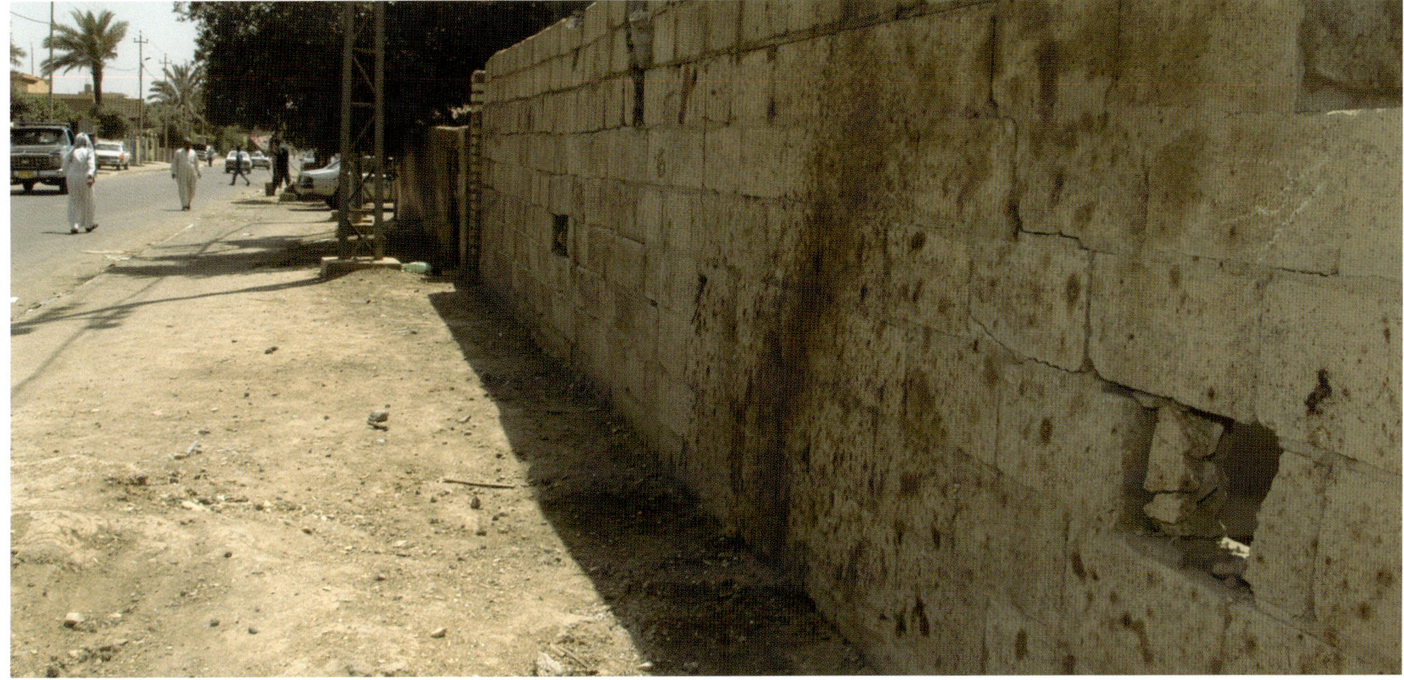

A child was blasted by the force of the exploding tank and thrown against this wall killing him. Blood splatters mark the exact site where he died

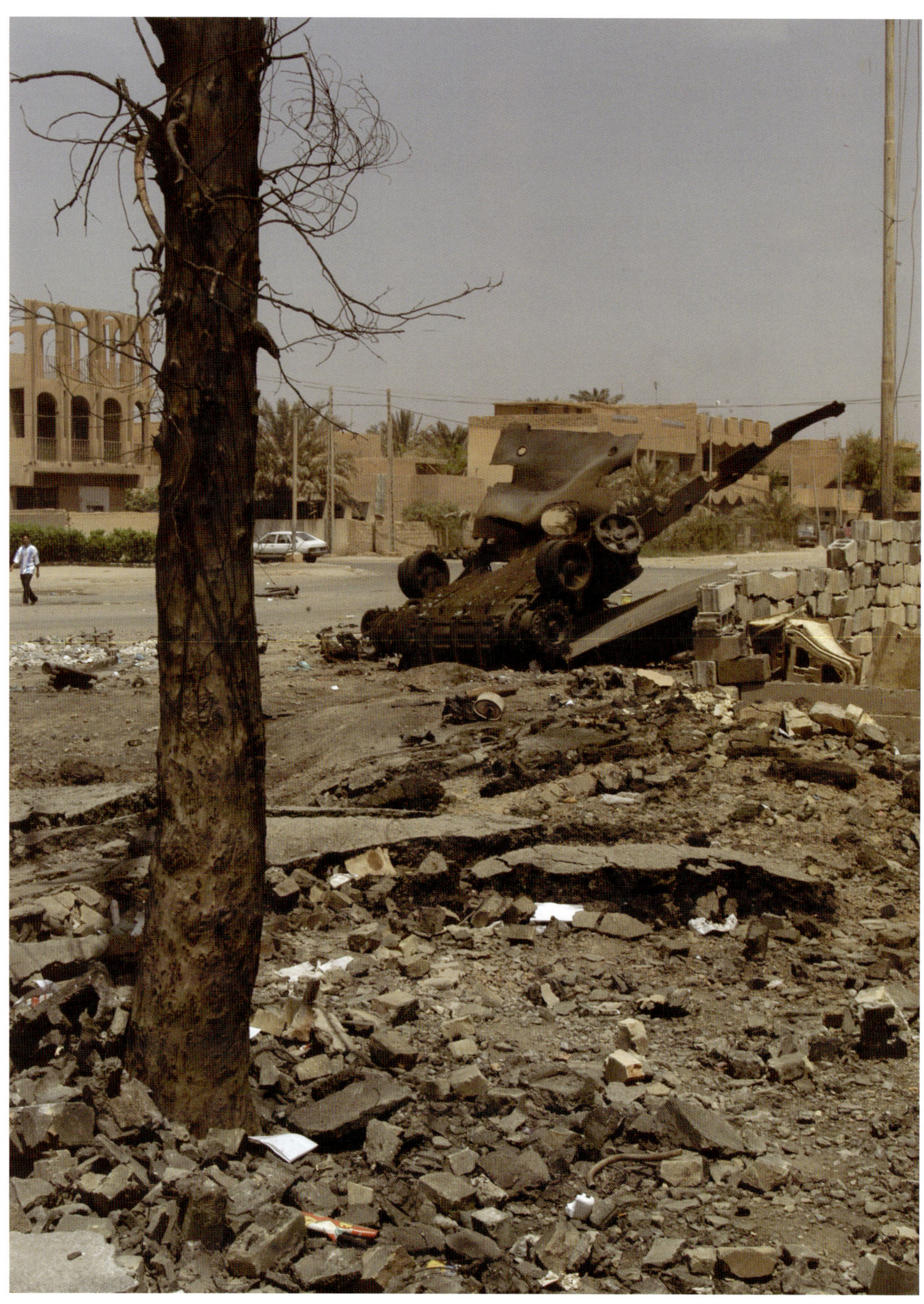

Tank hit by airstrike. The target was in a residential area right beside a school

The lobby is so busy with people that I decide to check again later in the evening. Wandering out in front of the hotel I take some pictures of the pedestal where the famous statue of Saddam stood in Firdos Square. The statue had been pulled down in front of an international television audience, just a couple of days before I arrived in Baghdad. All that remains of the statue are Saddam's bronze boots, bent and clinging from the top of the platform. The rest of his likeness has been broken apart for souvenirs.

I meet Tod, Tish, Sean, Simon and a Puerto Rican photographer friend of Simon's in the hotel lobby. We go out for supper at a restaurant next door to the Fanar. We order the special, Kentucky-Style Chicken. The food is good and fresh, with a good selection of salads and dips, which I indulge in. It is a nice gathering, with lots of laughing and discussion about Baghdad and the war. I slowly start to unwind after a brutal day of physical and psychological stress.

At the end of dinner I head over to the Palestine to try to find the Getty photographer. I search through the hotel ledger and ring up his room. But it is not the room of the photographer; the room numbers have been mixed up somehow. Instead, a cameraman with NBC News answers the phone. He tells me he has lived in the same room for a couple of weeks and does not know the photographer, but he asks if he can be of any help.

I tell the cameraman, who's name is Snora, that I am trying to locate the photog from Getty Images, to ask about catching a lift with him to Amman. Snora tells me that he happens to be leaving for Kuwait in morning, and if there is room (which he believes there should be) I can go with him to Kuwait. He is travelling with some colleagues in three Jimmys. Wanting to take advantage of a sure thing, I tell him that it sounds great, and I will be at the rendezvous spot outside the Sheraton Hotel at 5:30 a.m.

Walking back to the Fanar I hear sporadic gunfire a couple of miles to the south and stop to chat with a soldier manning a sentry post. He tells me that earlier in the day he had confiscated a 9-mm pistol from a civilian, at his checkpoint outside the Palestine. He said it was probably carried for self-defense, but he had no choice but to take the weapon from the man, then he let him continue into the hotel.

Back at the Fanar, I tell my roommates my plans to leave for Kuwait in the morning. They are really happy for me. My plan is to go to Kuwait for two days rest, then come back to Baghdad for a day or two, then head out of town with Tish and Sean to cover Kurdistan in northern Iraq.

I will also try to pick up a B-GAN Satellite transmitter in Kuwait. This transmitter would make all our transmission problems disappear and could make us some money. It will cost $2000, but Sean says he will foot the bill for the device. I tell them that I will be stopping in Basra for a day, to gather necessary material for the book. We are in a jovial mode, and end up chatting and munching on treats till 2 a.m.

Day 16. Friday, April 25th

(Meeting my travel companions; the road to Kuwait; six Scud missiles at Babylon exit ramp; a tour of Babylon; glazed brickwork; souvenir shop looted; rebuilding Babylon; Saddam's palace at Babylon; U.S. soldiers guard ancient city from looters; cuneiform inscriptions date to 4000 BC; the 'Lions of Babylon'; driving through Al Hillah; a break near the ancient city of Ur; repairing a flat tire; mile-long military convoys from Umm Qasr; ancient and modern farming practices; "Visa, what visa;" robbed at the border; the Kuwait Ministry of Information; tea from a chrome thermos; a personal insult; threatened with jail time; saved by a security agent; over ten hours to reach Kuwait City; the red carpet treatment; the glitzy Sheraton; thousand-dollar suits; journalist Tim Carlson; the opulent executive lounge; chocolate truffles and cappuccino; problems with e-mailing my images; I go to bed perplexed)

I am up at 4:30 a.m., quietly packing my gear, while Tish and Sean sleep. Twenty minutes before sunrise, I head over to the Sheraton where I meet Snora, Steve and Julie from NBC News. I am also introduced to three men from a Spanish TV network who will be travelling in their own Jimmy along with us.

In our Jimmy are Snora, Julie, Steve and the driver. A car will carry another NBC crew and a retired U.S. Colonel, who is the NBC military and security consultant. His job is to advise the team on security issues and act as a liaison between the team and any military we meet.

We leave Baghdad around 6:00 a.m., heading for the Kuwaiti border, ten hours away. Snora tells me that no one in the group has ever been out of Baghdad, their assignments have kept them in the city. It is a good gang to travel with and I feel welcome and right at home. The team decides it will be a good idea to make a side visit to Babylon, a suggestion I strongly agree with. It is just short of a two-hour drive (60 miles) from Baghdad.

We stop along the side of the road to photograph a blown-up tank. Twenty minutes later, we are taking the exit to Babylon. Positioned at the junction of these roads are three missile-carrying trucks, each carrying two 25-foot missiles.

They still have the nose cones and I wonder if they have been disarmed. Snora and I take some pictures of the missiles but do not venture close to them in case the surrounding area is mined. They look like Scuds but I cannot positively say for certain.

Five minutes later we park our vehicles and walk over to the Ishtar Gates of the ancient city of Babylon. There are two main brick towers flanking an archway, under which the main gate allows passage into the brick city. The brick towers and archway are painted medium-light blue, with a white and yellow geometric shaped trim. Mythical beasts (called Sirrush) with hawk feet, scales and a unicorn horn, seem to march across the gate walls. Just inside the gates, a mural of marching bulls, molded into the brickwork, are set into the walls. The city is enclosed within 50-foot tall walled fortifications made of a yellow brick.

We are hard pressed for time but have an hour to spare for our visit. As we pass through the gates, two young boys appear with a large cooler, asking if we want to buy some cold pop. Their cooler is crammed with Pepsi, canned juice drinks and some ice chunks. We enter the souvenir shop, just inside the gates and under the shadow of the lofty walls. All its windows and doors have been smashed and the building has been looted and burned. Inside, it is a burned shell with broken furniture and smashed display cases scattered about the floor. Postcards are strewn about the floor, a reminder of a more sane time.

Walking through the complex of re-built ruins, partial excavations and crumbling mud-brick buildings, it is hard to describe in words the effect the city has on a person, except to say that Babylon is not only visually stunning, but it is also a spiritual place, the seed where civilization was germinated – the first metropolis. Babylon was a small town that had sprung up by the beginning of the third millennium BC, at the dawn of the dynasties. Most of the city inside the high brick walls is clean and orderly. The ancient city was rebuilt by Saddam in the mid to late 1980's to recreate it as it was in the era of King Nebuchadnezzar, 600 BC. At that time the city had a perimeter of 11 miles.

Outside the city walls, large sections of eroded ruins stick out above the earth like large termite mounds. All indications are that excavation of some of the ruins continued right up until the time the war started (funded by a history-loving Saddam Hussein, who wanted Iraqis to be proud of their long history).

The city and surrounding area is a vast archaeological site. I find pottery shards, glazed brickwork and clay tablets with ancient writing pressed into them. For an amateur archaeologist like myself, it doesn't get much better! It is a feast of archaeological sites. There is so much to explore that it is difficult to decide what to go look at!

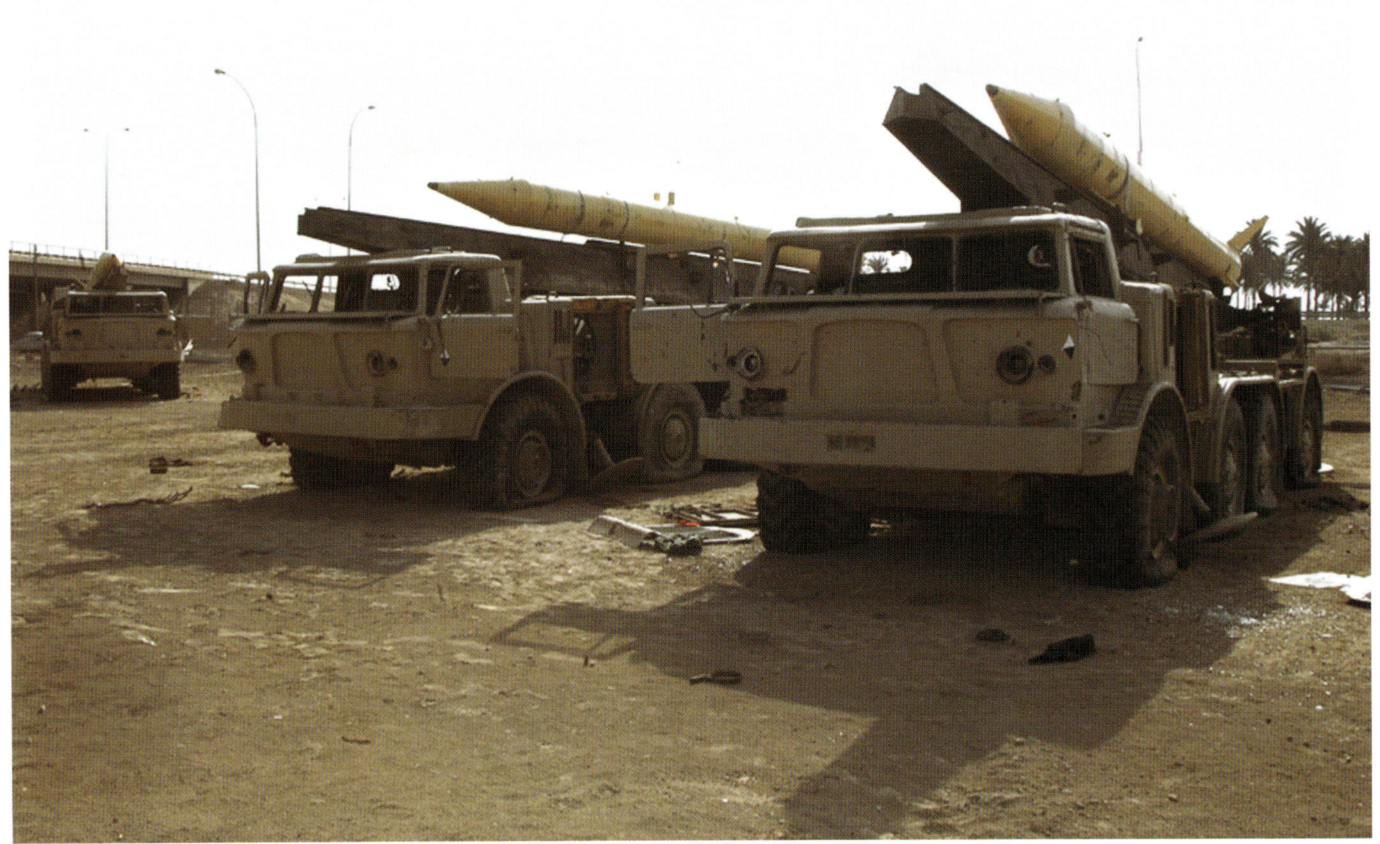

Live Scud missiles and launcher trucks near Al Hillah, a couple of miles from Saddam's Babylon palace.

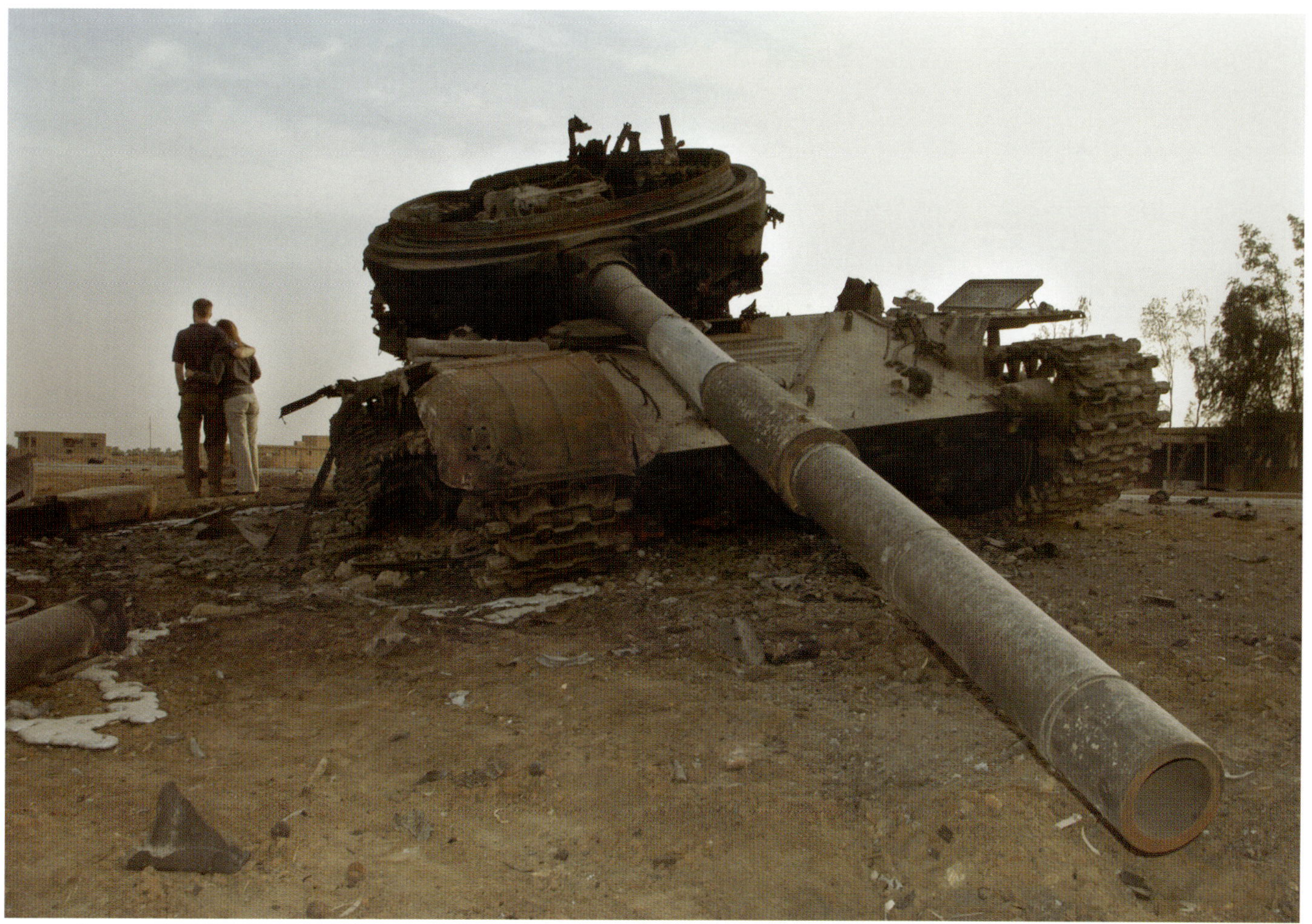

Destroyed Iraqi tank on the highway to Babylon, near Al Hillah. The aluminum components of the tank have melted onto the sand

I see Snora and Julie speaking with six American soldiers. I walk over to join them. I find out that the soldiers, Seabees from the 1st Marine Expeditionary Force, are guarding the city from looting and further pillage. Their unit is residing in Saddam's Palace, which sits on a bluff just outside the main walls overlooking Babylon.

The palace looms over the city, and is strikingly out of place. It is a beautiful finely carved sandstone castle, and looks like an Arabian palace. But that's the problem; it is obtrusive, misplaced and tacky to the limit. It appears that Saddam tried to buy his way into the history books by building his monument overlooking the ancient city. I wonder if Saddam would have built a palace beside the Giza pyramids, as a dictator in Egypt. But he is already guaranteed a place in history, for trying to destroy cultures like the Kurds, the Swamp people and other Muslims.

One of the soldiers holds up a large chunk of stone. It has primitive cuneiform symbols stamped into its face and is over 4000 years old. We explore more of the ruins, finding more cuneiform tablets and pottery fragments. Looking down from a mound of ruins, I see the figure of a lion carved in stone, mounted on a large basalt pedestal, situated outside the east gate of the city. It is the famous Lion of Babylon statue, written about in our world history books. I call Snora and Julie over to take a picture of them on the lion. I mention to Snora that over the millennia, many important people passed by this lion on the way into Babylon. This cast of historic personalities includes Alexander the Great, who died from malaria at Babylon in 323 BC (his body was carried to Alexandria, Egypt and buried in a mausoleum).

We leave Babylon (where I could have spent a week) driving south through the burning haze of the southern desert. Even though we have air conditioning, it is hard to breathe because of the relentless dust and sinister heat which engulfs us. Passing through the village of Al Hillah, residents gawk at us as though we are aliens. It is a dusty, hot village, and I feel that there is a disdainful tension in the people's faces. There is a Twilight Zone type of feeling to this region. We continue driving away from Al Hillah, as the brutal desert sun starts to take its toll, draining the energy from my body.

A few hours later we stop for a roadside snack near the ancient Sumerian ruins of Ur, which we can see as a high wide mound, 15 miles away. Ur is a city mentioned in the Bible as the home of Abraham, the patriarch of the Jewish, Muslim and Christian faiths. It is also where the alphabet is believed to have been conceived. This is such an important region of the world for our early history – but all I want to do is get out of the furnace-like, dusty environment.

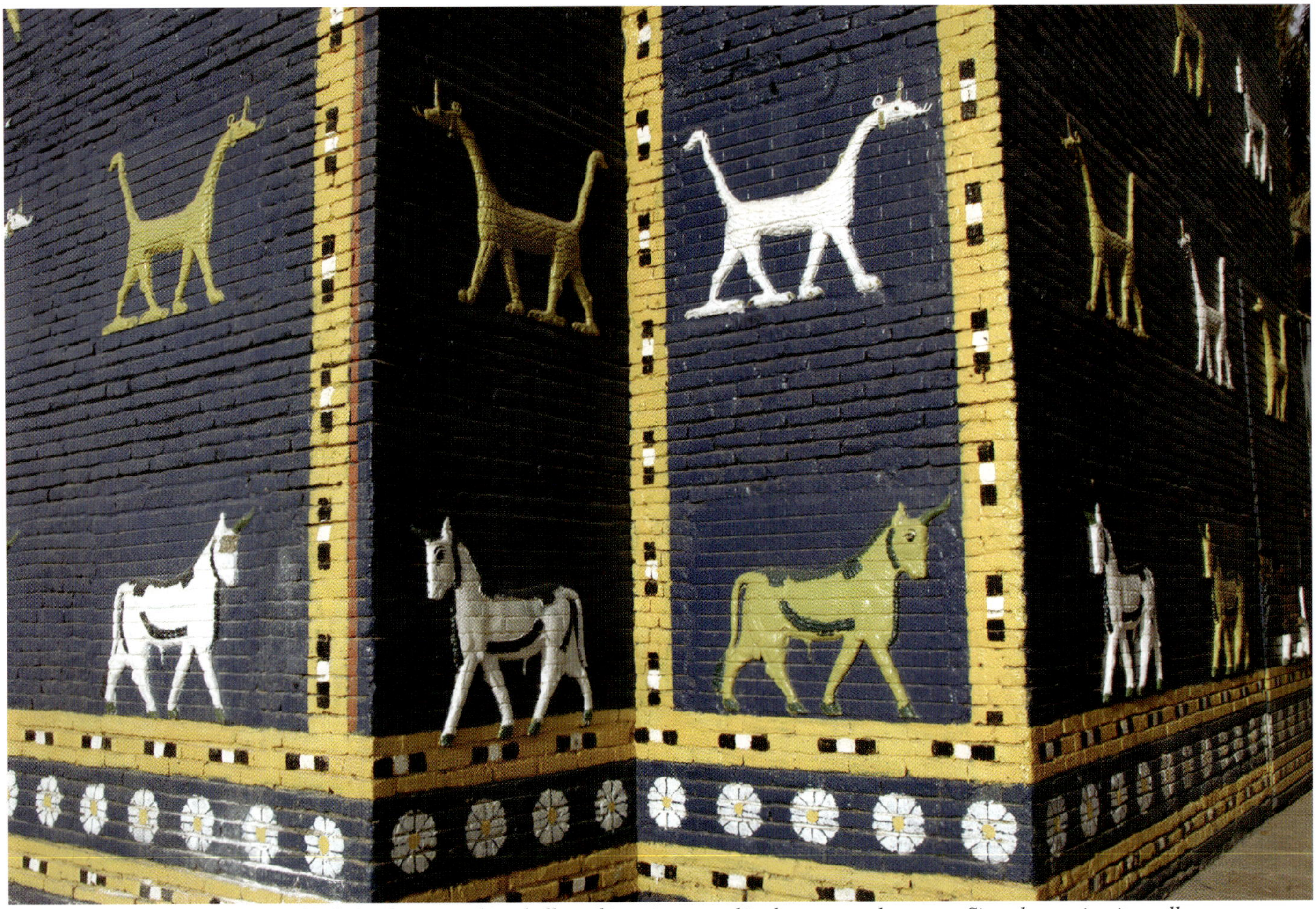

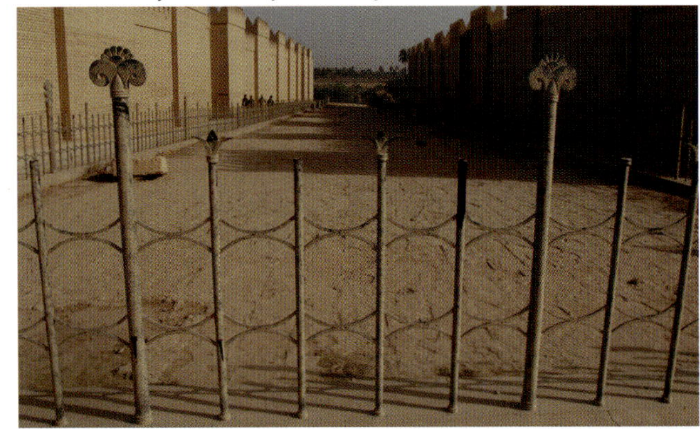

The Ishtar Gates of Babylon have marching bulls and imaginary mythical creatures, known as Sirrush, gracing its walls

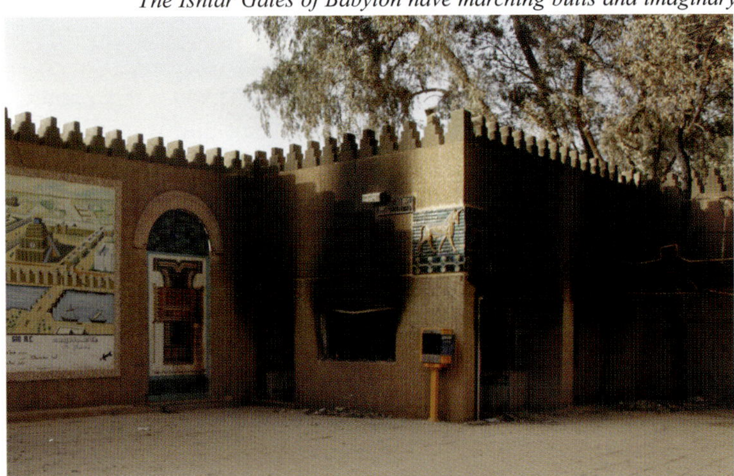

The souvenir shop has been looted and set ablaze

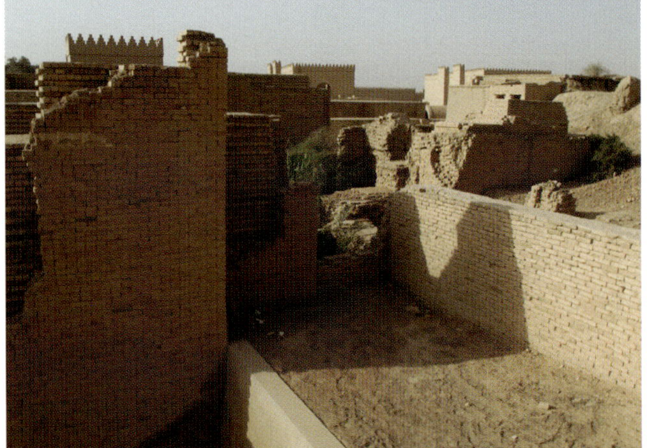

Babylon is a layer cake of ancient civilizations

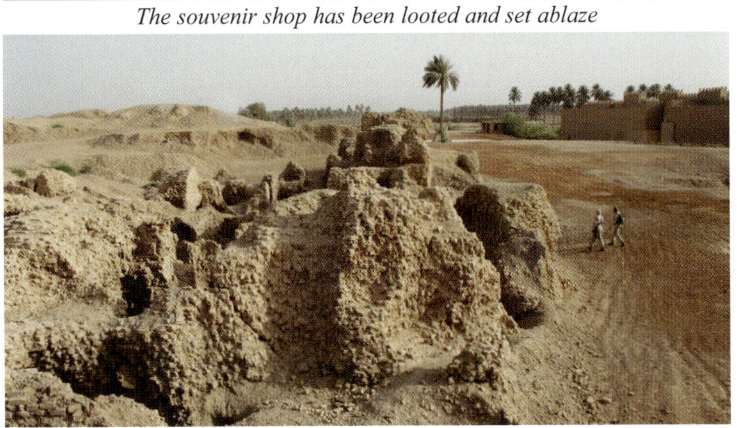

U.S. soldiers walk amongst the crumbling ruins outside the walled city

Plaza near the fabled Hanging Gardens of Babylon

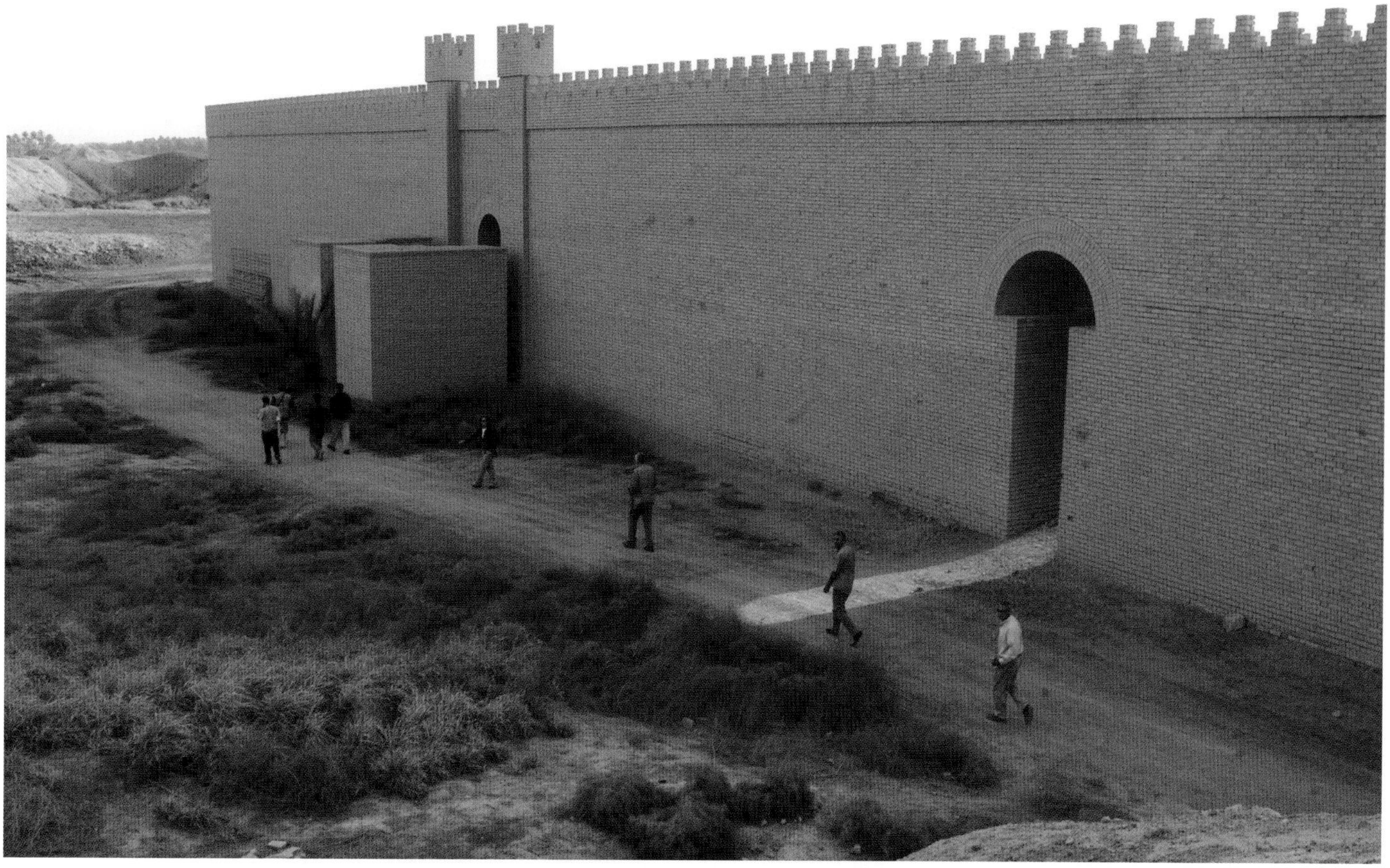

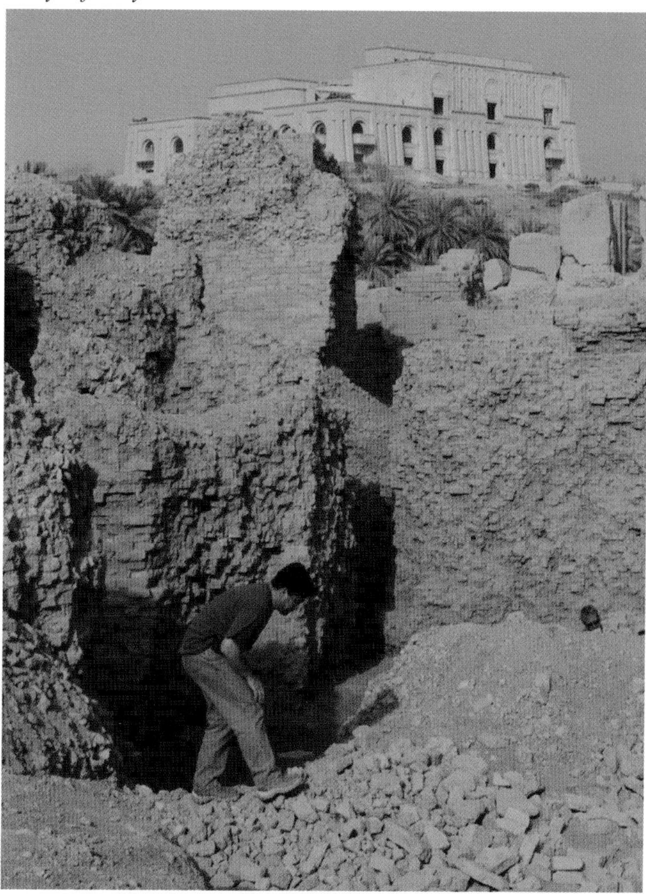

View of the east wall and gateways of Babylon

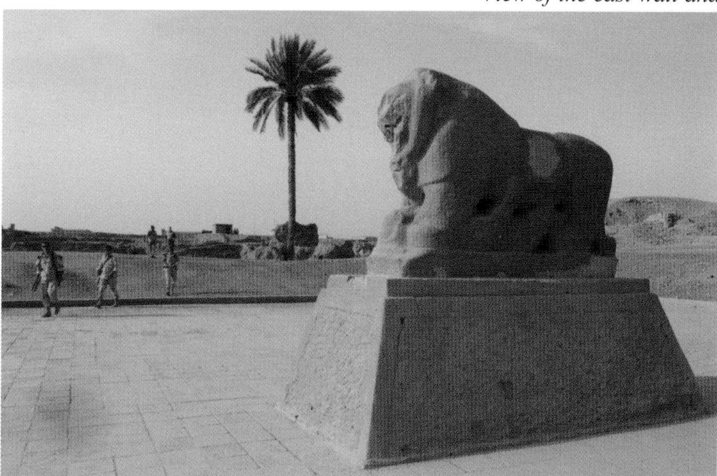

A Lion of Baghdad looks disdainfully at passing American troops

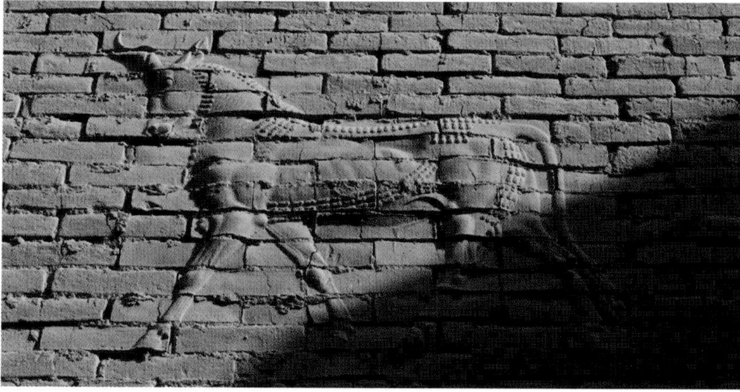

Relief of a mythical bull of Baghdad. These simple art forms are stunning

Saddam's palace rises above the ruins of Babylon

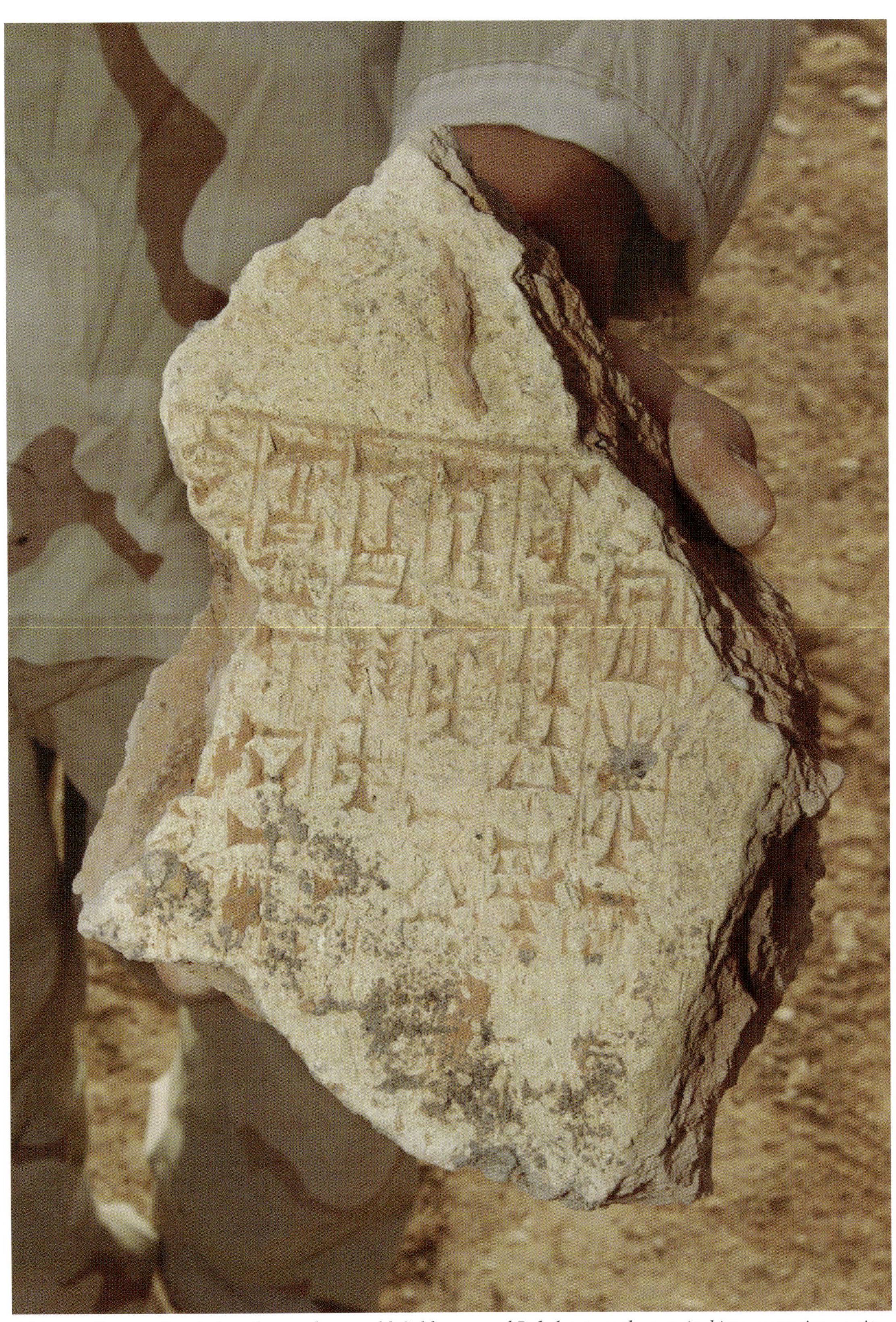

This cuneiform writing is four thousand years old. Soldiers guard Babylon to make sure its history remains on site

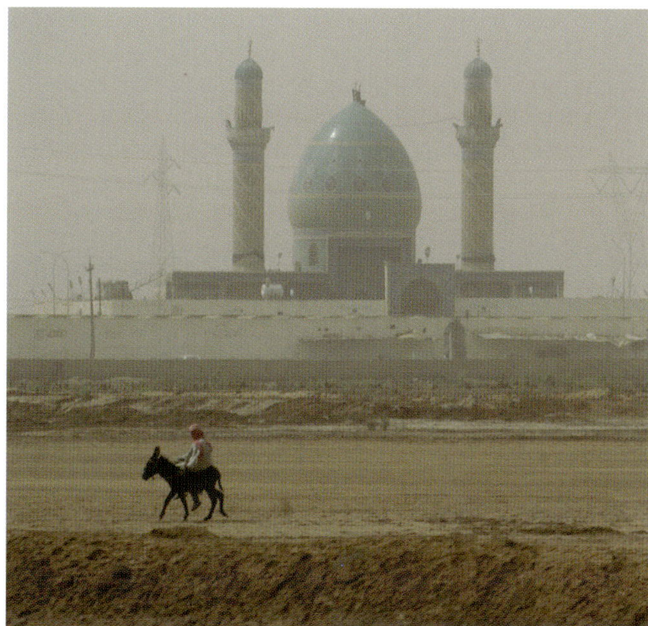

Scene near Najaf

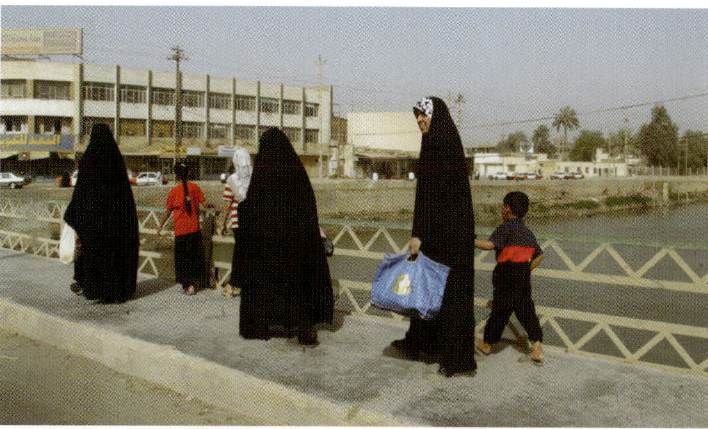

Bridge across the Euphrates River in Najaf

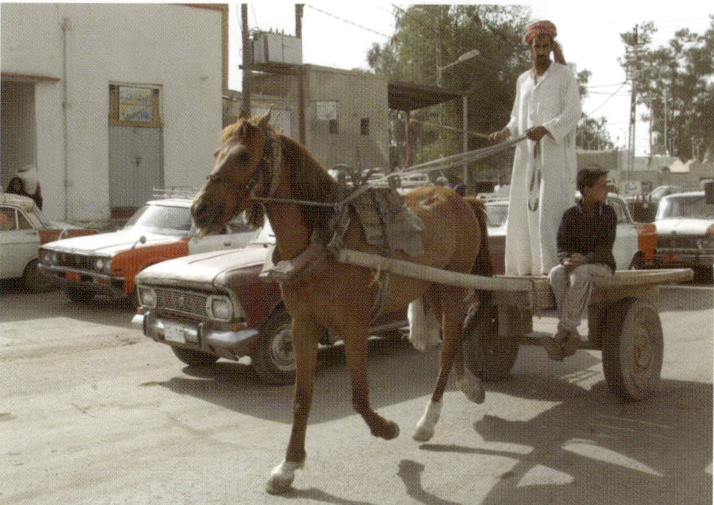

Horse and buggy in downtown Najaf

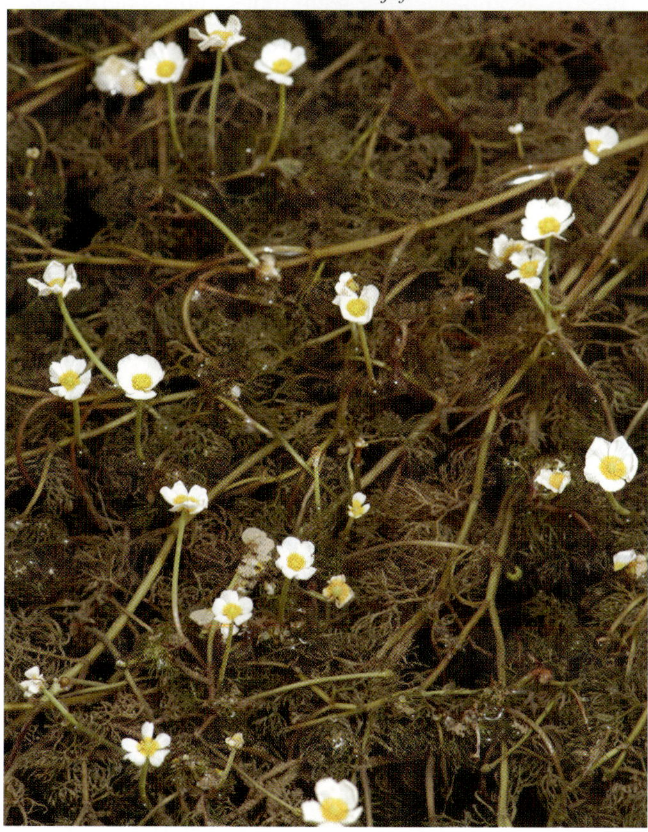

Water plants prosper in a roadside ditch

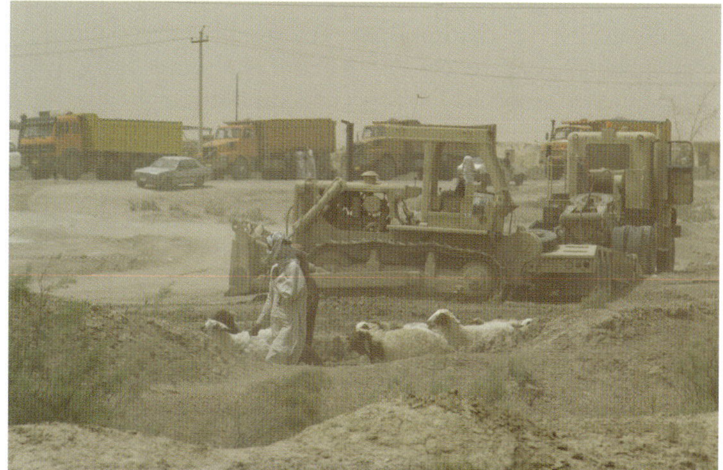

The sinister heat and wind cook those who venture from cover

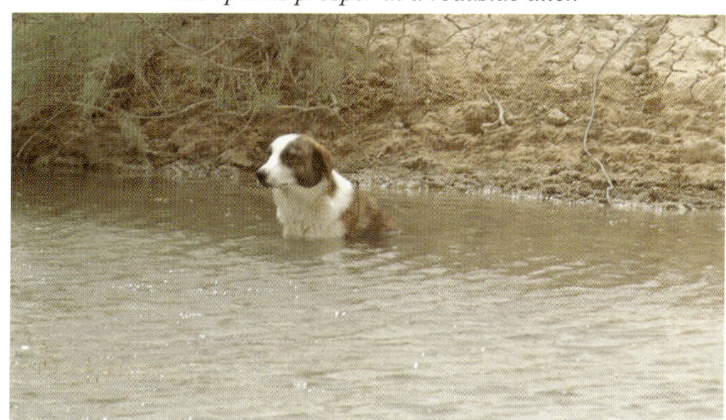

Dog takes a cooling soak in an irrigation ditch

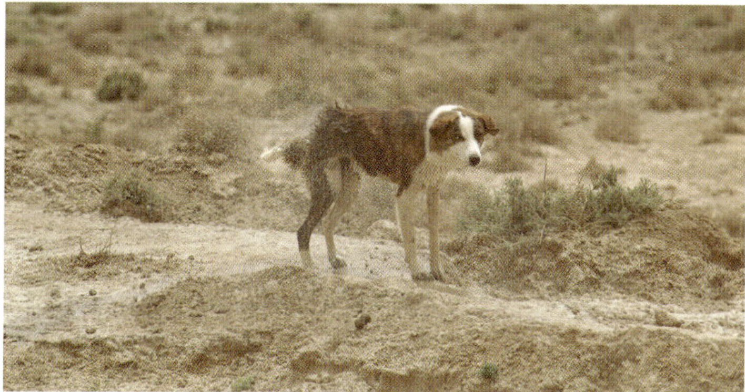

Shaking off the water

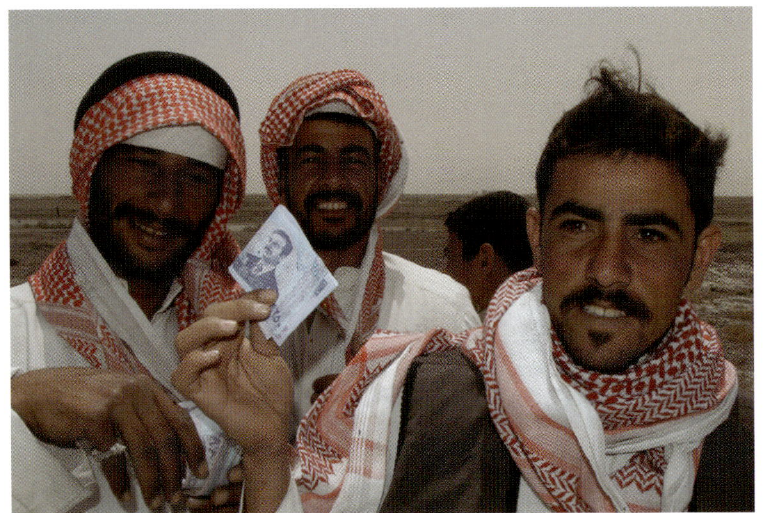

Money exchangers work the side of the highway

The wind is relentless and cutting, and we eat our snacks while trying to avoid getting sand into them. I brought along a couple of MREs, and share them with my friends. It is a little MRE buffet picnic in one of the most inhospitable areas I have ever visited.

Shortly after getting underway, we pull over to repair a flat tire on the second Jimmy. A mile-long convoy of military supplies head north on the other side of the highway. It transports supplies from the port City of Umm Qasr in Kuwait, to Baghdad.

There are farmers working along the Euphrates River floodplains near Jalibah, gathering golden sheaves of hand-cut wheat from their fields and carrying them to a waiting donkey cart. Others are using scythes to cut the grain by hand, grabbing an armful of standing wheat and slashing it with the curved knife. A half a mile down the highway, another farmer harvests his crop with a modern, diesel grain harvester (like those used in the prairies of North America). This machine, so familiar and a standard part of harvesting back home, cuts the plant and separates the grain. It is the meeting of ancient bronze-aged harvesting techniques and modern technology separated by a distance of less than a mile.

Hoping to take a side trip to Basra, we are running out of time and have to continue on. The conditions outside the vehicle are almost unliveable. To be left to die in this sea of burning, blowing sand, would be a horrible death, much worse than freezing to death. I would rather choose death by ice, than fire.

During the drive we sing Beatles and Rolling Stones songs to pass the time, but the day drags on. An hour before the Iraq-Kuwait border, someone mentions something about having your visas and passports ready at the border. I think for a second, "Visa? What Visa? There won't be a problem," I say to myself. I drop the concern from my head.

Approaching the Iraq-Kuwait border, we slow the vehicles to a crawl as we get within 100 feet of the border checkpoint. Suddenly, the back doors of our Jimmy are flung open. Two pre-teen boys have opened the doors and are stealing our luggage from the back of the Jimmy, while we are seated up front. We clue into what is happening, and hastily jump out of the Jimmy, chasing after the two punks. They immediately drop the suitcases and dart into the desert wasteland.

We pack it all back into the Jimmy, as the boys watch like jackals from a safe distance. But these two boys are not alone. There is a gang of other boys and older men who are lined up just

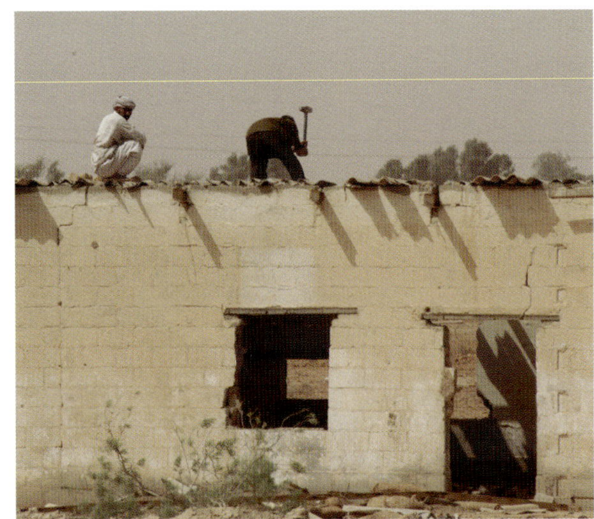

Men loot the tiles from the roof of a destroyed building

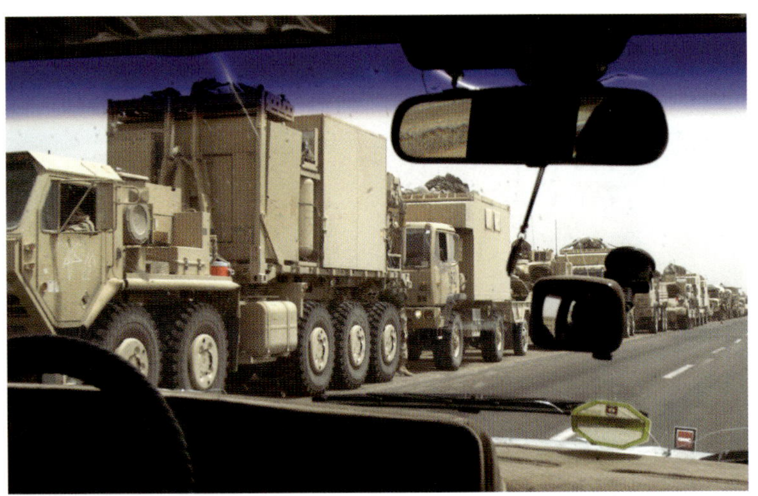

American supply convoy heads north from the Kuwaiti port of Umm Qasr

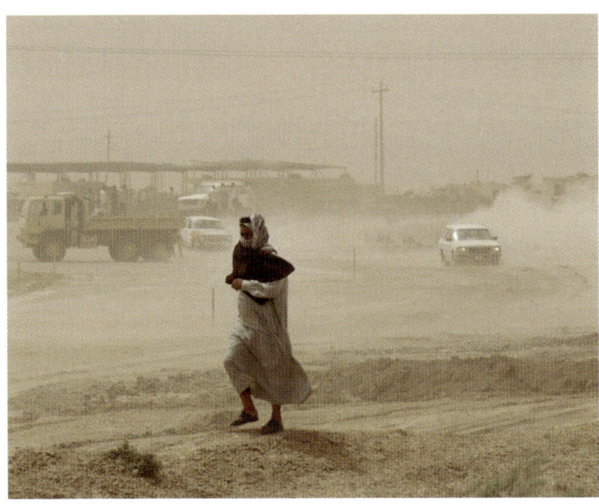

The talcum powder-like dust fills your pores and lungs

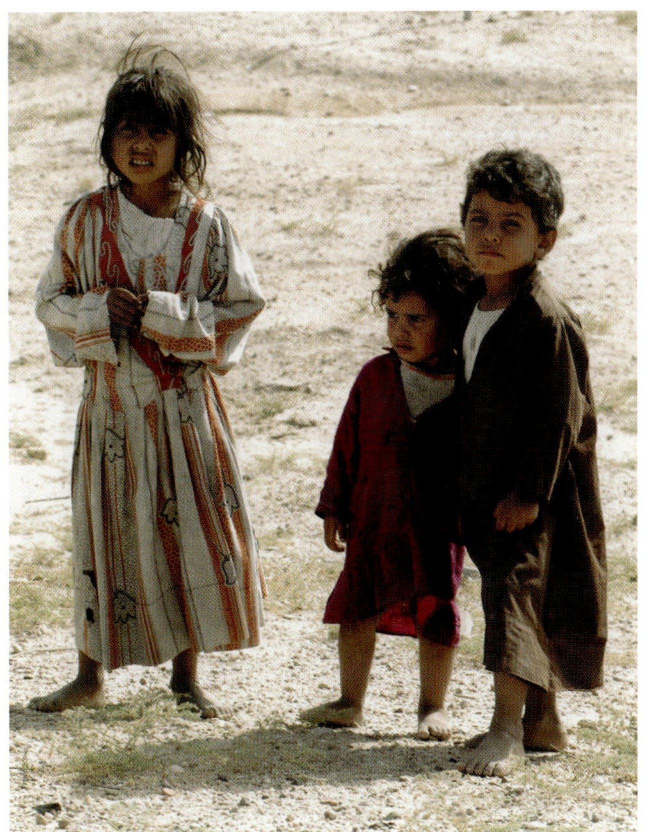

Children watch the traffic pass by near Al Nasiriyah

before the border. They beg from the roadside, while waiting for an opportunity to rip-off some unsuspecting voyager. We were being robbed less than 100 feet from the Kuwait border.

It is a scene of lawlessness, hopelessness and anguish, strung out along a quarter-mile frontier of sweltering sand and biting winds. On the Iraqi side of the border, a nation survives by the skin of its teeth; on the Kuwaiti side, a modern country of computers and vast material riches watches the downfall of their hated enemy Iraq. Iraq invaded Kuwait in 1991, but were eventually beaten back across the border. Kuwait's hatred of Iraq is not without reason, nor is their desire for revenge. There are always two sides to every story, and only the ignorant or naive listen with one ear open. Journalism is not just a job; it is about listening and separating truth from fiction and emotional knee-jerk reaction. And we are always learning.

We drive the last 100 feet and stop at the first of two Kuwaiti checkpoints. We step out of our vehicles and are ushered into a small trailer office where an official for the Kuwaiti Ministry of Information asks for our visas and passports.

He sits at a wooden desk, dressed in a white gown and headdress encircled by a black band. Thumbing through the documents he then hands them to two other white robed men, who ferry all our passports and visas from the office to another next door, where they photocopy the documents. A young boy, tucked in a corner of the office, offers us tea from a large cooler-sized chrome thermos. I drink down three glasses while smoking a bottomless package of Marlboros. I am not too worried about not having a visa; Kuwait is a modern nation, plus I was here in 1991 covering Operation Desert Storm. So I shouldn't have much of a problem. Hopefully it's just like Jordan, pay a few bucks and get a stamp.

Everyone passes scrutiny except for me. The stone-faced official, sipping his tea and smoking cheap cigarettes, grills me about why I don't have a visa. I tell him the truth, "I didn't know I needed to get one before I arrived at the border and I wouldn't have known where to get one had I known. I just yesterday decided on coming here." (Iraq is a war-ravaged country with no electrical power, telephones or government). In Jordan they gave me an entrance visa right at the airport, with no advance preparation.

I tell him about my time in Kuwait in 1991 as a journalist, covering the suffering of the Kuwaiti people. I show him my Desert Storm media press pass, issued by the American Armed Forces in 1991, in Riyhad, Saudi Arabia. But this is all irrelevant to the agent, who seems to be enjoying my discomfort. He is unconcerned that I am in Kuwait to cure my war fatigue, nightmares, hunger and a lack of sleep. I tell him I am just looking for a little compassion so I can get the rest I need.

It is as though everything before today never really happened to this man; no past, no tomorrow – just today! The Kuwaitis appear to have forgotten who their allies are, and that people from my country put their lives on the line for this nation in 1991. It is a personal insult to myself, the country I call home, and the Canadian men and women who risked their lives to protect this country.

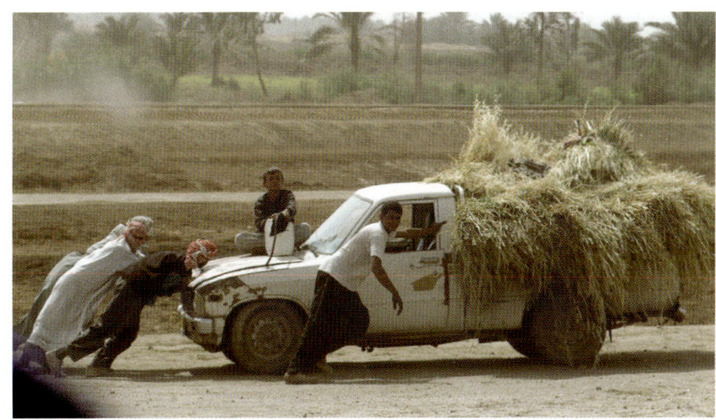

Truck makes a good push cart for a load of hay

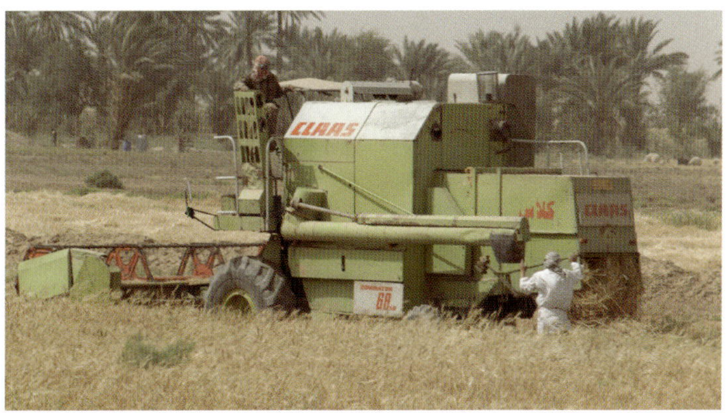

A combine harvester cuts grain

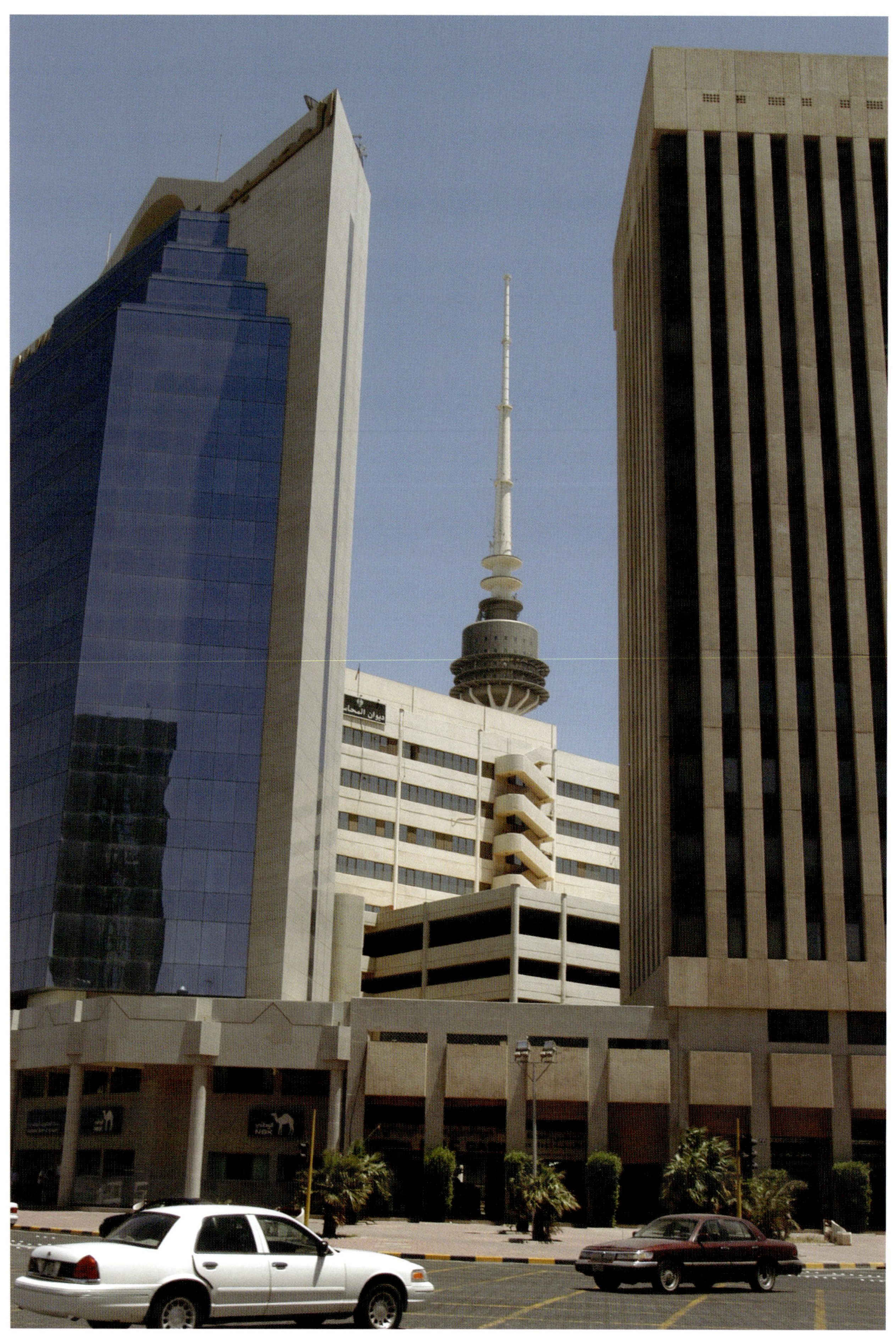

The modern metropolis of Kuwait is a jewel in the desert

I sip the boy's sweet tea, while trying to keep my wits about me. Speaking in a low, controlled, and polite tone, I try to reason with him, telling him that I realize my mistake about the proper channels for the visa, but there is a war going on, and I am at the breaking point of exhaustion from covering it.

Perhaps I should just turn around and go back to Baghdad, but that is out of the question. I am much too exhausted to even think at this moment. I am hurting bad. Surely the whole nation cannot be like this guy! He must think that I am some sort of threat to national security, but I am carrying my world on my back; how can I be a threat?

The man threatens to hold me overnight in a makeshift chamber. I tell him I would rather not spend the evening in a jail cell. At my saying the words 'jail cell,' the bureaucrat stumbles over himself trying to tell me and my colleagues, who are present, that it is not a jail cell, but a separate room at the back of this office. This threat changes my colleague's attitudes towards the official, from one of polite accommodation, to that of anger and urgency. There is much back-tracking by the official, who now seems to realize that he is not a deity and this time he might have bitten off more than he can chew.

I ask to borrow a satellite phone to call my wife. I tell her I am to be held in a Kuwaiti prison (making sure everyone in the room overhears what I am saying). I speak to her with sobbing words, in an attempt to try to butter up or break down the official. It is all part of the show of trying to get free of this shack and the bulldog behind the desk.

After two hours of sitting in the company of this arrogant, bullying clown, and having been put through his bureaucratic meat grinder, I get the green light to go on to Kuwait City with the rest of the crew. The official tells me that I must remain in Kuwait, and I need to get a visa and press accreditation at the Ministry of Immigration in Kuwait before leaving the country. He gives me a letter of introduction to present to the Immigration Ministry in Kuwait City. He holds onto my British passport, and that of Keith Rigby, a security officer for NBC who met the crew at the border and is interceding on my behalf. He tells us our passports are to be forwarded to the Immigration Ministry and will be waiting there for us in the morning. Without your passport, you are basically under house arrest, being unable to leave the country, or even withdraw money from a bank.

Keith, a retired member of the British Special Forces, helped save me from spending the night at the border by his intervention. I feel terrible that my companions had to wait two hours while my situation unfolded. Despite the gruelling 10-hour car journey, everyone is patient and supportive at the border, considering the circumstances.

We all climb into our vehicles and drive 300 feet to the second checkpoint. It is manned by three AK-47-clenching Kuwaiti soldiers. They search our baggage for contraband and find that Julie has a two-litre bottle of champagne hidden in one of her bags. The smiling soldier smashes it over some rocks, and hands the broken foil-covered top of the bottle to Julie. "Alcohol is not allowed in Kuwait," the crisply dressed soldier informs her.

The soldier insists on confiscating Steve's Iraqi war helmet, a souvenir that Steve wants to take home to the States. But he has had enough of this pettiness and tells the guard he is not leaving the border until he is allowed to bring his helmet with him.

Another half-hour passes as Steve tries to reason with the soldier. Finally, the soldier relents and lets Steve keep the helmet, telling him to keep it hidden. This frivolity is ridiculous beyond sane comprehension. I imagine these skirmishes with journalists are about the only action these soldiers ever see. They stand on guard, ready to protect their nation against war-fatigued journalists and souvenir smuggling newsmen.

We finally get under way and drive on to Kuwait City, an hour-and-a-half further down the road. Julie reaches into her baggage and pulls out another bottle she had hidden in the center of an extension cord bundle. We all laugh. We pass the bluffs where in 1991, I photographed the 'Highway To Death' massacre, but it is too dark to see. It takes over twelve hours of travel and delay to reach Kuwait City.

Pulling up to the glitzy Sheraton Hotel, I step out of the Jimmy and onto the red carpet winding across the polished marble floor to the reception desk. It seems like a royal palace, a dream. As I stand in the hotel reception line, a hostess comes over and offers me some freshly squeezed orange juice and fresh dates. I still have my plastic bottle of water clutched in my hands. Taking a glass, I drink down the cool, velvety orange juice. I can feel it go down, all the way to my toes. After completing my registration I am given the key to room # 959, at $120 a night.

It is a shock to the system to see, and be back in, a relatively familiar western setting. Silk tied businessmen in thousand-dollar suits chat on cell phones and drink from champagne goblets while enveloped in lush lobby couches. Impeccably dressed staff cart baggage from the reception area to the elevators. The place is abuzz, and I welcome the richness and opulence of the gold and marble that surround me.

I sink down into one of the lobby couches, and light up a Marlboro, while absorbing the pulse of normality going on about me. I feel as though I just stepped off a time machine. But I am starting to quickly unwind, knowing I am safe and away from the stresses of war photojournalism.

A tall slim man in his mid-forties comes over and starts to speak to me. He tells me his name is Tim Carlson, a journalist working for Lyons Publishing, out of L.A. Tim is documenting a book to be published on journalists during war. He asks if he can have a few words with me about my experiences in Iraq. I ask him to have a seat beside me, but warn him that I am a complete basket case, physically and mentally, and might seem somewhat incoherent. He apologizes for his intrusion but says it will take but a few minutes.

Tim takes a photograph of me slouched in the couch, then I offer him a brief explanation of what I have seen and done to cover the story and survive the adverse conditions in Baghdad. He is a soft-spoken kind man, with compassionate eyes. After about fifteen minutes he thanks me, then disappears into the bustle of the hotel activity. I head up to my room to grab a shower and a change of clothes before meeting the NBC people for dinner in the sixth floor executive lounge.

The lounge is laid out with deep couches and vases of flowers decorating the glass coffee and end tables, each of which has a bowl of delicious mixed nuts sitting upon it. Richly hung drapes cover the windows. A huge flat screen television rests in one corner beside a stall with two PCs and a printer available for the guests' use. Another section of the lounge has glass-topped counters, where a variety of snack foods and exotic fruits and chocolates are spread. It is high quality snob food, especially the chocolates, which include truffles. The hostess brings me a deep, foamy cappuccino with chocolate sprinkles.

What a difference a few hours can make. I feel like the guy in the old American Express television ads. The one where the marooned boater gets washed ashore in a rubber raft, with only his credit card in his torn pants pocket. A short time after, he reappears, tailored like James Bond and sipping brandy from a snifter in the hotel lounge. All thanks to the credit card.

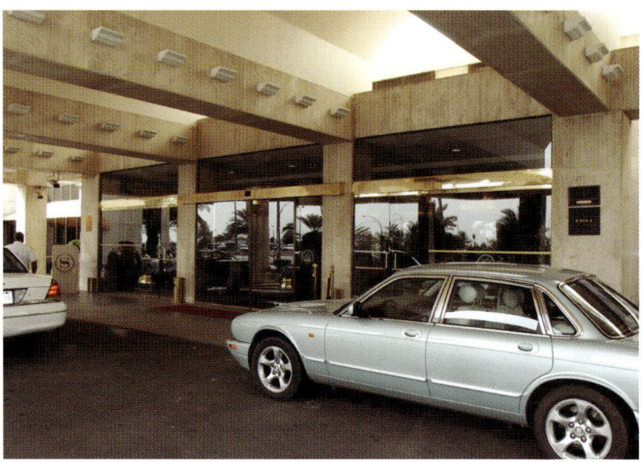
Entrance to the Sheraton. It is a very elegant hotel

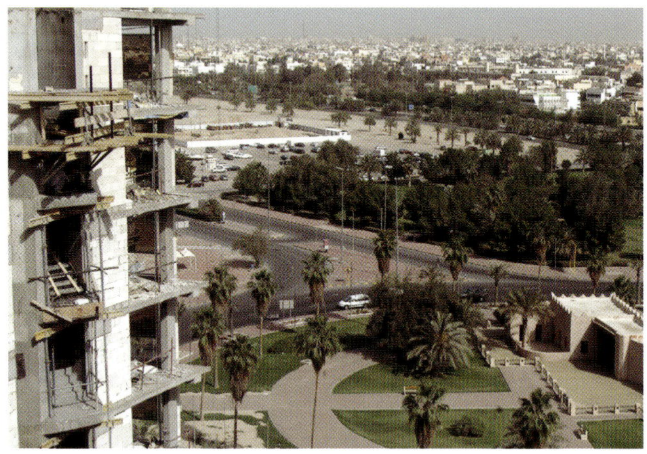
Kuwait City

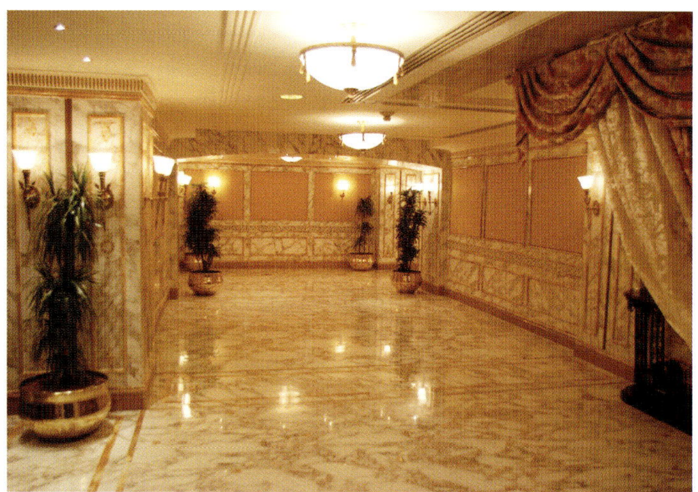
Lobby of the Kuwait Sheraton

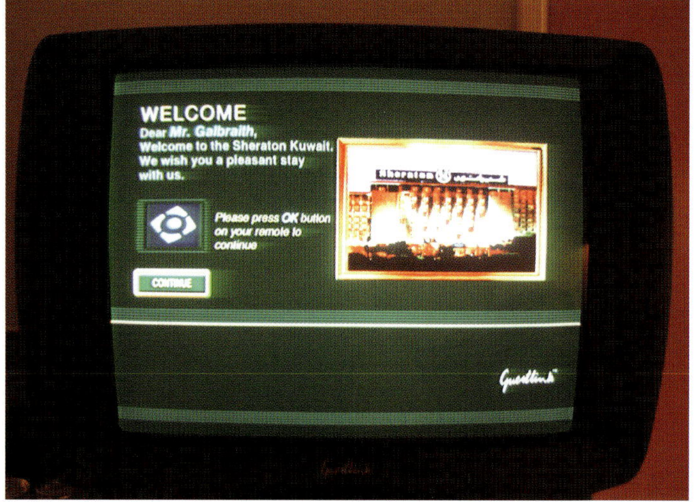

It's nice to feel welcome

After eating my way through the snack foods and drinking two large cappuccinos, I head back to my room. I grab a CD with the eight images on it that I need to send to the *Houston Chronicle*, and then head downstairs to the computer room, a small office off the lobby, to e-mail the images. The pics are to accompany John Otis' story, featuring upstart political parties in Baghdad. These include the Communist Party, amongst others. The feature is to run Sunday, so I have adequate time to send them for early layout in Houston.

The computer centre has eight PCs, printers and a photocopy machine. The manager works behind a counter, faxing and keeping track of the names and room numbers of the guests using the systems.

Asking the manager's help, I send my first e-mail with a small sized photo attachment. I send five more, back-to-back in separate e-mails. After this, I wait to make sure that all sent images are received, but the mails have all been returned and do not appear to be landing in Houston. An MSN message appears on my returned mails describing: Mail System Error – Check to make sure the destination address was spelled correctly. I check and re-check the addresses, they are all correct. I resend them, only to have them returned again.

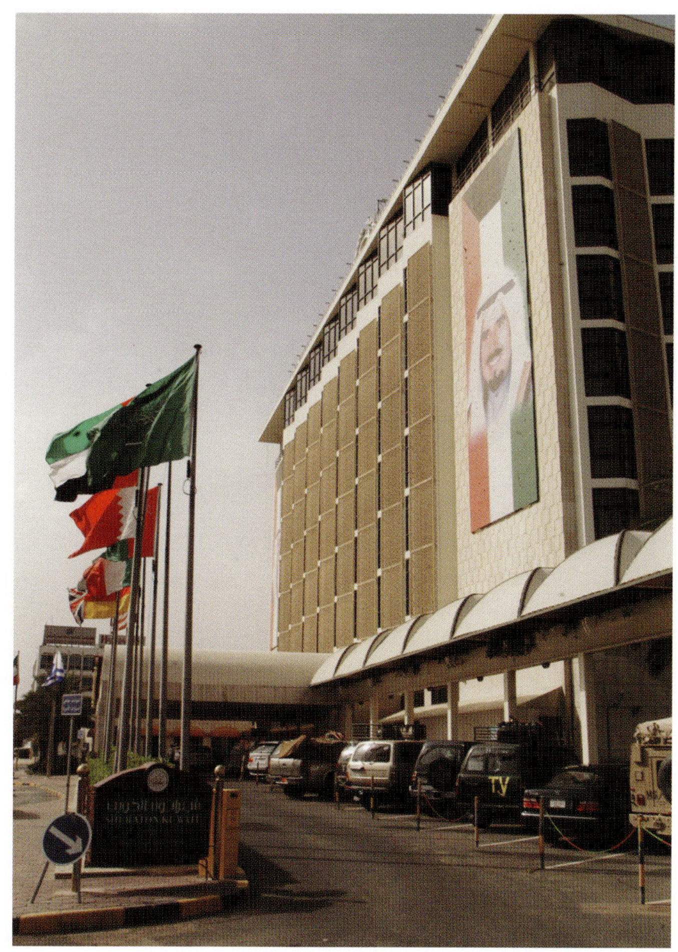

Kuwait Sheraton Hotel

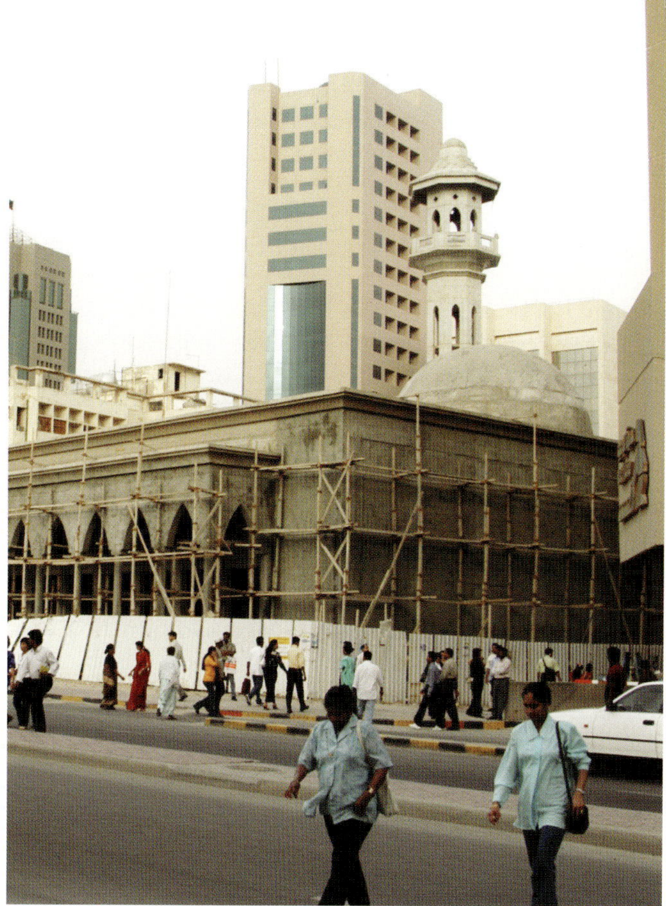

Kuwait has a large population of foreign workers

I am using the same e-mail (Hotmail and Yahoo) addresses that I successfully used a couple of days earlier in Baghdad, without any problems (by satellite from Baghdad). So I am baffled, and ask the manager if he has any suggestions. He replies, "There may be a glitch in the power system or network. Try it a little later."

So I go out and grab a sandwich at a local neon-drenched, take-out diner. Sitting outside, I watch the night traffic stream by. People pull their cars up to the sidewalk facing the grill, and a waiter runs over to take the orders. It's like American Graffiti, without the roller skates. There is a steady bustle of healthy tanned people in nice cars. You don't see any junk heaps on the streets of Kuwait; it is the land of Mercedes and Lexus.

Around 11 p.m., I return to the computer office and ask to speak with the hotel computer technician. We try to send the messages on a different computer, and then try using the technician's server, but that also fails. I play around trying to troubleshoot the problem, but it is nearly 4 a.m. and I am losing my strength.

I place a phone call to the *Houston Chronicle*, explaining my problem to the photo desk. They tell me their system is operating without problems and to try my best to get the photos through. They will be keeping an eye out for them. I phone my wife and let her know my present status, and the problems with the e-mail.

Perplexed with the network, and strung out on coffee and pistachio cookies, I head upstairs to have a bath and go to bed. I have been looking forward to a bath ever since my arrival in Iraq. It has been the longest day, and I have pushed myself to complete exhaustion. I lie in bed, concerned that the pics have not gotten through and knowing I cannot completely relax until they land in Houston.

I awaken at 7 a.m., and go downstairs to the computer room to try transmitting the picks again. But I have no luck and return to bed, thinking there should not be a problem later in the morning, and that the returned mails are just an inconvenient and untimely hitch.

Day 17. Saturday, April 26th

(A difficult sleep; my first full day in Kuwait; breakfast in the lounge; messages blocked?; meeting Yakoob from the Ministry of Information; Kuwaiti journalist Nora Dandashi; Yakoob wants copies of my photographs; I meet Rashid; going shopping with Rashid; avoiding the heat of Kuwait; living like a vampire; the Immigration Ministry; staying at the Plaza Hotel with my Canadian passport; no luck sending my e-mails from the Plaza computer)

I am awake at 9 a.m., after a difficult sleep. It is my first full day in Kuwait, and after eating a rich breakfast in the lounge I go down to the computer center to transmit my pics, but I get the same returned mails. I try on the manager's account but it also fails, then I try Yahoo (rather than Hotmail), but the same thing. No one seems to know why the messages aren't getting through. Not even simple text messages seem to be getting through.

I notice that there is a media office near the main lobby stairwell, so I go in to see what it offers. It is a small narrow room with a large table running down one side where two white-robed Kuwaitis sit working on computers. On another table, two large coffee percolators and an assortment of biscuits and dry sandwiches are all but inedible decorations. A large corkboard by the doorway has notes and notices stapled to it. This is the office where the media need to report for exit visas and a Kuwaiti press pass (which you need, even if you are not working as a journalist here). I need the visa and the press pass before I will be allowed to leave the country. It should only take a day or so, I would imagine.

One of the men behind the table introduces himself as Mr. Ya'aqoub A. A. Abdullah, a foreign media researcher with the Kuwait Ministry of Information's International Media Department. Mr. Abdullah (who goes by the nick-name Yakoob) runs the Sheraton-based Media Information Press Office.

We exchange courtesies and then he asks me about the situation in Iraq, and where I have been. A journalist named Nora Dandashi, (working for Kuwaiti newspaper publisher Dar Al Seyassah, who publish the Arabic Daily, English Daily, and the Arabic Weekly) asks if I would mind if she took some notes. She is interested in doing a story on my coverage of Iraq. Yakoob, Nora and a young western-dressed Kuwaiti man of about 22 years old (who had just dropped in to the office) sit around drinking coffee and listening to my adventures. The discussion goes on for about 30 minutes. I tell them I have taken thousands of photos for my book, and give them a small viewing of some of the pics on my laptop.

Yakoob is shocked but thankful for seeing the images, and asks me if he could get some copies of the CDs from me, as his government has nothing showing what it is really like in Iraq. He says the photos would be used in newsletters and small intergovernmental publications. I tell him it shouldn't be a problem, and I will give him some CDs before I leave Kuwait. Nora, the Kuwaiti journalist leaves the press office, thanking me for the interview and for making her

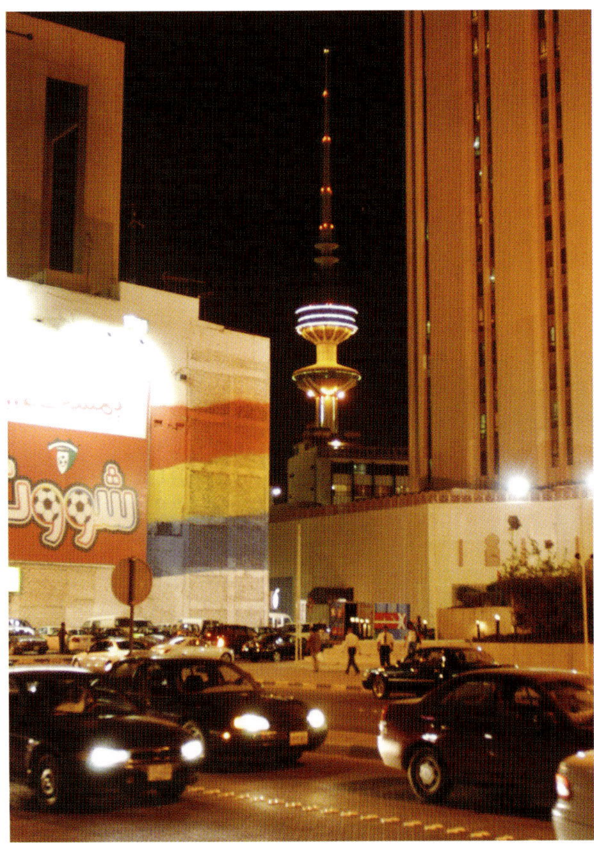

People fill the streets of downtown after the sun has set

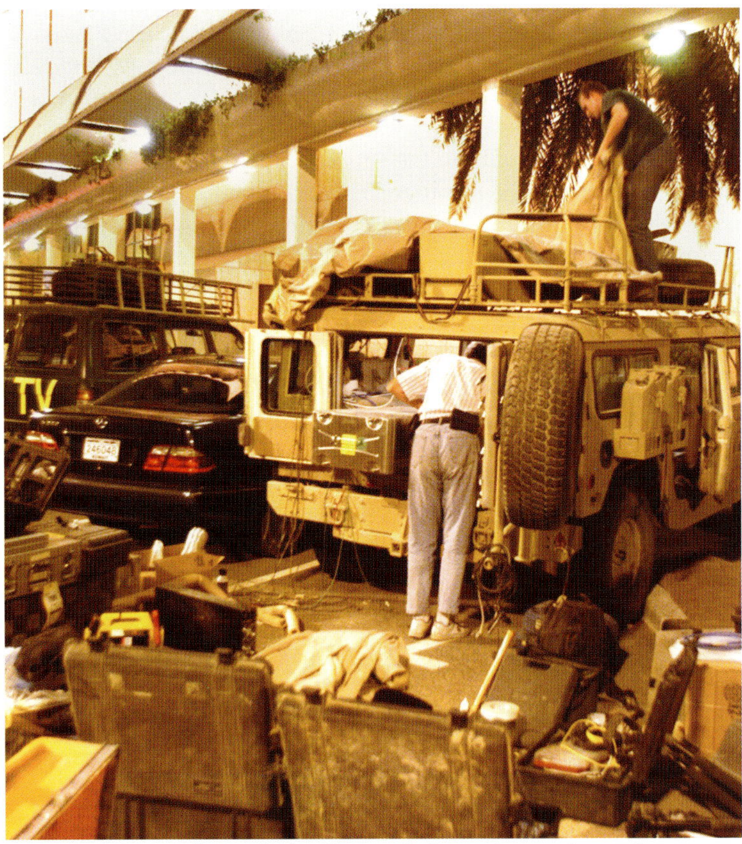

A journalist packs his Humvee before going on the road

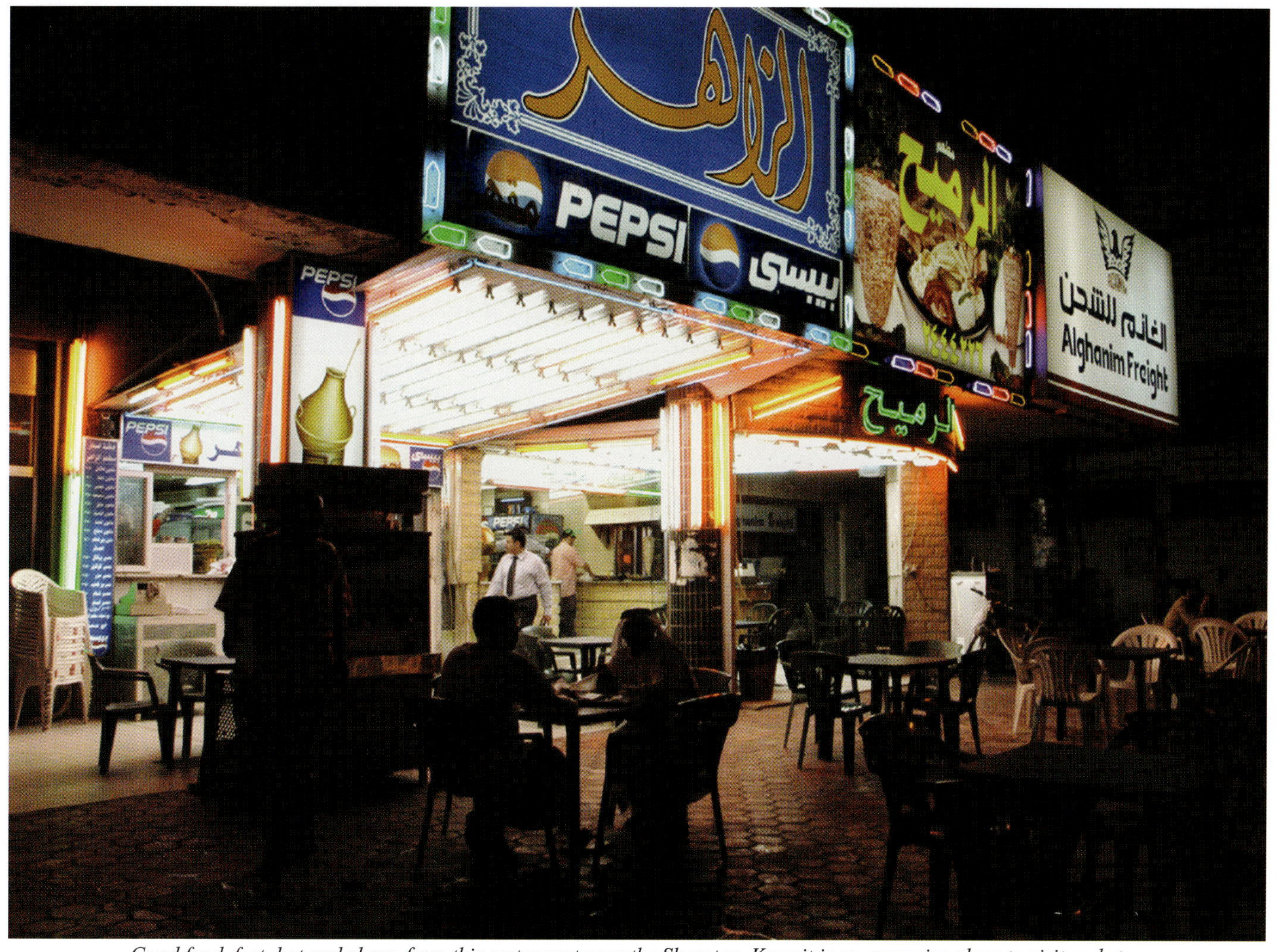

Good food, fast, hot and cheap from this restaurant near the Sheraton. Kuwait is an expensive place to visit and stay

aware of the situation in Iraq. All three are very friendly, and I take an immediate liking to Yakoob, Nora and the young man. Yakoob informs me that Mr. Rigby and I should bring my letter, which I received at the border, to the Immigration Ministry to get my visa process started.

Yakoob says he will get hold of Mr. Rigby and meet me in the office in an hour. I ask where I can find a photography shop to get my camera repaired. He waves over the young Arab man, (who had listened in on my account of Iraq). His name is Rashid, an employee for the Ministry of Information. His job could be compared to that of a copy boy in a news-room; (he's a gofer).

Rashid takes me to the camera shop, just around the corner from the Sheraton. After 30 minutes my camera is cleaned and my camera's hot shoe repaired. Rashid helps me find a bank to get some money withdrawn from my account. I cannot withdraw funds because I need a passport to carry out the transaction, and the Immigration Ministry still has mine. As an employee of the ministry, he must carry some clout as he clears the way for me to withdraw cash without a passport.

There is something weird about Rashid that I cannot seem to put my finger on. He is starting to become a little too accommodating (brown-nosing), while asking an increasing number of personal questions. Maybe I'm a little paranoid, but there seems to be something fishy about the guy.

Shopping in Kuwait is an experience. Going from the street (where the temperature hovers between 90 and 100 degrees) and into the air-conditioned shops and malls can give you a headache and a runny nose. Most Kuwaitis go from their air-conditioned homes, into their air-conditioned car, and then to air-conditioned shops and work places. The reverse is true in Montreal during the winter, when residents try to escape the mind-numbing cold by living in their climate-controlled world, while shopping in a network of miles of heated underground malls. I personally love the extremes of heat and cold, and try to live with them rather than fight them. But in Kuwait I am living like a vampire, ducking into air-conditioned shops and using the cover of storefront canopies to avoid exposure to the brutal heat of the asphalt and glaring sun.

Keith Rigby and I drive to the Ministry of Immigration to get our passports, and a letter, which I need to finish the processing of my visa and press pass. After an hour of being shuffled about from office to office, our passports are

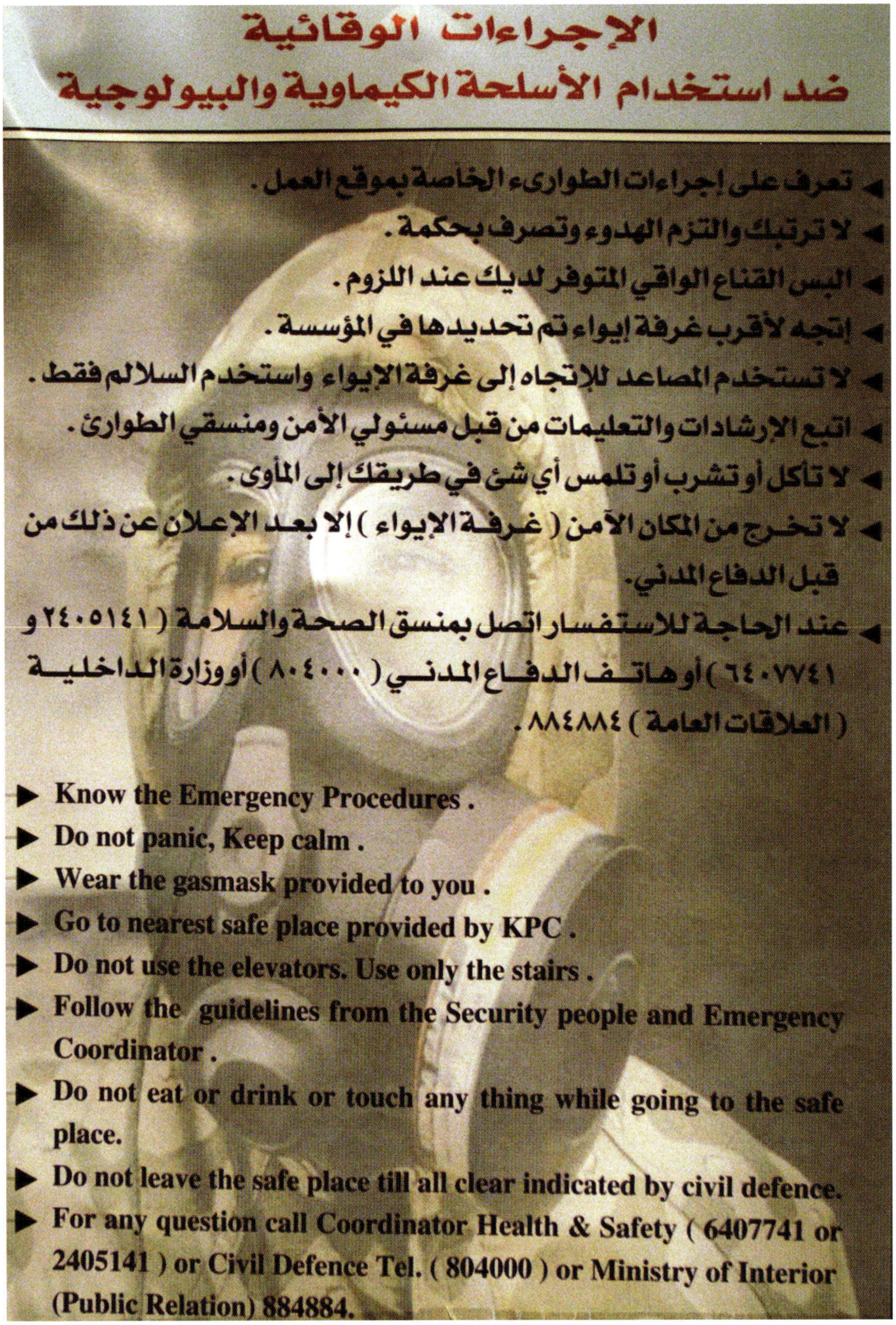

الإجراءات الوقائية
ضد استخدام الأسلحة الكيماوية والبيولوجية

◄ تعرف على إجراءات الطوارىء الخاصة بموقع العمل .

◄ لا ترتبك والتزم الهدوء وتصرف بحكمة .

◄ البس القناع الواقي المتوفر لديك عند اللزوم .

◄ إتجه لأقرب غرفة إيواء تم تحديدها في المؤسسة .

◄ لا تستخدم المصاعد للإتجاه إلى غرفة الإيواء واستخدم السلالم فقط .

◄ اتبع الإرشادات والتعليمات من قبل مسئولي الأمن ومنسقي الطوارئ .

◄ لا تأكل أوتشرب أوتلمس أي شئ في طريقك إلى المأوى .

◄ لا تخرج من المكان الآمن ((غرفة الإيواء)) إلا بعد الإعلان عن ذلك من قبل الدفاع المدني.

◄ عند الحاجة للاستفسار اتصل بمنسق الصحة والسلامة (٢٤٠٥١٤١ و ٦٤٠٧٧٤١) أو هاتف الدفاع المدني (٨٠٤٠٠٠) أو وزارة الداخلية (العلاقات العامة) ٨٨٤٨٨٤ .

▶ **Know the Emergency Procedures .**

▶ **Do not panic, Keep calm .**

▶ **Wear the gasmask provided to you .**

▶ **Go to nearest safe place provided by KPC .**

▶ **Do not use the elevators. Use only the stairs .**

▶ **Follow the guidelines from the Security people and Emergency Coordinator .**

▶ **Do not eat or drink or touch any thing while going to the safe place.**

▶ **Do not leave the safe place till all clear indicated by civil defence.**

▶ **For any question call Coordinator Health & Safety (6407741 or 2405141) or Civil Defence Tel. (804000) or Ministry of Interior (Public Relation) 884884.**

Instructions in case of a gas attack on the wall of a shopping center in downtown Kuwait City

returned to us. I am also given the letter to present to Yakoob, saying I passed immigration. Returning to the Sheraton, I give Yakoob my passport and the letter. He tells me to come back at 4 p.m., to see how the visa is progressing. I tell him I am having some trouble transmitting my pics, but I should be able to resolve it.

Worried about the network problems at the Sheraton, I decide to try again around 4 p.m. If it doesn't work at 4, then I will move out of the Sheraton and check in to the Kuwait Plaza Hotel, located a couple of blocks away from the Sheraton. I hope to be abler to transmit from the Plaza without any problems. If I fail to get my pics through to Houston, I will lose a thousand dollars, and leave a client without the photos they are expecting.

When 4 p.m. rolls around, I try to send my pics from the Sheraton, but once again they do not transmit through to Houston. Disappointed, I go to the pressroom to meet Yakoob and hopefully hear that my visa is rolling along. He tells me it might be ready by tomorrow afternoon, or Monday at the latest. I tell him I will be ready to leave Kuwait after a day or two of relaxation, and am looking forward to receiving my visa. He politely reminds me about the copies of the CDs he asked for.

After unsuccessfully trying to transmit my pics from the Sheraton, I decide to leave the hotel and check in to a room at the Plaza Hotel (using my Canadian passport which I have secretly stashed away for emergencies like this). As I mentioned previously, you need a passport to do just about anything in Kuwait. You need it to carry out any banking transaction, rent a car or stay in a hotel. So without it you are basically at the mercy of the system and the expediency of the system. This is where I stand; at the mercy of the system.

The Plaza lobby is covered wall-to-wall with marble. The accompanying furnishings are elaborate, but the rooms are small, musty and dull. It is a little bit of a shock to see the rooms compared to the lobby. I am staying in lucky room number 1303. For the extra $45 bucks it costs to stay at the Sheraton, I should have stayed put, especially after I try to send my e-mail from the Plaza business room and have them all returned. I will try again in the early morning, my last chance to get them through to Houston on time. I go to bed distraught about my transmission problems.

Day 18. Sunday, April 27th

> *(Staying at the Plaza Hotel; a good night's sleep; my e-mail nightmare continues; leaving the Plaza and moving back to the Sheraton; watching boats on the Arabian Gulf; ice on Missisquoi Bay; huge financial loss; I let the Houston Chronicle down; shopping at a book store; finding a map of Iraq; outdated maps; meeting architecture student Aroob; birdwatching with Tim Carlson; visa not ready; CNN vehicles attacked by bandits; CNN member shot in hand; like plundering a Spanish galleon; burning CDs)*

I wake up at about 10 a.m., feeling almost human after a solid sleep of seven hours. Getting dressed, I go downstairs to the Plaza business office to try to e-mail my pics, but once again I have no success. Now I really start to wonder what is happening, and begin to seriously consider the possibility that my e-mail, at least those carrying attachments (which are 0.5 megabytes, and easily sent through e-mail under normal circumstances) are somehow being censored and blocked. But they can't be.

After a small breakfast with bottomless coffee, I head up to my room to pack my baggage for the move back to the Sheraton. It just isn't worth staying here; it is very bland, and I can keep a closer eye on my visa progress from the Sheraton.

Checking back into the Sheraton, I am given room #305. Looking west from my room window, I can see the light blue waters of the Arabian Gulf. Powerboats and other watercraft motor across the calm Gulf waters, a billion miles away from the wretchedness of Iraq. From the number of watercraft, it is obvious that the Kuwaitis love their water sports. I can understand their love, as this is such a beautiful body of water. I start to reminisce about back home, wondering whether the ice has broken up on Missisquoi Bay, Lake Champlain where I spend so much of my time fishing at the family cottage.

It is now too late to get my photos to Houston for John Otis's piece on upstart political parties. The piece is running in today's paper and I needed to transmit the pics by noon Kuwait time. This really breaks my heart. I lost over a thousand dollars from the assignment, and let my colleague John Otis down. Not only this, but I have to pay for a high-priced hotel. I could have sent the pics from Baghdad, Thursday, but at the time it would have been a hassle. So I felt it would be a cinch to transmit from Kuwait, and held onto them until I got here. So far, I have lost out all around on this miserable visit to Kuwait.

I decide to go shopping for a few important articles that I need, such as a map of Baghdad and Iraq, and a field guide to the birds of the Middle East and Africa. I also want to get a small gift for Snora and Julie of the NBC gang. Luckily, I find a bookstore where I purchase all the articles I need.

Having a good map of Baghdad and Iraq will be a great help in my travels. Maps of Iraq are as rare as icebergs in that country, and if you happen to be lucky enough to find one, it most likely pre-dates Saddam's regime. Most of the government buildings, bridges and new development are not included in the outdated maps. Saddam does not want accurate maps of Iraq in circulation; this would identify possible targets to the attacking forces. I have been borrowing Sean's Iraq map since I arrived in Baghdad.

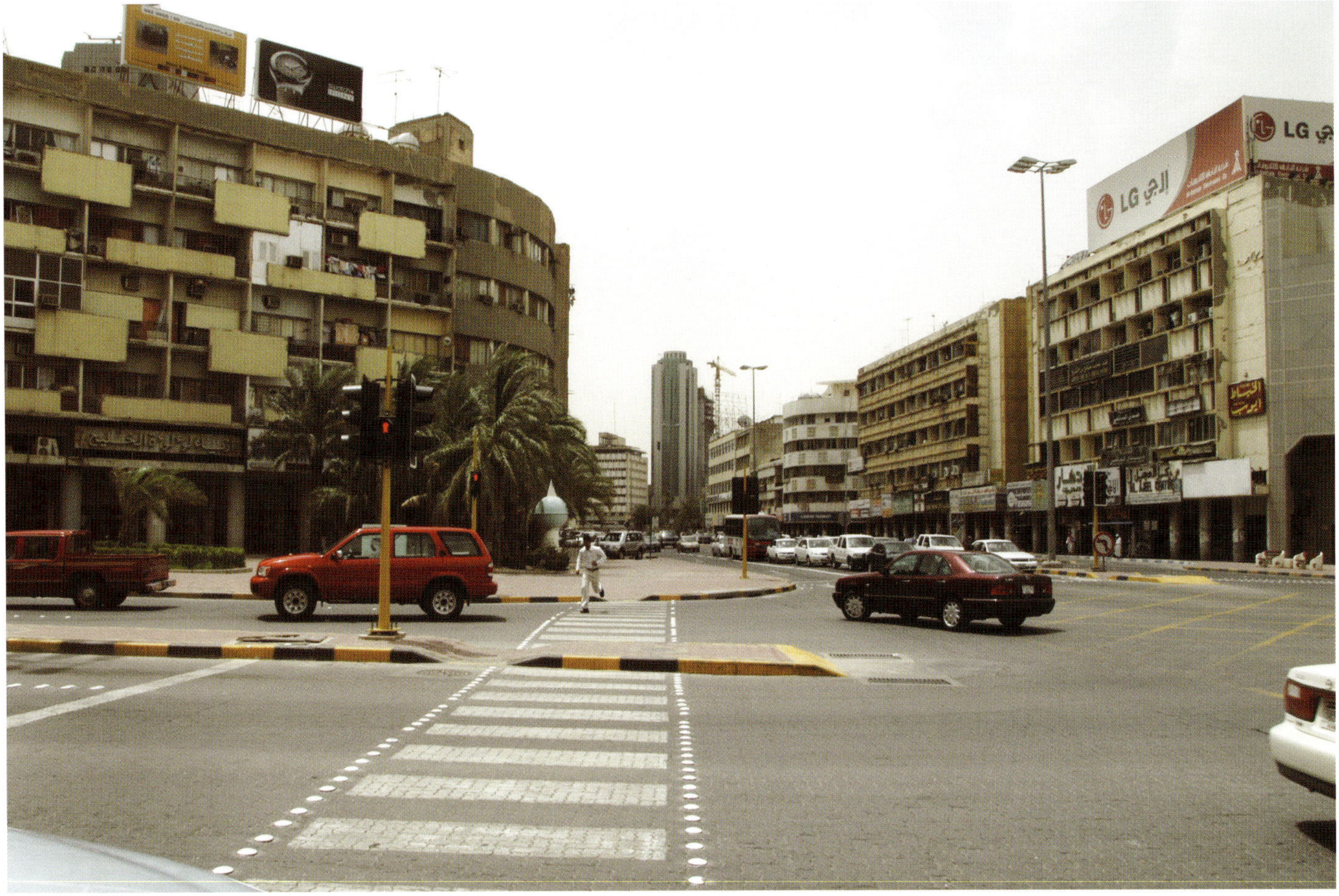

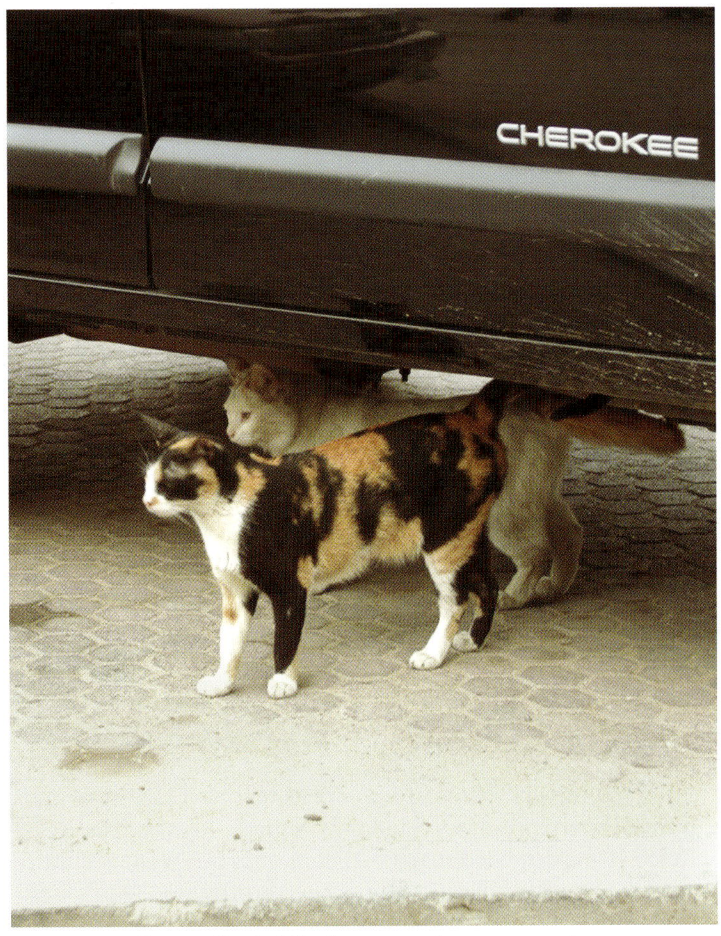

Kuwait City is full of stray cats, but not stray dogs

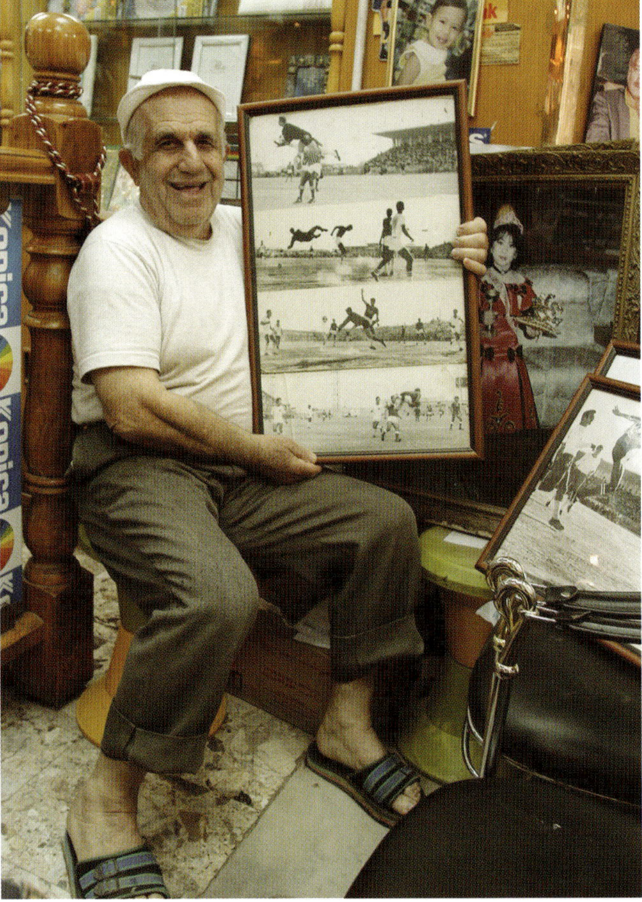

The owner of a film store shows off his soccer photos

Downtown Kuwait City

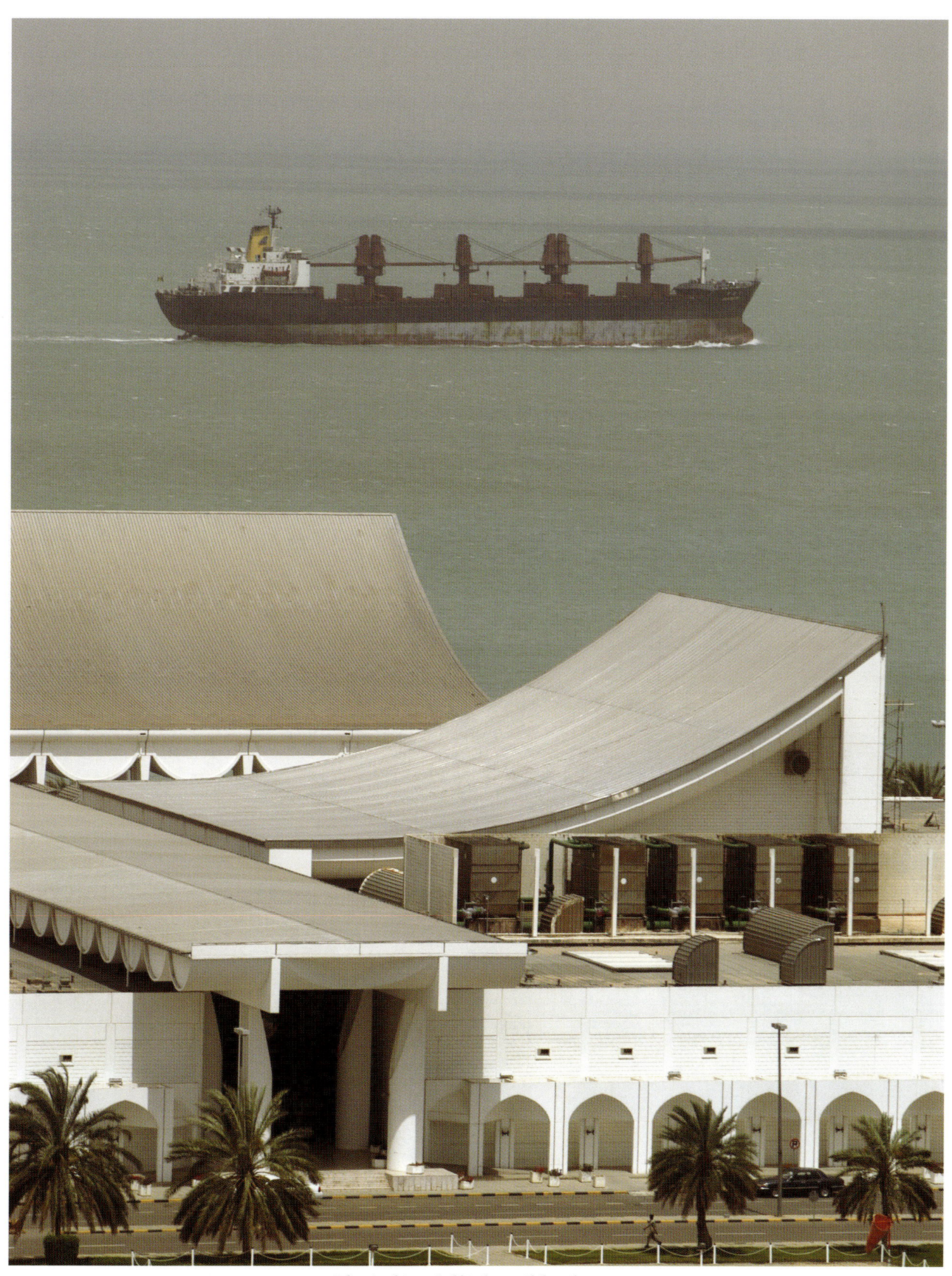

The Arabian Gulf is beautiful and warm

While in the bookstore I meet a young, twenty-something-year-old Kuwait University architecture student named Aroob. She starts chatting to me in the lineup at the store. She asks me all sorts of questions about my travels and life in Canada. I tell her I have a great interest in architecture, and try to show this love in my photography. She listens intently as I describe my love of French-Canadian architecture.

Aroob, who is extremely attractive, asks if I would consider speaking to her university classroom about war and architecture. I tell her it will depend on my visa situation, but she can call me later at the hotel to see how I am progressing. I would love to give these students a talk on art and war, and am flattered by her request. The reality is, that my life is in disarray at the moment, and I cannot really plan anything until I know the status of my visa.

At 1 p.m., I meet Yakoob in the press office. He tells me the visa is not ready but I should have it by Monday, or Tuesday, at the absolute latest. "I hope so, or I could go broke," I tell him.

I meet book author Tim Carlson in the lobby of the hotel. We go for a little walk around the downtown area, discussing our opinions and views of the war and how we believe it will inevitably unfold. I see a young fledgling sparrow hopping about on the sidewalk, chirping insistently for its parents to come down and feed it. Tim and I watch it for a little while, as the adults show up to feed it.

Back at the hotel, Tim is trying to find a ride to Baghdad. He has to interview more journalists in that city for his upcoming book, "Embedded." He is very concerned about finding a ride, and is on a very tight time schedule. Tim is a man on a mission; he has to get to Baghdad, whatever the cost or risk. I like his attitude and drive and wish him the best of success.

I bump into Snora, and he tells me about an incident the previous day where bandits in Iraq, near the Kuwait border, attacked a CNN convoy. One of the crew was shot in the hand; the vehicle they were driving in had seven bullet holes in it. The journalists escaped without any life-threatening injuries. Had the bandits stopped and robbed the convoy, it would have been like pirates plundering a Spanish galleon; the vehicles and personnel would have cash and equipment.

I start burning back-up CDs of my image files, which I will give to Snora in the morning. He and Julie leave for Amsterdam tomorrow afternoon, and I have kept them up on the visa problems. I ask Snora if he would mind taking some copies of my photo CDs out of Kuwait with him, to which he gladly agrees. It is necessary to have copies safe in another location should something happen to my master discs.

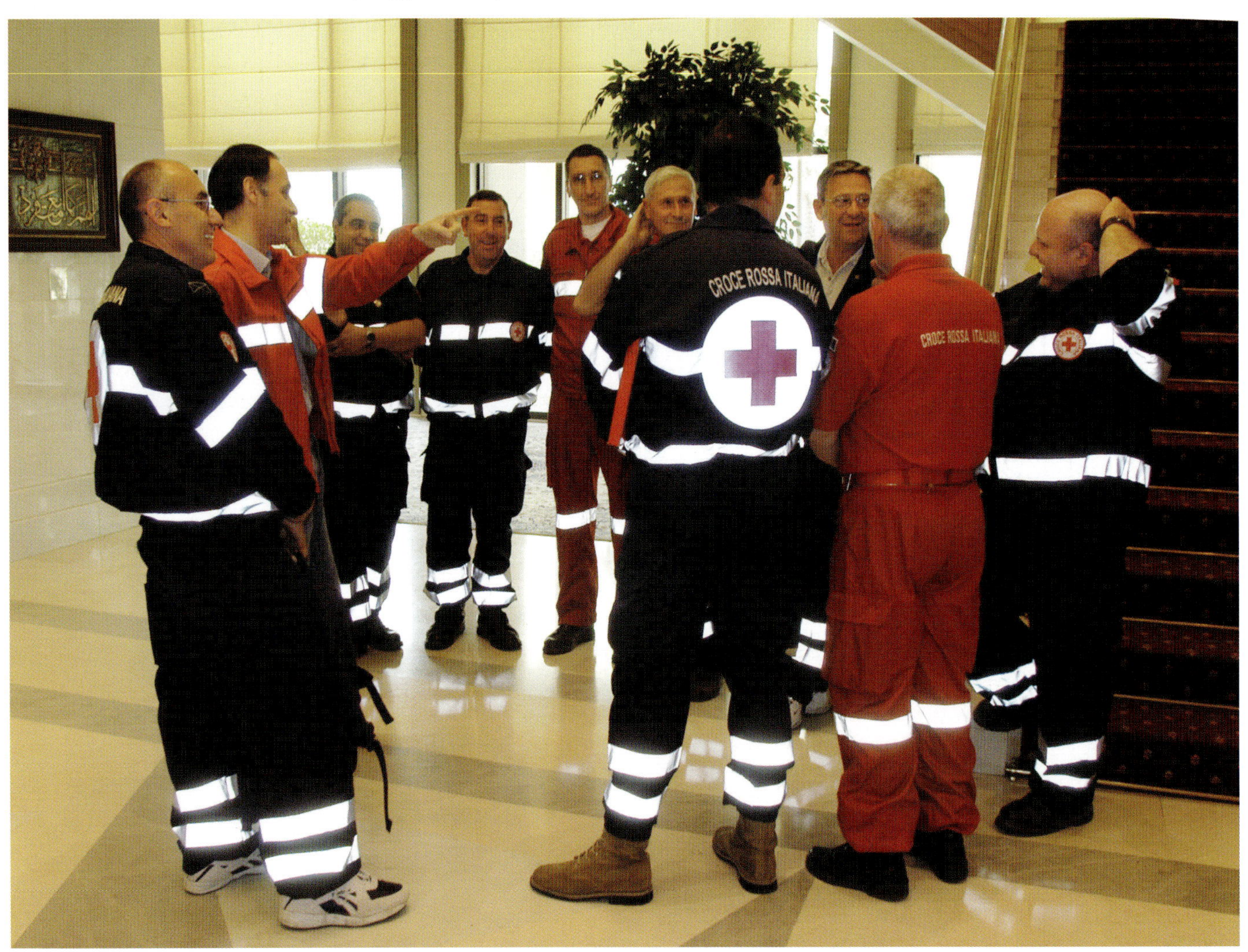

A team of Italian Red Cross personnel gather in the lobby of the Kuwait Marriott Hotel

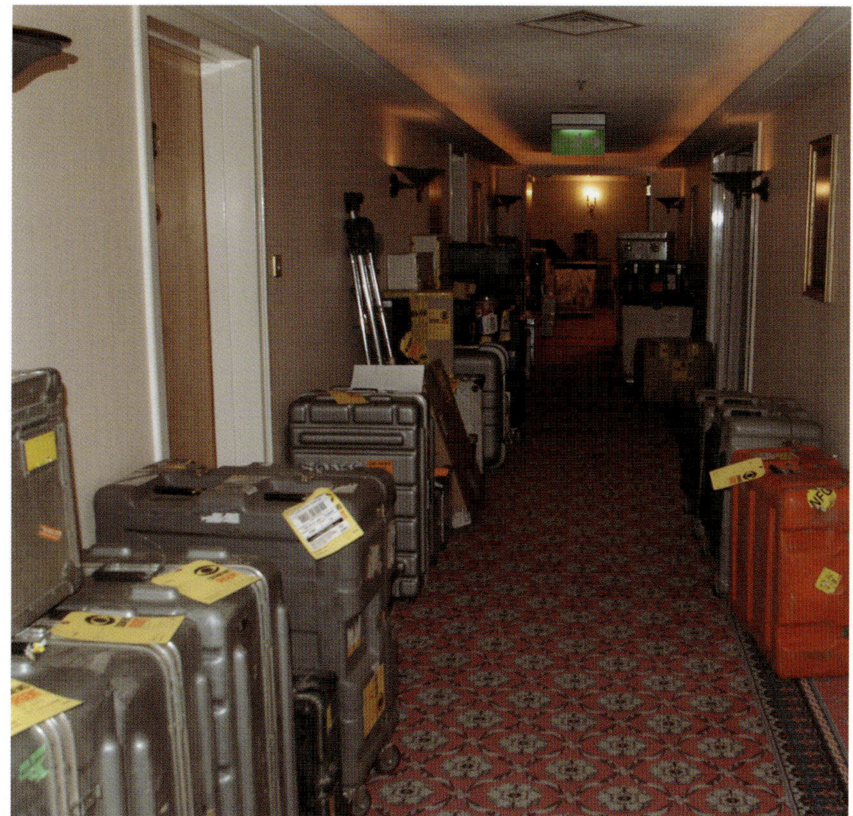

Luggage from the television networks line the hallways of the Kuwait Sheraton

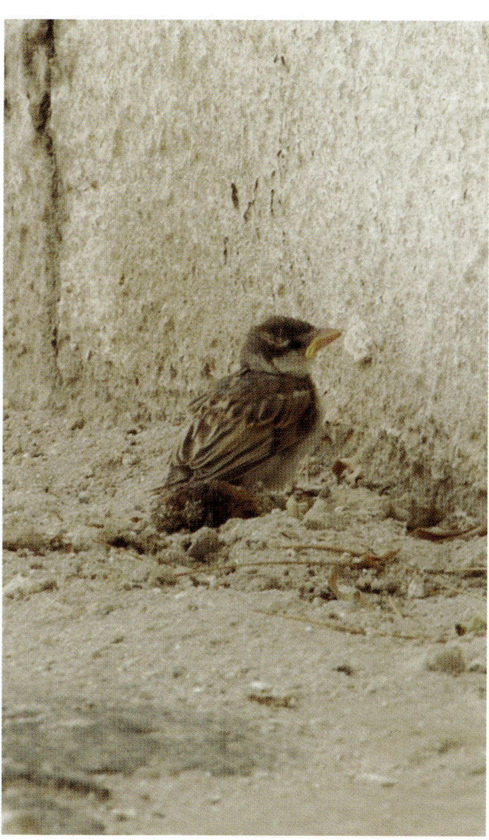

This fledgling house sparrow has just left the nest

Day 19. Monday, April 28th

(My visa isn't ready; I call my wife, Phyllis, and Don McKenzie (with the Canadian Press) to tell them of my situation; I give Snora my back-up CDs; Snora and Julie off to Amsterdam; I can't reach Sean or Tish; anorexic; the vulnerabilities of freelance journalism; I speak with Nino's mom in California; I call the Canadian Embassy in Kuwait; Bob Skrimes of the Canadian Embassy; things have changed since 9/11; fish or fresh-cut flowers; unprofessional and deceitful; will look into it; e-mail from home)

I wake up expecting that my visa will be ready today, and I can start planning the next stage of my trip back into Iraq. Yesterday, Yakoob told me it would be ready by 1 p.m., but when I go to pick it up, it is not ready. Yakoob apologizes and tells me the paper work is taking longer than expected. He reassures me that it will definitely be ready tomorrow by 4 p.m.

I am very concerned by my e-mail and visa problems and telephone my wife Phyllis and Don McKenzie (a friend with the Canadian Press in Montreal) to let them know of my predicament. I explain that I feel less than secure about my safety and felt that they should be made aware.

I finish burning my back-up CDs and give 16 discs (which together hold around 4000 photographs) to Snora to take out of Kuwait with him. He gives me his co-ordinates in the States, and asks me to call him when I get back. I also give him and Julie the small gift I bought at the bookstore, for their friendship towards me. It is a walking guide to Amsterdam.

I try phoning Sean and Tish, but cannot get through to their number because of bad reception. I hope they are not too concerned by my lack of communication, but there is no way I can let them know my status. Trying to get through to Tish's satellite phone is difficult at the best of times and she often shuts it off to save power.

One of the NBC hotel crew tells me that I look anorexic and should take better care of myself. He also tells me he is aware that our communications are being monitored, but he doesn't let it bother him, as it never gets in the way of his work.

The large news agencies like NBC or CNN are far less vulnerable to monitoring (compared to a solitary freelance journalist) because they are so powerful and can bite back hard if they feel someone is spying on their network or personal communications. So the Ministry of Information's policy may be to eavesdrop (and perhaps even interrupt messages) on independent non-mainstream journalists who work separately from the institutional news herd. Freelance journalists tend to work alone, with little backing or security. Because of this, we are easy to single out and abuse.

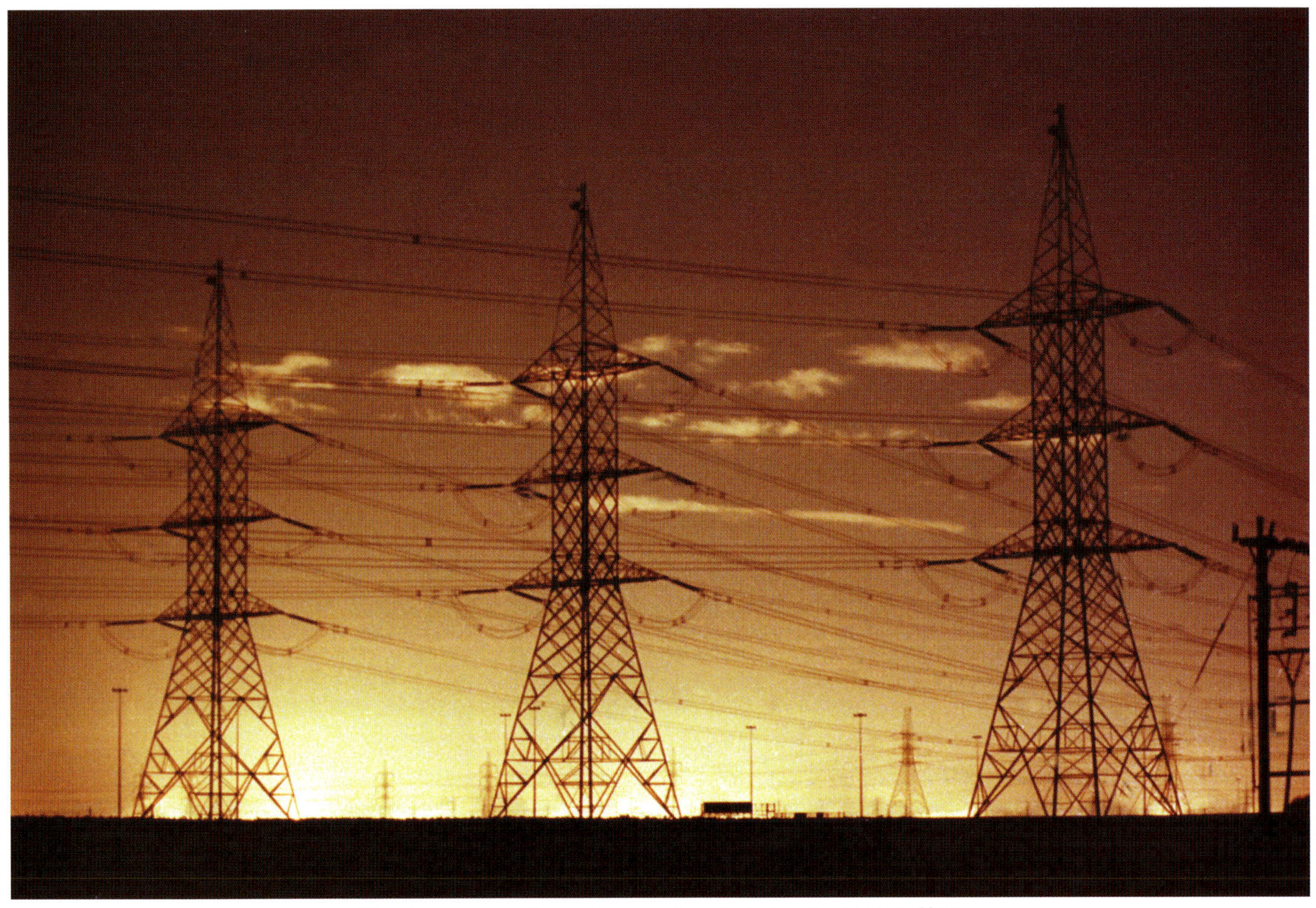

Oil wells burn out of control across Kuwait during the 1991 Gulf War

I decide to call Nino's mom, Rose, in California, to let her know about her son in Baghdad, and that he is healthy and in good spirits. Rose cries on the phone and sounds like a very nice lady. She tells me that if I am ever in California, to make sure to drop by and visit the Sanchez family, and they will treat me like a king! I miss Nino.

I phone Aroob to tell her that I am in the middle of a tricky situation and feel it better if I do not give a talk at the university.

To put some pressure on the Kuwaitis, I decide to place a phone call to the Canadian Embassy in Kuwait, to ask their help in getting my visa pushed through and to let them know my situation.

I talk on the phone with a Mr. Bob Skrimes, an embassy representative, to whom I relate my situation. He tells me that I should have had my visa granted and in hand before I reached Kuwait. I ask him how I was supposed to get a visa from a country at war and with little mode of communication with the outside world. I explain to him that my visit to Kuwait was unanticipated, and due to health concerns from war fatigue.

Skrimes doesn't seem to give a damn and is talking to me like I am some kind of pest that he has to get rid of. I demand to meet with him or another embassy official today, face to face. He tells me to calm down, and that he will meet me later in the afternoon at the hotel. I tell him that this is no time to calm down and that I need some help. I decide to push back a little and let him know that if I am abused any further by this Ministry of Information, I have asked my wife to be ready to call a press conference in Montreal to draw attention to my problem with the Kuwaiti Government and the lack of action by the Canadian Foreign Affairs Ministry on my behalf. Skrimes is the last guy you would ever want to meet in a time of need and is a typical example of all that is wrong with Canada's flawed Foreign Affairs Ministry.

Around 3 p.m., I meet Skrimes and an embassy assistant in the lobby of the Sheraton. We grab a seat on a lobby couch and I explain again what has happened to me. He tells me, in a condescending tone, that whatever happened previously, such as the Canadian involvement in Desert Storm and our country's past affiliations with Kuwait, is now changed and irrelevant since 9/11. I ask him how the Canadian soldiers who served during Desert Storm would feel about this supposed irrelevance, those who put their lives on the line for a nation with a short memory. "Well, let's not bring our flags into this little misunderstanding," he insists sheepishly.

Just out of interest, I ask him what the single largest trading commodity between Canada and Kuwait is. He responds saying, "I do not know the trade situation, or what the largest trade commodity is between our two countries." Not happy with his answer, I ask him sarcastically, "Well, is it fish, or fresh-cut flowers?" Skrimes replies, "I don't know about Canada-Kuwait trade, that's not my specialty. Does a brain specialist know how to remove teeth?"

I ask if he is aware that journalists' e-mails are being blocked. He pleads ignorance, but says he will look into it. He asks me to be calm and patient until tomorrow afternoon, when he will meet with me again. I tell him I will try my best.

Going to the computer office, I check my Hotmail address and am surprised to see a message from my wife. She tells me that the children are scared about my predicament and feel I could be harmed in Kuwait. She also tells me that their school is helping support the girls, by being very careful not to give them too much work or put them under pressure. I am very thankful for the school's handling of my two girls. The elementary school my son Brian attends is also treating him gently.

Day 20. Tuesday, April 29th

(Hurting all over; waiting for my visa; blackmailed for my photos by the Kuwaiti Government; panic and nausea; questioning my journalistic ethics; a covert reason for wanting my photos; my safety threatened; Rashid informs me my visa will be ready for tomorrow)

I wake up feeling like a truck ran over me while I slept. My body hurts all over, and I am sure it is from the stress and the heat of the city. I am just going to try take it easy till 4 p.m., when I am supposed to receive my visa. Going for a walk from the hotel, I return shortly after, as the heat outside is so stifling.

As 4 p.m. rolls around, I go down to the press office to see Yakoob. Seeing me, his downcast eyes tell the story. Looking up he tells me, "Sorry Mr. Galbraith, your visa is not ready. But you might have it tomorrow, if I receive the photo CDs you promised me, otherwise it could take longer." I did not promise this man anything. The bureaucrat turns the screw further when he nonchalantly comments that, "One journalist had to wait ten days for his visa." Yakoob looks up at me with the arrogance of a hangman.

This man is trying to blackmail me! Very upset, I walk out of the office without saying a word. I want nothing to do with either Yakoob or Rashid. I am overcome by a horrible feeling of hopelessness, panic and nausea. I go up to my room in a cold sweat, while wondering just how long they can hold me in tribalistic Kuwait. I am very concerned and anxious.

The pressure on me to hand over my photo files now conflicts with my journalistic ethics and I wonder if I made a mistake when I showed him the photos in the first place. There is definitely a covert reason for their wanting my photos and it is now clear that the Ministry of Information will not release me until they get the photos in their hand. I am under house – or city arrest, without my predicament being officially termed as such. I feel like a prisoner awaiting execution.

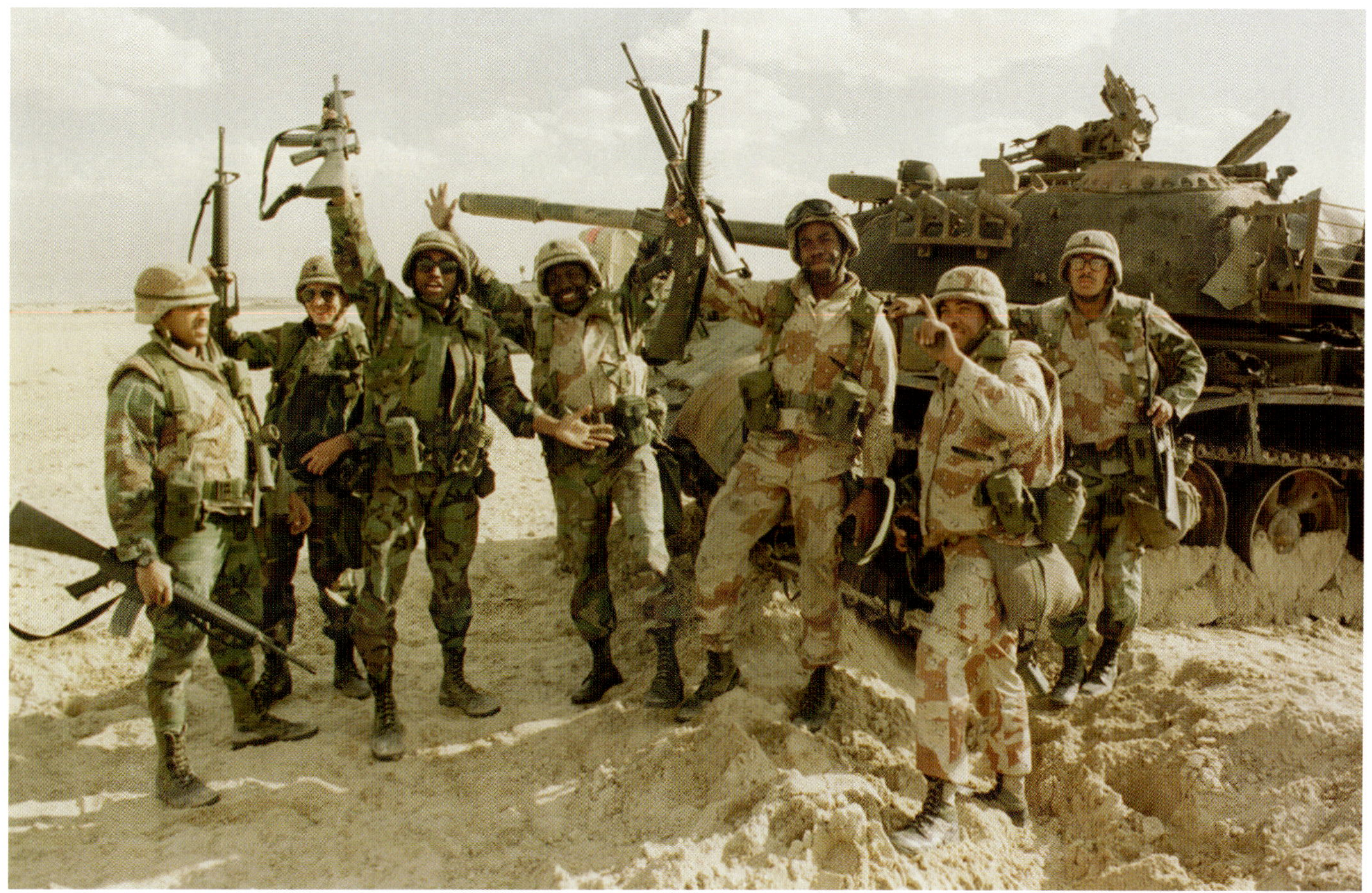

American soldiers pose beside a destroyed Iraqi tank on the outskirts of Kuwait City during the 1991 Gulf War

I reason that the ministry intends to identify individuals in the photos, thereby adding to their intelligence banks. Perhaps my photos (and there are thousands of faces in the photos) will lead to someone being detained, tortured or even outright murdered by Kuwaiti agents. Anything is possible in this part of the world.

It may be difficult for many to comprehend that a supposed modern nation like Kuwait would resort to such barbaric tactics to satisfy their revenge. All I can say is that unless you have visited this tormented region of the world, you are really only getting half the picture. There are no rules here, there is no real democracy, though the philosophy is tossed about about like a rag doll by nations who use the term for their own selfish ends.

The Kuwaiti hatred of Iraqi is unsatisfiable, and they will stop at nothing to get their pound of flesh, including using journalists to satisfy their blood vengeance. The Kuwaiti Government is blackmailing me for my freedom – and using me as their photographer spy/whore!

Supporting this summation is the fact that on Saturday, April 26th, Yakoob told me that the Kuwaiti Government had no idea what was going on inside Iraq and had seen only television and newspaper accounts of the war. When I showed him and Nora Dandashi my photos that afternoon, he was drooling all over them, asking me for copies and confessing shock at the situation in Baghdad. Now, everytime I converse with him, he clearly asks if his photo CDs are ready yet. Now my real fear becomes just how far they are willing to go to get the photographs. Might they just keep delaying my visa until I turn over the CDs?

I think back to Day 14 of my trip (April 23rd), when Sean and I visited the Baghdad Train Station and met the former Iraqi Ministry of Information's *Internet* and communications police. This Iraqi ministry monitored all incoming and out-going communications. It is so plainly obvious, from my meeting with the Iraqi *Internet* police (and from what I have learned from my talking to hotel staff and security personnel here in Kuwait) that the Government of Kuwait is using the same communications monitoring strategy as was used by the government of Iraq. So there are some very close similarities between the two enemies. I wonder if most visiting foreign journalists know that everytime they speak on a phone or send or receive an e-mail, it is being monitored and even blocked by the Kuwaiti Government (who cannot differentiate between a clear and present danger and the abuse of the press).

The rest of the day passes uncomfortably, and I feel vulnerable and fearful for my safety. I spot Rashid (who I now realize is a spook for the ministry) in the hotel lobby and try to avoid him, but he comes over and tells that my visa should be ready by 4 p.m. tomorrow. I answer him with a flat, "Thanks."

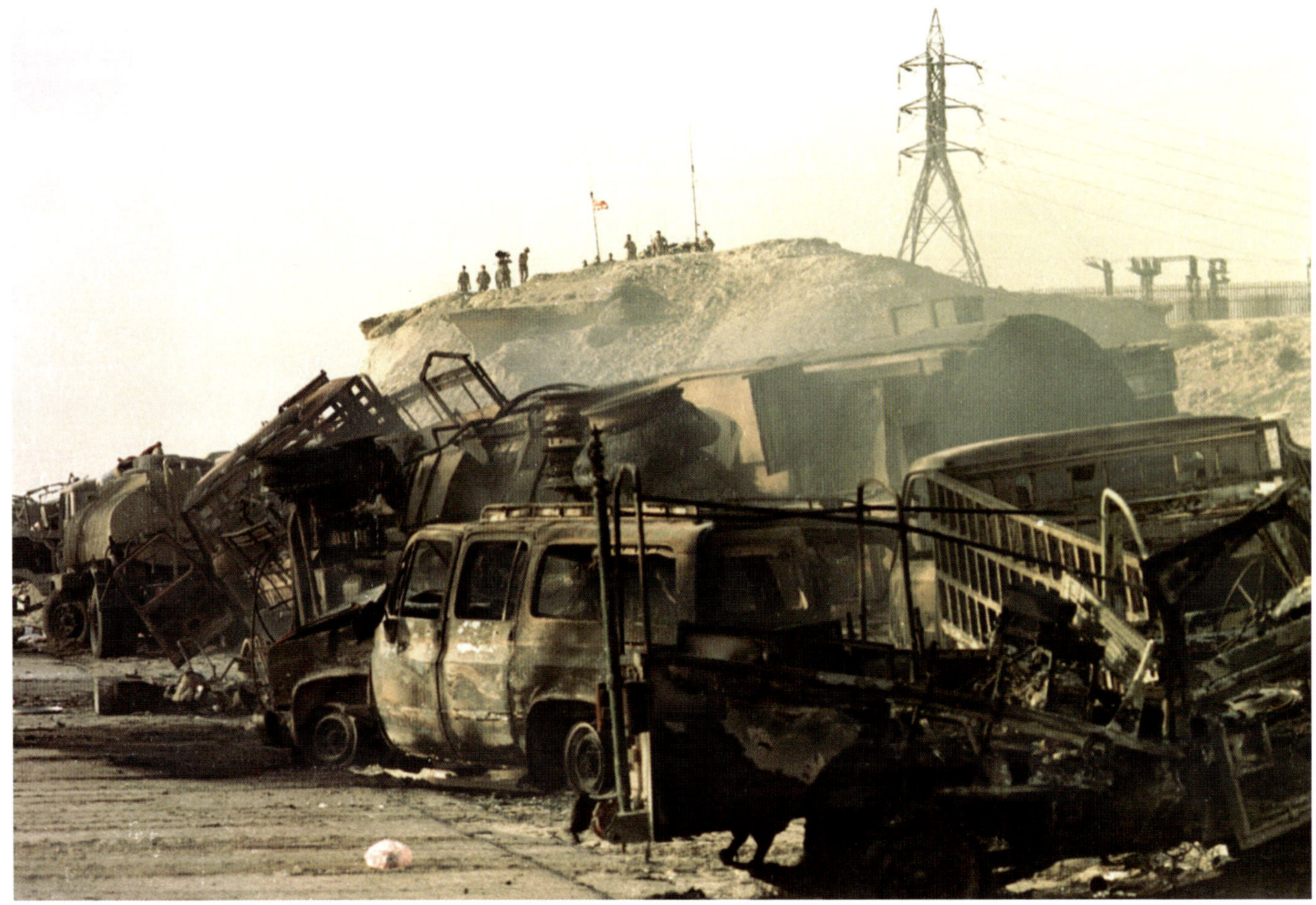

The highway from Kuwait City to Basra became a flaming inferno when the Iraqis were trapped between British and American forces in 1991

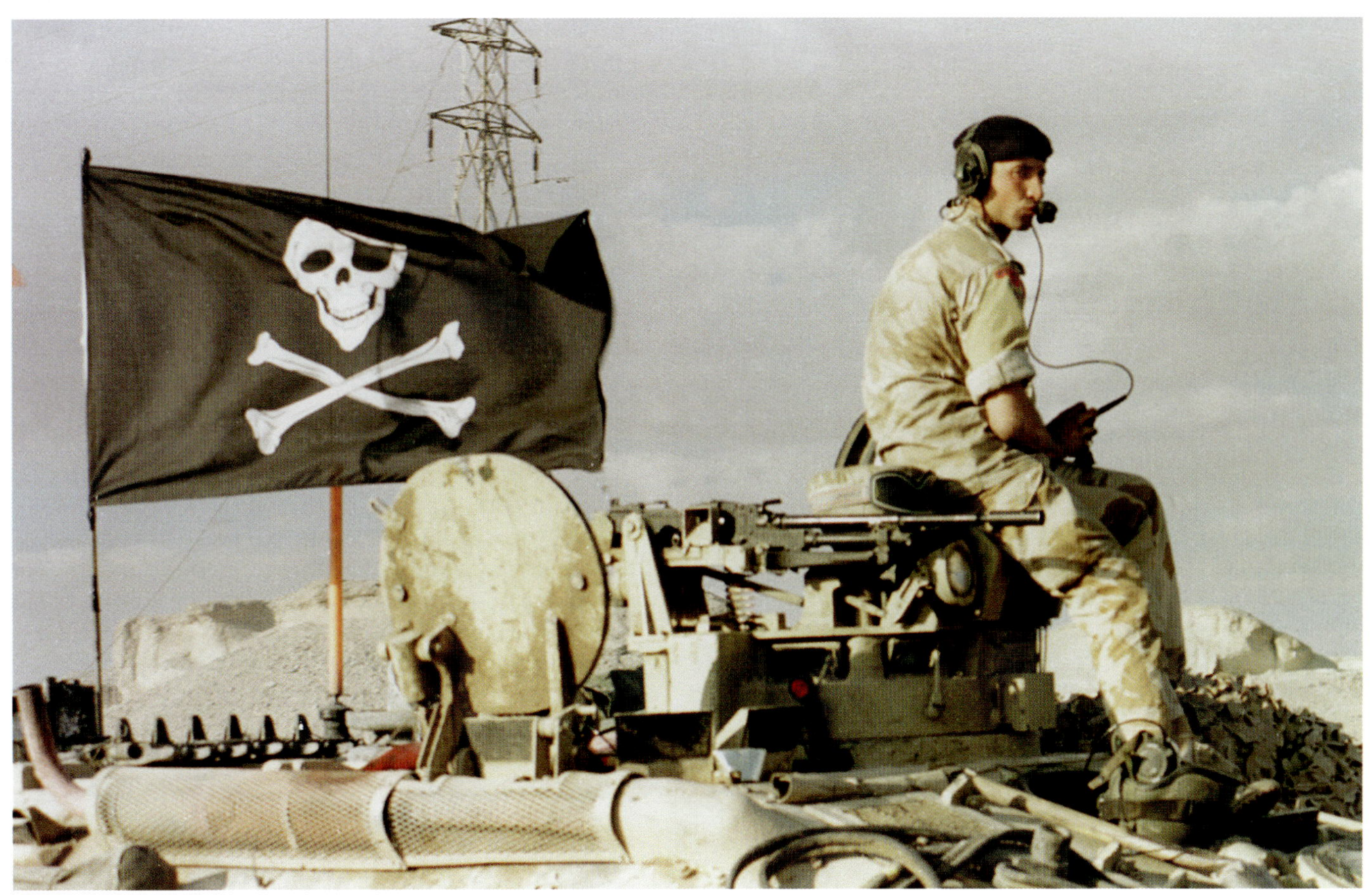

British soldier flies the Jolly Roger after the battle for Kuwait City and the annihilation of the Iraqi forces, during the 1991 Gulf War

Day 21. Wednesday, April 30th

(Looking for a room at the Marriott Hotel; message from Bob Skrimes; the beggar; population dynamics; censorship of books; controlling what people read; no room at the Marriott; I register at the Carlton Tower Hotel; visa ready at 4 p.m.; getting my CFLCC card at the Kuwait Hilton; I give Yakoob my photo CDs; your CDs are much appreciated by the Kuwaiti government; exhaustion and stress; gaming chips; I had to get out; this might be it; you are free to leave Kuwait anytime; I receive my Kuwaiti media pass and visa from Yakoob; press conference on hold till I leave country; drinking coffee and looking for a drive to Basra at the Marriott; $200 for a taxi to the border; working the Marriott lobby till midnight; witch hunt on the late show; eating blackberry jam and crackers; ants in my bed)

After a light breakfast I start packing my luggage. I leave them in the Sheraton lobby and head over to the Marriott looking for a room (for what I hope will be my last night in Kuwait). I want to stay at the Marriott to get away from the Sheraton and to try find a lift to Basra for tomorrow (should I get my visa).

As I leave the Sheraton, a bell boy hands me a message, it is from the Canadian Embassy. They want to know my plans. They will have to wait until 4 p.m. for the answer.

On the way to the Marriott, a middle-aged man of East Indian origin comes up to me with his hand extended, begging for spare change. I refuse to give him any money and am surprised to see a beggar on the streets of Kuwait.

According to a recent government poll, the population of Kuwait is 2,309,102. Thirty-eight percent, or 870,000, are Kuwaiti citizens; 1,438,819, or 62%, are expatriates, mainly Asians. The state employs about 93% of Kuwaitis. They enjoy high salaries and generous benefits. In the private sector, 98% of employees are expatriates, of which 60% are non-Arabs. The expatriates are mostly made up of Philippinos, Palestinians and East-Indians (from mainland India and Bangladesh).

I drop into a bookstore near the Marriott and ask the manager for any maps of Iraq or the Mid-East. (Although I have already bought a good map, it is nice to have a second different one). He tells me that just before the war, officials from the Ministry of Information came into the store and removed all books, maps, globes, magazines and children's books containing any reference to Iraq and Israel. He explains that they also removed similar material from the nations' teaching institutions and libraries. The censorship has all but killed his business and he is barely holding onto his store.

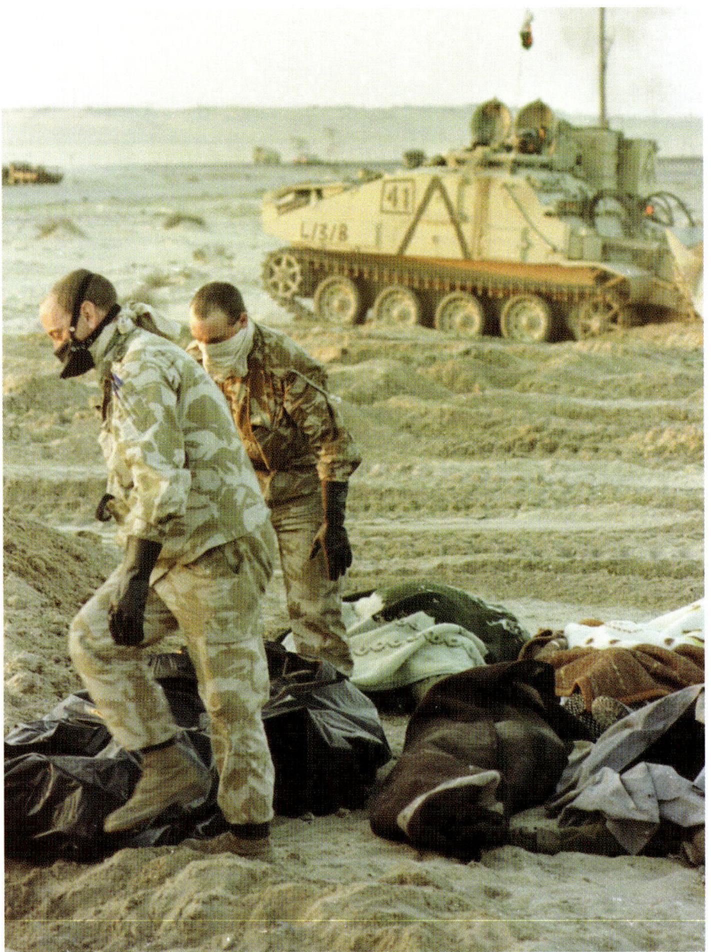

The British Welsh Guard bury dead Iraqis in long deep trenches, 1991

The Kuwaiti Government does not want any information on these two nations finding its way into the hands of Kuwaiti citizens. Perhaps the Kuwaiti government fears that if its citizens read about Israel, they might want to convert to Judaism or something. To control what people read or do not read is all about state enforced subjugation.

Reaching the Marriott, I find that there are no rooms available, so I cross the street and book myself a room at the Carlton Towers for $60 a night. It is a no frills two-star hotel, but it is clean and comfortable.

Returning to the Sheraton, I run into Yakoob in the lobby. He shakes my hand, and then enthusiastically tells me my visa will definitely be ready by 4 p.m. today. But before it is finalized, it is necessary for me to visit the American Armed Forces Command Headquarters, located in the Kuwait Hilton Hotel. I need to get a forces media accreditation, known as a CFLCC press card (Coalition Forces Land Component Command), pronounced; See-Flick. This, Yakoob says, will finalize the completion of my visa. He asks if the CDs are ready yet.

I take a taxi to the Hilton, about a twenty-minute drive north of downtown. The Hilton is a beautiful hotel, snuggled along the shores of the warm Arabian Gulf.

A soldier greets me at the forces media counter, and then asks me to fill out an application for the card. In ten minutes I have my CFLCC card and am leaving the hotel. In the lobby I see a table with brochures advertising B-GAN satellite transmitters. I stop and chat with the lady behind the counter. She says they have systems at their office in downtown Kuwait City. I grab a brochure and tell her I will visit their office when I get downtown.

Back at the Sheraton (I still have my room key) I grab some lunch and start burning a copy of my CDs for Yakoob. I take a break after I burn ten CDs, and then leave to visit the office of the B-GAN people. I have to forget about purchasing a satellite system when the manager tells me he has none in stock. This is disappointing, but not the end of the world by any means.

I return to the hotel and burn four more CDs, before reluctantly going downstairs and handing 14 Cds to Yakoob. I also hand him my CFLCC card, so he can complete my visa. He smiles upon receiving the CDs, then shakes my hand telling me that they will be much appreciated by his government. He then reassures me that my visa will be ready in an hour and he is just going over the final details; it is 2 p.m.

I feel like shit handing the CDs over to him, but at this point in my trip, I am in such a state of exhaustion and stress, that I would have done or given them almost anything to get out of this country and into Iraq. My photos are now just gaming chips – bartered away for my freedom. Nothing else matters to me right now but getting out of this sand trap.

Going up to the lounge, I drink a foamy cappuccino and help myself to the fresh chocolate truffles. Sitting back into a

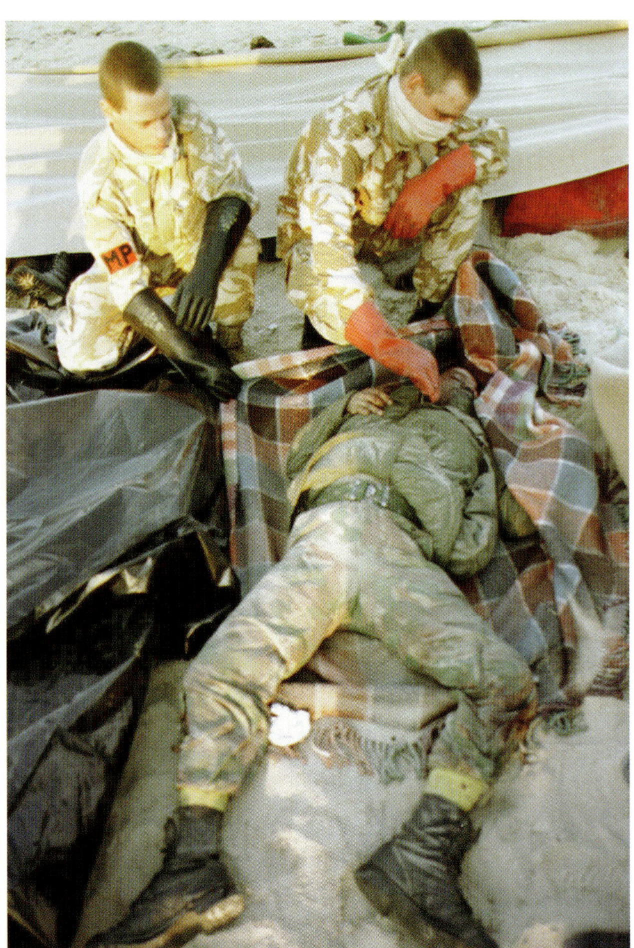

Removing dog tags from a dead Iraqi soldier, 1991

deep leather couch in the lounge, I suddenly realize that I might be allowed to leave Kuwait anytime after 3 p.m. The thought of actually leaving this country sends a rush of adrenaline bolting through my body. It brings on hidden resources of energy and positiveness from deep within me – my second wind is coming about!

I call Bob Skrimes at the embassy but he is on vacation (nice of him to let me know he would not be in the office for three days), so I leave a message on the answering machine explaining that I should receive my visa today. I also state that if I do not get out of Kuwait by Thursday, my wife will call the press conference in Montreal to denounce my treatment by Kuwait and the governmental theft (as I believe I had no choice but to hand them over) of my photographs.

After my call to the embassy, I call my wife to give her an update and let her know I am intent on leaving Kuwait tomorrow. The family is ecstatic about my impending release, and Phyllis says she will give Don McKenzie an update.

I meet a media friend in the lounge (who will remain nameless for her own security). She has been keeping an eye on my situation and my health, and is aware of the pressure I am under from the Information Ministry. She is not impressed by the Kuwaiti Government's treatment of foreigners and recently told me that she, "Can't wait to get out of Kuwait and into a free Iraq."

When 3 p.m. rolls around, I walk into the Sheraton press office. I am a man of mixed emotions, not knowing just what to expect. Yakoob stands up and shakes my hand. Wearing a large smile, he presents me with my passport, exit visa, Kuwaiti Press Pass and CFLCC card. "You are free to leave Kuwait anytime," he says. I thank him for the visa, then head upstairs to my room for a cigarette and to consider my next move towards getting out of Kuwait.

Soon after, I receive a call from a Canadian Embassy official asking me to reconsider calling the press conference. I tell him the conference is on, if I don't get out of Kuwait by tomorrow. (Because it is getting late in the day, I decide I will leave Kuwait tomorrow morning. I don't want to get stuck somewhere on the road to Basra with the sun setting).

I turn in my Sheraton room key, and then take a taxi to the Carlton Tower to drop off my gear. After this I walk over to the Marriott. I talk to guests and reception personnel, asking if they are planning to go, or know anyone who is planning to go to Basra tomorrow. Trying unsuccessfully for a couple of hours, I go for a walk, buying a few items I need.

I am just biding my time until I leave tomorrow, going over my plans for Basra and relaxing by window-shopping. It is the calm before the storm, and the storm is centered over Iraq. I cannot wait to cross the border and see my first looter and smoldering building. Then, I know I will be at home and on my own turf, so to speak.

Around 8 p.m. I am back at the Marriott looking for a lift. The hotel is a bustle of military officers, Red Crescent Society employees and other guests. I talk to many people but have no luck in procuring a lift to Basra. My other option is to hire a taxi to drive me to the border, but I am quoted a price of $200, a small fortune to me. This would be my last resort, should I not find a ride with someone with whom I can share the costs.

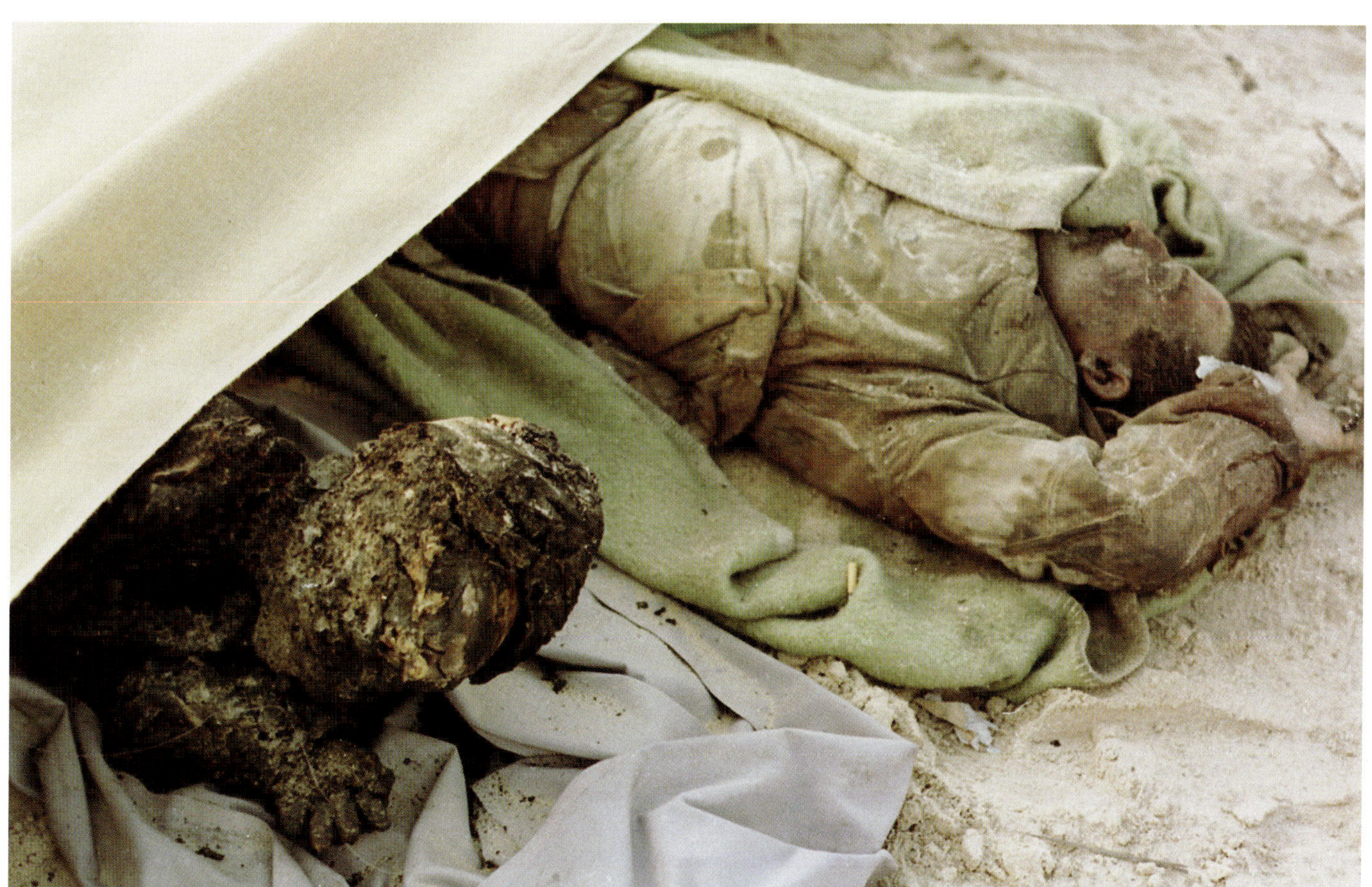

We should never forget that war is horrible. Dead Iraqis on the highway of death outside Kuwait City during Desert Storm, 1991

Nearing midnight, I decide to leave the Marriott and go to my room at the Carlton. I start packing my bags, then turn on the television. There is a great movie on about the Salem witch trials in Colonial America. I am fascinated by the similarities in the movie to my stay in Kuwait. I chuckle to myself, and then continue packing.

It is 2 a.m. and I am lying in bed eating the remnants of an MRE. Blackberry jam and crackers never tasted so good. After my late night snack I smoke my last cigarette, trying to calm my anticipation of tomorrow's journey. It feels as though my bed is full of ants, my stomach in knots. But it is just my impatience and desire to get on the road. With my bags packed and my body humming in anticipation, I finally drift off to sleep around 2:30 a.m., my last night in Kuwait.

Day 22. Thursday, May 1st

(I awaken at 4:30 a.m.; paying my bill at the Carlton; $100 taxi ride to the border; like the best of friends; visa stamped at border; between Kuwaiti guns and Iraqi thieves; no-mans-land; hitchhiking at the Iraqi border; "Thank-You For Visiting Kuwait"; barbed wire and tank traps; Canadian Embassy abandons bicyclist; drive into Basra; destroyed telecommunications centre; the abandoned Basra Prison; torture chambers; prison graffiti; Red Crescent Society; British refuse me a visit of Saddam's Basra palace; Basra International Airport; gorgeous women soldiers; the Brits aren't like the Marines; arrogant officers; from war to reconstruction; I meet two journalists from Iran's Urna News Agency; we find a hotel; phone family on satellite phone; electricity running in Basra; George Harrison brings me to life; my friend, the bird-sized cockroach; out for supper; we meet released Iraqi prisoners; blessed by the Iranians; burning CDs)

This is the day I will finally be leaving Kuwait, and I am up at 4:30 a.m., after only two hours of sleep. I pay the bill then walk over to the Marriott with all my baggage. I drink a couple of cups of coffee then chat with the doorman about arranging a cab to the Kuwait-Iraq border, should I not be able to find a hotel guest I can team up with. It is going on 10 a.m., and I am having no luck finding a lift. I ask the doorman if he can find me a taxi to the border. I let him know that I am a freelance journalist and could he find me a reasonable offer. He makes a couple of phone calls then tells me it will cost $100 to get to the border. I agree to the price, which is much better than the going rate of $200. I ask him to call the taxi right away.

The driver is a Palestinian refugee living and working in Kuwait, while his family lives in Israel. He is a level-headed, proud, polite man in his early 40's. We talk about the Iraqi war and the reasons behind it. We have a very similar under-

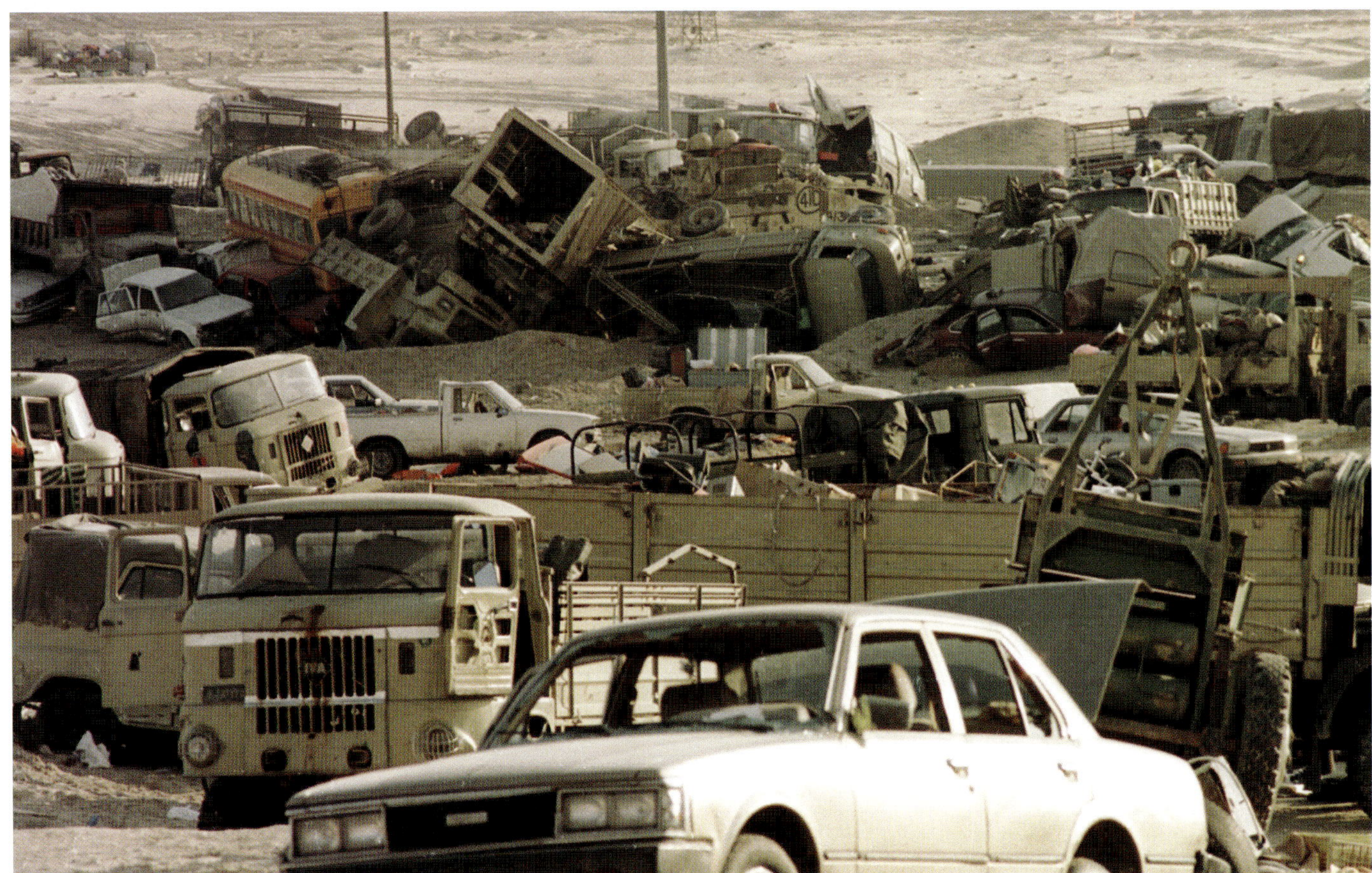

Trapped between British and American firepower and mines on each side of the highway, the Iraqi Army met a hellish death in 1991 Desert Storm

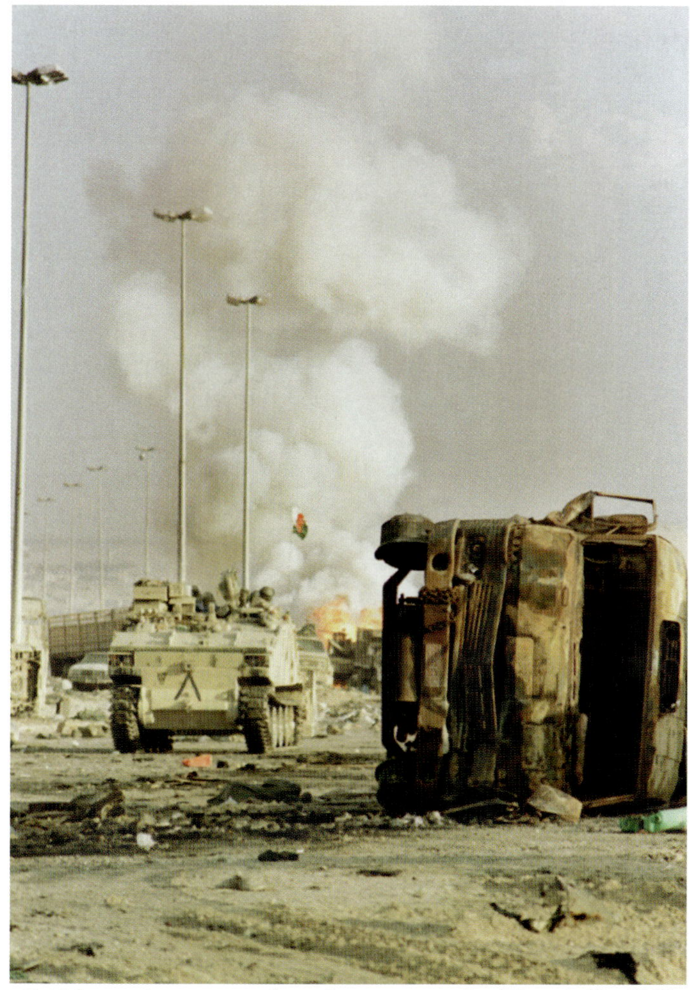
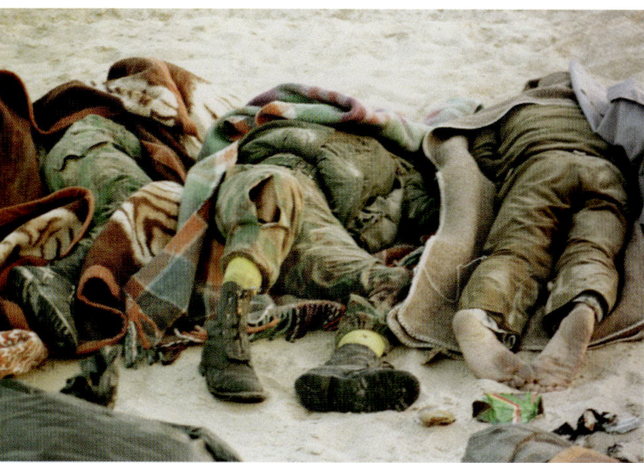

Iraqi dead await burial in mass graves, Desert Storm 1991

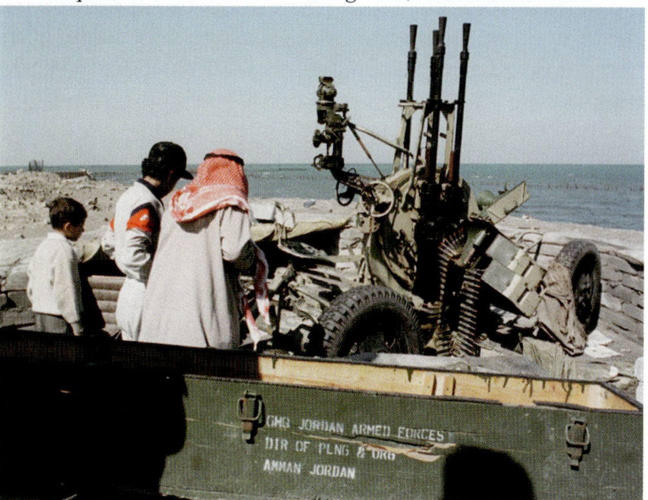

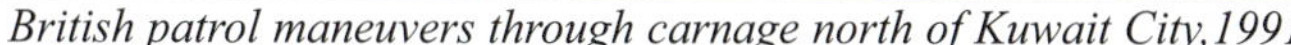

British patrol maneuvers through carnage north of Kuwait City,1991

Iraqi weaponry sits deserted along the Kuwait City beachfront,1991

standing of the war and Mid-East politics. He affirms what many people I have spoken to have told me, that the problems in the Mid-East will continue until the Palestinian issue has been resolved. He tells me that, "As long as the Americans keep supporting the Israelis with money and weapons, and turning a blind eye to the spread of Israeli settlements on Palestinian lands, animosity and violence towards Israel will continue."

The driver stops at a grocery store in the middle of the sandy wilderness. We buy water and some snack foods, and then continue north. As we pull up to the border crossing, I thank the driver for his companionship, then pay him the $100. I throw-in an extra $50, and ask him to buy his young nine-year-old daughter a new dress. He shakes my hand, kisses my cheeks, and then waves me good luck. I ask him to wait an extra ten minutes, just in case I have some border problem and have to go back to Kuwait City. We are like the best of friends, but I know I will never see or hear from him again. Life as a journalist is like that.

I walk over to the first of two border checkpoints manned by Kuwaiti soldiers. I ask how I get to Basra from the border, as there are no buses or taxis. One of them tells me that there is an American checkpoint 400 feet across the border. "They will take you to Basra," he tells me.

He sends me marching to the second and last checkpoint. I walk along the hot asphalt with my entire luggage on my back and in my hands. All I can think about is driving back into smoldering Baghdad – a city I love and hate.

Finally, I reach the checkpoint and walking into the same trailer, I see the same official who dragged me over the coals when I first arrived at the Kuwait border, on April 24th. Sitting at his desk smoking a cigarette, he smiles and stands up holding out his outstretched hand (like the best of old friends), which I am loath to shake. The tea boy offers me some tea while the official rubber-stamps my papers. The official passes me my papers and wishes me good luck. No guards at either checkpoint inspect my baggage.

From the trailer a soldier ushers me over to a 50-foot strip of gravel and sand, a sort of demilitarized strip of land separating Kuwait from Iraq. I ask where the American checkpoint is located, but this guy tells me there is no American checkpoint and that I will have to flag down a ride to get to Basra. Well, there is an American checkpoint. I can see it a mile away in the distance, on another road leaving from Kuwait. But it is for military purposes only and off limits to all but the military.

I stand trapped in this no-man's-land, stuck between the machine gunners at the checkpoint and a sign that reads Thank-You for Visiting Kuwait. Pass this sign, and you are in Iraq, where half a dozen Iraqi beggars and thieves stand motioning me for food and water. In front of the checkpoint runs a continuous fence of barbwire, stretching as far as the eye can see in both directions along the frontier. In front of the fence a tank trap, 12 feet deep, 8 feet wide runs in both directions along the border. So here I am, stuck between the Kuwaiti machine gunners and rabid Iraqi bandits. A merciless sun cooks me from above, while a sharp, relentless wind cuts across my face like sandpaper.

But I do have some company, miserable as it is. A schoolteacher from Ottawa, Canada, Alexander Saikaley, who has pedaled his bicycle from Amman, Jordan, across Iraq to the Kuwaiti border, is now trying to get into Kuwait for a flight home to Canada. He is sort of in the same boat (or camel) as I was. He does not have an entrance visa.

He is an unusual man, though a typically inquisitive Canadian, making this dangerous journey to see first-hand the suffering of the Iraqi people. But the Kuwaiti border officials are telling him he cannot enter without a visa.

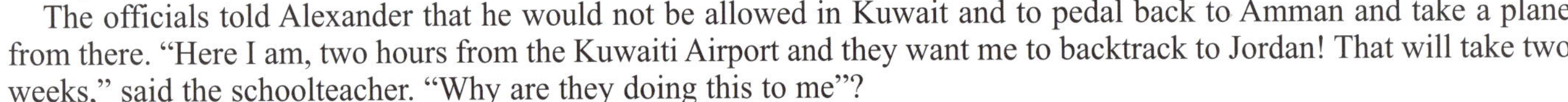
A small lake of oil on the Iraqi side of the border

The officials told Alexander that he would not be allowed in Kuwait and to pedal back to Amman and take a plane from there. "Here I am, two hours from the Kuwaiti Airport and they want me to backtrack to Jordan! That will take two weeks," said the schoolteacher. "Why are they doing this to me"?

He tells me he has been camped at the border for the last two days, waiting for the papers to gain entry into Kuwait. He keeps looking down at the sand, mumbling about his situation. Another day in this heat and Alexander will just shrivel up and blow away, I think to myself. Suddenly he looks up at me with squinting eyes and with the conviction of a preacher, asks, "Are they going to shoot down some guy on a bicycle if I walk across their border?" Waiting for my reply, I announce, "Anything is possible. But give me a heads up if you decide to walk and I will have my camera ready in case they shoot you or rough you up."

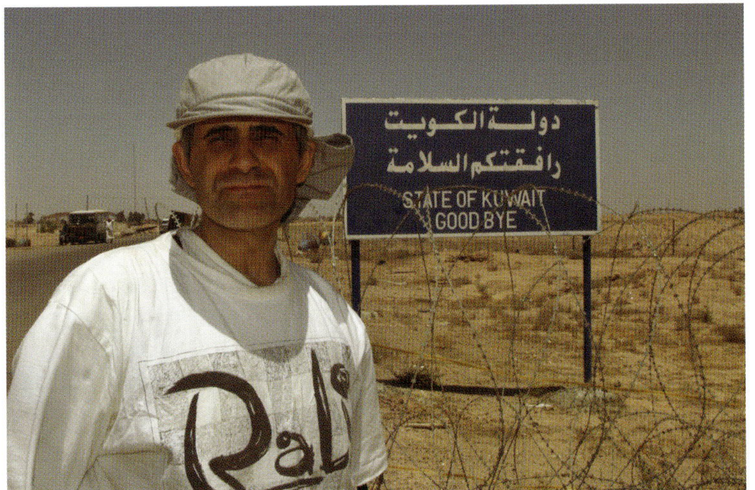
Canadian schoolteacher, Alexander Saikaley is left stranded at the Kuwaiti border

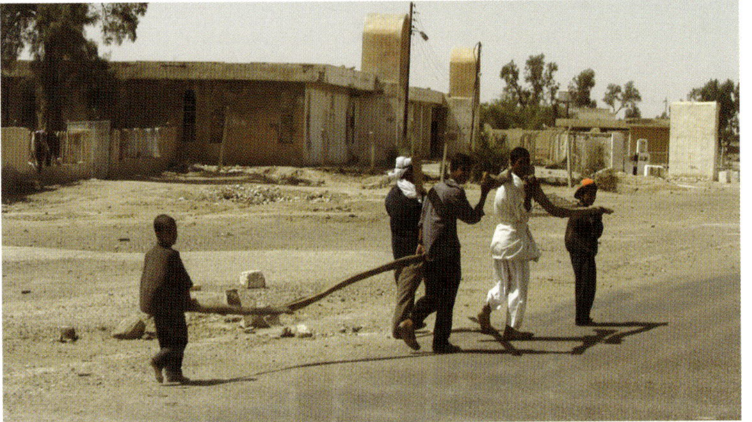
These Iraqi boys will sell this lead pipe, looted from buildings along the border

I give him the phone number of Bob Skrimes, at the Canadian Embassy in Kuwait. But I tell him not to hold his breath. Saikaley says he contacted the embassy earlier in the day (by borrowing a satellite phone), but as yet no one had shown up to assist him. He is furious at the Kuwaitis for their steel-heartedness and at the Canadian Embassy for taking their time to come to his assistance.

I have been standing in the void between the two borders, trying to flag a ride for over two hours, and am growing very impatient. I start holding up my British passport (it is more recognizable and the Brits rule this area) and flashing it in front of passing vehicles slowly trickling over the border. One hand holds my passport, the other my outstretched thumb. I am hitchhiking from a no-mans-land to a war zone. This has to be the most adverse travel situation I have ever been in.

The bicyclist and I gulp down copious amounts of water, while talking about the war and Canadian foreign policy. We are two angry hornets, and all I can think about is how many other Canadians out their have been screwed over and abandoned by their own government like this, and worse.

Finally, a Jordanian news photographer named Tarak pulls over in his air-conditioned Ford Explorer and offers me a lift to Basra. He works for a Kuwaiti news agency and does not speak very much English, but we communicate well – we are journalists.

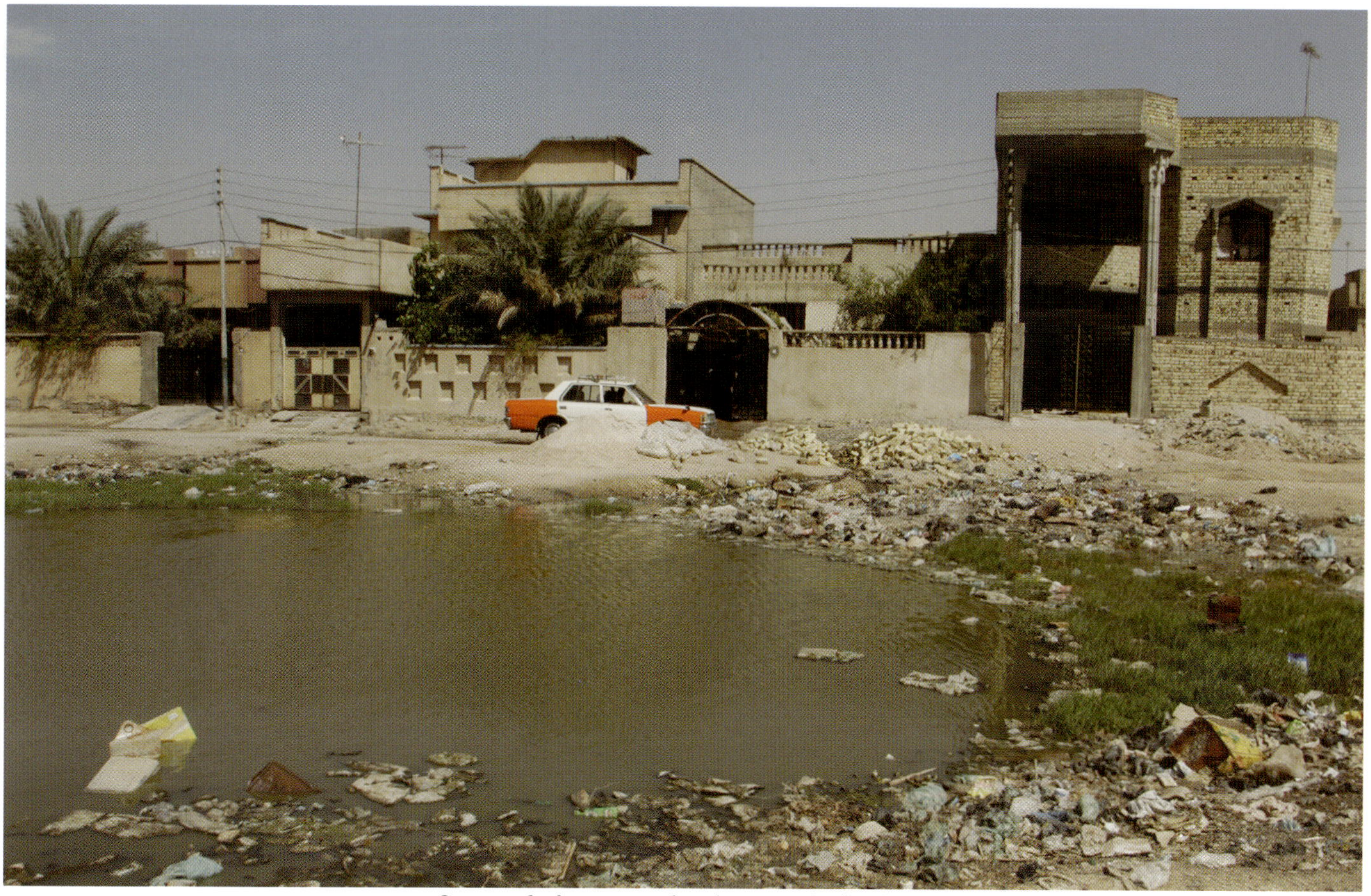

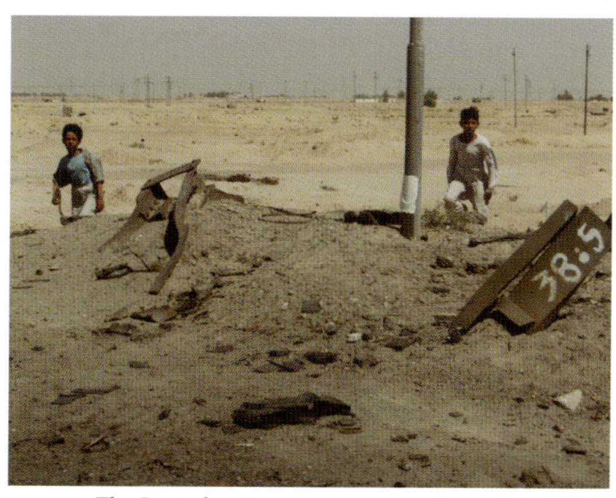

Open pool of sewage and garbage in suburban Basra

Jumping into the Explorer, I leave a flask of bottled water with Alexander and wish him luck. I tell him I will try to reach the Canadian Embassy to insist they take care of him, if I find the opportunity and the means to call them. The feeling as I drive away from that border crossing is extremely uplifting, and I feel like the weight of the world is being lifted from my shoulders. I am ecstatic about being out of Kuwait and driving into Iraq. At least in Iraq, I know who my enemies are and the rules of engagement.

Just into Iraq, I see four tattered looters, just boys, carrying a twenty-foot section of lead piping. It looks as though they carry a huge anaconda.

The first stop we make is at a telecommunications centre on the outskirts of Basra. Stepping out of the car I bend down on my knee and kiss the hot Iraqi sand, I am so happy to be back.

The communications building has been heavily bombed, looted and torched, but its remains are still being picked over by looters. Working in teams of two or more, they are busy removing wheels and rims from vehicles. Even the suspension bars are being removed. Elsewhere on the site, adults and teens walk through the rubble of cinder-block and twisted metal, with white sacks in their hands, picking out anything (metal siding, support columns, fences etc.) that is re-usable or recyclable. Well, that's one good thing about the looters, they are recyclers. In fact, one must not overlook the value of some looting. This metal will be sold and food will be placed on the table.

Looting is the only form of employment for many of these impoverished folks, and in some cases, the only means of feeding their family. Stealing to keep one's family alive is one thing, but looting financial institutions or your neighbor's home for blatant greed is wrong. My own hungry, crying son would be all the incentive I would need as a father, to turn into a thief to feed him. And this is the present situation for millions of Iraqis. This is the question I ask the reader to keep in mind – what would you do, in a similar situation, if your hungry little baby was crying and you had no money to feed him, nor a job, nor family nor government support? Now what if you had seven kids, and you could not rely on other family members because they are in the same predicament as you. How far would you go to provide? How much crying could you stand before you would be driven to steal to feed your infants?

The Iraqi frontier is a war-torn wasteland

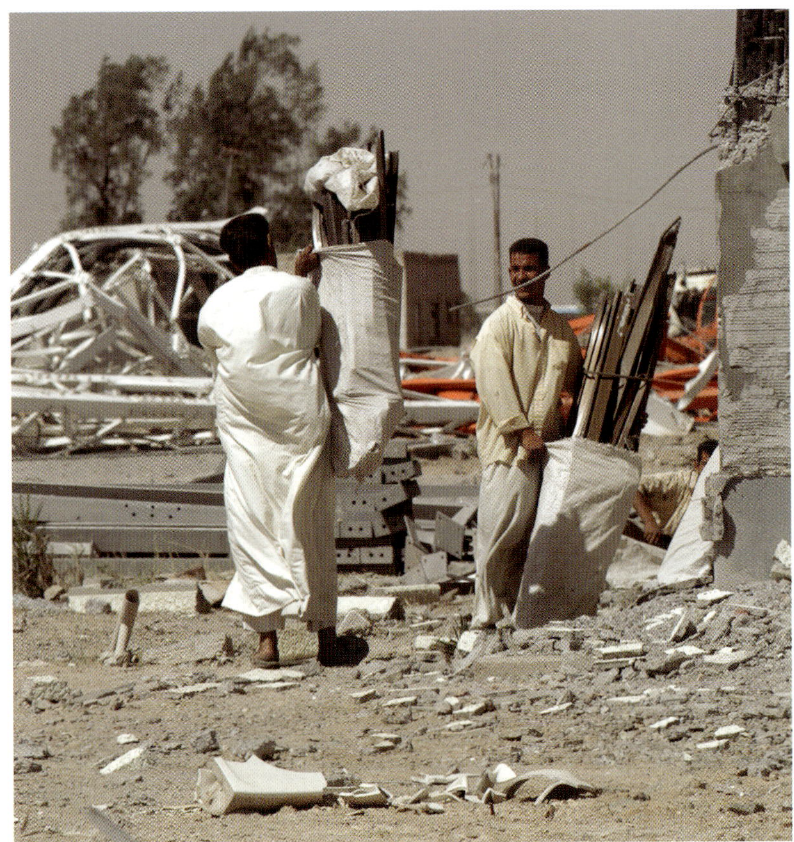

Looters stripping iron and aluminum from the communication center

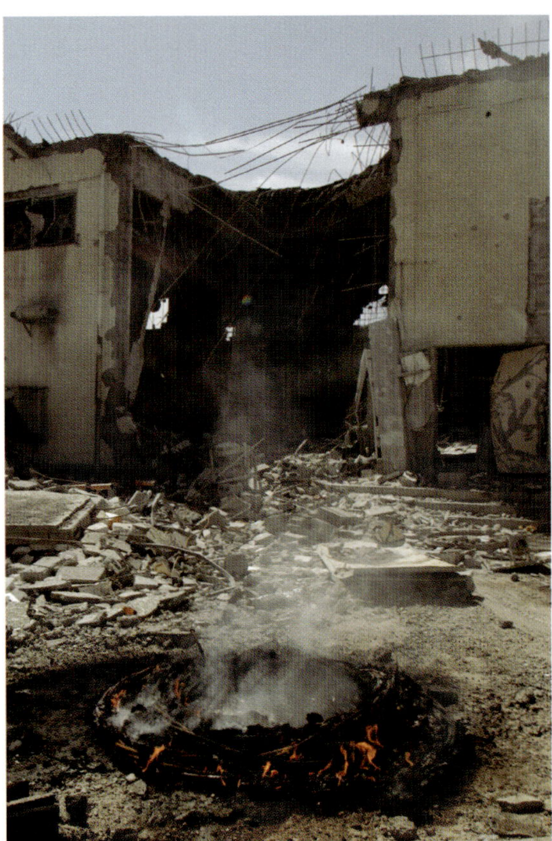

Communications center has been shelled and stripped

The communication center's 150-foot tall transmitter tower lies crumpled and twisted on the ground. The walls of the main building have been blasted by tank and rifle fire. Inside, it is a burned useless mess. We just have a short stay, taking a few snapshots. As we are leaving, we wave at the looters, who smile and jubilantly wave back. The looters know we mean no harm. To them, we are just doing our job, as they are.

We stop in a suburb of Basra and pick up a former Basra police officer, a friend of the driver. This area has open sewers flowing through the laneways, but is by no means a poor area. Some of the wastewater has backed up into swimming-pool-sized reservoirs of foul smelling raw sewage. I can't understand why the local residents do not try to clean up their own neighborhood. But maybe it is a mindset. With Saddam as leader-despot, any form of organization would be considered a threat.

Silly as it may seem to a Westerner, perhaps these people are used to having a government official plan every facet of everyday life for them, including unclogging sewage lagoons or burning trash. The people of Iraq must re-learn how to think for themselves, but that will not take long. I find the Iraqis highly intelligent, humorous, and willing to work.

The three of us drive along a main Basra street where we reach a large walled prison complex (according to Tarak, Saddam's goons murdered 3000 prisoners here just before the war started).

The Basra Prison, which looks like an unassuming Spanish villa from the road, is a maze of medieval cellblocks, guards' quarters and an exercise yard. The dilapidated complex had held both male and female prisoners. We walk through heavily barred cells and suspected torture chambers, where ropes and metal hooks hang from the ceiling (prisoners were hung by the wrists, and then beaten with heavy sticks).

Other jail cells or dorms have cloth rope hanging from the window bars. Prisoners were forced to balance on their tiptoes with a window cord pulled tight around their necks. By tightening the cord, the neck was stretched. It was like slow death by hanging. This is one method, according to Tarak and his policeman friend, used in extracting confessions from prisoners.

Up to 300 prisoners were held in rooms meant for 25. Their iron sleeping cots are laced with torn clothing and plastic or nylon rope,

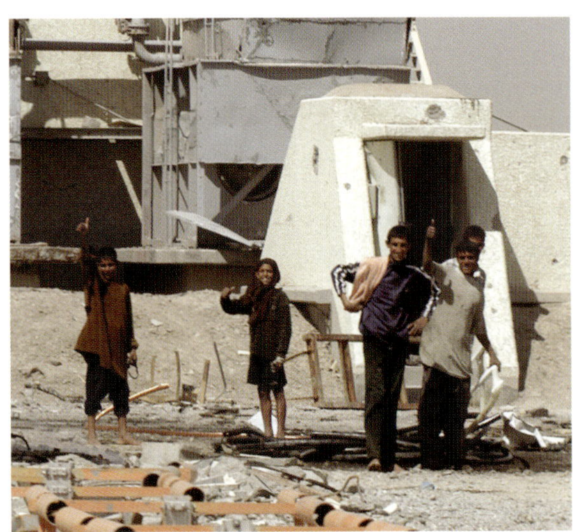

Young looters wave at us as we leave center

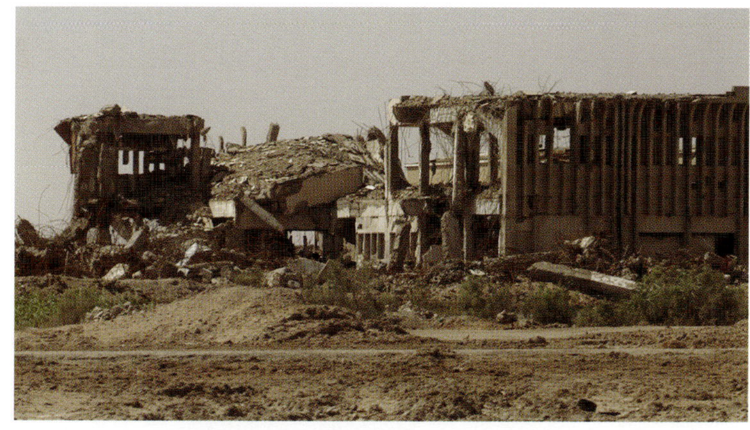
Ministry building hit by aerial strikes

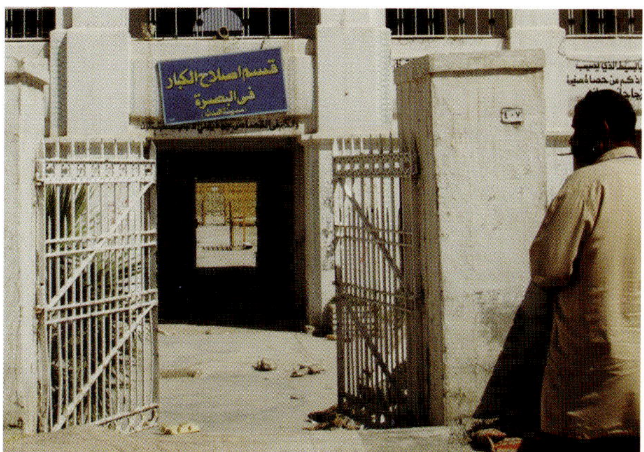
Front entrance of the Basra Prison

forming the base on which to rest their cardboard box mattresses. I don't see any blankets or covers anywhere. Perhaps they covered themselves with their clothing or other sections of cardboard.

Graffiti scribbled onto the cell walls show the number of days a prisoners had spent in captivity, or show a self-portrait. Other more elaborate artwork, mostly in the women's sectors, show colorfully painted scenes of waterfront settings with boats and flowers.

It would have been an extremely overcrowded, dirty, hot place to be locked up in. Some areas, like the exercise yard, are enclosed by a heavy iron-bar fence with sharpened tips. A number of cellblocks have woven barbwire mesh instead of a ceiling. Dozens of discarded bed cots and other prison debris clutter the exercise yard, where a solitary basketball hoop stands in the middle of the half-acre asphalt square. The basketball hoop and the cell locks are stamped with Made in the USA.

The small, one-room medical clinic has a toppled and smashed x-ray machine lying on the floor. Syringes, medical records and broken bottles of medicine litter the floor and counters. Mats of black hair cover the floor (the clinic also served as the barbershop).

The building housing the guards' and officers' quarters has been freshly painted, and is a palace compared to the prisoners' cellblocks.

We leave the prison and its secrets, heading further up the road until we reach the Basra Red Crescent Society Headquarters. On the way, we pass an open market where all sorts of looted items (such as office furnishings, metal poles and computers) are for sale. Other vendors sell blocks of ice or an array of fresh fruits. At least there are fruits and vegetables for the inhabitants. Even frozen slush cones are for sale. I am tempted to have a slush cone, but I can't chance it; the ice would have been made from local water, and therefore possibly contaminated.

Basra appears to have at least a limited supply of electricity, and shows little sign of war damage or looting in the downtown area, compared with Baghdad. There are a few ministerial buildings that I have seen rendered useless by bombing, and these have suffered precision or direct hits by Smart Bombs. The streets are relatively clean and the residents are openly friendly and cheerful.

The Red Crescent Society is housed in a large, well-kept two-storey building, separated from the main road by a wide lawn of withered grass. A throng of 150 desperate men women and children stand outside pleading for food. I attempt to take some pics from a balcony, but the crowd grows angry and motions me to put my camera down. Being respectful of their wishes, I stop and go inside the building to talk with some of the staff. They tell me the residents are in dire need of flour, rice and cooking oil, and say there is no excuse for a lack of supplies, as the port of Umm Qasr (where the brunt of the coalition relief supplies are unloaded) is less than a two hour's drive away. Somehow, they say, Basra has missed out on the food aid.

The people begging for aid look cleanly clothed, and full faced, compared with the long drawn-out faces of hunger I had seen in Baghdad. I have to wonder if these Iraqis are perhaps better off than most. Their city stands virtually undamaged and there are fruits and vegetables in the market.

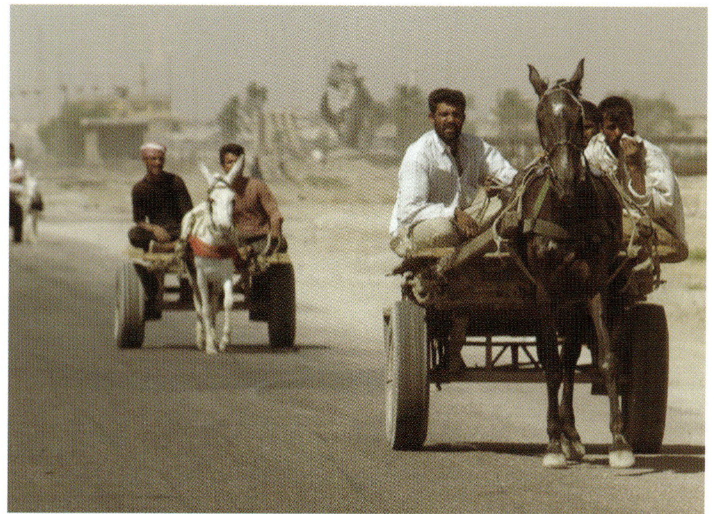
Donkey and horse carts are commonly used for transport in Basra

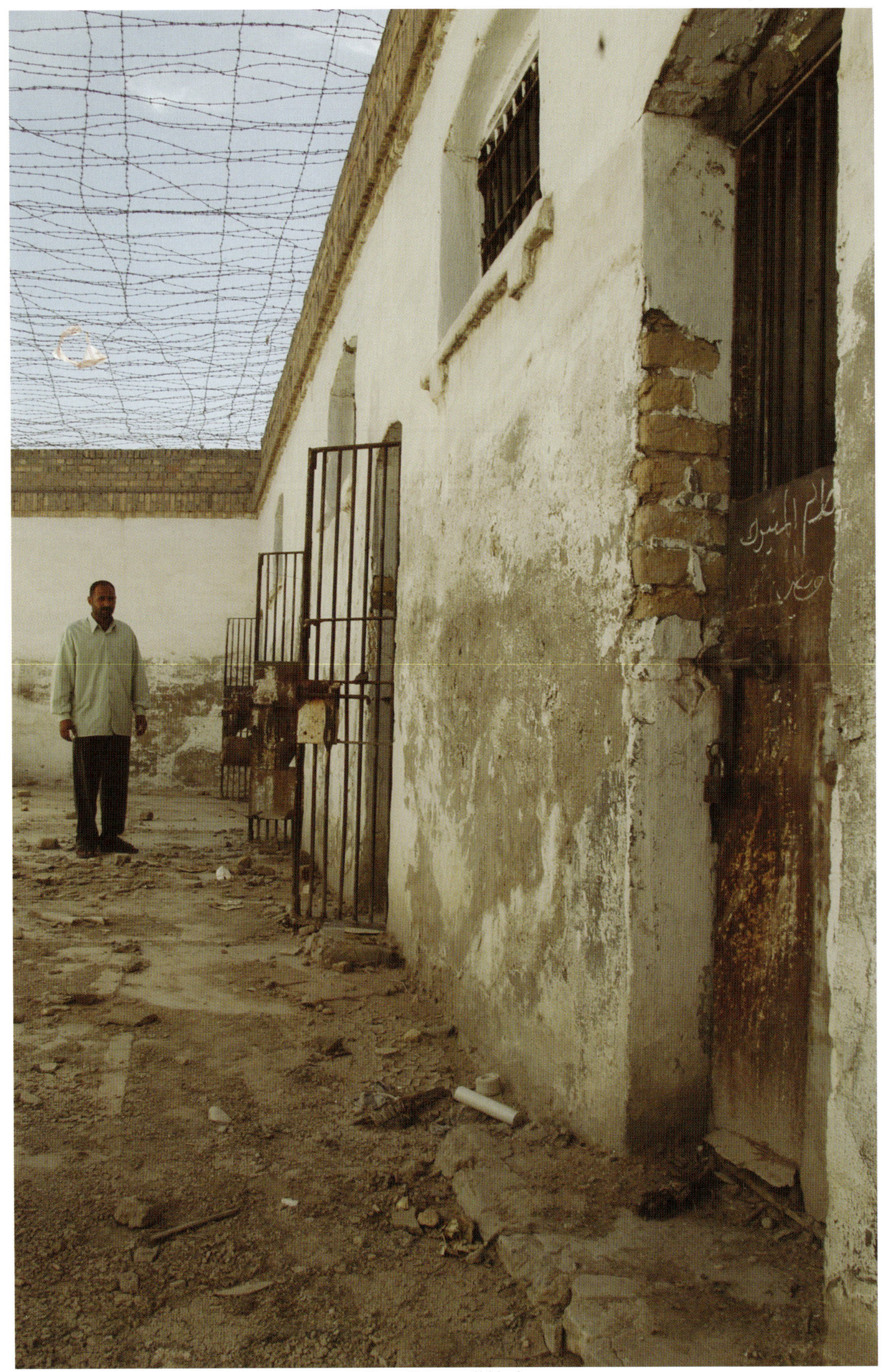

Basra Prison cell block

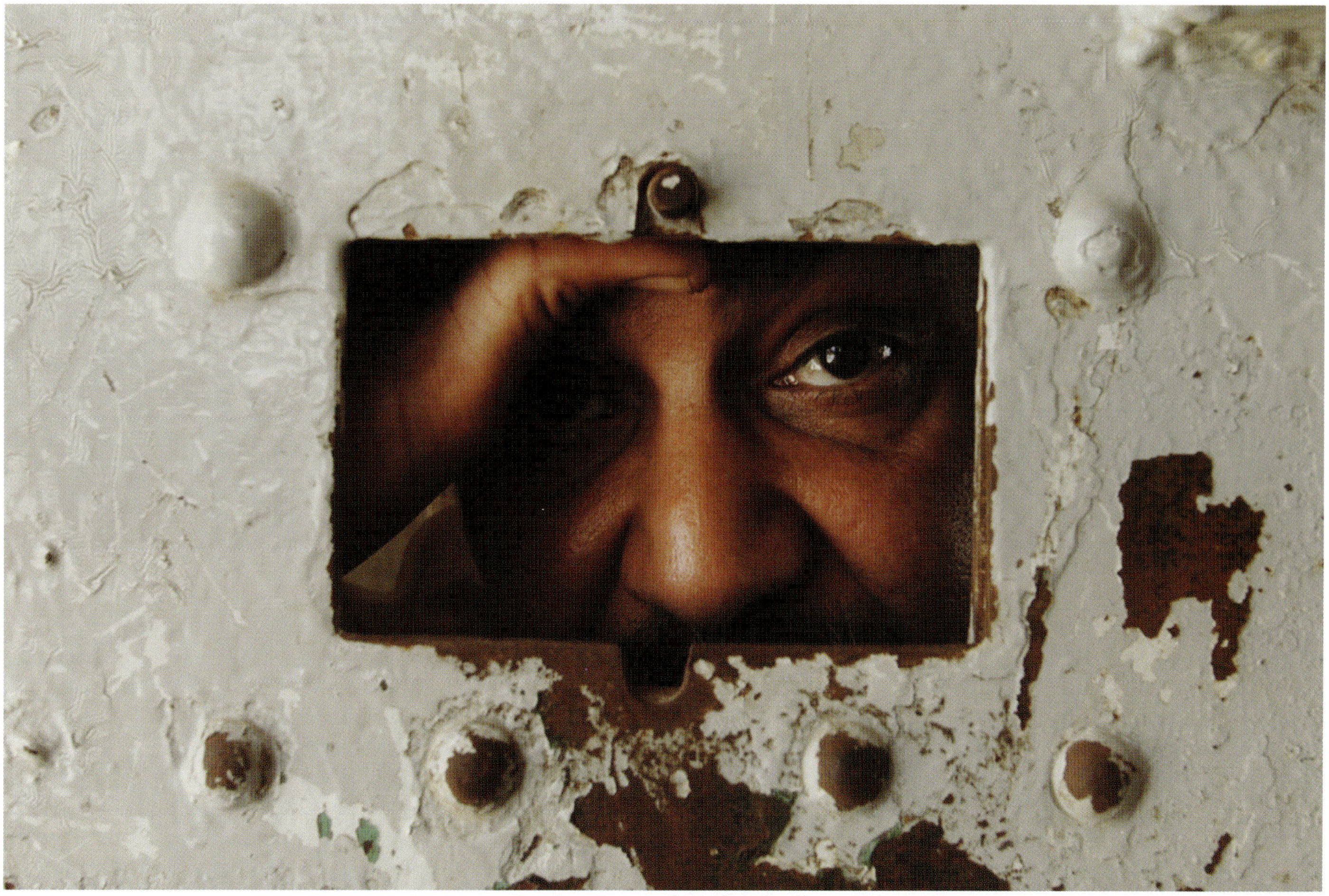

A journalist friend peers through jail cell peephole

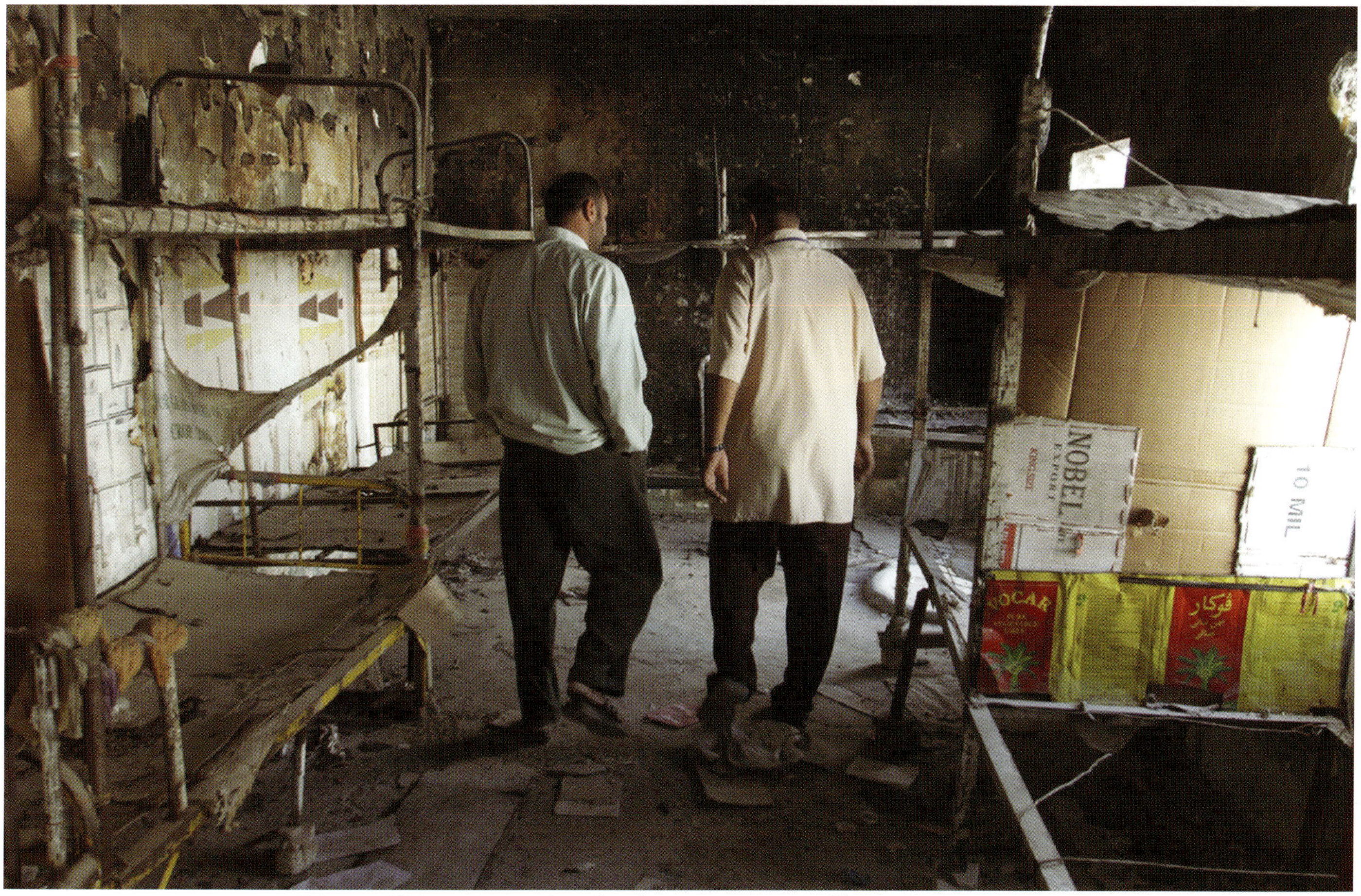

Prisoners' living quarters show that this prison was more like a concentration camp

Leaving the Red Crescent Society, we drive along the shore of the Tigris River, stopping at the entranceway to Saddam's riverside Basra Palace. We ask permission to visit the palace, but the British soldiers guarding the entranceway tell us that we have to go to the airport and ask central command for permission. So we drive to Basra International Airport, 10 miles north of town. On the way we pass the main port area, where ships should be unloading and loading, but there is no activity; it has been shut down and partially damaged by bombing. Tugboats, barges and some private craft are moored along the docks. There is a line of huge cargo cranes lining one section of the river. They look like giant iron storks dipping their beaks towards the fabulous Tigris.

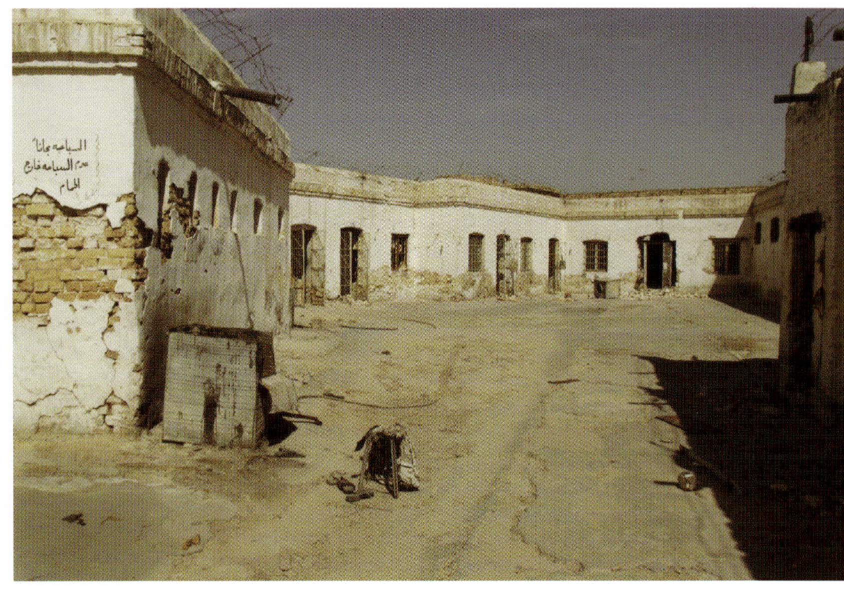
A wing of Basra Prison

The airport route takes us through a large expanse of open, inhospitable desert. About a mile from the control tower, we pass a massive concentration of British military vehicles (tanks, troop carriers, communications trucks etc.). They are strung out for over a mile along a raised embankment that cuts across and dominates the south flank of the airport. There are a few remnants of destroyed Iraqi vehicles along the roadway leading to the airport, but much of the destruction looks like it has been cleaned up by the British.

I can see a number of large black patches and burned debris on the highway and at the side of the road, where vehicles have been destroyed and burned (a major battle for control of the airport had been fought here in the first weeks of the war). It is now under the control of the British 7th Brigade. Just before the terminal, we pull over at a checkpoint where the sentry asks us to wait for an escort.

Following the escort vehicle, we are led into the parking lot in front of the departures terminal, now British Forces Headquarters. Climbing out of the Explorer, I see a couple of joggers dressed in t-shirts, shorts and running shoes jogging past the front of the terminal building. This is a shock to me. One of the joggers is a gorgeous woman, a soldier, with her blonde hair done up in a ponytail. A narrow red halter-top covers her above, and tight butt-enhancing shorts below. This place has the air of an English country club. The Marines weren't like this.

We enter the main building (after dodging another jogger) and make our way to the second floor where a soldier speaks up from behind a long wooden desk. "Sir, there is no smoking allowed in this facility," she barks. "Yes ma'am!" I reply. It is another gorgeous woman soldier, this time manning the welcome desk. I head downstairs to find an ashtray outside the main doors.

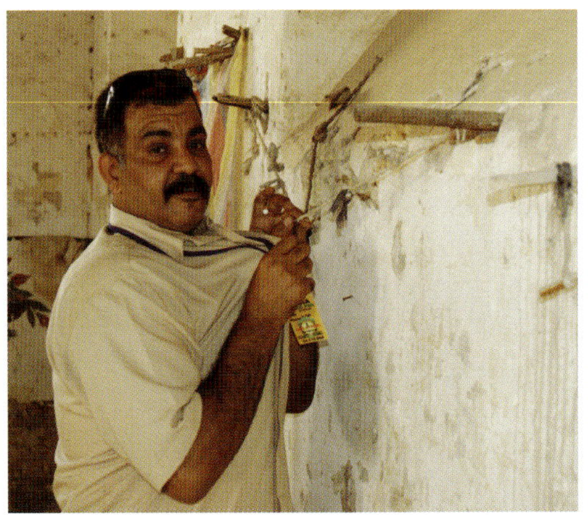
Tarak shows how prisoners were hung by cords

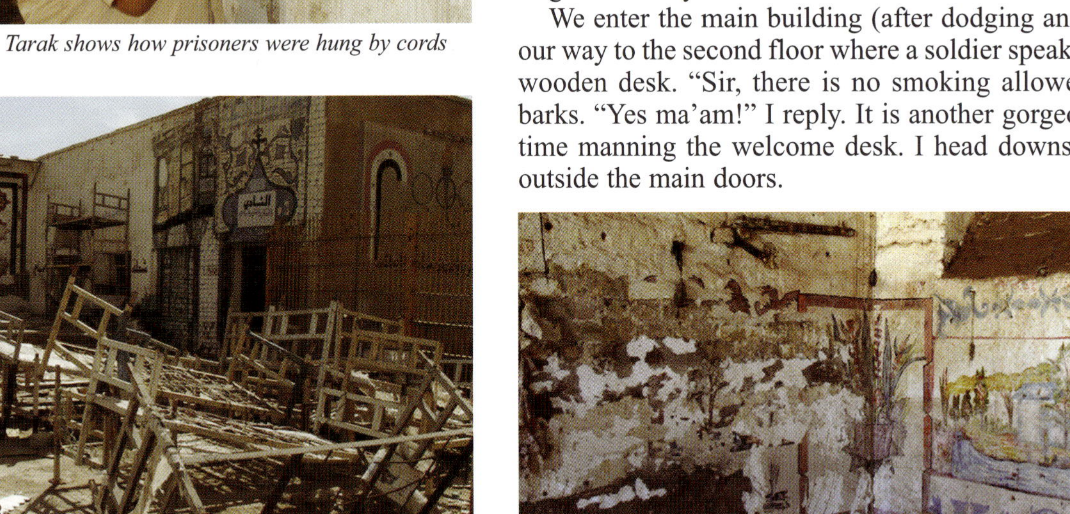
Bed cots are piled up in the prison yard

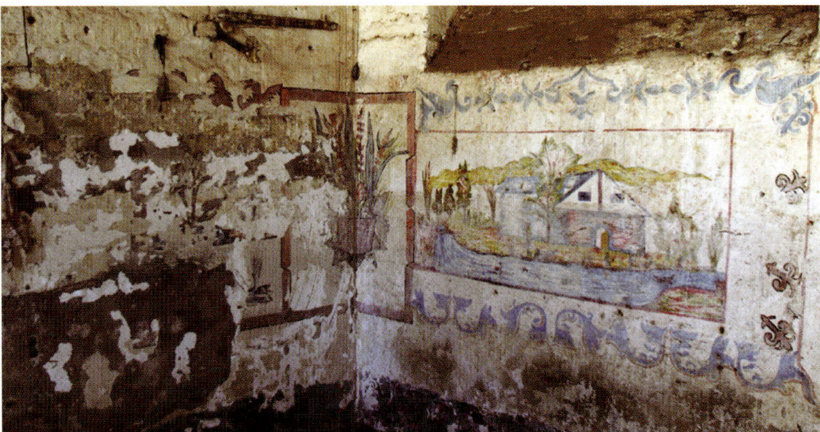
Female prisoner's drawing of her home in the marshlands of southern Iraq

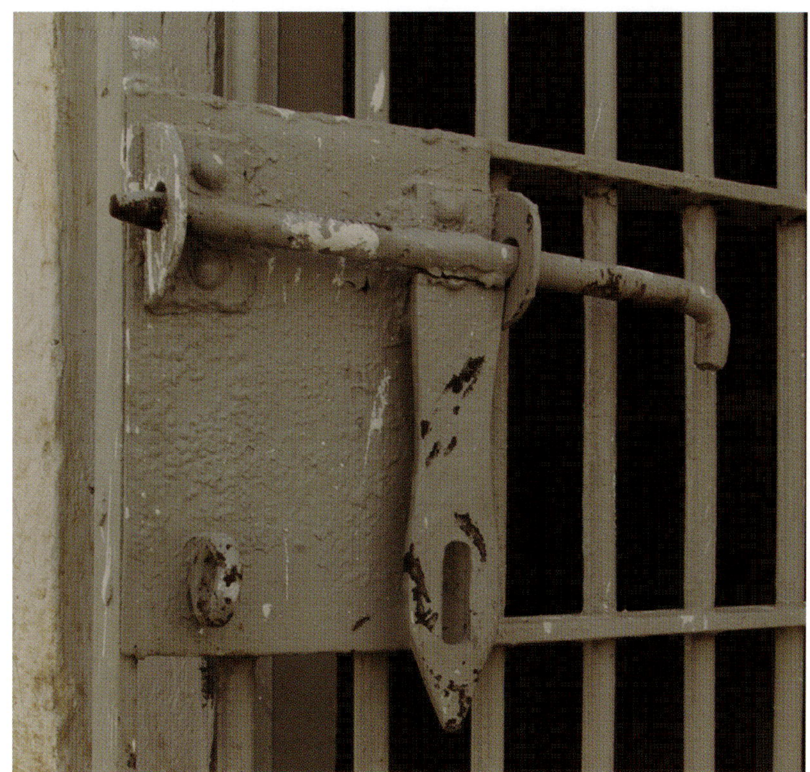

Thousands of former prisoners, murderers and sex offenders are now roaming Iraq

I head back upstairs and end up talking with an officer who outlines the British plan in the region. Two other journalists are taking part in the interview; they are Iranian. While the interview is going on, I drink three cups of their tea, topped off with sugar and real milk. There is also a bowl full of colorful hard candies to suck on. I reflect on how sophisticated these Brits appear to be; joggers, beautiful soldiers and real milk in your tea!

Suddenly the officer notices my tape recorder up by his face. He becomes agitated by its presence and turns to me saying, "I'm not going to give you an interview." I ask him what the problem is. He says that I interrupted him. I apologize and explain to him that I have difficulty writing and taking photos at the same time, so I use a microphone.

He does not respond, but just nods his head and continues explaining the British strategy. The officer tells us, "The thing that is happening now is we're making a transition from war-fighting, to what we call phase four, when humanitarian organizations will come in and the reconstruction of the country can begin. As a force, we are applying ourselves to the internal security situation, and day by day, it is what the British Army is good at. We are trying to reduce the lawlessness."

Tarak and his cop friend tell me they have to go back to town, so they ask me if I can find a ride back to town with someone else. I thank them for their hospitality and tell them not to worry; I will find a ride. Tarak is a good companion and very accommodating to my strategy of coverage. We enjoyed each other's company, but now we part ways.

I ask the two journalists who are participating in the interview if they would mind taking me to Basra. They tell me I am welcome to join them, if I can squeeze into their equipment-jammed car. They work for the Iranian news station, Urna News Agency. After wrapping up the interview, the three of us head back to Basra to look for a hotel.

Driving through Basra, I tell them about my experience in Kuwait. They agree my treatment was outrageous, and ask if I would mind being interviewed for a news feature. I agree, and they start to ask me how I got to Basra and what I think about the war, and the people I have met.

They tell me they had crossed into Iraq from Kuwait earlier in the day, and met Canadian bicyclist, Alexander Saikaley stranded at the border. They had called the Canadian Embassy in Kuwait from the border (so it was their phone Alexander called the embassy on), for an interview to ask why they had not taken care of this Canadian citizen.

We chat continuously as we drive around Basra and its beautiful riverfront, while keeping an eye open for a hotel.

As the sun sets over Basra, we stop to take some pictures on a rickety bridge spanning the Tigris River. The three of us have become good friends; another instance of how war can bring cultures together. The war has made me a much richer man in knowledge, while at the same time picked my pockets.

We find a not-so-bad hotel along the main road, a mile from the British checkpoint at Saddam's palace. Outside the hotel, a local man is selling airtime on his satellite phone for $2 a minute, (compared to $10 a minute in Baghdad). I call the family but they are not at home, so I call my brother-in-law, Peter McLaine, in Ottawa. I tell him that I am out of Kuwait and safe, and to contact Phyllis to tell her the press conference is off. It is great talking to Peter, and kind of him to help me.

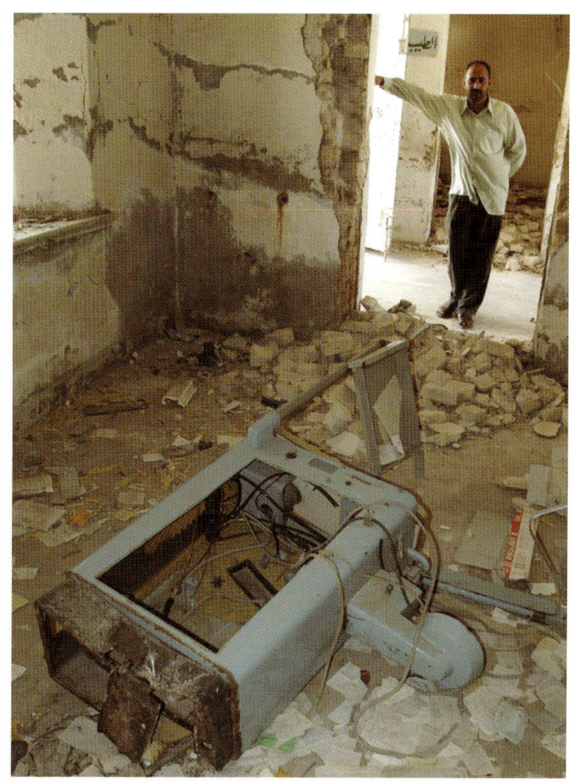

X-ray machine lies broken in prison clinic

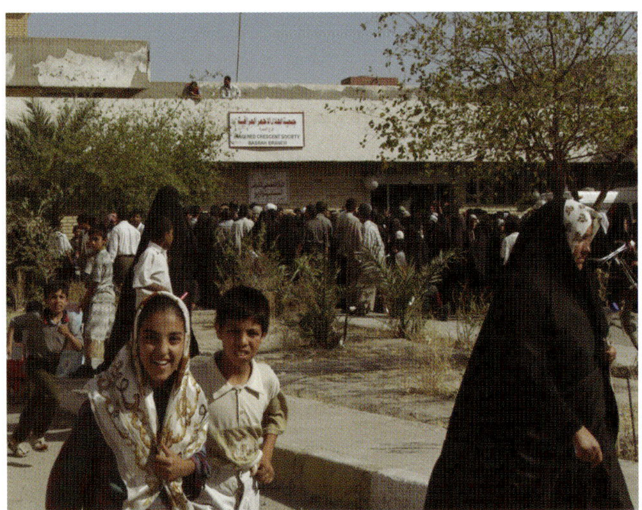
People line up for aid outside the Basra Red Crescent Society

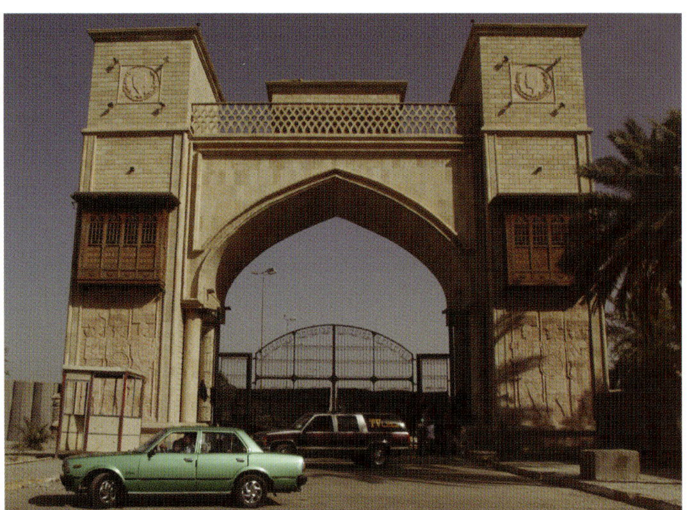
The entranceway to Saddam's Basra Palace

Finishing with my phone call, I check-in and head upstairs to my room. The Urna News guys are rooming together next door to me. My room is a one bed, no-frills accommodation. It even has a TV, but it doesn't work (it makes a nice ornament).

After unpacking, I put George Harrison's "All Things Must Pass" CD into my laptop and crank it up. I have not heard my favorite tape since I left Baghdad. The tunes pour out from my laptop like waves of electricity, charging me with a massive surge of energy and buoyancy. I'm alive again, and ready for the world!

I look out my window to see that the streetlights and storefront signs are on. The manager of the hotel tells me that the electricity has been up and running for a week now.

Walking into the washroom, I start washing my face and glance up from the basin to see a bird-sized cockroach clinging to the tiled walls, one foot away from my dripping face. It is a huge, light brown-colored, antenna-twitching critter, like something out of a Brazilian rain forest. The 'hulk-of-a-bug' remains motionless, proudly standing its ground. I think about killing it, but I wouldn't want to miss and have it escape under my bed holding a grudge!

I start talking to it, as though it is an old friend. "Why should I kill you; you deserve to live here as much as I do. What makes me any holier than you, to take your life? Just stay off my face tonight and we will get along!"

My simple philosophy is that we both have our jobs to do in this short span of life; sometimes they even have their similarities, man and cockroach. The roach has become my instant friend, and I brush my teeth and wash myself while it clings to the wall watching me. I tell it again not to fear me, unless it invades my bed. I decide to take a different approach to negotiation – man as an equal to cockroach. I strike up a bargain, a contract of sorts, with my creepy friend.

Finishing off an apple (compliments of the Sheraton in Kuwait), I place the juicy core in the bathroom wastebasket on top of a bed of discarded papers. I talk to the roach, telling him (and any of his hidden friends), that he is more than welcome to stay in his room, and I will stay in mine. Pushing the basket to the middle of the bathroom floor I wish him bon appetite! Leaving the lights on, I close the bathroom door behind me. I sit on my bed relaxing with a cigarette and tea, thinking about life and cockroaches. I am happy to meet this creature. My life has changed, I don't have much faith in my fellow man at this point, though I am trying to convince myself that I do. God help us!

After taking a shower (the roach does not move), I go next door to see if my Iranian friends are ready to go out for supper. A British tank patrol passes outside the hotel, its rumbling highly audible. The British presence is well established in the city, with a sandbagged checkpoint just down the road from us, and regular tank patrols. From what I can see, this town is very peaceful and very friendly.

We drive around looking for a restaurant, but most of them are already closed, as it going on 9 p.m. We finally find an open diner, illuminated with a large colorful neon sign. I order a

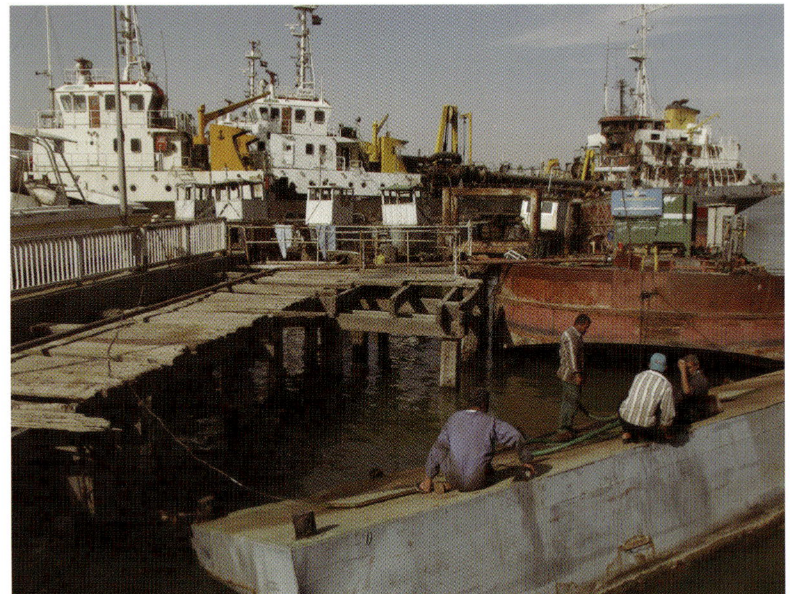
The Tigris River is the economic soul of Basra

kabob, tea, and a cold Pepsi. It is a bright, bustling place, filled with activity and the smell of broiled meat and vegetables.

While we are leaning over eating our kabobs at the stand-up counter, five men enter the eatery. Four are dressed in blue coveralls the other in a standard white gown and sandals. They have stubbly unkempt beards and are very thin, but fit. They have the appearance of factory workers, just finishing their shift on some assembly line and coming in for a snack; but in reality, they have just now been released from an American prisoner of war camp.

The former P.O.W.s are soldiers from the Baghdad area, and speak as though they have just awakened from a long, deep sleep, and now want to make up for it. As soon as they walk into the place I make eye contact and bow their way while smiling. They return the gesture and before I know it, I am shaking their hands and they are embracing me. They are desperate to speak to someone, to hear a voice from free Basra, to communicate with the outside.

The five explain to me (as translated through the Iranian journalists) that they have been held as prisoners of war for over a month, interred at the Kasra Military Camp, south of Al Nasiriyah. Most of the 1500 prisoners that the prison held, have been released over the

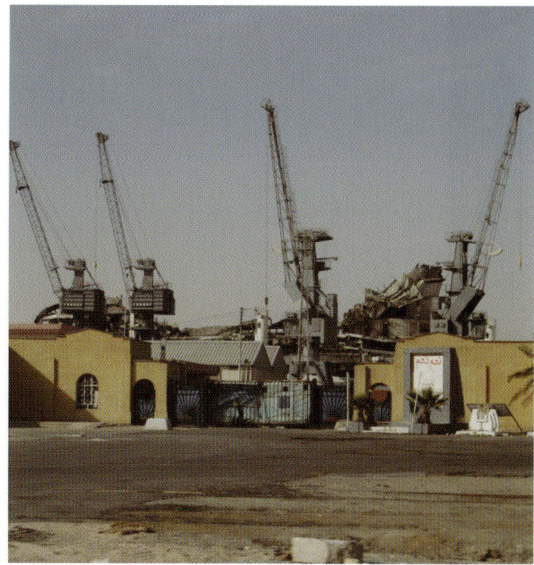

Cranes line the Basra docks

last couple of days, except for 500 who remain in custody. We are told that the remaining prisoners are being held because they have information that the Americans want, such as witnessing or partaking in crimes against humanity, or being suspected as part of Saddam's former administrative structure.

Without hesitation, I get the attention of the waiter and order the liberated five a Pepsi and a kabob. I am ecstatic at seeing these men smiling and filling their faces. What a fantastic feeling this is! We chat using the usual sign and body language and with the help of my Iranian friends. A little into the meal, I hand them a crisp $20 banknote. Using my hands, I explain that I want it shared amongst the five. They hug and kiss me. I wish them peace.

They tell me of their surrender to the Americans without a fight, after seeing the massive force and firepower up against them. It doesn't matter to me whether they are Iraqi or American prisoners, I would have done the same for either. They are soldiers, and I have a huge respect for the soldier.

The Iranian journalists later tell me that they were deeply touched by my compassion for the ex-prisoners, and for the courage to show it. I tell them that all men are soldiers in some form or another, and we have to start re-building broken fences, no matter how small the fence. I tell them that I also was treated like a prisoner not that many hours ago, so seeing these men free had a special meaning for me as well. We drive back to the hotel feeling enlightened and invigorated by the events at the restaurant.

I lie in my bed burning back-up CDs of my pics and planning how and when to get back to Baghdad. I fall asleep feeling safe, relaxed and extremely happy.

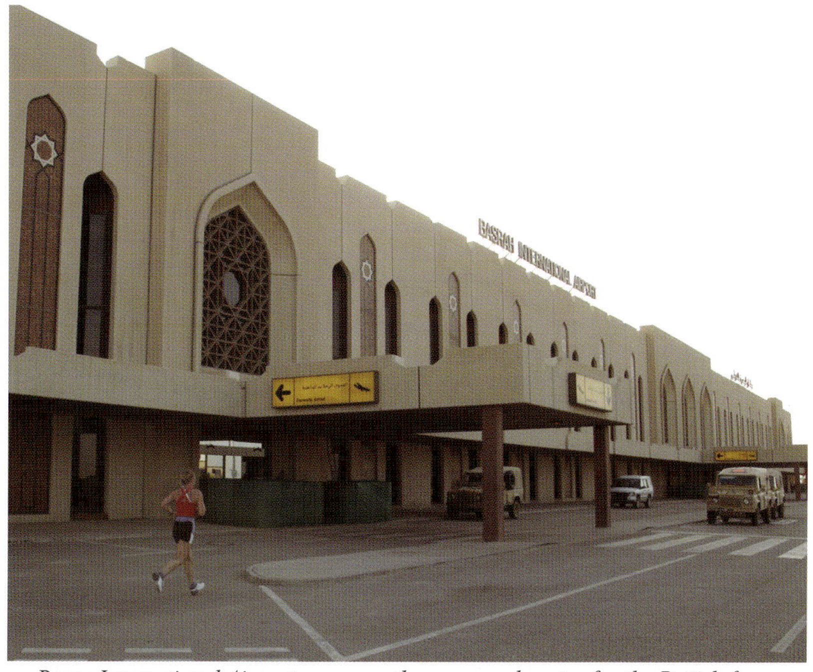

Basra International Airport serves as the command center for the British forces

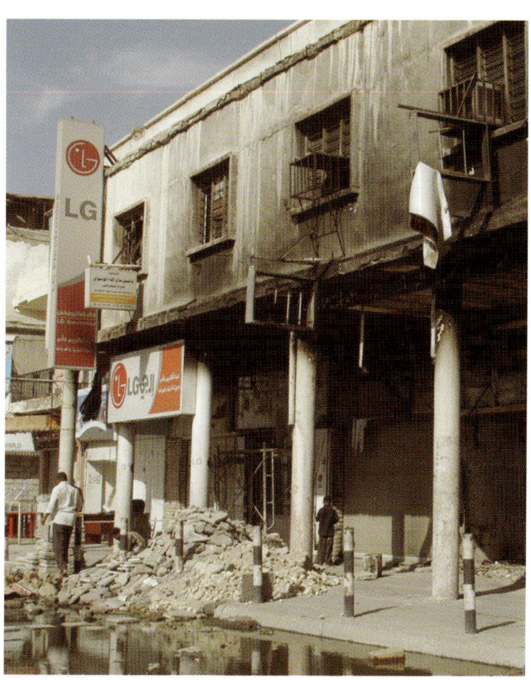

A small number of shops are damaged by war

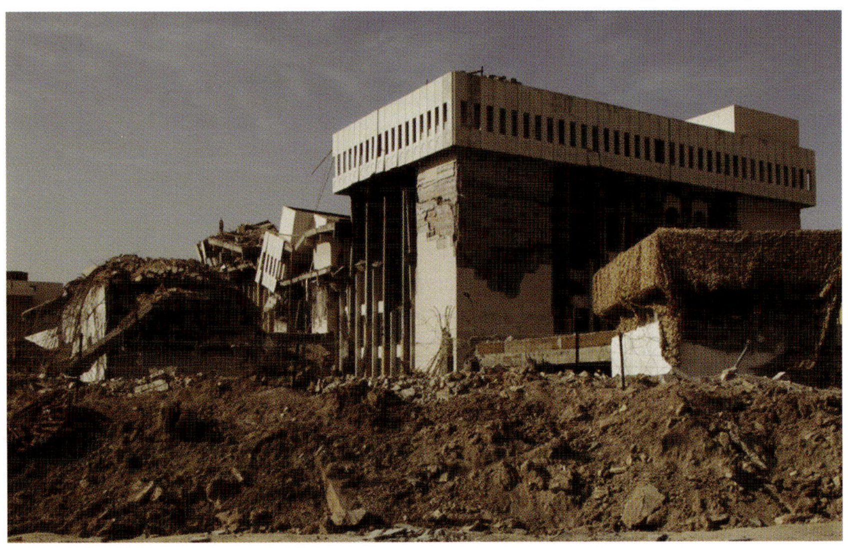

This destroyed ministry building has a camouflaged pillbox in front of it

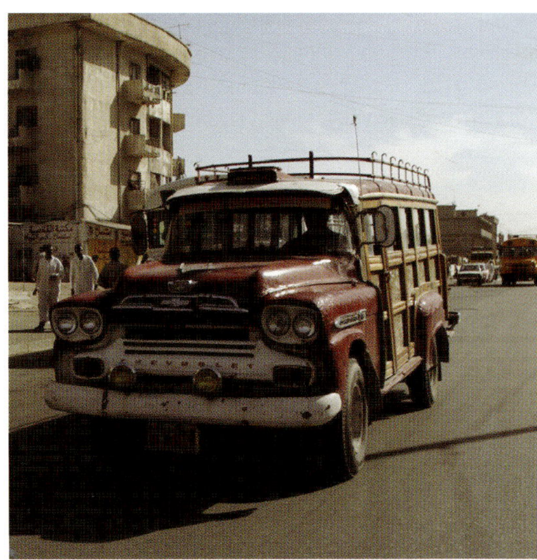

Automobiles, like this classic Woodie, last long in Iraq

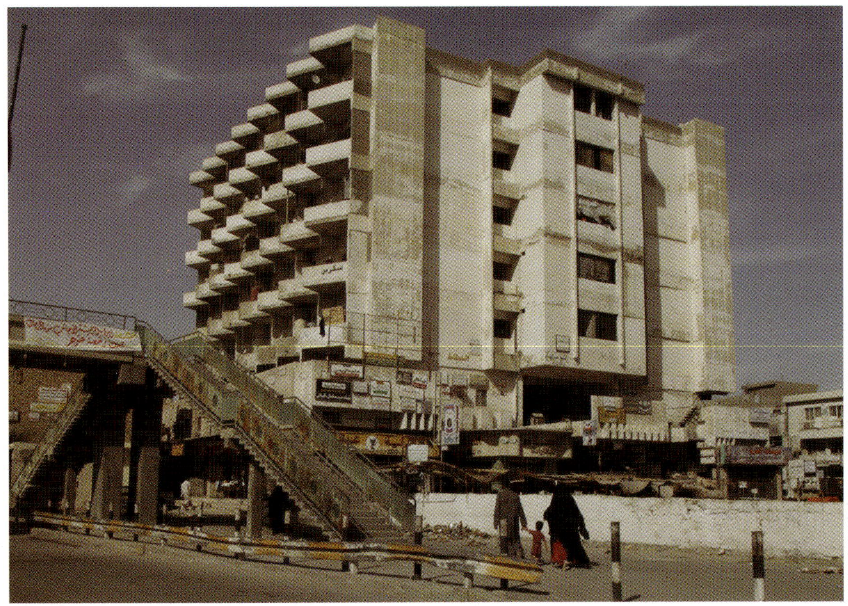

Basra has a variety of architecture and is a very pretty city

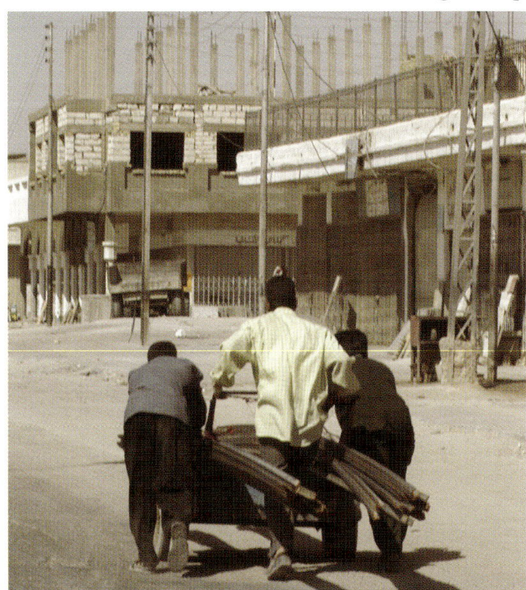

A cartload of pilfered iron posts goes to market

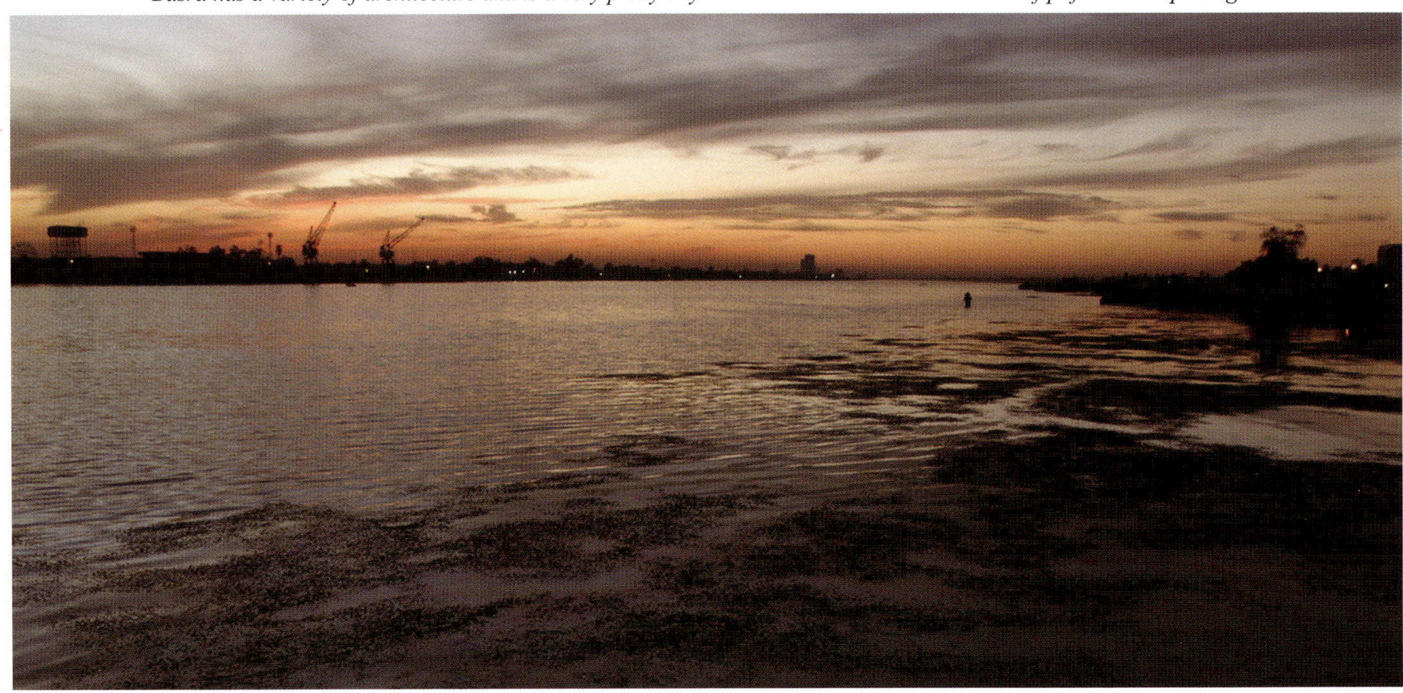

The Tigris River runs through Basra

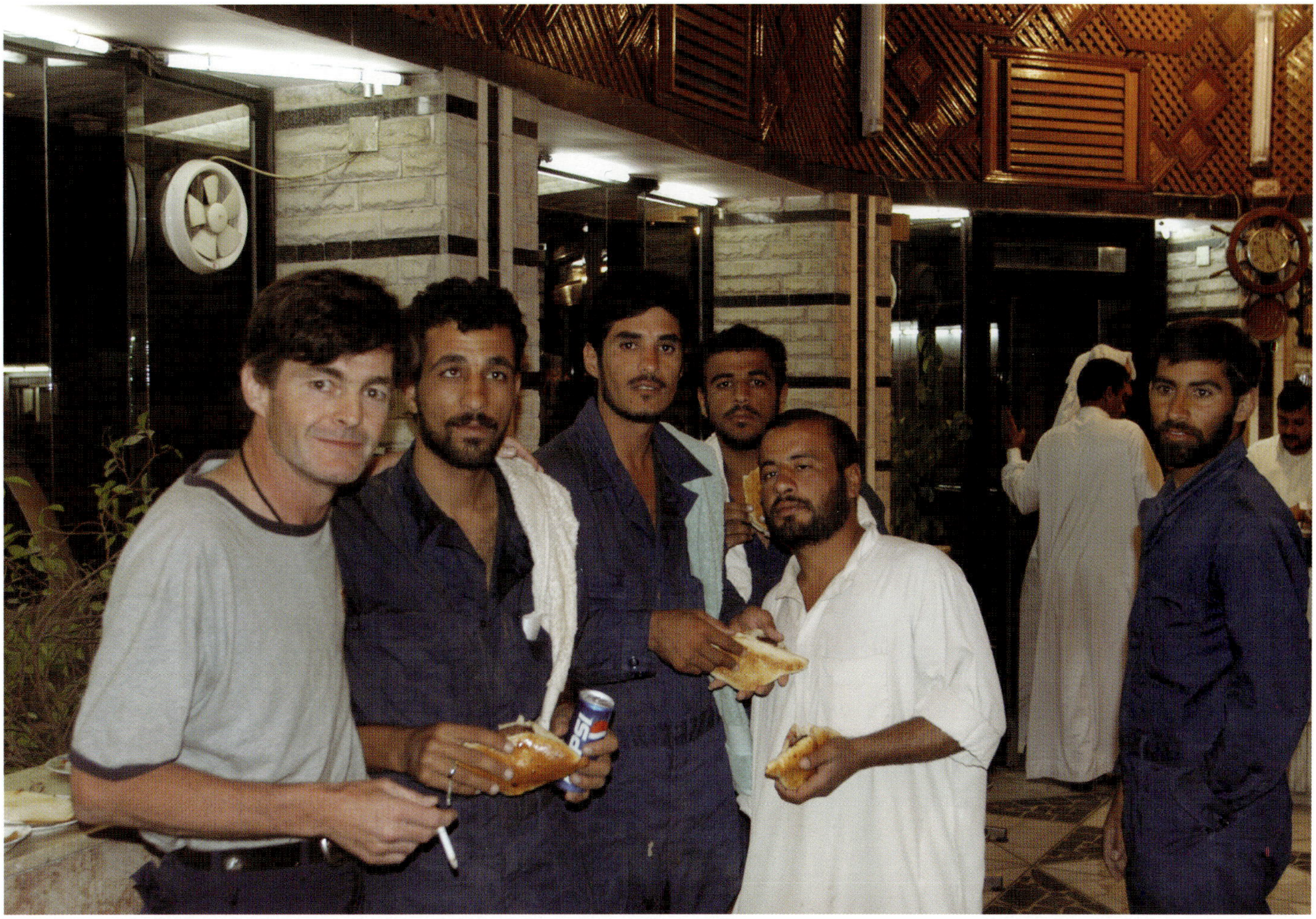

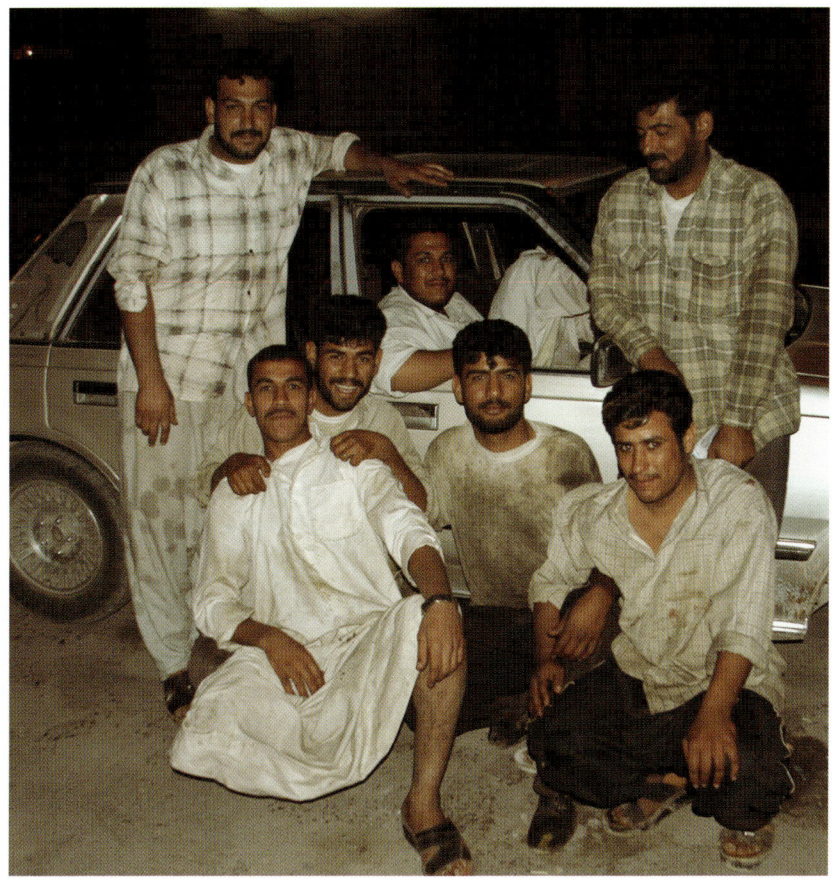
The author (left), stands with five P.O.W.s just released that evening from the American-run Kasra Military Camp

These teenagers urged me to take their picture

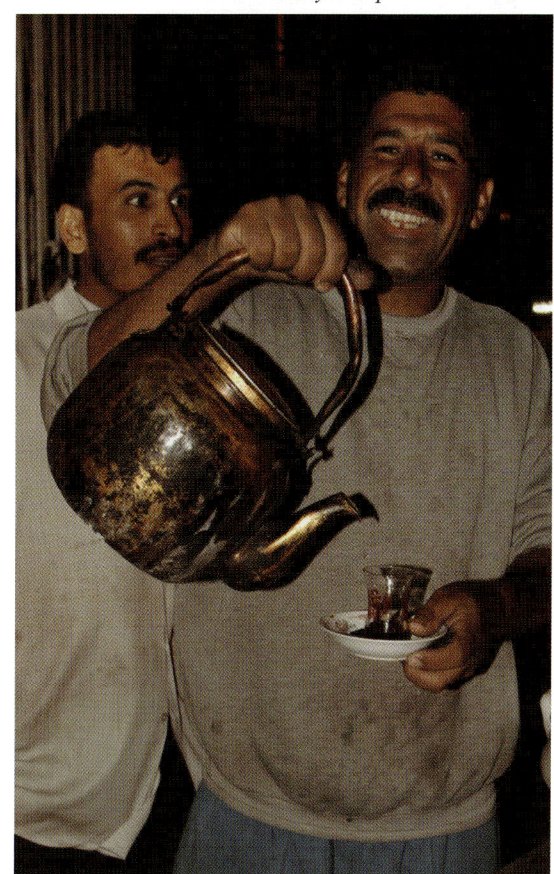
A man on the street offers me some hot chai

Day 23. Friday, May 2nd

I am up at 5 a.m., itching to get out and take the pics I need of Basra. The roach has stayed true to the terms I laid
down last night and has kept away from me. By 5:30, I am out of the hotel and lucky to flag down a taxi on the desolate street. It is a taxi driven by a former Olympic boxer from Russia. We drive two streets over to the waterfront, where
I photograph fishermen in dugout canoes. While one fisherman manoeuvres the canoe with his paddle, the other stands
to cast the net by hand into the golden Tigris. It is a beautiful sunrise on the river, fringed by date palms and reeds.

It is from near here that the southern wetlands of Iraq once spread north, east and west along the Tigris, encompass-
ing an area the size of Massachusetts. It is also the region of Iraq that biblical scholars believe is the setting for the
Garden of Eden. But the marsh region has been nearly drained out of existence by Saddam, in his persistence to destroy
the people whose life depends on the marshes; the Marsh People. They are Shi'a Muslims, a non-conforming thorn in
Saddam's side. The dictator's plan was simple, and in the early 1990's he launched a massive program to drain the
marshlands. Get rid of the marsh and you get rid of the Marsh People.

A similar strategy was used in 19th century America, to rid the prairies of the Plains Indians (who were resisting white
expansion across their lands of the American Midwest). The government supported the plan to exterminate the buffalo,
the main food source of the Plains Indians. Once the buffalo were gone, the indians became reliant on government handouts and lost their homelands.

Arriving at the checkpoint guarding Saddam's massive waterfront palace, I ask if I can gain entry to take some photographs, but the sentries tell me the officer in charge will not be available until late morning. I knew this was a long
shot, but I am driving past the palace anyway. I take some pics of the guards and palace entrance, and then continue on.

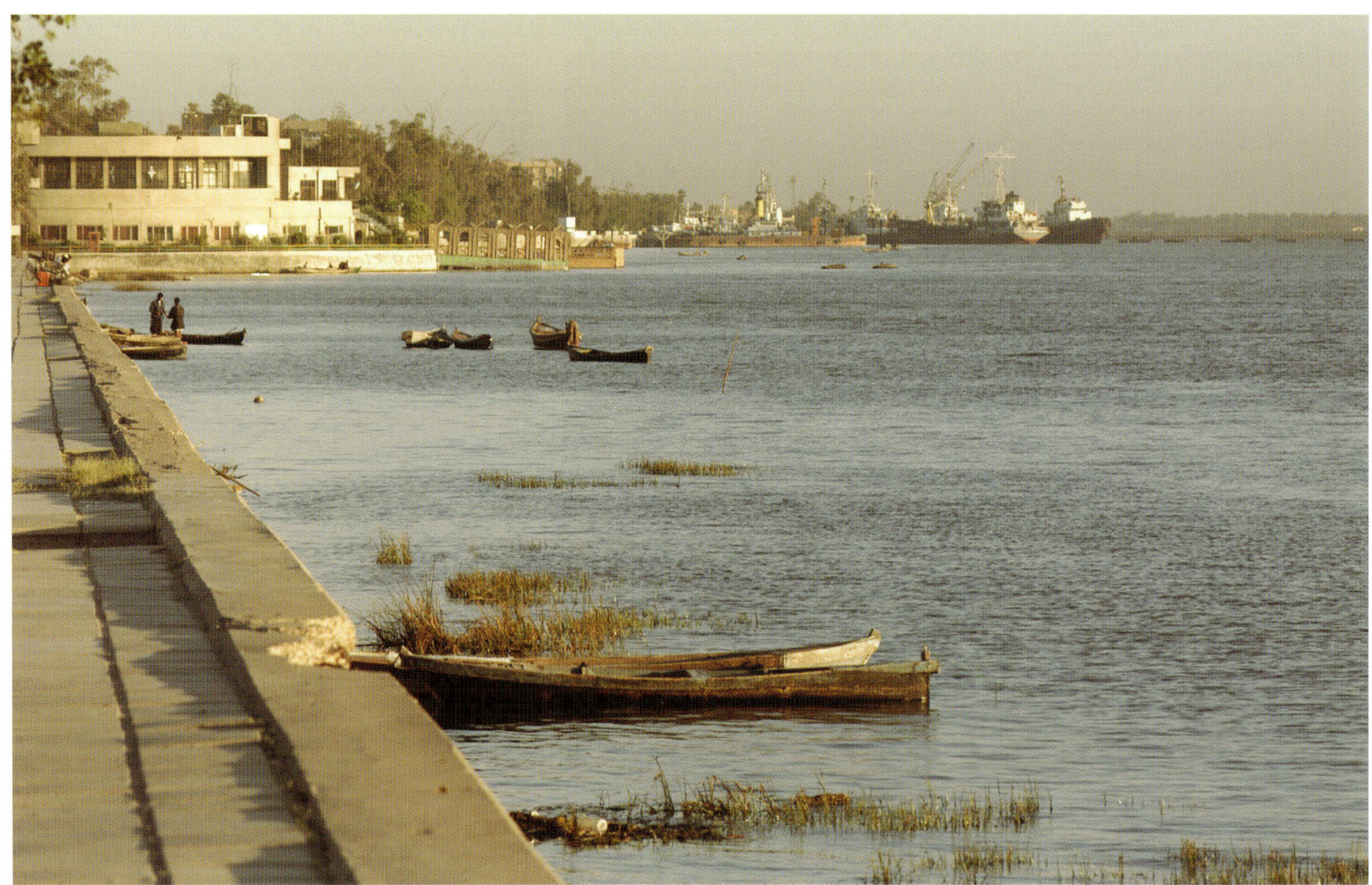

The western shoreline of the Tigris River looking north

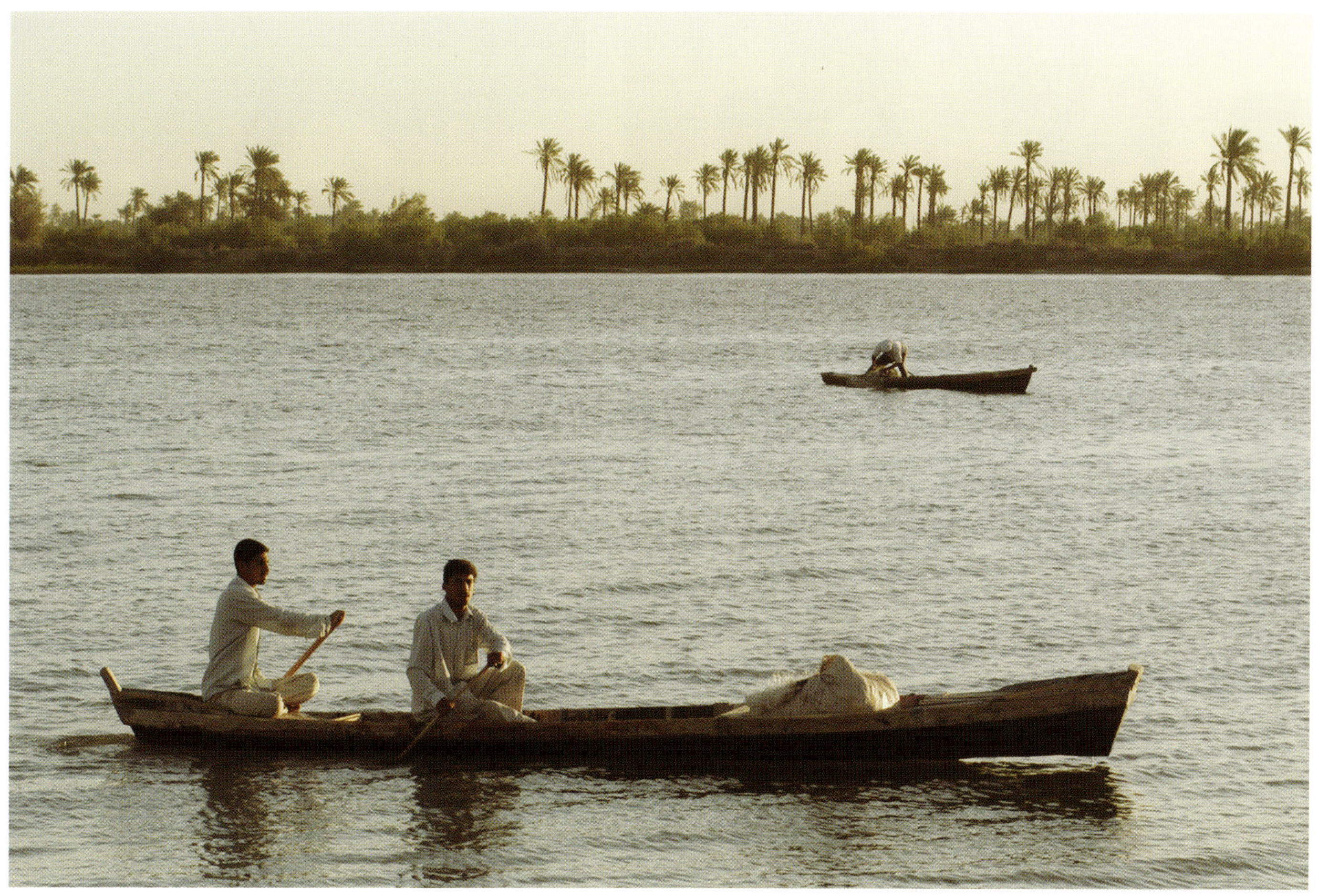

Looking towards the eastern shore of Basra. Fishermen have worked the Tigris River for thousands of years.

A half mile down the road we stop at the six-storey Basra Sheraton Hotel, now a looted and burned-out wreck of a hotel. The outer walls of the hotel have been blackened by the smoke. The place is now an ugly eyesore. The lobby is blocked by a crush of fallen structure and debris. Broken furniture sticks out from the smashed windows of the rooms and patios. The hotel grounds, with its beautiful flowering roses and sunflowers, are strewn with broken light fixtures, chairs, couches and other furnishings tossed from the hotel windows. A soiled and tattered Iraqi flag droops limply at the top of the hotel flagpole.

I would like to have a look around inside the hotel but it is not worth the risk of falling through the floor or having a wall fall on me. Having taken some necessary photos, I head back to my hotel to meet my Iranian friends. I tell them I am thinking about catching a bus to Baghdad later in the morning or early afternoon.

My friends and I have been invited to have breakfast with the hotel management. It is a nice breakfast, even though I pick at it like a bird (as I always do this early in the morning). There is yogurt, fresh fruit, flat bread, jam and tea. Eight of us sit around a low circular table talking about the war, Canada and the people of Iraq.

One of the men (who had visited Canada a few years earlier), brings me a couple of photos of the town of Banff, Alberta, in the Rocky Mountains (I met my wife in Banff and it is one of the most beautiful places on earth). Looking at the images, I begin to get all choked up, and my eyes start to water. I tell my hosts that just last autumn I lived in the Rockies for three months, and the sight of one of my most adored parts of Canada makes me homesick.

The man, seeing that the photos are stirring my emotions, apologizes for bringing them to my attention. I tell him not to apologize for trying to bring me some comfort and that I am honored at being in their company and seeing the photos.

At the end of breakfast the manager tells me that I am the first Westerner he has ever invited for a meal to his home/business. The look in his eyes as he tells me this, is so warm and comforting. Here we are, 5 hotel staff and three journalists, no one knowing much of each other, becoming close friends after only a short breakfast. Back in my room I start packing my bags, making ready to leave Basra.

After I pay the $15 room fee, the manager asks if I need a ride to the bus depot. Accepting his offer, myself, the manager and another hotel employee drive through Basra heading towards the bus depot. We stop at a cemetery situated just off the main road running through downtown Basra. There are clusters of grieving men and women burying their dead, while grave diggers hunch over with small shovels in their hands, digging new graves. It is an extremely sensitive and personal situation, and I use all my courtesies and polite mannerisms to not seem like an intruder. I must reflect the best example of my society.

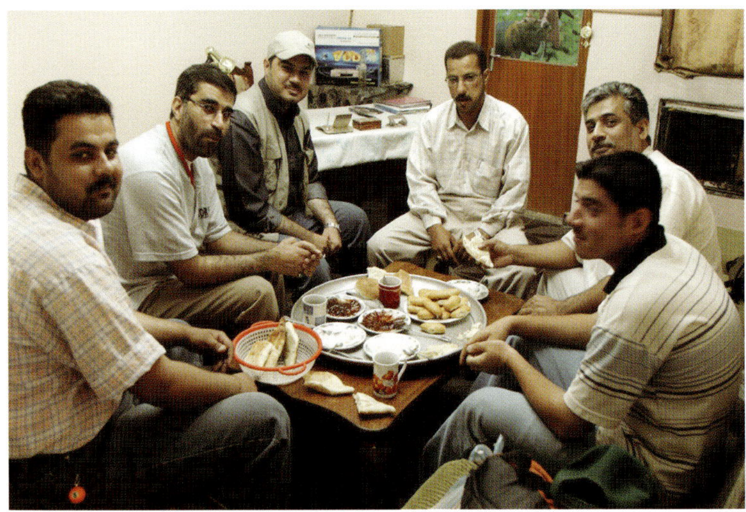

Breakfast in Basra

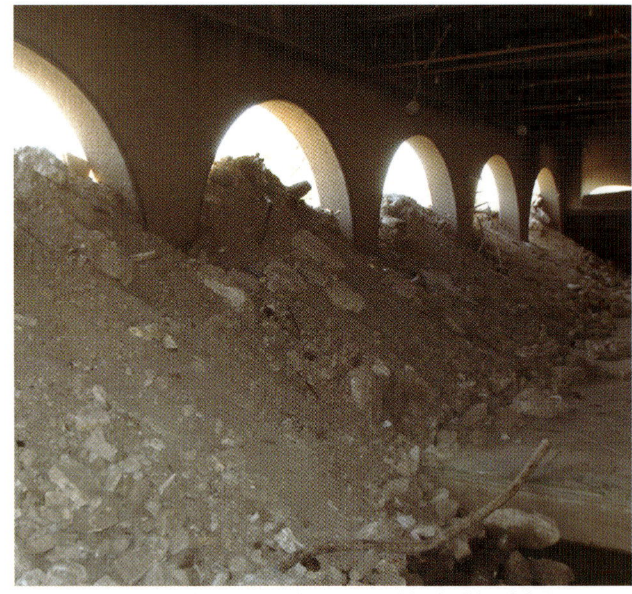

Access to the Basra Sheraton is blocked by debris

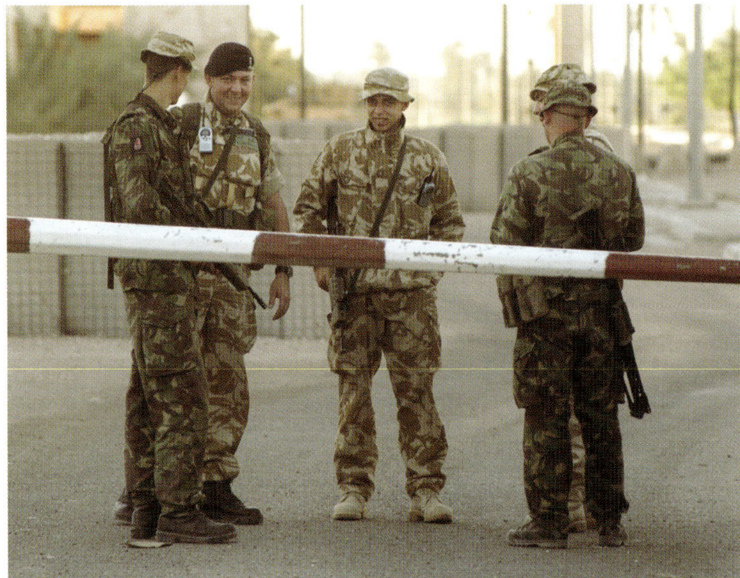

British soldiers guard the checkpoint outside Saddam's Basra palace

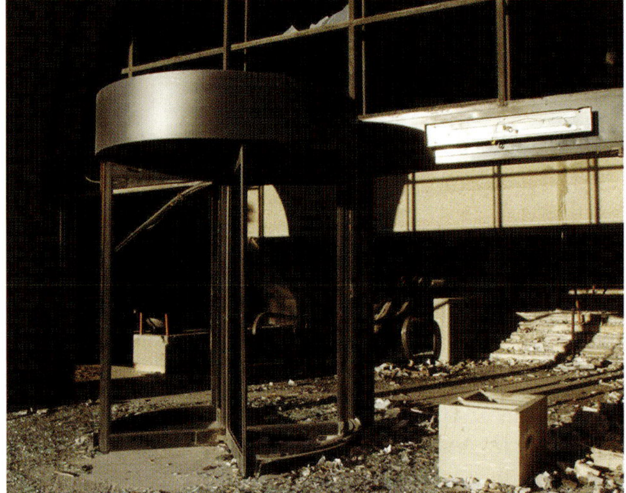

Front entrance to the Sheraton

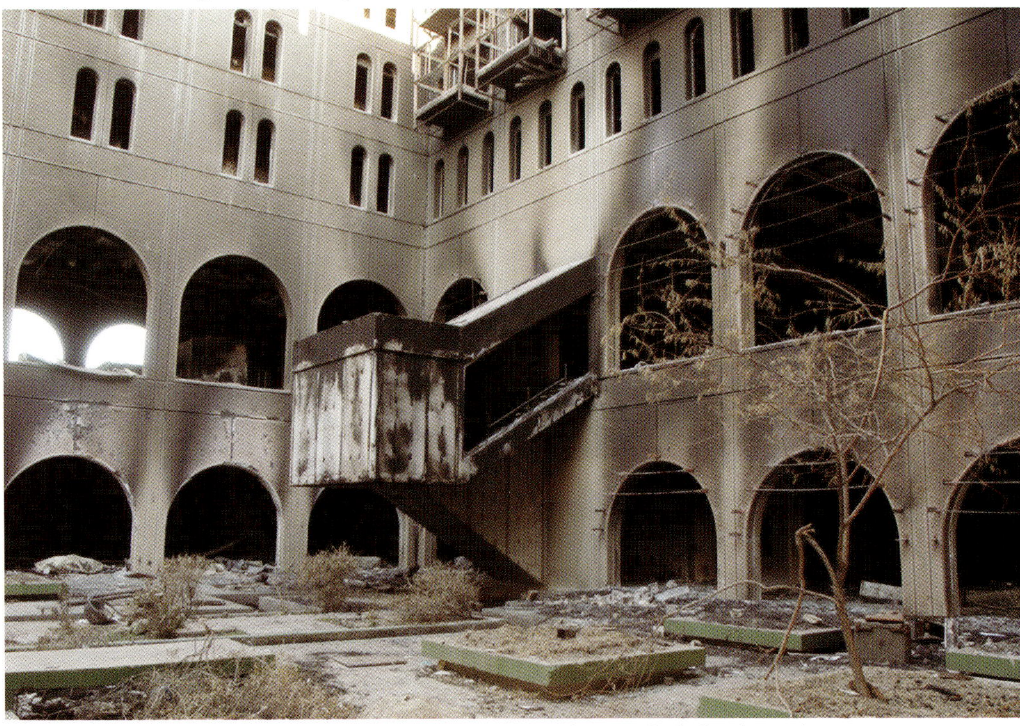

The Basra Sheraton has been looted, ransacked, then burned

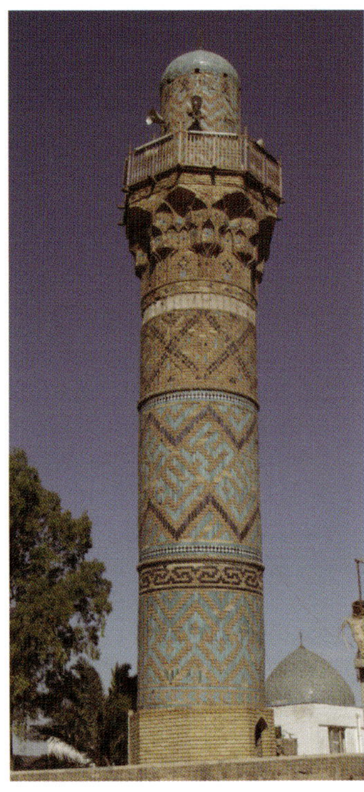

Basra mosque tower

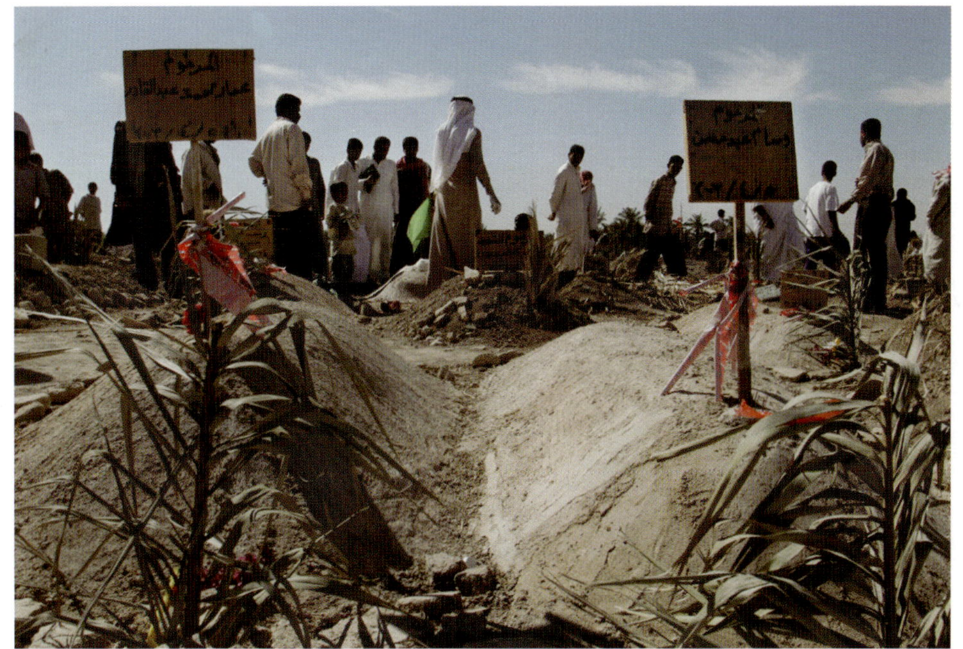

Fresh graves fill a graveyard in Basra

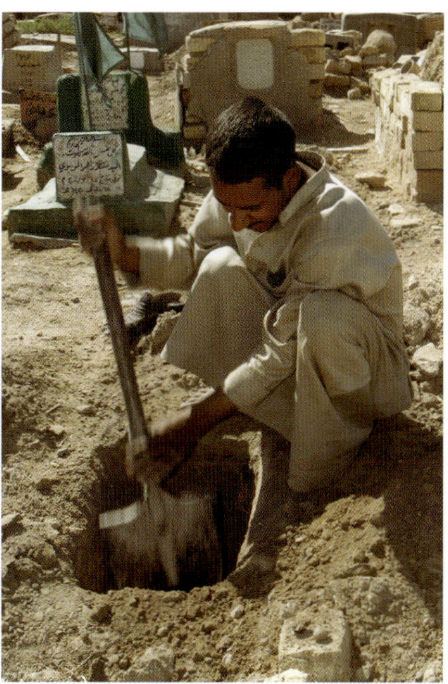

A grave is dug for an infant

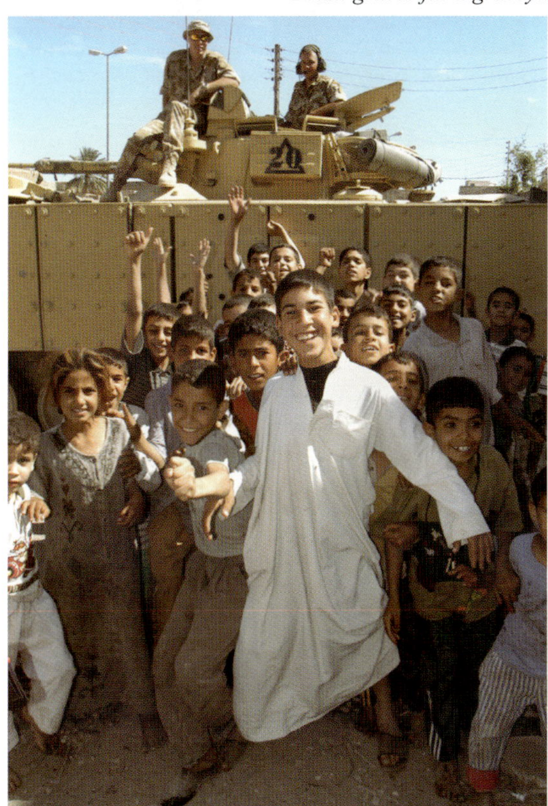

Kids love being near the soldiers

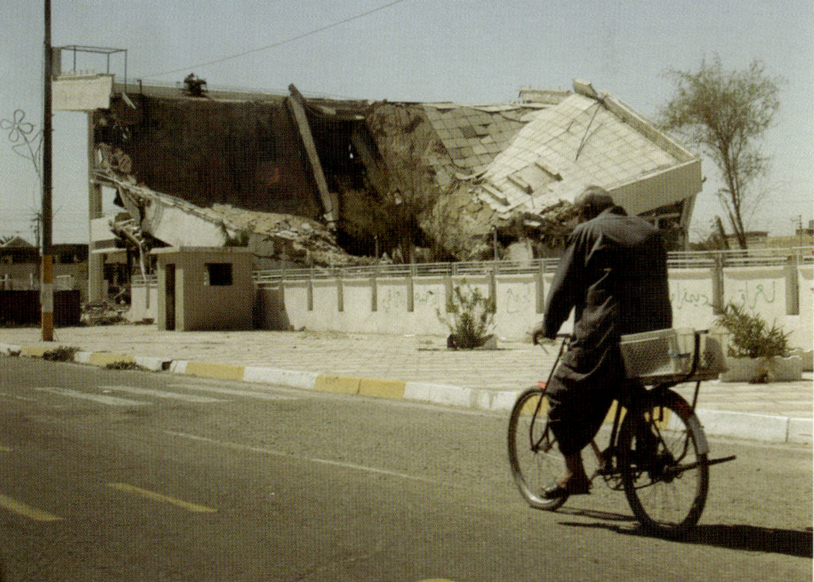

There is little war damage in Basra. This structure was part of a sports complex

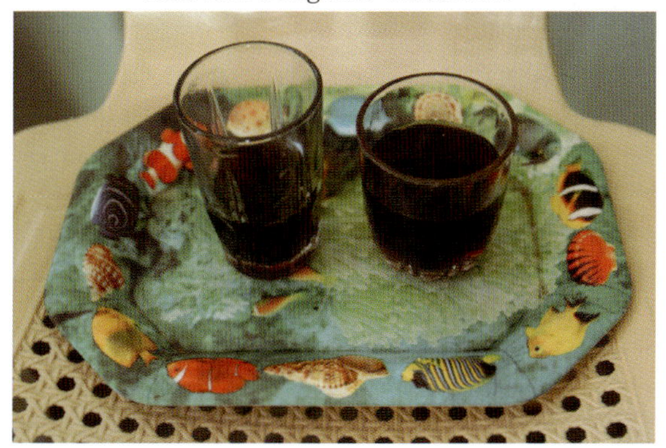

I always order two glasses of chai at a time

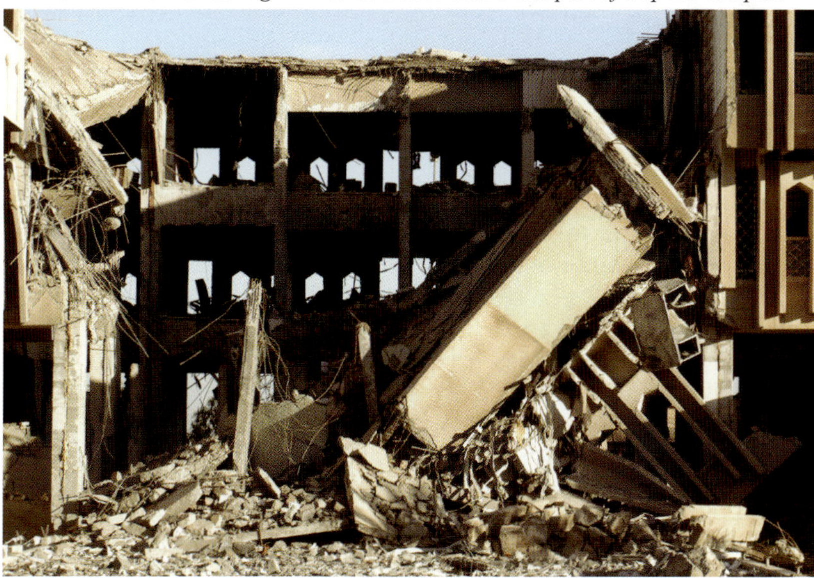

This Iraqi ministry building has been totally destroyed

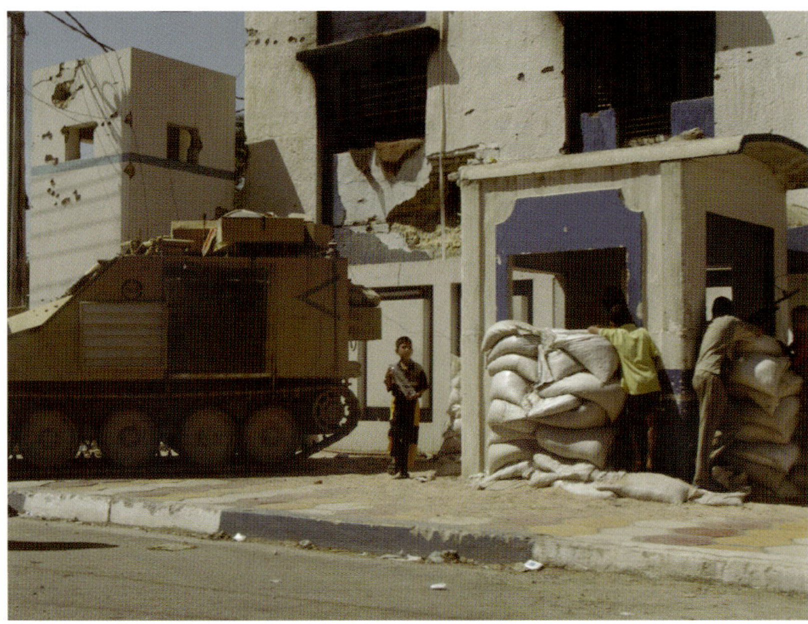

British security checkpoint in Basra. Note the bullet and shell damage to building

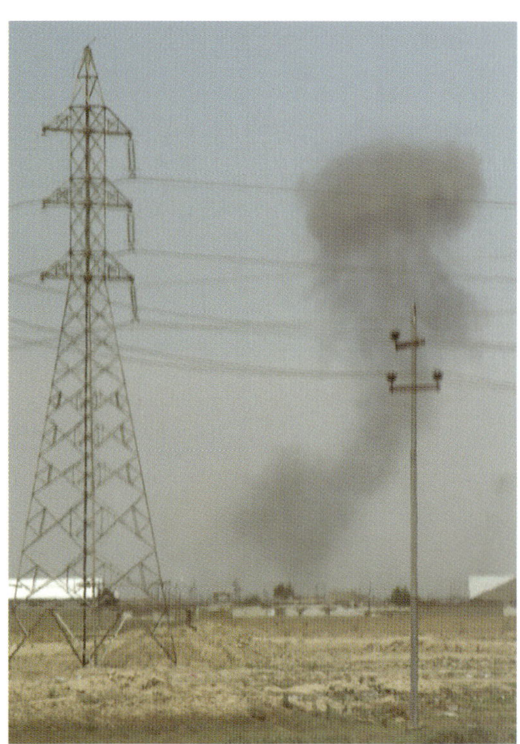

Mushroom cloud rises from a destroyed arms cache

A prism forms in the skies above the southern Iraq desert

None of the grieving families appear distraught at my presence, as I slowly move about the plots taking my pics and watching their body language. A man comes over to me and tells me that he is busy burying nine members of his family who were accidentally killed when a bomb fell next to his home. Looking into the man's eyes, I see a father at peace with himself and the world. He has no hate in his eyes, no sense of grudge or revenge in his soft-spoken words. He has fully given his heart and soul over to his God, and is being guided by that secret understanding. As he shakes my hand and bids me peace, a powdery brown dust from his hands envelopes our grasp. He had just finished burying one of his children.

We leave the cemetery, stopping shortly after to photograph a swarm of 30 children hanging out next to a British tank and its two-man crew. Kids and soldiers seem to go together hand in hand. Whenever you see a parked military vehicle, there is a good chance you will see children hanging around talking with the soldiers. They definitely enjoy each other's company. But man, how these children like to be photographed! They are all over me, asking to have their pics taken then re-taken. I grab some nice pics then move on to the bus depot.

At the terminal, one of my two friends offers me a gift of a Muslim prayer stone. He tells me the stone is placed in front the worshipper as he kneels in prayer. When bowing, the top of the head touches the stone. This is said to bring the worshipper closer to Allah. It is quite a gift of friendship and respect, and I am truly touched once again.

The trip to Basra has been an extremely spiritual experience from many aspects. But it is a spiritual place, and a very ancient place. As I sit alone at the bus depot waiting for a bus in the relentless late-morning sun, I cannot help but feel how the hours I have spent here have been an oasis for my tired spirit. Someday, I would love to come back, but most of all I would love to bring my family back with me, when life is more settled.

An old man, who I think works at the depot, tells me the bus will be leaving in an hour-and-a-half. I ask another person and he seems to believe it leaves in four hours. Moments later I am offered a ride in a taxi (a Caprice) to Baghdad for $60. It is rather expensive but I do not have a choice if I want to arrive in Baghdad before sundown. I am told that the car's air-conditioning works and there will be two other people taking the trip, including the driver. I buy some extra jugs of water, chug a couple of glasses of steaming-hot tea, and then climb into the cab. I gladly accept the offer of the front passenger seat. This will allow me to take pics from the car window with lots of elbowroom. It is going on high noon and the intensity of the sun is so unbearable.

As we drive through the dusty streets I discover that the car air-conditioning is not working. I try opening the window a little, but the driver does not want the dust getting inside the car, so the windows will stay up for a good part of the trip. We pass the collapsed Ministry of Oil building, which caved in on itself after being hit by a bunker buster bomb. A large mosaic mural of Saddam graces the outside of the building and has, along with all the others I have seen in Basra, been torn down or mutilated.

There is not much said between us until we are well out of Basra. One of the two men in the back, a slim middle-aged man in Arab dress, starts asking, in broken English, what I think about the war and the reasons behind it. He is rather aggressive and keeps peppering me with political questions about the American occupation. I don't mind answering his questions, in fact I relish hearing different viewpoints, but he is a little too much 'in your face.'

After what seems like an eternity responding to his inquisition, the driver says something to him in Arabic, and he stops questioning me. I think he was starting to make the others feel uncomfortable and getting on their nerves. This is a relief as it is so damned hot in car. The other passenger in the back seat is an elderly Palestinian of about 60. He is quiet and polite and keeps to himself.

A hundred kilometers to our east, the mountains of Iran disappear, and then reappear, floating on a watery ocean of illusion. The desert is a movie screen of endless mirages. In the sky I see a type of rainbow, but it is not a rainbow; it is a prism of light bouncing off, or through the light veil of high cirrus clouds. Since cirrus clouds are formed from ice crystals, the sun striking the ice cloud at a certain angle can cause these flaring effects. It is an unusual phenomenon.

At 2 p.m., I hear and feel a thunderous boom, and I look out the window to see a huge mushroom cloud rising in the desert ahead of our taxi, about 3 miles away. The explosion is from a weapons or ammunition cache being destroyed by the coalition. The grey-black mushroom cloud curls upwards for half a mile, looking much like a mini nuclear explosion. (On Thursday, the British officer at the airport had told me that their explosives units would be blowing up confiscated arms and ammunition on the hour. This way the forces would not confuse the blast as an attack by the enemy).

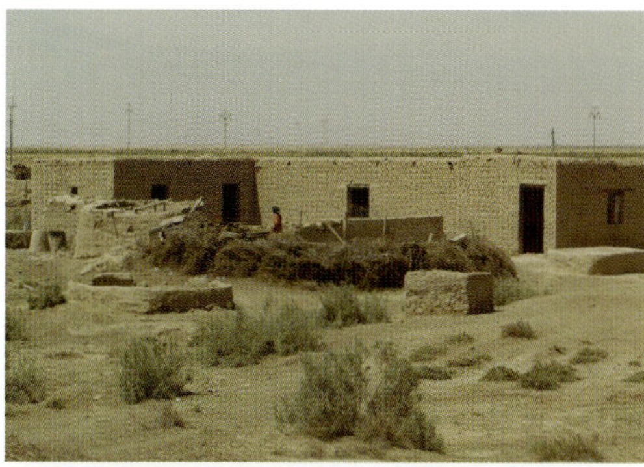

Mud-brick home near Al Nasiriyah

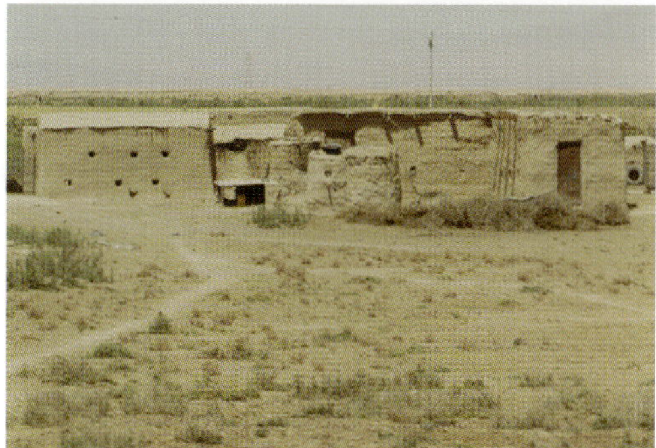

This home is coated in a layer of mud

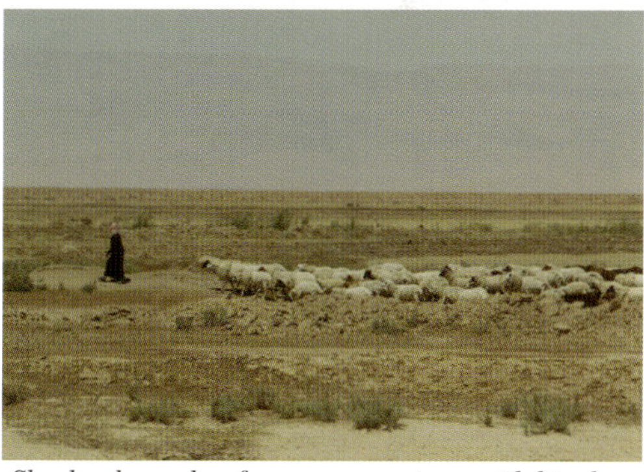

Shepherd searches for greener pastures with his sheep

Continuing along the highway, we slow down as we approach an American checkpoint. A soldier motions the taxi to pull over to the side of the road, to be inspected for weapons or wanted persons. At the same time, I hold up my CFLCC media card to the soldier. Upon seeing the military endorsed pass, he motions us through the checkpoint without having us come to a full stop. As the taxi passes, the soldier courteously nods his head at me, and I nod and smile back. Simple courtesies can say so much at times like this. There is a line of cars waiting to be inspected, but we are spared the wait.

As we drive on, my fellow travellers are dumbstruck. They stare at me as though asking who I am and what the magic card is. They realize that I just saved them more than an hour's delay of getting all our gear removed and the car inspected, under a burning sun. All of us start laughing and chatting back and forth. The chuckling passengers and driver, with their hands flying, are whisked away from the misery of heat in this animation of distraction. They realize that I am not just some misplaced desert vagabond with white skin. Now we are all the best of buddies. I have been accepted by these men, these strangers.

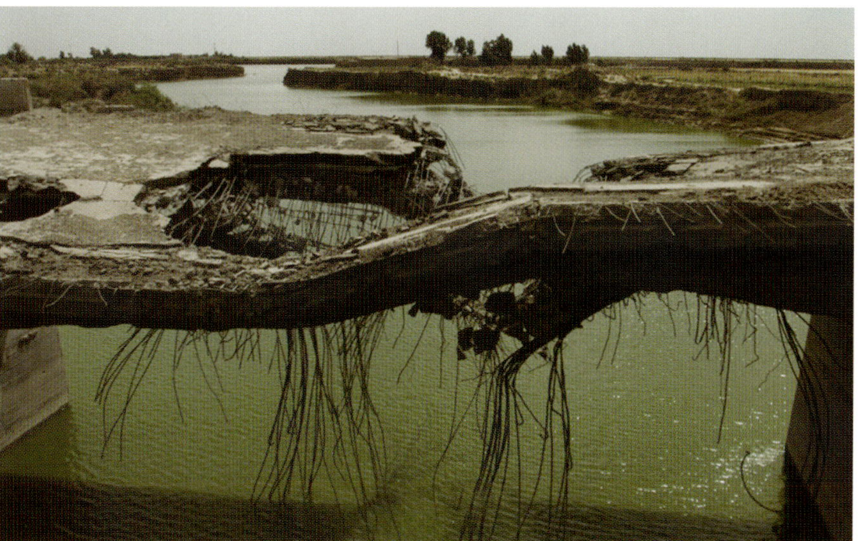

Bridge over a tributary of the Euphrates River destroyed by aerial bombing

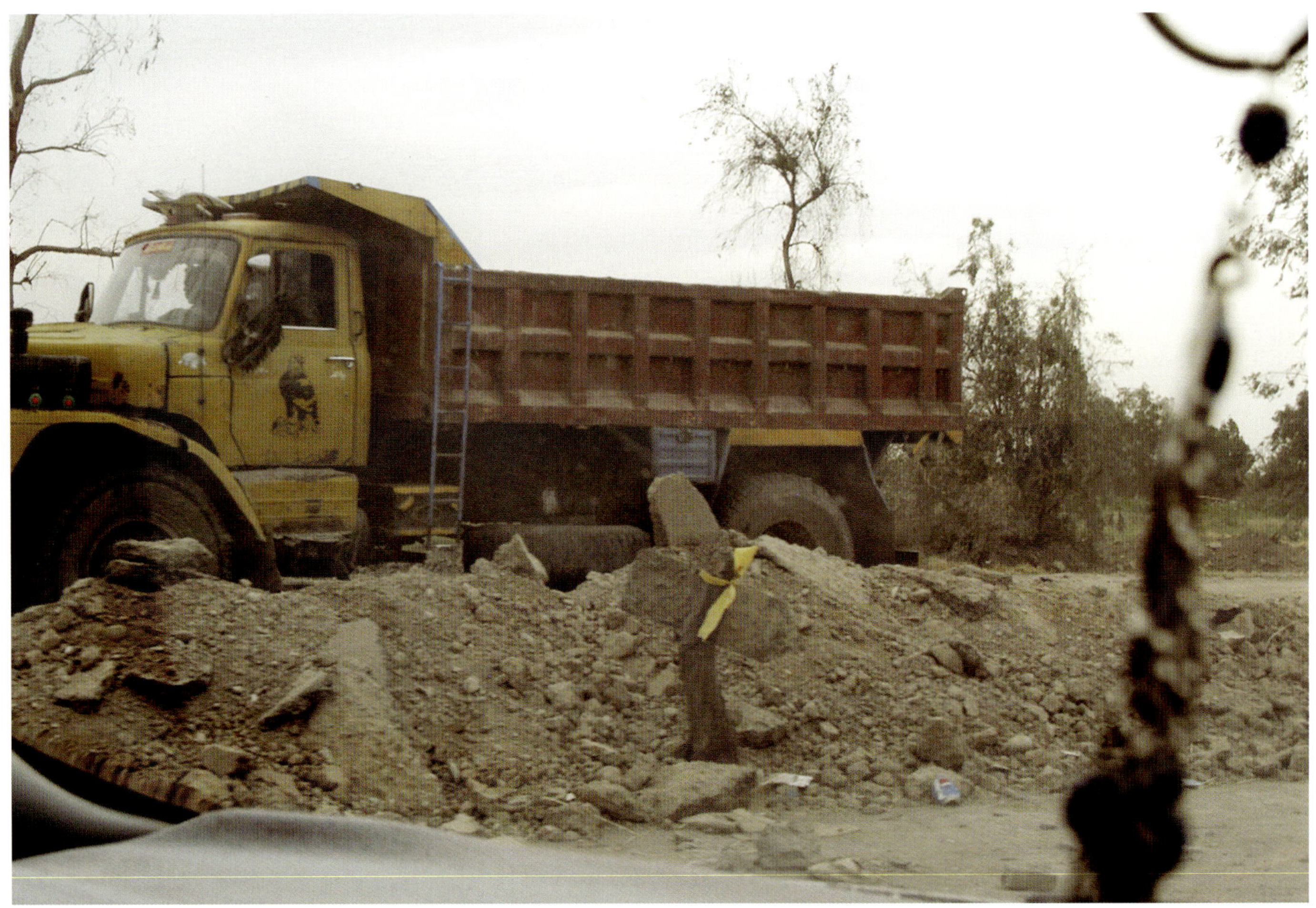

A simple stone and yellow ribbon mark a makeshift graveyard of Iraqi soldiers, crudely buried along a highway median near Baghdad

We pass over a bridge spanning the Euphrates River near Al Nasiriyah. It has been hit by a large bomb, leaving a 30-foot gaping hole in the bridge. Cement-encrusted iron support beams dangle from the hole down into the river. Here is another reason why you do not drive at night in war-ravaged Iraq.

A short time later I take out my field guide to the Birds of Europe, Africa and the Middle-East, and start thumbing through the pages. Looking out the window I see small oases of life in the lower areas of the desert, especially along the roadside. Here moisture collects from wells and irrigation ditches. A lot of this water is undrinkable due to heavy concentrations of salty minerals, which leach into the water from the earth. But it is heaven for birds like waders and terns, which eke out a living feeding on small fish, crustaceans and insects. Larks, doves, bee-eaters and shrikes also flourish here, under the most inhospitable conditions. But as long as there is some sort of brush coverage and a little moisture, nature will adapt and proliferate. Many types of desert birds are able to get a good amount of their daily moisture from their prey.

I watch out the window, looking ahead of the car for the little green pockets of wet along the roadside. This is where you see the lapwings and stilts walking through the shallow pools fringed by reeds and other water plants. Black-winged terns dive into the open pools for minnows, as the wood pigeons fly overhead. There are two different worlds at work here – the clock of nature ticking on as it always has, and the arrogance of man against man.

It doesn't take long before the driver looks over at the field guide in my hand. He smiles, then says what I imagine is the Arabic word for birds. I show him the guide and tell him that I am a bird watcher, and point to some wood pigeons flying near the car. The guy in the back seat leans forward and looks at the book, then starts asking me questions about the birds in Canada. Before long, my travel companions are talking and pointing at passing birds.

Nature, like the dialect of music, is a universal language. Everyone has a natural attraction towards the mystery of nature; to hunt it, watch it, or protect it (or a combination of all three). I don't know if these people have ever met a real birdwatcher, but it sure breaks the monotony of the drive and lets them see a different side of my Canadian personality. I break out some fresh buns purchased in Basra, and we all have a little snack of sweet buns.

A few hours into the drive, we stop for lunch at a truck stop, in the absolute middle of nowhere. It is a large open restaurant, with long picnic tables. A man in a small room just off to the side of the dining room is on his knees praying. Most public places have separate rooms like this for prayer, and I personally feel very comfortable and enjoy seeing worshippers praying in public (whether at a restaurant or in the open desert). Diners sit at the long tables eating their meals of chicken or lamb and flatbread, along with pickles and other garnishes. What a relaxing break from the car this is.

Finishing up, I try to pay the dinner bill for the driver and passengers. The passengers kindly refuse my offer, but I insist on paying the driver's bill. I tell him that I have a tradition when I travel, of paying for the driver's meal. The driver accepts, and we climb back into the automotive oven for the last leg of the journey to Baghdad.

Three brutal hours later we are driving through the southern reaches of Baghdad. I start to catch whiffs of war. It invigorates me and snaps me to attention like a noseful of smelling salts and is a good indication that I am close to where I need to be.

We drive across a heavily damaged bridge, on both sides of which a major amount of carnage lies about, (like the North Gate, this is part of Saddam's last line of defense encircling Baghdad). On the median separating the north and southbound traffic lie the graves of Iraqi soldiers, buried in a long thin line. There are at least a dozen, but it is hard to tell the exact number, as only a handful of the graves (crude mounds of rock and dirt), are marked with large stones or metal bars with ribbons tied to them.

Fifteen minutes later, the driver drops me off in southern Baghdad near Mechanics City. I flag down another taxi, and ask to be taken to the Fanar. It is a badly beaten Russian boxcar, driven by a small, smiling man. The drive home to the Fanar, through the now familiar streets of Baghdad, fills my heart with great joy and relief. Finally I am home! The looters are still looting and the buildings are still smoldering.

I walk into the Fanar and its warm surroundings; it feels fantastic to be back, but I am in immediate need of some strong coffee and something sweet. Some of the staff notice me and come over smiling. They shake my hand and kiss me gently on the cheek, asking where I have been and if I am alright. I feel right at home and at ease, even after the punishing 8-hour drive. I chat with the personnel (who listen with great interest as I explain the condition of Basra, and what life is like in Kuwait) then head upstairs to meet Tish and Sean, but they are out.

Returning to the dining room, I sit down for another coffee when three earth-shaking explosions go off, one right after the other. I turn my face away from the glass panel windows as the shock waves swell through the hotel; a wall of energy. No one knows what the explosions are, but I suspect it is ordinance being destroyed. When the earth moves like that it really perks your attention and, for a brief moment, it leaves me with a scary, helpless feeling.

The blast was not on the hour, but the Americans who run Baghdad may not use the same system as the Brits do in southern Iraq. Relaxing with my coffee and chocolate bars, I watch the young street urchins begging for money and selling their cigarettes and candies on the street. God, it's good to be back in Baghdad!

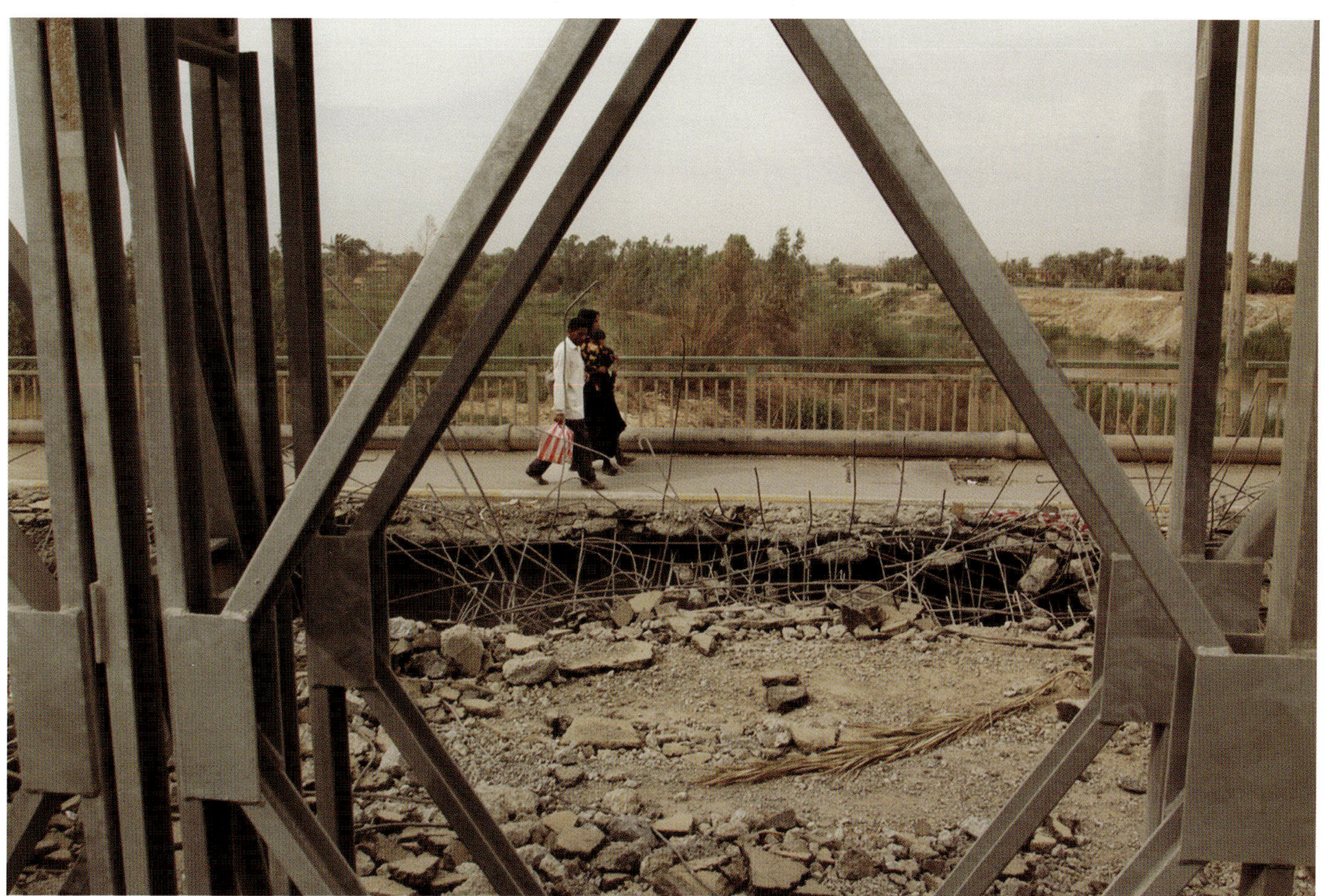

Damage to a highway overpass, an hour south of central Baghdad

As I take a short walk around the hotel complex, a soldier runs up towards me calling out my name. It's Paul, the young soldier I lent $10 to last week before I left for Kuwait. He shakes my hand and gives me a huge smile, then hands me a $10 bill saying, "Am I glad I found you my friend, to repay you this ten bucks."

I go for a walk along the riverbank, to suck up the slow flowing beauty of the Tigris and organize my thoughts. I stop to look at one of a line of abandoned Iraqi trenches stretching along the banks, where I photograph some discarded Iraqi items, like helmets, gas masks and chemical retardant suits. A group of young children, from 4 to 9 years, come up to me insisting that I take their pictures. So I entertain these little kids by taking their picture then letting them see the picture on the viewer of my digital camera. They are well groomed and have clean clothes and shoes. They live at home with their parents, somewhere near the Fanar. These kids are fortunate, unlike the poor wretches who live off the streets. It is nice to be around the kids, their smiling and playing about helps me unwind from the drive. I take some pictures of a soldier pedaling a bicycle past the front of the Fanar. He has his rifle slung over his back.

I walk upstairs and knock on my room door and Sean opens it. He and Tish have been in the room all along sleeping, not hearing my knock the first time. We all embrace with hugs and smiles. It is just fantastic to be back with my close friends.

Sean, Tish, Tod and I decide to go out for supper at a restaurant next door to the Fanar. The gang wants to know the details of my trip. Everyone is in a happy, jovial, mood. Tod, Sean, Tish and I eat a good meal, while I describe my adventures, accompanied with lots of laughter and cheer.

Tod tells me that Jim left Baghdad a couple of days ago and is now somewhere in Kurdistan, covering the war from there. Simon has left Iraq and returned to England. I will miss Simon; he is a good friend and I really liked his character. I hope to meet him again some day.

After supper, Sean, Tish and I sit up till 1 a.m., discussing our strategy for travelling to Mosul, in northern Kurdistan. Now that I have covered Basra, I need to cover the northern region of Iraq, to see the effects of war there. We decide to leave tomorrow morning by bus for Kurdistan.

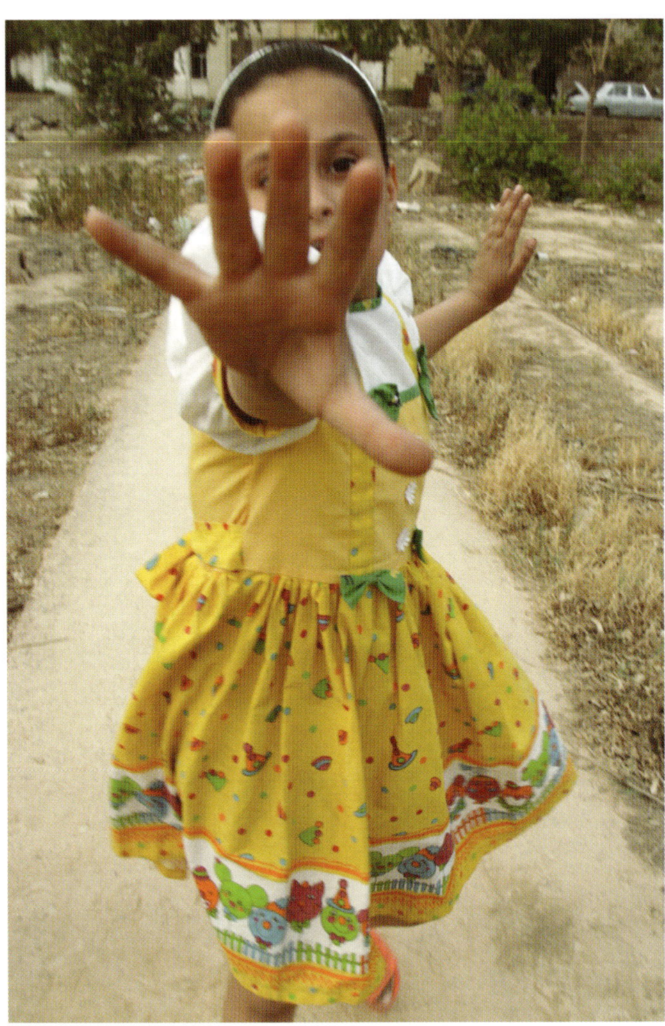

This girl wants a chance to fix her hair before I take her photo

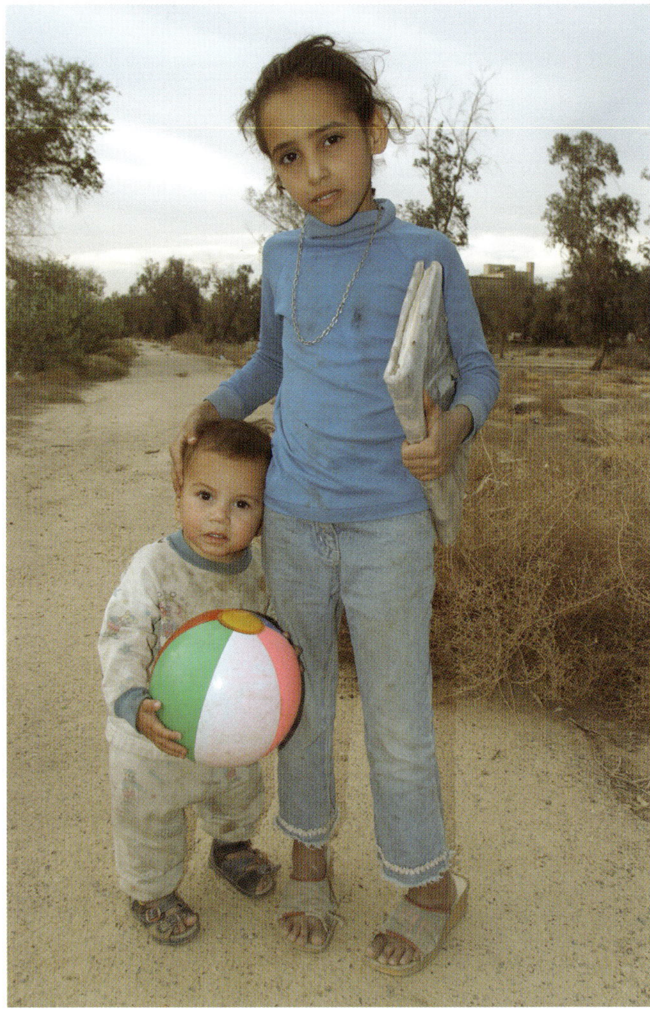

Sister and brother pose on land between the Fanar and river

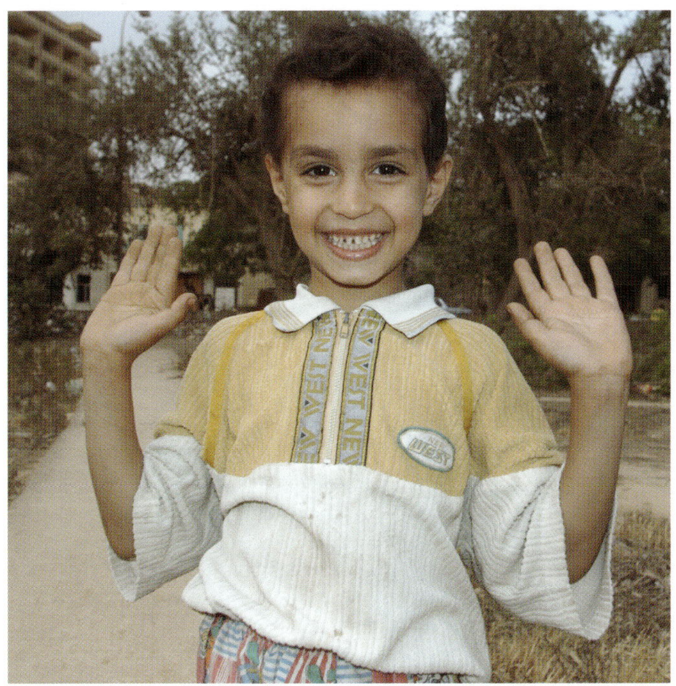
Iraqi children loved being photographed

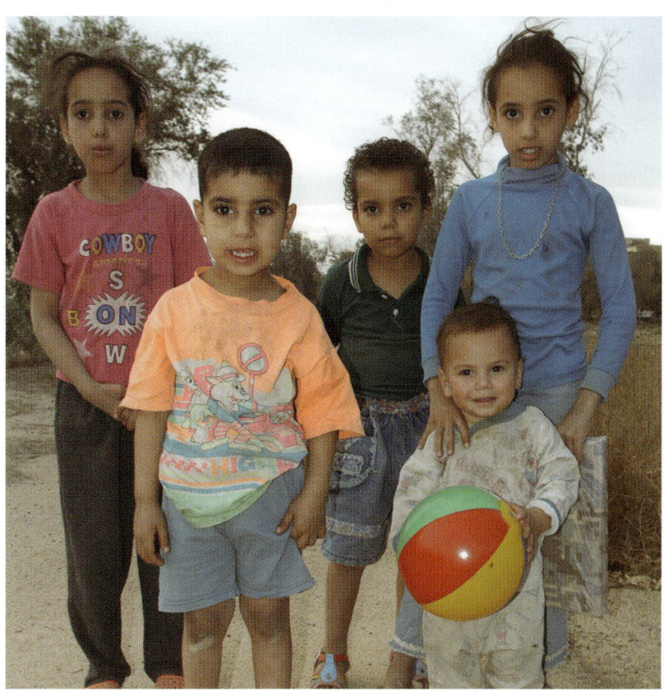
These children are the future of Iraq. Will they die in another war?

Day 24. Saturday, May 3rd

(Early morning gunfire; not in a good mood; air-conditioned bus to Mosul; alien curiosities; rudimentary graves; bomb or missile factory; soldiers search bus; naptime; lunch in Baiji; the only woman; Turkish influenced dress style; desert changes to a green oasis; mountainous ridges; Baiji Oil Refinery; river of oil; Kingfishers, bee-eaters and Blackhawks; Mosul in good shape; the 101st Airborne guard Hotel Mosul; hotel looted and burned; well-off kids; Captain Henry Morgan; sleeping with the soldiers; great coffee and company; letters from home; a night in the casino; peshmerga looted hotel; nature is my medicine; looking for scorpions; MREs for supper; cooking lessons with Sean O'Sullivan; possible targets; watching television; from Skittles to toilet paper; wanting to get closer to the action; long underwear worn at night)

This morning, while having a late breakfast, I hear five or six rifle blasts fired close to the Fanar. It is unusual to hear gunfire in the morning, but it is a comforting sound that I have not heard for over a week – morbid as this may seem. It is like I lost all remnants of fear the moment I crossed into Iraq from Kuwait. Nothing but nothing will ever scare or intimidate me again. I will have to temper my new bulletproof attitude, or it could get me killed. But I am better off with it, than not.

I am not in a good mood this morning. The long, hot trip across the desert from Basra and a lack of sleep, have left me very grouchy and impatient. My body is exhausted, I feel beaten and bruised. You might be surprised, unless you have done it, how a long drive in the desert can knock you off your feet and sap you of your energy.

Tish, Sean and I leave the Fanar around 1 p.m., taking a taxi to the Baghdad bus depot. Our destination is the northern Iraqi city of Mosul, in Kurdistan. The public buses I have been seeing are barely operable, hot and packed tight with travellers, but when I see the bus we will be travelling on, all my fears fade away. It is a recent model, air-conditioned Toyota mini-bus. It is in better shape than most buses in Canada, very clean and comfortable. The price is also more than reasonable, costing only $20 per person, for the five-hour drive.

Before departing I clean the outside of my passenger window so I can shoot unobstructed through the glass. Sean and Tish's decision about the bus turns out to be the best one for the three of us.

We leave behind another sweltering hot day and start our adventure north to Kurdistan. The bus is full, but not crowded, and the passengers look at us with hidden glimpses. But they are not being rude, they are just interested in our culture and who we are; a human curiosity. Many of these people have never seen a Westerner, so it's West meets East!

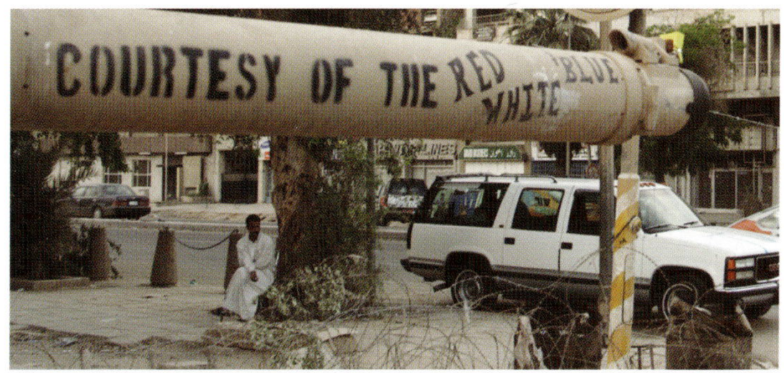

The United States continues to change the face of the Middle-East

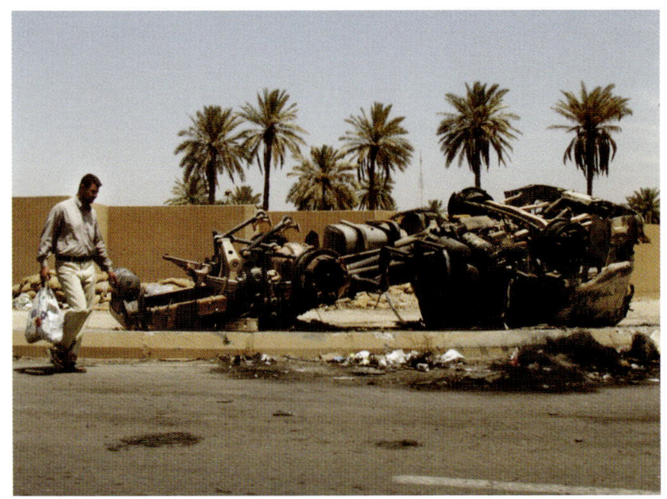

Wreckage in Baghdad

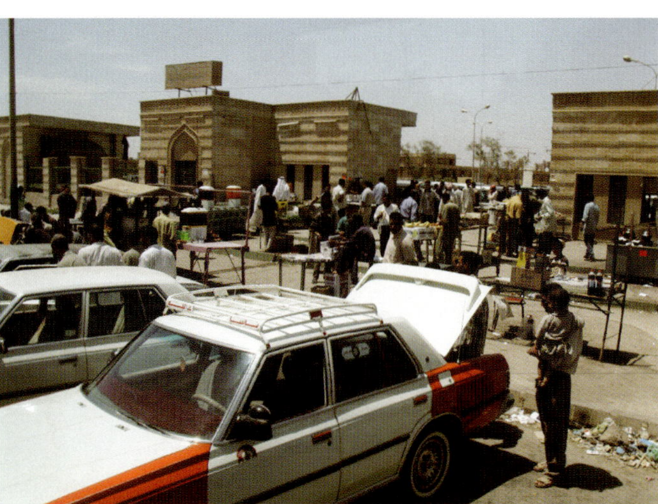

Baghdad's main bus depot

On some occasions I have overheard people refer to me as George Bush, just a local term referring to Westerners. I try to explain to them that back in Canada, we do not point at a person of Mid-Eastern origin and call them Osama Bin Laden. I ask them to please try not stereotype people, to be more open and accepting. I also try to explain that Canada is a society of mixed marriages of all colors and religious freedom.

We drive through Baghdad heading north, passing the badly damaged North Gate, (as we did on our way to and from Tikrit on April 15th). As we pass the fields of destroyed military hardware, a creepy unsettling chill goes up my spine. It is haunted by the spirits of the dead; I can sense something horrible here. The rudimentary graves of the dead Iraqi soldiers lining the median of the highway, with their simple pole markers, all seem so impersonal; like garbage tossed from cars.

A half hour north of the gate we pass a huge military depot. There are stacks of large, twelve-foot-long missiles or bombs piled outside some green warehouses. I cannot tell exactly what type of bomb they are, but they look like fat cigars. There are at least 100 of them stacked on top of each other in a pyramid shape. They do not have a tail fin, perhaps because they are not completely assembled, or they are in the process of being prepared for transport. Maybe this installation is a bomb or missile factory, as some of the bombs are painted light green while others are bare shiny metal, like gigantic silver bullets. It all flashes past my face from the bus window, but it really piques my attention. I make a note that I will have to visit this facility when I return to Baghdad.

We stop at an American Army checkpoint where an armed soldier boards the bus and walks to the back. He reaches up and takes a passenger's duffel bag from the overhead storage area and carries it off the bus. He and another soldier unzip the bag and take a quick look inside, without even moving the articles inside the bag. He closes it up and brings it back on the bus and gives the driver the O.K. to move on. As the bus pulls away, the two soldiers stand outside the bus looking at each other and smiling, as though asking, "Is that what I am supposed to do?" It is almost comedic. Obviously these soldiers have never done this sort of thing before, but they go through the motions, useless as it is.

I fall asleep for half an hour, then wake up with a sore neck. At the best of times, I have an extremely difficult time napping, so my little nap indicated to me how tired and exhausted I really am.

About two hours out of Baghdad we stop for lunch at a truck stop in the oil region of Baiji. But this is no ordinary Iraqi restaurant. It is a brightly illuminated place with a large colorful sign. Inside it is a clean and bustling place full of people. It reminds me of my favorite diner in Montreal on a Friday night. Right away we feel refreshed by the brightness and bustle of this place and the people in it. There are a half dozen cleanly dressed waiters ferrying heaping plates of kabobs, veggies and pickles to waiting travellers. Graced with all the food, our table looks like a huge plate. There is way

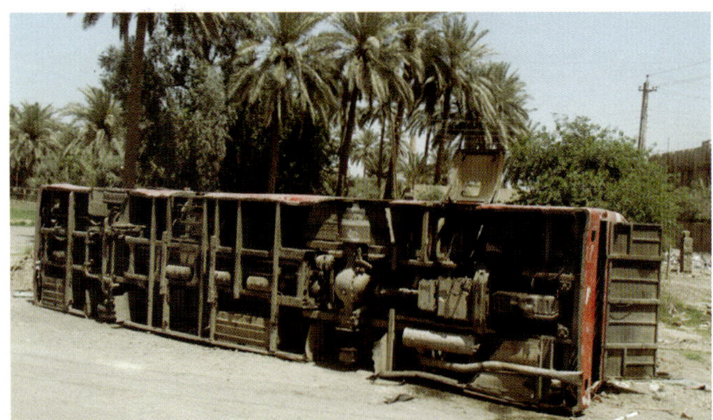

A city bus stripped by looters lies like a beached whale on the road

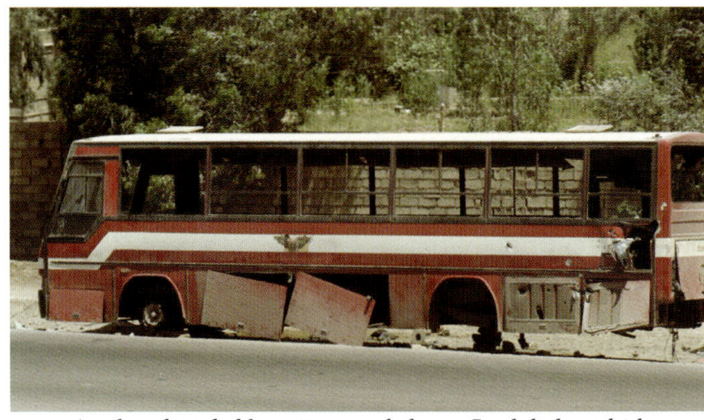

Another denuded bus sits stranded on a Baghdad roadside

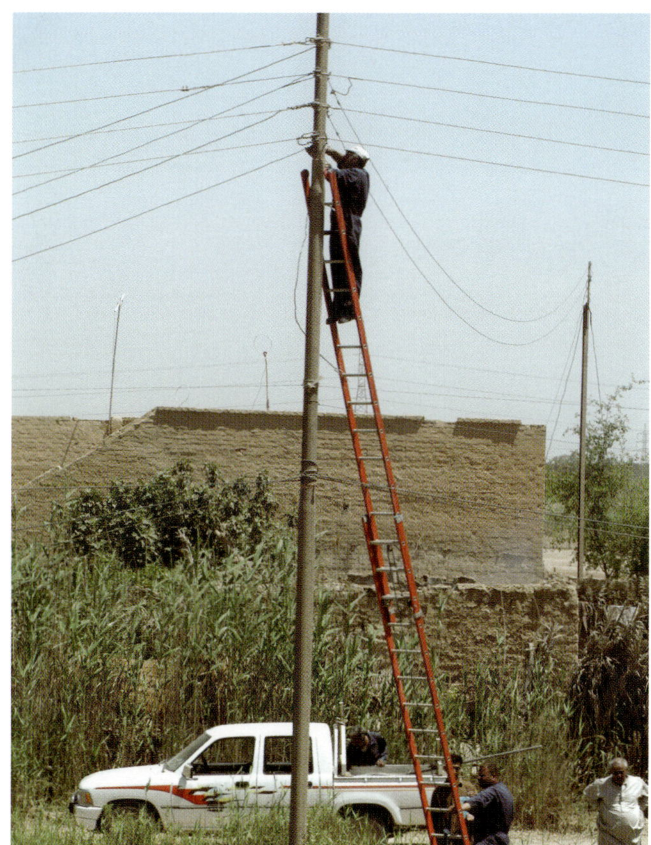

Technicians repairing hydro wires in north Baghdad

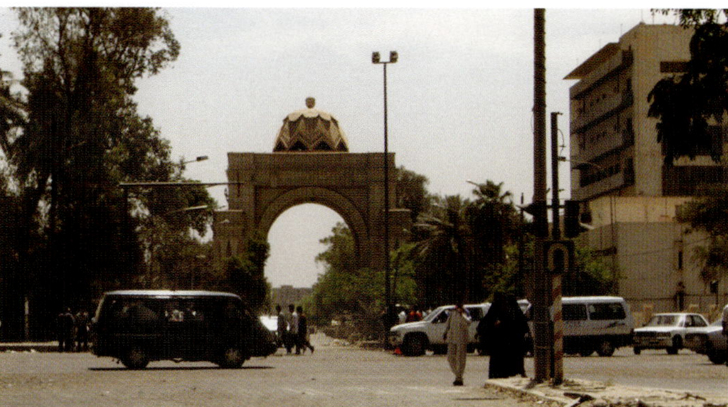

Passing the north gate of the Republican Palace, on the way to bus depot

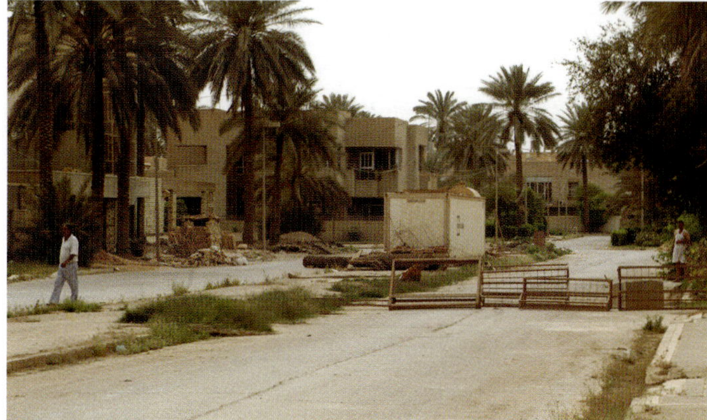

Residents of Al Mansour have barricaded some streets to keep out looters

too much for the three of us. Pickles, garnishes, dipping sauces, salads and our large plates of food cover the table. It mesmerizes us, and looks about equal to the total amount of food we have eaten during our entire stay in Iraq.

Diners gawk over at us with polite glimpses, trying to catch a look at the Westerners. Tish must have been an unusual site to them, a blond-haired, white-skinned woman without a head covering. She is the only woman in the place, as far as I can see.

The people in the restaurant appear genuinely very friendly and effervescent; there is an air about them and this restaurant that is different. They look healthier, fuller faced, and more handsome than any people I have seen so far in Iraq. Some sport well-kept handlebar mustaches. Their eyes and body language beam strength and confidence. They are not the usual gaunt, hopeless figures I am used to seeing in the city.

Their style of dress is also different from that worn in Baghdad. They wear bloomer style pants, pulled in tight at the ankles, with a sash across the midriff. On their head they wear small turbans, rather than head covers with circular bands to hold them in place. There is a strong hint of Turkish influence in their dress, rather than Arabian. I wonder why they are so much better off than their southern cousins? To my surprise, the answer is just outside the window.

The desert is changing from an endless hot dustbowl to a rolling, greening pastureland. This is largely due to the mountainous ridges and bluffs rising in the east along the border with Iran (50 miles distant). Mountains change weather patterns. For the first time in Iraq, I see fluffy pillows of cumulus clouds drifting overhead from the east. This type of cloud carries rain! It is a stunning geographical and meteorological transformation, within just a handful of miles.

Just outside the restaurant, looking north, we see the huge oil processing facilities of the Baiji Oil Refinery. Flames and thick black smoke belch out of the large smokestacks, indicating the refinery is producing petroleum products. Oil is the backbone of the Iraqi economy and this working refinery is a good sign. The refinery is set back from the highway and is surrounded by a high, barbwire fence. Lookout towers are manned by armed guards.

As we drive away from the diner, I see a 15-foot wide river of flowing oil. It is running under a highway overpass and along a dry riverbed. I cannot tell where the black river flows to, but it is flowing away from the refinery. It may be low-quality oil being dumped somewhere out of the way. It really is an unusual scene; a river of oil.

The bus continues north, through sheep and goat-filled prairies, planted with alfalfa, wheat, oats, barley and mustard. The countryside is starting to look as fertile as the Canadian prairies in late spring. A large abandoned pipeline project runs along the east side of the highway, leading out from the Baiji Refinery. Large sections of pipeline lie beside excavated trenches, resembling large black liquorice sticks.

I see a European kingfisher sitting on a fence post. On other posts I see bee-eaters and shrikes. They drop down from the posts into the grassy fields, capturing bugs, then fly back up to their perches where they dismantle and eat the insects. Beautiful pink flowering rhododendrons line the median of the highway. Half an hour from Mosul I see six Blackhawk helicopters flying far off to the side of the highway.

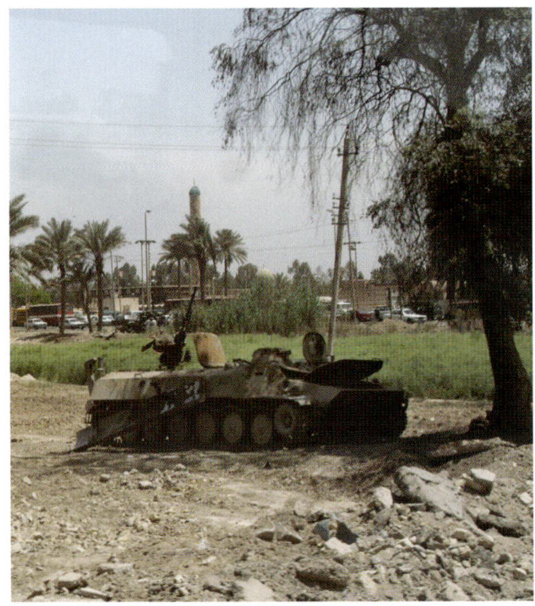

Burned remains of an Iraqi tank

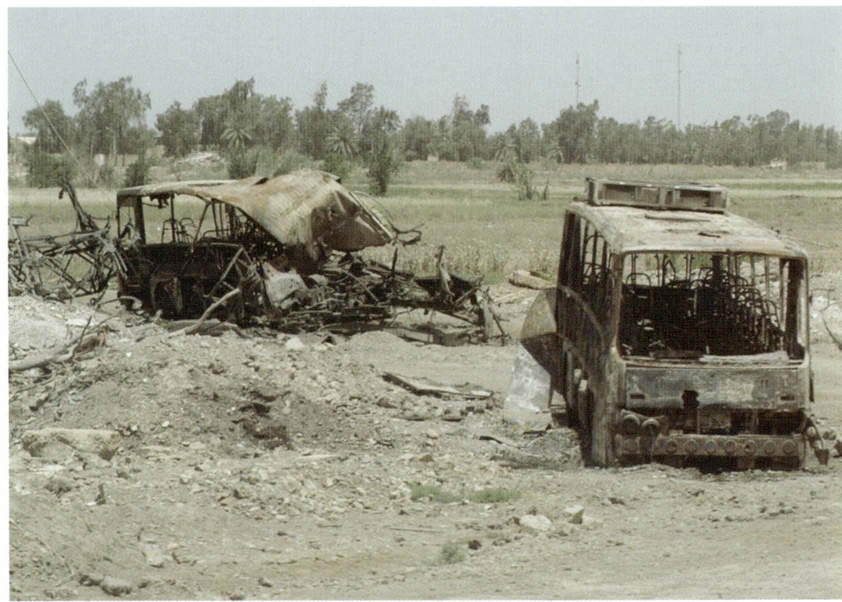

Buses used for carrying Iraqi troops lie pulverized on the road to Mosul

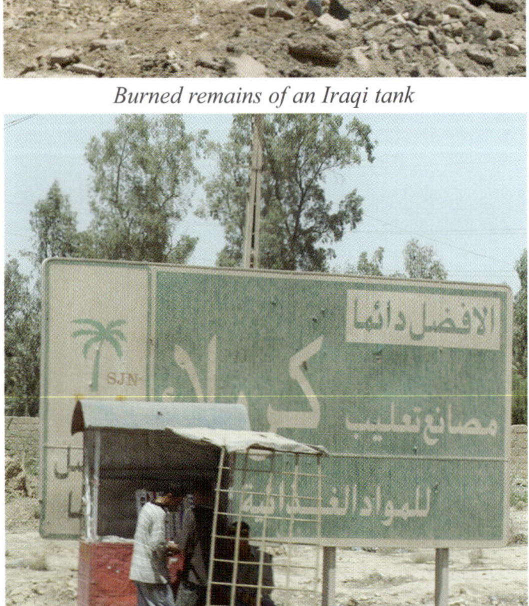

A cigarette vendor shields his smokes from the sun

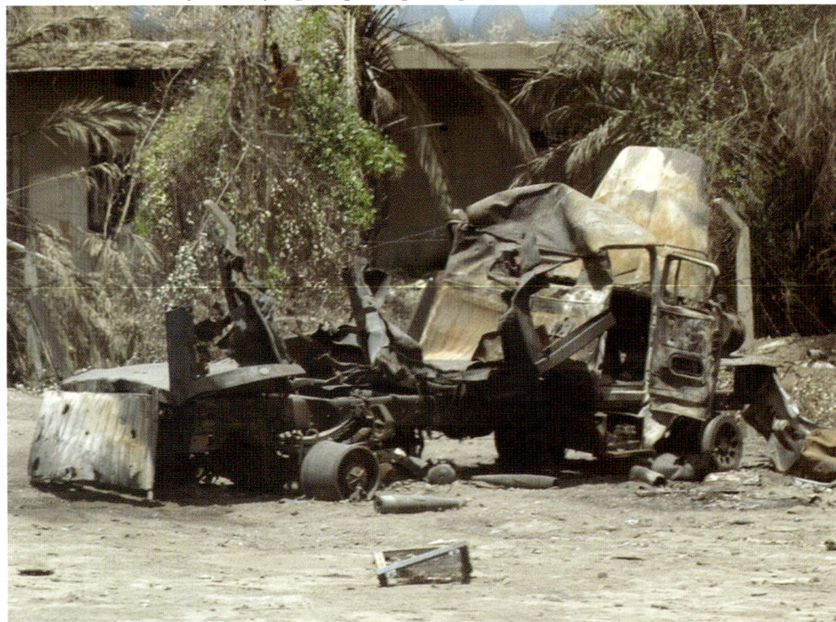

This truck was carrying artillery shells when it was blown to bits

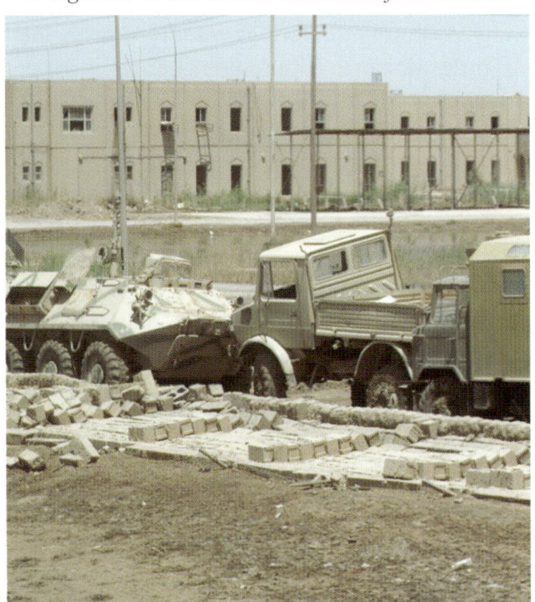

These vehicles were abandoned by their drivers

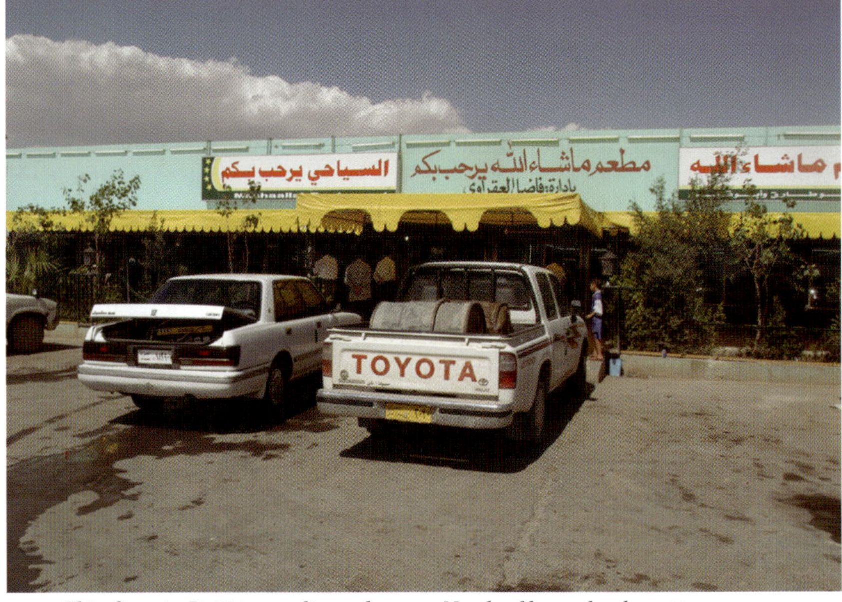

This diner in Baiji is a culinary heaven. North of here, the desert turns green

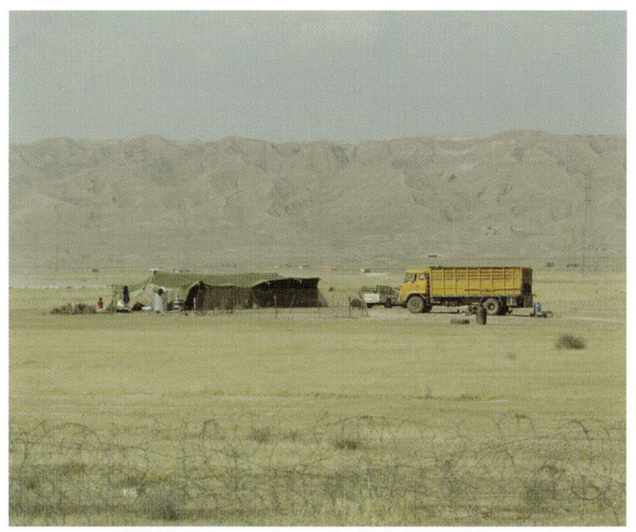

Shepherds' camp near the Baiji Oil Refinery

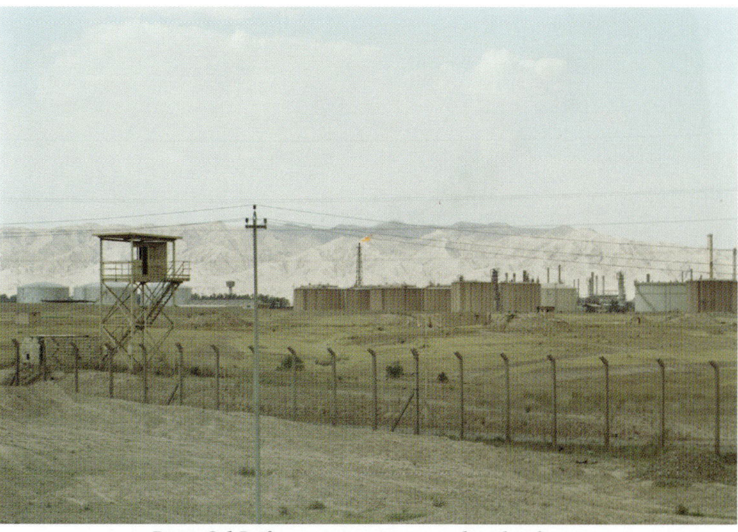

Baiji Oil Refinery is a major crude oil refinery

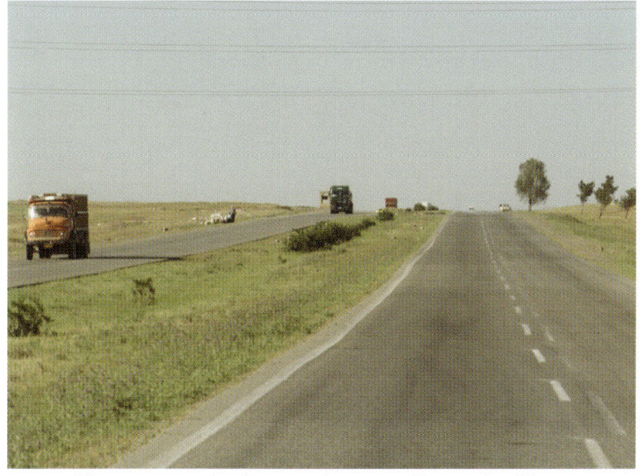

The countryside changes dramatically north of Baiji

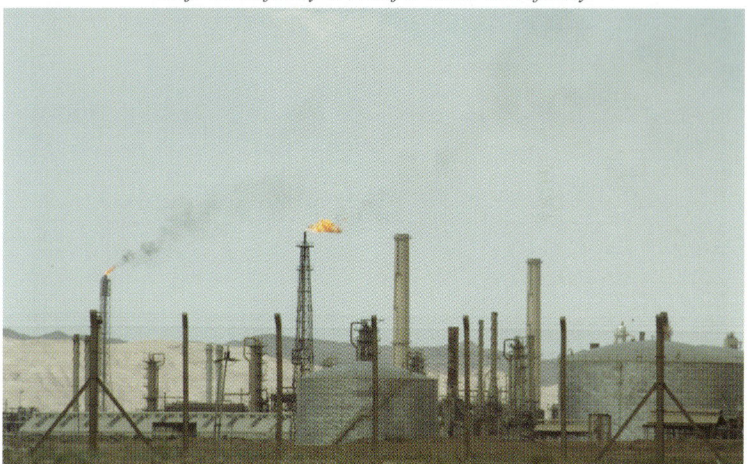

Smoke and flaming smokestacks mean a boost to the Iraqi economy

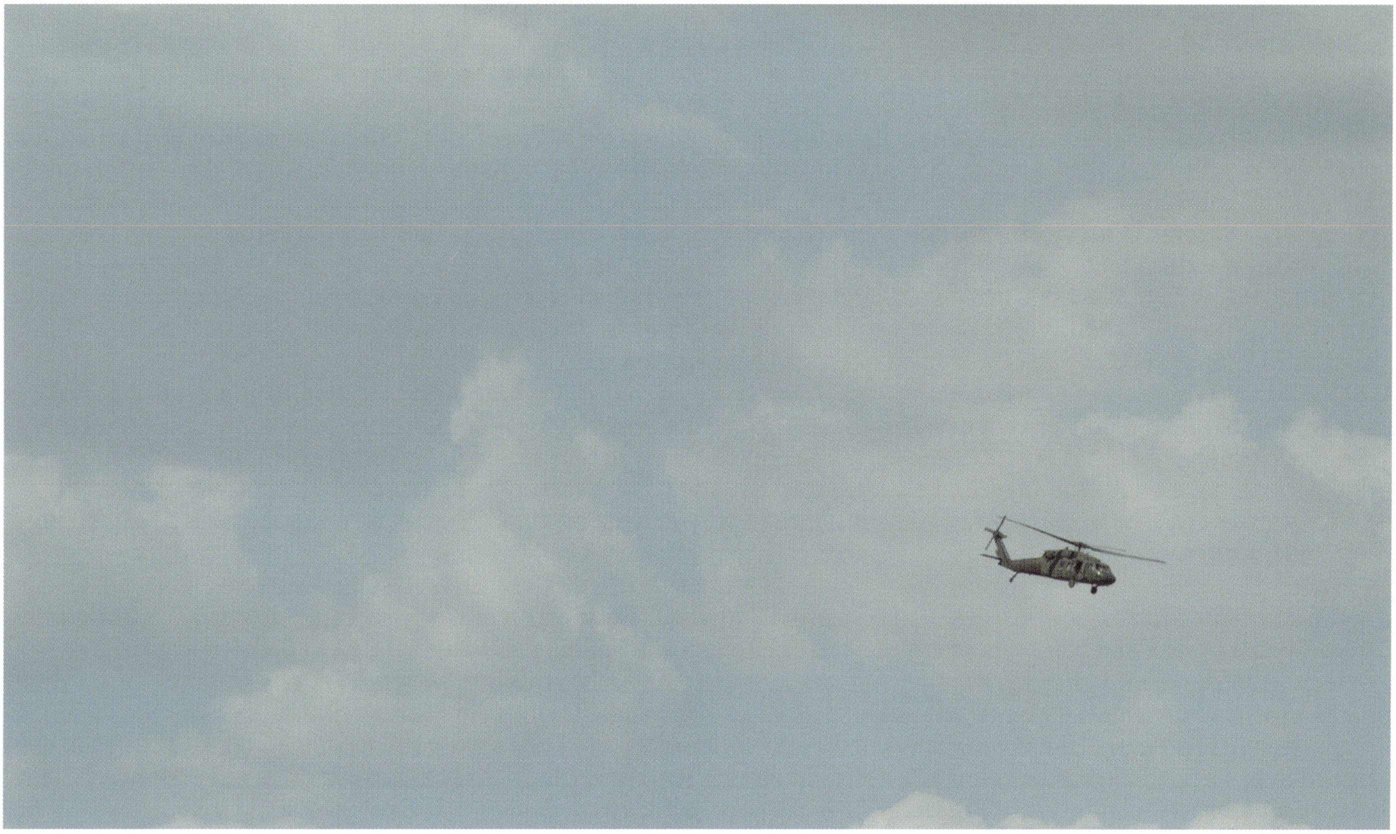

A Black Hawk helicopter patrols the skies near Mosul

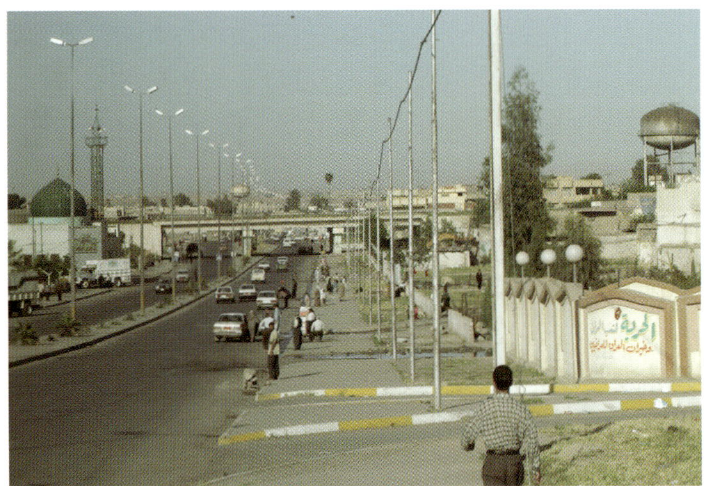

Entering Mosul

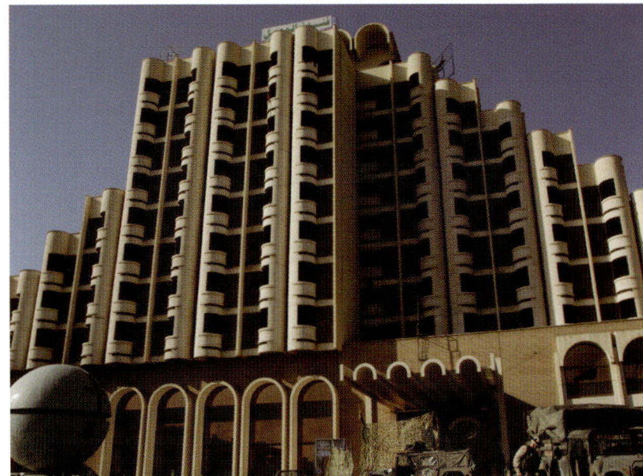

The looted and ransacked Hotel Mosul

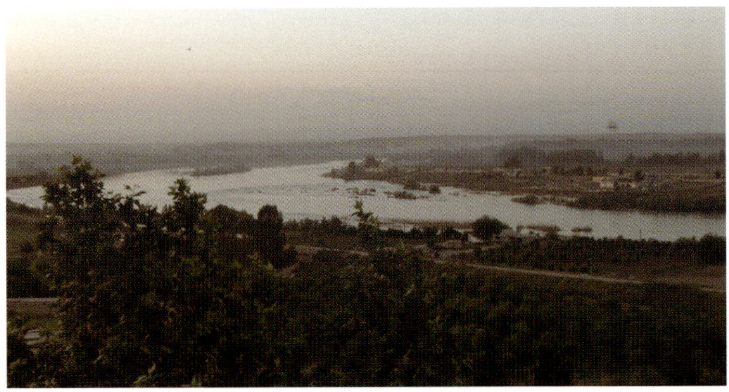

Looking north-west towards the mountains of Turkey

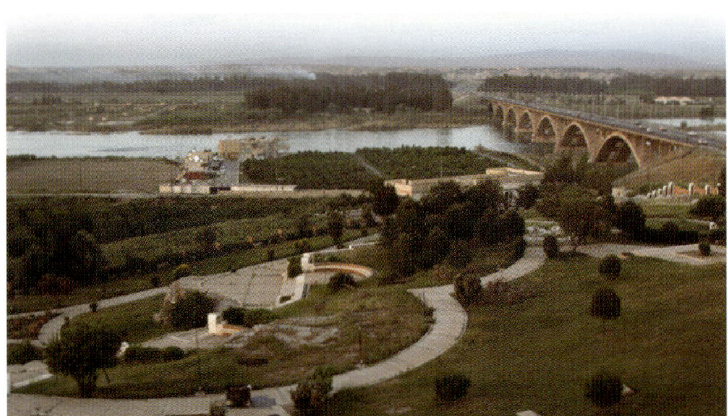

Looking north-east towards Turkey and Iran

No wonder these northern people look so healthy and are dressed so well – they have agriculture! Kurdistan looks like a Garden of Eden. But not only do these semi-autonomous people have agriculture – they have oil! Saddam was concerned by the Kurdistani independence movement, and so he should have been. They are the breadbasket and oil patch that greases a huge chunk of the economy.

Just before 6 p.m., we arrive on the outskirts of Mosul. The bus pulls over and we climb out and flag a taxi. We ask the cabbie to take us to the best hotel in town, and he starts driving through the winding streets of old Mosul. We had planned this trip as a working vacation, and are willing to splurge on a good hotel for a couple of days.

The market area is clean and bustling with shoppers. The shops are all open and stocked with all kinds of goods. Its laneways and roads are clean and in order, with literally no sign of looting or burning. It looks like the war never reached Mosul. The architecture is a pleasant mix of ancient and modern, and everything in between. In one area the ruins of a crumbling old fortress occupy a sandstone bluff. Below this, a row of busy shops has facades decorated with beautiful old Persian woodcarving.

Mosul, population 1,789,000 is the third largest city in Iraq. Built on a large upward sweeping ridge of land, and bordered below by the Tigris River, it is a beautiful setting, with a great green plain fanning north towards Turkey, where a distant ridge of mountains rise. This region has a spectacular history.

The driver takes us to the best hotel in Mosul, the Nineveh, but it has been looted, gutted then abandoned. Well, I guess Mosul is not completely untouched by war. You would think the local taxi driver would know about the hotel's closure. Next he takes us to the Hotel Mosul, a modern ten-storey hotel situated on the outskirts of the city, overlooking the Tigris River. The hotel is shaped like a large triangle, and is very attractive, until we get closer look, that is.

We walk over to the main gateway and are surprised to see two American soldiers guarding the hotel. They are just inside the gates on a sandbag riser, manning a 50-calibre machine gun.

We tell the soldiers we are looking for a hotel to stay in, and could they recommend something to us. They tell us this hotel is not in operation and has been looted and badly gutted. Looking up at the front of the hotel, I see that all the windows are broken and black smoke has stained the front of the building. It's a mess!

One of the soldiers radios his superior to come out and talk with us. While waiting, I watch a throng of children hanging around the gates, trying to sell chocolate bars or beg handouts from the soldiers. But these kids, boys ranging in age from 5 to 12 years, are not orphans and they do not need to beg. They are a fairly healthy looking, well fed bunch of children. They all have shoes (which most of the street youth in Baghdad do not) and are dressed in relatively clean clothing with neatly combed hair. These are the lucky ones. All they are doing is what kids would do anywhere, hanging out where the action is and trying to sell a few candy bars for extra change. The army presence is like the circus in town to these young boys; it is an exciting time for them. There are no young girls in this adolescent gang.

A few minutes later, an officer appears at the gates. He is a very friendly, upbeat officer named Captain Henry Morgan, of the Second Battalion, 502nd Infantry of the 101st Airborne (Air Assault) Division. (Airborne Command Headquarters is located ten minutes away in downtown Mosul). We tell Capt. Morgan that we have just arrived from Baghdad and are looking for accommodations, and wonder if he can recommend something. He tells us he doesn't know of any other hotels that are operating; then, out-of-the-blue, he invites us to stay the evening with his men in the hotel. We are happily shocked at his offer, and jump at the opportunity to get a close look at the life of the soldier.

He tells us that only two floors of the hotel are livable, the rest has been turned upside-down by looters, and is unfit for human occupation.

We walk through the hotel's front doors and into the lobby and reception area, now devoid of most furnishings, except for a few large couches and two coffee tables. It is a large open space with the walls, ceiling and floor covered by a lovely orange-pink marble.

The check-in office has been taken over by the soldiers and is full of all sorts of military gear, with the exception of weaponry. Bedding, radio equipment, rations, kit boxes and crates of other assorted necessities are piled inside the office. Soldiers lounge about on the couches, reading letters and chatting. One man is deeply entranced by his Gameboy video game. There is a folding table set up with a tankard of fresh-perked coffee, chai and cookies. The Captain asks us to help ourselves to the goodies. Their coffee is some of the best I ever drank; it is delicious. I joke with the Captain that the Airborne should open a Starbucks in the hotel.

The walls are covered by colorful cards, drawn and sent by the students of an elementary school in Wisconsin. A rainbow of crayoned colors wish the soldiers a safe return and proclaiming the children's admiration for them. Flags and self-portraits decorate some; tanks firing shells are sketched on another. A soldier tells me that the cards mean so much to the men; it is hard to describe how they bolster morale and make everyone feel closer to home. Many of the soldiers had sent thank-you letters back to the school.

A first-floor wing of the hotel is being cleaned up by a group of six soldiers with brooms and shovels. The main living quarters are on the second floor (though there are some soldiers living in a back wing of the first floor) where the hotel casino used to be located. We are told that the second floor was completely busted-up and littered with debris when the Airborne first arrived. The only furniture left standing and undamaged was a solitary blackjack table that still stands in one corner of the large, open gambling floor.

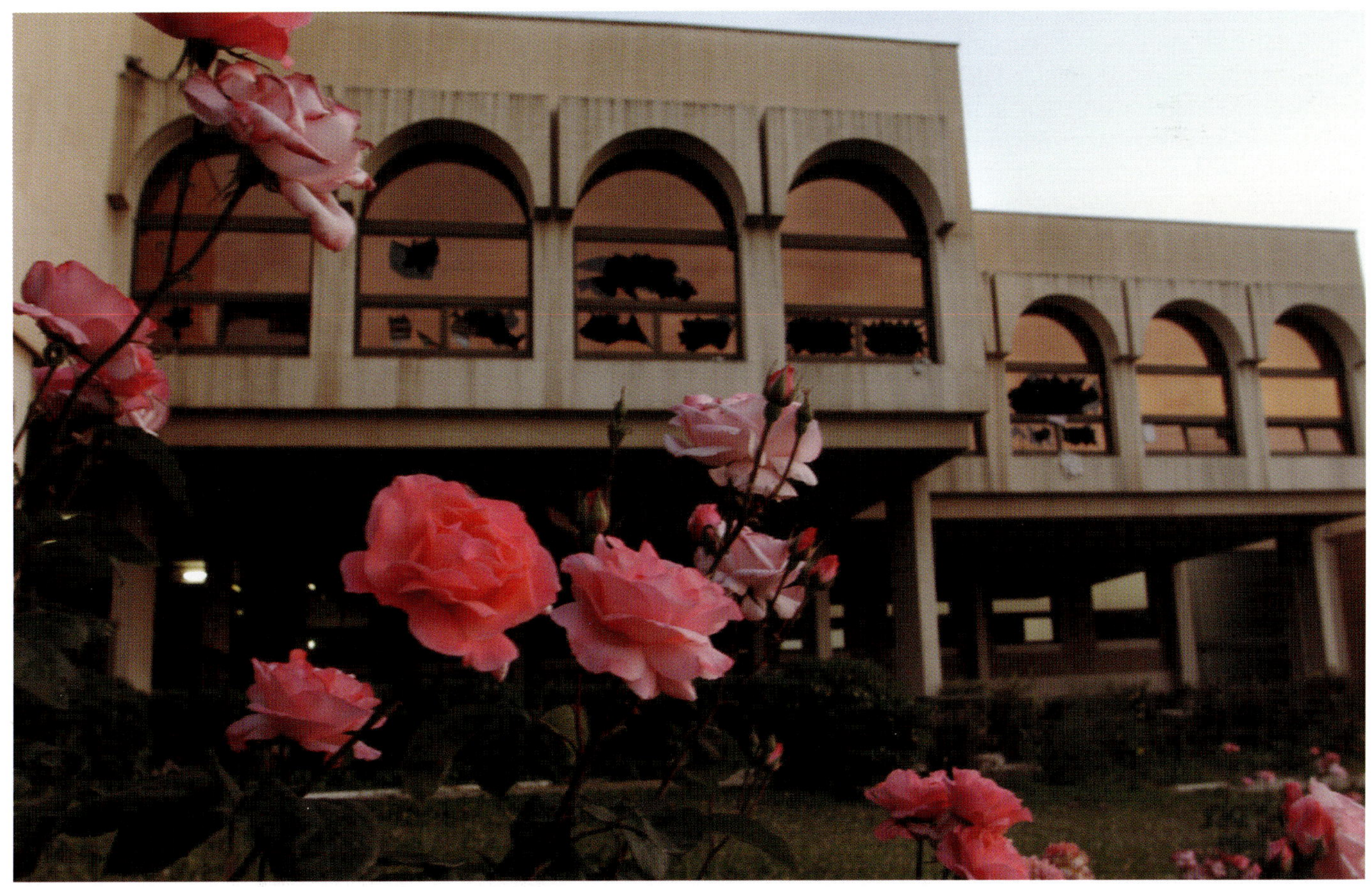

The patio, or north side of the Hotel Mosul has a beautiful rose garden

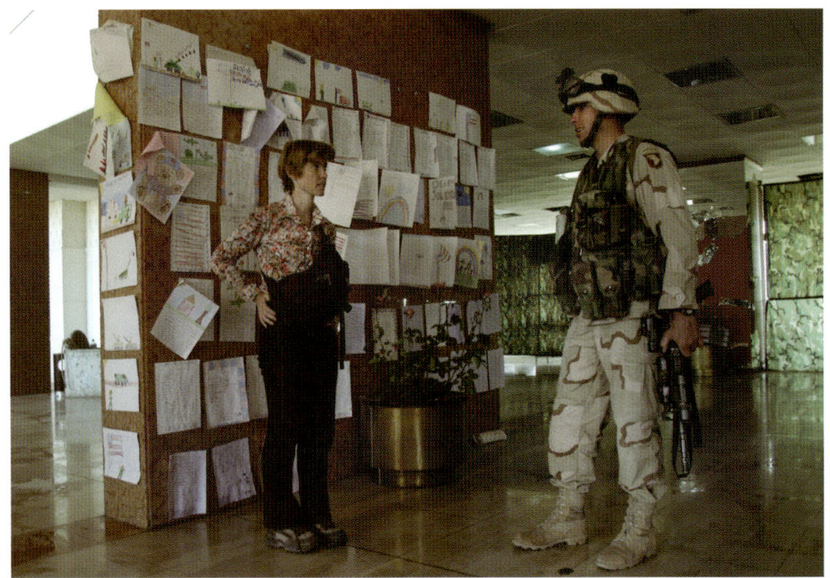

Journalist Tish Durkin talks with a member of the 101st Airborne in hotel lobby

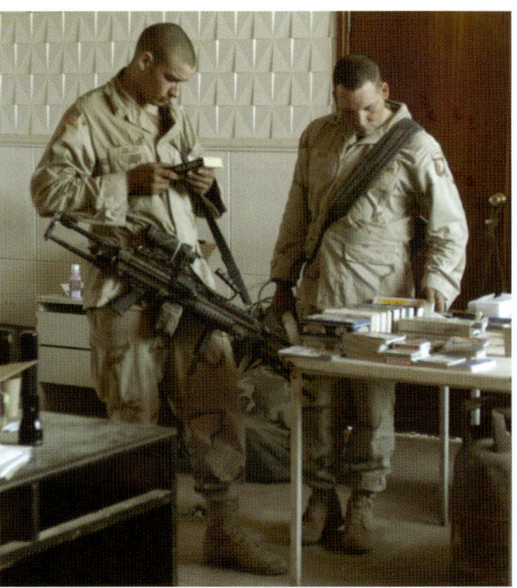

Soldiers are never apart from their weapon

A hundred men reside on this floor. They sleep inside sleeping bags on top of foam mats, with their weapons and personal gear neatly organized by their bedside. It is not what I would call over-crowded, but free space is very limited. Sean, Tish and I are shown a bed space on the floor beside the elevators, where eight soldiers are already living. Since we don't have any of our own bedding, the Captain gives us each a light blanket to cover ourselves. He asks if we have eaten and kindly offers us an MRE each, which we gratefully accept.

The Captain, who is making us feel very welcome and right at home, starts to explain the circumstances leading up to their occupation of the hotel. His tells us his orders had been to liberate and occupy the city of Mosul and surrounding area. His company invaded from the south, and during their sweep of the city, found the *peshmerga Army* occupying the hotel (the *peshmerga* are the northern members of the coalition forces and are also referred to as the Kurdistani Army). When the Airborne arrived at the hotel, the *peshmerga* were in the act of savagely looting and destroying the hotel, breaking and burning anything they could not steal.

Captain Morgan demanded that the *peshmerga* leave the hotel immediately, telling their officers that his orders were to occupy the city, and that included the hotel. Infuriated and disgusted by the wanton destruction, Captain Morgan told them they had five minutes to evacuate their men from the building, or else face the brute force of American weaponry. "The *peshmerga* knew they were outgunned and that they would have been totally destroyed, very quickly," said Morgan. He said the Kurdistani soldiers hesitated at first, but by the time five minutes had passed, they had cleared out and were fleeing north across the Tigris, where they disappeared into the foothills of the mountains. Morgan confirmed that he was unquestionably ready to open fire on them had they refused to leave. "Luckily for them," he said, "they retreated."

The *peshmerga* left behind the destroyed shell of what used to be a five star hotel. Every window is shattered, and holes have been kicked into most of the walls. Furnishings have been tossed through the windows or burned in the rooms. It is completely trashed, but that isn't the worst of it. The Captain tells us, with a healthy dose of disgust, that the *peshmerga* soldiers had defecated in every room, staircase, office and hallway of the hotel (this is particularly repulsive to Morgan, a man highly respected by his troops as a 'soldiers officer'). He tells us that nobody is allowed above the second floor, as it poses a health hazard. Beside what I have seen at the Hotel Mosul and Hotel Nineveh, very little other war damage is evident in Mosul.

It is starting to look as though foreign-owned hotels are a favorite target of the looters (e.g., the Sheraton Hotel in Basra looted and burned). Perhaps it is because they are owned by Western companies and therefore (at least in the looters' or *peshmergas'* minds) are the symbols of Western opulence.

This hotel is in a picturesque setting, with large rose gardens and magnificent flowering trees. It sits on a bluff, the back side facing north and overlooking the fast and clean Tigris River, the front towards Mosul. A beautiful, large arched bridge spans the Tigris. On the far side of the bridge, the roadway leads north towards the distant mountains and Turkey. The main city sits two miles to the east. It is a beautiful, ancient Mesopotamian city clinging to the crest of the high river bluffs. It is an impressive panorama, with lush green farmland fanning out from the river, and a huge orange setting sun. The view down towards the river and the mountains distracts me from any thoughts or images of war.

I ask a soldier if he has seen any scorpions near the hotel (the habitat looks perfect for them). He tells me that there are some living under the rocks in the gardens. I thank him, then try to find one to photograph, but I have no luck. These critters are active at night and remain hidden during the day.

Sean, Tish and I sit in the TV room (a separate room off the Casino playing floor). We are preparing our MREs. Sean shows me how to use the MRE meal-warming package. You take the included heating pouch (about the size of an envelope) and tear it open across the top (it has heating pads incorporated into it) then add two tablespoons of water into the open pouch. The sealed meal bag is then inserted into the heating pouch and the top of the pouch is folded over. The pouch is propped upright at a 30-degree angle, so the water does not escape but partially immerses the meal pack inside it.

In a matter of seconds the water is steaming, then boiling. In five minutes the meal package is piping hot, as if boiled in a pot of water. It is my favorite meal I am preparing, the noodles and chicken dinner! It is amazing technology; a hot meal without fire or electricity. Backwoods skiers would be wise to carry a couple of these in their packs. They could melt and heat-up snow in an emergency situation.

As a side dish, I have crackers and blueberry jam, then for dessert I share two Tootsie Rolls with Sean and Tish. All these foodstuffs and more are found in a single MRE. It is a good meal for tired journalists, and saves us from going out to blindly find a restaurant after dark. It is not that it is dark or possibly dangerous, it's just that we are very tired. But even in tidy, well-fed Mosul, anti-Western sentiments are a reality, and it would be foolhardy to dismiss it.

We chat with some of the troops who are coming in to watch TV. They are good men who believe they are fighting for a just cause, but there is little admiration amongst the soldiers for Mosul, or the type of soldicry thcy arc practicing. They would rather be on the warpath, hot on the heels of the enemy, than shacked-up in a hotel performing picket duty or keeping swarms of children away from the checkpoints.

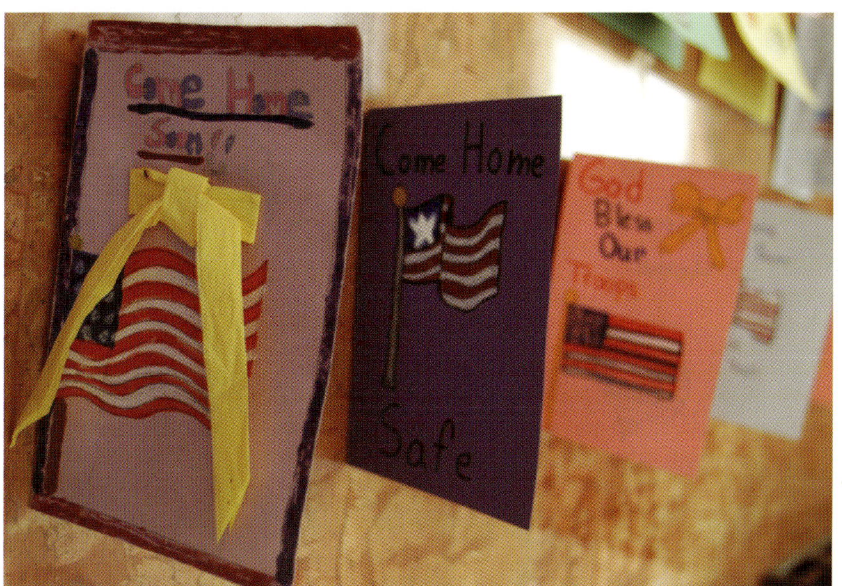
Students of an elementary school in Wisconsin sent these cards to the troops

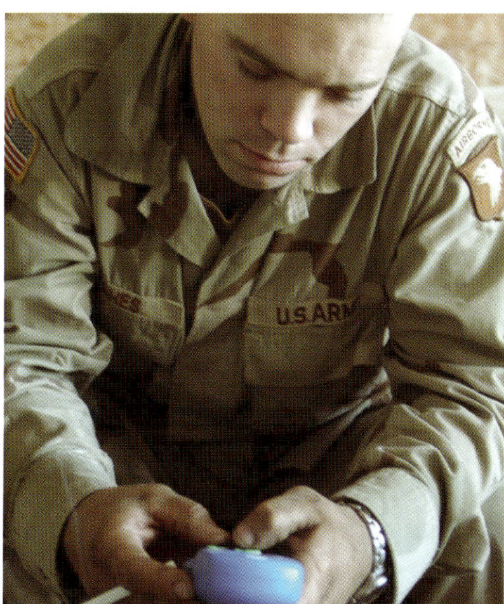
Relaxing with a little game on Gameboy

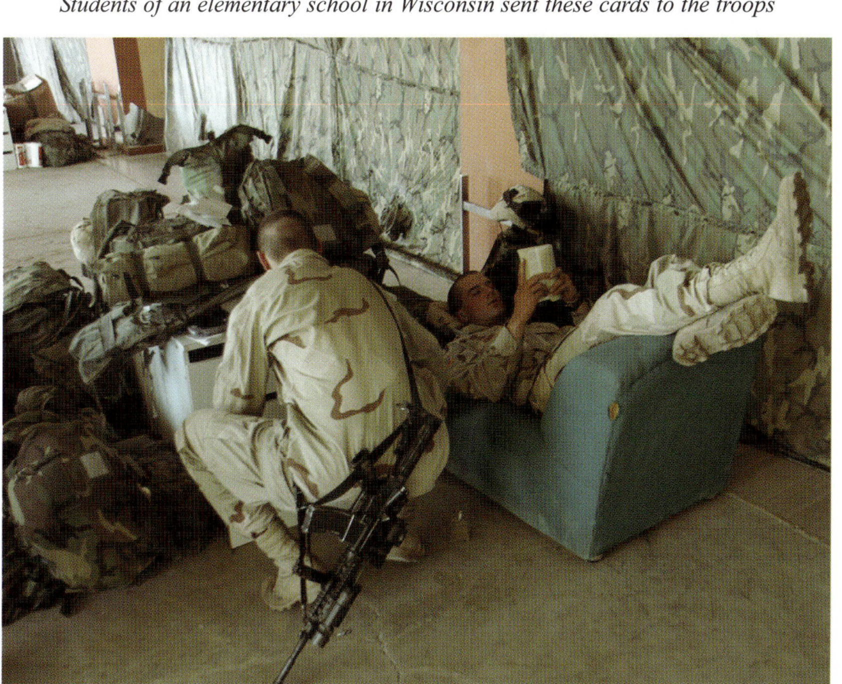
Time for a little reading between shifts

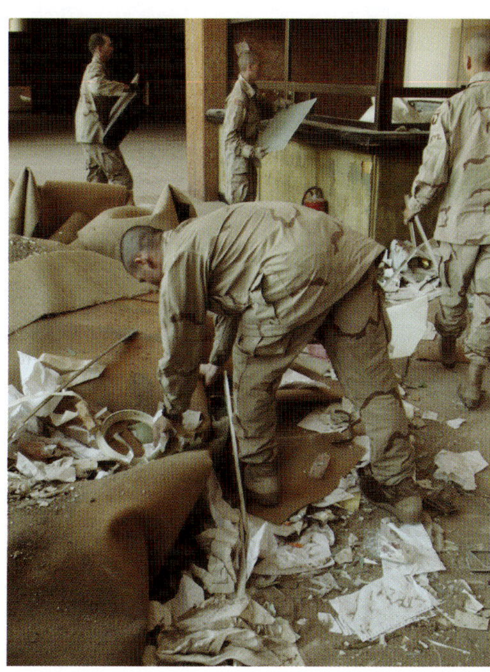
Members of the 101st Airborne clean the Hotel Mosul

During down time, the soldiers clean their weapons, write and read letters, eat, sleep and do their laundry. They laugh when they see us gleefully enjoying our MREs. They say the food tastes like paste. The only way to improve the meals, according to the soldiers, is to mix together different meal packages, for a more diverse taste. Little do they know how little we have eaten since our arrival in Iraq. An MRE is like a banquet.

Just before bed, I give a group of soldiers a slide show of my pics from Baghdad and Basra, inside the TV room. They are thankful to see what is going on in other parts of Iraq and comment that they wish they were closer to the action. The soldiers tell us they admire us for what we are doing, and how we go about doing it.

Tish, Sean and I finally get to sleep after conversing (with hushed voices) into the early hours of the morning. It gets so cold during the night that I am awakened by it and have to get up to put on my long underwear. I did not expect this range of temperature fluctuation, but I am glad I brought my long johns. I sleep well after I put them on.

Day 25. Sunday, May 4th

(Burning CDs; breakfast at the Mosul Hotel; visiting a gas station; huge line-ups for fuel; even day odd day distribution of gas; Airborne Headquarters; Army media personnel; local newscasts aired; 1st Sgt. Ken Heller; interim government; pushing the transmissions further; American strategy in Mosul; soldiers' displeasure; low morale; gun dealers brought to jail; a game of cat and mouse; the police station; Iraqis don't trust police force; a road map to disaster; school yard bullies; patrolling for black market gas dealers; drinking gasoline; machine gun on roof of gas station; CIA command post; supper with the general; great food; ice cream for the troops; satellite dish; Fox News is hated by American soldiers; BBC news admired by American soldiers; rap star 'Eminem' on Much Music; Burn the House Down; thinking of home; plans to move on to Arbil; just over a week left in Iraq)

I get up around 8 a.m. and start burning a CD of my Baghdad pics for Captain Morgan. This is under the condition that he makes the CD available to the soldiers, so they can make their own copy. I consider this a minor form of payment to the soldiers for the room and board.

By the time I finish and head downstairs, breakfast in the lobby is just about over. I grab a coffee and biscuit, after missing out on the pudding, and cereal with real milk.

Captain Morgan invites us to go out on a Humvee to see how gasoline is being doled out to the public at one of the few open gas stations. Walking out to the front of the hotel, Sean, Tish and I hop into the back of a Humvee and we drive off to the station, ten minutes from the hotel.

On our arrival, we see cars lined up two abreast, and backed up for two miles. The system of distributing gasoline is slow and methodical, but at least it shows that the Americans are trying to make sure that everyone gets their fair share. When it is their turn for gas, the car owner gives the attendant a coupon, which is matched to a list showing the drivers name and license plate

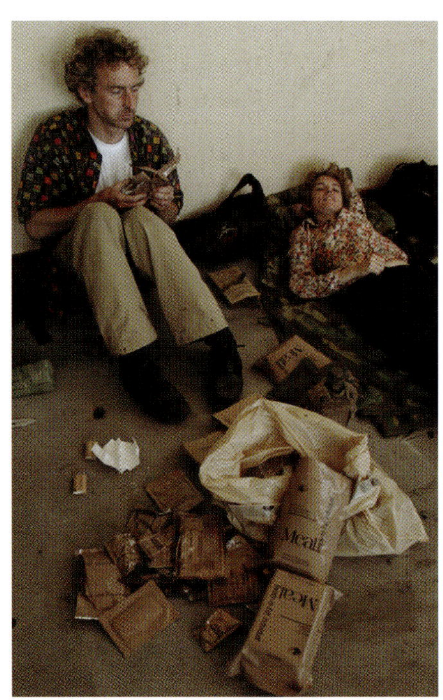

Sean and Tish enjoy a buffet of M.R.E.s

Soldiers of the 101st Airborne in Mosul. Any one of them could be the kid from next door

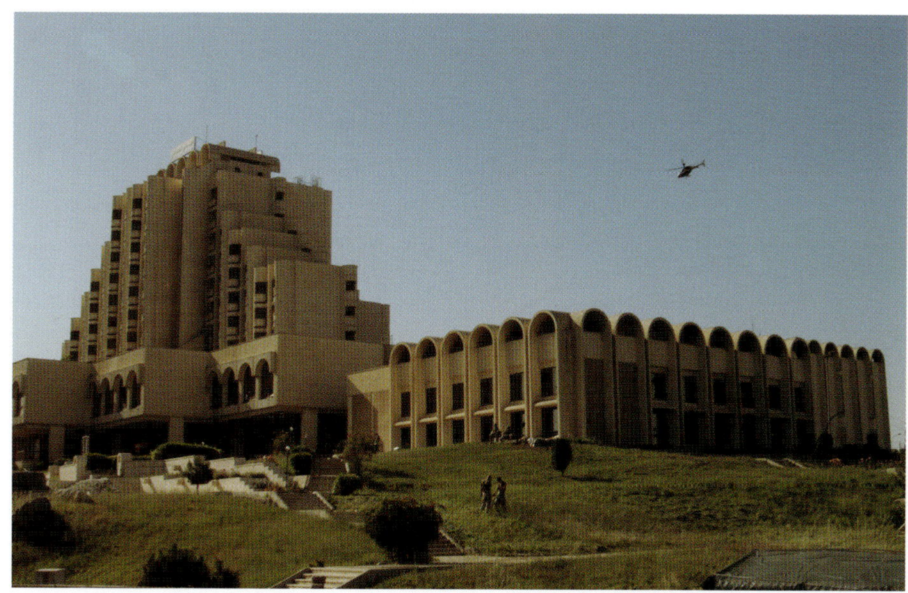

The formerly beautiful Hotel Mosul was looted and trashed by Kurdistans' peshmerga army

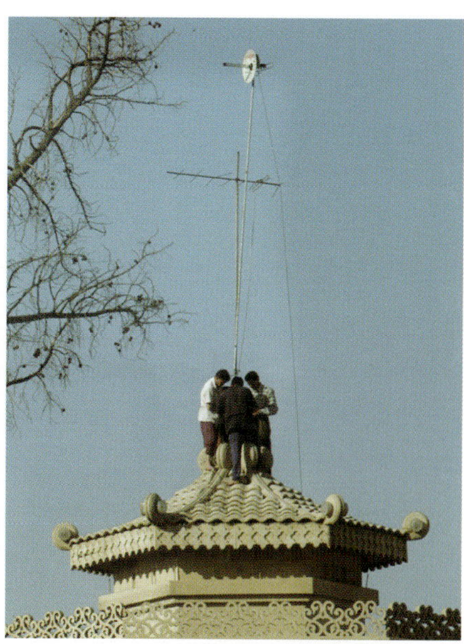

Mosul residents raise a satellite antenna

number. Those with license plates that have an even number plate are given their allotment of 25 litres of gas for 1000 Dinars, or about 50 cents. The following day, those with odd-numbered license plates are allowed their 25 litres. So on paper you should receive your 25 litres every other day. The problem is that the lines are so long, some 3.5 miles, that it sometimes takes two days of waiting in line to get a chance to get gas. If your number falls on the wrong day, you have to get out of line and wait until it is your day. So this leads to confusion and frustration. But at least the rules are the same for everybody.

Sometimes police officers or influential people will try to cut the line, but they, like all the others, are told to take their place in the line – with no exceptions. This is the message the soldiers want to send out; that no man is above another. It is a good strategy.

The reason for the fuel shortage was that fuel production had been shut down prior to the war, and some of the oil-producing infrastructure was destroyed or heavily damaged by war. Even before that, production was heavily curtailed because it was difficult to procure replacement parts used in the industry, due to the sanctions. So much of the machinery used in the refining process is outdated and in need of replacement or upgrading. It will take years to get the industry up to full capacity.

Now, the problem is not as much getting the oil out of the ground, but in refining it, which takes a massive amount of electricity. There is little electricity available, and what there is, is inconsistent. Most of the refined gasoline in Iraq is being trucked in from neighboring countries.

After seeing how the gasoline (called Benzene by Iraqis) is being rationed, we drive off to Airborne Command Headquarters near the center of town. We are led into headquarters, where we meet with the media staff. One of their tasks is to put out a newsletter to inform the troops of the latest developments in the conflict; another is to try to answer our questions.

Perhaps their most important task is getting the local Mosul television station up and running, with the help of former Mosul TV station staff. Last night they aired their first television broadcast, since the outbreak of war.

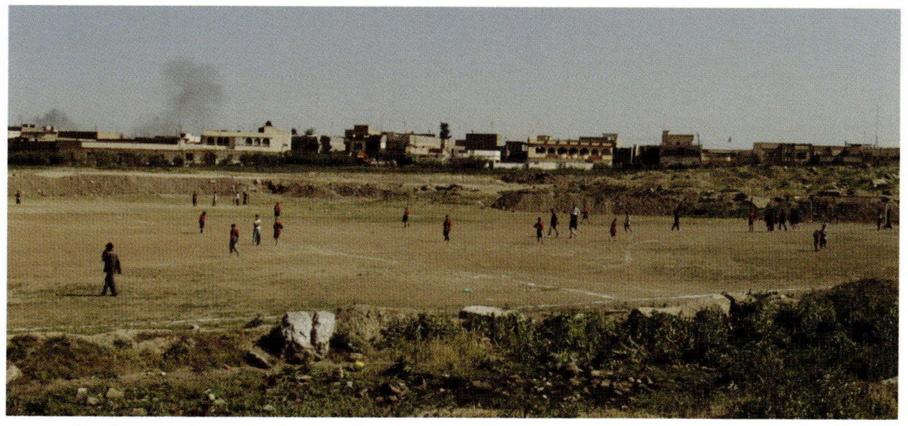

Smoke rises in the background as these residents enjoy a game of soccer in Mosul

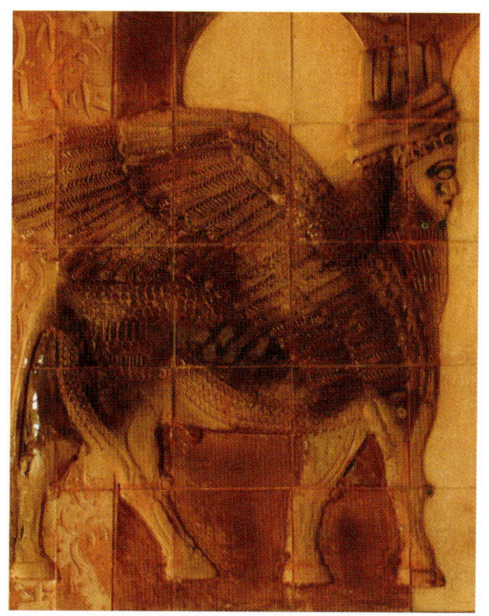

Flying lion wall art in hotel

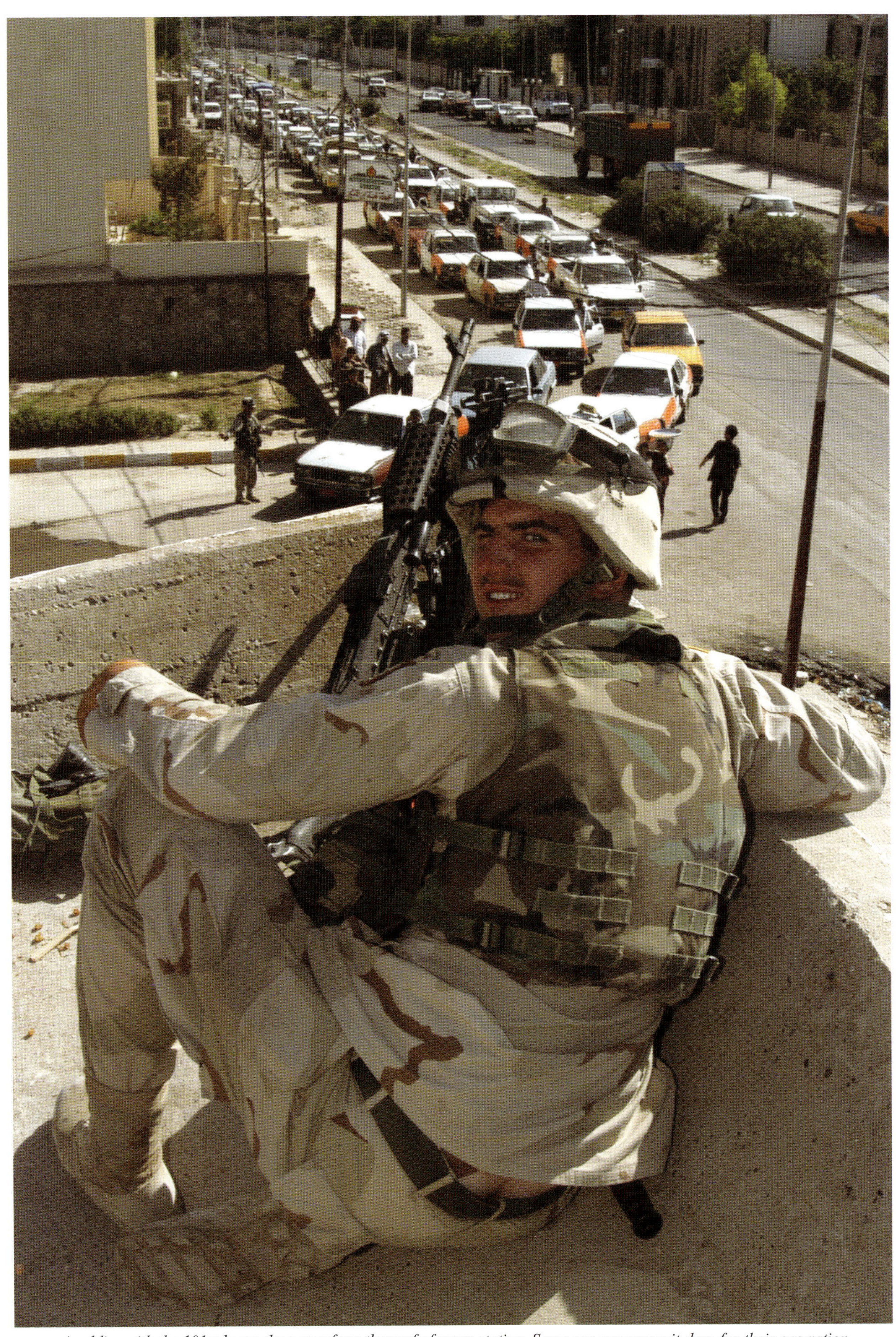

A soldier with the 101st keeps the peace from the roof of a gas station. Some car owners wait days for their gas ration

"They aired a twenty-minute local newscast which featured a chief judge being sworn in," said 1st Sgt. Ken Heller, of Army Communications and Media. "They also had a piece with the manager of a propane-fuel company in the north of Mosul." The company manager told the viewers about the status of fuel, and the problems with getting it to the public, and how they were trying to alleviate these problems.

"The lead piece was about the formation of the new interim government; it's actually more of a caucus than an election," explained Sgt. Heller. "The station gave each of the 7 candidates 5 minutes to air their policies. They aired everything they said, which was unusual because the public is used to getting only one opinion from only one political representative," he said.

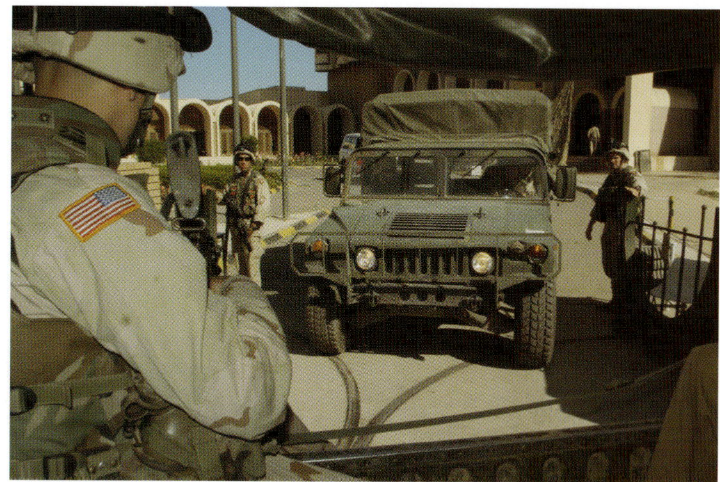
Humvee patrol leaves the Hotel Mosul

Sgt. Heller explains that there is only a one-kilowatt transmitter operating. This one transmitter only covered the City of Mosul, reaching 750,000 viewers. "They were trying to upgrade that so they could push the transmissions further," said Heller. "It was a great new concept for the producers, they didn't understand that they could play anything. Somebody doesn't have to tell them what to play. It was phenomenal for them to understand that", concluded Sgt. Heller (prior to this, censorship ruled).

A colleague of Heller's takes over and starts to outline the American strategy in Mosul. "What we first started to do was attempt a system of law and order, which included fire and police services; that was our number one priority. Number two was to get a system of civil administration in place, so the people could govern themselves," he continued. "The next step was to try to get some of the infrastructure going; to make sure we had, fuel, water, electricity; to make sure the schools could open; to make sure the hospitals were operational. But first and foremost was security," said the officer. "Now we are trying to get people to run the city for themselves."

I ask the officer what is significant about the city of Mosul. "As we would say in America, it's a melting pot of many different ethnic and religious groups, which makes it a very unique city, not unlike many of our American cities," he said. "It is a beautiful city; the people are very friendly, and again, there are many walks of life here from all kinds of backgrounds that live together, but have been broken apart. And now we are seeing that all come back together again."

I ask Sgt. Heller if he could e-mail a message back home to my family to let them know I am in Kurdistan. He told me it would not present a problem, and will send it later in the afternoon.

On the subject of e-mail, last night a group of soldiers voiced their displeasure to me at not being able to phone or e-mail their families. Most of them had not talked to their families in months (though they are allowed to write home). I ask an officer why the troops were not allowed to phone their families, even if only once a month. He explained that, if the soldier was told something bad had happened to a family member, his morale could be affected. This could make it difficult for the soldier to concentrate on his/her duties, possibly upsetting the morale of other troops. "What if the soldier found out, through a phone call, that his wife back home was leaving him for another man? He wouldn't be able to perform as well as he should, and this may endanger his fellow soldiers, especially for the smaller platoons."

He explained if anything bad did happen to a soldier's family member, then the American Red Cross would contact him or her through army headquarters. The soldier would then be able to speak with his family and even head back home if the situation warranted (such as a dying parent).

Sean and Tish leave H.Q. and drive over to Mosul City Hall, to look into the story of the new Iraqi coalition government that is being formed. Members of the coalition are meeting to discuss policy issues before their official inauguration tomorrow. I head back to the hotel in the Humvee for a break.

I am walking through the hotel lobby when a soldier asks me if I want to go with them on a patrol to arrest black market gas dealers. I tell them to count me in. First we have to pick up some gun dealers from the other side of the hotel where they are being held, and bring them to police headquarters. They were caught selling guns and ammunition at a local market.

The weapons trade here is nothing like Baghdad, where you can buy almost any type and amount of weaponry. Here, the black-market weapons trade is very small, a pin-

A soldier's best friend is his weapon

prick, and usually only a handful of small arms and ammunition are found. After a few days of raids, the dealers are getting smarter, using kids or other vendors as lookouts. "It's like a game of cat and mouse," one soldier tells me, "but it's kind of fun."

Our two Humvees leave the front of the hotel and drive to the side entrance where the prisoners are being held. Under the arches of a hanging rose garden, four Iraqi prisoners sit with their hands bound behind their backs by plastic straps. This fragrant garden would have been a beautiful place to hold a wedding reception, or a social tea party, had this been peacetime. But presently, a soldier stands guard over the detainees, a high power sniper rifle cradled in his arms. A nine-year-old boy cries hysterically while clinging to his father's smock, one of the prisoners. A pathetic sight, but the boy had been with his father when he was arrested, and the soldiers had to bring him along, otherwise the boy would have been left alone.

The prisoners are loaded into the back of the Humvee and I jump aboard, sandwiched between the prisoners and two armed soldiers. The detainees try to keep their heads covered while I take pictures of them and the soldiers as we drive to the police station. I feel so bad for the kid, but this would be a lesson he will never forget. The problem is whether he will hold a grudge against the Americans, or learn from this that it is wrong to break the law. None of them speaks a word during the ten-minute drive; only the whines of the boy's crying are heard above the grinding of the Humvee engine.

We pull up to the police station and the prisoners are led in to a large open square where a group of ten police officers, in snappy green uniforms, stand around chatting with each other. A police officer comes over and asks me what I am doing at the station taking pictures and that I should stop. He is agitated and bitter at my presence, and acts as though he is used to having things his way. The soldier tells him that I am with them, and that I have complete access to use my camera. The officer abides by the soldier's wishes and disappears into the crowded square.

The Iraqi public does not like the very real possibility that some of the worst element of the old police guard might be re-instated, and eventually seek revenge on those they don't like.

The prisoners are lined up against the prison wall and frisked by the Americans before being interned into individual cells by the police. The soldiers and police discuss what to do with the boy, and ask his father if there are any other family members who can take care of the boy. I leave before that situation is resolved.

Being able to patrol with the Humvees gives me insight into the structure and teamwork amongst soldiers. It also gives me a good view of how the locals feel towards the soldiers.

From what I have seen so far, I personally doubt this operation in Iraq will succeed. It is like reading a road map to disaster, then seeing it unfold in front of my eyes. It is too massive an undertaking for the Americans to have taken on alone – right from the start. But I am not solely blaming the Americans, though they bear the brunt of responsibility for what will inevitably unfold in Iraq. The American plan in Iraq would have and could have worked, with the U.N.s backing. The fragmented U.N. has become a powerful lobby group to the anti-American sentiments of the European Community leaders, who jealously take swipes at the American empire. Now is the time they should be here.

How many hundreds of thousands of people have died in civil wars in Africa while the U.N. became smothered in their own bureaucracy and bad decision making. Where is the U.N. compassion towards the people of Iraq? They have done nothing to relieve the anguish of Iraq. And while the in-fighting between the U.N. and USA continues, millions are living a miserable existence. The Iraqis want answers, solutions and peace – not more accusations and hair-pulling by the world's schoolyard bullies!

Our two Humvees start patrolling the main streets, looking to catch the black-market gas dealers who undermine the American attempts at controlling the distribution of gasoline. It does not take long to find those selling illegal gas right in Mosul.

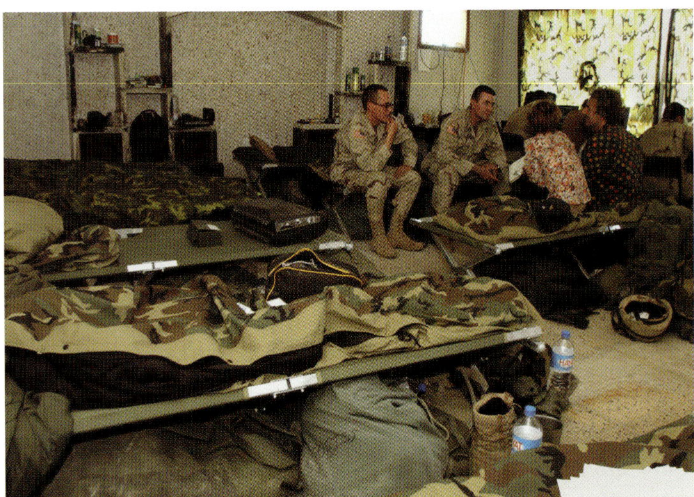

The media center and residence of the 101st Airborne in Mosul

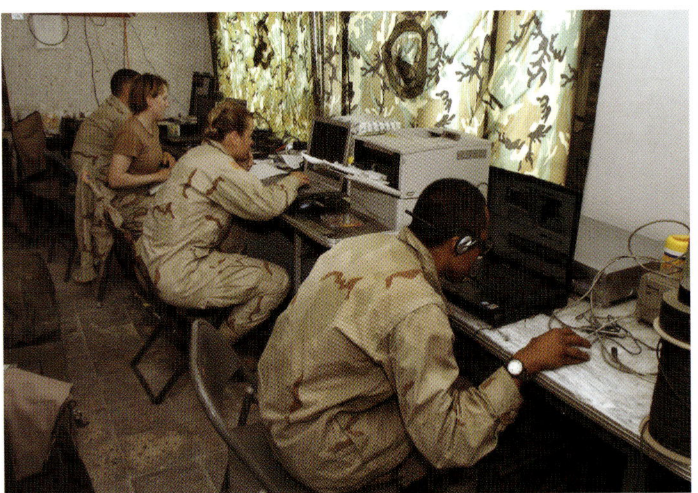

Media team keeps troops informed by publishing a newsletter

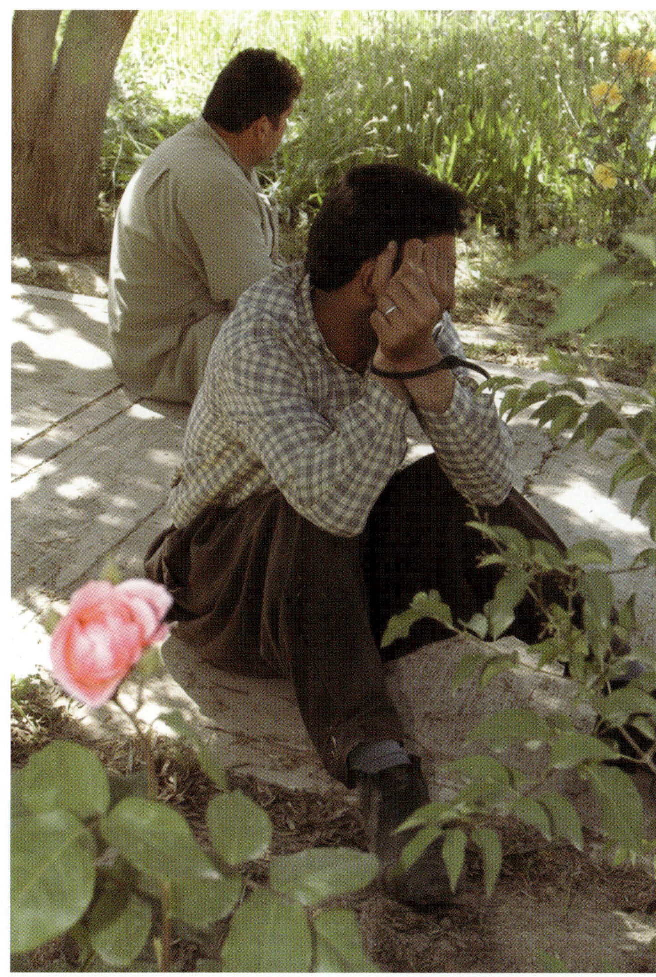

Suspected weapons dealers are held in the hotel garden

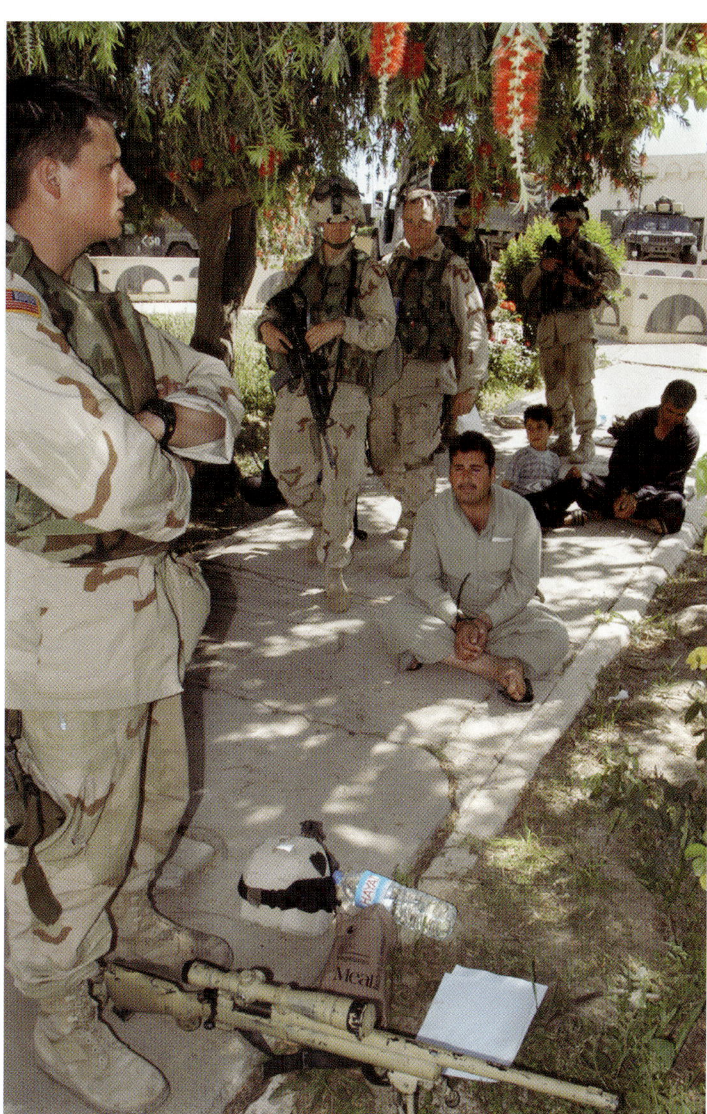

Soldiers hold suspects before they are transported to the police station

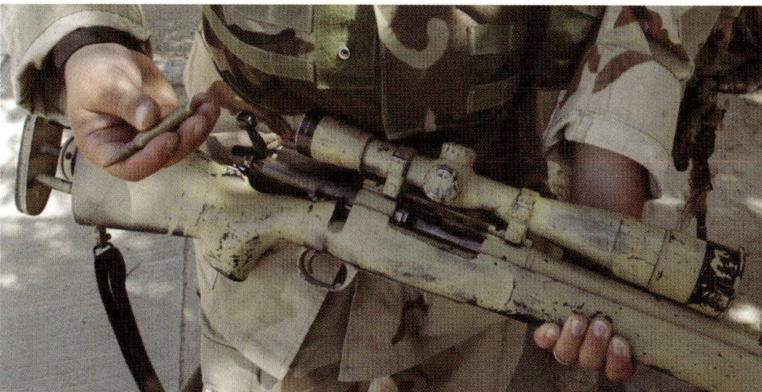

A sniper rifle

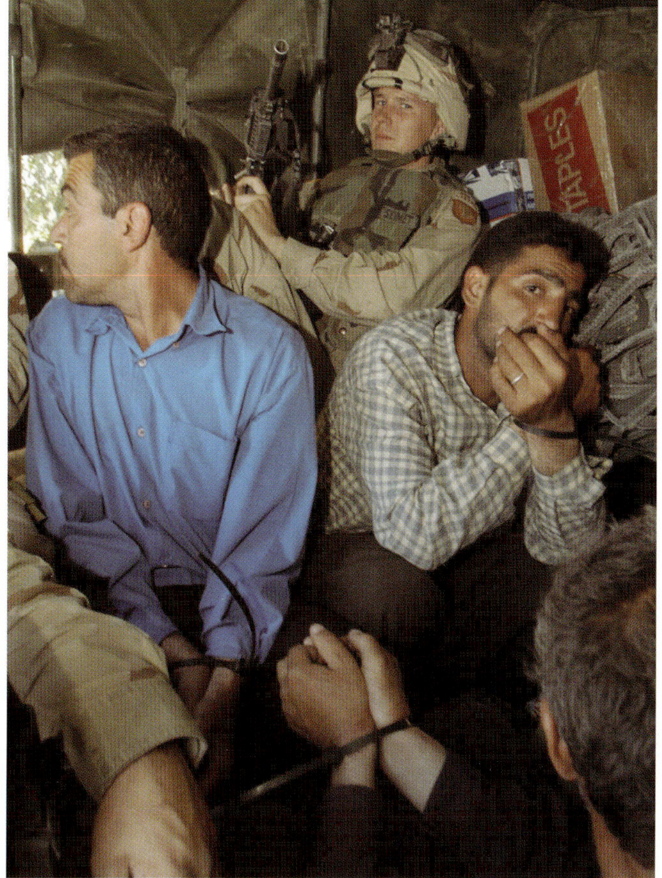

Four cuffed prisoners head to the police station for internment

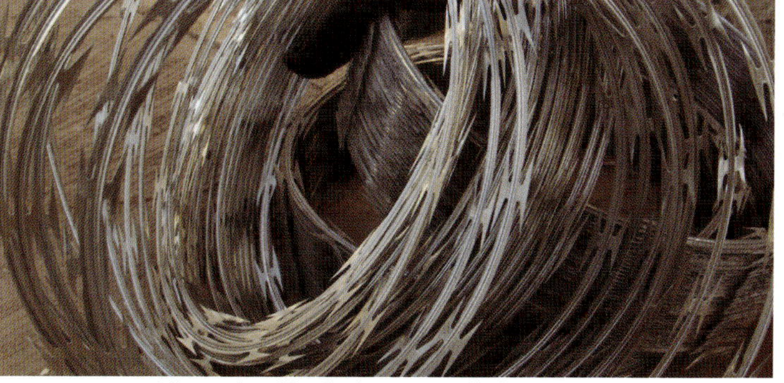

This style of barbed wire is called razor wire

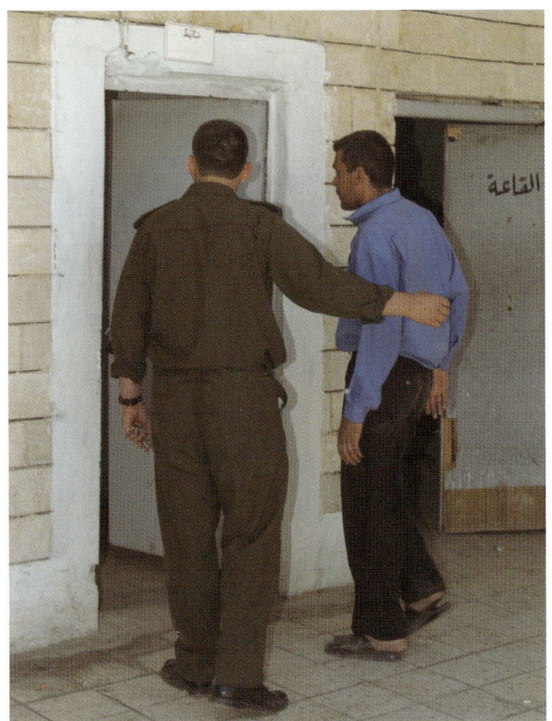

Prisoner led into a jail cell by policeman

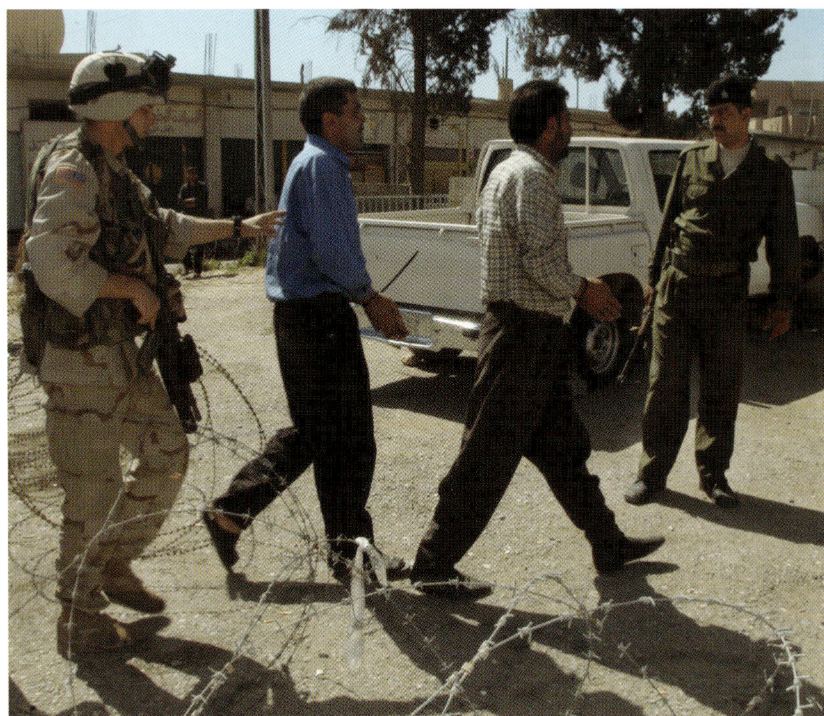

Soldier and policeman escort prisoners into the station

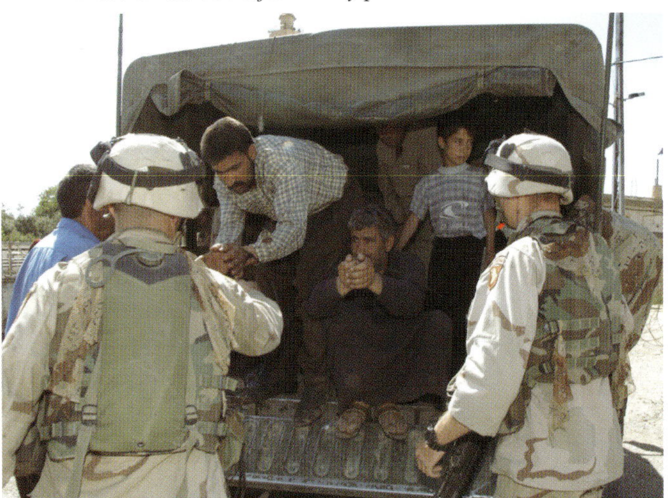

Prisoners out of Humvee

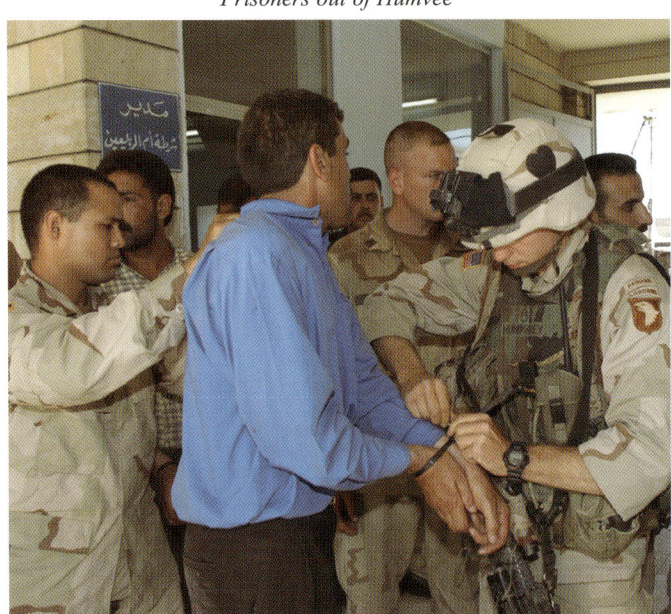

Prisoner uncuffed on prison property

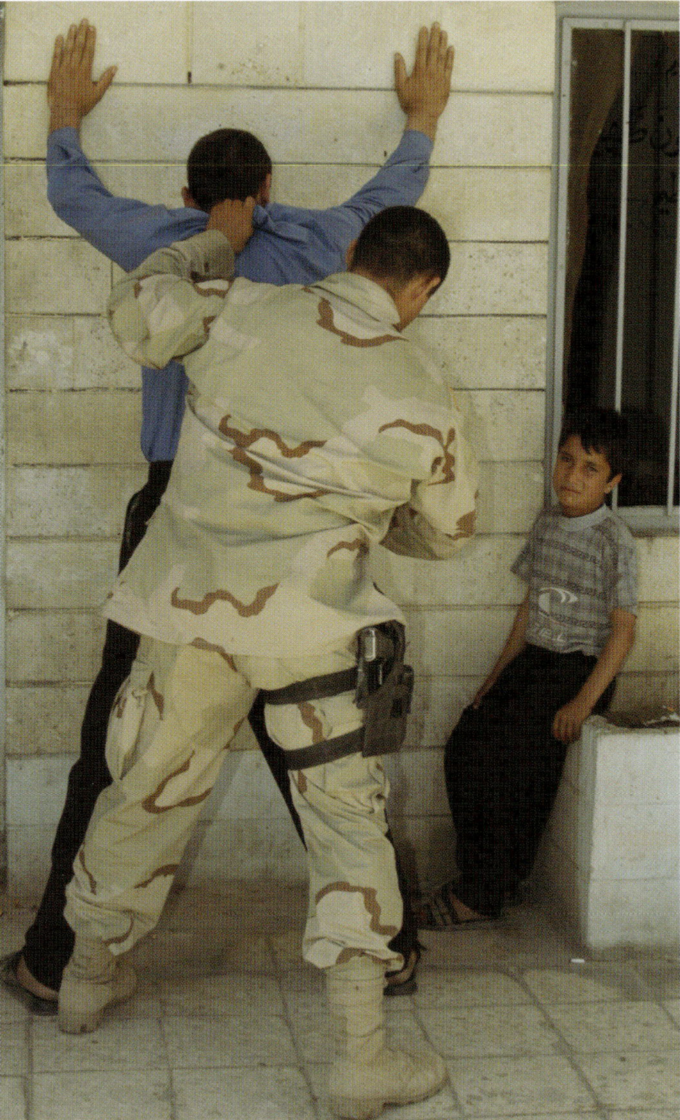

This young boy was with his father when he was arrested

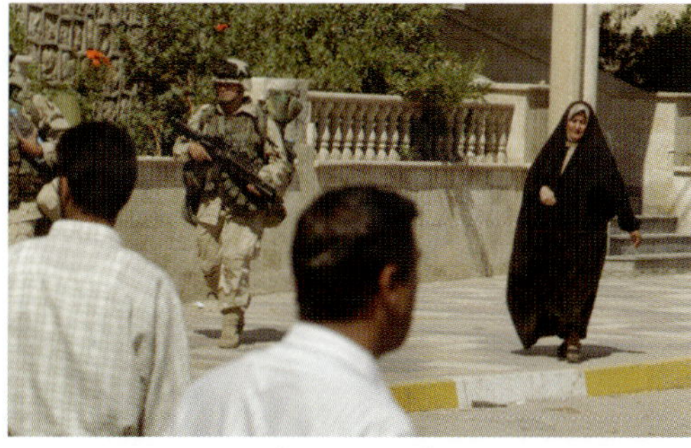

Street patrol

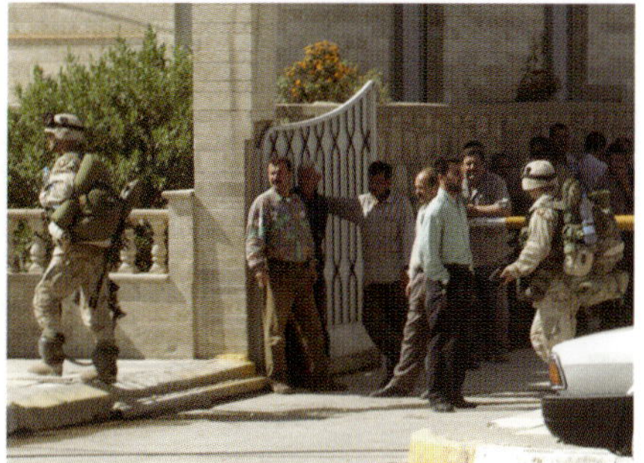

Street patrol

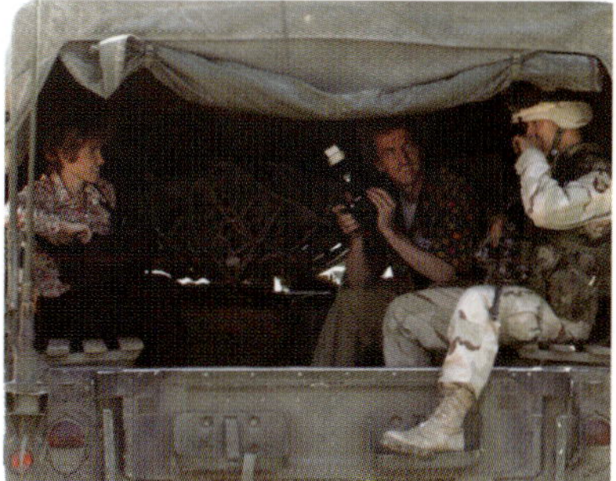

Sean and Tish on patrol

Three men with four 10-litre and two 50-litre plastic containers of gas, stand along the curb of the road. In one hand they hold a four-foot section of rubber hose, which they wave at passing motorists to let them know they have gasoline for sale. The vendors are set up just down the road from a gas station with a two-mile line-up of people waiting for their legal gas allotment.

Our Humvee pulls over beside the dealers and two soldiers jump out with weapons ready (the driver remains in the vehicle). One soldier stands off to the side, covering the Humvee and his colleague, while the other soldier confiscates all their hoses and gas. They frisk the dealers and check their vehicle for hidden weapons, then tell them to get lost and do not come back. The containers and hoses are put into the back of the Humvee, and we drive on to another location.

At the next illegal gas stop, it is basically the same deal; jump out, grab the hoses and gas, listen to the dealers' excuses for why they are selling the gas, then confiscate it and tell the dealers to get lost. We break up four separate operations, if you want to call them operations (more like roadside fruit vendors – only with gasoline).

Should you have money to afford illegal gas, the dealers would stick one end of a rubber hose into the gas jugs, and suck on the other end until the gas started flowing. The desired amount of gas would be siphoned into the customer's gas pipeline. It doesn't take long to siphon ten or twenty litres, making it difficult to catch the dealers actually selling and serving the gas. But all the soldiers need is evidence of the intent to sell. The hoses and jugs, even if empty, provide that.

Those waiting in the long lines at the stations endorse the soldier's actions. They have to wait in line; so everyone else should. The only exception is emergency vehicles.

The soldiers tell me that some dealers, when confronted, actually drank from the gas jugs, saying they were only filled with water (trying to outwit the soldiers). In cases like this the soldiers would ask the suspect to breathe into a lit cigarette lighter. At this challenge, the dealers backed down and confessed that it was gas, rather than being turned into a flaming torch. Some of the soldiers told me they were impressed by the dealers' entrepreneurship.

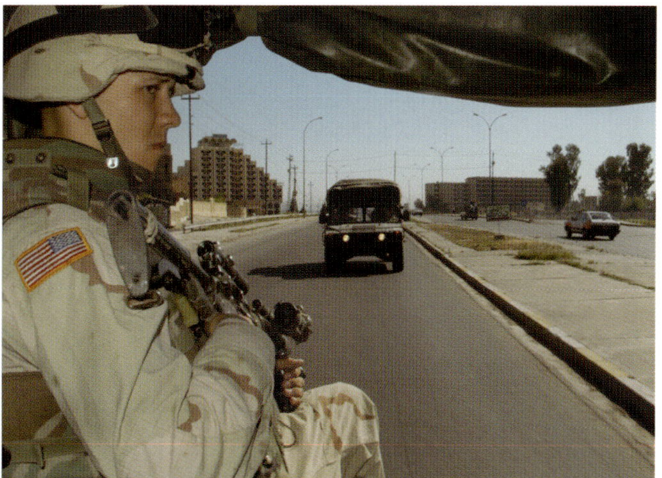

Patrolling in Mosul

We drive to a gas station which serves as a center where confiscated gas containers and hoses are unloaded and kept. On the roof of the station, a soldier sits behind a 50-calibre machine gun, overlooking the two-mile long line-up of cars. He is positioned there to ensure that a gunfight does not break out, should some motorist try to retaliate against someone cutting in line.

I can understand the American policy for its distribution of the gas. It is a bureaucratic system, and tries the motorists' patience, but it has to be done this way to show that the Americans are at least trying to ensure a fair distribution system, and everyone is on the same playing field. If not for the rationing, the high cost of black market gas would put it out of reach of most Iraqis.

On the main highway in and out of Mosul, you can buy all the black-market gas you can haul. There the roads are lined with concession after concession of illegal gas. The Americans cannot possibly control it all; it is too over-

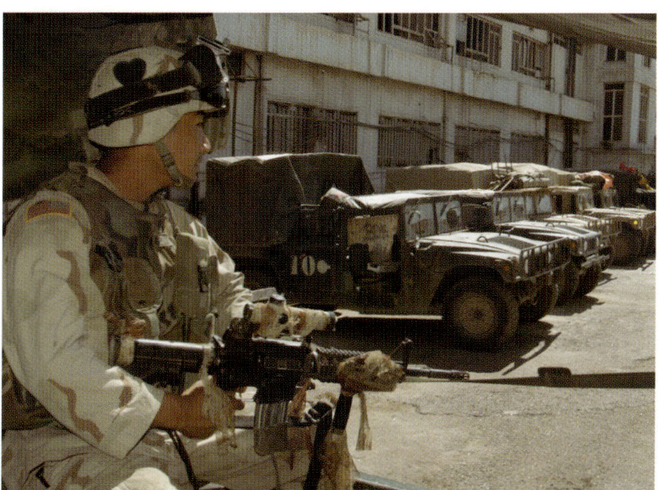

Keeping guard outside Airborne headquarters

whelming. But they can keep a partial lid on it in the city itself. The Americans do not want to become gasoline cops. This is one reason why members of the former Mosul City Police Force are being asked to return to their jobs; to help curb the illegal gas market and free-up the soldiers for other important tasks.

The Americans are also trying to train and clothe members of the new Iraqi Army, known as the F.I.F or Free Iraqi Forces. They are already assisting the Americans by manning checkpoints and taking over dangerous policing duties. It is hoped that the F.I.F. will take over the responsibility for soldiering the nation, once the Americans leave Iraq. There is just a handful in Mosul, but from my conversations with them, they have the drive and

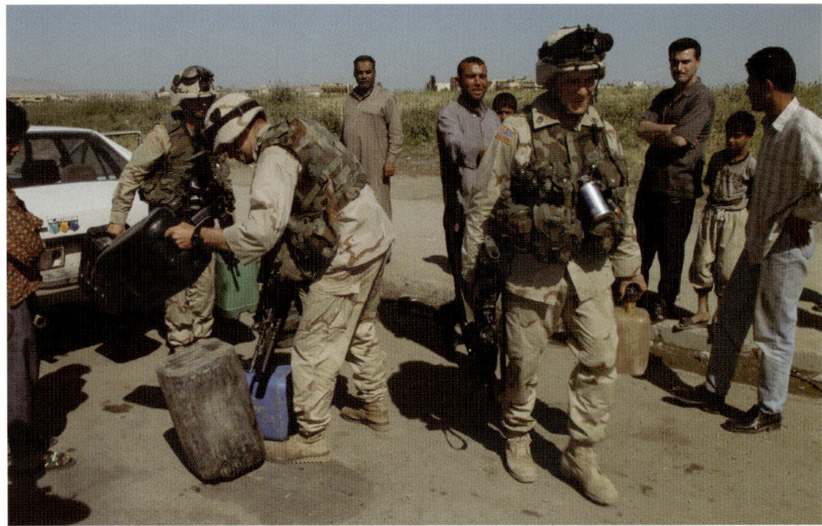
Gas dealers are free to go after their gas is confiscated

desire to improve the situation in their country, and are readying to lead it in the right direction. I found most of them to be honest, hard working people.

The Americans are attempting to supply them with uniforms, as most have only parts of old outdated uniforms. Some wear running shoes, because they do not have army boots. They are bedraggled, but an energetic group of men who love their country.

With the gas patrol over for the day, I head back to the hotel with the Humvee crew. A soldier tells me that the American CIA has a small command post below the big arched bridge spanning the Tigris. It is hidden from view under the arches, and is off limits to all but the exclusive members. He explains that the CIA members drive GMC Jimmys, and many of the personnel wear blue jeans or a mix of civilian clothing and military uniforms. Many of them are bearded, and look like undercover narcotics officers.

Late in the day, Sean and Tish return to the hotel. We start talking about going out for supper, but it is getting dark. Captain Morgan introduces us to Hakim Mallaleh, a former Iraqi Air Force General and helicopter pilot, who is at the hotel looking for some work as an advisor or interpreter (this shows how difficult it is to find work in Mosul, even for generals). We ask him if he can recommend a restaurant. He, with his 16 year-old son, offer to drive us downtown to a restaurant across the street from the Mosul Foreign University. We agree, as long as they join us for dinner as our guests.

The restaurant is full of bustle and activity and great-looking food. We eat like kings. During supper the general tells us that he hopes the Americans stay in Iraq for at least a year, or longer, to help stabilize the country while it is being rebuilt. I am hearing this same opinion from the majority of locals I talk with, or at least two-thirds of the voices. Most of the others just want the Yankees to leave; they do not want them in their country at all, regardless of the outcome.

After dinner, we walk along the people-filled streets. They are lined with rows of busy shops and kiosks, brightly lit with an overdose of neon. There are many different items that we have not yet seen in Iraq, including great ice cream. We stop at an ice cream shop and buy six large bricks of chocolate and strawberry ice cream. We want to give the bricks to the soldiers back at the hotel, for being accommodating to us.

Back at the hotel we hand out the ice cream, making sure that all the soldiers receive at least a small portion, including the six members of the F.I.F. who are also bivouacked on the casino floor.

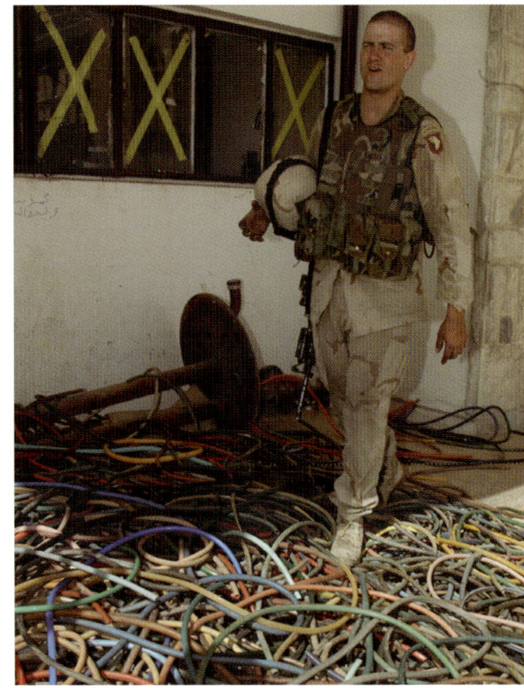

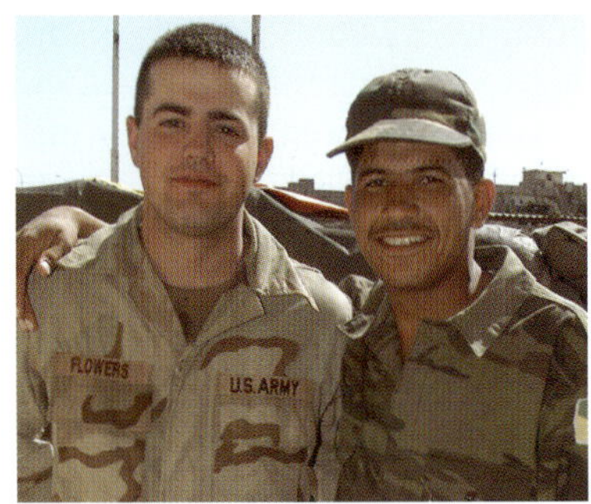
The F.I.F. helping the Airborne

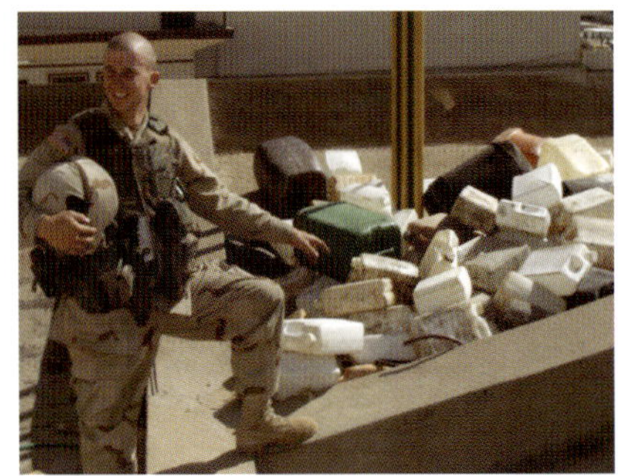
Empty gas jugs on roof of gas station

Pile of hoses seized from black market gas dealers

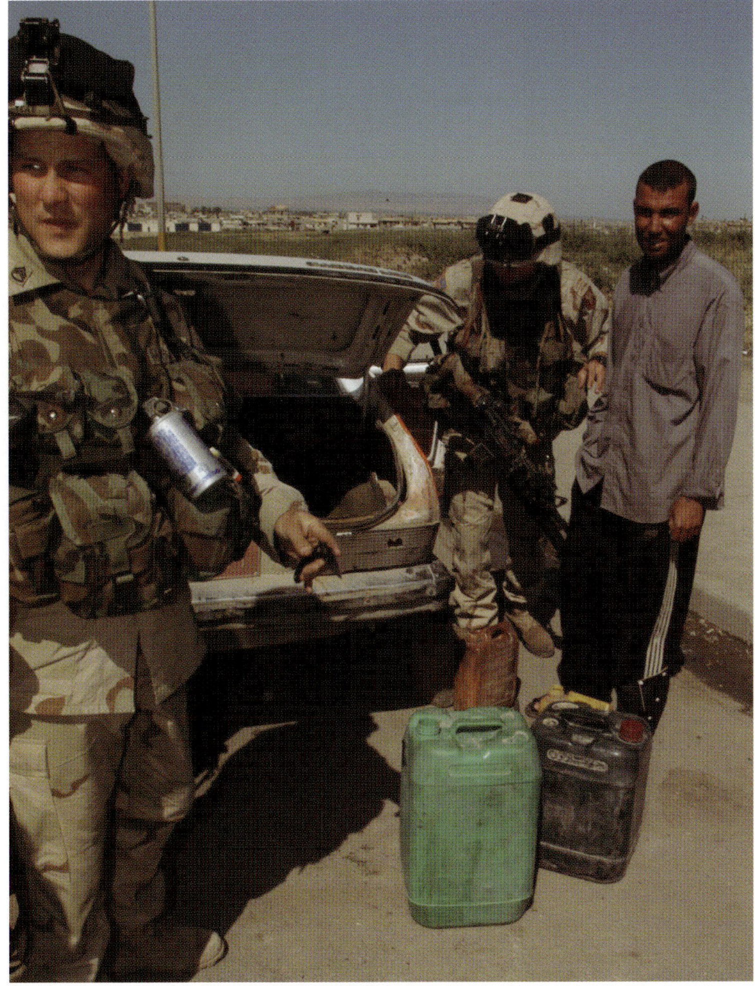

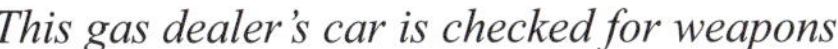
This gas dealer's car is checked for weapons

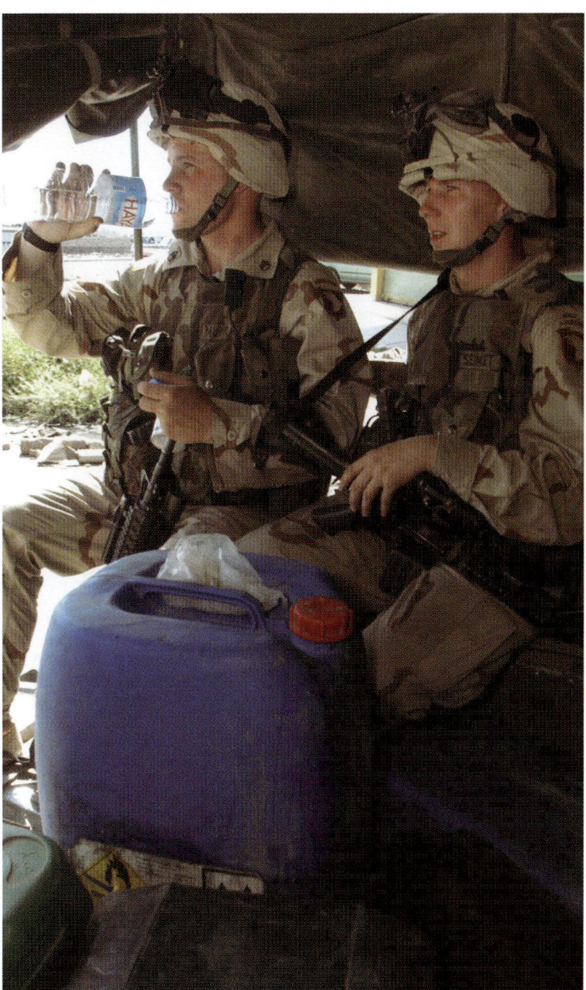
Soldiers pause as the Humvee fills up with gas jugs

A technician is at work in the TV room hooking up a satellite dish. The three of us, and eight soldiers are lounging around on couches and chairs 'shooting the bull' and smoking cigarettes. A cheer goes up from the soldiers as the technician tells them the satellite works. The soldier grabs the remote and starts channel surfing. He pauses long enough to watch a news clip on the Fox News Network.

The broadcast mentions something negative about whether the presence of the Americans in Iraq will come to any good. The whole upbeat mood in the room crashes down to one of disgust and disenchantment. One of the soldiers gets up and changes the station to Much Music while commenting, "Fu…ing Fox assholes; now we have them fighting against us."

They curse the network for the attack. After a few moments of cursing, they get up and start leaving the room when one turns to us and comments scornfully, "We are only soldiers – now our own country is attacking us!"

If you think that negative media coverage like this does not affect the morale of the troops, then think again. I saw it first hand.

The soldiers tell us that the BBC coverage is the best for getting a balanced report. I have to agree with them, though I try to avoid watching the news.

I glance back at the TV to see rap star Eminem on the MTV channel. He is performing his hit video and song; Tear the House Down. I turn up the volume and a couple of soldiers re-enter the room to hear the tune. My kids are big fans of this rapper and listen to his CDs back home in Montreal. I suck up the music like a sponge, while closing my eyes and thinking of my family.

Sean, Tish and I lie in our beds quietly gabbing until 1:30 in the morning. We talk about our strategy for tomorrow's coverage in Mosul and what else needs to be covered here. Sean and Tish are going to cover the official signing-in of the new coalition government in the morning. I will sniff around and look for something else, as I do not want to cover a bunch of talking heads, even though the coalition is huge news. I tell my companions that I might travel south to Arbil tomorrow afternoon, depending on whether I find something to cover here. I have covered what I need in Mosul, and with just over a week left in Iraq, I still have lots to do. I sleep through the entire night without awakening.

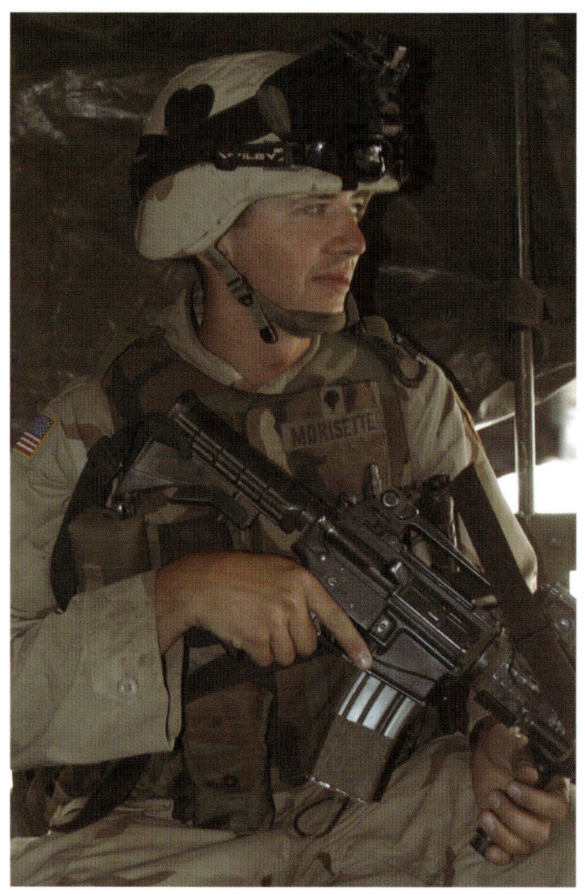
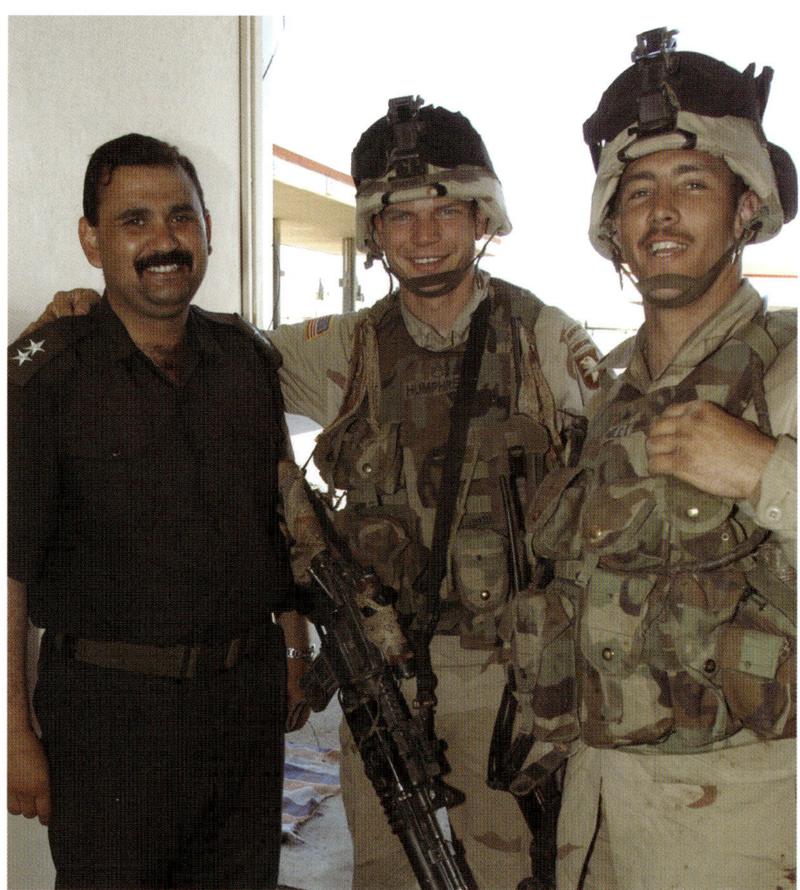

On guard in the back of the Humvee

This policeman, a cheery fellow, helps administer the gasoline rations

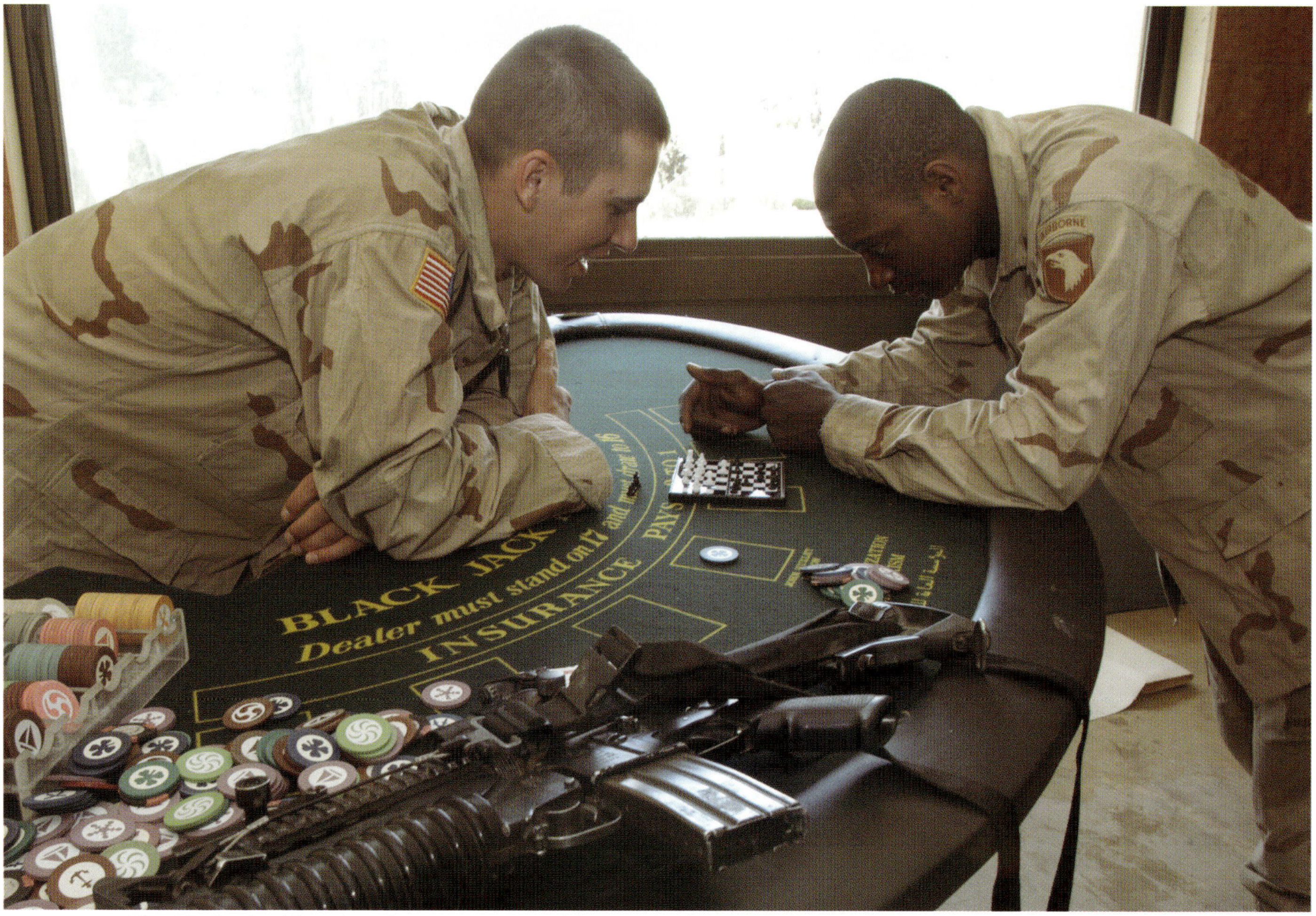

This Blackjack table is the only surviving piece of furniture on the Casino floor. The rifle goes wherever the soldier goes

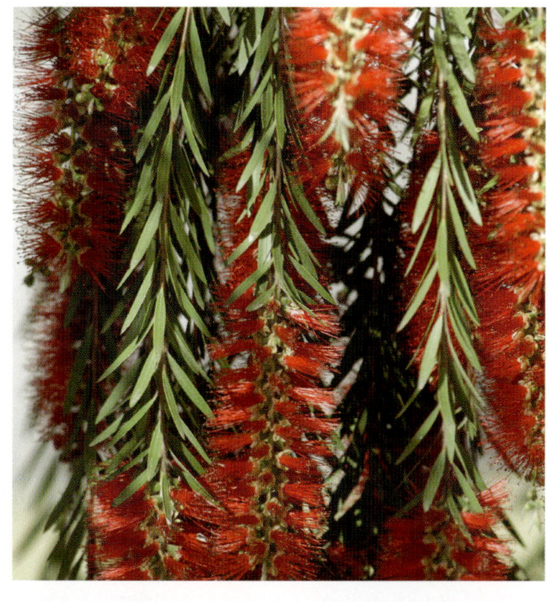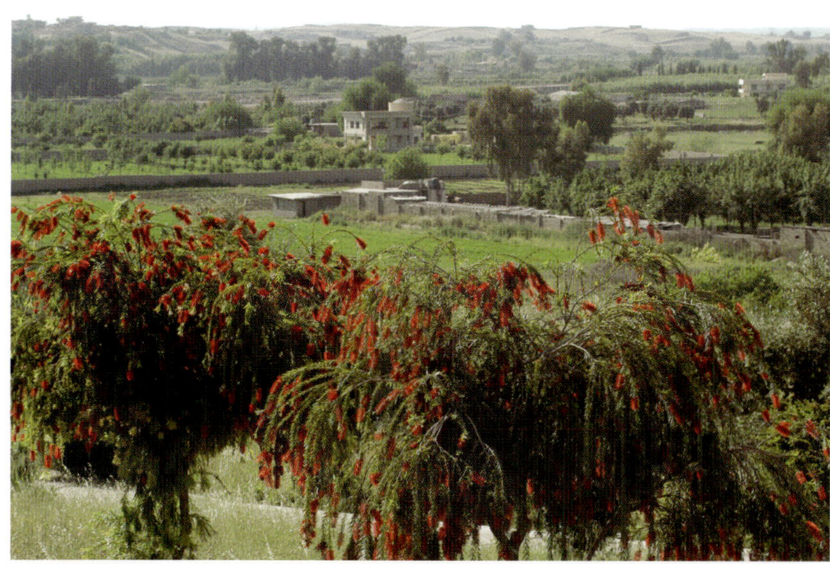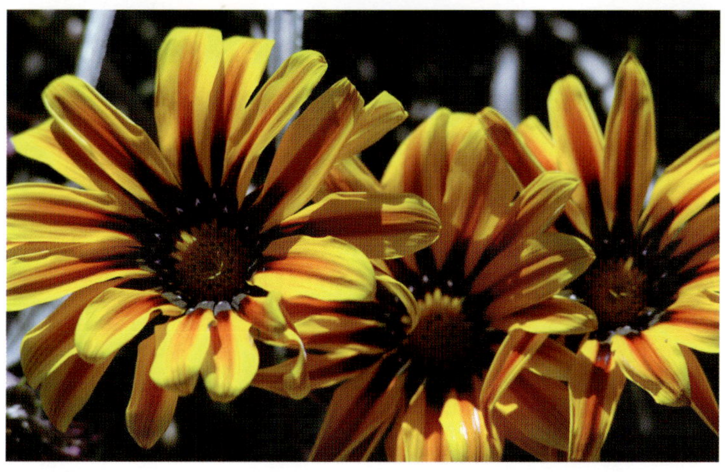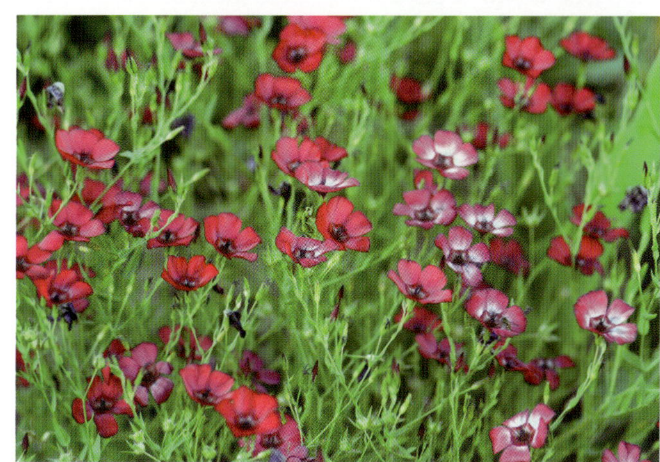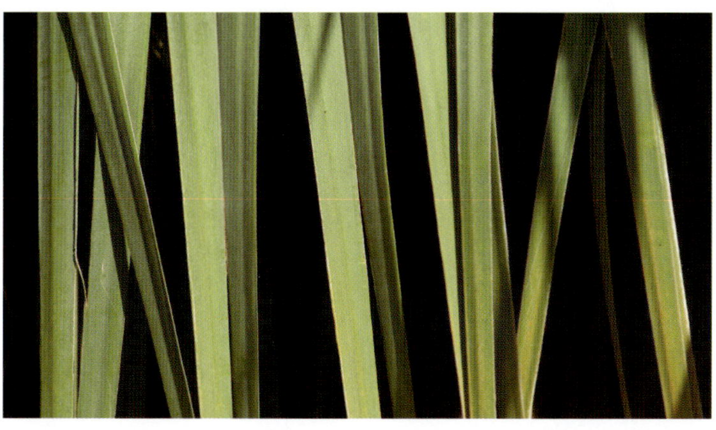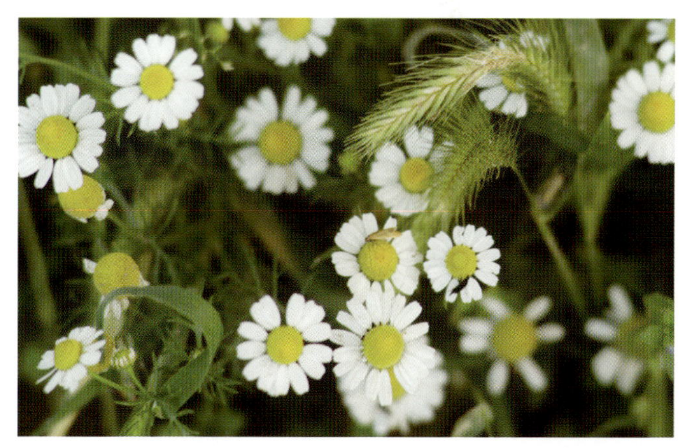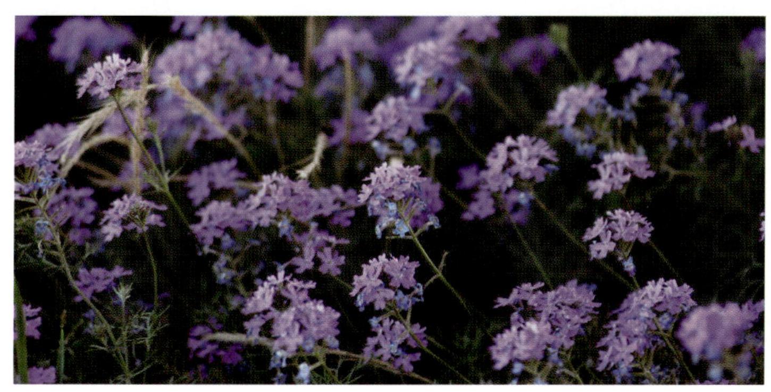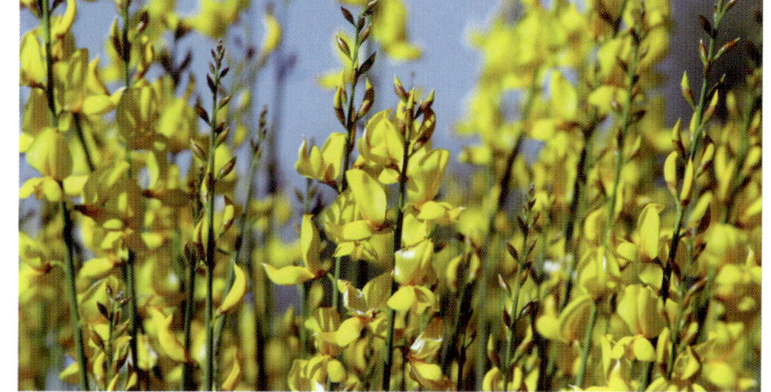

Day 26. Monday, May 5th

(Washday at the Hotel Mosul; Blackhawk helicopters thread the needle; F.I.F. soldiers clean weapons; F.I.F. soldiers present me with a bayonet; Blackhawks on the lawn; helicopter crews haven't seen any action; Kevlar armor removed from copters; Sean and Tish to stay in Mosul while I catch the bus to Arbil; eating Arabic style; younger Kurds prefer modern Western dress; liberal minded people; joking on the bus; tampons and Cheesies; oil-derrick lighter for $2; "He's from Canada"; these people are so vain; breaking down barriers; MRE Christmas; untouched by war; Arbil's Sheraton Hotel burned and looted; staying at the Arbil Towers Hotel; the Citadel; Internet café; the phone exchange; brightly lit streets; friendly folks; kids play soccer under street lights; an AK-47 on his lap; chai and sweeties at the Chra Hotel; I decide to leave tomorrow for Kirkuk)

I get up at 6 a.m. and spend part of the cool early morning washing some clothes at the backside patio area of the hotel. A couple of stainless steel wash sinks and a clothesline have been set up by the soldiers. After doing the laundry I grab a towel and go for a walk, looking for the showers somewhere in the west sector of the hotel. Mortar cannons stand ready to fire on the back lawn, covered by rain ponchos. Ammunition canisters are stored along the inside walkway of the emptied swimming pool. I finally find the solitary shower and enjoy a much needed cleanup. It is a gorgeous morning in Mosul.

Back on the second floor I hear the thumping of incoming helicopters. Three Blackhawk helicopters thunder past the back side of the hotel. They fly under one of the narrow archways of the bridge, just above the river, and then disappear downstream towards Mosul. I go back into the hotel and see three F.I.F. soldiers cleaning their weapons under the instruction of an American soldier.

Parts of different rifles lie dis-assembled about the floor, though in an organized manner. Each rifle piece is individually cleaned with a rag, then oiled and re-assembled. A ramrod with a wad of rag is pushed through the barrel chamber to clean it of dirt and carbon. I finish photographing the cleaning session then meander over to the TV room to burn a CD of the pics I just took for the F.I.F. crew.

Ten minutes after taking their pictures, I stick a CD into the laptop and show the F.I.F. crew the photos of them cleaning their weapons. Then I hand them the CD. They are very thankful and amazed by the digital technology. Moments later, one of the F.I.F. soldiers presents me with a gift of an Iraqi bayonet and sheath, which I gratefully accept. I get along well with the upbeat and always smiling F.I.F. soldiers.

I go out to the back of the hotel where I see that the three Blackhawks have returned, and are parked on the back lawn of the hotel. The crews are outside their helicopters talking with Captain Morgan. I walk down the patio stairs to meet

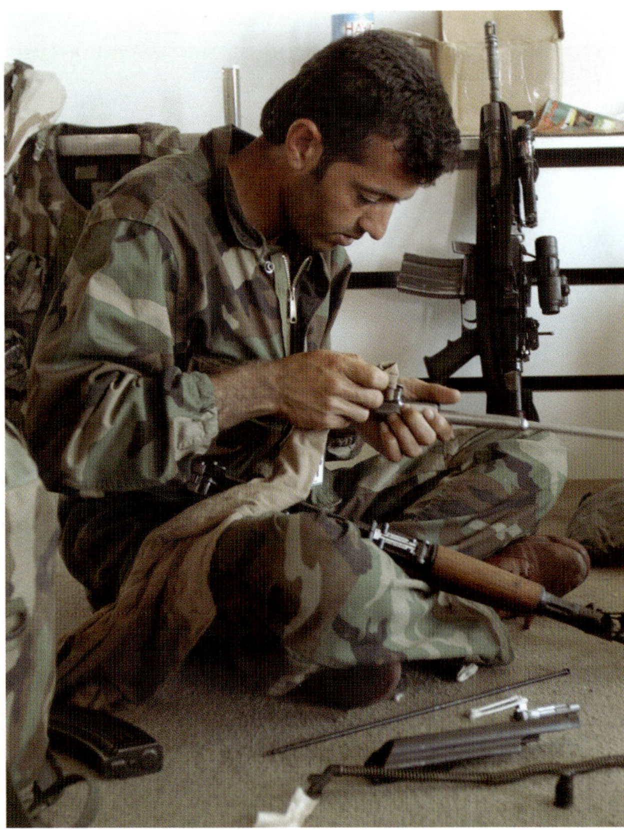

Member of the Friendly Iraqi Forces, (F.I.F.)

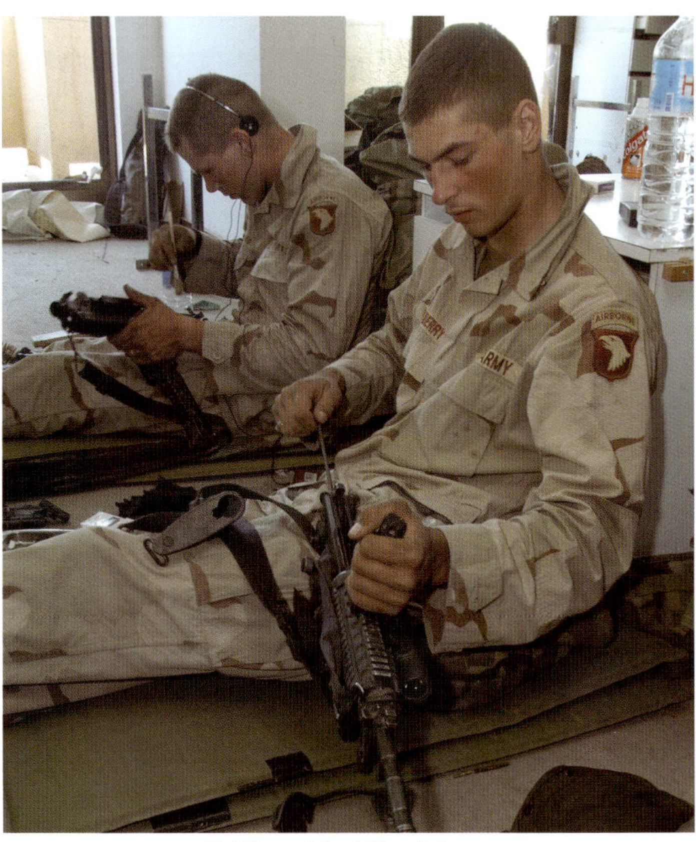

Soldiers of the 101st Airborne

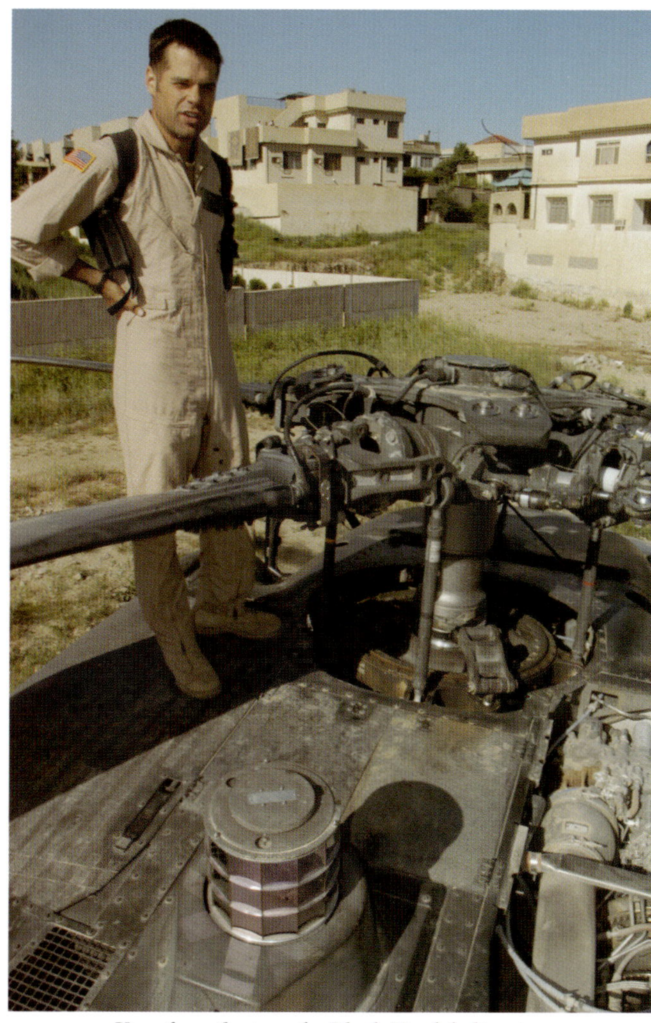
View from the top of a Black Hawk helicopter

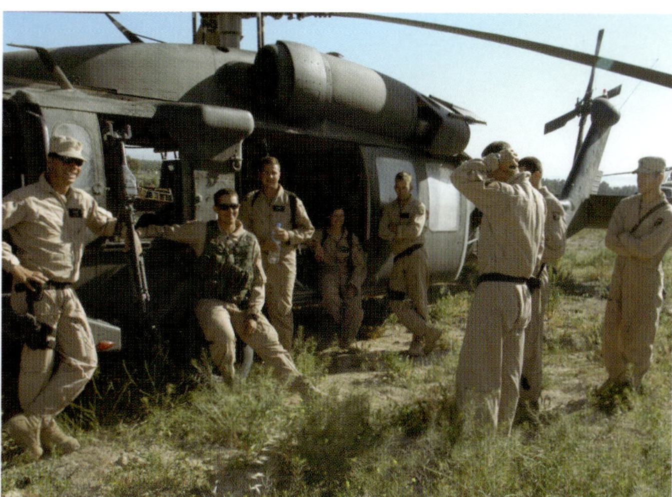
Black Hawk crews from two helicopters drop in on the hotel lawn

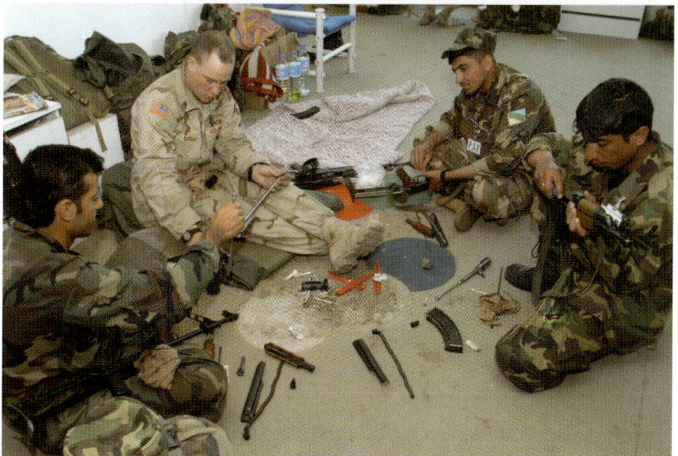
F.I.F. learn refined gun cleaning from an American soldier

them and ask if they would mind me taking some pics. One of the crew, the engineer, takes me on an overall tour of his copter, or "his bird", as they call their flying machines.

Chatting with the crews, they tell me they have not even fired a single round during the hostilities. They listen with interest as I tell them about the goings-on in Baghdad and Basra. They curse under their breath when I explain some of the situations we have been in and what we have seen. "I should have been a damned journalist," one of them sarcastically comments.

One crew member tells me they have been given orders to remove the Kevlar plates that protect the vulnerable shell of the bird. "This means a termination of hostilities," the pilot confirms. Like other soldiers I have talked to who had not seen action, they are upset and wish for a chance to put their training into action. They desire an opportunity to fire their guns and try out their high-tech equipment in a war situation. This is the way the soldier thinks – and it is the only way to think if you are a true warrior. To not engage the enemy is discouraging to these men and women. They are trained to be fighters and to kill the enemy.

I have a chat with Tish and Sean about heading to Arbil this afternoon. I figure that there isn't much more for me to do in Mosul and it is time to move on.

Sean and Tish have decided to stay in Mosul for a day or two longer, to work on the story of the new coalition government. I agree to meet up with them in Kirkuk, two days from now. I feel a little apprehensive about leaving my friends, but I do not have much choice if I want to finish my work and cover all the bases. I am in the home stretch now, so to speak, and need to schedule my coverage frugally.

Taking a taxi to the bus station, I grab an Arbil-bound bus. The bus fare is around $2 and takes under two hours to reach Arbil. The compact and clean Toyota bus drives through Mosul and the outskirts of town. We pass a chain of black-market stands selling gasoline and propane. I shake my head as I think about the Americans trying to curtail this trade. It will take a long while, with more manpower and better organization.

We stop at a diner for lunch on the outskirts of Mosul. It is a bright, clean restaurant and I eat heartily, under the glances of the other diners. I try to eat Arabic style, using the fingers of my right hand to put the food in my mouth, as is the custom. I find it difficult, and have to concentrate on not using my left hand to touch the food.

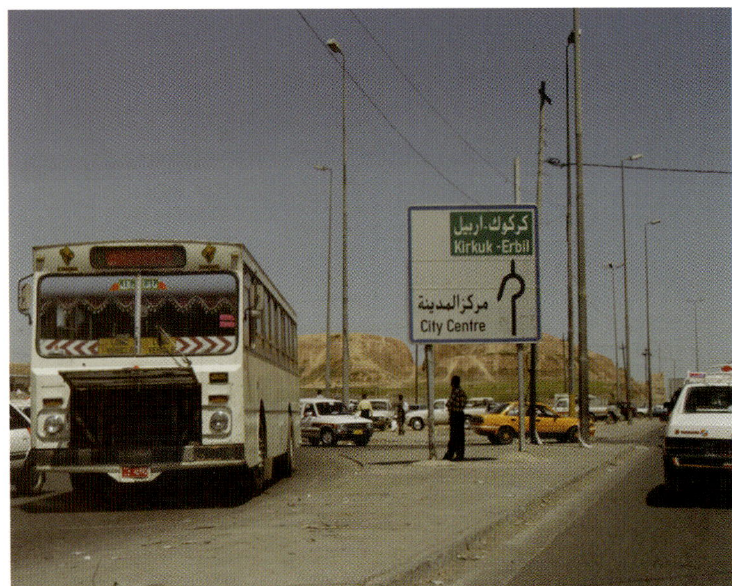
Leaving Mosul and heading south to Arbil

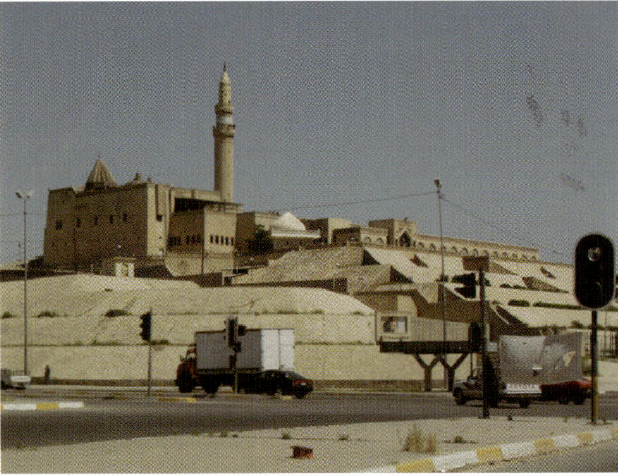
Mosque on the outskirts of Mosul

Most of the passengers on the bus are Kurdish men going to Arbil on business or to meet family. There are no women onboard. The more traditional style dress, with bloomers tied at the waist by a sash, is not as readily worn by many of the younger Kurds, who seem to prefer more modern, Western-style clothing.

The Kurds are a handsome people who smile frequently and show a childlike curiosity towards visitors like myself. Many of the men wear a moustache, and have one long unbroken eyebrow, running from one side of the brow across to the other. This characteristic seems to be a mark of beauty to these people, as tattoos or body piercing are to other cultures.

After I nod and smile at the passengers, the inquisitive passengers start asking me many questions, mostly about my work and Canada. To me, their open curiosity indicates the characteristics of a free, confident and liberal-minded people. This independent attitude is further proof that Saddam had less control over the Kurdish people, compared to those south of Kurdistan, who are so busy surviving that there is no time to be nice.

Everyone on the bus has a question to ask me (translated through two English speaking passengers) and they laugh and joke animatedly with me. It is like a little festival on our happy bus tour. I make a friendly joke about one man, who has four pillow-sized plastic bags of yellow Cheesies on his lap. He offers me one of the large Cheesies, being a courteous and kind

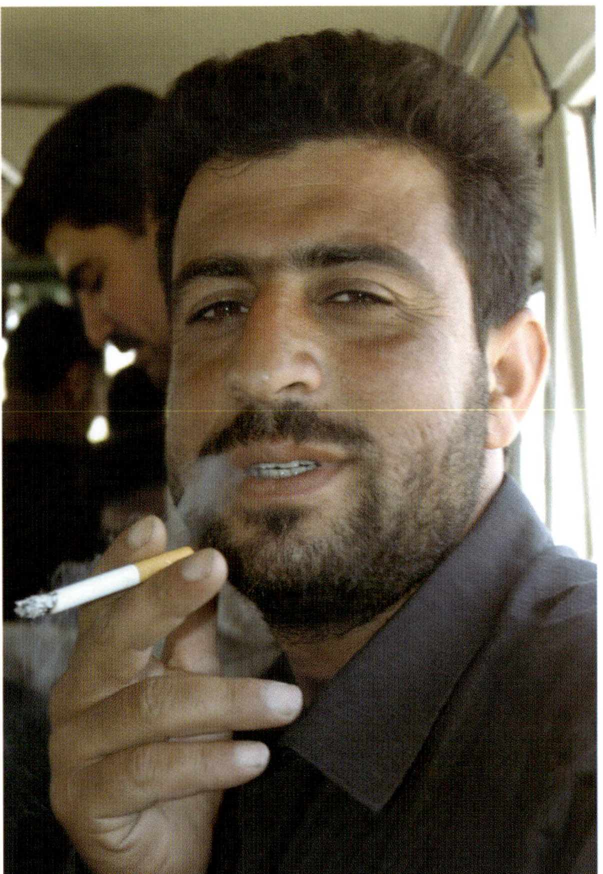
Iraqis, such as this Mosul Kurd, love being photographed

person. I turn to another man, who spoke in broken English, and ask if they are tampons for women, and why does this Kurds want me to eat a tampon? "Doesn't he like me," I jokingly ask? The man soon catches on to my joke, and in a few seconds the entire bus is in stitches, all laughing hysterically. As the laughter dies down a bit, I raise a Cheesie to my mouth and crunch down on it (to show that I am just joking and mean no disrespect). The laughter starts again. We are all one big happy family – laughing and joking as the baby-blue bus continues across the desert. It is locker-room talk, and the Kurds love my warped humour.

By this time, the passengers have really warmed up to me and are offering me cigarettes and candy goodies. I am so happy to be able to laugh a little, and to see these other travellers laugh with me.

Putting a cigarette in my mouth, I search for my matches. A young teen, in the seat behind me, leans over and pushes his wristwatch at me, as though offering me the time. I say, "No thank-you," and indicate that I need a match. At the same time he presses a button on his watch, and a one-inch flame shoots up from a hole in its face. I light my cigarette with it and start laughing at the site of my first oil-derrick lighter. The whole bus is laughing again; it is now contagious. I ask if I can buy it from him, and for how much. He responds, "Ten dollars mister." His friend playfully nudges him while saying, "No no, two dollars! He from Canada!" His friend agrees, and I hand him two crisp American dollar bills. He undoes the watch and hands it to me. I thank him and give him a friendly hug.

I ask if I can take a picture of the guy who sold me the watch. He sticks his smiling face in front of me saying, "Yes, yes mister, take my picture." These people are so vain! I take a shot of him and show him his image on the digital LCD. He bursts out laughing, pointing at his image. His friend starts laughing.

They grab at the camera to see the instant image, but I have to politely push their hands away, as I don't want them handling my camera. Before long, I have taken pictures of most of the passengers, who will not stop bothering me till I do. But I like these people, and they like me. I guess this bus trip could be compared to a school field trip; I am learning about them, and they are learning about me. The lesson we learned together is that we are not all that different from one another.

The character of the Kurds reminds me of the aboriginal Mohawk people of North America, a people I admire. The Mohawk are very like the Kurds, witty and humorous. I feel partly responsible to try to break the fear barrier between East and West, and this is my opportunity to show the warm friendly face and humor of a Westerner. It is diplomacy, but it is also courtesy. I am probably the only Westerner these people have ever met face to face. I can only imagine the stereotypical brand which they have been taught about us, as we have about them.

With the idea of offering the passengers a little treat, I take out one of my partially used MRE packages (where I stash my sugar, juice crystals, coffee and other condiments). I start handing out the packages to the passengers, but they start grabbing at the MRE like a bunch of hungry crows. I close the package and tell them there is something for everyone, and that I want everyone to have a little something. They understand what I am trying to say, and calm down.

There are smiles all around, as they look at their little packaged treats. The whole affair has a feeling of Christmas about it, and they smile while comparing what each other received. I tell them jokingly, while holding up a coffee and cream pack, that at least the Americans are good for something. We all laugh together.

I get dropped-off in Arbil, a clean, tidy city of about 840,000. I flag a taxi and drive around looking for a hotel. There are no signs of war damage, except for the burned shell of the Arbil Sheraton Hotel (another looted and burned Sheraton). This hotel is being overhauled, and has construction scaffolding covering its sides that reach half way up the 12-storey building. It is unusual that they are repairing this hotel so fast.

Stopping at the beautiful Chra Hotel, I find it booked solid. It is of English-Arabian architectural style, with a large, beautiful fountain on the spacious front lawn. The lawn also doubles as a garden-restaurant. It reminds me of an Indian hotel from the era of the 1800's, complete with crisply dressed waiters and a fine choice of pastries. Too bad it is full.

Next, the taxi driver takes me to the Arbil Tower Hotel, in the center of town. I check in to a clean comfortable room on the seventh floor, at $37 a night. The

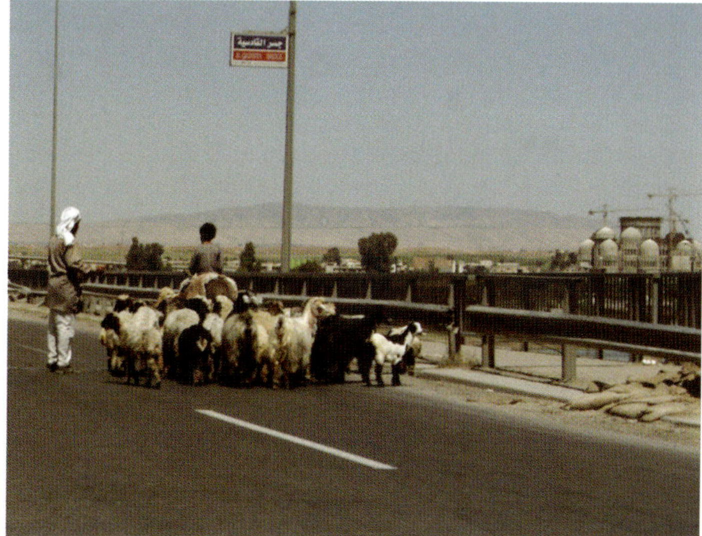

Herding sheep on highway overpass. Note huge mosque under construction

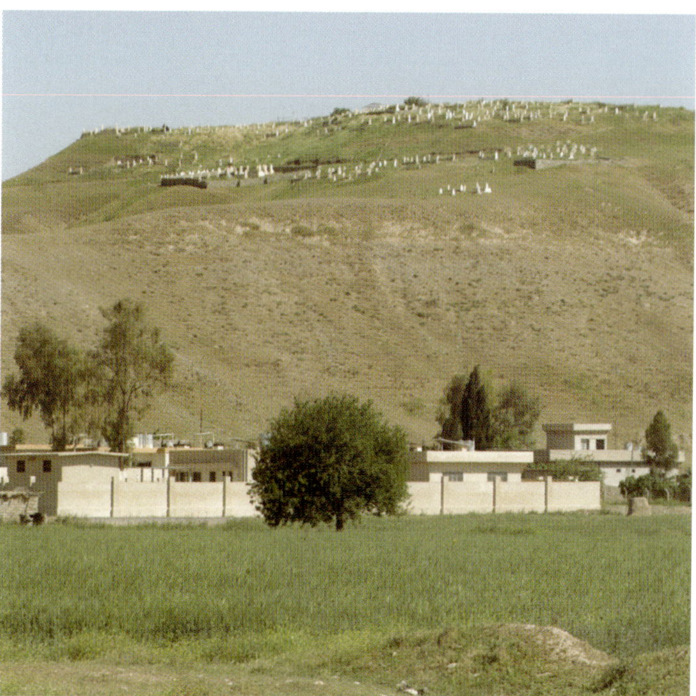

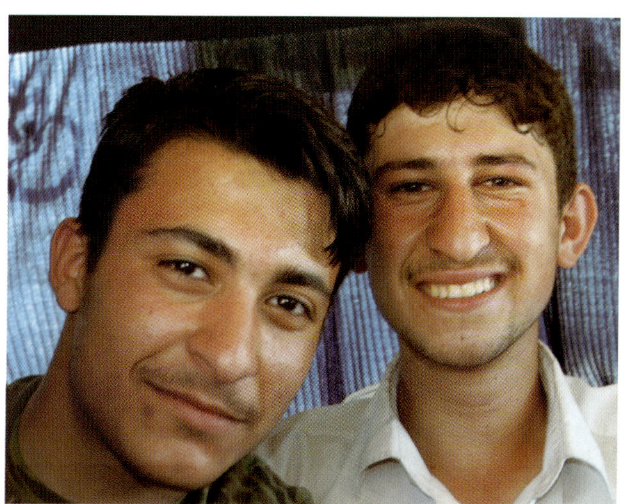

These Kurdish teens sold me a cigarette lighter watch for $2

This village in beautiful Kurdistan has a cemetery on a hill above it

room has a grand view of the city and surrounding countryside. A huge castle-like fortress, called the Citadel by the locals, rests on top of a mile square central plateau in the heart of the city. The Citadel sits like the hub of a bicycle wheel, and from here, the city fans out 360 degrees to the edges of the panoramic countryside, five miles distant and tinged in an almost fluorescent green. The lie of the land reminds me of photos I have seen of the Steppes region of Mongolia. It is quite a spectacular city, with its castle and panoramic, emerald views.

I take a shower, and then head out to find the Internet café (which someone told me about while in Mosul). Outside the hotel lobby I see an elderly man sitting on a chair, traditionally dressed in Kurdish attire, with a huge handlebar moustache. I figure he must be the doorman, but he is probably on break. His style of dress is very distinct and attractive.

A block away from the hotel I find the café. It is very modern, with a dozen PCs and a small snack counter. It serves coffee, chai, cookies and candy bars. I relax, drinking a few glasses of chai and some chocolate biscuits, before trying to get online with my laptop. After trying for ten minutes, the manager and I cannot get my laptop online, so I use a PC to send a message to my family, letting them know where I am and that I will try calling them in a short while.

I walk around the corner to the telephone exchange office (a phone centre where international telephone calls are placed from) to call my family. At the exchange office, you have to give the phone number to an attendant, and it is dialed for you. Meanwhile you are asked to go into one of ten little telephone booths to take the call. I chat for ten minutes with my wife and family. The chat gives me a new breath of energy and the drive to continue on with my pace of work.

As the sun sets, I go out for a walk around the downtown area, to get a feel for the city and its people. Walking along a road below the steep embankments of the Citadel (which is less than a block away from the hotel) I reach a brightly lit street. It is like a market bazaar, bustling with shops, stalls and sidewalk vendors. The electricity is on in Arbil, as in Mosul, and all the shops and streets lights are dazzling, like an arcade.

I buy a fresh grilled kabob and veggies from a roadside vendor. He has a small charcoal cooker set up on the curb, with a little electric fan blowing a stream of air under the coals, keeping it fired and hot. I sit at a sidewalk table eating this delicious meal, watching the crowds of people passing by. The locals are extremely friendly and outgoing. They bow their heads slightly and smile at me as they pass, a symbolic gesture of welcome and respect. Some of the pedestrians stop to say hello, shake my hand and ask where I am from. I feel very welcome and at home. These people are some of the friendliest folks that I have met in Iraq.

I walk back towards the hotel, about a ten-minute walk, stopping to buy a short-sleeved shirt, some Turkish delight candy and some baklava pastries. There are a bunch of kids playing soccer on the road, illuminated by the streetlights. When a car passes, all the kids stand by the side of the road until it passes, then continue their game. It is just like kids playing street hockey back home.

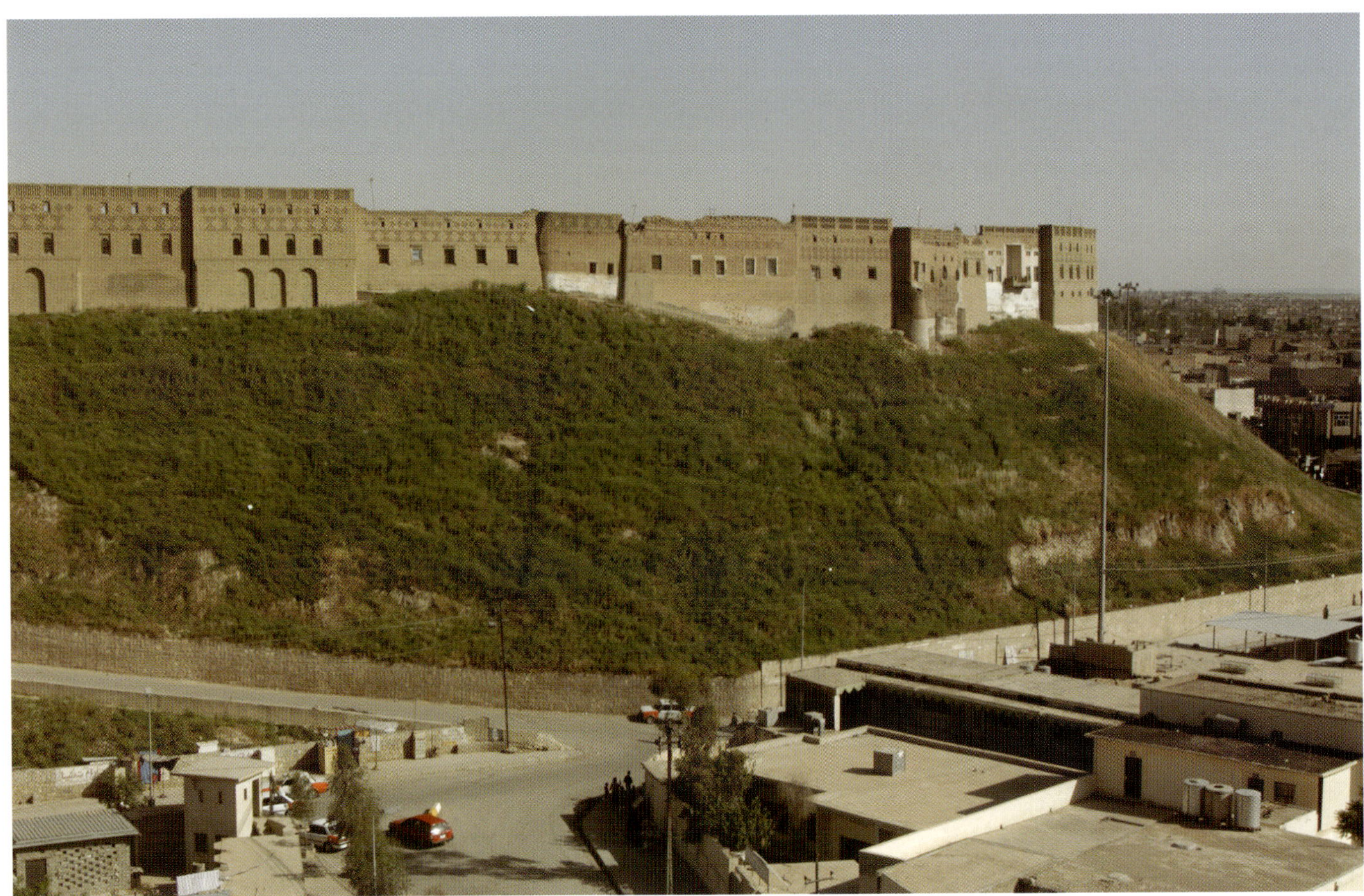

For well over a thousand years the ancient city of Arbil has been built, then rebuilt by successive occupiers

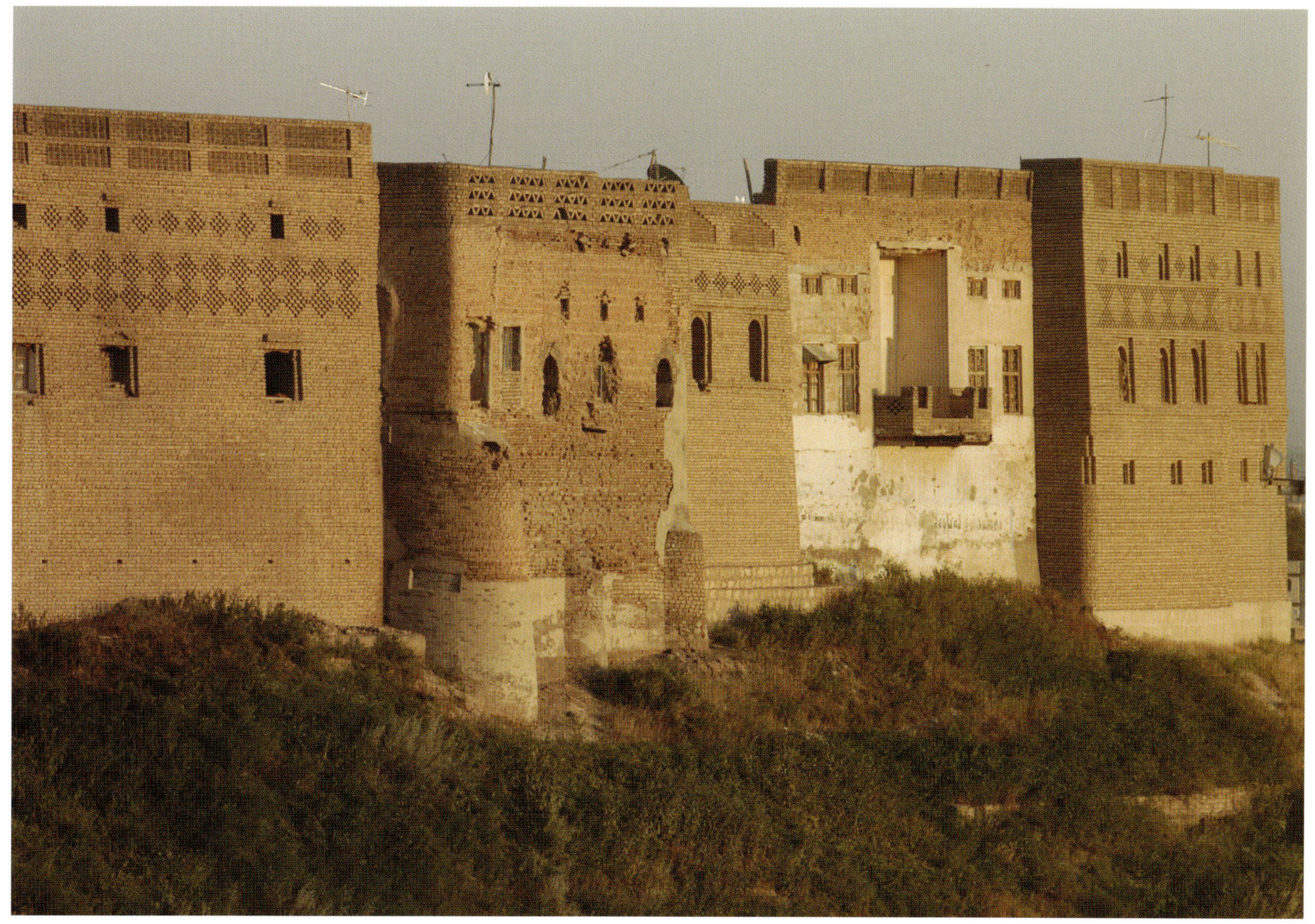

The Citadel stands on a high plateau in the heart of Arbil. It is a spectacular piece of architecture

Everyday life is so familiar to me here (though the culture is very different), and the warmth I feel from the people is very touching. At the front entrance of the hotel I see the same elderly man I had seen earlier, sitting on his chair. But he now has an AK-47 lying across his lap. He is the hotel security man. He smiles and says good evening to me, and I return the courtesy.

It is getting late, but I decide to hire a taxi to take me to the Chra Hotel for some chai and cookies, and to see if I can meet any other journalists. I drink my coffee and cookies at a table on the lawn, while organizing my notes and CDs. It is so nice to relax and take in the view of this classy-looking hotel, but I do not meet any other journalists.

Returning to my hotel, I eat some of the sweet goodies I purchased earlier at the market, then watch a little of the sports channel on TV. I decide to stay for just one evening in Arbil, and will move on to Kirkuk by mid-day tomorrow. By 1 a.m. I am in bed and drifting off to sleep, completely relaxed and well fed.

Day 27. Tuesday, May 6th

(Visiting the Kurdistani Parliament; Arbil Sheraton burned in 1991 civil war; for the control of Kurdistan; the peshmerga; "Some people do bad things"; American reconnaissance patrol in Arbil; no American forces in Arbil; leaving Arbil by bus for Kirkuk; massive thunderstorm; desert forts; dense black smoke; Hotel Kirkuk; 'Thank-You USA'; I meet Kenji from Japan's Yomiuri Shimbun newspaper; Kenji trying to get access to visit the Kirkuk Refinery; 'Take commands directly from me'; peshmerga turned military police; do not volunteer any information or documentation unless asked; touring the refinery; "You're the Boss"; flaming pipes and smokestacks; no room for second guessing; this guy could get us killed; trench oil fire; heat singed hair; invited to dinner by locals; Saddam statue of shoes; bubbling with excitement; out for dinner; let the chips fall as they may)

Up early, I turn on the TV to see Avril Lavigne singing on Much Music. I turn up the volume and think of my kids who love this talented young singer. I leave the hotel and take a taxi to the Kurdistani Parliament buildings on the far side of town.

Entering the main building, I meet with a Kurdish Government media representative who gives me a tour of Parliament, while at the same time describing Kurdistani politics. He tells me Kurdistan's three main political parties,

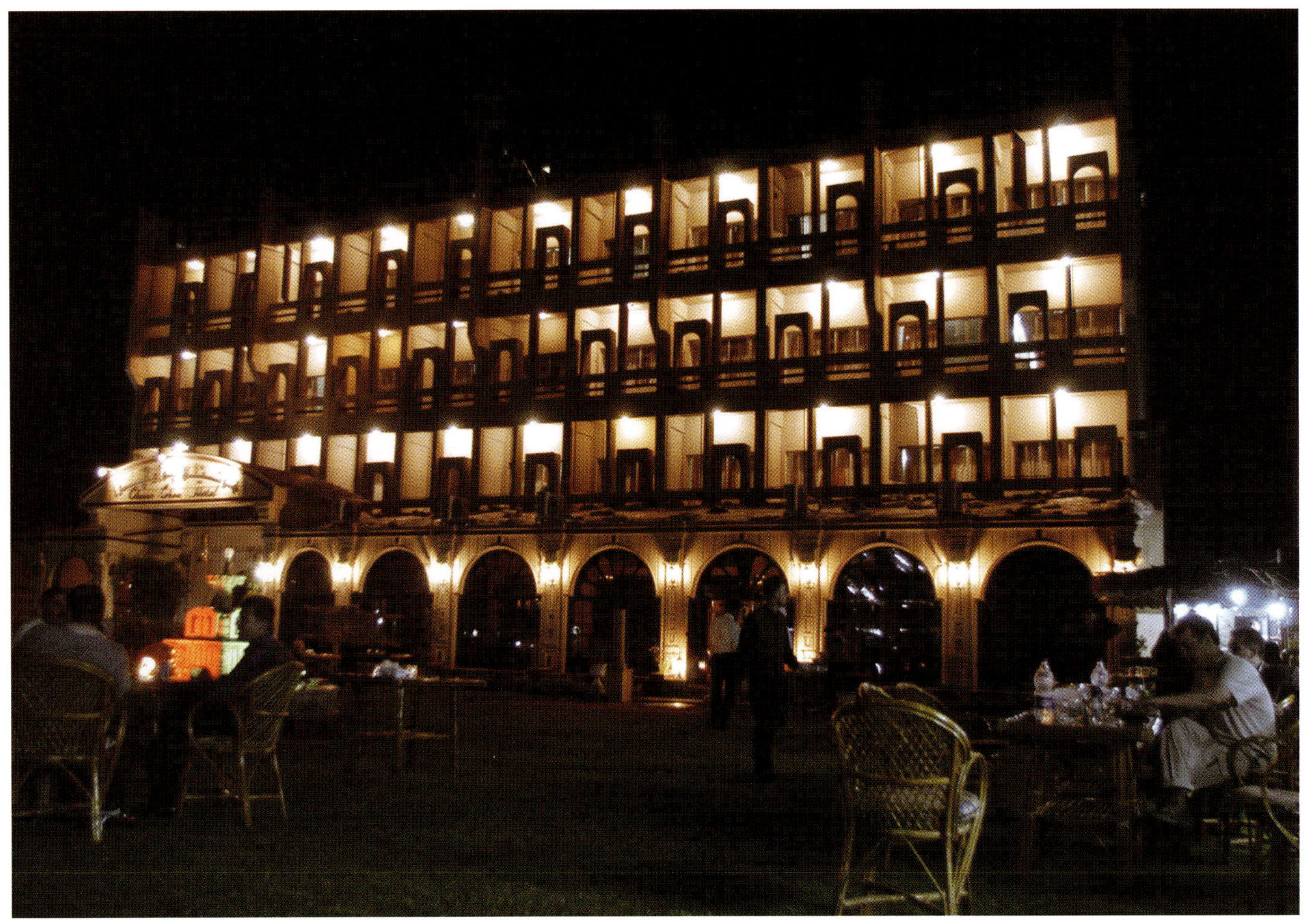

The elegant Chra Hotel in downtown Arbil

the *peshmerga* (PUK Party), the PKK, and the Christian Party (Assyrian Christian Party) formed a coalition government in 1992 after years of fighting and killing each other. Now, all three parties share the 105 seats (with the PKK and PUK holding the majority) and run the government of Kurdistan together. He says the Americans have been protecting his government from Saddam's forces since the coalition formed in 1992.

I ask him who is responsible for burning the Arbil Sheraton Hotel. He explains that it burned in the 1991-92 civil war between the *peshmerga* and the PKK. I point out that it is the only looted and burned building that I have seen in Arbil. He suggests that, "It may have been a symbol of Western wealth, and a target for the more radical Kurds".

The *peshmerga* presence in the north is cited as being the reason for minimum looting and mayhem in Kurdistan. I would have to agree with this assumption.

I ask him about the character of the *peshmerga* in light of their looting and burning of the Mosul Hotel. Contrary to Captain Morgan's description, the official tells me that the *peshmerga* could not have destroyed the hotel. "They would not do that sort of warfare. They don't do bad things. They don't need to. They are a professional army," he explains. I ask why Captain Morgan would want to lie to me about it. He dodges the question at first, but then answers in an apologetic manner, "Some people do bad things, but not all. They are good people."

This man probably knows that the *peshmerga* looted the Mosul Sheraton, but does not want to confront it. The visit to the parliament proves an interesting distraction.

I catch a taxi back to the hotel, pack my bags and pay the bill. Checking out of the hotel with all my gear on my back, I stop to have lunch at a nearby restaurant. I am seated outside at a patio table when two Humvees pull up outside the eatery. A group of soldiers leave the vehicles and go inside to eat, while I sit outside enjoying a very good lunch. As I am paying the bill, I talk with one of the soldiers. He tells me his team is on a reconnaissance operation, to see if Arbil is safe for the Americans to enter and set up a base of operations for the region. (I hadn't even noticed, during this brief stay in Arbil, that there are no American troops in the city). There is a large police station a stone's throw from the hotel, but no Americans.

The restaurant owner asks where I am travelling to. I tell him Kirkuk. He suggests that his cousin, a taxi driver, could drive me there for a fair price. I tell him I will take him up on his offer, and five minutes later the cousin shows up at the restaurant and offers to take me to Kirkuk for $15. This is a good price as I will be the only passenger in the cab, so I gladly accept.

Leaving the outskirts of Arbil, I see huge, dark thunderhead clouds moving towards our direction, just a couple of miles to the south. A thick dark curtain of rain sweeps across the quivering desert, pushed onward by the fast advancing storm front. It is a spectacular sight to behold.

In a matter of a few minutes, we are overcome by thick pulsating waves of hard driven rain, like living curtains of water. Dust devils quickly form in front of the deluge, and then are sucked into the moving mass of water. A barrage of oversized lightning bolts start spearing the earth randomly around us, as shepherds run for cover with their flocks of sheep and goats. It is an awesome storm, and the first lightning I have seen since last September, in Montreal.

The land is slowly changing, still rich with crops and animals, but not as lush as the area north of Arbil.

We drive past two beautiful 19th century desert forts, built of stone, brick and mortar. They look similar to those fortresses used in the great movie, Lawrence of Arabia, with gun slits cut into their thick walls, and high corner towers. Though old, they are resilient, and employed right up until the first days of the war. Black smoke pours out of one due to fires set by looters.

There is some old tank and truck wreckage, possibly from the Kurdish civil war, lying rusting and twisted along the side of the road, but the area is void of any recent destruction.

As we continue south, the landscape starts turning into wide, dry expanses of sand, interspersed with a loose patch-works of green croplands. The further you travel west, away from the eastern mountains, the drier the climate. Five miles north of Kirkuk, I start to see large plumes of dense black smoke belching skyward from the vicinity of the city. They look like oil fires and are a welcome greeting.

We drive through Kirkuk (population 850,000), a dusty working-class town built on and by oil. It's quite a nice town. We pass one bombed and burned ministry building, but I can't make out which one. Children and teens play soccer on a large dirt soccer pitch, some with local team jerseys on. Soccer is the sport of choice in Iraq.

The driver lets me off at the Hotel Kirkuk, a five star hotel (that is more of a three star rating) costing $50 a night. But the room is fine and the staff very friendly (which are the most important requirements to this traveller). I unpack my gear in my room then head downstairs to the lobby for some chai, a cigarette and to chill-out from the drive.

I ask the reception if Sean or Tish have checked in, but they haven't. I try phoning the other two hotels in town, but they are not there. I imagine that they are staying another night in Mosul.

Out in front of the hotel, I see a huge column of black smoke rising from the west side of the city. Another plume of black rises from an eastern suburb, but I can't tell if they are buildings burning, or oil fires, but the smoke is pitch black and intense. Graffiti painted on a wall across the street from the hotel reads, Thank-You USA.

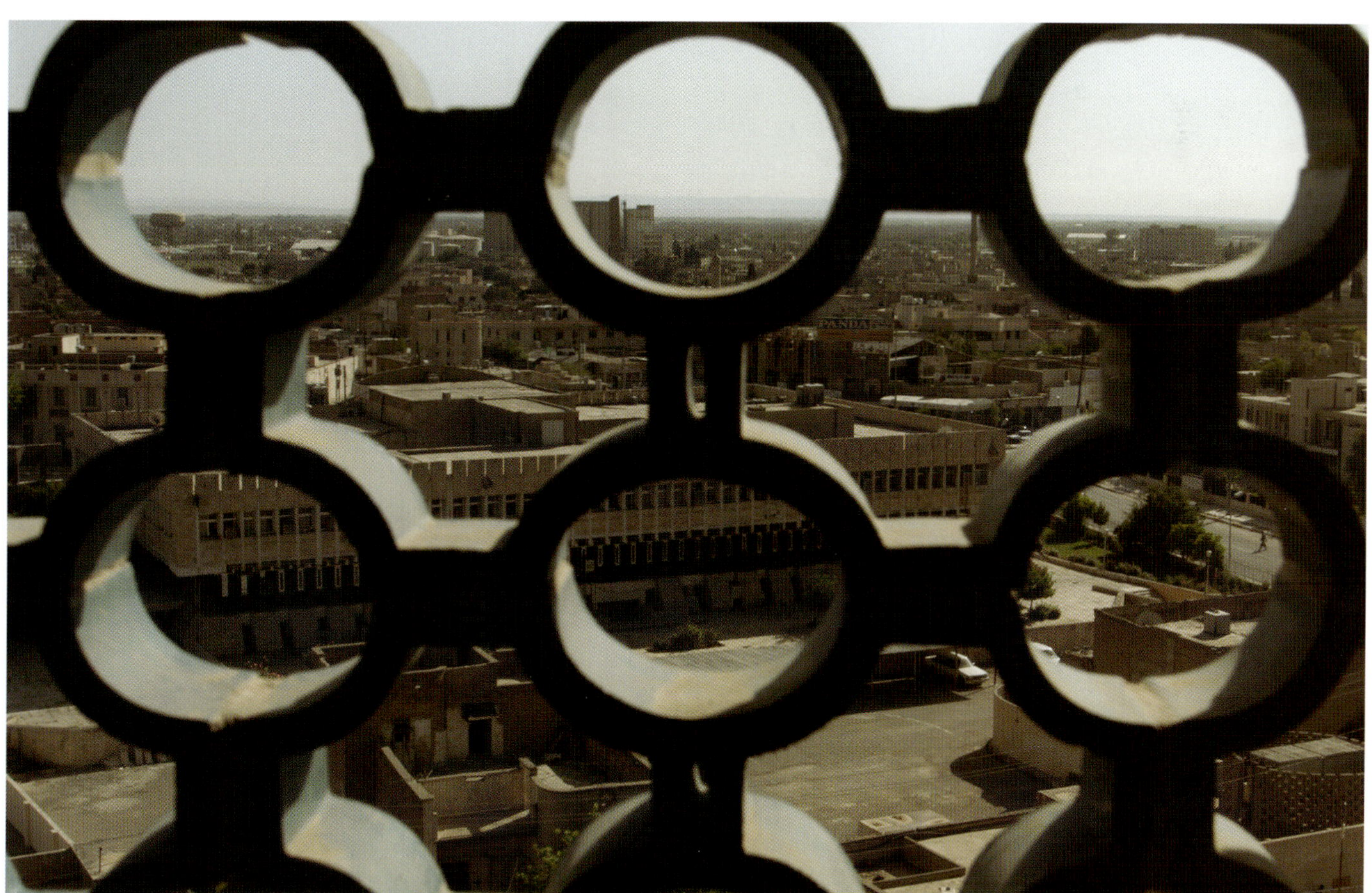

Looking southeast from my hotel balcony

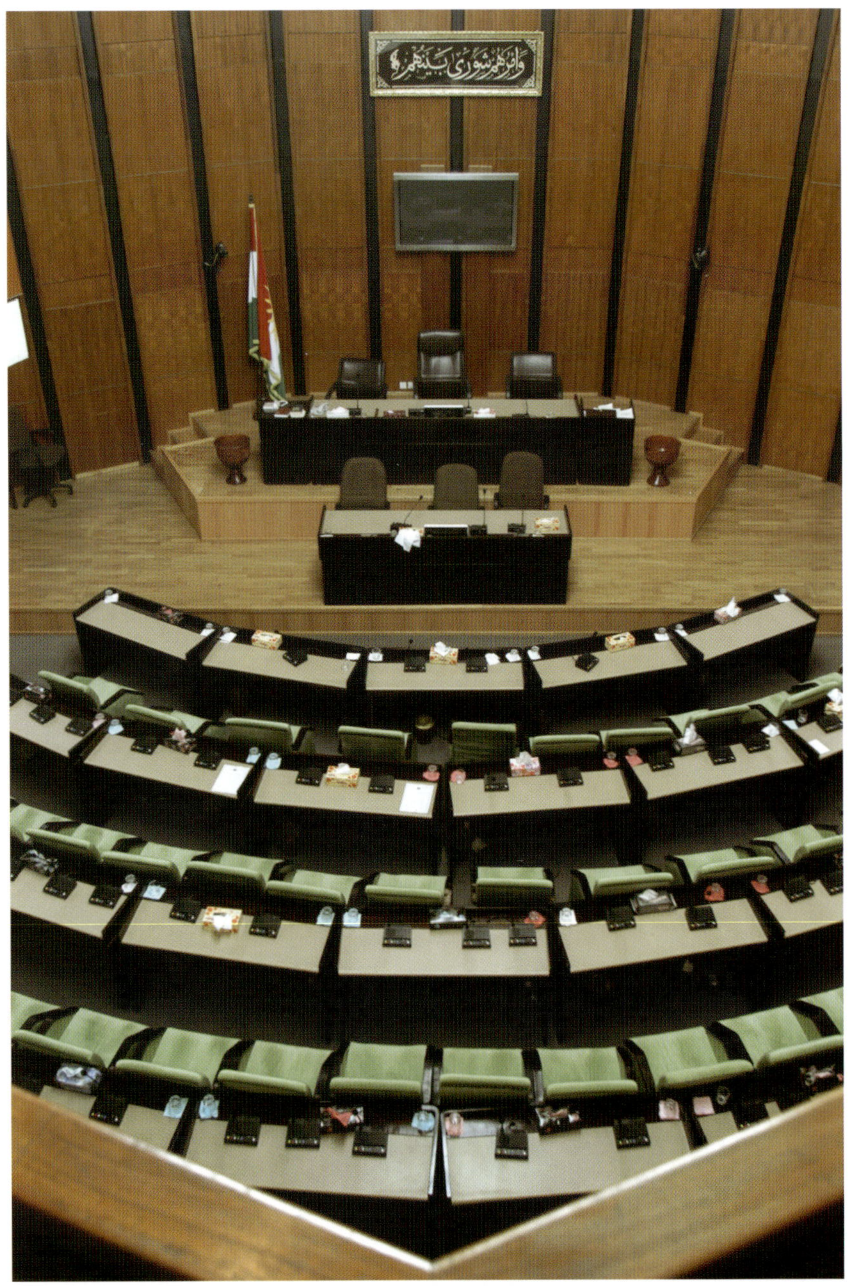

Inside the Kurdistani Parliament, Arbil

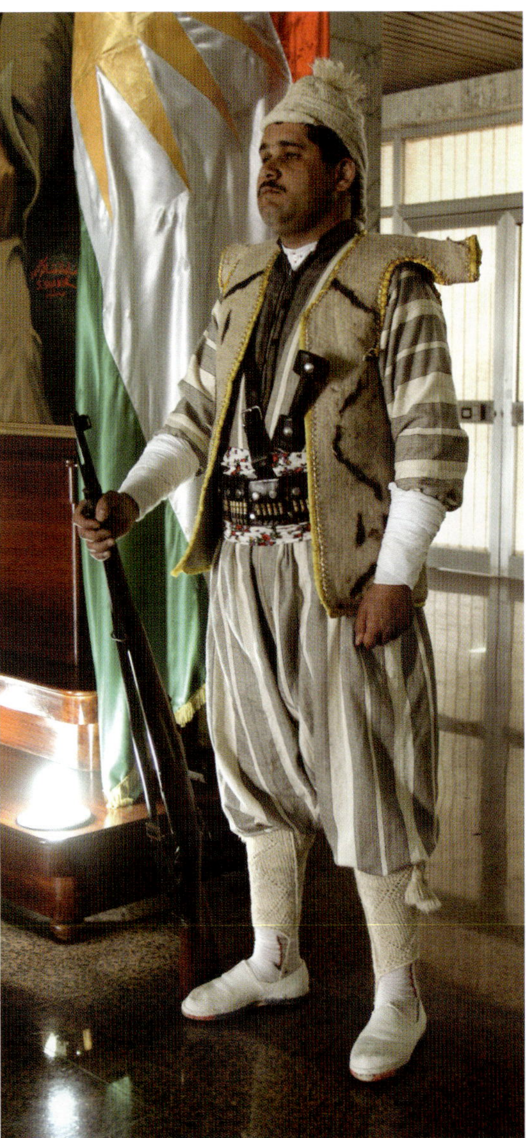

Kurdish Honor Guard in traditional dress

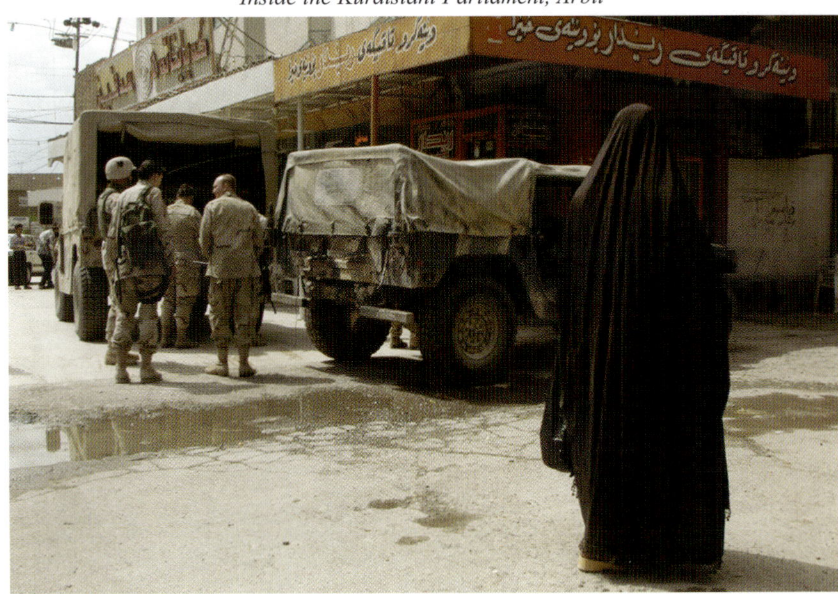

An American reconnaissance patrol in Arbil

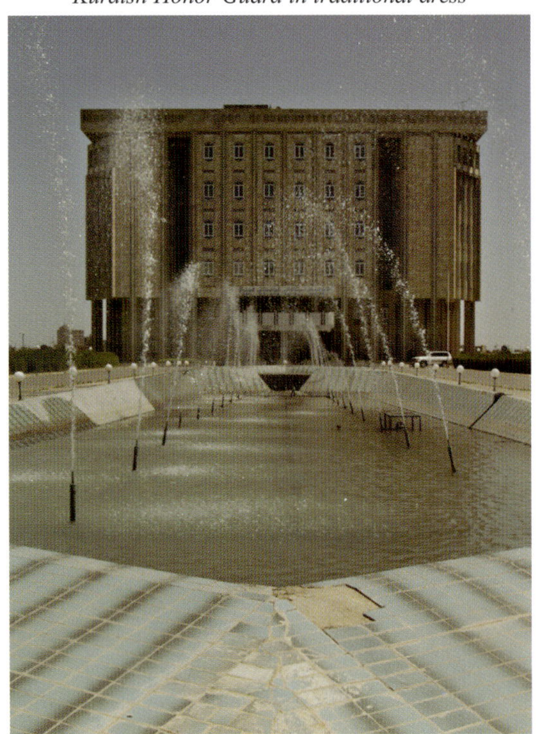

Front of Kurdish Parliament in Arbil

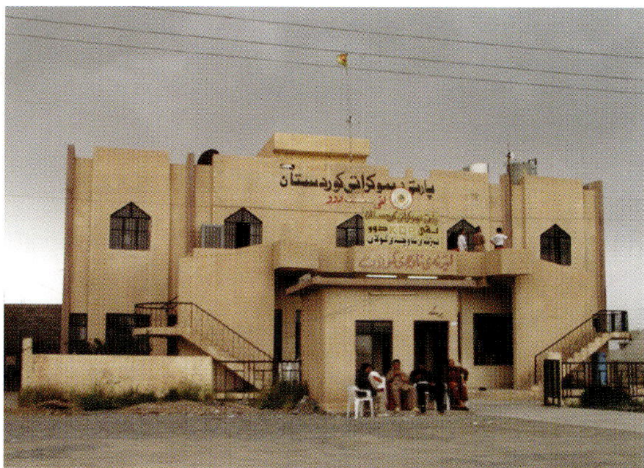

Kurdistani Democratic Party office just south of Arbil

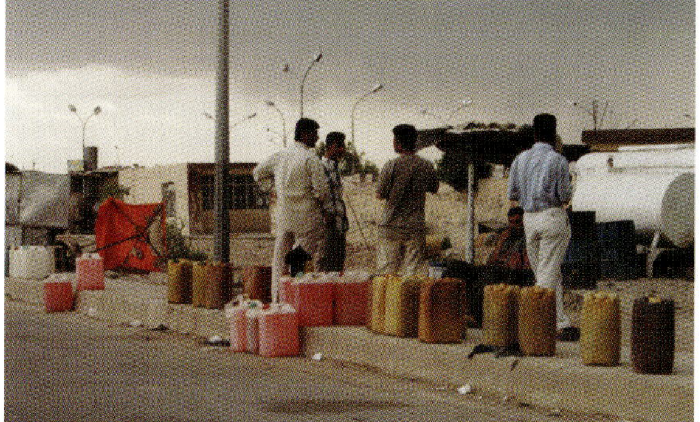

Black market gas for sale on outskirts of Arbil

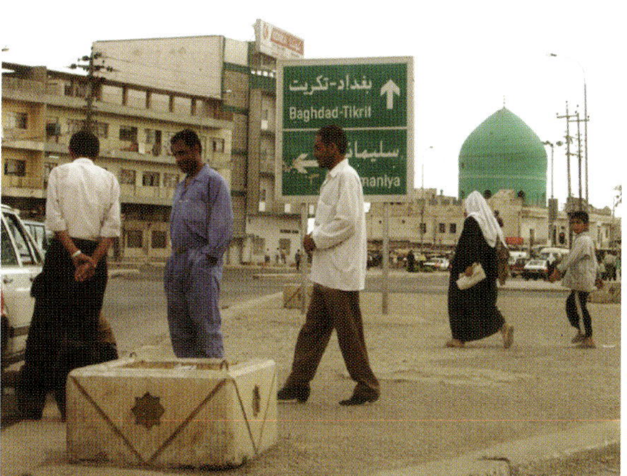

Downtown Kirkuk

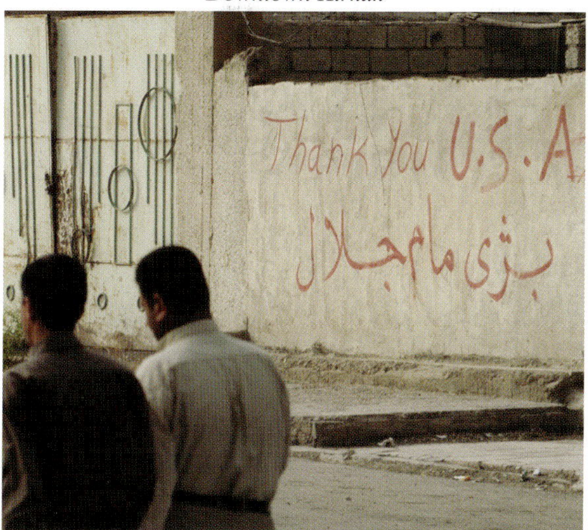

Pro-American graffiti in downtown Kirkuk

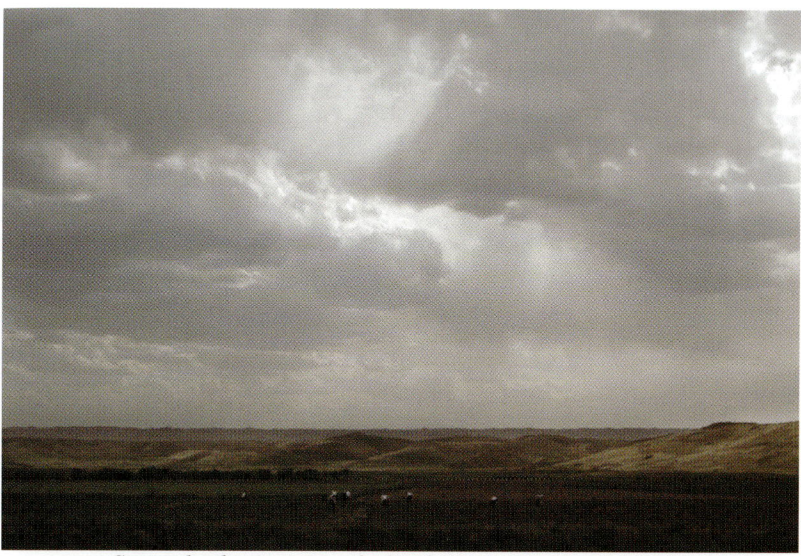

Storm clouds sweep over the Kurdistani steppes south of Arbil

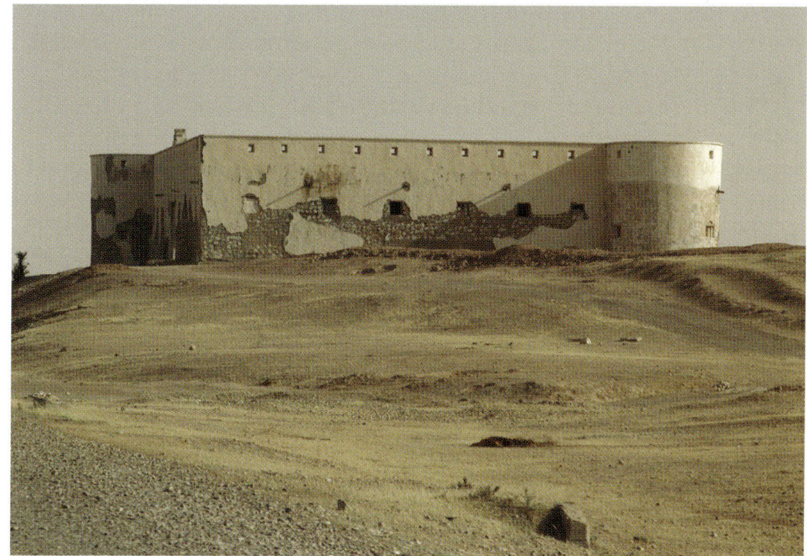

This impressive fortress is located on the main highway, ten miles north of Kirkuk

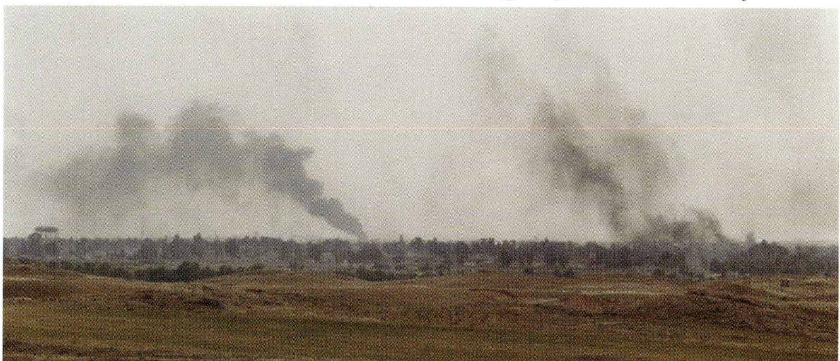

Smoke rises from Kirkuk as we drive into the city from the north

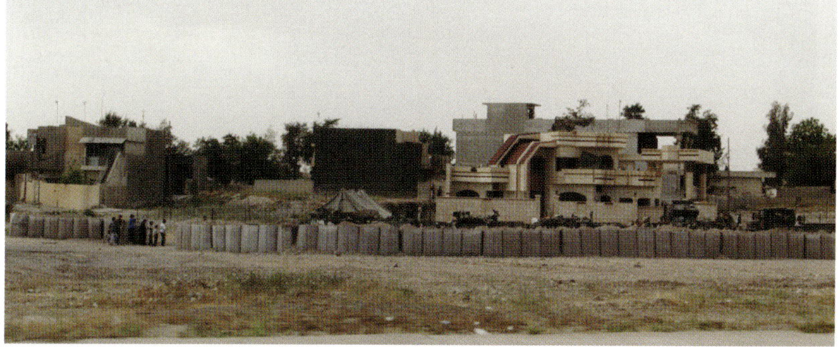

American military installation surrounded by a wall of protective barriers

The smell of war starts to percolate up through my nostrils. My head twitches. Goosebumps push up on my arms and neck, my heart is racing, and I feel like I am about to explode with anticipation. I have been keeping up a tread-mill-pace since I first arrived in Jordan, and it is difficult for me to truly relax, I can't sit still as long as there is light enough to take pictures. I have no 'off' switch but the darkness.

A Japanese photographer and his Kurdish translator enter the lobby and sit down on a neighboring couch for a chai. After a few minutes we start talking about Kirkuk and the war.

The photographer introduces himself as Kenji Shimizu, a staff photographer for The Yomiuri Shimbun, Japan's largest daily newspaper (with a circulation of 10 million). The interpreter's name is Dana, a Kurd from Sulaymaniyah, Kurdistan's most picturesque mountain town. It is nice to converse with them, especially Kenji, whom I take an immediate liking to.

They tell me they are waiting for a call from Airborne Headquarters to get permission to photograph the Kirkuk Oil Refinery. Some of the black smoke is coming from this refinery, indicating that it is up and running.

I ask Kenji when he called headquarters; he tells me yesterday. I am very blunt with him, saying that I don't think he has a hope in hell of getting access to the refinery, if he has not heard from H.Q. by now. It is going on 4 p.m., with about three hours of daylight left.

I tell Kenji that I have a CFLCC press pass from Army Command in Kuwait, and that I would be willing to go with them to the refinery to try and get access with it (therefore circumventing headquarters), but there is no guarantee. I reason with them that, rather than sitting around waiting for a phone call, we should drive to the refinery and try talk our way in from there. I am really determined to take some photos and make the best of the lingering light before the sun sets.

Giving Kenji and Dana ten minutes to think about my proposal, I go out to the front of the hotel to watch the traffic and pedestrians. A few minutes later Kenji approaches me saying, "Let's go!"

I hop aboard their brand new white GMC Jimmy. Kenji has all the toys; digital cameras, an interpreter and a driver, but not the street smarts that are needed in a situation like this. But a combination of street smarts and toys might get us on the refinery grounds. The smart looking Jimmy gives us a good image and credibility, along with the hired help of a driver and Dana, who are both locals. On the way, I tell Kenji that we could be looking at either wasting a half a day, or getting our cameras filled with fresh news photos, but at least we will give it a shot. Kenji needs something to send to his paper and I need the refinery and some burning oil shots for the book.

As we drive towards the refinery, I tell Kenji, Dana and the driver, to have complete faith in me, and that I will do all the talking. But most important of all, I ask that the driver take directions from me, doing exactly what I say, regardless of what he may think!

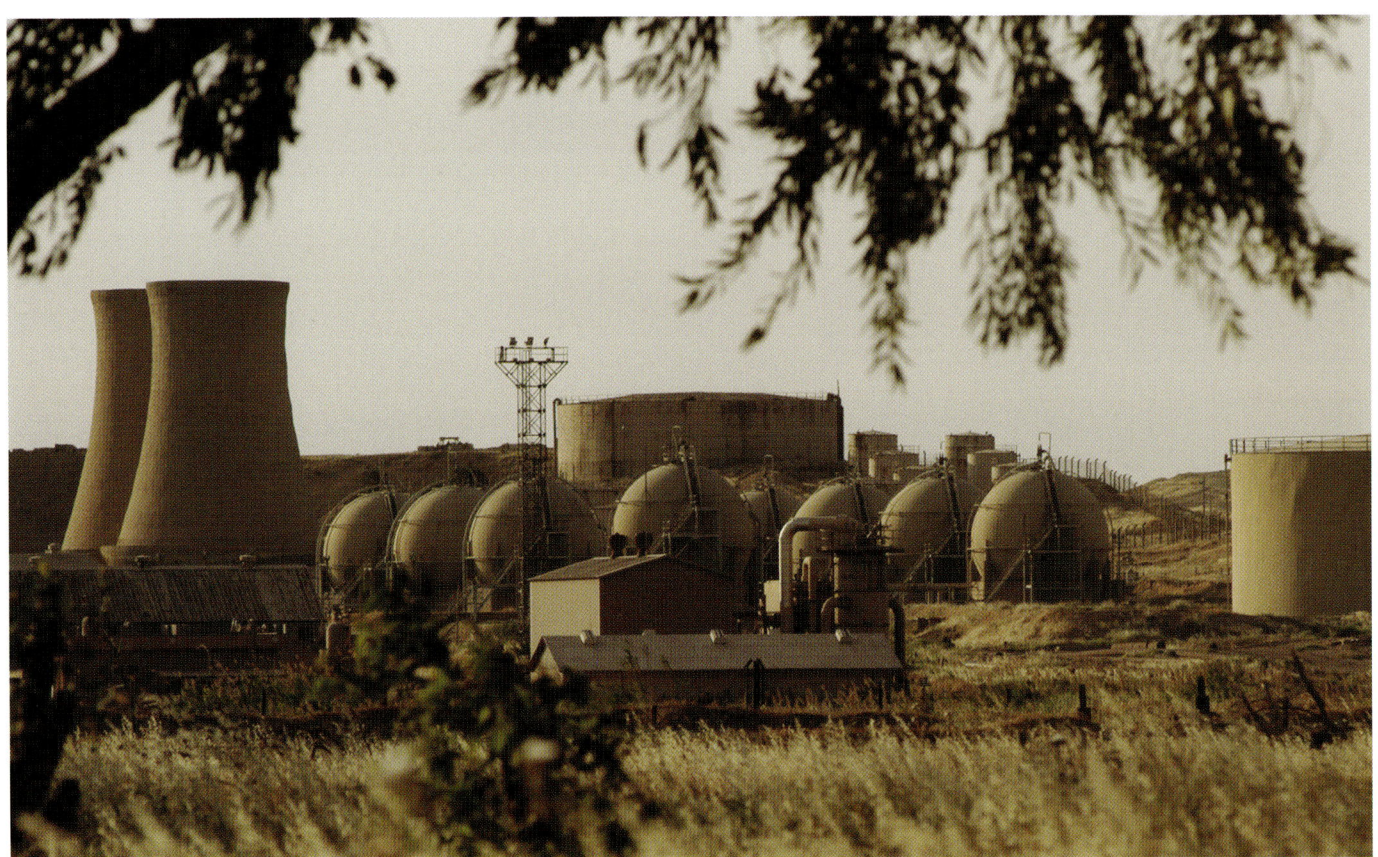

Tanks used in the storage and processing of oil products. With its vast oil reserves and agricultural capabilities, Kurdistan is very rich

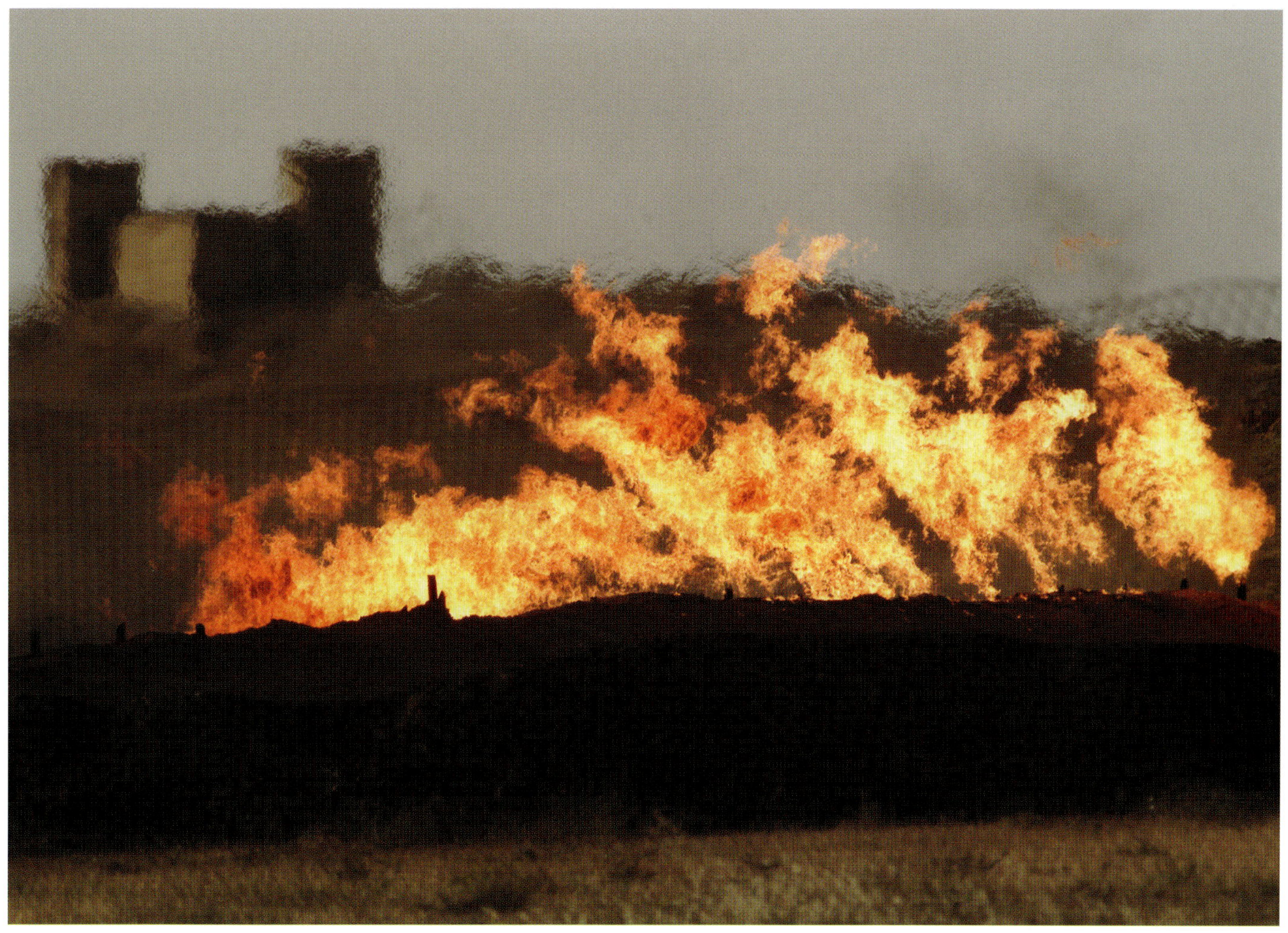

Waste gas is burned off at the Kirkuk Oil Refinery. The 19th century castle is no mirage. Kirkuk has always been a strategic prize

They all agree to my terms, though I think I upset the driver's feelings. But I don't care; my life could be on the line here. This attitude may seem extremely arrogant, but I know what I am doing, and I do not want to get shot, or arrested. Sometimes an individual has to take command of a situation, because of experience and knowledge, and I am the individual for this situation.

A mile before the refinery, we are motioned by an Iraqi cop to pull over at a police-army checkpoint. An F.I.F. officer comes over and leans his head into the front passenger seat where I am seated. I bid him a cheerful 'Salaam' while raising my CFLCC pass in front of him. He asks where we are going and I tell him Major Gowan directed us to the refinery (Kenji indicated earlier that he is the media contact at H.Q.). He motions us on, without pulling us out of the vehicle or asking for any other credentials. Dana leans over and tells me that some of the police are former *peshmerga* soldiers, now turned police officers.

As we approach the main gate to the refinery, I tell Kenji that it's show time, and to be alert and confident! I ask everyone to stay in the vehicle and to refrain from making eye contact or speaking to the soldiers. I specifically warn them not to speak with or hand over any papers unless asked for by the soldier. Saying the wrong word, or an unconfident response, could sink our plans.

While still seated in the vehicle, I tie up the bottom of my dock pants, high against my U.S. Army-issue desert boots, so they bloom out like a soldier's combat pants. Leaving my camera in the Jimmy (some soldiers don't like cameras), I step slowly and methodically out of the car, and pull a cigarette out of my pack of Marlboro's. Sticking it in the corner of my mouth, I walk confidently towards the guards at the sentry post, then stopping fifteen feet away from the front of the sentries, I raise my oil-derrick watch lighter and spark its large flame to light the smoke protruding from my lips.

I approach the fenced gate, with the cigarette dangling from the corner of my mouth, and ask a guard if I can speak with the officer in charge of the post. The guard comments, "Nice lighter. I've never seen one like it!" An officer steps forward and introduces himself as 1st Lieutenant Nash.

I offer him my hand while asking, "How are your men sir, are they all in good health?" He replies, "Just fine, and how are you sir?" "Couldn't be better," I respond, "Unless I was back home at the cottage in my bass boat." He lets out a laugh and asks where I am from. I tell him I live in Canada, along the New York-Canada border, on the shores of Lake Champlain.

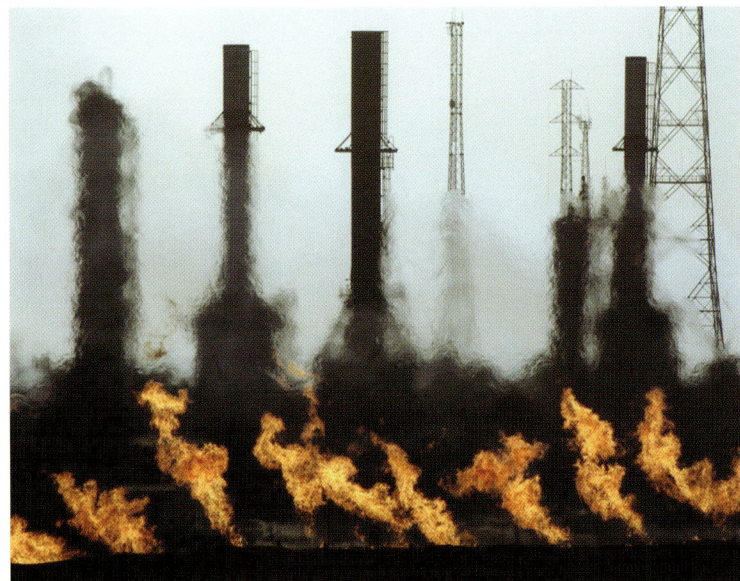

A wave of flames inside the Kirkuk Oil Refinery

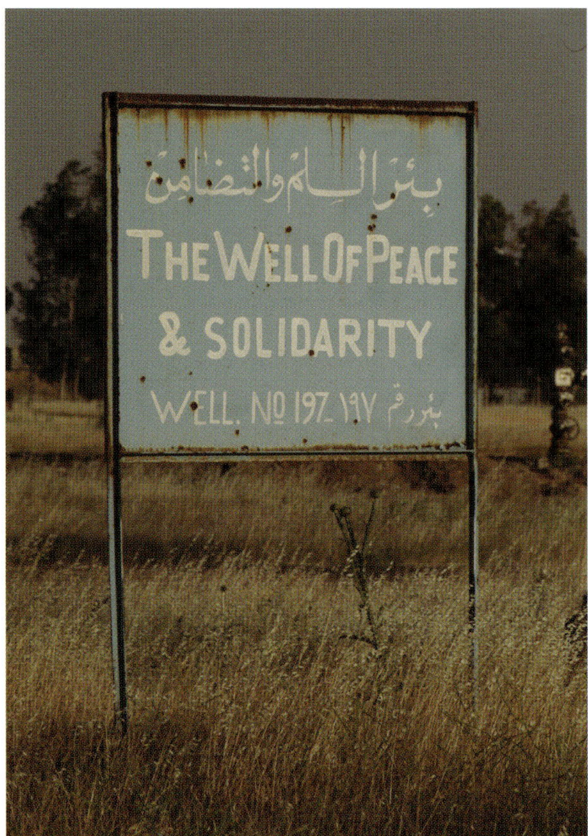

A sign at the refinery

He sees the CFLCC pass hanging from my neck and asks to see it. He has never seen one, though he has heard of them. I tell him I picked it up in Kuwait at forces command. I notice the soldier is wearing Airborne insignia, and I tell him about the good job his comrades are doing in Mosul, and that I spent two days bivouacked with Captain Henry Morgan and his men. He is glad to get an update on Mosul and asks me what Kuwait is like. I tell him expensive, arrogant, and boring – with no action. He laughs, and then asks how he can help me. I ask if it would be a problem if my Japanese colleague and I take some photos of the refinery. I comment that the burning-off of gases is a positive sign of coming prosperity to Iraq, and symbolizes the re-building of the economy. "I need to document this for my book," I tell him.

Surprisingly, the soldier agrees with my request and says, "That won't be a problem, as long as you stay on the main road and don't go off road, for your own security." He does not want us to be mistaken for the enemy, which is understandable. As both of us walk over to the Jimmy, he asks if my colleagues have clearance. Kenji, upon hearing this, gets ready to hand his passport to the officer. Before the officer sees him, I abruptly motion to Kenji to put it away. I tell the soldier they are with me, and we work the war together as a team, for security purposes. "That's fine, just stay on the main road."

We shake hands and I tell him to keep safe, and I hope he and his men are homebound soon. 1st Lieutenant Nash and his men are good people, and treat us with respect and courtesy.

I get back into the Jimmy and tell the driver to turn on his lights and drive ahead towards the flaming pipes. He looks inquiringly at me, as though asking why the lights should be turned on in the daylight. I tell him that it shows that we do not have bad intentions and that we are not trying to hide or be inconspicuous.

As we drive away I tell my friends that we can photograph whatever we want. Kenji and the others are astonished and they spontaneously break out in laughter. "You're the boss!" says Kenji. The Jimmy is one happy truck!

The refinery is a maze of pipelines, massive oil tanks, smokestacks and flaming pipes. A large blue sign reads, The Well of Peace and Solidarity. We stop to photograph the flaming pipes and smokestacks. Some of the pipes run low along the ground, with smaller pipes coming out from their sides. All these are alight, forming a continuous 50-foot wall of yellow and orange flame. Another medieval-style castle (like the two on the way from Arbil), stands high on a bluff running along the northeast side of the refinery. It is a beautiful sight, with the burning wall of flames highlighting the starkness of the medieval-style bastion.

The sun is sinking quickly, with about an hour-and-a-half of shooting time left. Looking over at the huge plume of black smoke curling about five miles distant to the southeast, I tell Kenji that it

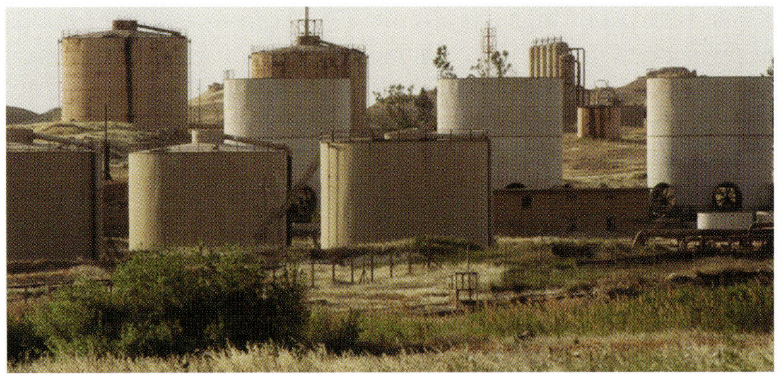

Petroleum storage tanks

may be a burning oil trench or oilrig. If it is an oil trench, then it could be burned out by morning, and we would miss out on some necessary pics if we don't try to get to it now. I tell Kenji that if we leave right now, we might be able to get there in time to photograph it. Dana and the driver are a little hesitant, but I tell them there is no room for indecision, and that we must leave now. "We must at least try, like we just did at the refinery," I tell them. I know that if we can pull this off, it will be the cherry on top of a great photo day. This is how things work when covering a war; you try to grab what you can while you can, as if there is no tomorrow.

We head out of the refinery (after spending an hour photographing the facility) driving towards the tower of black smoke. I tell the driver which roads to take, but he ends up taking his own route, going where he thinks we should go. Before long we are disoriented and lost in a maze of suburbia, where we are vulnerable to possible assault from rooftops and alleyways, as well as wasting precious time.

I am furiously pissed-off at the driver, and have a quick word with Kenji about it, telling him that things have worked out so far, and he has to have complete faith in my instincts, or this guy could screw-up our plans. Kenji angrily tells the driver to turn when I say turn. We get that settled and before long we are driving out of the mess the driver got us into. Now we are on the main road to the fire.

Sometimes simple things, like groups of trees or a concentration of buildings indicate that there must be a main connecting road nearby. By looking at the pattern of distant trees and structures, I am able to get an overall two-dimensional map of the area. This is where a hobby such as bird watching (or a profession as it once was) comes in very handy. Even whale watch-

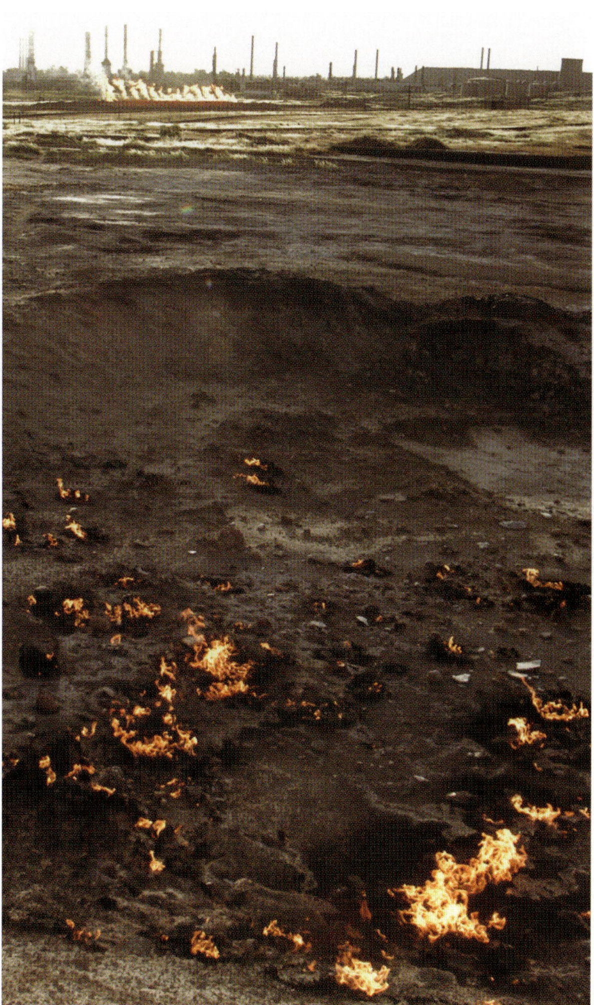

Rock-sized chunks of crude oil burn in pit at the refinery

ing, believe it or not, can sharpen the eye and train it to decipher mirage from whale. Both these hobbies have increased my powers of observation well beyond the average person's abilities. I am a professional observer.

The driver and interpreter tell me they have never met anyone like me, and they feel a bit intimidated and shocked by the way I work. Kenji knows what I am attempting to accomplish in this short afternoon, to both our benefits. He is just sitting back, watching me carry the ball. He is a great companion, and like me, he has a passionate love for his job.

We arrive at the site of the curling black smoke to see that it is an oil trench fire, a horrendous blaze of burning crude. It brings back memories of the flaming oil wells in Kuwait in 1991. The trench is 300 feet long, ten feet wide and five feet deep. Thick, choking black smoke spews out of the entire length of the trench. Concerned about our vehicle, I tell the driver to move the Jimmy further away from the fire, in case the wind changes direction and blows the fire and smoke towards the vehicle. The driver tells me it is a good idea and complies with my request. I think this is when he realizes that I have all bases covered, including a concern for his vehicle.

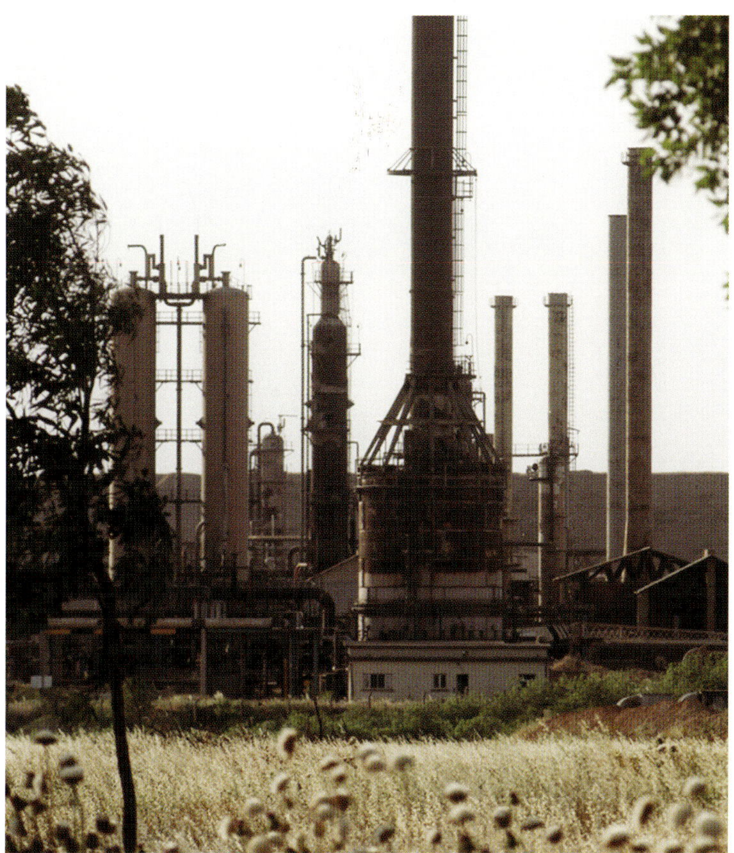

Kirkuk Oil Refinery

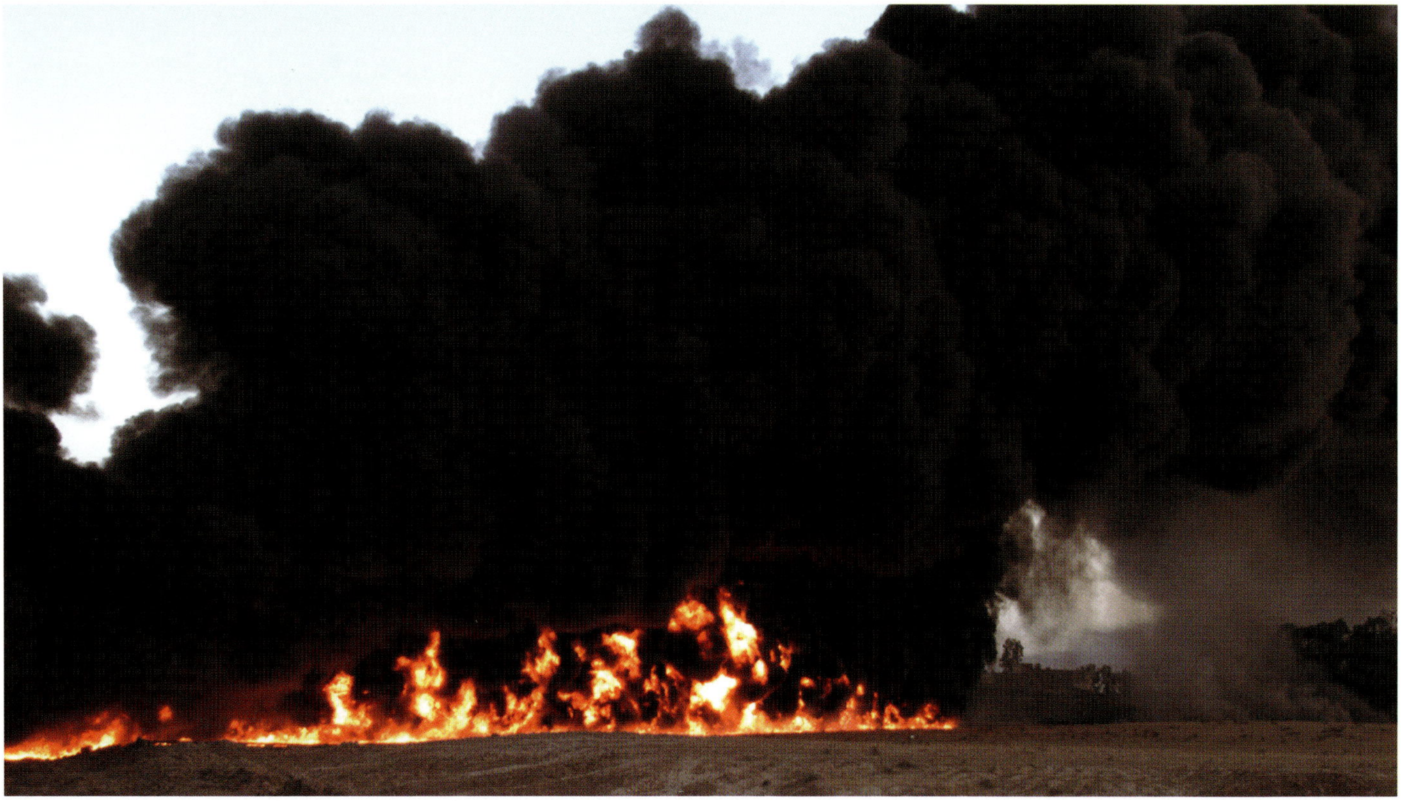

A three-hundred-foot long wall of fire burns in an oil trench. The oil, when lit at night, is meant to confuse enemy bombers

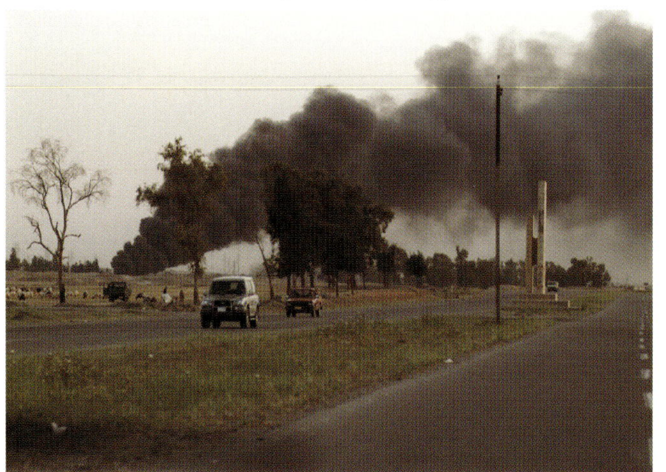

Driving to the oil fire

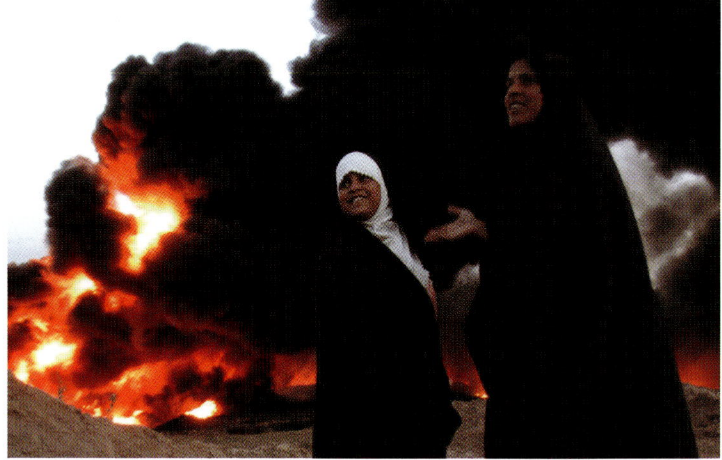

These women came to see the fire

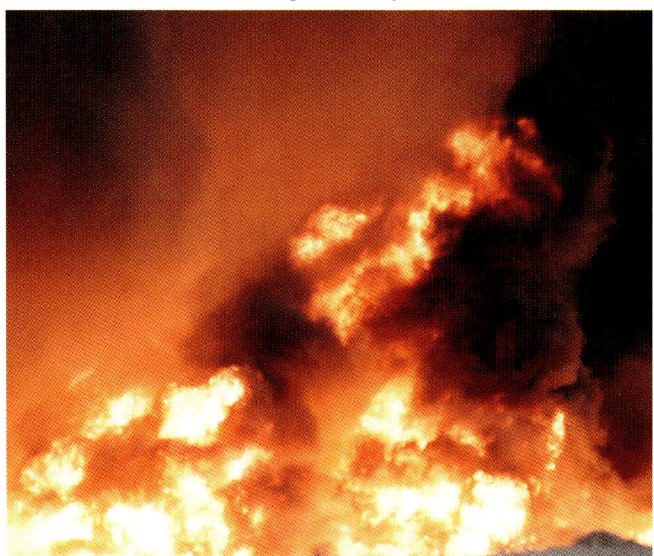

When you can smell your own hair, you know you are too close

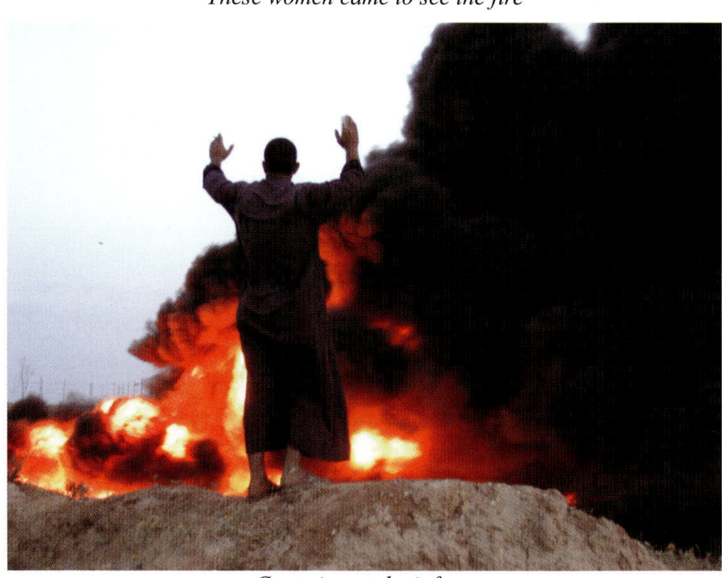

Gesturing at the inferno

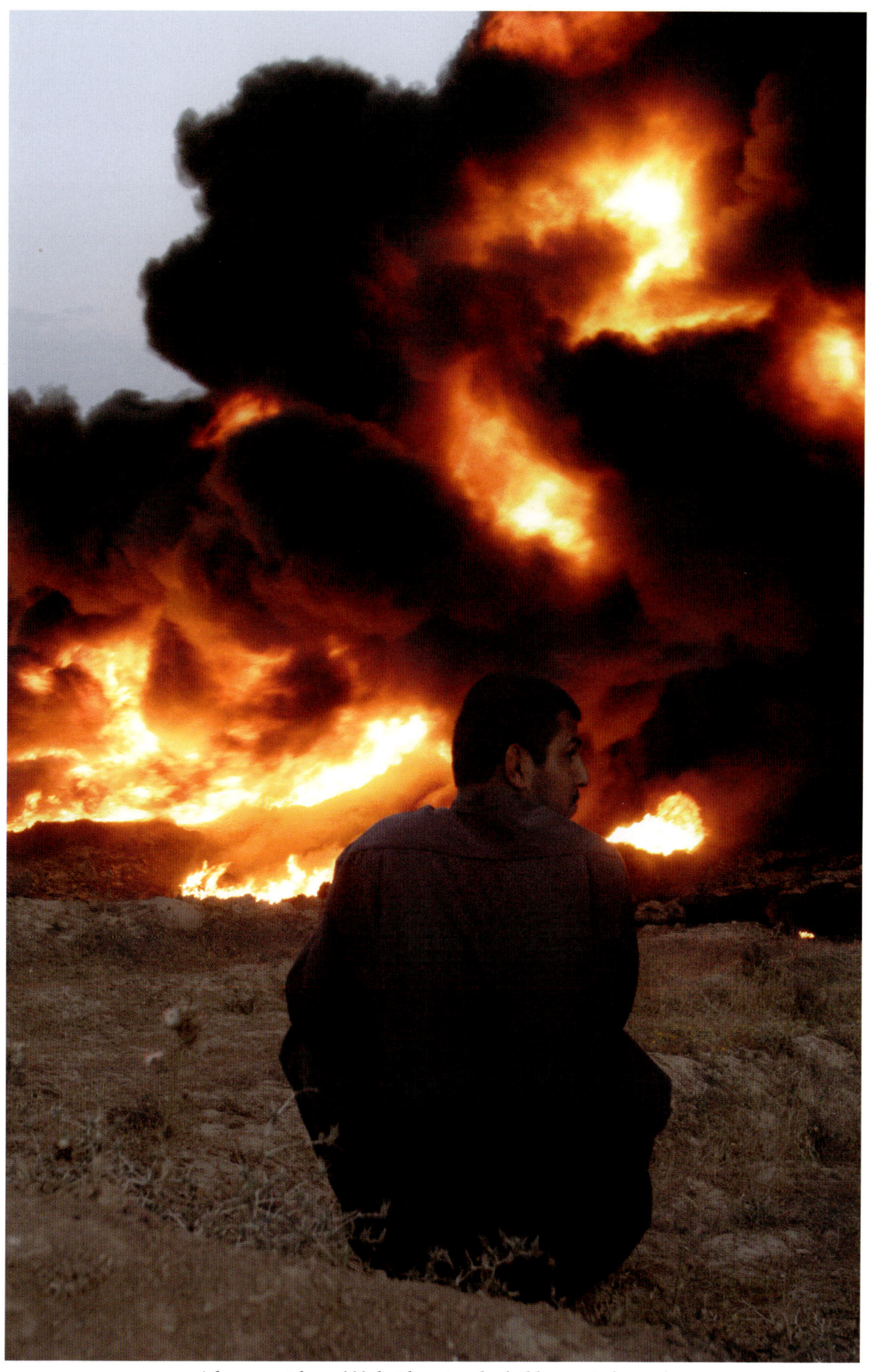

A farmer watches a 300-foot-long trench of oil burn out of control

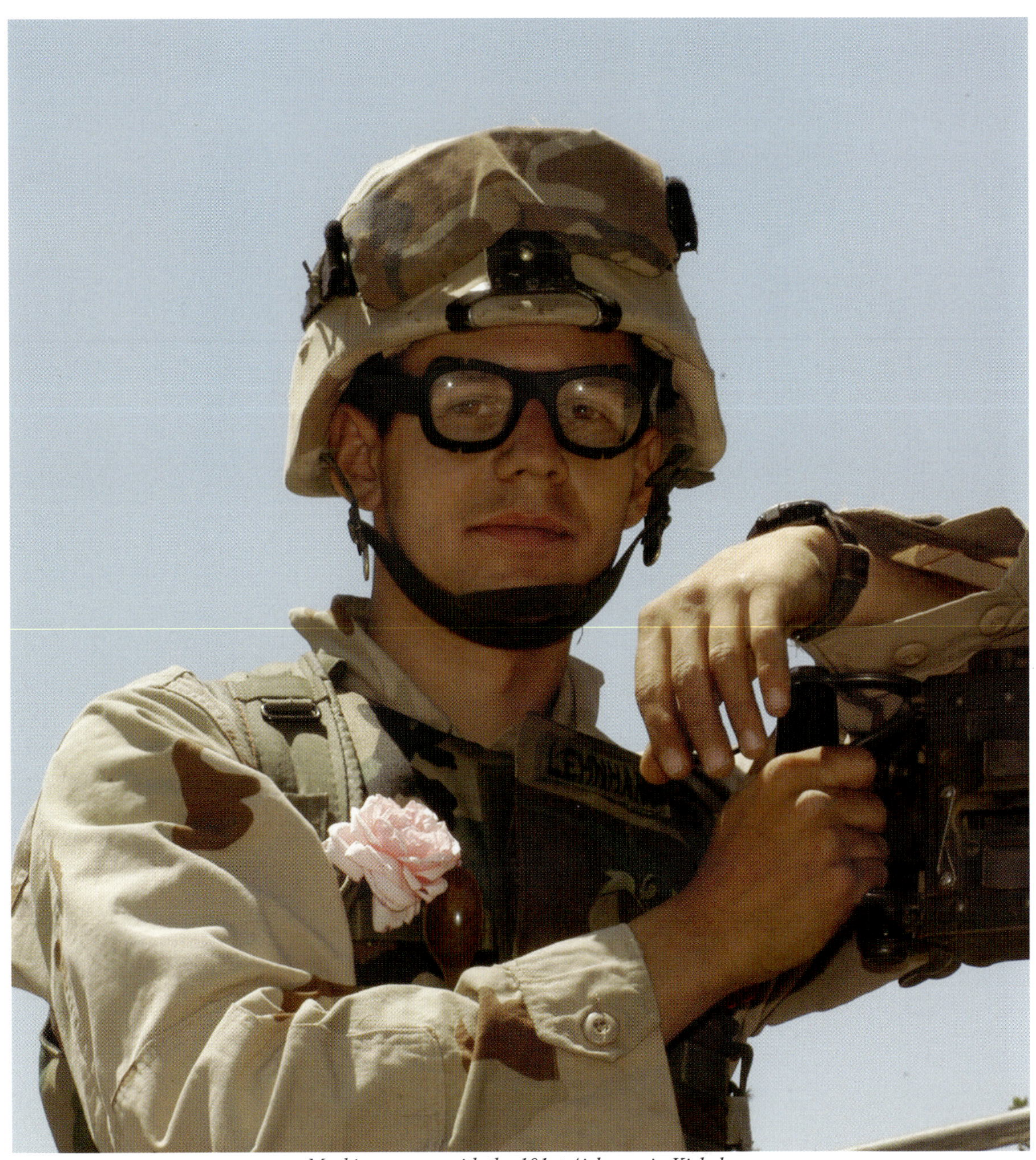

Machine gunner with the 101st Airborne in Kirkuk

There is so much to be aware of when covering such a huge blaze. There is the danger of being burned, as well as the possibility of inhaling toxic fumes. It is important to watch out for your companions; teamwork is vital to preventing injury.

Kenji and I go about our work like a couple of brain surgeons, analyzing what position will make the best pic, while trying to avoid heat waves churning off from the inferno. Reading the flame and wind direction, we are able to get within a few of yards of the inferno. The heat singes the hair on my arms, so it is time to back off a little.

While we are working, a small family of locals come over to welcome us and see what we are doing. They tell us *peshmerga* is responsible for starting the fire earlier this morning. The soldiers shot at the oil, intentionally igniting it. The civilians don't know why the oil was set on fire.

These trenches were dug and filled with crude oil by Saddam's forces. When set afire at night, during a bombing raid, they are meant to confuse the American bombers' targeting systems. But the American bombers were not needed in Kirkuk, because there was little resistance when the Airborne arrived to capture the area.

The family asks if we would like to join them for a meal at their home. We have to refuse their kind offer because we have had a long day, and Kenji needs to transmit his pics to Japan. They want to show us some Iraqi friendship, and to learn about us. They are so kind and open.

Before long, Kenji and I have all the pics we need, and we head back to the hotel. On the way, I see a 12-foot statue of Saddam, made of old cast-off shoes. The actual metal casing of the Saddam statue has been broken into pieces, and the shoes tied by their shoelaces onto the steel skeleton (which had supported Saddam's larger-than-life image). Showing or exposing the sole (with or without a shoe) of one's foot to another is considered an insult in this part of the world. So this is the ultimate insult to Saddam by the people of Kirkuk – a statue of shoes.

We are all ecstatic at what we have accomplished in these few short hours. The oil fire was the source of even better pics than the refinery. We bubble with excitement, on a special high, the high of camaraderie and accomplishment. It is one of the most exiting days I have spent in Iraq. Kenji is overjoyed with his bounty, and I with mine.

Back at the hotel, Kenji invites me out for supper with him, Dana and the driver. I accept his offer and grab a fast shower before we leave. I am covered by a thin veil of black soot.

The restaurant is a bustling eatery lit by a what seems like a thousand green and white neon bulbs. Locals dine alongside tables seated with American soldiers, all eating huge plates of kabobs, chicken, rice and vegetables. Once again, our table is spread out in front of us like a Sunday buffet table. Dana and Kenji did the ordering.

We feast like conquering kings, while laughing and recounting our afternoon's successes. We are extremely happy, and, because Kenji is happy, the driver and Dana are happy. Even the driver compliments me on my work strategy and unconventional style. We are a smiling team of success. Life doesn't get much better!

Back at the hotel, I burn my day's photos onto a back-up CD. This way I don't use up any memory on the laptop with image files. I try to decide what I will cover tomorrow, but conclude that it is best just to let the chips fall as they may, and keep all options open, including heading back to Baghdad. If the morning is short of good opportunities and the afternoon is uncertain, I definitely will be heading for the big city. I call it a day, and settle down to a good night's sleep.

Day 28. Wednesday, May 7th

> *(Government House in Kirkuk; Major Gowan; Iraqis in serious need of employment; the American strategy in Kirkuk; the peshmerga and Special Forces; clearing the airfield; schools used to store ammunitions; 500 police officers; "God has sent you to save us;" troop morale; army cracks bank vaults; occupied by squatters; do not photograph the Turkish military officer; Canadians at war in Iraq; taking the 3 p.m. bus to Baghdad; Tish stays in Kurdistan; our friend and team member Jim Rupert returns to the USA; cyber-journalists drink lavishly and hate America; like arguing with a ten-year-old; security changes at the Fanar; open to attack; Sean leaves for Jordan tomorrow; just Tod and I left in Baghdad)*

I meet Kenji in the lobby of the hotel, after getting back from having a shave and a few glasses of chai at the local barber shop. Kenji and I discuss what to do with the morning. We decide to head to Army-Police Headquarters (also referred to as Government House) to see if we can sniff out any good story leads.

Arriving at the front of Government House, we find a scene of confusion and frustration. Long lines of civilians wait for a chance to meet with civil representatives who are in charge of hiring the staff needed to run the city. Some of those in line are former civil workers and police officers, others are women laborers with children, but all are in serious need of work.

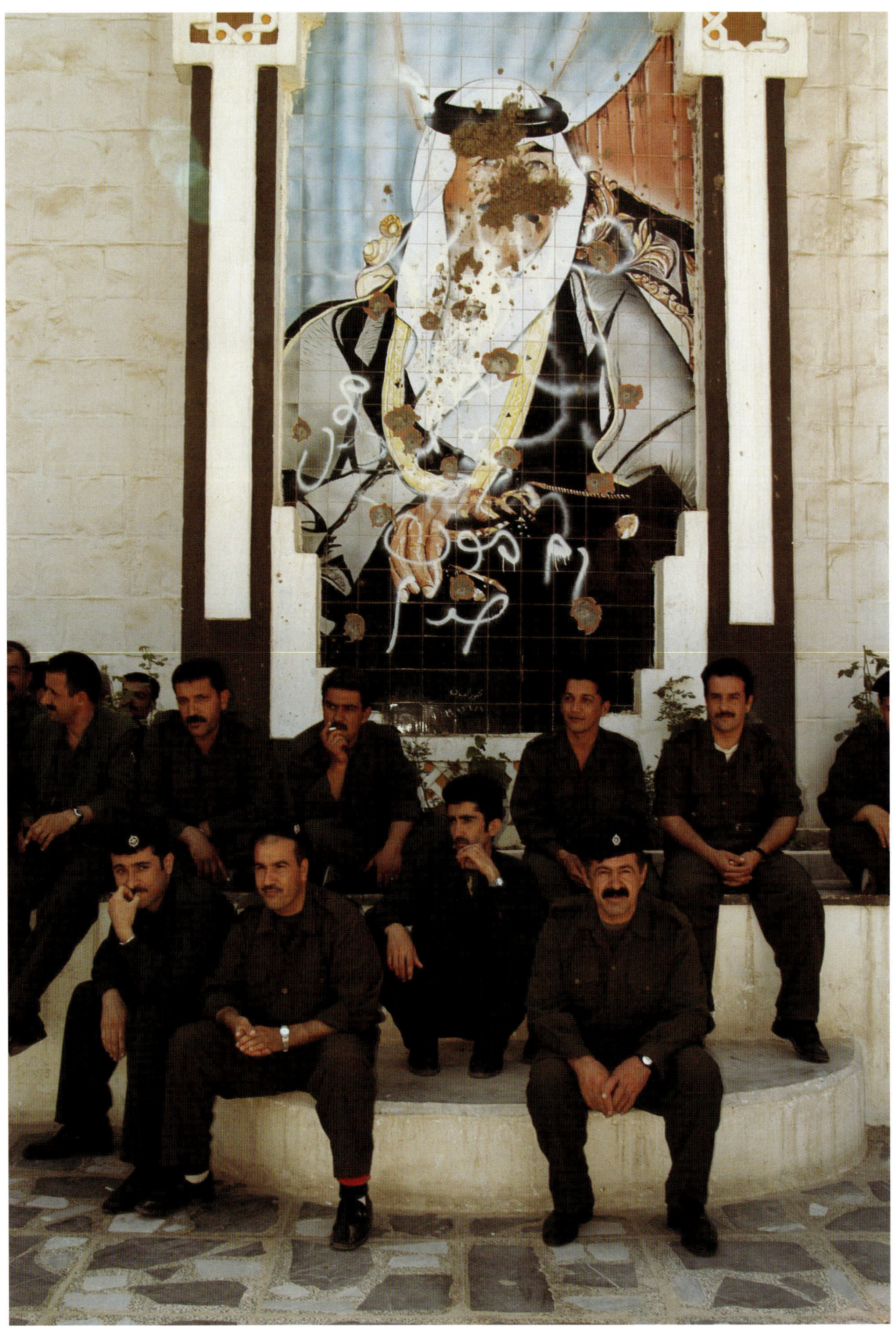

New recruits and former police members gather outside Government House in Kirkuk. Mural of Saddam is shot and disfigured

Before entering the building (which could involve hours of waiting), each person is searched by a soldier and asked to show proper identification. An armed Iraqi policeman stands by the soldier's side, serving as a translator and armed back-up. Once inside the front doorway, an armed sentry checks credentials again. With the proper credentials, the job seeker is directed to either military, civil or police representatives to be interviewed for possible employment. The thought enters my mind that this busy building, with its civil and military brass, could all be wiped out by a well-placed bomb or a couple of lucky mortar strikes.

A group of twenty newly enlisted police officers are gathered outside by the front rose garden, smoking cigarettes while leaning against a bed-sized mosaic of Saddam, built into the front wall of Government House. It is quite a beautiful piece of glazed stone craftsmanship, except that Saddam's smiling face is peppered with bullet holes and splattered with mud and paint. The cops seem a little nervous as I photograph them, with Saddam's image at their backs.

We have been waiting outside the Government House for close to an hour, when finally we are allowed in to speak with the Major. He is as busy as a basketball coach before the big game, trying to get all his players organized.

Major Gowan takes us into a large, comfortable conference room, where he gives us an outline of the American strategy in Kirkuk. He tells us that the 173rd Airborne Brigade captured the Kirkuk airfield a couple of days earlier, and that five Bradley and Abraham tanks are presently guarding the airfield. "At first, Airborne Command expected a refugee crisis, but that didn't materialize. Food was available for those in need and the town was secure. So the rush of refugees never happened," stated Major Gowan.

He explains that their first objective was to secure the airfield for incoming flights. This presented very little resistance, as the enemy had retreated before the advancing troops. "We thought we were going into combat in Kirkuk, but it never happened," said Gowan. "The *peshmerga* and Special Forces secured the drop zone, and worked very closely together." He indicated the paratroopers saw no action because the hostile forces fled. In fact, they retreated so fast that, "When the *peshmerga* cleared the airfield, there was fresh food still cooking in the pots of Saddam's troops," explained Gowan. He further stated that, "Our involvement with the *peshmerga* has been a huge success story, there were many good vibes."

He proudly tells us that the two Kirkuk hospitals are now in better shape than before the war, after being re-supplied by the Americans. And schools are open for the students. "Some of these efforts involved supplying schools with chalk boards, desks and making sure the schools were safe for the return of the children," said Gowan. "Many of the school buildings were used by Saddam's forces to house ammunitions and equipment." The number of bunkers full of ammunition "was overwhelming," said Gowan. "We are trying to secure or disarm the munitions so they cannot be used against us. We are also storing some of the weapons to be used by the future Iraqi military, when that is up and running."

Gowan is also trying to establish a city government, with 24 delegates representing the four political parties, but cautions, "There is potential for violence because of the ethnic diversity of the population." As if to buffer this potential, he tells that by the end of the day, "there will be 500 police officers patrolling the city."

But all is not going as well as expected. "We are on the verge of a fuel crisis," he said. "We need more help and money. The pipelines and machinery are unsafe, and without continual power supplies, we are at minimal productivity from the oil fields." Optimistically, he foretold that, "Everything should be back to normal in two to three weeks."

Gowan believes the American forces are a welcome face in Kirkuk. "I think the people of Kirkuk are very grateful and if the Americans were not here, Kirkuk would have been a blood bath," says Gowan. "One of the local religious clerics told me that; God has sent you here to save us!"

The Major admits that it is not going to be easy getting Kirkuk on a democratic track. "We will make mistakes but we're trying to do the right things, and the morale of our troops is very high. They're doing great work – almost like a peacekeeping role," he said. "They see they have made a difference; that's what it's all about." He says that troop morale has recently been boosted with the implementation of barbershops, latrines, hot showers, and mobile kitchens providing hot chow.

I ask how the army has been able to pay the cops and civil employees. He explains that his troops have been visiting banks and blowing open the safes and removing the cash (this sounds like the Clint Eastwood movie, "Kelly's Heroes"). "This cash is then being distributed to the new police force members, oil refinery workers, schoolteachers and other civil servants and workers, to keep them doing their jobs." He said all the removed money is being documented. At the same time, another team is working throughout the northern part of the country to get those banks tidied-up and open to the public.

The Major tells us where the Humvee patrol is located that is cracking the bank vaults in Kikuk. He gives us directions and we drive off looking for them. But when we find the patrol, they tell us all the banks have been emptied, and we are too late.

The patrol leader, seeing our disappointment at missing out on the safe cracking, asks us if we would be interested in going out on another operation. Apparently, residents have been returning to their homes (after escaping the advance of the war), only to find their homes occupied by squatters, some of whom are soldiers or former government officials and police. Some of the squatters are threatening the residents with retaliation, after being forced out from their squats. So the troops are visiting the homes to see how they can help the families and ease the threat.

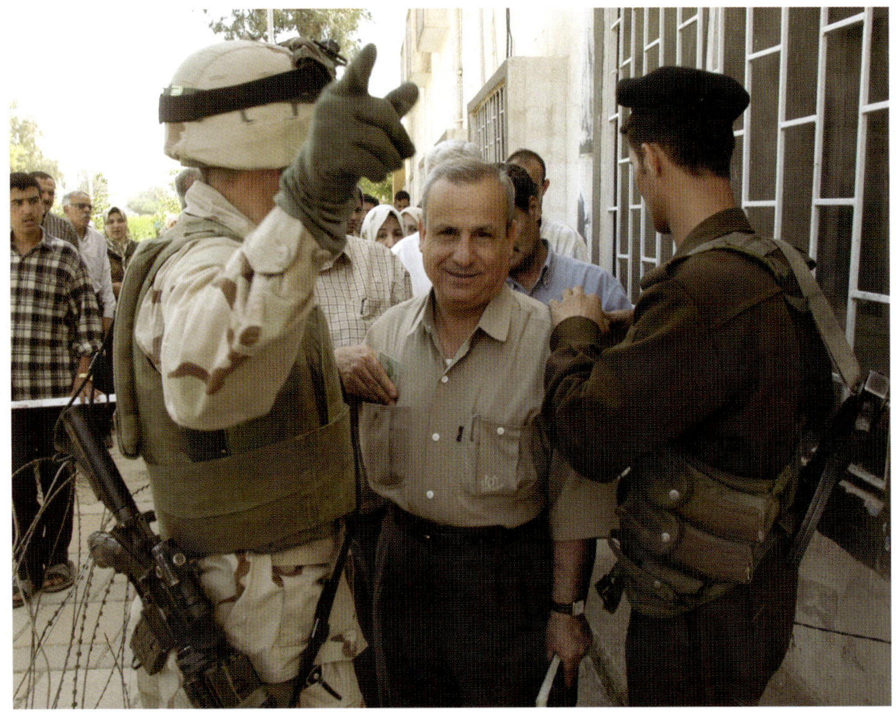

Security screen at Government House. An Iraqi cop and soldier keep order

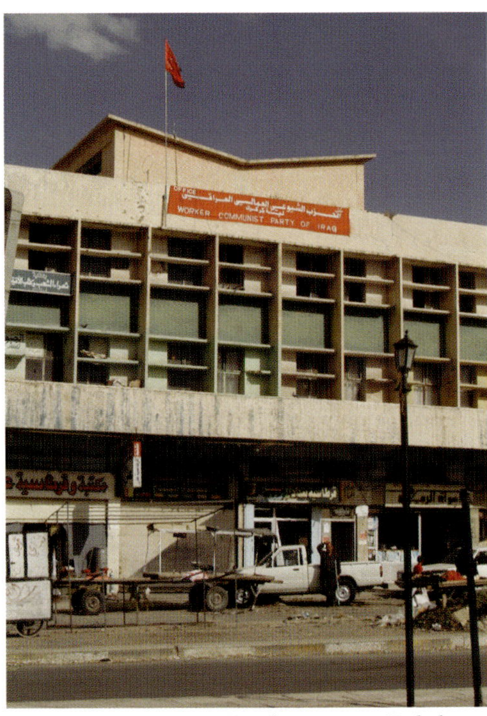

Communist Party Headquarters in Kirkuk

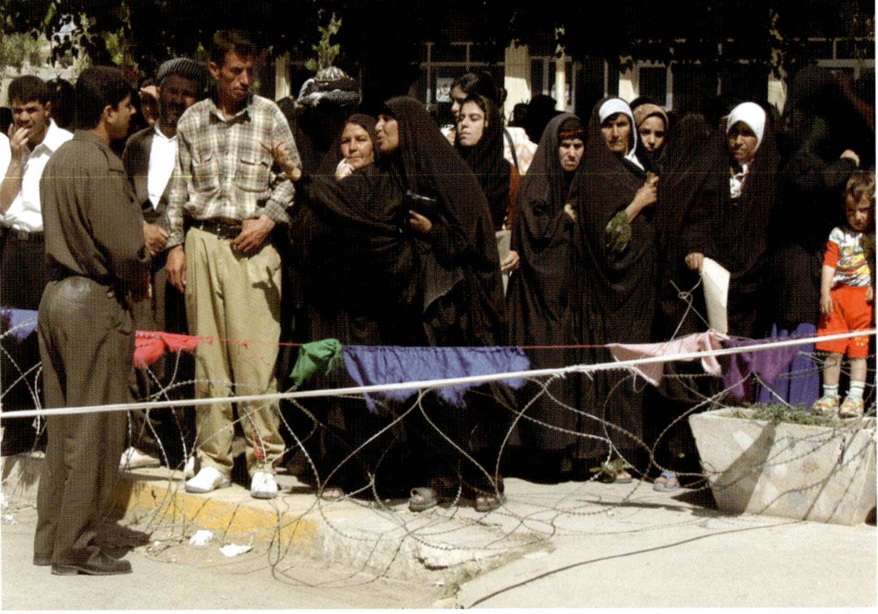

Waiting outside Government House for hours to get a chance at employment, with few jobs

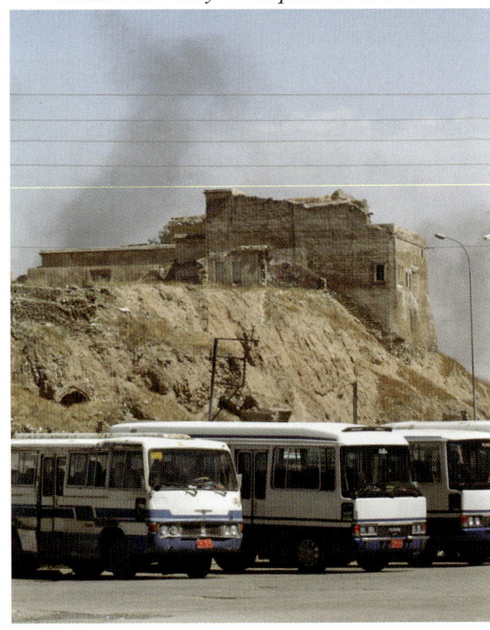

Ruins of an ancient castle near the bus depot

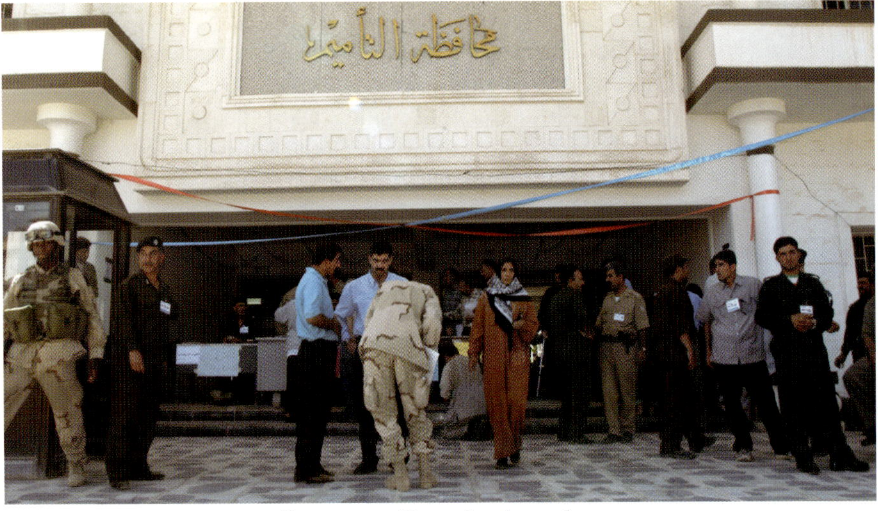

Government House is a busy place

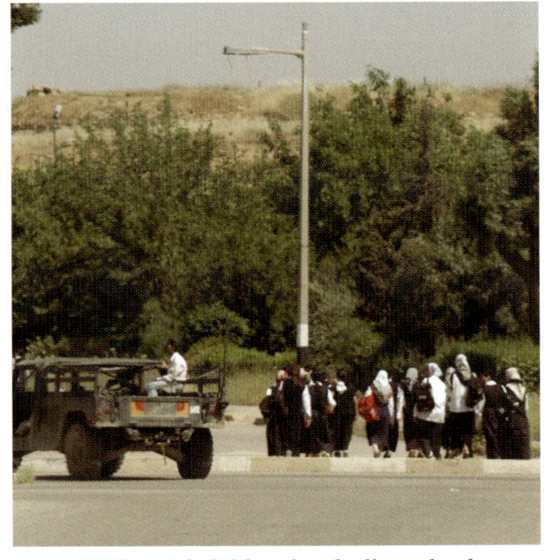

Uniformed children head off to school

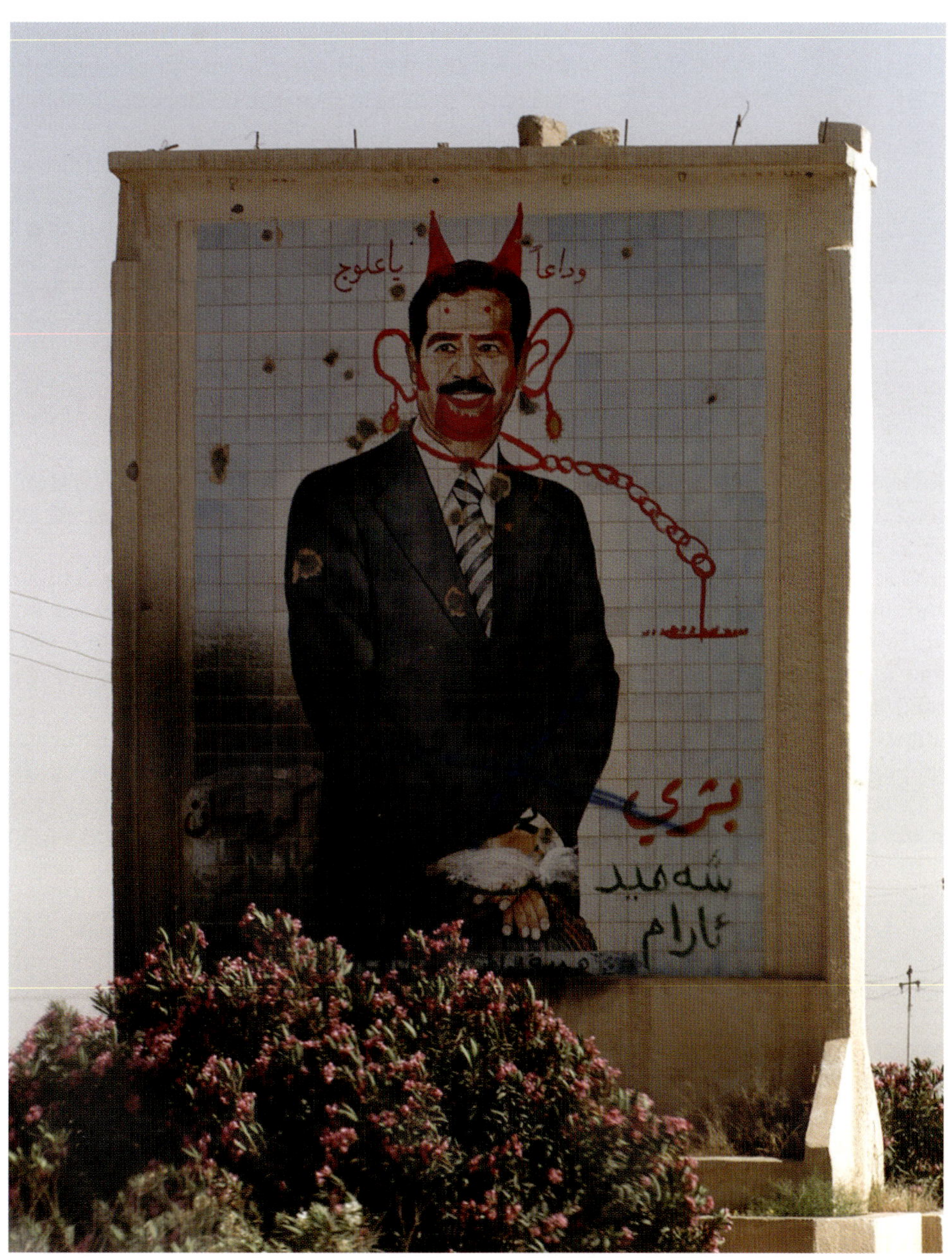

The best example of mural alteration to be seen in Iraq. This mural is just south of Kirkuk

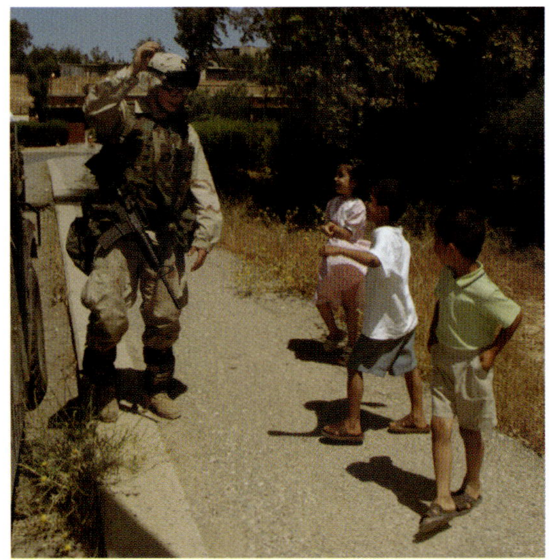

Meeting the locals during patrol

It is all pretty boring stuff, more diplomacy than anything, but I go along just in case we run into some aggressive squatters. Kenji and Dana are happy to be on their first Humvee patrol, and are enjoying the drive through the streets with the troops. I am glad they are having a good time, but I am starting to think about leaving for Baghdad this afternoon.

Accompanying us on the two Humvee patrol is a Turkish Army officer, dressed in a dark green uniform. Neither his beret nor uniform have any identifying flashes of rank or nation. The American patrol leader informs us that he is an observer from the Turkish Military, and we are not allowed to photograph or speak with him during the patrol (the Americans are double-dating the Kurds and the Turks. This takes a fine balancing act).

The 'politics of war' has brought this officer to Kirkuk. The Turks are concerned about the Kurdish drive for statehood in Iraq. Should this occur, it could ignite unrest amongst the large population of Turkish Kurds, perhaps starting a civil war in Turkey.

Even Canada has observers in Iraq. They are here to assist the Americans with certain weapons guidance systems and other electronics.

We get back to the hotel around 2 p.m., after a largely wasteful morning. But I did get a few useful pics, and met some bass fisherman from Tennessee. They also hunt wild turkey, which requires a good knowledge of the bird's habits to successfully stalk.

Saying my goodbyes to Kenji, Dana and the driver, I grab my gear and take a taxi to the bus depot. Kenji tells me he will return to Baghdad in a couple of days and will look me up. I catch a 3 p.m. bus to Baghdad, hoping that Sean and Tish made their way to Baghdad from Mosul and are already there waiting for me.

The drive to Baghdad takes a couple of hours and is largely uneventful. Walking into the Al Fanar, I go looking for Sean and Tish, though they are not in the room. So I go to Tod's room on the second floor. After our greetings, he says that he hasn't heard from Tish for a couple of days (last time he knew, she was in Sulaymaniyah, Kurdistan). Sean is back in Baghdad, but just happens to be out for the afternoon. He also tells me that our good friend Jim Rupert, of Newsday, has returned to the States.

I am happy for Jim, and glad to have made his acquaintance. I will miss his teamwork. He is the only journalist I know who works with two pens in one hand, switching from one colored pen to another mid-sentence, like a majorette. The text is written with a standard blue pen, while names and places are written in red. A great way to organize your notes.

I go for a chai at the Casino Café, by the riverbank across the street from the Fanar. I start organizing a final list of what stories I need to cover before leaving Iraq. If my luck persists, I should be able squeeze it all in before I leave Baghdad. In seven days I should be flying over the Atlantic, heading home to my family.

While at the café I see Ken, the New York Daily News stringer. I go over and say hello and ask him what has been going on in Baghdad over the last few days. He is seated with a man and a woman, both in their mid-thirties who I have not seen before. They claim to be journalists who work for a cyber newspaper.

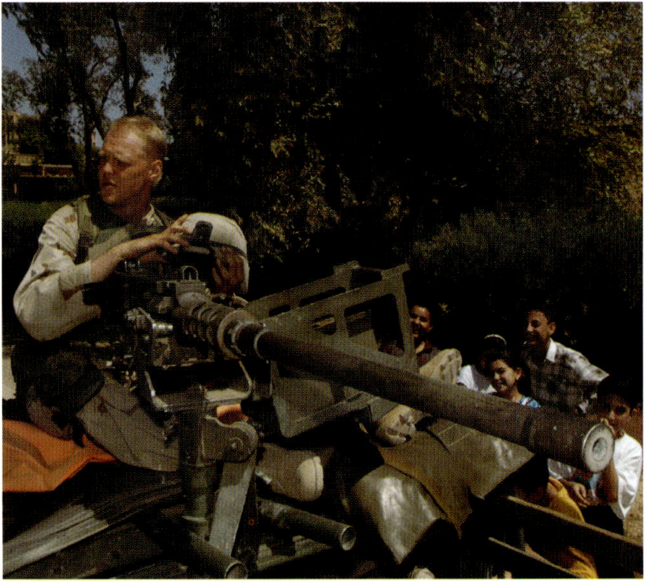

Machine gunner keeps alert during patrol

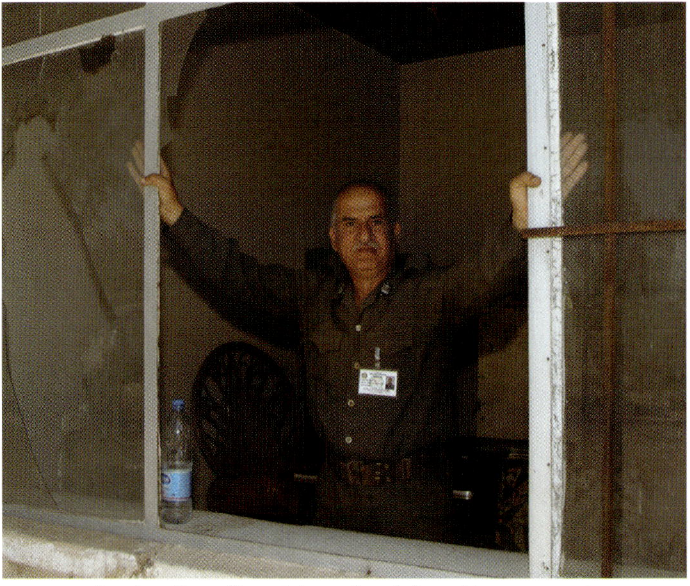

Iraqi police officer takes a break from his paperwork

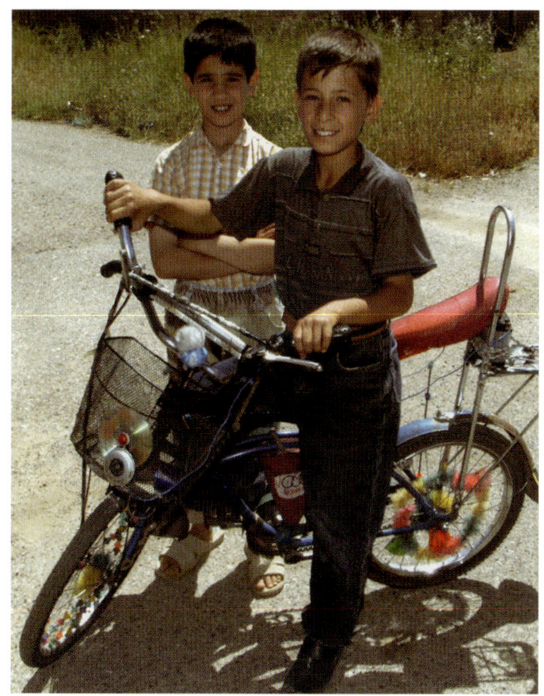

The children of Kirkuk are well taken care of

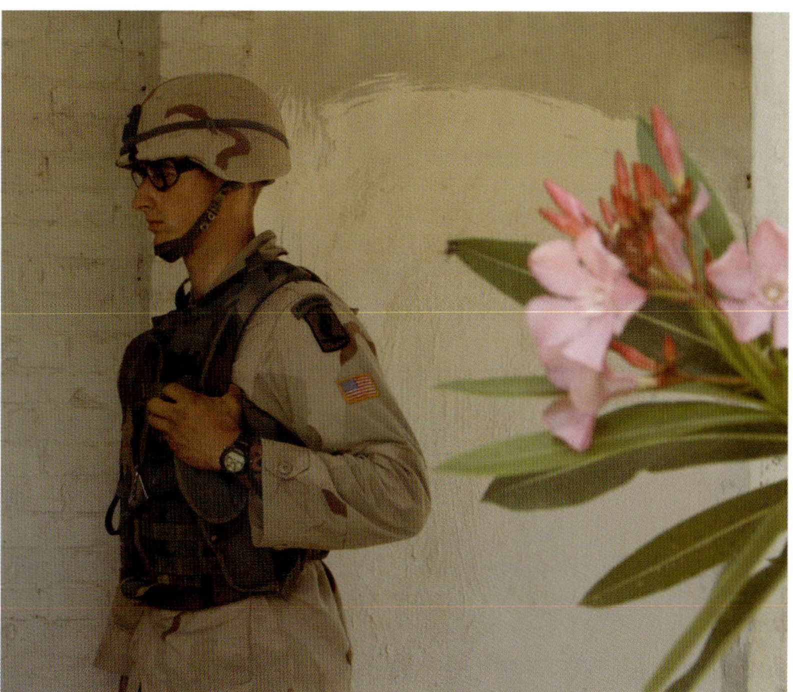

Soldiering can be a boring occupation

From the very moment I start speaking to the two strangers, it becomes clear they have been pressed from the same mould as the Italian woman from Voices in the Wilderness and the Iraqi journalist. They are very rude to me, and tell me that I am a pro-American puppet, spreading lies with my reporting. I do not know what they are trying to accomplish with their aggressive attack. They are not going to change the way I think, or influence me by acting like they are.

They interrogate me about my book project and insult the idea behind it. Their arguments and reasoning go far beyond honest criticism, and after a short while I start toying with them and leading them on.

Then I tell them I stayed for a couple of days with the Airborne in Mosul, to find out what makes the soldiers tick. They respond by saying, "If you want to kill people, why don't you just pick up a gun and join them?" It is like arguing with two seven-year-olds. I don't need to hear this from these two clowns. They order their third round of imported German beer, as I excuse myself and get up to leave. At $6 a tin, each beer is equivalent to about a month's wages to the average Iraqi. This type of people remind me of cult members; they all talk the same talk and walk the same walk.

Just after dark, Sean shows up at the hotel. We have dinner downstairs in the Fanar dining room. He tells me that both he and Tish left Mosul the same day as I, only they travelled to Sulaymaniyah, where Tish remains. Sean arrived in Baghdad yesterday.

The whole security set-up outside the Fanar and the Palestine Hotel has changed again. There is a barbwire fence strung right across the road, just outside the Fanar front doors. This fence sections us off from the residential area running north along the river road, and it encloses us within the Palestine complex. A small checkpoint has been set up on the road at an opening in the barbed wire, where three soldiers are stopping all cars and checking them and their occupants before they enter the hotel complex. A tank is parked on our side of the fence, just 100 feet from the checkpoint, and 50 feet from the hotel. It has its cannon pointed at the checkpoint.

While it looks good and might keep a car bomber out of range, we are now more vulnerable to attack and assault. The public can now freely wander inside the complex, after a light frisking or look-over. I cannot figure out why the army is letting the public into the area, as it just increases the chance of attack. On top of this, a new deluge of hawkers, beggars and street orphans now plague the street in front of the Fanar, or anywhere else you walk within the complex. We are all caged in together.

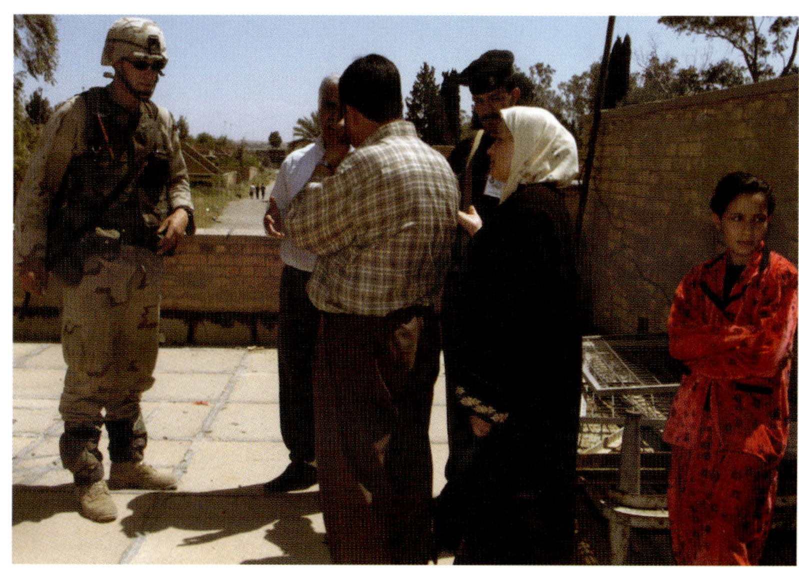

These residents fear retaliation from squatters who had taken over their home

The soldiers aren't checking vehicles for our safety, but for the safety of the political, military and governmental movers and shakers who meet daily to discuss strategy at the Palestine Hotel. They don't want a suicide bomber taking out their officers. It is nice to be back home in Baghdad, but it is much less secure.

Sean is packing his gear for his early morning departure to Amman. From Amman he will fly to Cannes, France to work as an usher at the Cannes Film Festival, which starts in just over a week. After the festival, he will return to Texas to begin working on his film documentary. He also tells me that Tish should be back in a day or two, and is having an enjoyable stay in Sulaymaniyah.

It will be extremely sad to see Sean go. He has been such a good supportive friend, and a principal member of my Baghdad family. Soon it will be just Tod and myself left. I just have to hang in and concentrate on the task ahead of me. It has been a long day, and I head to bed exhausted – but happy to be back home.

Day 29. Thursday, May 8th

(Up at 5 a.m. to help Sean leave for Jordan; horrendous nightmare shakes me severely; changing my room; cockroaches on the carpet; loudest explosion of the war; a taxi to the missile factory; a maze of traffic jams; large ground-to-air missile and launcher by the side of the road; the Al Taji Air Force Base; French manufactured fuel tanks; soldier tells me no photos at facility; 4th Infantry Division; voracious biting fleas attack soldiers; 44th Chemical Division visit airport; Haider is a great friend; two honorable men; introducing civil law; the lost patrol; "You aren't going to shoot me – are you?"; "Oops, sorry buddy"; a soldiers paranoia; looters brought to holding cells; crocodile tears; "Everyone is innocent"; anything could happen; Jennifer the budding journalist; street journalism; pizza at the Fanar; Sean safe in France; Tish in Kurdistan; I have been in Baghdad for over a hundred years; staccato of rifle fire)

I awaken at 5 a.m. and start helping Sean carry his gear downstairs to the lobby of the Fanar. In the darkness of early morning we sit outside, hauling on a cigarette and chatting about what life will bring us next; then the Jimmy shows up. We finish the loading then embrace. Sean waves back at me as the Jimmy disappears into the dark Baghdad night.

Feeling very spaced-out and weak (I think we finally got to sleep around 2 a.m.) I head back upstairs to get some more sleep. A couple of hours later I awaken from the most horrendous nightmare. It is no ordinary nightmare, but a ghastly experience of warped psychological torture. I will not go into describing it, except to say that I take it as danger signal that it is soon time to leave Iraq. I get out of bed and try to snap the jitters out of me, but am I seriously shaken up. It is as though I have a nauseating fever. I realize that if I cannot drop the nightmares, I could have a really difficult week ahead.

Since Sean has gone, the room is open if I want to take it over. But I decide to see if there is something else available. I ask the manager if I can look at another, and he shows me a small room on the second floor. I tell him that it looks fine, but after spending fifteen minutes watching a bunch of small cockroaches running around the bathroom

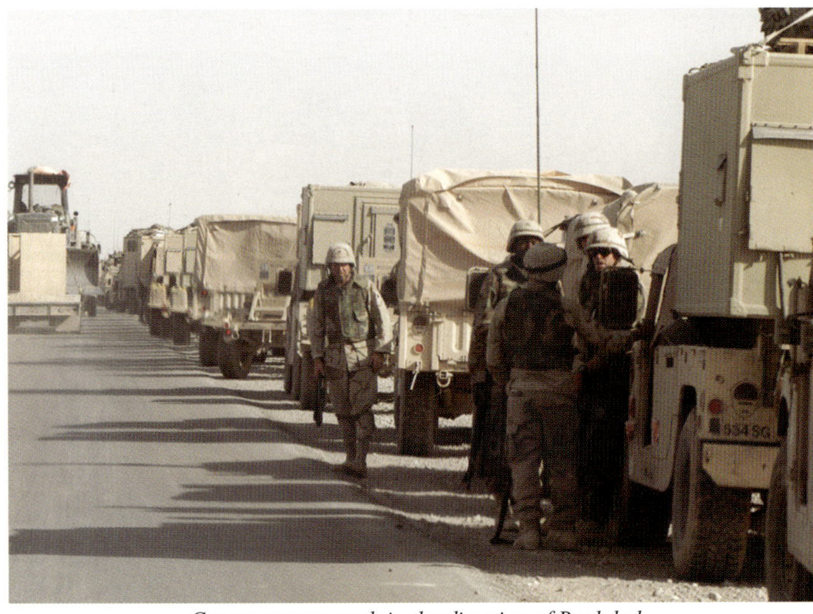

Convoy moves south in the direction of Baghdad

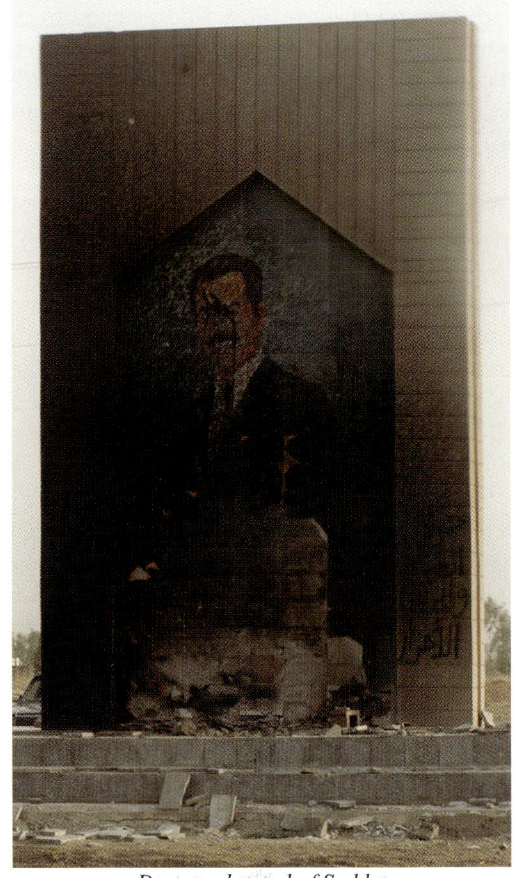

Destroyed mural of Saddam

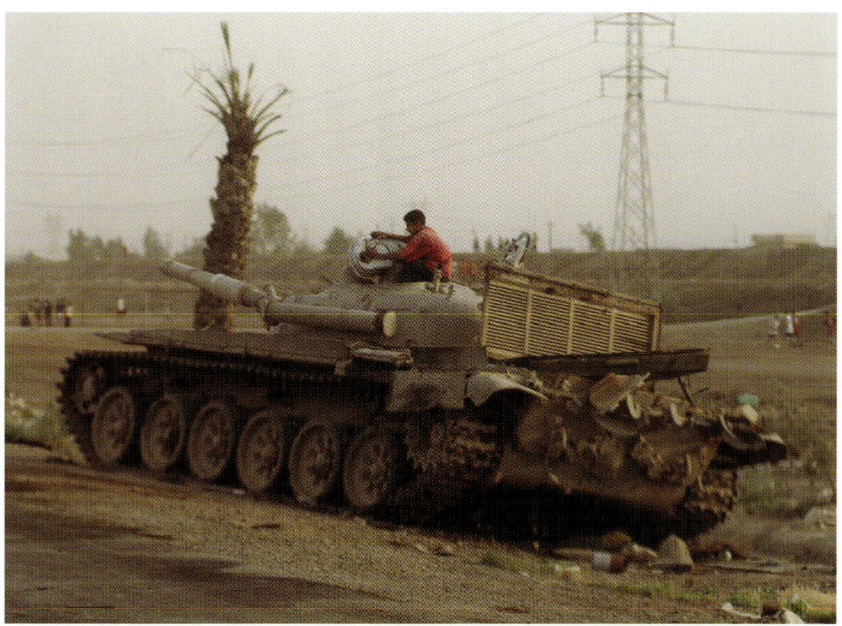

A young looter strips parts from a destroyed Iraqi tank near Injana

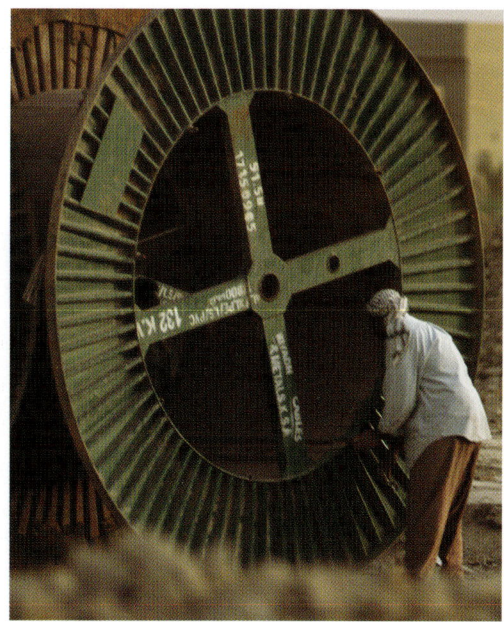

Looter strips bolts from a cable spooler

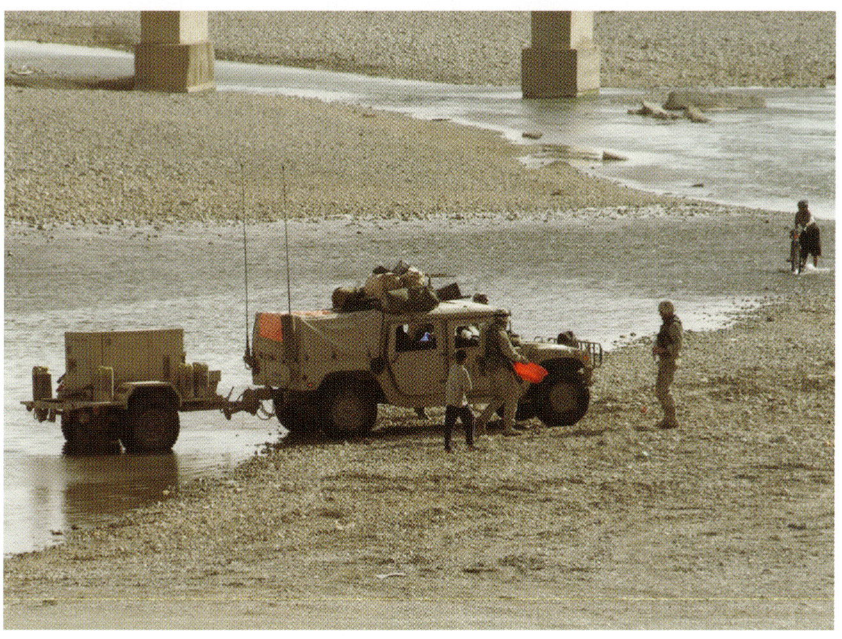

A Humvee crew stops along the Adhaim River near Tuz Khurmantu

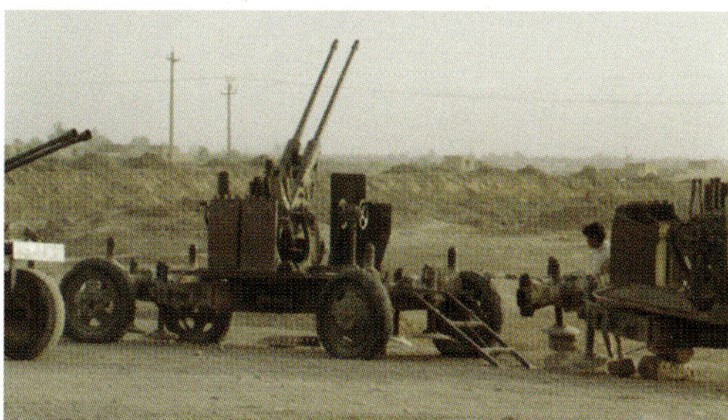

Anti-aircraft guns are now outdated scrap

and carpet flooring, I go downstairs and complain about the bugs. I am not too happy about having been offered this room and wonder if the roaches are this active in the day, what will it be like after dark. I don't like little cockroaches.

The manager apologizes about the critters, and then shows me a nice large room on the seventh floor. I collect my gear from the third floor and immediately move in. It faces south along the river road and banks of the Tigris. I put my George Harrison CD into the laptop, hoping the tunes can help pull me together from the nightmare.

I decide to go for a taxi drive to check out the missile or bomb factory that I saw on May 3rd, when Sean, Tish and I were on the bus going to Mosul. All I know is that it is located north of the North Gate.

Driving out of the downtown area, we enter a maze of traffic jams. Cars are driving up, and backing down the merge onto the highway, causing a huge gridlock. There is no order; it is traffic hell. A few traffic police, in white and green uniforms, are trying to untangle the haystack of traffic chaos. Even civilians are standing in the middle of the mayhem, trying to assist, as angry motorists muscle them out of the way with their cars.

I stop for a brief moment at the site of the Black Hole in Al Maghrib (along the main road leading north from central Baghdad) and grab a few snap shots of the devastation then continue north.

Just before we reach the North Gate, I take some quick photos from the car window of a huge ground-to-air missile lying on the back of a launching truck parked in vacant field. This missile, about 35 feet long, is the largest I have ever seen. It has extra extensions or segments (possibly fuel tanks) built into it, making it look extremely long and jury-rigged in appearance. Judging from the length of it, I would imagine it has great range capabilities. It looks similar to a Scud missile, only larger.

Finally, a good hour-and-a-half after leaving the Fanar, I reach the location of the bomb or missile factory. The driver tells me that the site is called the, Al Taji Military Airfield, on the outskirts of the village of Al Taji. The installation is

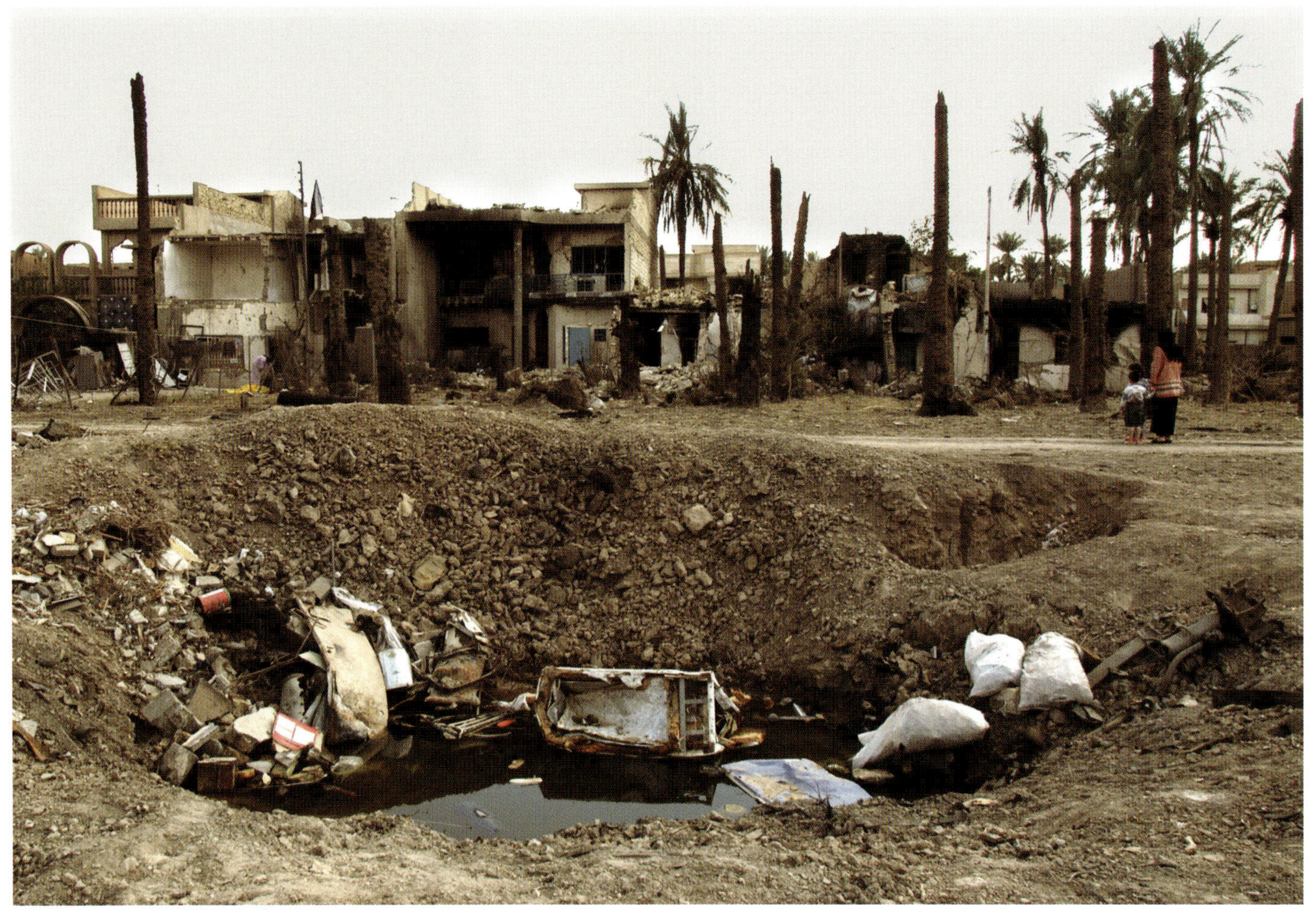

Devastation at the Black Hole in the Al Maghrib district

huge, but all I can see from the highway is a small part of its front. I can't see any runways or anything else to identify it as an airport. A high cinder-block fence, covered with barbed wire, surrounds the grounds. Luckily, a section of the fence has been knocked down just enough for me to see the bombs/missiles. Three large warehouses stand back about 100 yards from the highway. I now see that the weapons are not missiles at all, but bombs – huge bombs. There are over 50 of them stacked up against the outside walls of the warehouses.

Approximately 12 feet long and tapered at the ends, they look like gigantic fat cigars. Some are painted light green; others are unpainted, their naked skin shining in the sun like glistening silver bullets. The tail fins are not attached to the bombs, and sit close by in their own wooden crates, ready to be attached when needed (the bombs were probably built elsewhere and shipped to the air base partially assembled and unpainted). These are bombs that would need to be dropped from aircraft, and Iraq's air force has been basically non-existent since the late 1980's. So the bombs are just expensive piles of explosive junk.

Two disposable fuel containers for jets lie just in front of me on the ground. Red lettering painted onto the side of the containers indicates pressurization ports. The language is in French and English. They are probably French-manufactured containers.

I use my 80-200mm zoom lens with a 1.5 converter to get some close-up shots of the bombs by the warehouses. I grab about ten frames, when a U.S. soldier walks up to me telling me that the facility is a restricted site, and I am not allowed to photograph it. I apologize to him if I caused him any inconvenience, then ask where I should go to get permission to take photos or gain access to the site. He tells me to ask at the main checkpoint, just off a side road from the highway that leads into the facility.

I am happy that the soldier does not hassle me about my camera. So I walk away confident, knowing that if I am not allowed onto the site, at least I have some usable pics of the bombs.

I drive over to the checkpoint, which is manned by six soldiers and a tank from the 4th Infantry Division. Barbed wire is stretched across the roadway and a wall of sandbags partially encircles the tank. A large section of camouflaged netting is strung over it, protecting its crew from the sun and wind.

It is a dusty-hot place to be stuck in. I feel sorry for the soldiers at this miserable post. When I ask for permission to go onto the site, a soldier phones command and I wait for a response. I start talking with the sentry guards, asking how the men are making out. One of them tells me of an attack by a plague of chiggers, a small though voracious biting flea. Some of the soldiers walk over to me, and lifting off their Kevlar helmets, show me their badly bitten foreheads. They look beaten about the face and slightly bloodied . I ask the soldiers why they didn't use their insect repellent. The sentry replies, "We did – but it was like gravy on the meat for these bugs!"

They are a friendly bunch of soldiers, who all crowd around to ask me where I have been in Iraq. We are smoking and chatting when the radioman on the tank shouts over to me. He tells me that command says I need a military escort if I want to visit the site. Surprised by this reply, I ask him if they are sending me an escort. He radios back to command then tells me, "They don't know where you can find an escort; it's up to you." It is a 'Catch 22' response to my request. The only people who could provide me with a military escort are the military. Their reply, in bureaucratic terms, means they do not want me on the airfield grounds.

By this time I have a good chatty relationship going on with one soldier. I take his home phone number and tell him I will contact his family to tell them that their son is doing well and surviving the war. The soldier tells me that he would be forever grateful. I shake their hands and bid them a quick return home to their loved ones. They do not like how I am being treated by command; though the soldiers are real gentlemen, courteous and friendly.

Just as I am leaving, four military trucks stocked with equipment and crew stop at the checkpoint. I overhear them identifying themselves to the sentry as the 44th Chemical Division. I guess they are going to check the airport for possible weapons of mass destruction. Perhaps this is why they did not want me on the site; they hadn't checked the airport for chemical weapons yet, or perhaps the chemical unit is using the airport as their base.

I head back to the hotel, glad to have found the site and to have got some photos. The round trip cost about $30 because of the distance and all the waiting. It was expensive, but very worthwhile.

After having a refreshing shower and a few glasses of hot chai, I meet Tod and Haider in the lobby of the Fanar.

Tod wants to visit a police station to talk to police about the re-introduction of civil law and how it will work. We drive towards a police station in the desolate east side of Baghdad. On the way, we see a small army truck, with hand-cuffed prisoners in the back, parked at the side of the road. Two soldiers, who appear to be lost, stand outside the vehicle looking over a map.

We stop near the vehicle and Tod climbs out of the car and walks over to assist the soldiers, while we wait in the car watching out the back window. Seeing Tod approach, one of the soldiers turns, and raising his pistol in his clenched hands, aims it directly at Tod and shouts, "Stop – place your hands above your head!" Tod stops dead in his tracks, and raising

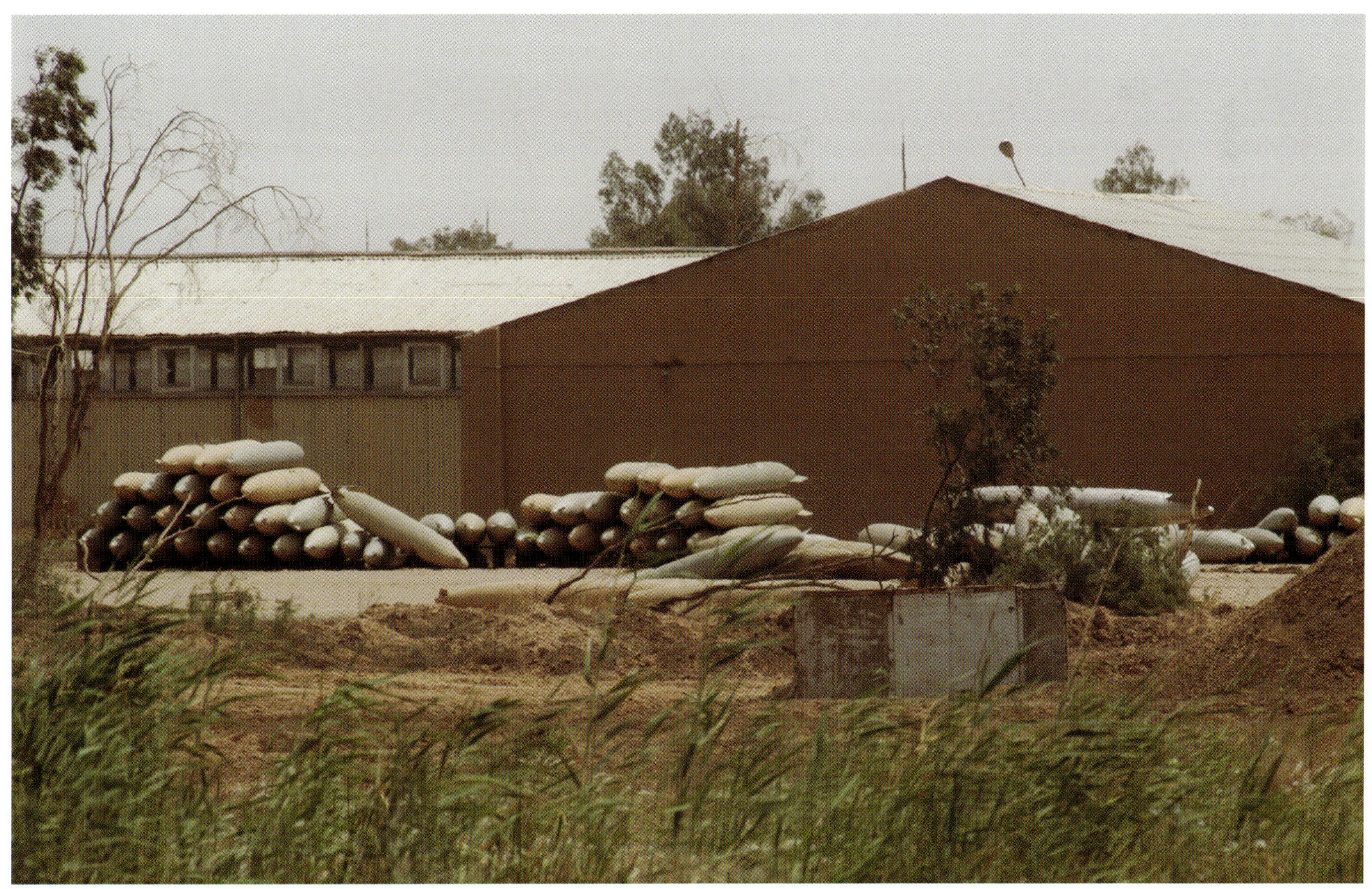

Large bombs at the Al Taji Air Base north of Baghdad

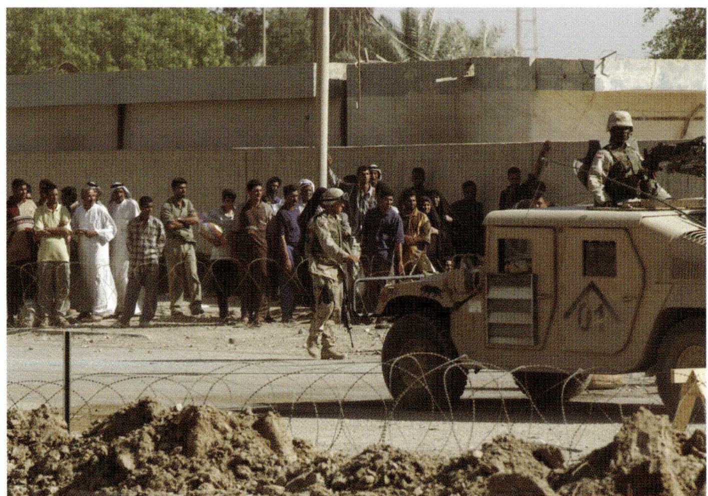
Family members wait for their kin to be released from jail

his hands slowly into the air speaks out in a heavy Texan twang, "You aren't going to shoot me – are you?" The soldier, suddenly realizing the suspect is media, drops his weapon and says, "Oops – sorry buddy, I didn't know you were with the press!" Tod drops his arms and starts laughing; we start laughing and then the soldiers in the truck start laughing.

Tod does not have his press pass visible around his neck, and is dressed in partial military-style clothing (which is hard to avoid, as some of the best desert clothing is only available in military colors or issue, like my Army-issue desert combat boots). I can understand the soldier's paranoia, but Tod came a little too close to getting blown away. One misjudgment, and you're dead, mistaken for the enemy and a victim of friendly fire. It was an innocent mistake on both sides, an almost comical and deadly mistake.

The soldier holsters his sidearm and walks over to Tod and shakes his hand, apologizing further. He tells Tod that his patrol is lost, and looking for the same police station we are heading to. We tell him to follow behind us; our driver knows the way.

A few minutes later we drive up to the sprawling police station, which also doubles as a large prison. The six handcuffed prisoners (who were caught looting), are unloaded, brought inside the walled compound and placed in holding cells. It is now the job of the police to process them and to see if the charges warrant them being held in confinement, and for how long. Chances are, they will be warned not to loot again, then set free. There are too many thieves and not enough of a security force, police or military, to put a dent in the thievery and anarchy which rules in this city of five million.

An angry crowd of over 150 impatient civilians are gathered outside the police station, waiting for their family members to be released, or for word of their status. Crying mothers plead with the armed police and army sentries for the release of their sons and husbands. They swear that their sons are innocent. But the crocodile tears and hand gesturing does not fool the police; they have seen it all before. "Everyone is innocent," says a police officer in a sarcastic laugh, as he throws up his hands. Then in a serious tone he adds, "They always say 'It wasn't my son, he was watching, he wasn't involved in the looting.' It's never their son! It's always someone else's son!"

It is a killer hot day, and the civilians standing outside the station are restless. They heave against the barbwire fences, shouting at the soldiers to release their family members. The soldiers are tense and alert, gripping their rifles tightly in sweaty hands, squinting at the crowd, alert to any danger. Soldiers on Humvees armed with 50-calibre machine guns look down over the crowd. The barbwire fencing is keeping them back from the station and in a controlled area, rather than roaming all around the road in front of the facility. It is one of those situations where anything can happen. I feel like waiting around a little longer to see if anything pops, but Tod isn't into 'ambulance chasing,' so we return to the Fanar.

I have a chai and then go for a walk to the waterfront with Jennifer, a former Gulf War Veteran, now a budding journalist. She is in Baghdad to cover the

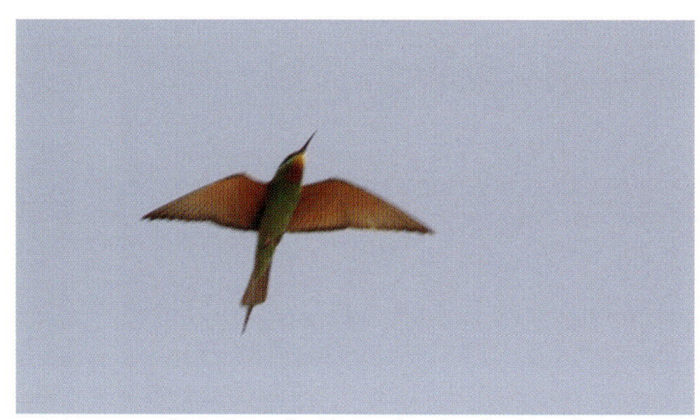
A bee-eater flies along the Tigris shoreline looking for insects

Once inside the prison walls, the police escort suspects to cells

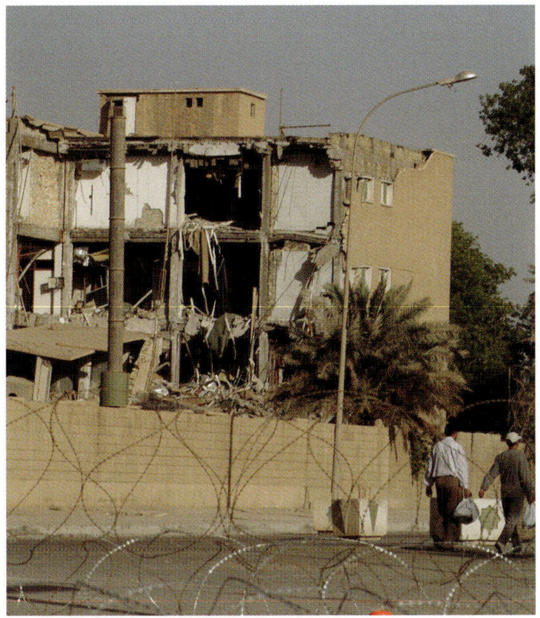

Damaged apartment building in Al Maghrib

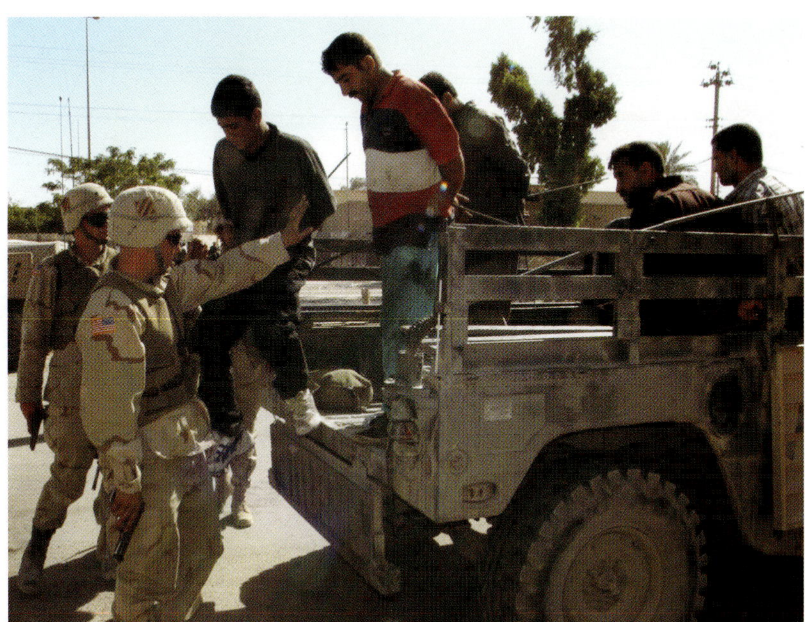

Prisoners are unloaded from Humvee. Note the soldiers carry pistols in hand

news for an American west coast newspaper. I had met her briefly yesterday in the dining room of the Fanar. She asks if she can tag along with me, to help her learn the ropes of street journalism, so to speak. She is a very nice, soft-spoken person, and willing to take risks to get real stories.

I tell her there are no rules, and no guarantees. Photo-journalism is all about street smarts, adaptability, courage, wit, control of body and mind, humour, honor, a pinch of bullshit, and a talent for finding news.

After our walk, Tod and Jennifer and I share a pizza supper in the Fanar dining room. It's not a bad pizza, but it is missing a few toppings, like pepperoni, mushrooms and peppers. I ask Tod if he is aware that a small handful of NGOs and some individuals parading as journalists, are using press I.D.s or organizational names to assist in spreading their anti-Western hatreds. He tells me that he has had similar experiences, and is strongly considering writing a story about those who abuse NGO or journalistic status, and who they really are. He is especially interested in who 'Voices in the Wilderness' are (myself included), and what they are supposed to be accomplishing in Iraq. As many readers already know, the first fatality of war is the truth.

I am happy to hear he feels the same way I do about some of these organizations. I believe they should be more responsible, ensuring that contributors' money does not go towards groups or media that are, perhaps unknowingly to the organization, being used by anti-American or anti-Western insurgents, who have infiltrated the organizations.

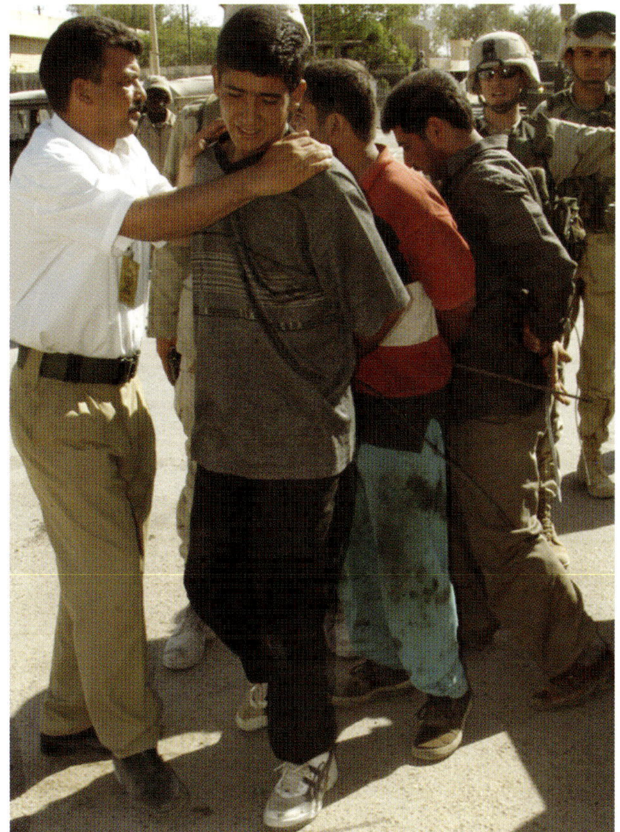

A police officer takes control of prisoners

This sort of activity is happening right now in Baghdad as I speak. The problem is that there are many credible NGO groups who have sacrificed much personal suffering in their desire to help the unfortunate. Tod tells me that the presence of NGO groups in Kabul, Afghanistan has become the leading industry there, an industry that feeds on itself and protects itself from those who would expose their secrets or their financial structure. People, or NGO groups who use the impoverished for their own justification, and then claim legitimacy, are simply evil. And they are a number of them out there.

Tod tells me that he received an e-mail from Sean today, saying that he arrived safely in France, and one from Tish, saying that she is having a great time relaxing in Sulymaniyah.

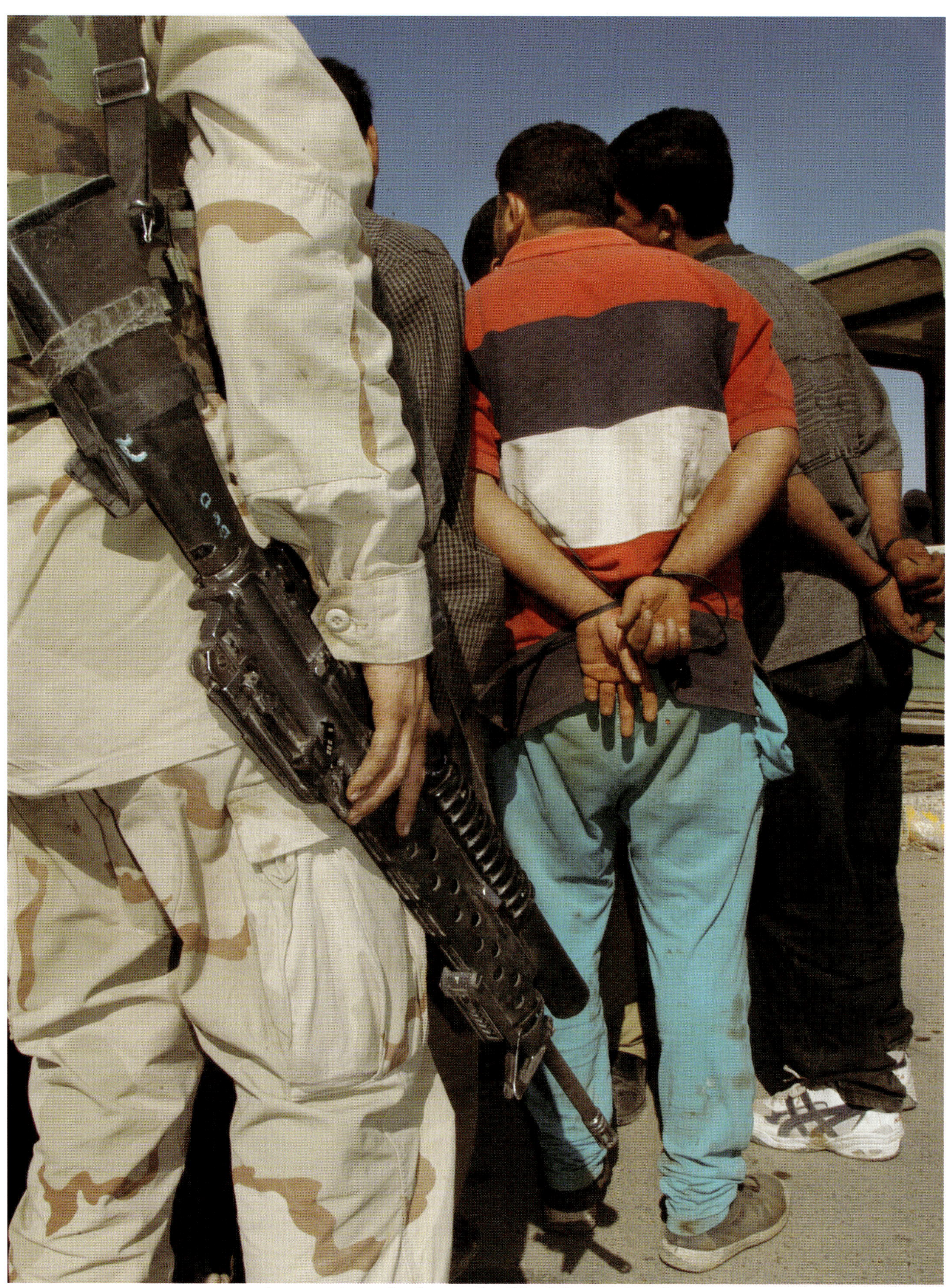

Looters are kept under close guard until handed over to the police

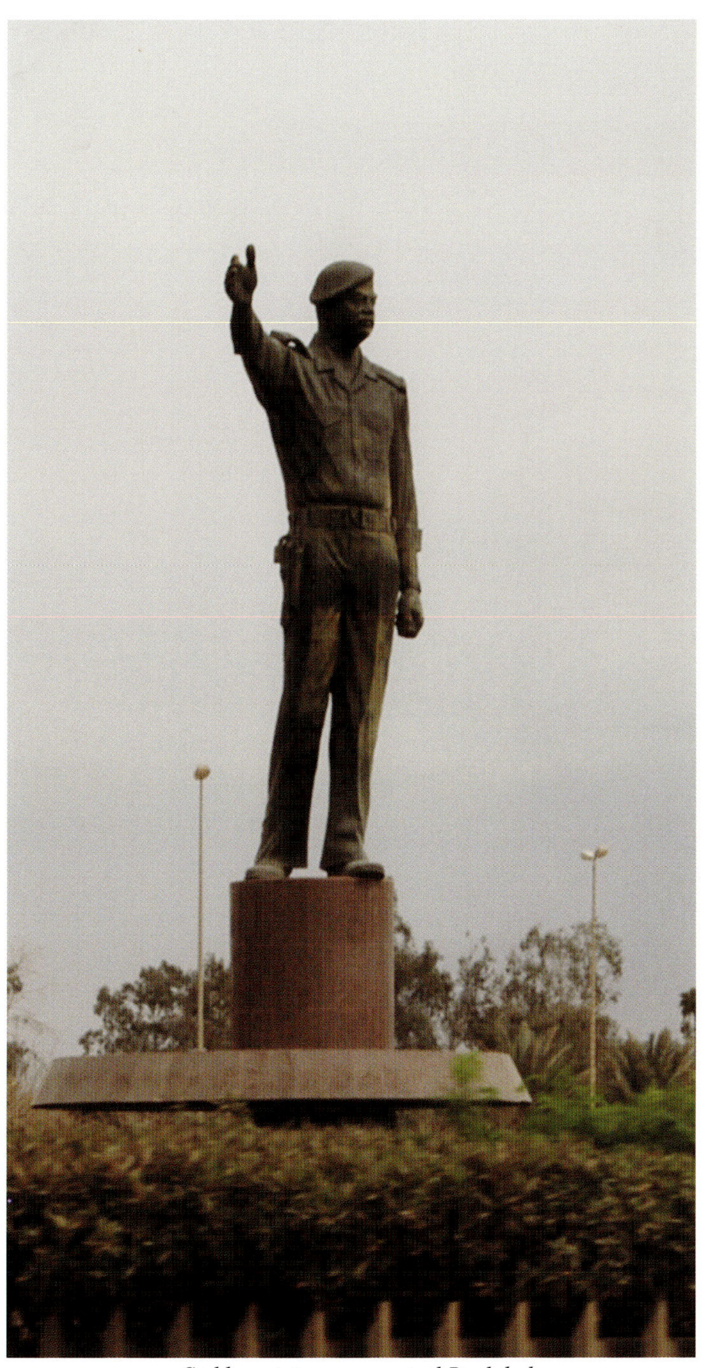

Saddam statue near central Baghdad

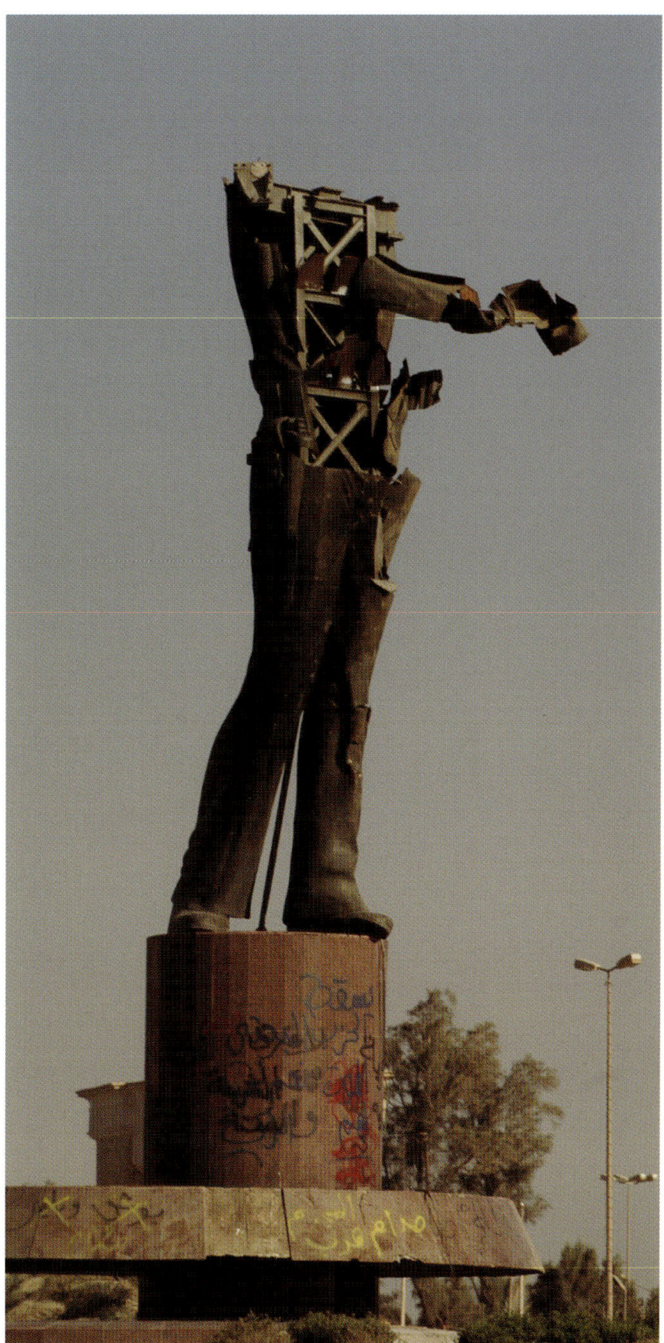

A week later and his bronze shell is being stripped bare

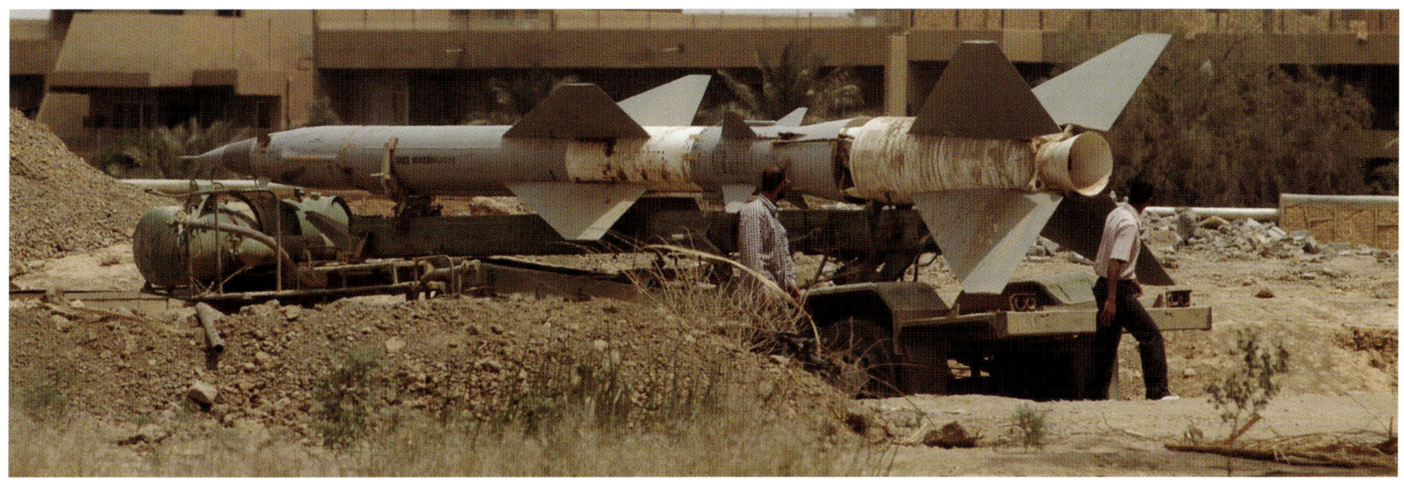

This ground-to-air missile lies in a vacant field in north Baghdad

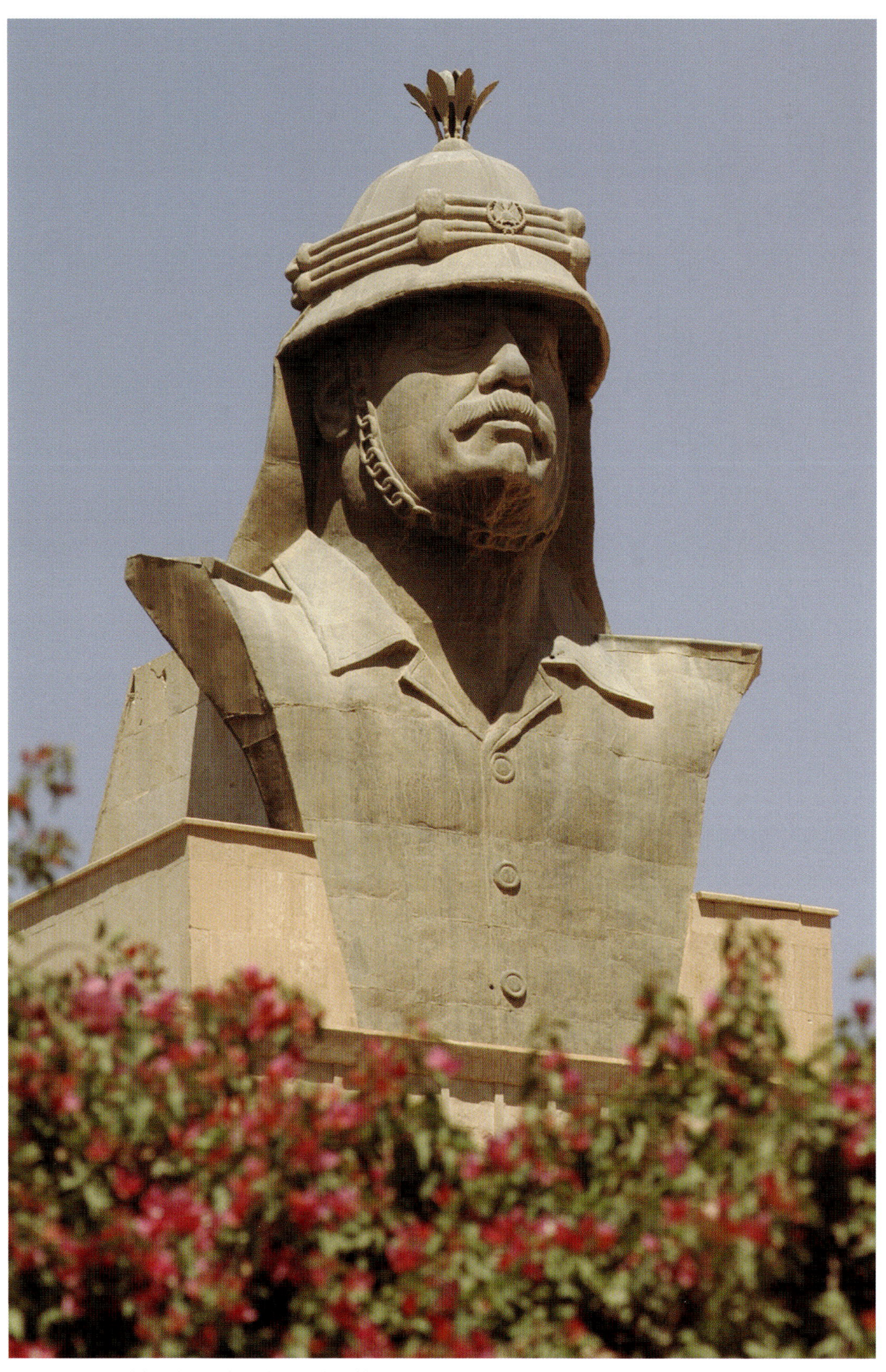

One of four huge metal busts of Saddam Hussein that overlook the Republican Guard Palace

After dinner, I sit outside the Fanar, watching the soldiers checking people as they pass through the barbwire security perimeter. The streetlights are on (at least within our block), and a group of hotel staff are eating their dinner on the front patio of the Fanar.

I feel as though I have been in Baghdad for over a hundred years! I can't wait to get my material completed and head out of this crumbling city. As I lie in bed, the wild dogs of Baghdad serenade me to sleep with their yelping and scuffling. For some reason I find that the dogs' howling sedates me, like a bedtime story. A crescendo of rifle fire echoes through the thick night air – home sweet home!

Day 30. Friday, May 9th

(Visit Saddam's palaces; the looting continues; looking for human remains; Saddam's Republican Guard Palace; barbwire and metal spikes; a Forbidden City; tacky architecture; stone busts of Saddam; jogging soldiers with guns on their backs; Special Forces; "No more pictures"; "What is this – Disneyland?"; touring Al Adamia Palace; Jennifer forgets credentials; a sad sight to witness; hit by Smart Bombs; like wildflowers in a landfill site; a masterpiece of art; soldiers living in palace; bombs dropped to destroy Saddam – not the palace; American patrol boats on the Tigris; heat exhaustion; panoramas from the Palestine roof; picking pink flowers; abandoned trench network; equipment used in gas attacks; well-dressed children; AK-47 in a garbage bag and a pistol in his pants; looming danger; carjacking phenomenon sweeps city; black market for stolen cars; meeting Stephan of 'Animal Care'; a lion of Baghdad gives birth; journalist shot in hand; increased tension from the soldiers; from bad to worse; looters threaten to steal generator; Stephan witnesses a carjacking; guns in the driver's face; hordes of beggars and homeless; Dr. Rafal Badri of the Americares Humanitarian Agency; relief flight of medical aid; a credible NGO agency; "They need medical supplies – rather than doctors"; Peter Tomarczyck inspires me; difficult to find a job; pray I have no nightmares)

It is another sweltering hot morning in Baghdad and I sit having a coffee with Jennifer. We are discussing plans to visit one or more of Saddam's luxurious palaces. These will be very important photos for the diary.

Hiring a taxi, we drive west across the Tigris, heading for Saddam's Republican Guard Palace, also known as Al Salaam Palace, his main palace in Baghdad. Situated directly across the Tigris River from the Al Fanar Towers, it is a massive complex of buildings and palaces from where Saddam ran Iraq.

As we drive through the debris-cluttered streets of Baghdad, the looting is still going on in broad daylight. Looters wheel office tables and chairs from smoldering buildings. Derelict cars and trucks are being stripped to the frame. Nothing has changed, except the city looks uglier.

At a main intersection near the palace grounds, I see four blue-uniformed men wearing white latex gloves and face-masks. They are searching the bombed wreckage of a building for human remains. This is very close to the palace and I wonder if a stray bomb hit the building. It looks like it was once a small apartment building.

We reach the main gate to the Republican Palace compound where we talk with one of the soldiers at the checkpoint. He tells us to drive ahead until we reach a second palace gate, a few minutes further ahead. Driving through the grounds, the compound unfolds as a massive complex of palaces, residences, gardens and outbuildings, all encircled by a high yellow brick wall topped off with barbed wire and sharp metal spikes.

It is like a beautiful, quiet little city inside the city, a Forbidden City! Most of Saddam's closest advisors and family lived here. The main palace is sprawling and spectacularly decorated with fine stonework. The overall design is kitschy and cartoon-like, at least for my taste in architecture. It is a sand colored castle of the finest masonry and linear design. What destroys the beauty of it are the four corners of the palace, each topped by an imposing stone tower, and crowned with a massive bronze bust of Saddam, The Mother of All Narcissists. What an egomaniac! The heads loom above the palace grounds like permanently tethered hot air balloons, and are visible from a great distance across Baghdad. An attractive wrought-iron fence encloses the modest garden, filled with roses and pink flowering rhododendrons.

I see four jogging soldiers dressed in white T shirts, dark shorts, running shoes, and a rifle slung over their backs. Soldiering involves common sense and a respect for your fellow soldier. A real soldier would not jog in front of an army of men, or women, looking like a piece of cheesecake! The Brits are good people, and have their own way of conducting themselves. But I just tell it like I see it, good or bad.

This complex is where, on my arrival in Baghdad on April 12th, the firefight on the waterfront began. (I photographed it from the other side of the river, next to the Fanar).

We ask the soldiers guarding the front of the palace if we can get permission to visit inside the castle. One soldier radios headquarters and they tell him to send us to a side entrance, where we are to meet with an army media person named John. Just as we are starting to walk to the side entrance, a Humvee pulls up and a soldier jumps out telling us not to take any pictures on the complex grounds. They look like Special Forces or CIA (luckily, I had taken most of the photos I needed before they showed up). I just smile at him and respond, "Sure thing."

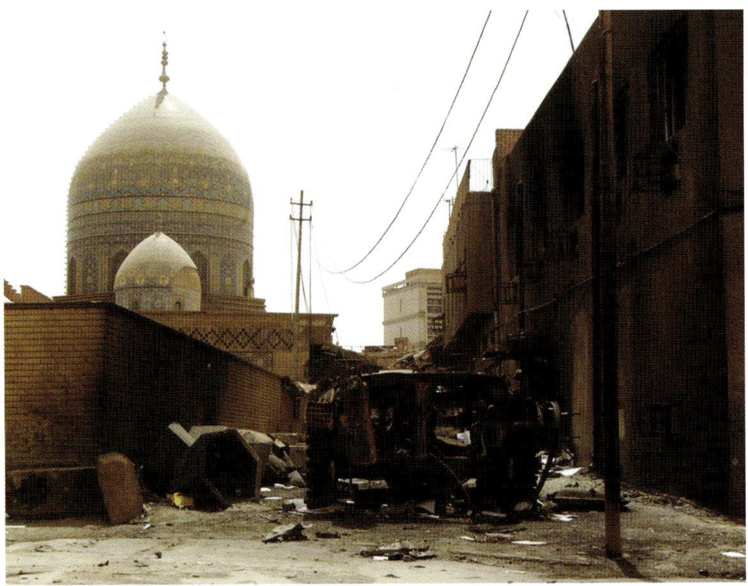

Driving through Baghdad to the Republican Palace

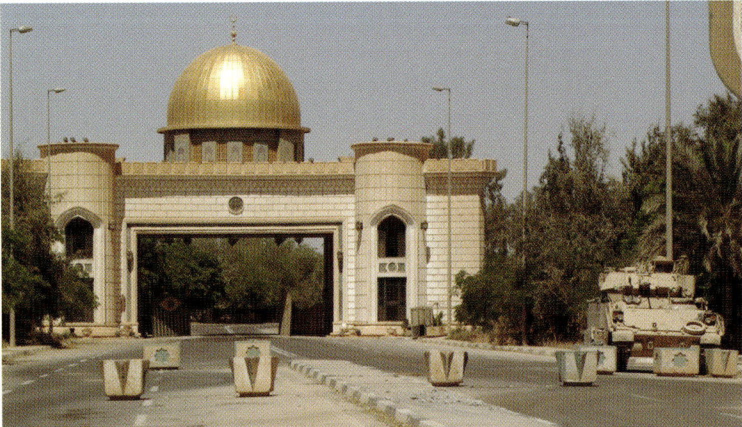

The north entrance to Saddam's Republican Palace

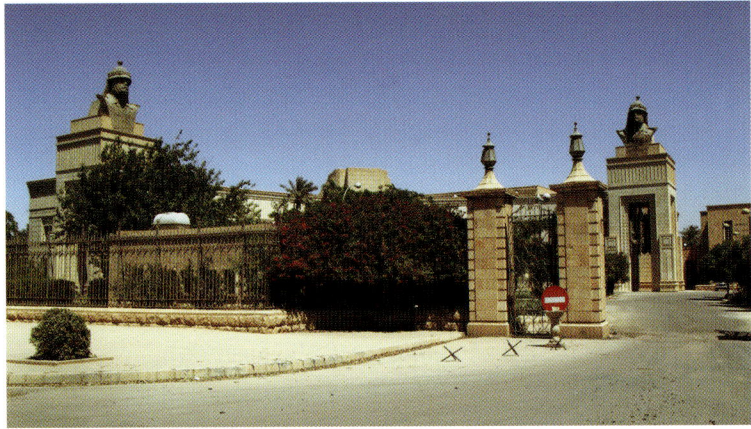

Saddam's own personal retreat inside the sprawling palace complex

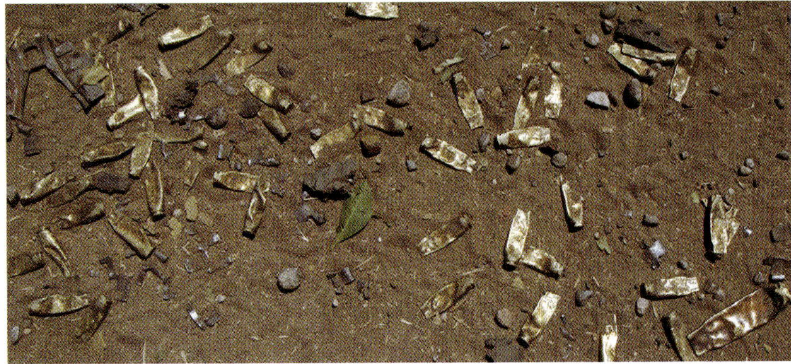

Spent bullet cartridges lie scattered about the grounds of the palace

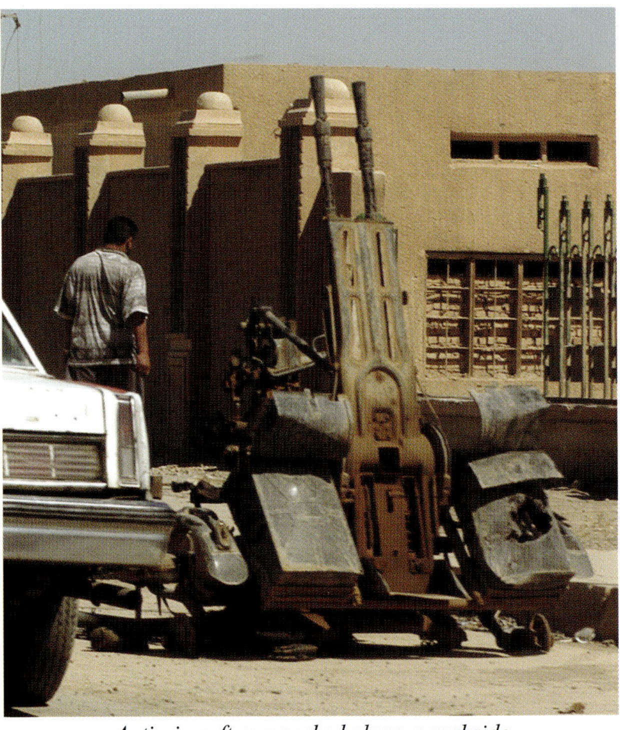

Anti-aircraft gun parked along a curbside

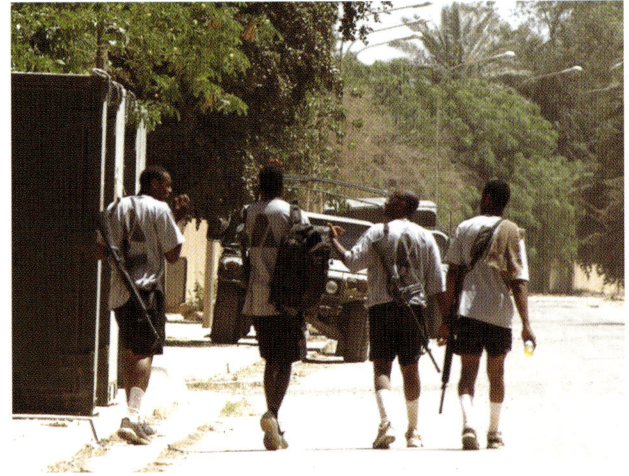

These soldiers just finished jogging

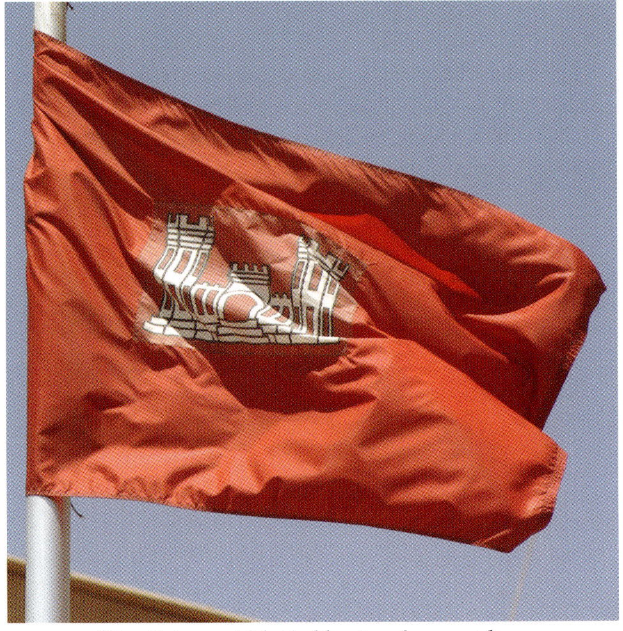

Flag flying outside Saddam's palace residence

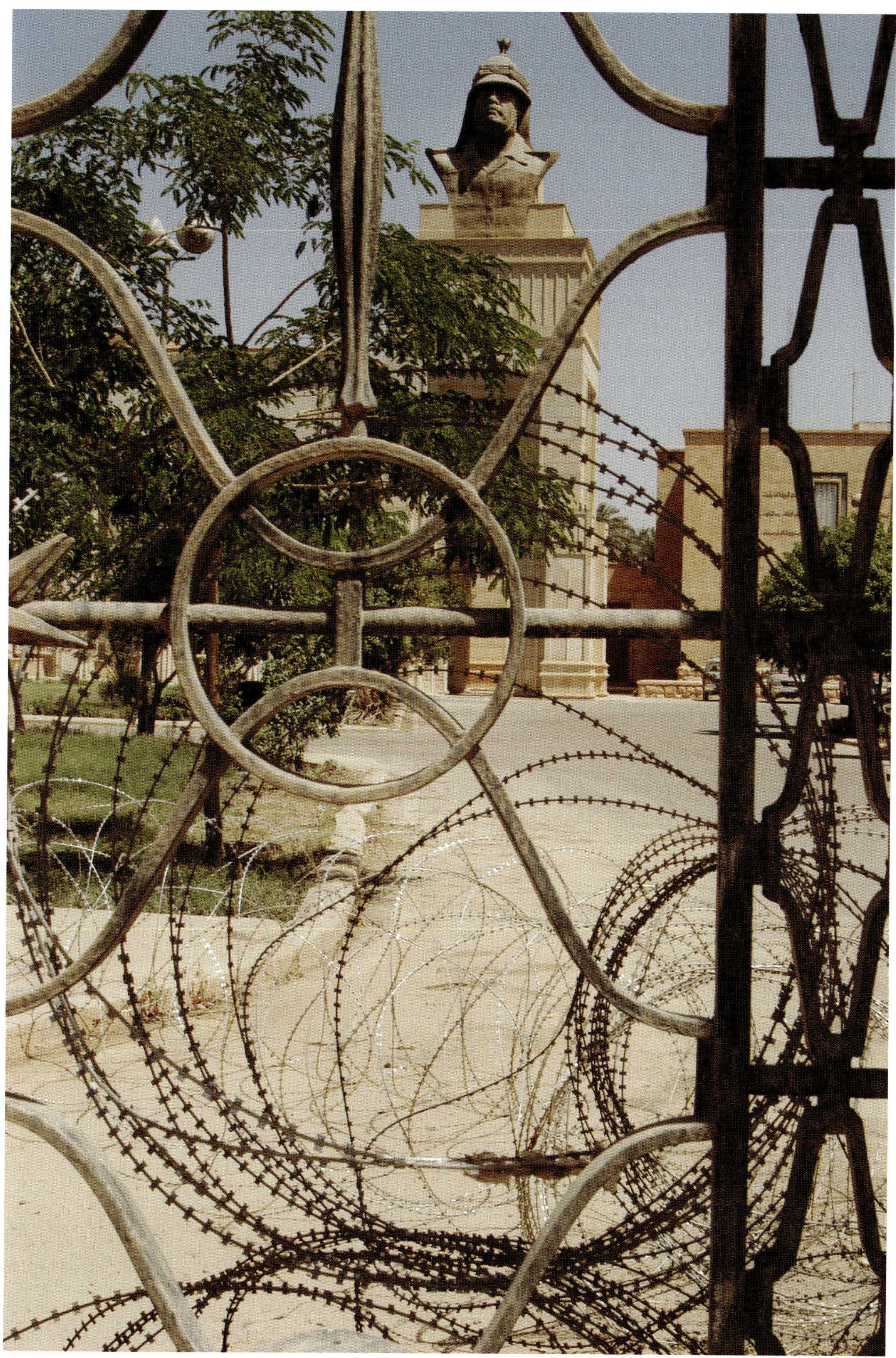

Looking through the iron fence that surrounds Saddam's personal residence inside the immense palace compound

We meet John the media officer outside the palace side entrance. He tells us that the palace is off-limits to the media at the moment, but if we come back in a couple of days there will be organized tours for the media.

I speak under my breath saying, "What is this, Disneyland – do we have to buy a ticket?" We tell him thanks a lot. There is no point in pushing the issue so we leave the oasis-like serenity of the royal palace grounds and its new inhabitants, and drive back onto the deceitful streets of Baghdad.

Had we been with a large news affiliation especially television, we would have been guaranteed the royal tour, but command does not care about small fry like us freelance journalists (the main news organizations had already visited the palace). This is another good example of media favoritism in the military and the same crap I experienced with the Brits at Saddam's Basra palace.

Perhaps the coalition forces did not want any more embarrassing photos in the newspapers, showing soldiers and generals lounging around in palaces decorated with gold leaf ceilings and lead-crystal chandeliers. I don't give a damn where or how they live, I just wanted to be treated fairly and get the pics I need.

We drive east, back across the river to another of Saddam's palaces, the Al Adamia Palace. It is located about fifteen minutes north of the Fanar, along the east bank of the Tigris (Simon and I were refused access to this place a couple of weeks ago). Jennifer and I walk over to the sentry post and ask a soldier to radio his superior for us, for permission to enter the palace and take some photos.

I get the green light (thanks to my CFLCC pass), but Jennifer doesn't even have a press pass! She has forgotten to bring any documents showing that she works for a newspaper. (I remember reminding her this morning, while getting ready at the Fanar, to make sure she has these documents with her whenever leaving the hotel). Right now, I am prepared to abandon her outside and go into the palace solo; I need the shots and don't have the patience to baby-sit at this time. The soldier reconsiders, and allows her to enter with me (for which he might have been reprimanded had his superior found out).

He leads us onto the palace grounds, located behind a 12-foot high brick wall that surrounds the complex. Inside, date trees shade and cool a network of garden pathways and rose gardens from the sun. It is a much smaller complex than the Republican Palace, but not lacking in its opulence.

The palace's architectural style is similar to the other palaces I have seen; very fine stonework and beautifully outlined facades. The same stonemasons must have been hired to construct all of these palaces, or so it would seem. Viewed from the street, the complex appears untouched by war. Inside the walled complex, only a broken safe lying by the front doors of the palace main doors indicates that something is amiss here.

Stepping in through the grand, shell-inlaid wooden doors leading into the palace interior, my eyes behold a sight of complete and total destruction. The entire interior of the palace looks like a hurricane hit it, and sucked everything inside out, leaving behind an interior of bare cement support

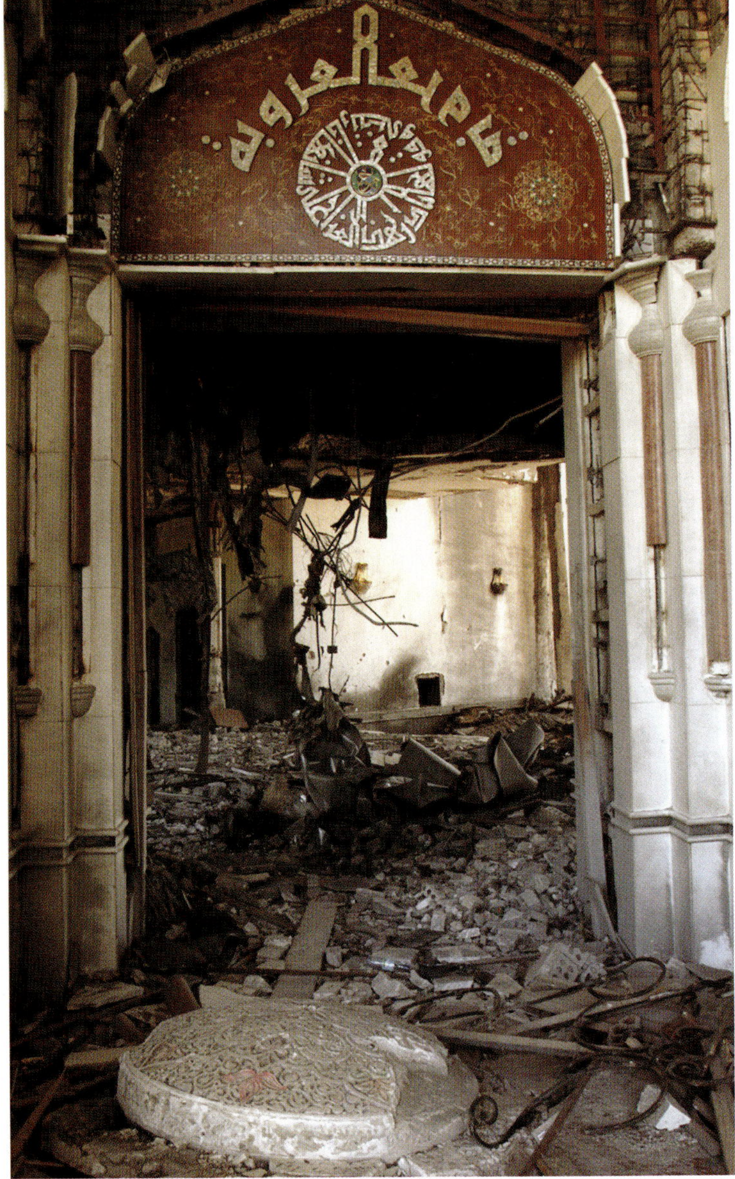

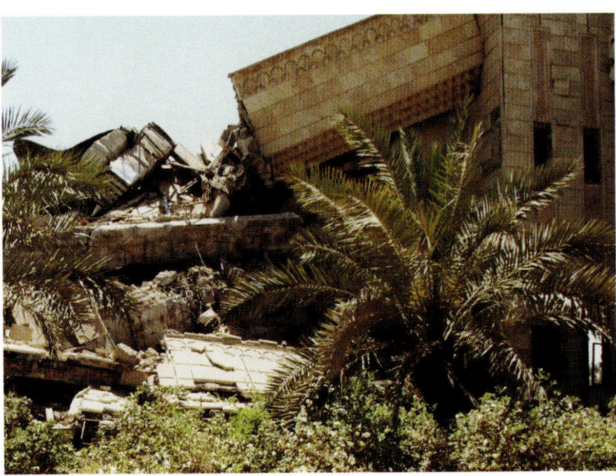

The front of the palace shows some damage

Main palace doorway gives a hint of the destruction that awaits inside

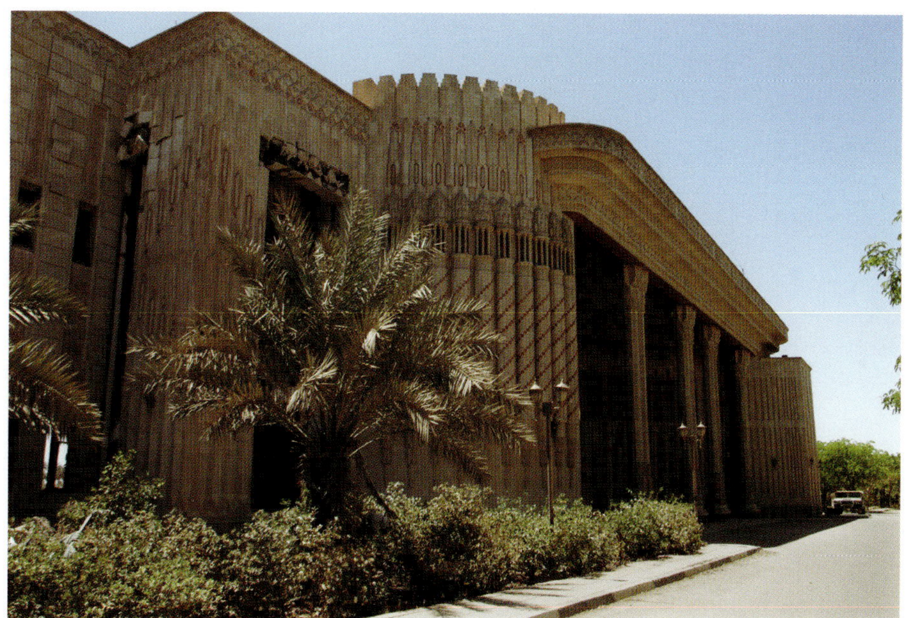

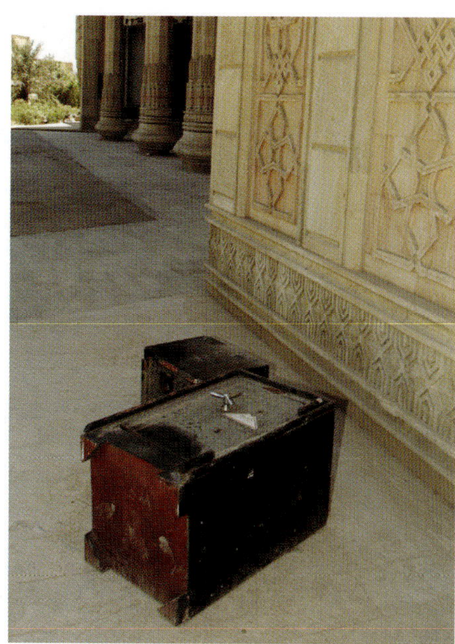

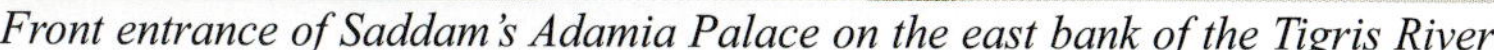

Front entrance of Saddam's Adamia Palace on the east bank of the Tigris River

A looted safe lies outside the palace doors

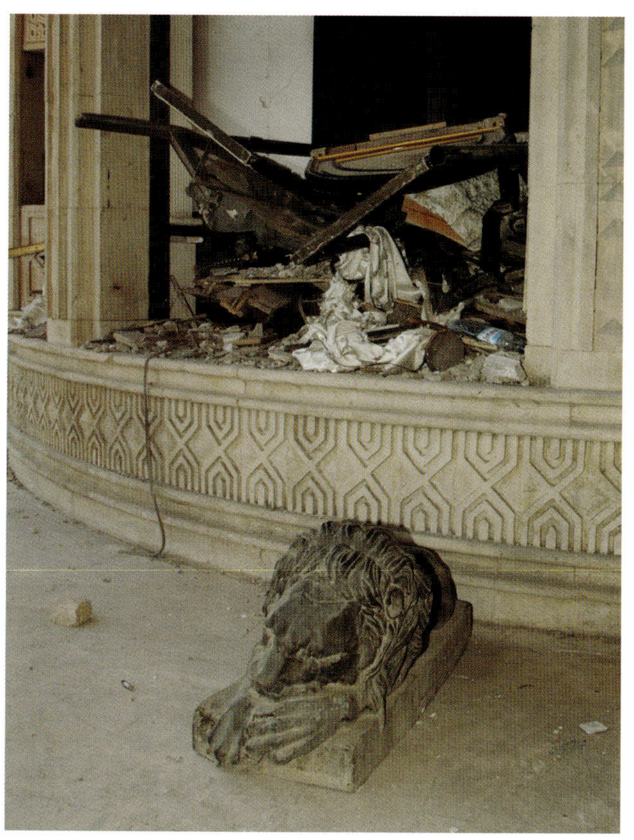

Sculpture of a sleeping lion guards the carnage

columns and stripped crumbling walls. However, it was not hit by a hurricane, but by a Smart Bomb. The facade is just a cracked sandstone eggshell, concealing the destruction inside.

But remnants of its former beauty still shine through the clutter and dust, like wildflowers in a landfill site. From the rubble of the marble floor, chunks of intricately carved woodwork, and shell-inlaid mosaics poke through the ruins. A glittering gold and crystal chandelier still dangles from a wire clinging to the edge of a gaping hole in the ceiling. Much of its gold trim and crystal teardrops lie scattered and glistening amongst the wreckage on the floor, like diamonds in the rough. Exquisitely etched brass wall trimmings, crumpled and bent, add a flash of formerly warm elegance amongst the wreckage of antique furniture and other broken treasures.

A spectacular winding staircase leads to the open blue sky of the bombed-out top floor. One of two such magnificent staircases, this one has hand-blown Italian glass railings and posts. They are broken into twisted metal and glass pretzels, still attached to their bases. Before the bombing, this palace would have been a masterpiece of ancient and modern Mid-Eastern art and architecture (everything the highest quality and craftsmanship). Just the shattered dregs of the palace dazzle me.

The two side wings of the main palace are not as heavily devastated, but looters have gotten in and broken or stolen all the antique French Renaissance furniture.

In another outbuilding, connected by an enclosed walkway, a dozen American soldiers have set up living quarters. They are here to guard the palace complex, while using it as a residence. It is a large windowed room similar to a tearoom, facing a beautiful expanse of lawn and gardens that lead down to the Tigris River. The soldiers' cots and equipment are spread along the walls of the room, some covered by a raised sheet of green mosquito mesh. Two soldiers sit writing letters, while a poker game goes on in the corner. A couple of others doze on large plush couches, and another hangs his laundry on a rope tied across the outside balcony. It is a little like the Beverly Hillbillies TV series, with the soldiers, who are used to sleeping on a bed of sand, moving into this lavish, multi-million-dollar palace. The soldiers are not too cheerful or friendly. I don't think they like house sitting, and appear slightly embarrassed by it.

It is outside by the riverside that the complex shows its true size and opulence. Beautifully decorated and pristine residences, separate from the palace, grace the immaculately gardened property. A crescent-shaped goldfish pond, the size of a small lake, shimmers in the middle of the complex.

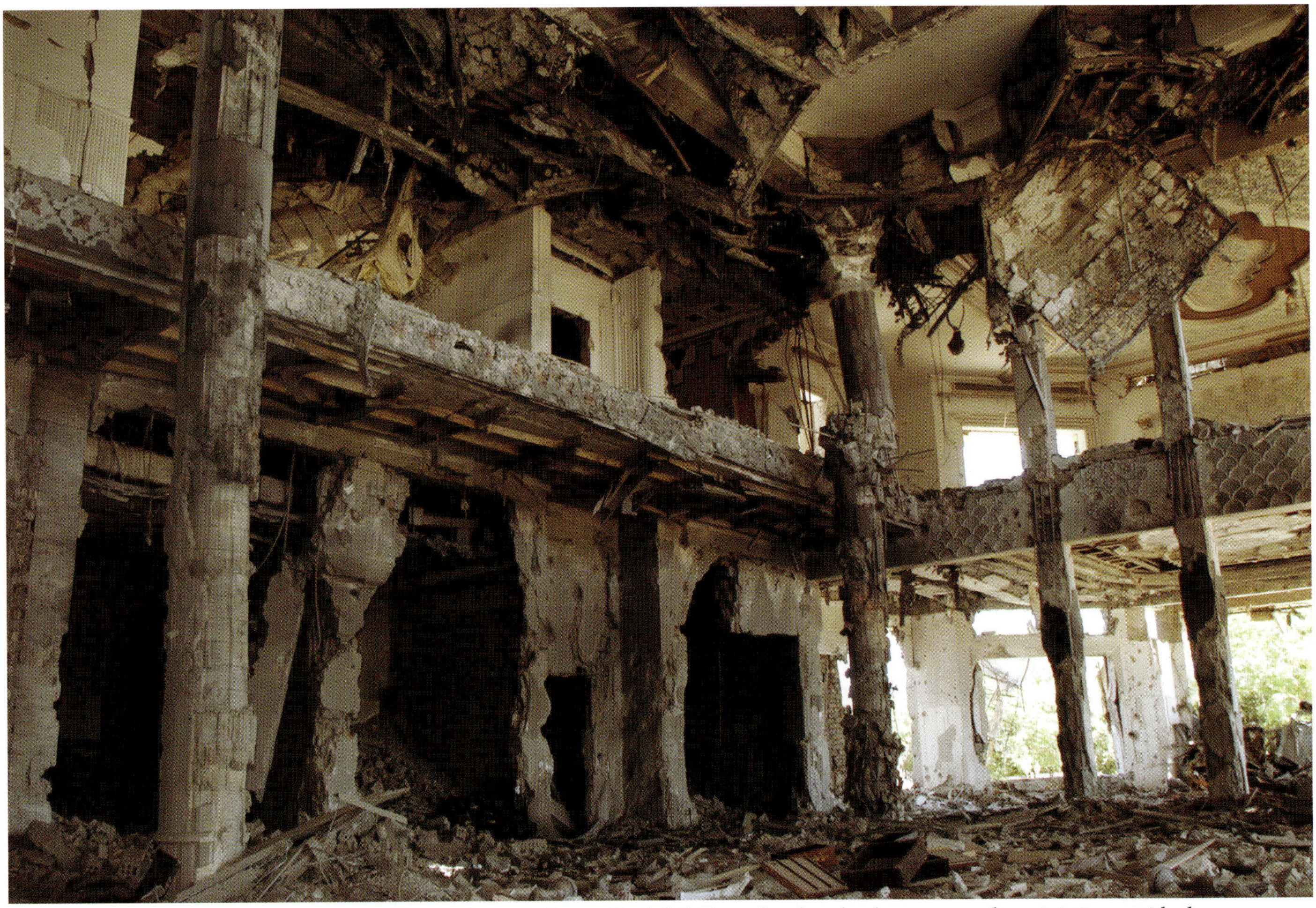

Destruction in the main foyer of Saddam's Adamia Palace in Baghdad. Smart bomb technology was used to minimize outside damage

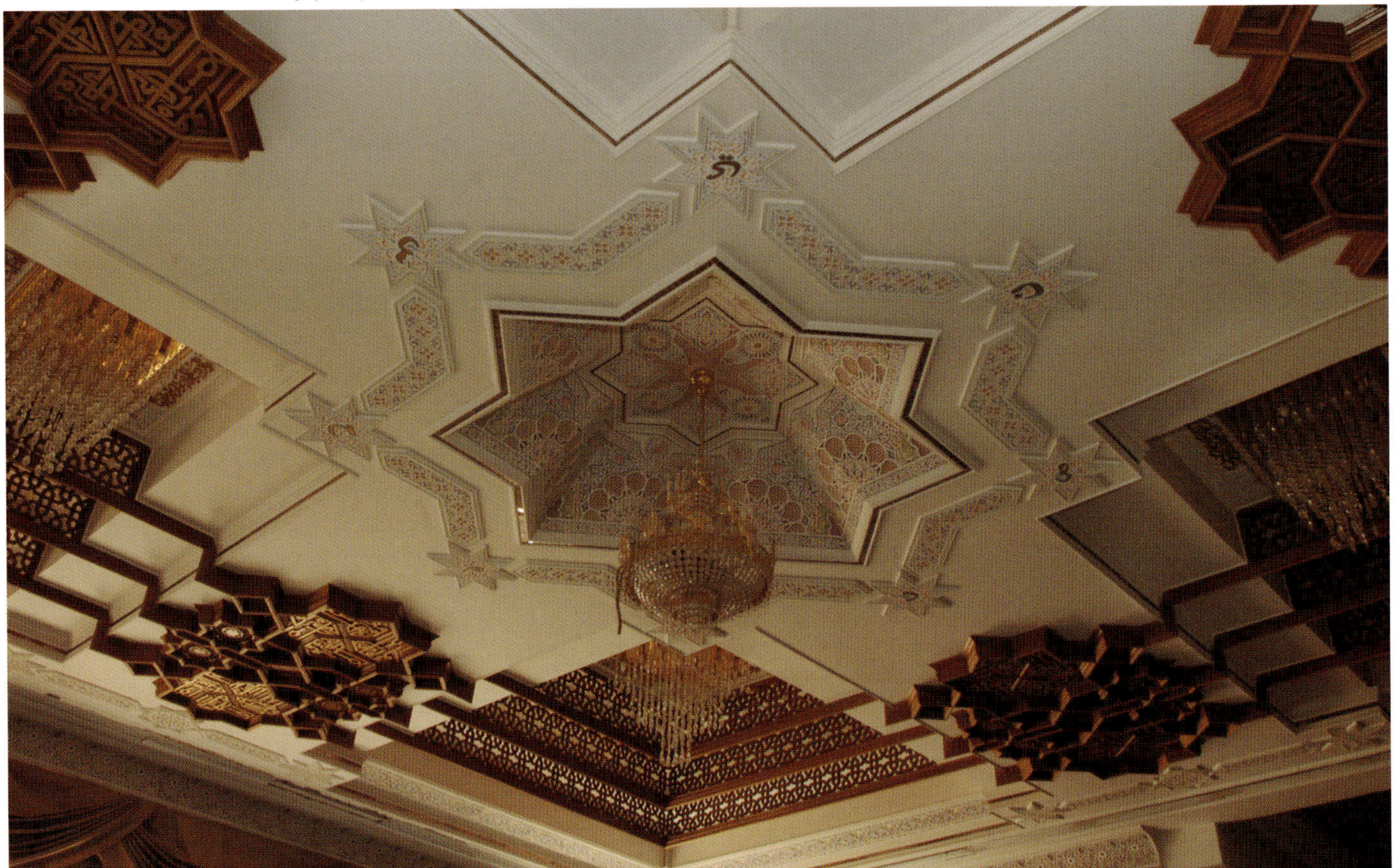

A small area of fine detailing and giltwork that escaped destruction from the bombing. The main palace is in danger of collapse

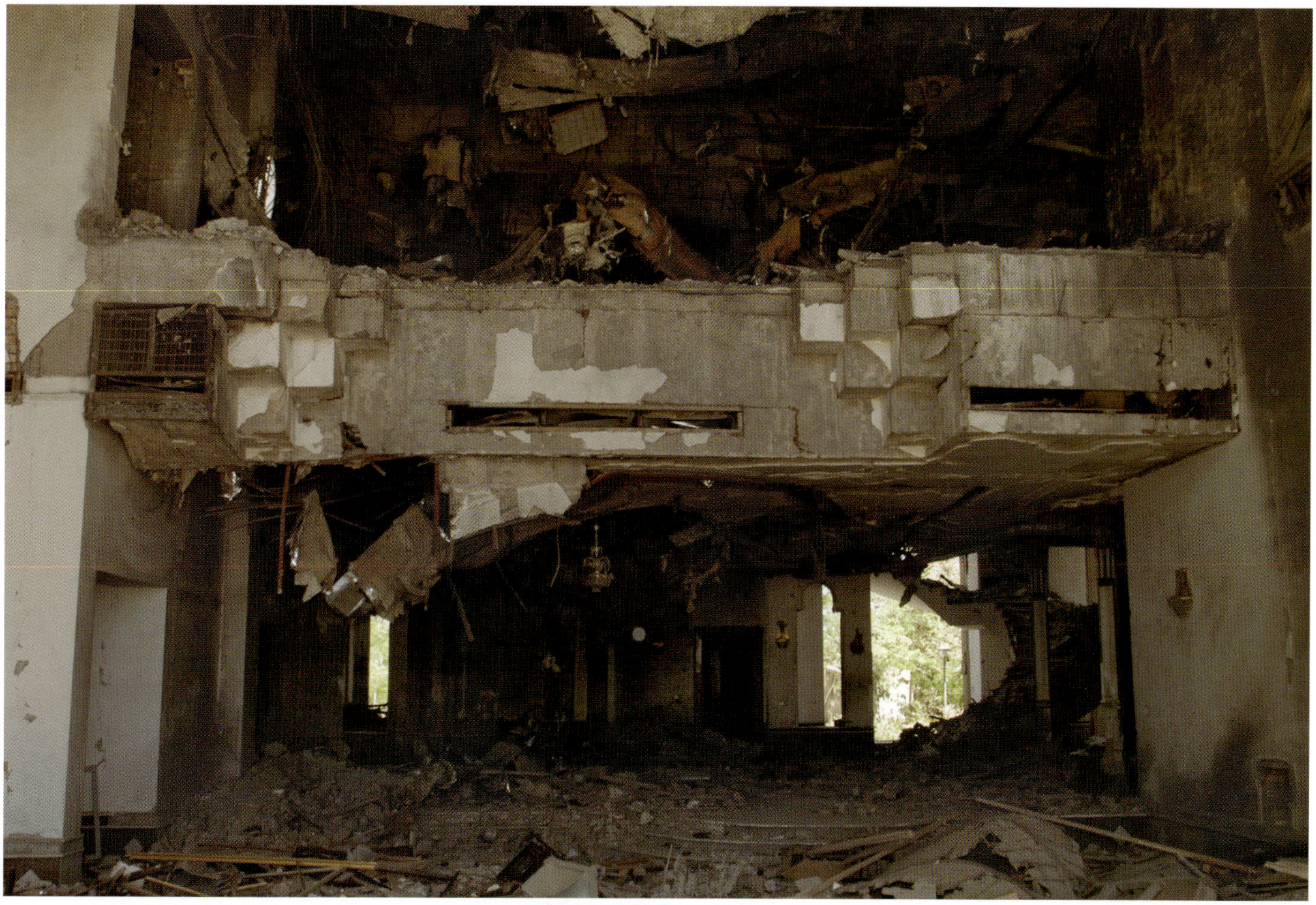

Interior of Adamia Palace

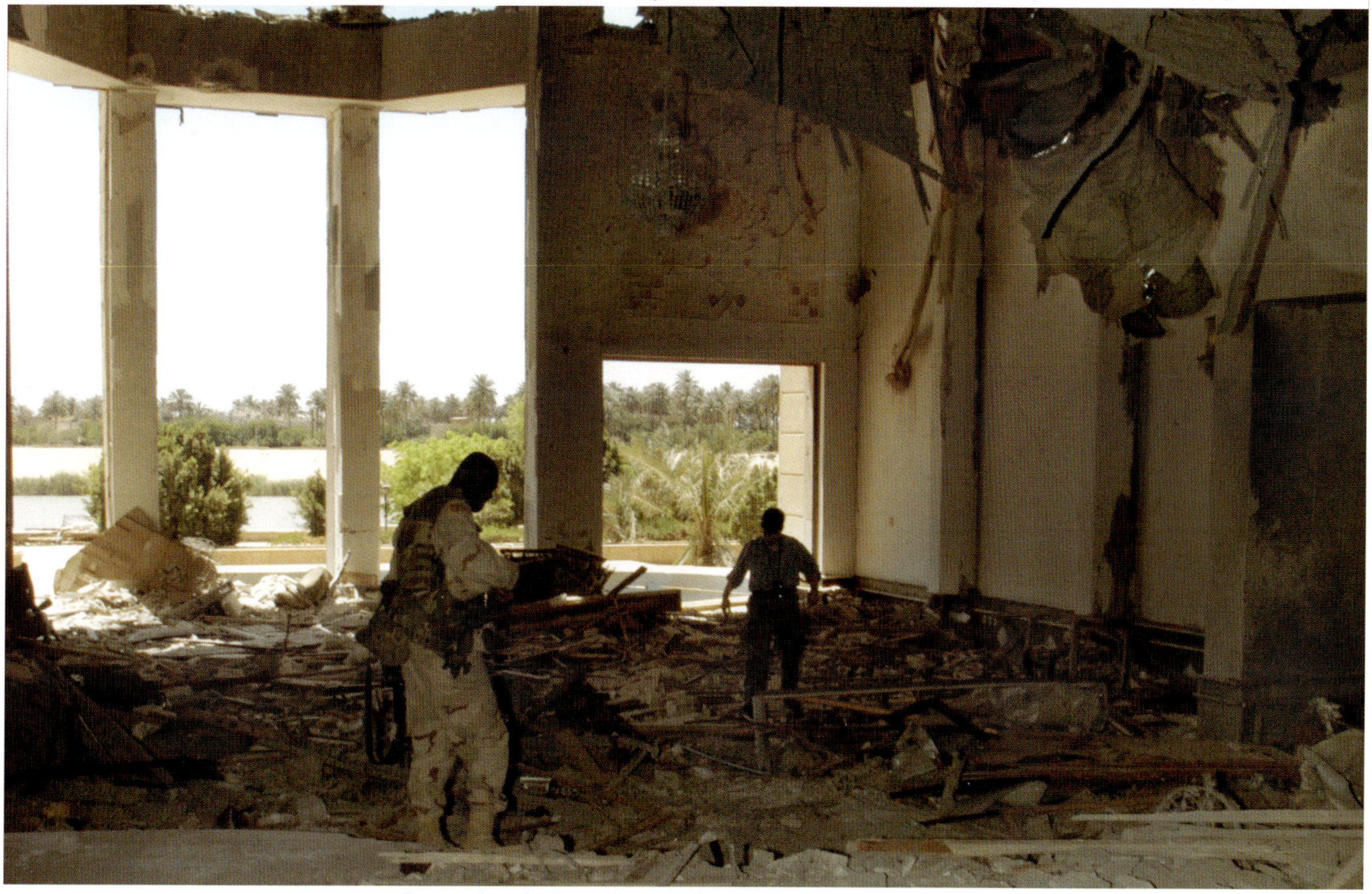

It is as though a tornado sucked out the interior of the palace

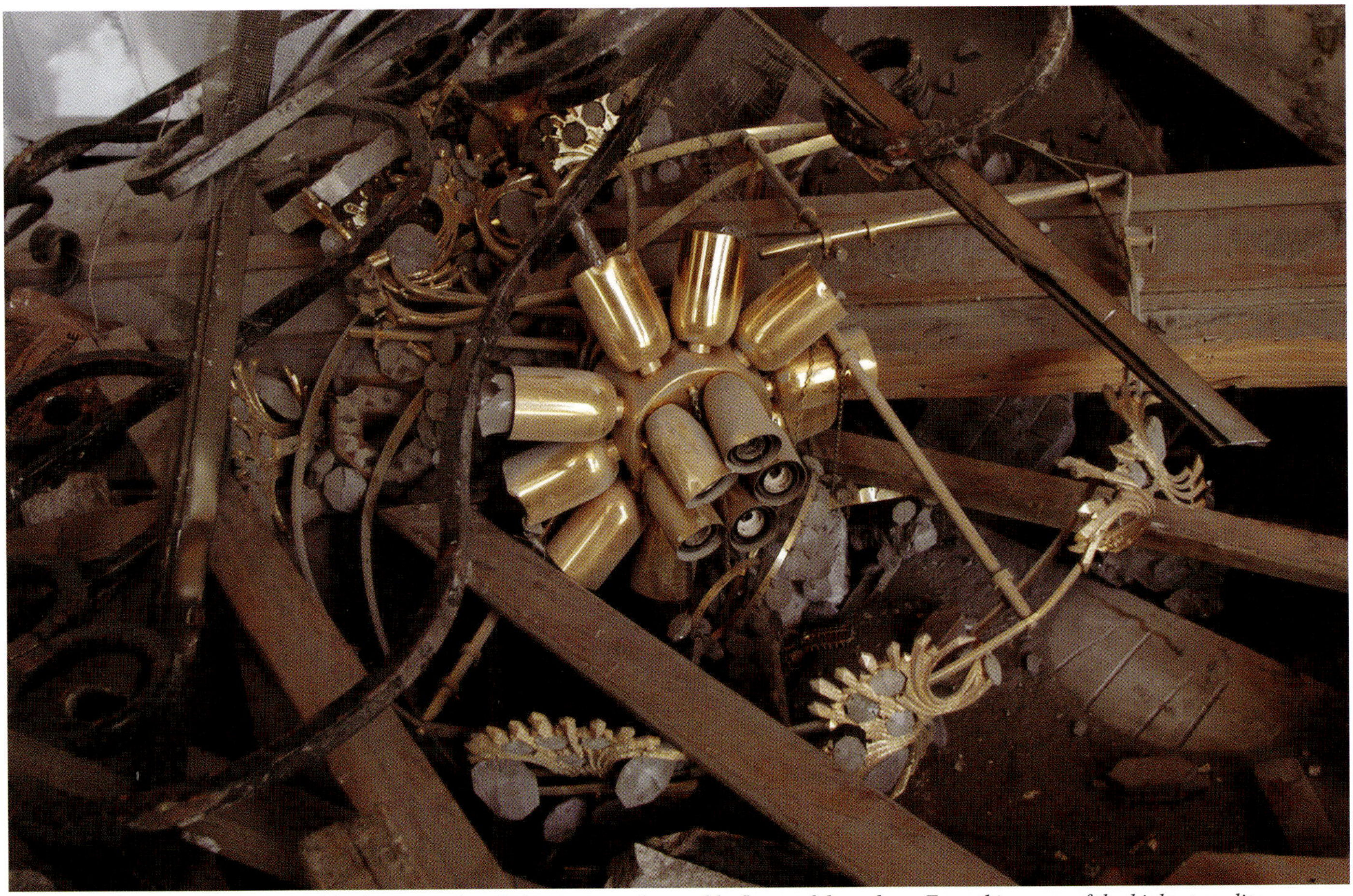

Rich woods, mosaics, gold gilt, ironwork and plaster cover the marble floors of the palace. Everything was of the highest quality

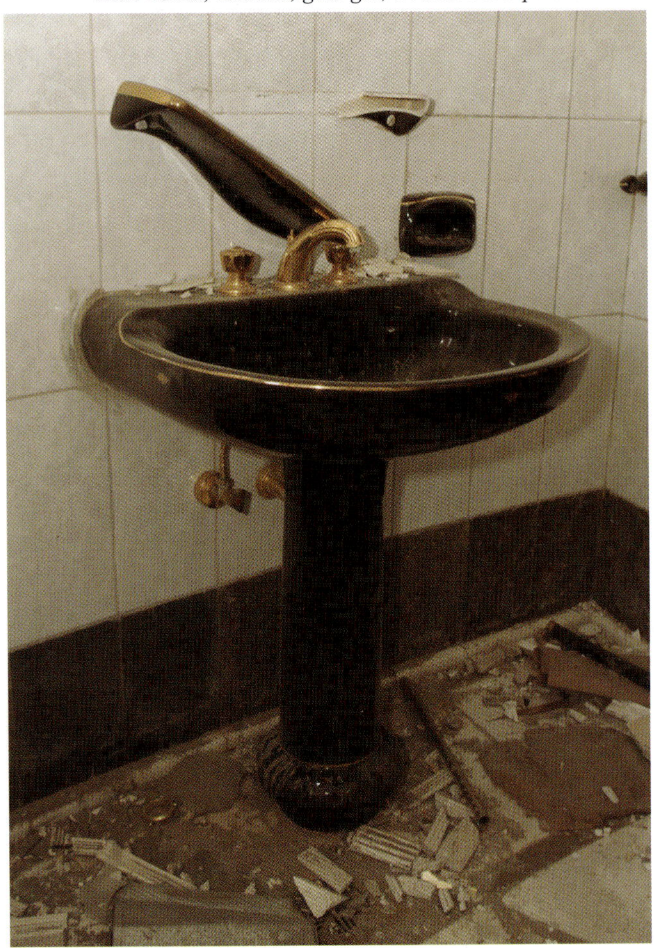

Gold shines throughout the palace, from sinks to chandeliers

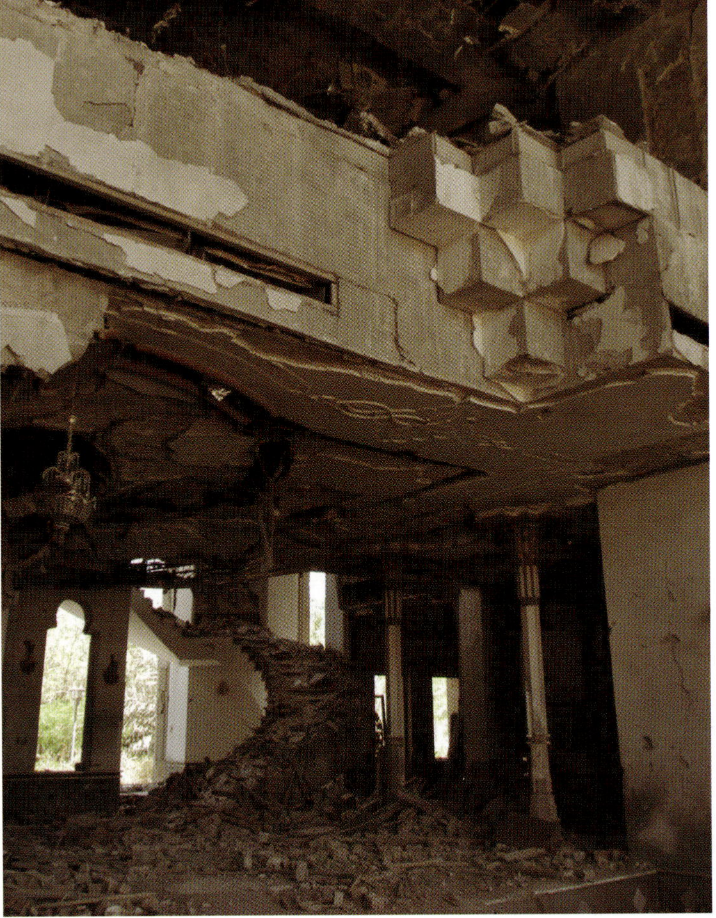

Saddam had sixty palaces throughout Iraq.

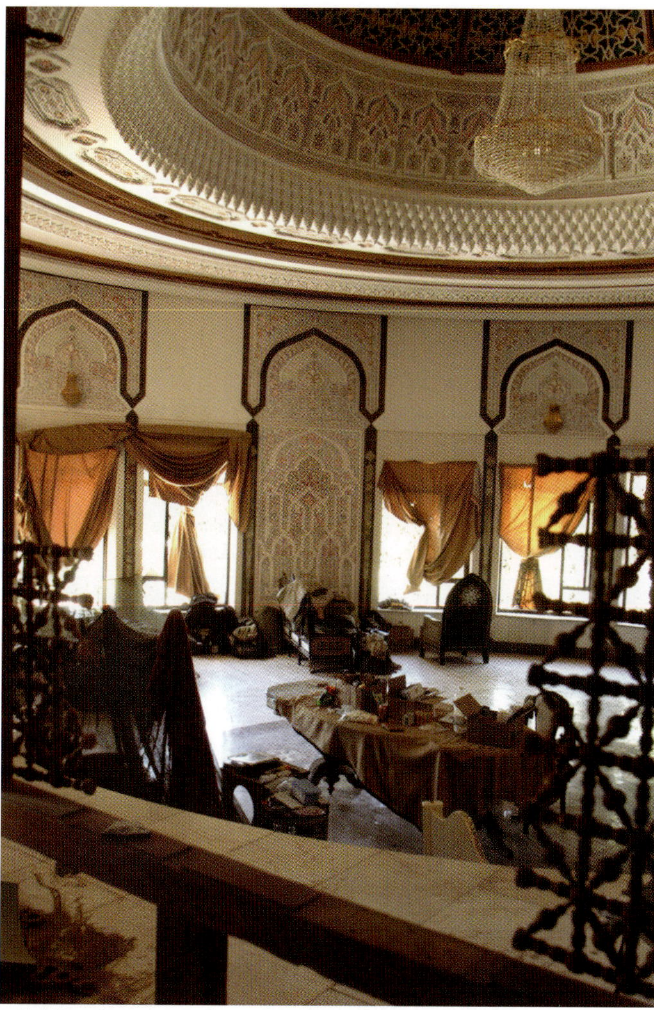

Soldiers have moved into the Adamia Palace and now reside there

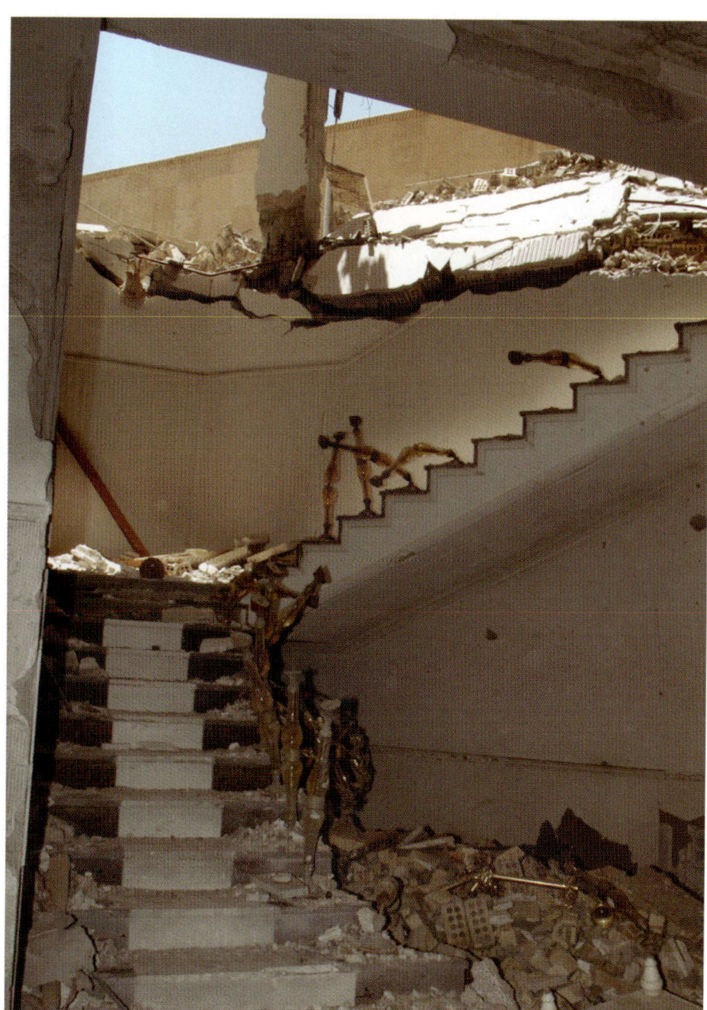

Glass railings line this staircase to nowhere

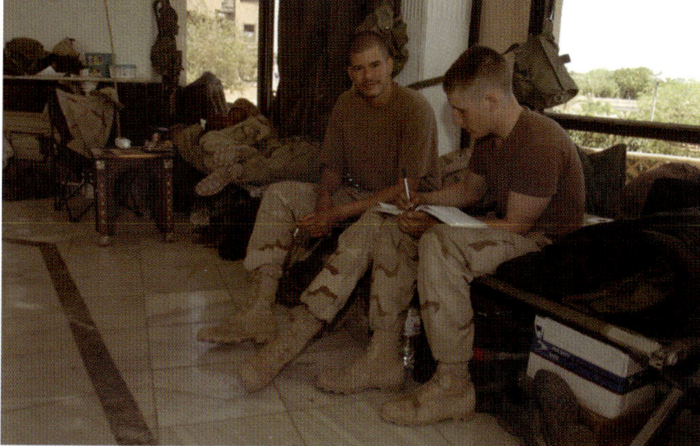

These soldiers know there's no place like home, palace or no palace

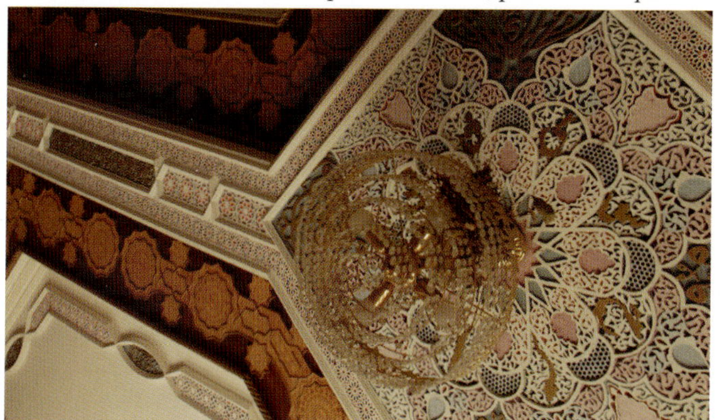

The immaculate details of a section of the palace ceiling

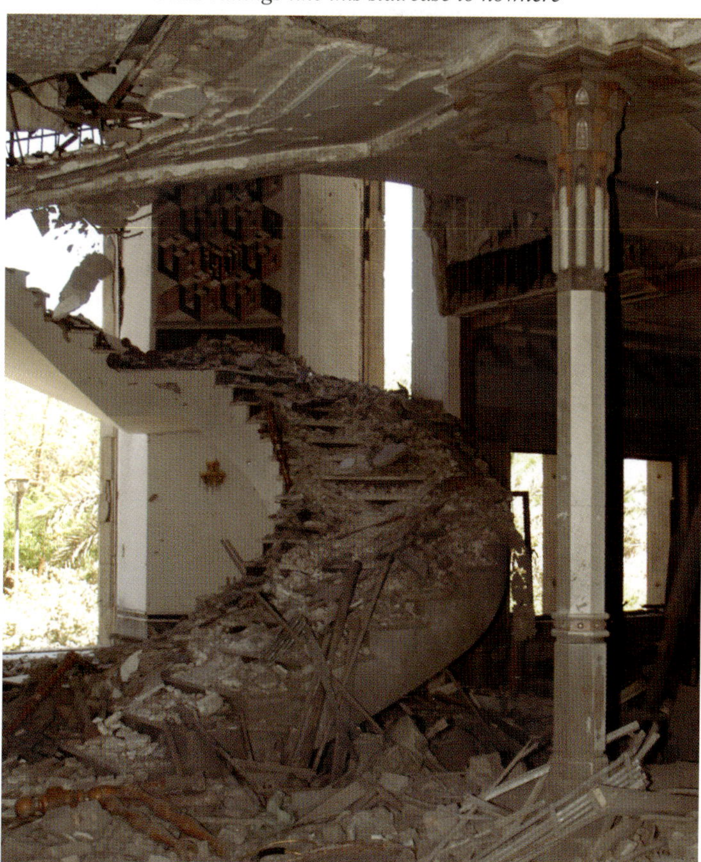

Saddam's palaces rival those of European royalty

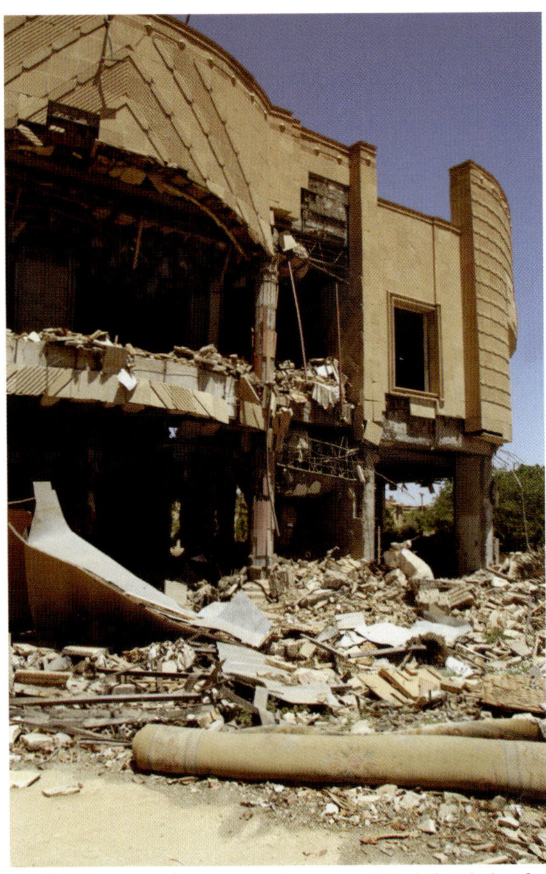

A looter started to remove large rug but left it behind

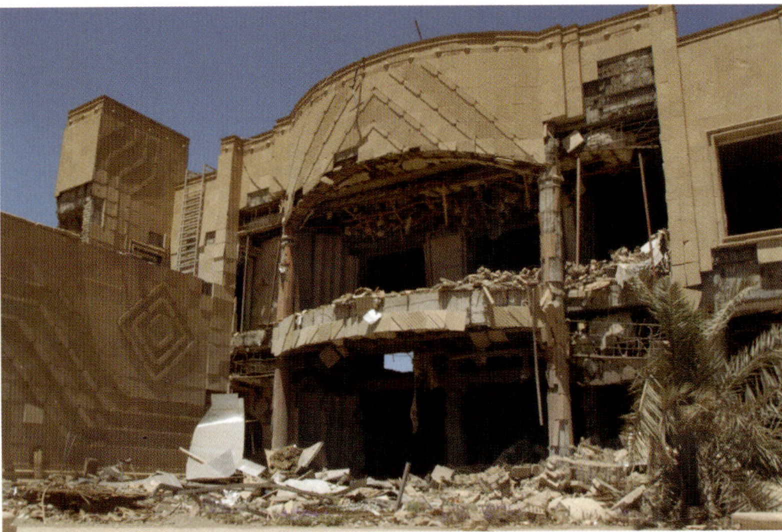

The west face of Al Adamia Palace showing damage

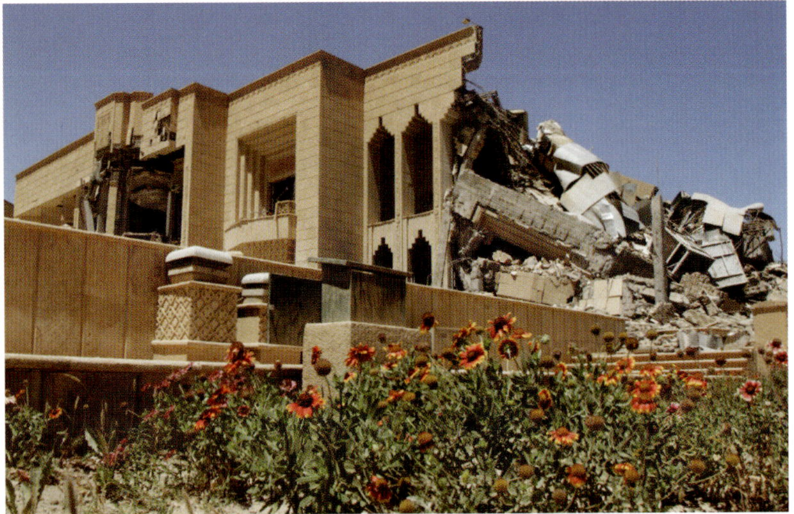

The palace is now just a fragile shell filled with debris

Looking at the palace from the riverside, it is half standing, half caved-in. All that remains is the fractured husk of a once grand building. All the other outbuildings are untouched by the bombing. (The smart bombs were dropped to destroy Saddam, not necessarily the palace).

Scanning the Tigris, I see four American patrol boats, about 30 feet long, motoring north along the Tigris. These are the first military boats I have seen in Iraq.

We thank the soldier for the tour, then Jennifer and I head back to the Fanar for chai and to re-group. An extra-productive shoot, I now have a large selection of interior and exterior shots of one of Saddam's destroyed palaces. I check it off on my list of things to do.

Jennifer is showing symptoms of heat exhaustion (energy draining fatigue, flush skin and headaches). I tell her to force herself to drink more water than she feels she needs. Since leaving this morning to cover the palaces, I have drunk at least two, and maybe even three litres of bottled water. I notice that her bottle has hardly been touched. I emphasize the importance of over-drinking, warning her that if she does not, she could be in for a bad case of debilitating heat exhaustion. But it may already be too late for her, as she appears to be suffering quite badly.

I decide to go over to the Palestine, and ask Jennifer if she wants to come along. I need some panoramic photos of the city, and the hotel rooftop makes the best vantage point. A hotel staff member leads us to the roof, where we take our panoramas of the city, sweeping out as far as the eye can see. These are also very important photos for me to have and I check these off my list.

After the Palestine visit, we walk back across the street to the Fanar for another chai break. We have to drink continuously as it is so devilishly hot. I go for a walk by myself to the riverfront and end up picking some beautiful rhododendrons for my new room.

A small group of well-dressed children (aged 6-9 years) follow me about, asking to have their pictures taken. I snap their photos then show them their digital image on the camera screen. They laugh and giggle at each photo. How I miss my own children!

These kids are well cared for, compared to the bedraggled street orphans. Their faces are clean, their hair combed, their clothes washed and orderly. I have seen these kids before; they live with their parents in one of the houses fronting the river, close to the Fanar. The father is a pleasant man, and obviously a good father. I have seen him and his wife keeping an eye on the kids from his doorstep. He always smiles at me when I walk past. It is so comforting to see a happy family in Baghdad. They are a satellite of sanity in this insane theatre of war.

Returning to the Fanar, I go upstairs and arrange the flowers in my room (which really bring the room to life), then head downstairs to the outside patio for a strong coffee. Sitting, having my coffee and a smoke, I see one of the hotel managers carrying a concealed AK-47, wrapped in a green garbage bag from his car to the hotel reception desk. He stashes the weapon in a room to the side of the reception.

Seeing this, I snap out of my siesta mood and start wondering if the hotel has been threatened with attack. Ten minutes later, I see that the same manager is now wearing a holstered pistol at his side! I wonder what he knows that I do not. My curiosity is sharply piqued, as these two observations suggest to me that the danger level has just reached a new high.

The atmosphere around the hotel is becoming tense and unpredictable, especially since the security perimeter has been changed and weakened. We are now very vulnerable to attack and the weapons in the hotel confirm this. I feel more alone and less secure without my team of friends to talk and strategize with. It is an eerie sort of a feeling, a feeling of increased vulnerability and looming danger. The air is becoming thick with uncertainty and paranoia.

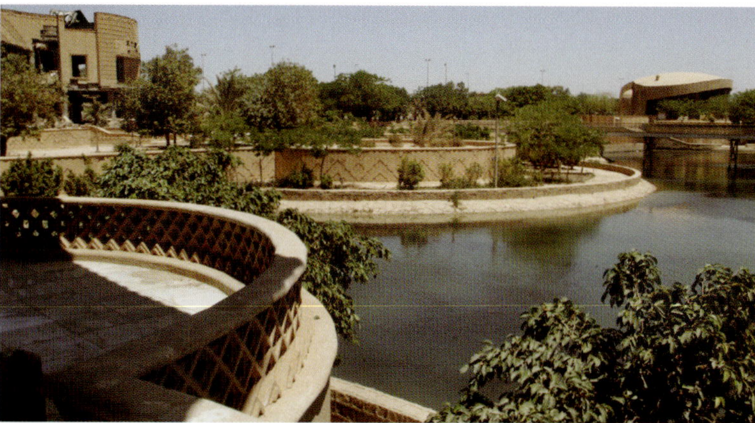
A huge outdoor goldfish pond, as large as a small lake, graces the west side

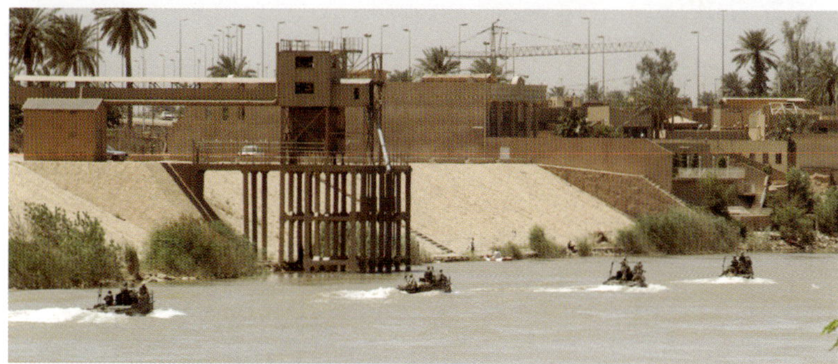
American patrol boats head north along the west bank of the Tigris

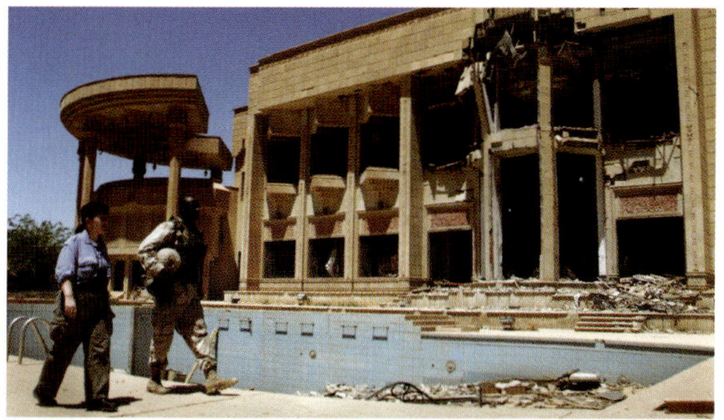
Large swimming pool on west side of palace

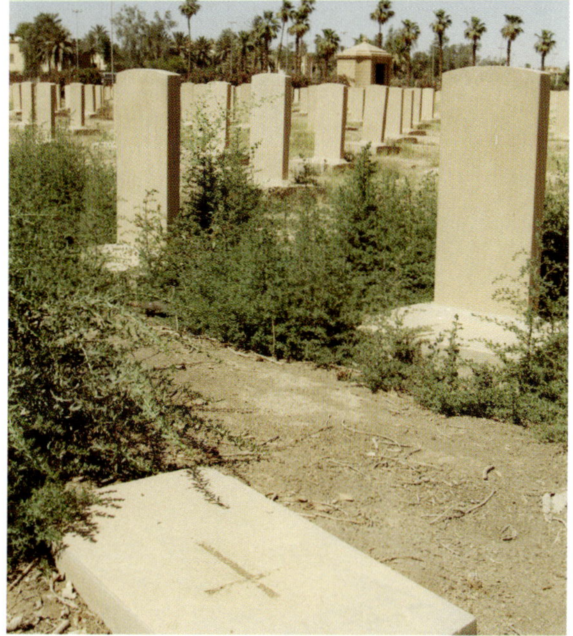
British Veterans' Cemetery. Victims of earlier wars

I ask around if the security level has been officially raised, or if there have been any recent attacks on the military or journalists that I might not have heard about. Tod tells me that carjacking is the brand new phenomenon sweeping the city, and he is aware of at least three of them over the last couple of days.

It would appear that the looters' strategy is changing from smash-and-dash, to gun-and-run, as the sources of easy plunder become exhausted. Carjacking can be a very lucrative business, if you have no conscience.

Tod says a black-market for stolen vehicles is in operation just 15 minutes north of the Fanar. Here you can buy a 2002 Toyota Land Cruiser, with 180 miles on the odometer for $8,000 dollars or less. New Peugeots, looted from Saddam's ministries, sell for half that. Other highly sought-after vehicles include BMW's, Mercedes Benz and Toyota pick-up trucks. You can order a vehicle, and someone will steal it for you. If you have the money, you can buy anything in this city.

I meet a man named Stephan, in the lobby of the hotel. He tells me he is with a non-profit animal welfare group, named Animal Care. Stephan is now in charge of the lions, tigers and bears at the all-but-destroyed Baghdad Zoo. His group has taken over zoo security from the Americans (whom I met on April 20th during my tour of the facilities). He tells me that one of the two lions gave birth to six lion cubs last week, all of which are doing fine. Animal Care has a budget set aside for the zoo, allowing them to hire four armed guards to protect the few remaining animals from the looters.

The animal rights advocate also tells me of a CNN journalist being shot in the hand during an attempted robbery of a convoy as it drove into Baghdad from Amman. Stephan agrees with me that the security situation is rapidly getting worse, along with a feeling of increased tension from the soldiers. The atmosphere has certainly changed in this once-magnificent city. Baghdad is a city in transition, from bad to terrible!

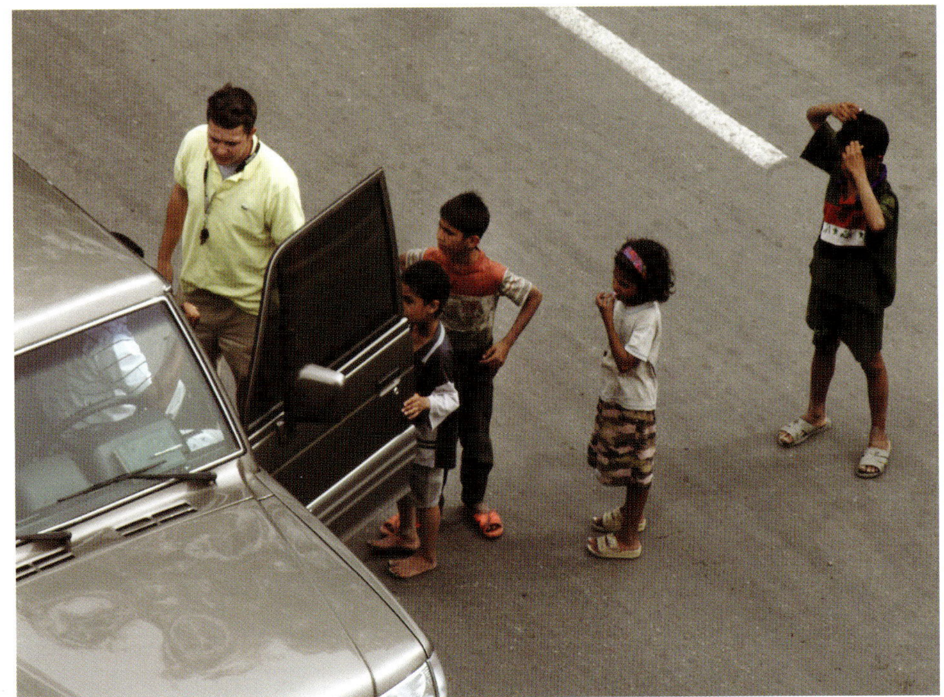

Street children beg for money from journalists outside the Fanar

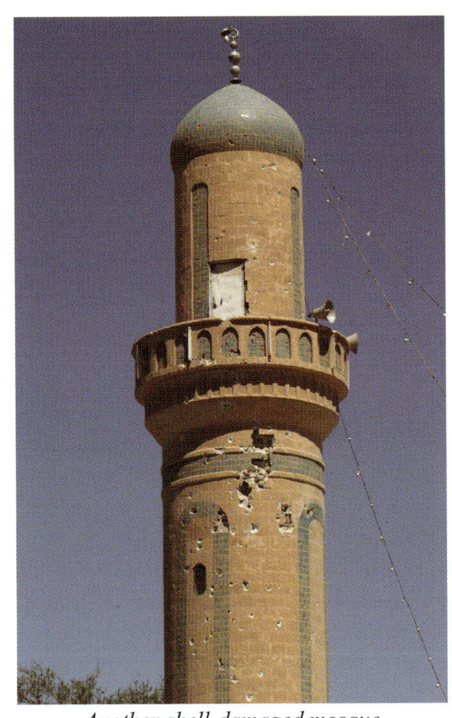

Another shell-damaged mosque

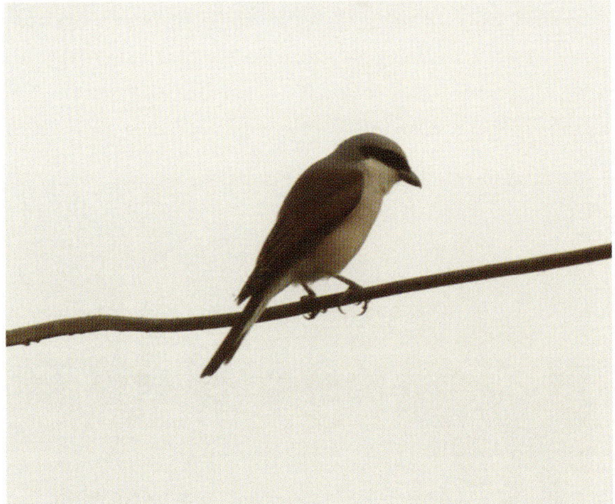

This shrike hunts insects along the Tigris shoreline

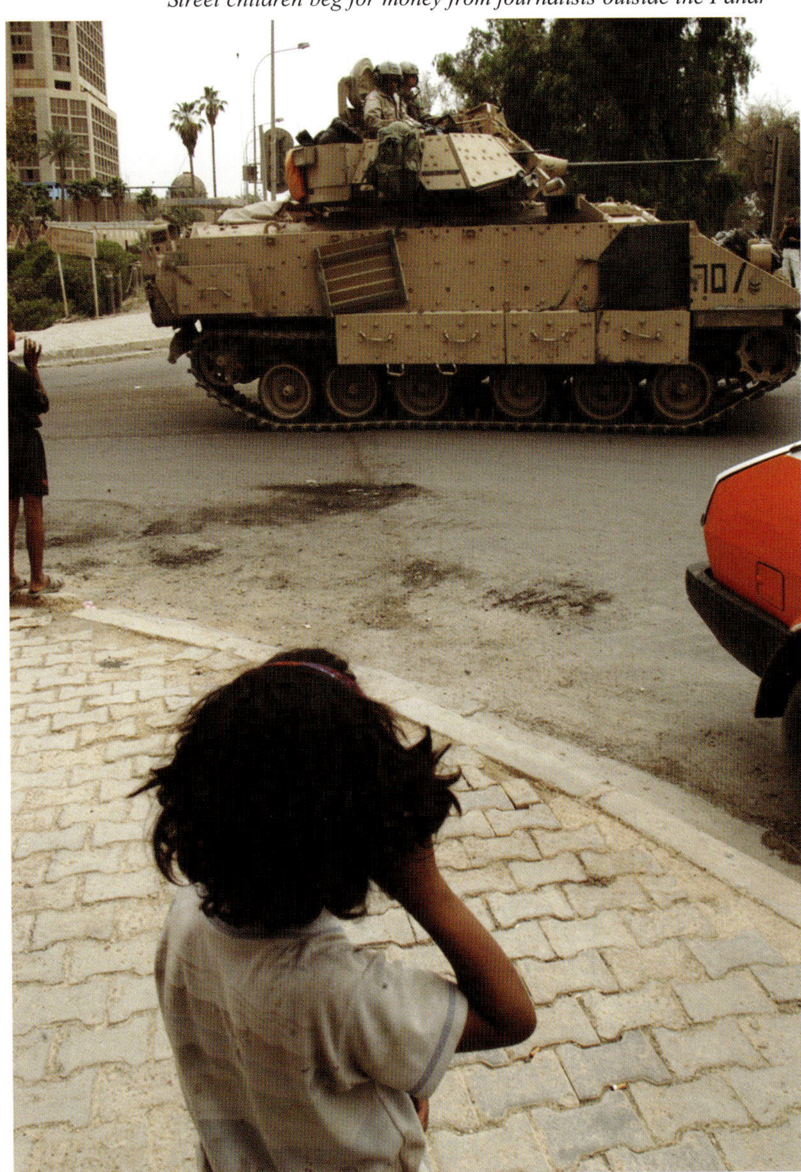

A young street girl pauses from begging long enough to watch a tank pass

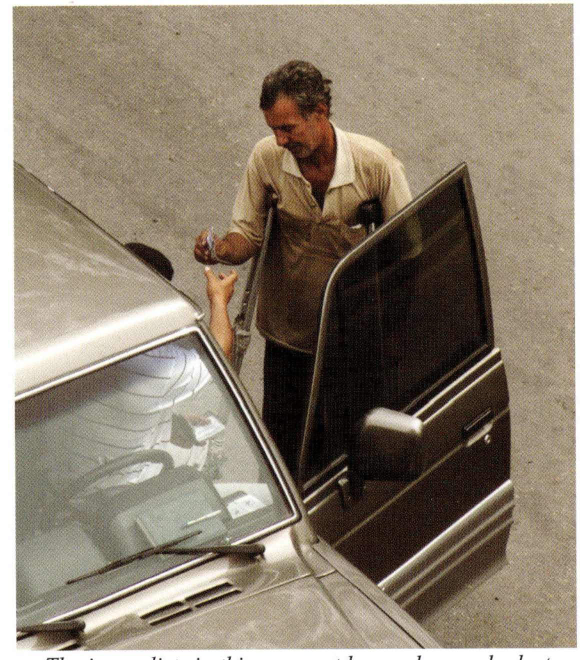

The journalists in this car must have a beggar budget

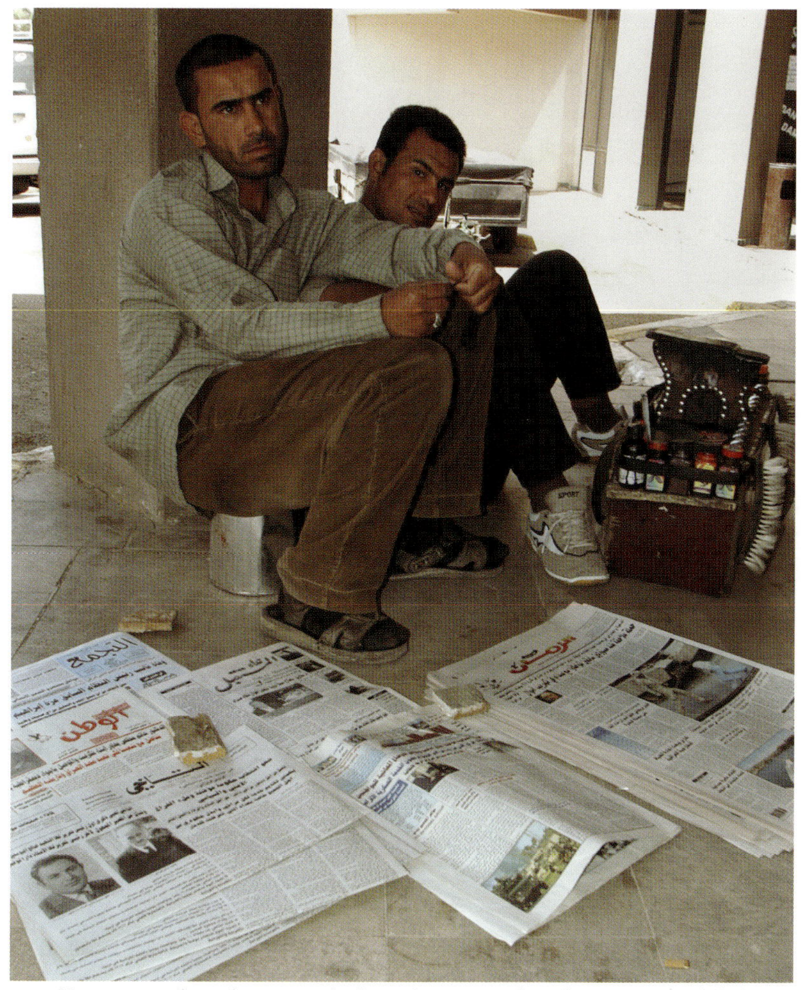

Newspapers have been on sale for at least a week in downtown Baghdad

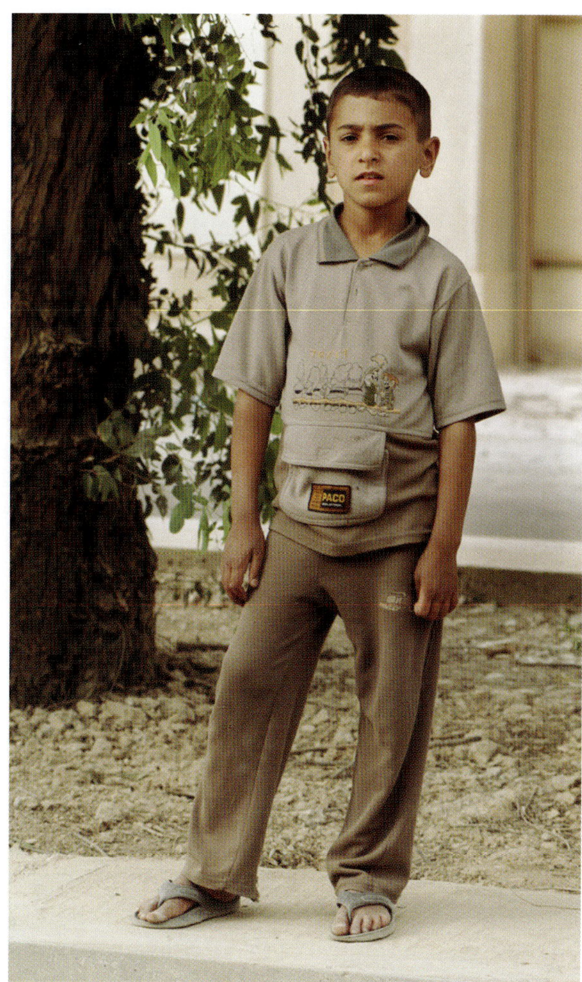

This young boy stands relaxed and healthy looking

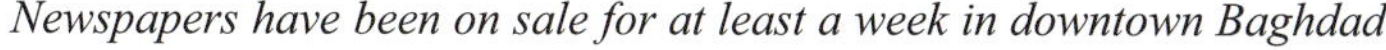

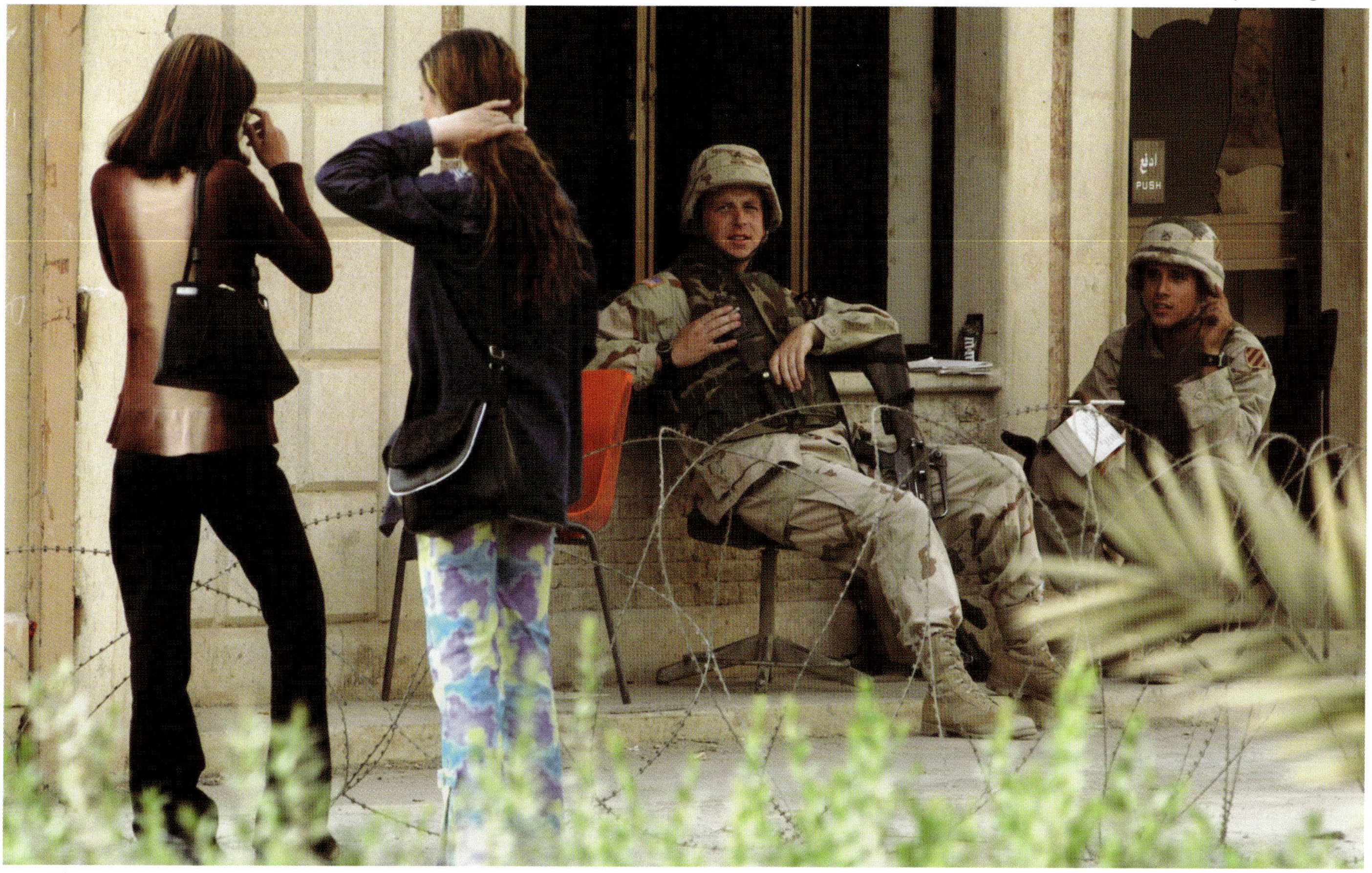

These gorgeous young women are a sight for very sore eyes in war-ravaged Baghdad. Next time these grunts may volunteer for sentry duty

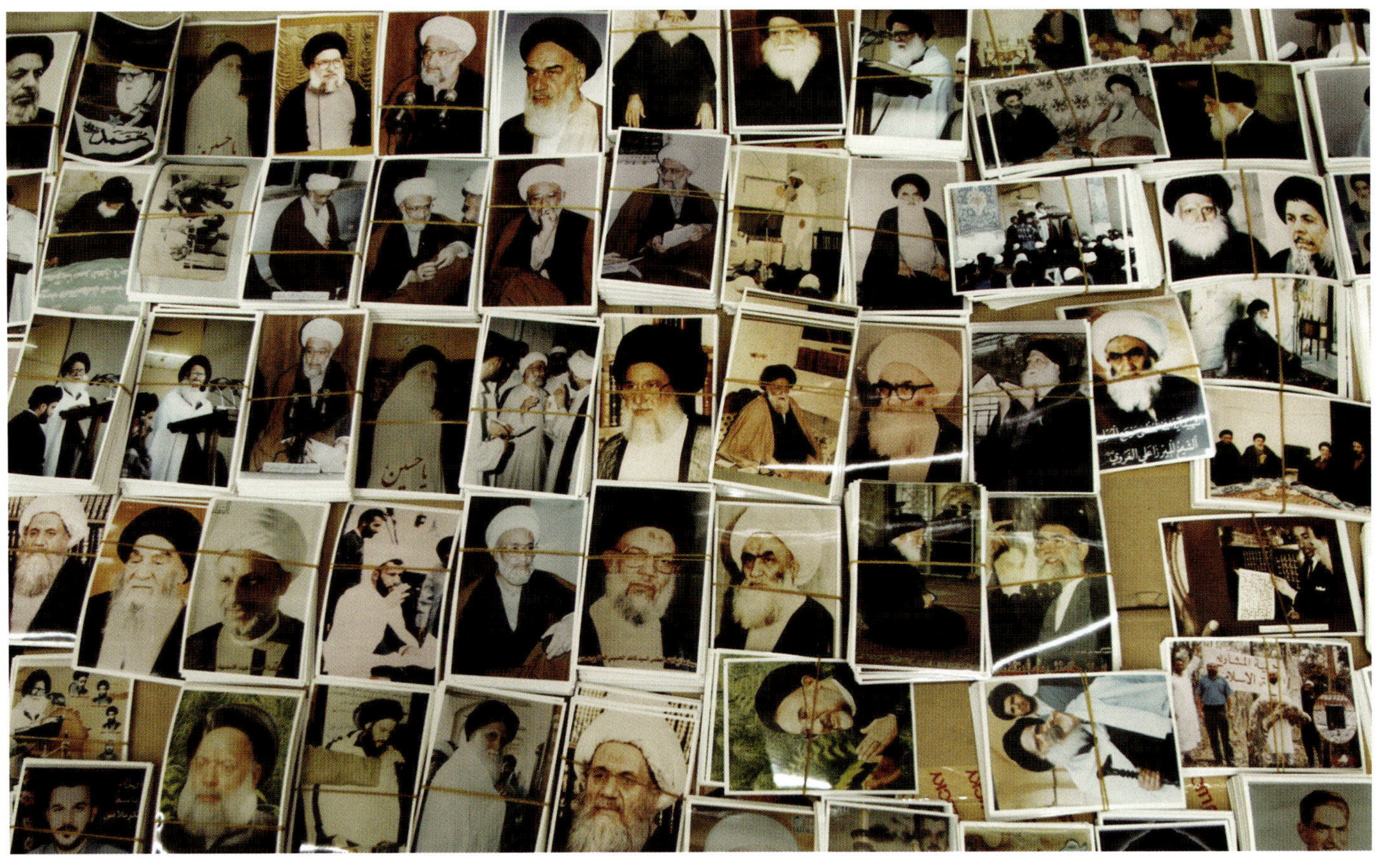

Color pocket cards of religious leaders for sale at a downtown camera shop. Women hold little influence in a Muslim world

A local resident rushes into the hotel lobby in a panic, asking if someone can get a soldier to help him. He explains that a group of looters are trying to steal the large generator from the apartment building he lives in, just a few hundred feet north of the Fanar. This generator is the building's only source of power, and many young families live there. There is nothing we at the hotel can really do, except to send him over to the Palestine where we hoped the soldiers could assist him.

This is an example of how ravenous the looters are becoming. Well over a hundred people; mothers, fathers and their children, live a precarious existence in this apartment building. Now, their only source of lighting for security, and heat for cooking their meals, is being stolen from right under their feet. A situation like this is so sad, but it is happening all over Baghdad.

Stephan informs me that around 11 a.m. this morning he witnessed a carjacking that happened right in front of his eyes, while driving near the stolen car market. He gave me an account of the incident.

He was stopped in a large traffic snarl, when three machine gun-toting men jumped out of a car and swarmed over a pickup truck (the truck was stopped in front of Stephane's car). Reaching through the truck's open window with his rifle, he pushes the weapon into the driver's face, while the other two bandits drag him out of the vehicle and push him down onto the road. One man drives away in the pickup as the two others release the driver and screech off in their car. They leave the owner of the truck shaken and trembling at the side of the road.

Carjacking is one of the most obvious next steps in the evolution of crime and anarchy in Baghdad. Extortion, murder and kidnapping are some of the others. The looters are morphing into a more refined and adept animal, and Baghdad is their jungle.

Since my return from Kirkuk two days ago, a new horde of beggars, street vendors and homeless orphans have invaded the neighborhood. Now you can't walk ten paces without being accosted by the dregs of Baghdad, (they are, by no fault of their own, collateral damage victims of this war; wounded by the shrapnel of circumstance). Some of these are not your regular beggars, but pushy, rude bastards, who curse you if you do not give them money. The hotel complex has become beggar command headquarters, and this new force has taken their place alongside the military, civil and media command that currently occupy the complex.

But there is an element of structure to this insanity, and if Charles Darwin joined me on the Fanar patio for a sweet coffee, I could explain to him my 'theory of devolution'. As I sit in front of the Fanar drinking a coffee and eating some crackers and jam (left over from my MREs) three cats meow and rub at my feet and legs, each one fighting the other for my table scraps. Fifty-feet across the street, a pack of eight wild dogs fight over territory and status within the pack, a cloud of hanging dust is kicked up from their scuffling as they yelp and snap at each other. Stepping off the patio, beggars of all ages, including four-year-old solvent-sniffing boys and girls and one-legged cripples push their open hands into the faces of Westerners and Iraqi's alike. Whiskey and cigarette-dealing street vendors, taxi drivers and interpreters push and snarl over who gets our business. Then there are the journalists; holding out our notepads and cameras in outstretched hands, begging for clues to exclusive news. We are 'news beggars'. We need a daily feeding for our family too, the readers and viewers back home.

A man seated at the table next to me introduces himself as Doctor Rafal Badri, from Edmonton, Canada. He is seated with his colleague and friend, Peter Tomarczyck. Both work for the NGO humanitarian group *Americares*, based in the United States. It is a non-profit agency that provides free medical aid to survivors of natural disasters and war. They tell me they are arranging the groundwork for the arrival of 30 tons of medical aid from Europe, due to arrive at Baghdad International Airport on Sunday, May 11th. Peter, the field agent for the organization, tells me there is a good chance I can photograph the unloading if I am interested. I definitely am interested. He just has to OK it with the military at the airport.

A couple more of their colleagues show up on the patio and join our conversation. I find them all very honest, dedicated and compassionate people. A great group of people! This is so very refreshing and gives me great hope that all NGO groups are not like those I have met up until now. I ask the *Americares* gang (who are staying at the Fanar) to keep me up on the details of the flight. This photo op could be a very timely wrap-up to my coverage in Iraq, as it will be the first major medical relief flight to land in Baghdad, and it arrives the day before I leave for Amman.

The calm-speaking Dr. Badri describes to me the present status of doctors and medical supplies in Baghdad. "I've talked to plenty of doctors in Baghdad's hospitals, and they tell me they need medical supplies, rather than more doctors. They already have a good number of doctors," he confirms. "But our hurdle is that there are no medical supplies in the institutions."

An Iraqi civilian, drinking his coffee next to our table, leans over and matter-of-factly comments to me about the employment situation in Baghdad. "Things are now much worse than when Saddam was in power, the administrative delays of the army and police is making it difficult to find a job." I head upstairs to record my daily audiotape.

It's another gunfire and dog lullaby night, and as I lie in bed smoking my last Marlboro, I feel very alone and somewhat lost. I pray I have no nightmares.

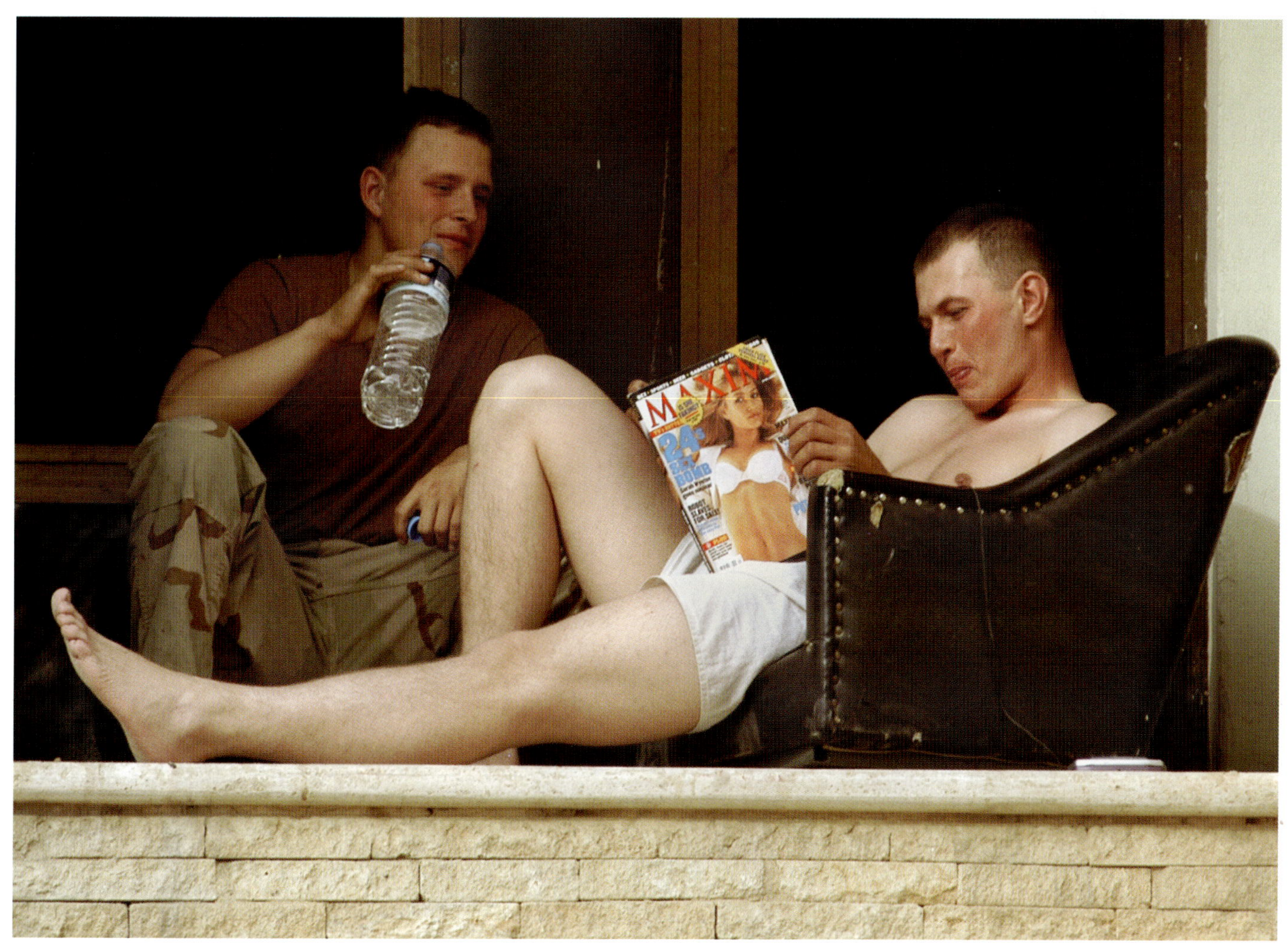

Mothers hide your daughters when these young men arrive back home stateside. A soldier's life is lived day by day, hour by hour

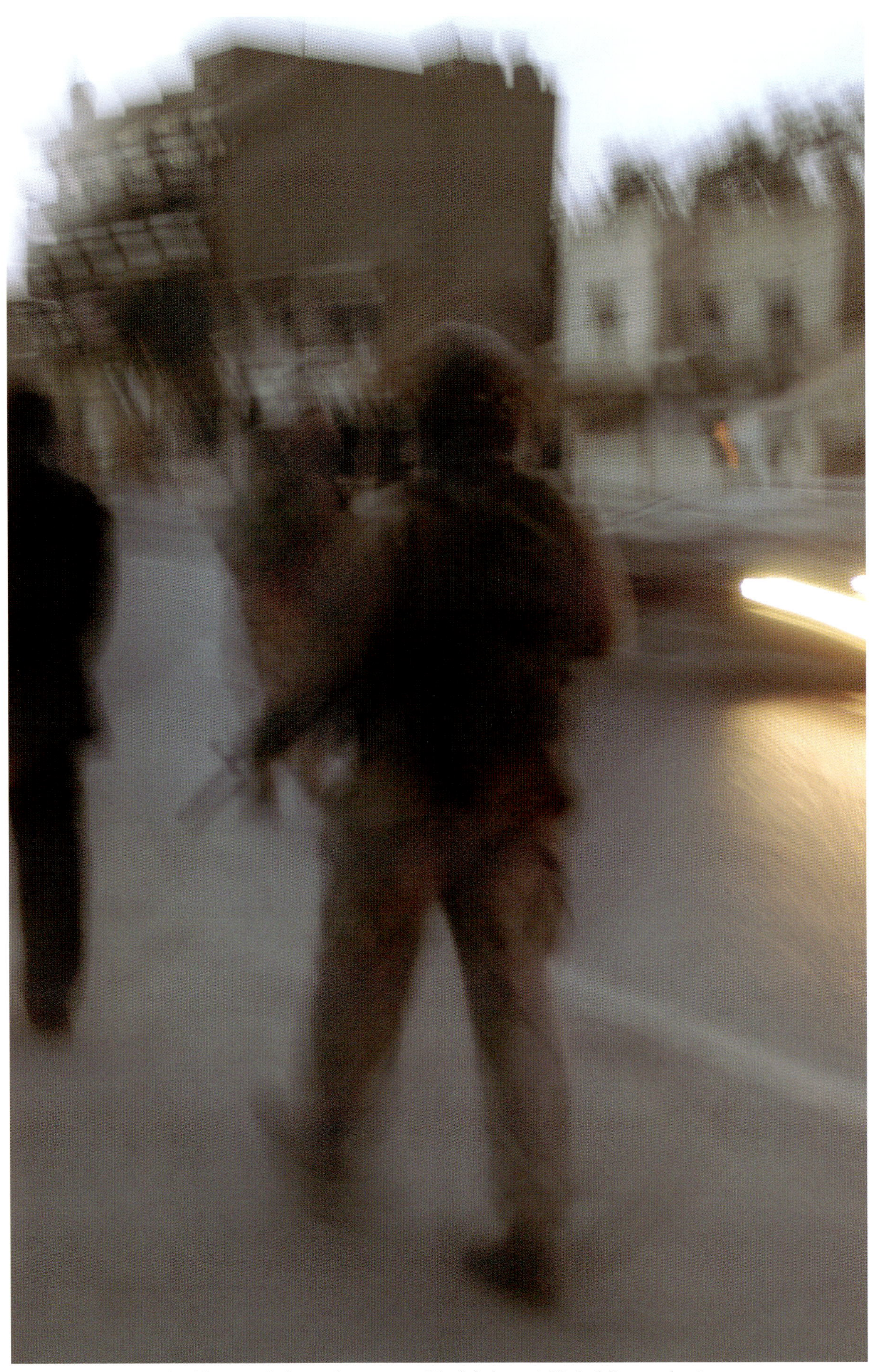

A soldier patrols the perilous streets of Baghdad as twighlight falls over the city

Day 31. Saturday, May 10th

(Tod briefs me on the shooting of two American soldiers by unknown assailants; carjackers kidnap female occupant; stone-faced soldiers; Paranoia City; I meet Kenji and Dana outside the Fanar; I carry a bayonet for protection; 'they might try rip us off'; clenching the knife and ready for a fight; the dangers of a trip to the camera shop; losing self-confidence; a game of Russian roulette; stolen shirt; like the Mafia; no honor amongst thieves; kids sniffing glue; tattered clothing and no shoes; Mother Goose soldiers; a Dickens novel; the love of one another; kid gang beats boy; a hand on my camera; an Iraqi journalist; "You want some mister"; indiscernible breast; kiddie sex; children shouldn't beat children; forgotten memories; despondent and confused; the downfall of civilization; human wreckage; shoeless beauty; still hope for them; my last story; stuck in the elevators; a little claustrophobic; little kid sandwiches)

I meet Tod on the Fanar patio for a coffee. He starts telling me about an unsettling situation regarding two soldiers who were shot in two separate incidents yesterday in Baghdad.

One of the soldiers was apparently on sentinel duty on a bridge in downtown Baghdad, when a solitary gunman, armed with a pistol, approached from a crowd and fired a bullet into his head, mortally wounding him. The gunman then disappeared back into the crowd. In the other incident, a soldier was seriously wounded when shot through the neck by a sniper. Both shootings happened in broad daylight in Baghdad.

These are the first incidents of soldiers being wounded or killed by gunmen in post-capture Baghdad that I have heard of. This introduces a distinct new level of violence and paranoia to the streets of Baghdad, and I believe that these shootings, and the carjackings, are the beginning of a new wave of targeted violence, particularly in the shooting of the American soldiers.

In the hotel dining room, the journalists are discussing a gut-wrenching piece of news over breakfast. It involves another carjacking that happened early this morning in Baghdad.

A man and his family were driving in their Toyota pickup truck when it was stopped and carjacked. The armed thieves pulled the family members from the car, but constrained the man's wife in her seat. Jumping into the truck, they kidnapped the wife along with the truck. I wonder if the poor woman will ever be found alive again, and what evil intentions the thieves have in mind for her.

There is a different attitude in the faces of the soldiers as they pass by the hotel in their tanks and Humvees. The troops are now as stone-faced as the busts of Saddam at the Republican Palace, no longer are they very outgoing and waving at the children and civilians. Wearing their war faces, they methodically pivot their heads from side to side with their weapons bristling, looking out for possible ambush. This is a complete change of character. The troops must have been briefed about the two shootings and told to be on high alert. Baghdad is now Paranoia City.

Walking over to the Palestine to buy some cigarettes, I bump into my good friends Kenji and Dana, who have just arrived in Baghdad from Kirkuk. It is great to see them, and I welcome them back with hugs and smiles. They are just getting settled, so I tell them I will meet them later in the day.

There is a demonstration of Iraqi war amputees just breaking up in front of the Palestine. They are former soldiers who fought in the Iranian and Gulf wars, and are demanding that their sick benefits, withdrawn at the start of the war, be reinstated. The demonstrators, about 50 of them, are sitting in wheelchairs or propped up by crutches. Some are missing an arm or a leg, are blind, or had a large area of flesh and bone burned or blown from their bodies. Their sacrifice must seem so misspent to them now.

These people must be having an extremely difficult time surviving without any rations or aid. Survival is difficult enough here as a complete human, but being handicapped must be an absolutely gruelling nightmare.

Getting back to the Fanar, I decide to go for a walk along the riverfront with Jennifer. Due to the increased tension, the closeness of the public, and the reduced security situation around the hotel, I have decided to carry a concealed bayonet with me when away from the hotel. With only one more full day left for me in Baghdad, I want to have at least some minimal protection on me. This is the first time I have carried a weapon in Iraq. I wear it concealed away from peering eyes, tucked under the back of my shirt. That blade, about a foot long, is my security blanket. And as fate might have it, as soon as I wear it, I have a need for it.

Walking along the dusty plain of partially treed land that separates the roadway from the riverbank, I spot a group of five teenagers making their way toward Jennifer and me. Suspicious of their intent, we walk more to the right towards the roadway, but they shadow our movements and approach closer. They seem to want to ask us something, but judging by their body language, and the fact that I am alone with a woman in a desolate location, I conclude that they may be thinking of ripping us off. If they get any closer they might just have the opportunity to mug us, so I decide to go with my gut instincts and carry the battle to them, hopefully catching them off guard.

When they are about thirty feet in front of us, I stop abruptly and turn slightly to the side. Raising my arm, I point aggressively towards the largest member of the gang shouting, "You! I want you!" Waving him to come closer with one hand, my other hand reaches behind my back and lifting up my shirt, I slowly draw the long silver blade three-quarters of the way out of the sheath, while twitching it from side to side, to make sure he knows exactly what I have in hand.

The gang stands frozen and startled in their tracks, their faces painted by uncertainty. I continue waving him closer, as I now start baby stepping towards the group. "You want some!" I say, challenging him to make a move.

The punk raises both his hands open in submission, while shouting "No, No mister." They start to slowly back off, but I am royally pissed-off and enraged. I growl at them to come closer. But suddenly, like a herd of startled deer (and as fast), they break into a sprint, running in the opposite direction away from Jennifer and me. Slipping the bayonet back into its scabbard, I smile at Jennifer and tell her that survival here is all about adaptability, knowing when to make the first move and knowing when to run.

Jennifer and I go back to the Fanar and grab a cab to take us to a local camera shop where she needs to look for a lens. I am extremely reluctant to leave the area of the hotel complex unless absolutely necessary, but I promised her yesterday that I would go with her. The blade comes along for the drive.

Even a drive to the camera store is risky. We slouch down low in the taxi, keeping a low profile from any desperados who might be out looking for an easy target. Anyone, and everyone is suspect to me. The city is coming apart at the seams. We return to the hotel without finding a lens, relieved to have had no problems during the drive.

I ask the Fanar receptionist to bring my laundered clothing to my room, and when they are delivered, it is missing my new short-sleeved-shirt I bought in Arbil. They look all over the laundry room but the shirt is gone. It appears it has been stolen. I will not let this upset me; I have other shirts and am willing to share, even to petty thievery. How can I complain about a shirt when there are children roaming the street with no shoes and no home.

Institutional theft has been a part of life in Iraq for decades, and this attitude long ago seeped into the psyche of the society. Pay-offs, extortion, blackmail and murder have been the way things have always worked in Saddam-ruled Iraq. His web of power held an iron grip over all, and on every important transaction of cash and products coming into and leaving the country.

Sitting outside drinking a chai, I notice a group of about seven kids wandering along the street toward the Fanar. As they approach closer, I notice that some of them are sniffing glue from plastic and paper bags. It is one of three or four gangs of little girl and boy street orphans that I have been seeing over the last couple of days. They are between four and eight years old.

I remember seeing a few of these kids a couple of weeks ago, hanging out around the Palestine, begging off the soldiers and journalists. I remember seeing the oldest boy (perhaps eight-years-old), being chased out of the Sheraton Hotel by an angry staff member. The cheery, smiling kid, unwashed and shoeless and wearing tattered clothing, was enjoying his game of chase with the security men. I like the kid's spirit, he turned misery and want into a playful game.

Some of the soldiers manning the complex checkpoints have become almost surrogate parents to certain children. I have nicknamed them 'Mother Goose soldiers.' The sight of a soldier with a rifle in one hand and a bedraggled little kid clinging to the other is just so stirring. The kid is looking up to the soldier for the momentary feeling of security offered by an embracing hand. The soldier (perhaps being a father or brother to someone back home) is doing what he knows best, even better than killing. He is showing the kid a little love. It is a moving mix of soldier and orphan, love and uncertainty.

The little squad of glue-sniffers passes in front of the Fanar. A young boy of eight walks over to me with his four-year-old brother tagging behind him. The older boy raises his cupped hand at me – still sucking on the glue bag in the other hand. The paper bag inflates then deflates, as the boy inhales the numbing vapors of glue. Keeping the bag to his mouth, he uses his eyes as a voice; glancing at his open hand then back up at me. He is an eight-year-old glue addict, who uses glue to anaesthetize his reality and stave off hunger.

Both boys are filthy, and dressed in mismatched, grubby, worn clothing, with no shoes on their feet. Their hair has never seen a comb. Smears and streaks of dried glue cake the front of their sweatshirts and paint their dirt-mottled hands. The younger one (who is now holding onto one of my hands while looking up at me) has a white-grey halo of dried glue encircling his mouth and across his cheeks. His little twinkling eyes are red and watery, pushed back into their black sockets from the continual exposure to the toxicity of the solvent. Both their faces are gaunt and puffy.

Regardless of their unforgiving nomadic life, both children are smiling and joyful, and they beam large smiles as I offer them some sticks of gum. I refuse to give them any money; I know where it will end up – in the bag.

The four-year-old tugs at my sleeve and points to my water bottle, then motions for a drink by pointing into his mouth and grunting, 'ah-ah.' I pour it directly into his gaping mouth (like feeding a baby bird) being careful not to have the bottle neck touch his gluey lips or snotty, running nose (the boy is a Petri dish of microbes). I accidentally spill some down his neck, and the child giggles like a baby. I have not heard that sound since my own children were his age or younger; it throws my thoughts back to my own children. I give them both a couple of extra sticks of gum and send them away to join the rest of the rootless gang of sniffers. My heart is in my stomach, my hopes are with them.

Their only crime was that of being born. Now they serve out their time, living day-by-day, hour-by-hour, searching for love from the family of man. They have become the whores of my conscience, a nightmare in the day. How can we let the most innocent of souls be trapped in this collapsing theatre of Shock and Awe. How can the world turn its back on these children? Have we not learned from our past failures. It is the innocents that suffer most during war. Shame on the world!

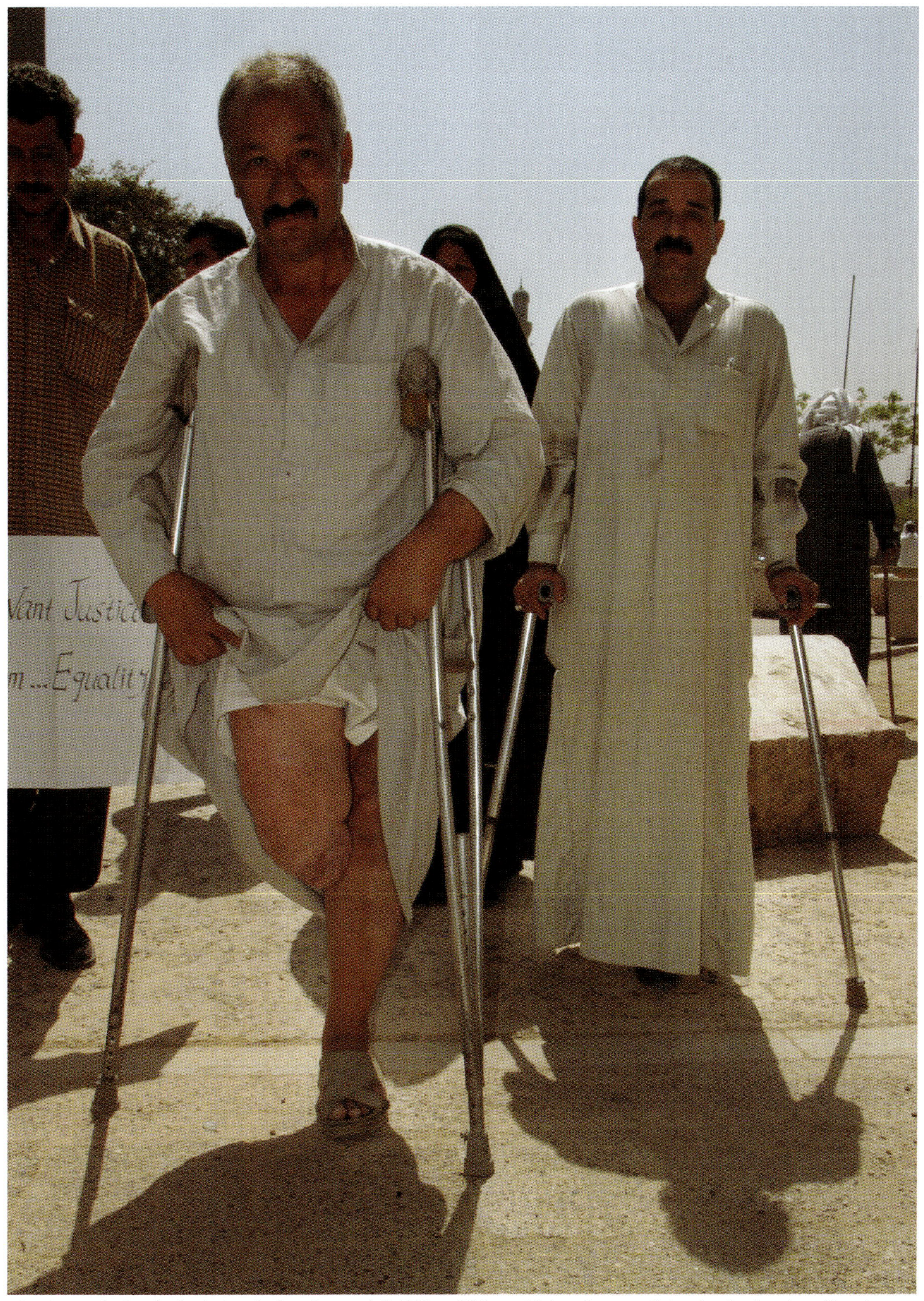

Iraqi vets who lost limbs during the Iran-Iraq and Gulf Wars. Without sick benefits or medicine they lead a miserable existence

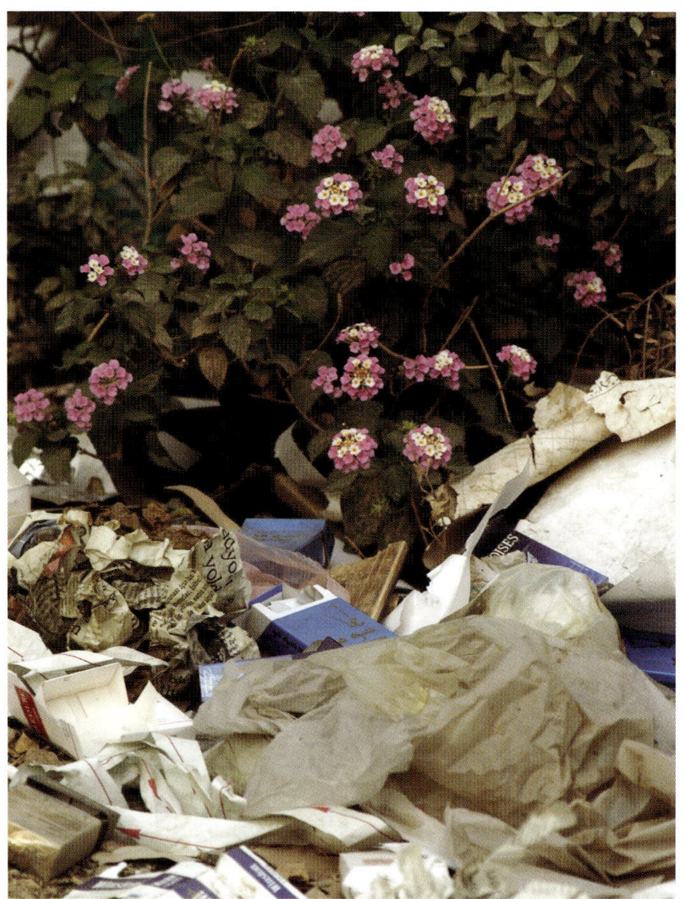

Litter fills the streets of Baghdad

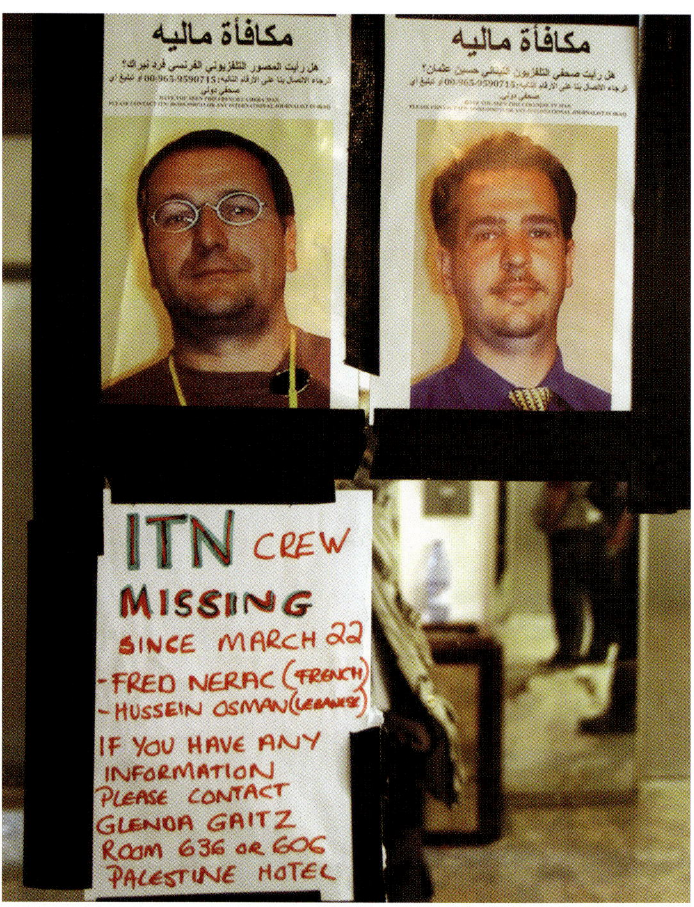

Missing journalists Fred Nerac and Hussein Osman

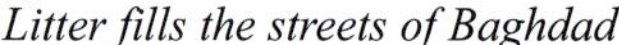

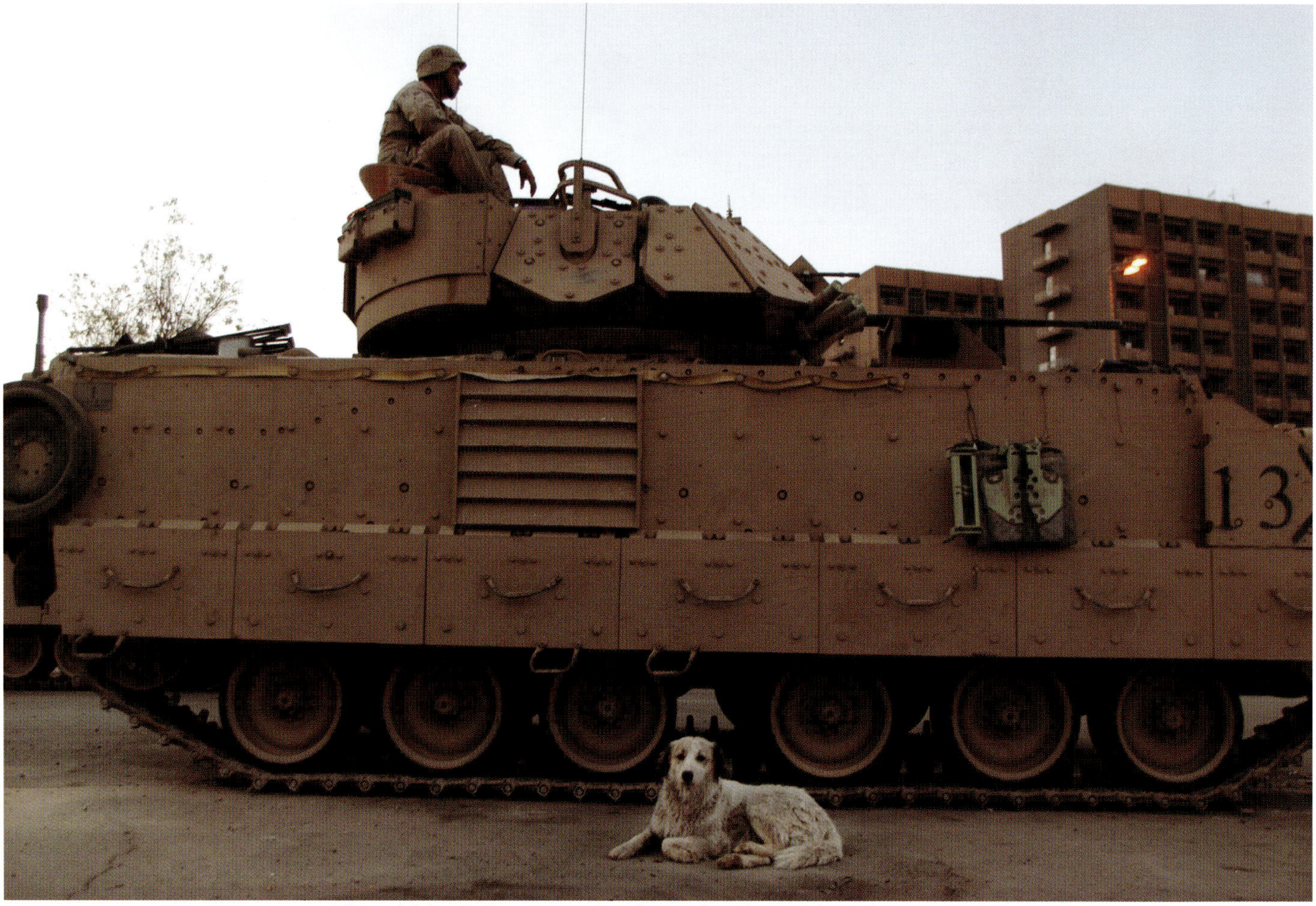

This wild dog finds some rest beside a tank in front of the Palestine Hotel

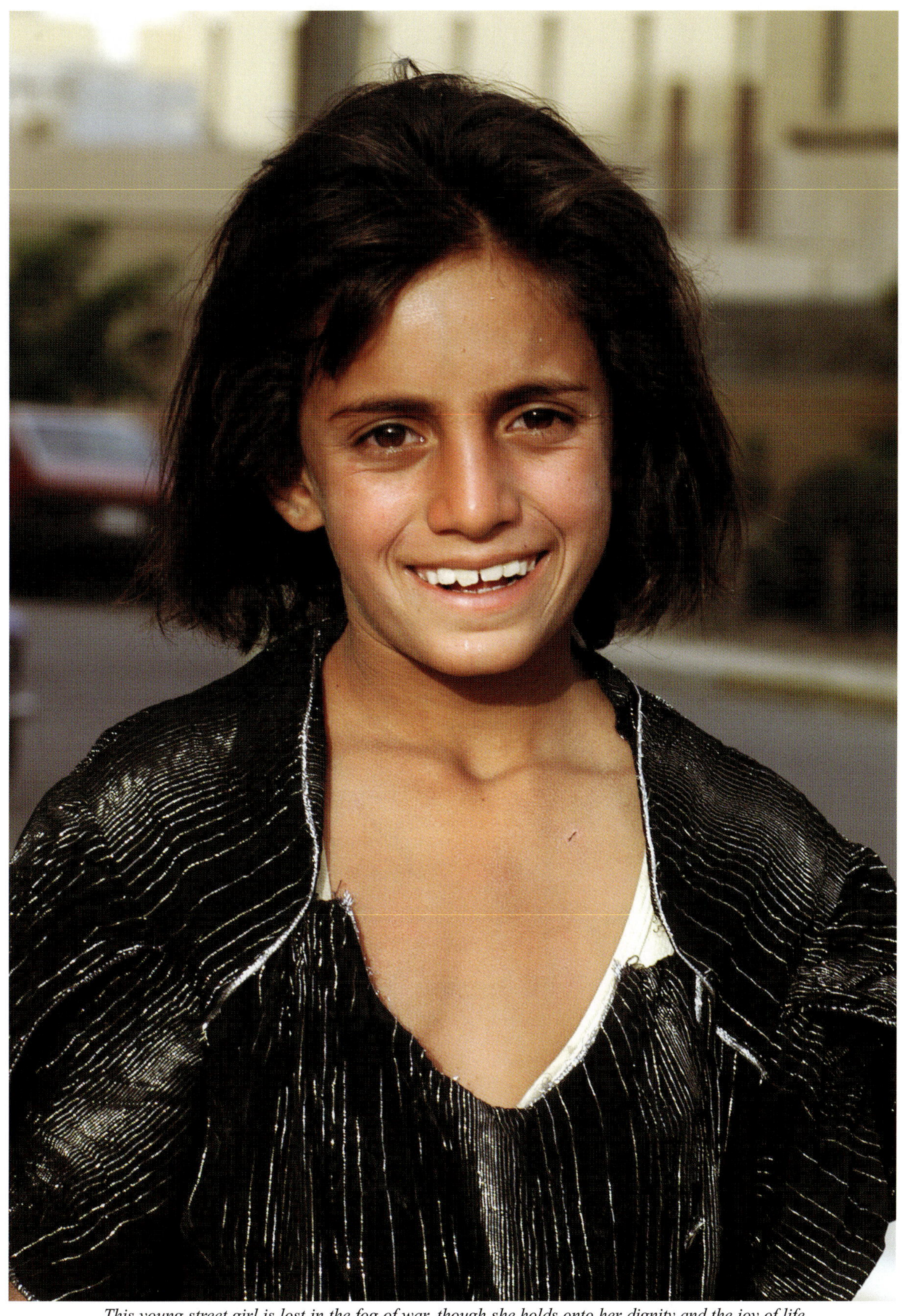

This young street girl is lost in the fog of war, though she holds onto her dignity and the joy of life

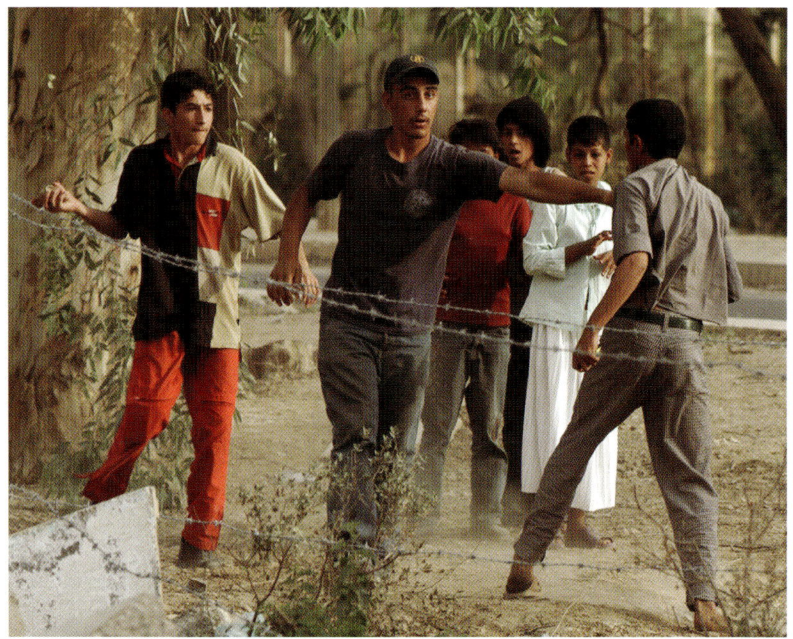

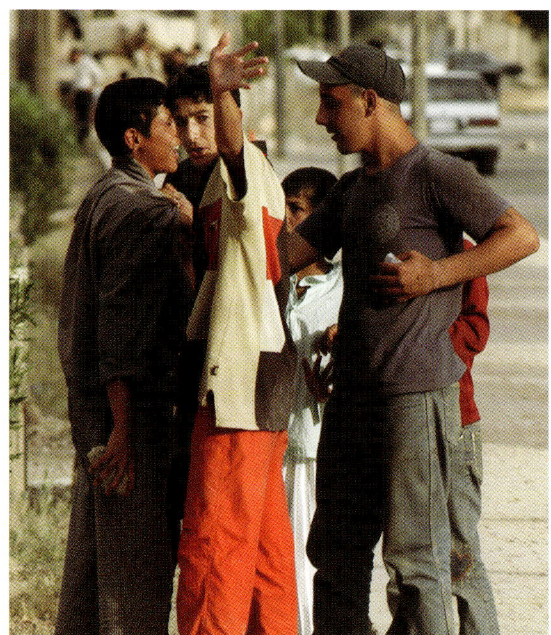

The daily brutality of life on the streets is a war of survival and confrontation

The child on the left is being extorted by older kids

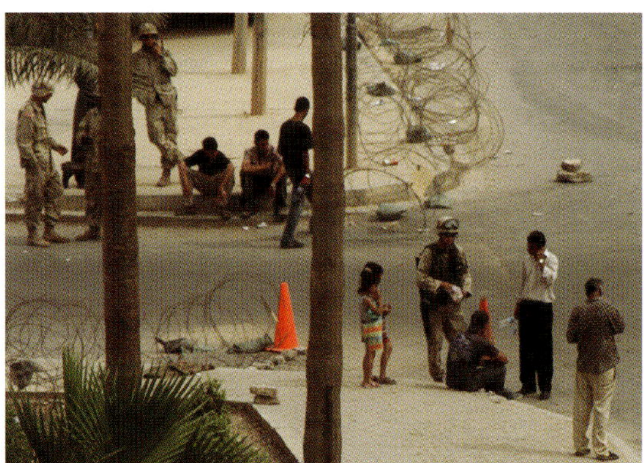

West checkpoint guarding the Palestine Hotel

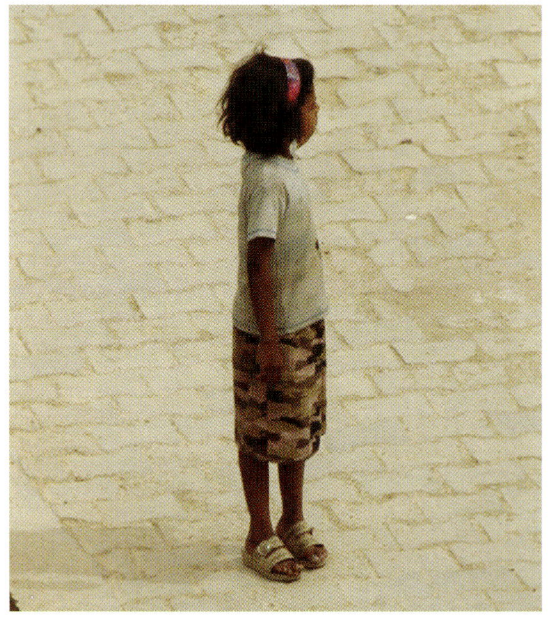

This little kid sleeps under the bushes wrapped in a box

About a half hour later, while outside the Fanar having a coffee, I see a small group of six children accosting a young boy. One of the six kids has a large rock in his hand, and is swinging it at the boy's head, while the largest and oldest (maybe 14 years old) holds the kid tight by the shirt collar. This looks really ugly. The other kids (boys and girls), are taking sucker-shots at the boy's face, but most of them miss.

I walk over with my camera in hand, and shouting at them to get their attention, I start taking pictures of the scuffle. Using sign language, I let them know that if they harm the child, I will bring the photos over to the soldiers and they will come and take them to jail. The ruffian starts waving his hands at me shouting, "No pictures mister!" But I continue shooting while he waves.

One young girl of perhaps 11 or 12, with her hair shaved off to look like a boy, walks over to me and tries to block my camera with her open hand. I tell her to not touch the camera, but she persists. I tell her again. She persists. Having enough, I grab her forearm and twist it sharply to the side, at which point she backs off immediately and keeps her distance.

The scuffling and wrestling continues, then I catch site of the Iraqi journalist who bad-mouthed me when I first met him at the Fanar on April 23rd. He is watching the barbaric show from the side of the road. When I call him over to help me break up the fight, he backs down and refuses to become involved. I call him a liar, a hypocrite, and a coward. "Where is all your journalistic bravado now you coward?" I shout across the street at him. "You know the language, you are from here, get over here and help break it up!" I jibe him.

Hearing this barrage of embarrassing verbal abuse, he comes over and starts talking to the kids in Arabic, but they continue to take swings at the kid. Another close-shaved young girl, who also dresses like a boy, comes over to me and takes my hand in her hand. Looking up at me, she winks and motions with her head towards the bushes just behind us. "You want some mister," she says, while rubbing her small indiscernible breast. I don't even say a word or react to her comments, but simply walk a couple of feet away from her and continue shooting the scuffle.

This kid is offering me sex, she is younger than my thirteen-year-old daughter! This gives me a horrible sinking feeling, and makes this hellish stage even more appalling. The kids continue tangling, until another person comes over from the Fanar to assist breaking it up. Shortly after this, the kids calm down and the scuffling stops.

Later, I see the victim and attackers all sitting calmly together on the curb, as though nothing had happened (they had been extorting the boy). By keeping my camera fixed on the scuffle, I deterred them from smashing the boy's head in. If they started hitting him on the head with the rock, I would have physically entered the fray. I would have had no choice, or else I would be witness to a child murder. Life on the streets of Baghdad is a dog-eat-dog world where the weak do not survive long.

I look back at the Fanar, 50 yards away, to see Tod looking out from his second floor apartment. I wonder what he thinks of this savage exhibit of street law. I don't care about what anyone thinks about my trying to break it up. Men killing men is one thing, but I am not going to stand aside while a kid is being pummeled to death. Here I draw the line, children will not beat children if I can prevent it.

This street theatre burned deep into me, and touched a raw nerve in my past, personal life. I suddenly feel despondent and confused. The wheels are starting to seriously fall off my buggy, and every day I spend here, is more difficult than the last.

My emotions are becoming a roller coaster of extremes, which flip-flop from happiness to depressing sadness in the span of just a few minutes. I am fast becoming just another piece of human wreckage in this city of anguish, a victim of my own compassion. But I don't want to crash and burn; that means failure. I start to doubt myself as a journalist. What am I trying to accomplish, what am I doing here? Why even care? Why? I have to hang on!

A beautiful young street girl of perhaps eight, with a flowing black and silver-trimmed dress, comes over to say hello to me. The same girl I chatted with yesterday and the day before. I find her to be quite a sweetie, and intelligent. I have also seen her sniffing glue. Neither her long, matted black hair, nor the misery of the street, can cover over her big bright smile and friendly, open character. I give her some pieces of bubble gum, which she unwraps, then reads the comic the gum is folded-in. She giggles as she reads it, and then passes it to me while smiling and chuckling. The wrapper shows two cupids hugging, as two big red hearts float above them. Above the hearts it reads, "I love you!"

She reaches for my hand, and sheepishly glancing up, smiles and says, "Thank-you mister." The shoeless beauty then skips back to her little gang of friends, turning to wave back at me. I don't know if she is thanking me for the gum, or for breaking up the scuffle (which she was involved in). I hope she is thanking me for not wanting to see a kid get hurt.

Under my breath, I say a little wish for her and her friends, then return to my room to escape the stifling heat of the street.

I lie on my bed thinking about this little gang of lost children and my own childhood. Who would ever think that these street-wise orphans might grow up to be journalists, or accountants? For them, their predicament isn't the end, but a beginning. I take a couple of deep gulps of air, then head downstairs for a coffee.

That evening I am having supper at the Fanar with the *Americares* crew. The chicken tastes old and rubbery, so I just pick at it, stick-handling the peas with my fork. Peter, the field agent for *Americares*, informs me that I will be allowed to photograph the unloading of the relief flight tomorrow. This is great news! It will be the last story I will cover in Iraq, and a good one to wrap up my entire trip on, as this plane brings hope. Peter tells me of their last relief mission in Afghanistan.

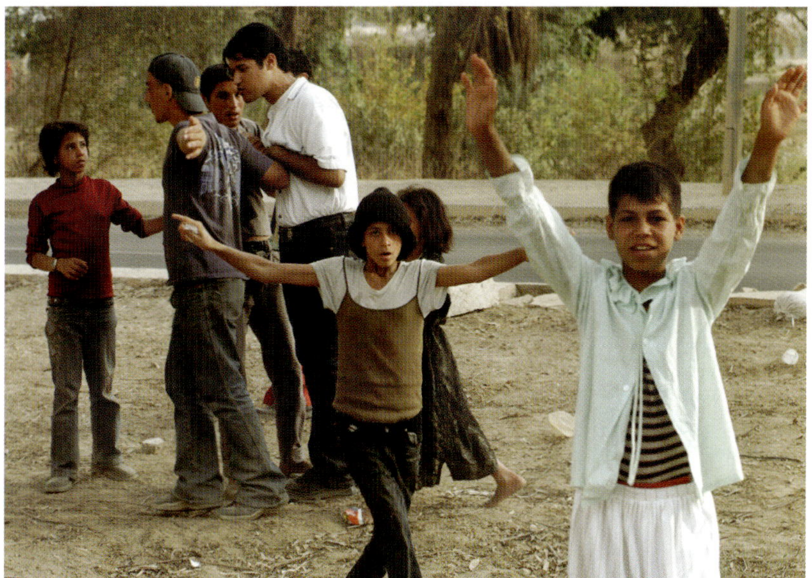

Iraqi journalist helps break-up fight. Street girls shave their heads to look like boys

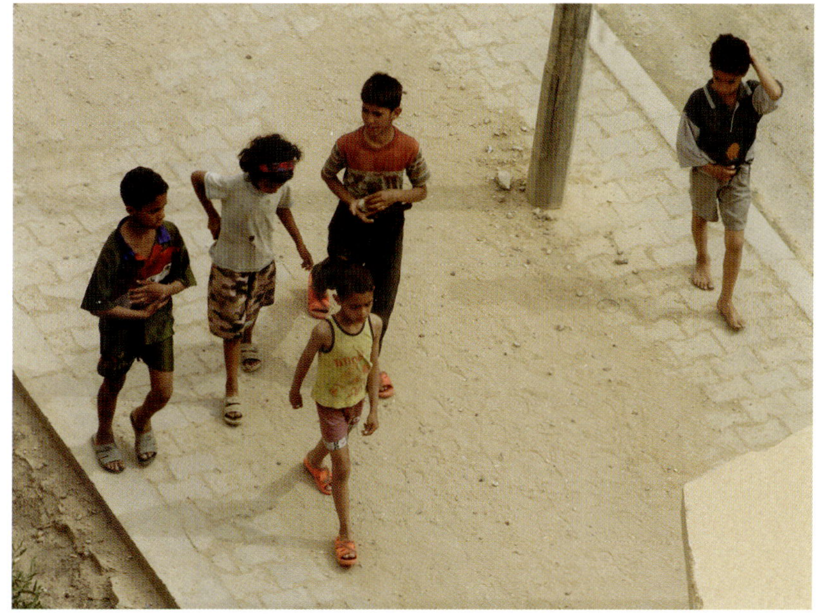

Younger street kids are preyed upon by the older gangs and perverts

Ken, from the *New York Daily News*, asks me if I would be able to take some pics tomorrow of an upstart new business in Baghdad, offering *Internet* access. It is called the *Internet* Café. This is the only place for the public to transmit material out of Baghdad that I have heard of, unless you have a B-GAN or other satellite transmitter at your disposal.

Kenji and Dana show up and join me at the outside patio table. We drink coffee and chat about our time in Kirkuk. Kenji asks about joining me at the airport for the shoot tomorrow, but I tell him that Peter has already completed the paperwork, and the military will not allow another photographer onto the tarmac for security reasons. Had I known a day earlier, it would have worked out for him. It is almost 1 a.m. and I head upstairs.

While recording my diary on the 7th floor patio of my room, I look onto the street and see the same group of glue-sniffing orphans from earlier today. They are sandwiched together under large sheets of cardboard, tucked under the hedgerow that encircles the Palestine. They look like 'little kid sandwiches,' with their tiny heads and feet sticking out from the ends of the folded cardboard sheets. I try to fall asleep, so alone, thinking about these disposable children sleeping in the dirt and litter seven floors below me. Jesus we're messed-up!

Day 32. Sunday, May 11th

> *(Up early for relief flight; Baghdad International Airport; gaping jaws of a whale; Air Force helpers; 30 tons of medical aid unloaded and re-loaded in two hours; very dangerous and getting worse; soldier describes placing dead comrade onto plane; "This young boy didn't deserve it"; classified photos; Red Cross in a Lear jet; "Welcome to the Hotel California"; Kenji and I discuss trip to Jordan; an unexploded grenade in his luggage; USA Today photo shoot; driving to the U.N. building; delivering a soldier's letter; Mother's Day; returning the loot; humiliating the looters; punch the guy in the face; winning the war by politeness; to psychologically drain the country; army of looters; tipping the Fanar staff; stealing the tip for himself; happy to get their share; foot soldiers watch amorous shadow boxers; sunflowers stretching for light; ready for drive to Amman Monday; rape of a young girl; the muffled crying of barefoot kids; lessons of war and the barbarity of humanity; lonely and confused)*

This is my last full day in Baghdad, and I am up at 5:30 a.m., preparing to head off to Baghdad International Airport with the *Americares* people. The relief flight lands at 8:30 a.m., but before this, we have to rendezvous with a convoy of three 18-wheeler trucks and 25 helpers near the airport. We finally leave the hotel around 7:00 a.m., and start the 30-minute drive west, crossing the Tigris.

At our rendezvous, Peter makes sure everyone has the papers required by the military, so everything goes smoothly at the entrance checkpoint. With everything in order, we move off in a convoy towards the airport, 5 minutes down the road. Receiving clearance at the checkpoint, we move onto a runway and park beside a huge hangar facing the main landing strip.

Climbing out of the Jimmy, I see the Russian-made IL-76 cargo plane touch down and taxi towards us. I grab a few quick frames before it comes to a stop right in front of us. There is handshaking and hugging amongst the *Americares* crew as the gigantic cargo plane shuts down its screaming engines.

The back doors of the plane open up like the gaping jaws of a humpback whale. It is packed with all sorts of medical supplies, from medicines to IV units, stacked high on wooden skids and each wrapped in a shroud of shrink wrap.

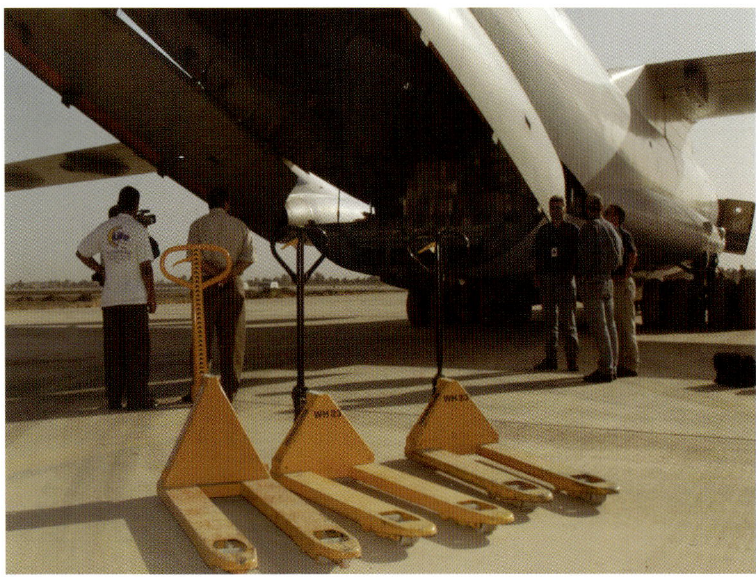

The calm before unloading begins

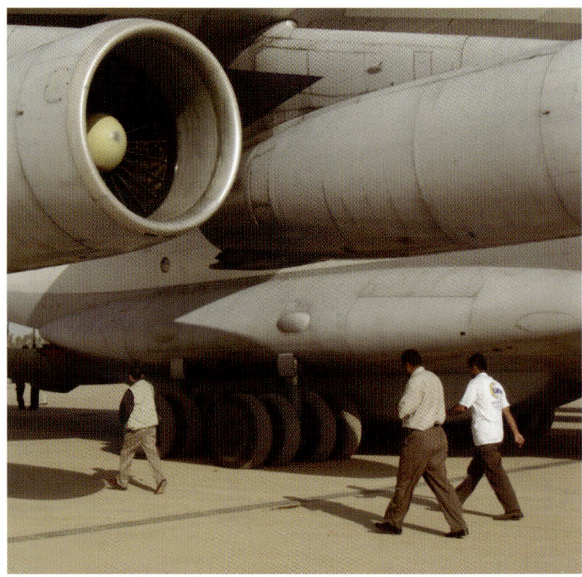

The gigantic engines of the cargo plane

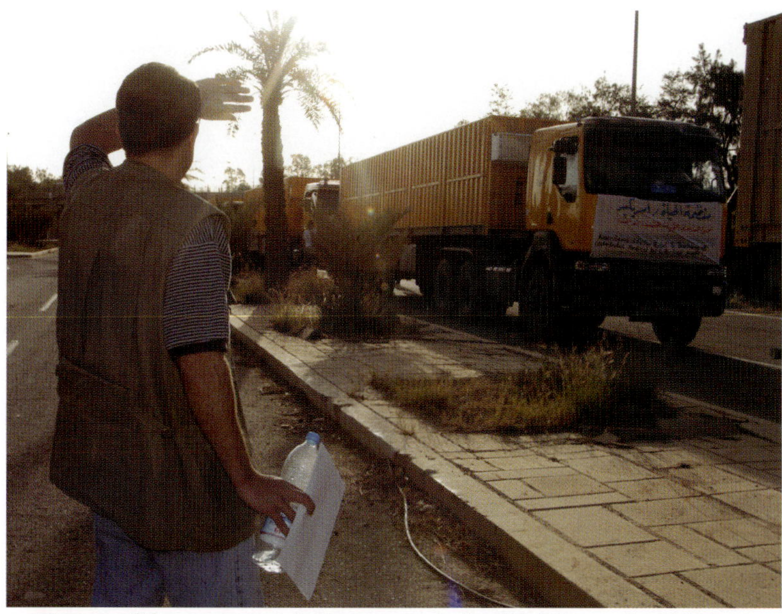
Convoy of three transport trucks en route to Baghdad International Airport

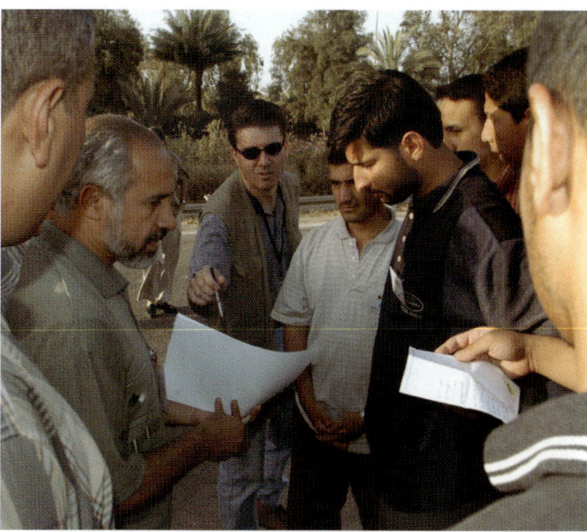
Making sure everyone has the required identification

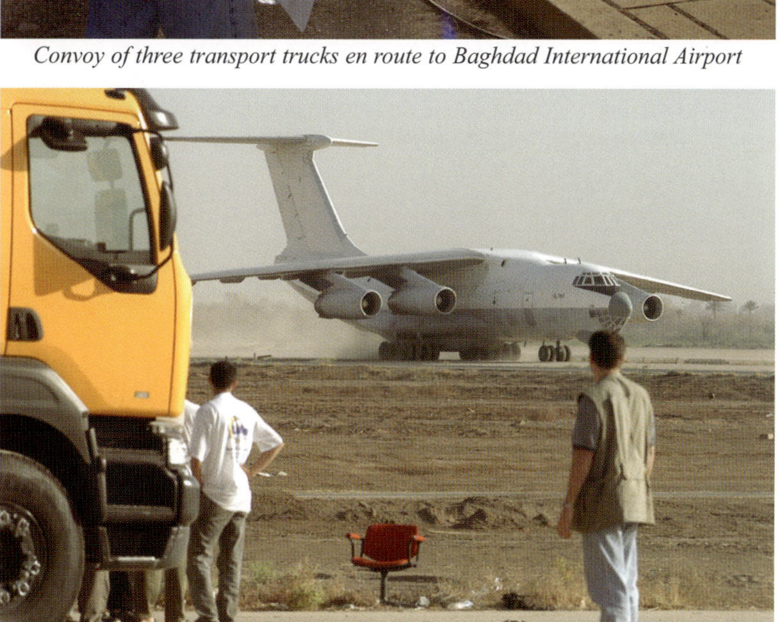
Thirty tons of medical supplies arrive on a Russian-made IL-76 cargo plane

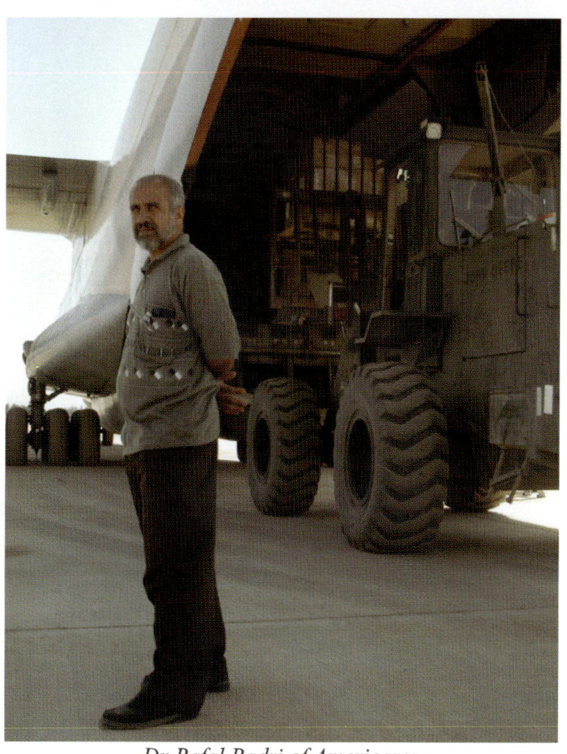
Dr Rafal Badri of Americares

A crew of eight soldiers with two large forklift trucks appear (while Peter and I are staring into the full belly of the monstrous airplane). The soldiers come over to Peter and, shaking his hand, offer their assistance in unloading the plane. This is unexpected, though greatly appreciated, and will cut the work time by half, if not more.

With the two industrial-sized forklifts outside the plane, and two heavy-duty dollies inside its belly, the plane's 30 tons of medical aid is unloaded, and then reloaded onto the three trucks in two hours.

Near the end of the unloading, I talk with one of the soldiers in the emptying belly of the plane. He asks me what it is like in Baghdad. He has been stationed at the airport for two months, and has been so busy he has not had a chance to visit the city yet. I tell him it is very dangerous, and getting worse, especially for the soldiers patrolling the streets.

The soldier lowers his head and, in a hushed voice, starts telling me about the dead soldier he loaded onto a U.S.-bound plane yesterday. It was the body of the young soldier who was shot in the head at point blank range Friday (the shooting that Tod had told me about).

"It was the first time I ever stood out on a runway and saluted when a plane was taking off," the soldier confessed. "This young boy didn't deserve it. He didn't have a chance."

I hear gunshots and machine gun fire along the northeast perimeter of the airport. There is a cloud of dust being stirred up by the shooting, but I can't make out what is going on. It appears to be a small skirmish.

Alongside the runway, I see Patriot missile installations. I am restricted to shooting the relief effort only and have been warned not to photograph any weaponry or layout of the buildings and runways. I respect this demand, and although I

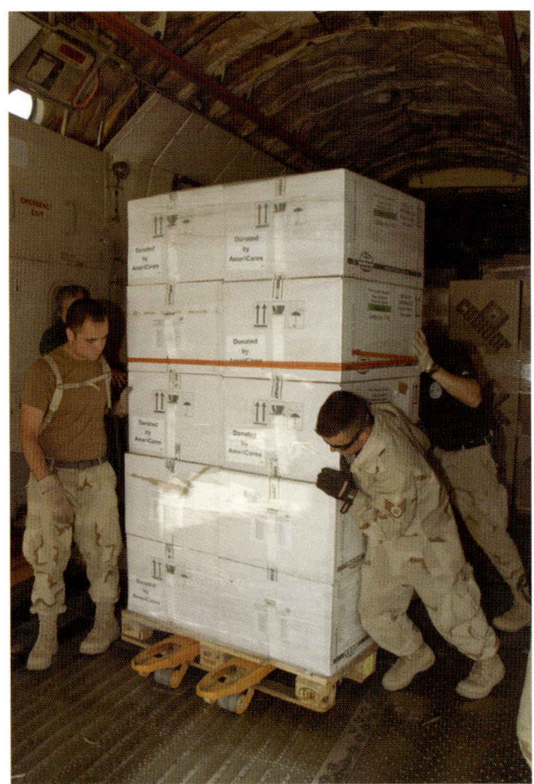

Shrink-wrap secures this load

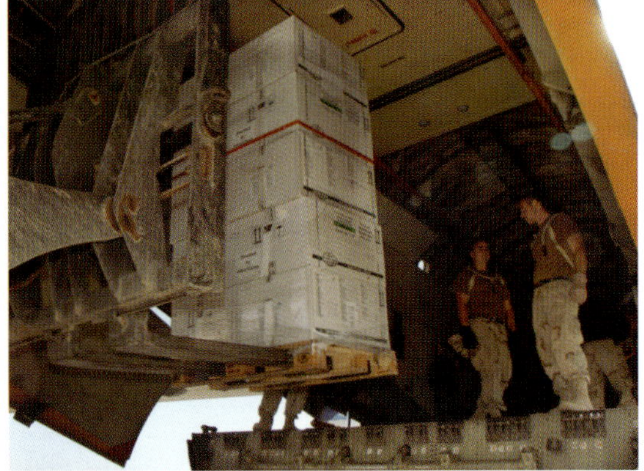

The belly of the plane is as hot as an oven

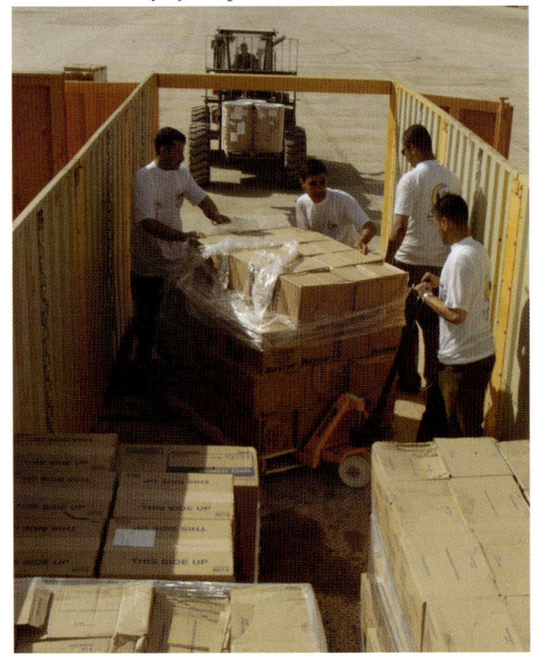

Loading the transport trucks

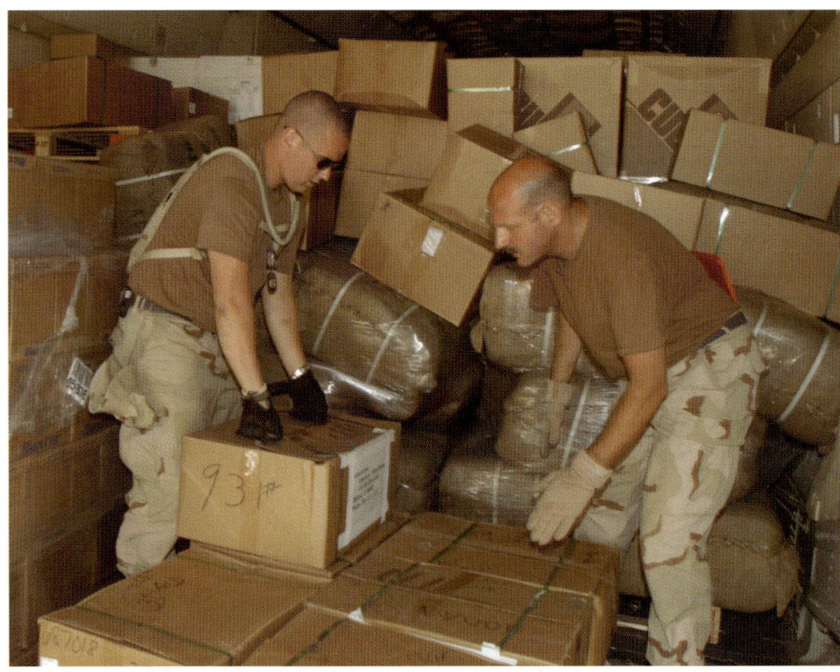

Some of the supplies shifted during flight and had to be re-stacked on skids

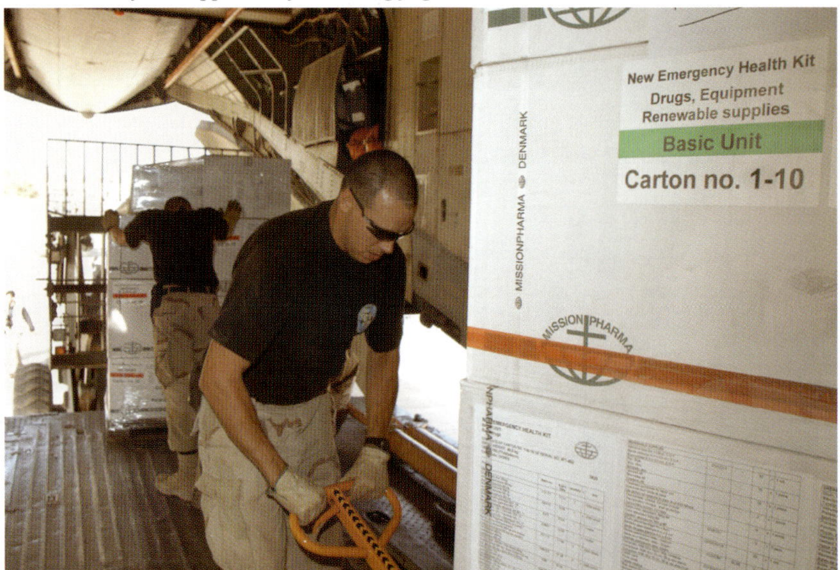

The soldiers choreographed the unloading to an art, and were real gentlemen

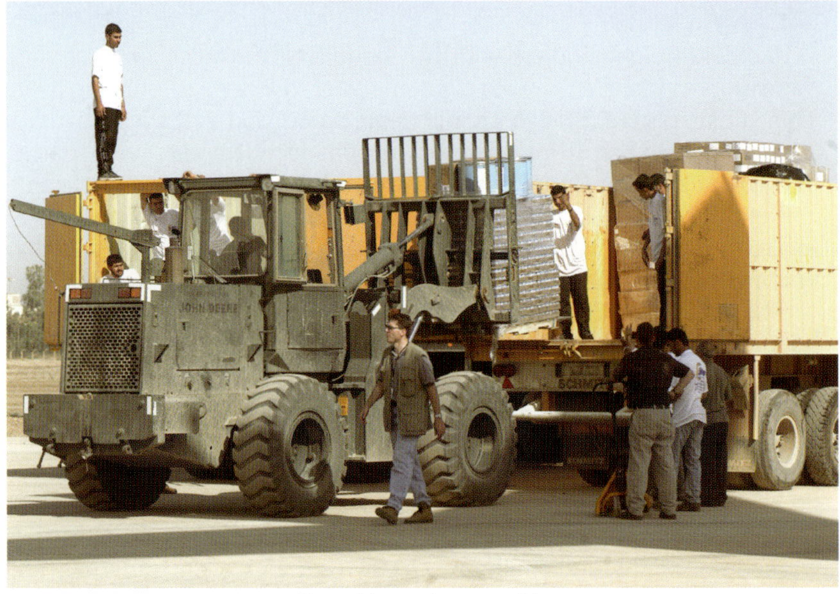

Everything going smoothly

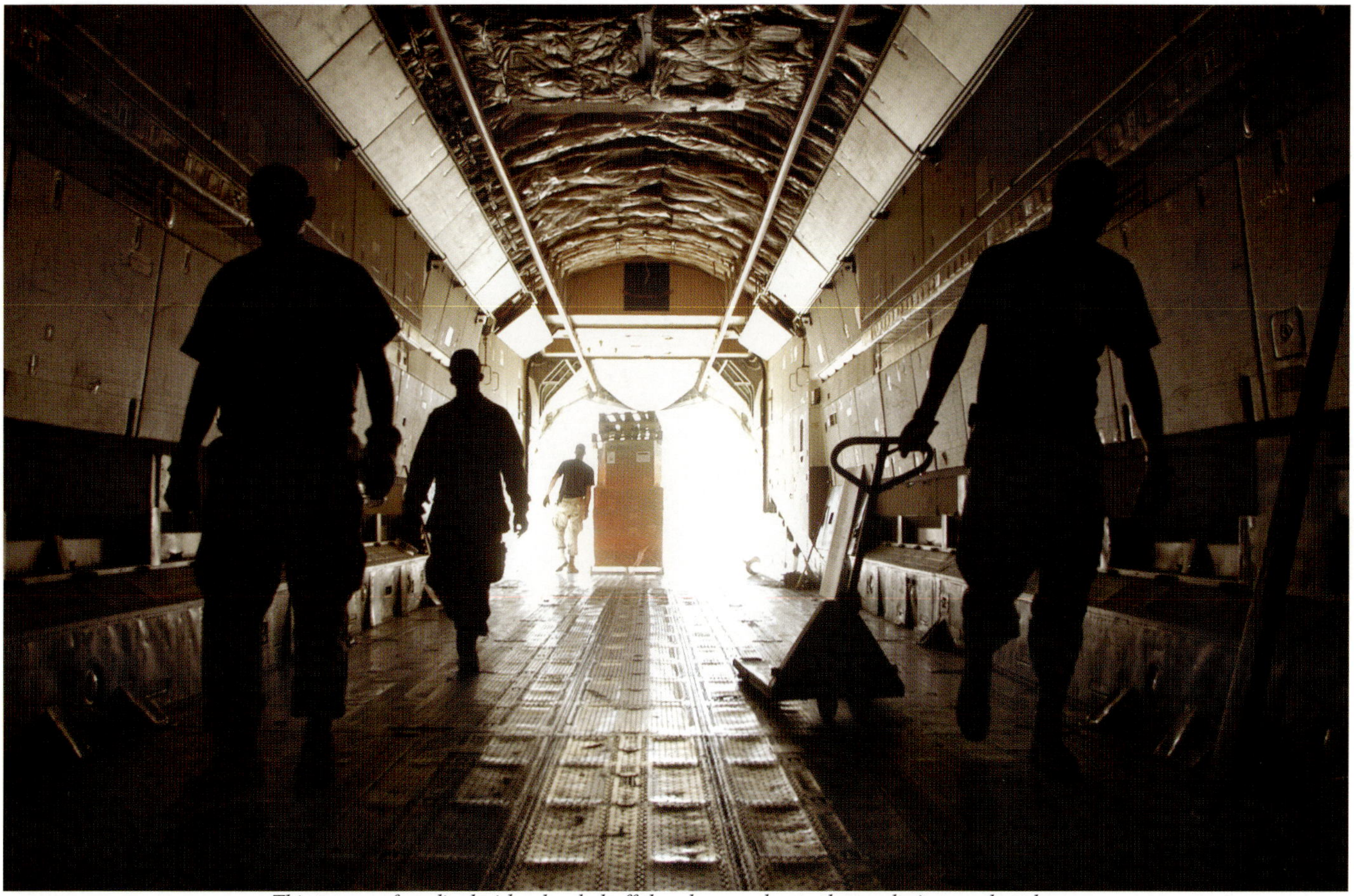

Thirty tons of medical aid unloaded off the plane and onto the trucks in two short hours

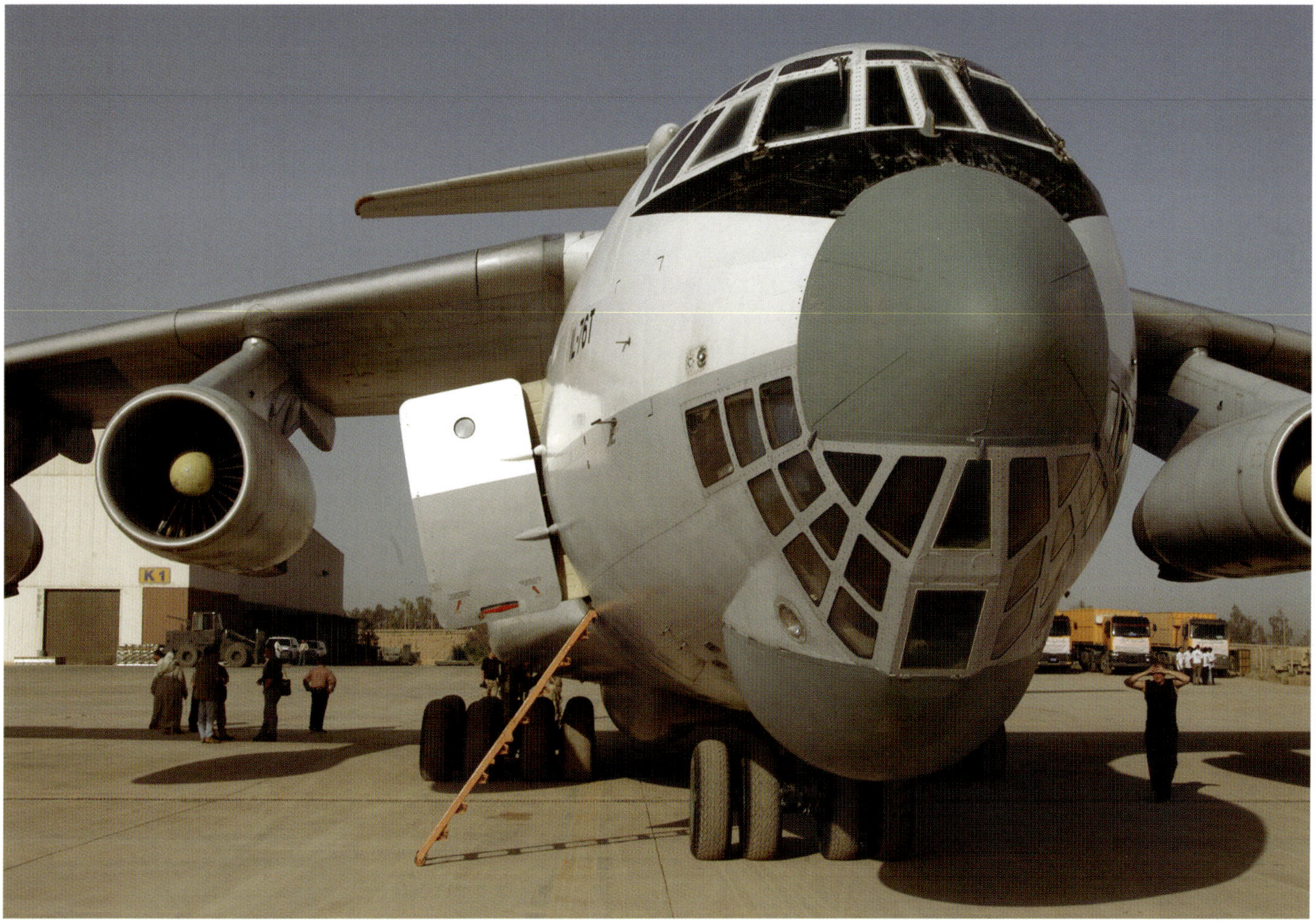

The plane is readied for the return trip to Europe

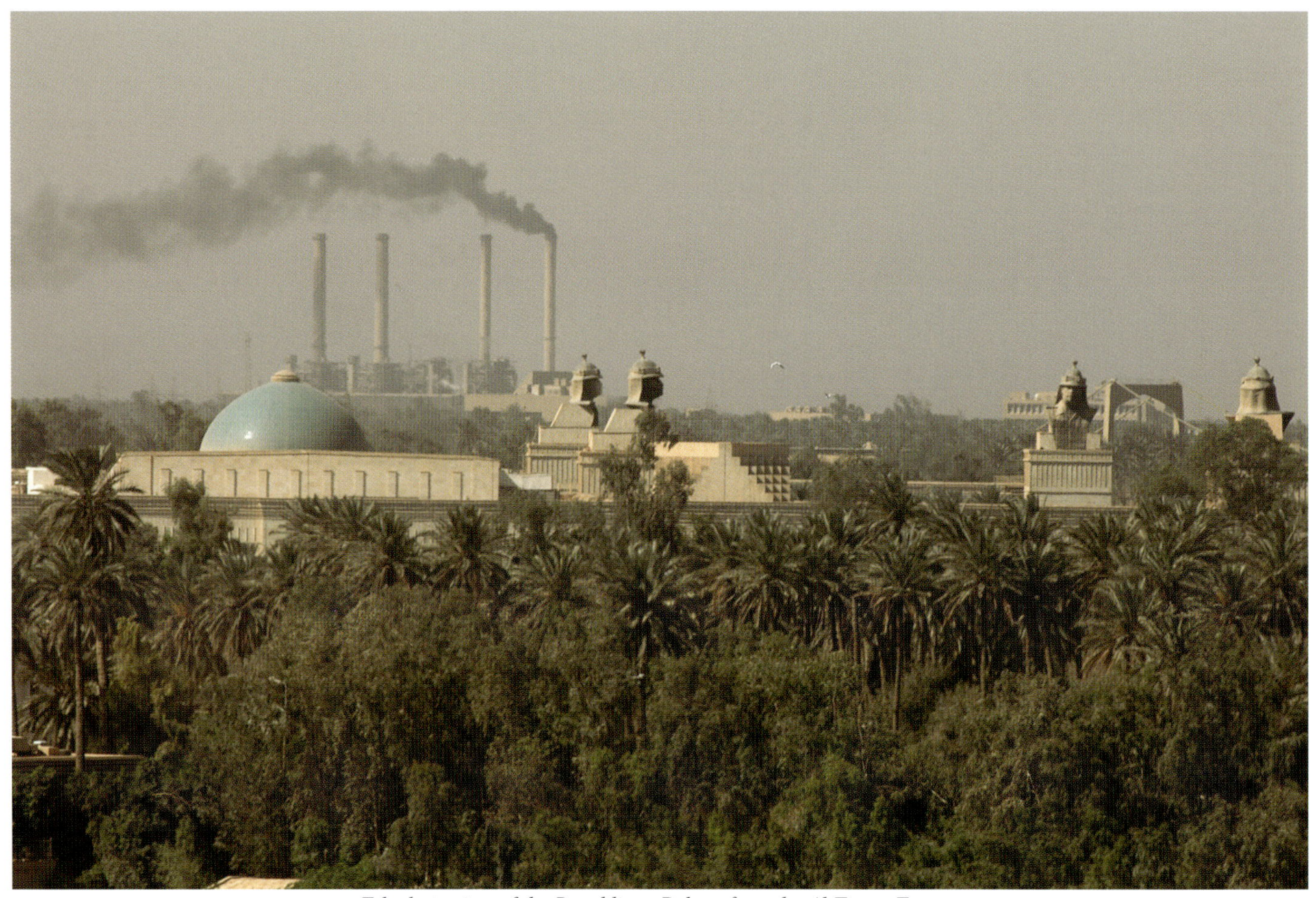

Telephoto view of the Republican Palace from the Al Fanar Towers

could easily take shots of the missiles and other stuff, I do not want to take the chance of discrediting the *Americares* staff, or breaking my word. There is a very strong military presence here, with tanks and other hardware along the runways and tucked along service roads and under trees.

We stand outside the empty plane, chatting with the soldiers who helped us. They tell us that they have ever been to Baghdad (some have been stationed at the airport for over three months), nor have they seen an Iraqi dinar note. Hearing this, we reach into our pockets and start passing out dinar notes. It is nice to repay them in some small way for their help. They are very happy to receive the Saddam banknotes and the update of what is happening outside of the airport.

Just before the convoy is set to leave, a beautiful, shiny Lear jet, with a large red cross painted on its side, lands and careens over beside our trucks. It is a flight from Europe carrying officials of the Red Cross Society. The officials emerge from the plane dressed in well-fitting business suits and finely sculpted hair. They resemble extraterrestrials, 'beamed down' from Wall Street. They are going to have a surprise when they see what Baghdad has become. At the same time I notice a blue Jeep, with the lettering U.N. emblazoned in orange on its side doors. This is the first time I have seen a U.N. vehicle in Iraq. Perhaps it is here to bring the Red Cross personnel into Baghdad.

Leaving the base, I see a group of administrative buildings inside a large walled compound. A white bed sheet is draped down the face of one of the buildings. Painted on it in huge lettering is the phrase, Welcome to the Hotel California. Beside it hangs a 50-foot tall portrait of Saddam, wearing his fedora and clutching a shotgun. This image of Saddam is a famous one, and is seen on billboards and posters throughout Iraq. From the way the two murals hang beside each other (intentional I imagine), it looks as though Saddam is welcoming the American soldiers to the Hotel California.

These buildings are part of Saddam's former airport palace complex. The place is huge, but because of a high brick and barbed-wire topped fence surrounding the complex, we are unable to get a good look at it. A large number of Humvees, tanks, troop carriers and support vehicles are tightly packed into a four-acre parking lot at the foot of the buildings. Soldiers go about their leisure activities, hanging laundry, inspecting their vehicles and lounging about.

A short distance from the airport, the convoy of trucks heads off in another direction to a waiting warehouse, while we continue downtown. Over the next two to three days, the supplies are to be inventoried and readied for shipment to needy hospitals and clinics.

After returning to the hotel, I meet Kenji and Dana in front of the Fanar. We sit drinking coffee, discussing our drive to Amman tomorrow morning (Kenji and I have decided to leave together, and are trying to finalize details with the owner of the shuttle service). The Al-Wafid Transport Company has been running a shuttle service between Amman and Baghdad.

We walk up the street to the transport office, minutes from the Fanar. Kenji and I sit in the office talking with the owner, who says there will be seven Jimmys full of journalists in our early morning convoy. The cost is $300 per Jimmy, and is to be split by up to 3 passengers. This sounds good, perhaps too good.

I want to be certain that I will have no problem bringing my two bayonets into Jordan. So I have a chat with the owner, emphasizing that he must be certain that the border guards will not take the items from me should I bring them. I do not want any trouble at the border, and I do not want to lose my gifts. I tell him I will try to find another way to send them back, such as the TNT courier service in the Palestine, if necessary. The owner promises that there will be no problem. "The border patrols are only restricting firearms from crossing the border, not knives. As long as you have no firearms or bombs you'll be OK my friend! I promise you!"

Just last week a Japanese photographer crossing the Iraqi border into Jordan, was carrying a live grenade in his luggage. During a search of his bags it exploded, killing a border guard.

Kenji knows the photographer, and says he is just your regular type guy. He cannot believe that he would have knowingly carried a live grenade in his luggage, and wonders how he could have been so careless. It is because of this tragedy, that I want to be sure that there will be no problem at the border with my bayonets.

I leave Kenji and head off to do the *USA Today* shoot at the *Internet* Café with Ken. After the shoot, I transmit my pics directly to the paper from the café. Ken and I take a taxi back to the complex, but we decide to get out for a short walk before reaching the hotel. We pass a small shop with a large handgun painted on its front window. A sign announces, Guns For Sale. We walk inside and talk to the owner, who tells us that before the war you needed a license to buy a gun; but now you don't. There is not a large stock in the display cases, but there is a small selection of shotguns, handguns, and two tiny derringers. His business is hurting because the whole of Baghdad has become one super-sized gun shop.

Returning to the Fanar, Ken hands me $175 for the photo shoot. I thank him for the job, then relax on the hotel patio with some coffee and chocolate bars. I am not in Baghdad to make money, but the spare cash will come in handy.

It has already been a long blistering hot day, and by late afternoon the city is like an oven. But there is one last commitment that I have to follow through with before wrapping up in Iraq.

Just before dark, I grab a taxi in front of the Fanar. My destination is the United Nations Building, about a thirty-minute drive east of the hotel.

It was five days ago that I had met and promised a soldier at the Taji Air Force Base, that I would try to carry a message to his brother, a soldier with U.S. Army Logistics stationed at the U.N. building in Baghdad.

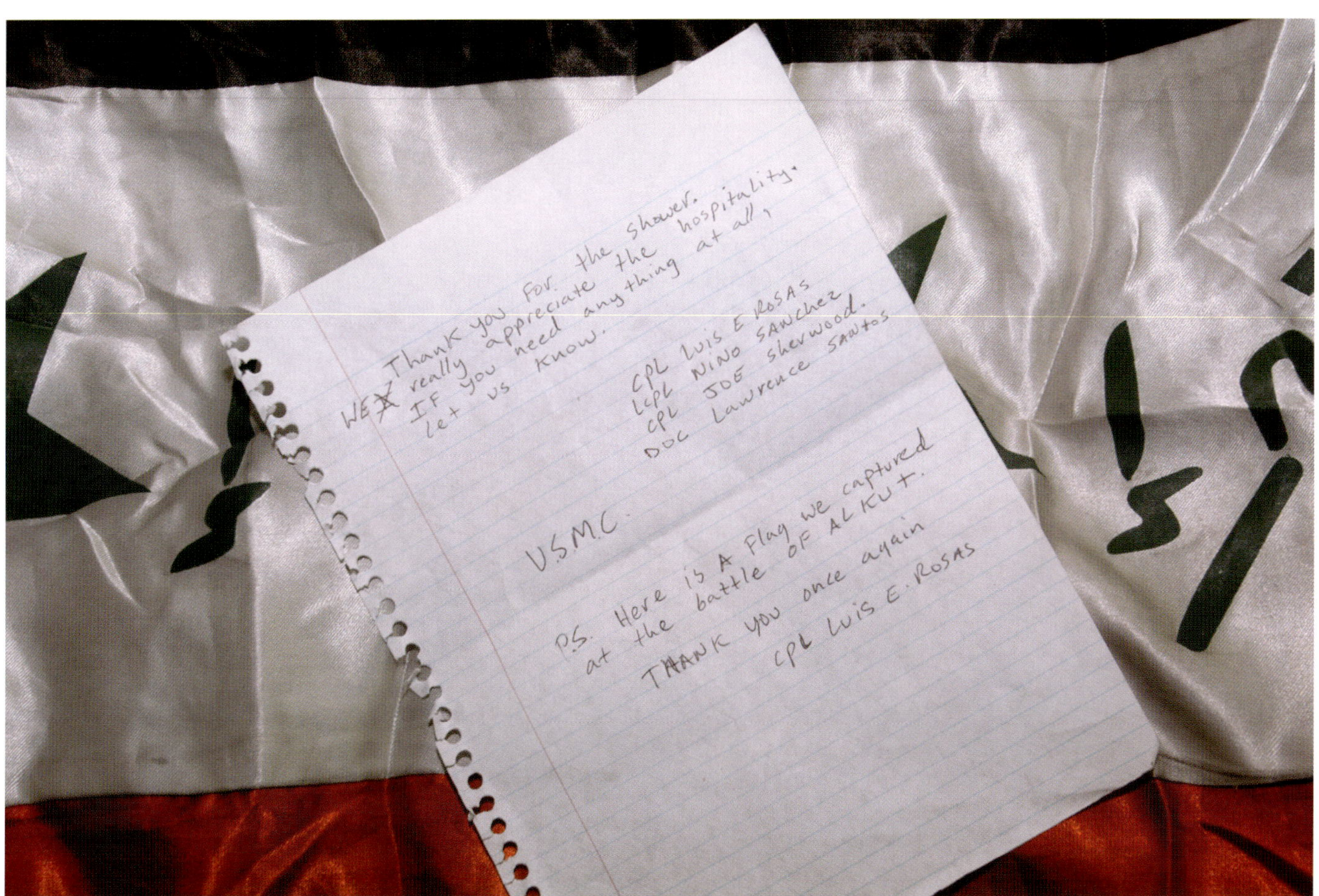

Flag given me by Nino and his fellow Marines

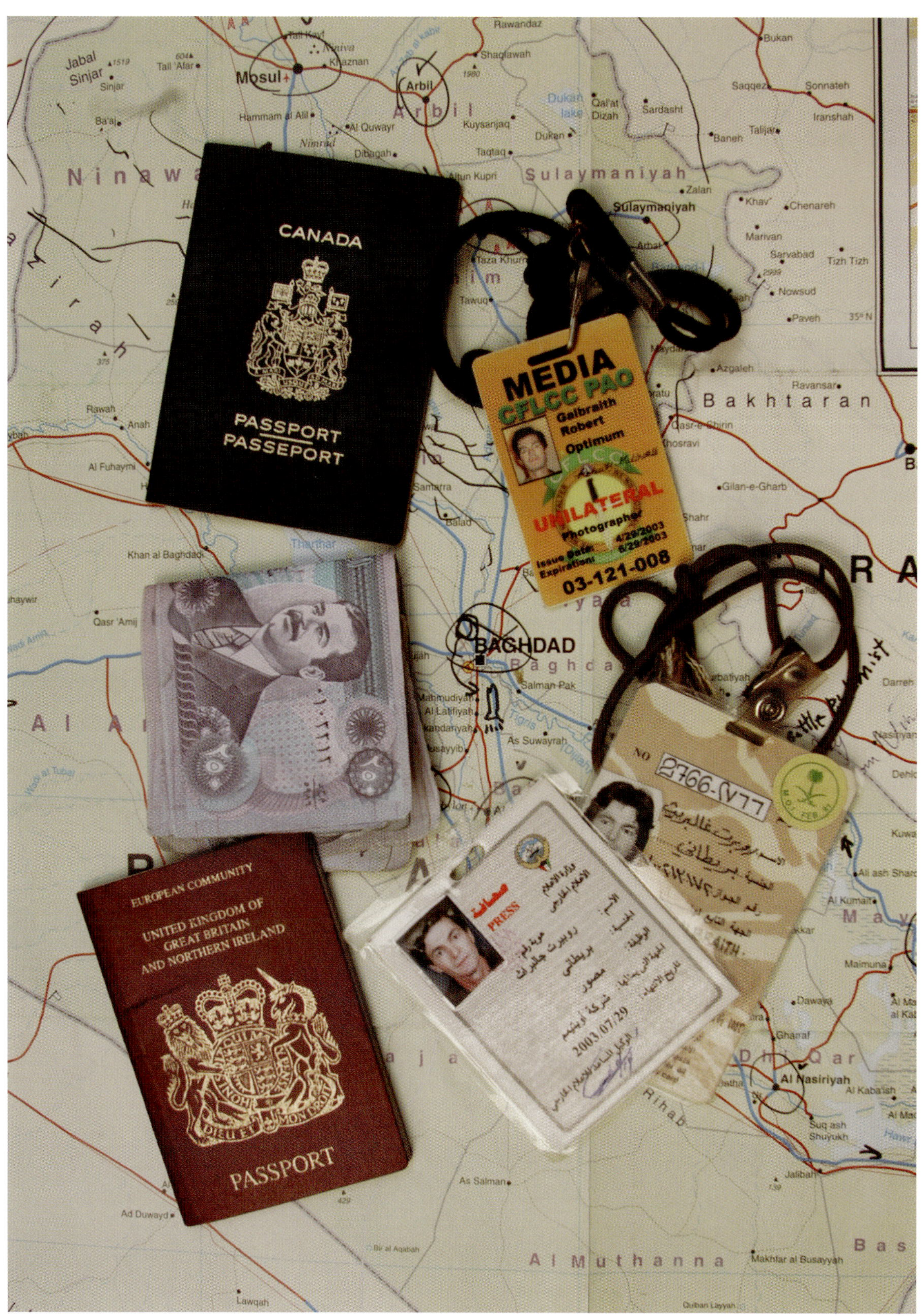

Some of the credentials used during the daily coverage

We manoeuvre through a wasteland of suburbia, interspersed by large empty fields of sand and smoldering garbage. It's like driving into hell.

Arriving at the front gates, I speak to a sentry who tells me that the soldier's unit has moved to another location, a couple of miles from where we are. With darkness spreading its cloak over the city, I stand in the middle of nowhere, a very dangerous nowhere. It would be just too risky and foolhardy to continue trying to find him in the twilight. I decide to head back to the Fanar. I have kept my promise to the soldier, and to myself. There is nothing else I can do, except mail the note to the soldier who first gave me the note; I have his home address.

As the taxi driver turns the ignition key, the engine fails to turn over. Three more attempts, and the vehicle's engine grunts back to life. Feeling like a helpless target, the driver and I make our way back through the outskirts of Baghdad. I keep my head low, to avoid being seen by people in passing vehicles. It would be so easy to get killed out here in "no-Westerners-land." The last few days in Baghdad have been extremely unnerving, and I hope this will be the last time I risk my life in this country. But in Baghdad, hope is just a four-letter-word.

The taxi driver is the Turk who accompanied us during the uprising of the vigilantes in front of the Red Crescent Society on April 13th. Ever since that day, our news team has tried to avoid this man at every opportunity. Unfortunately, he is the only taxicab available.

As we pull up to the Fanar, I am extremely happy to be safely back home. Today is Mother's Day, so I borrow a satellite phone and call my wife in Montreal. She is not home, so I leave her a 'caring husband message.' How ironic, wishing my wife a happy Mother's Day, while my life is a living nightmare! But I have to put on a brave face on the phone, so as not to panic my family. I also ask her to call my mother in Hamilton, Ontario, to let her know that I am still in Baghdad and I wish her a happy Mother's Day.

I am sitting in front of the Fanar, having a coffee and sharing some laughs with my good friend and colleague Tod, when he starts to describe an unusual situation he ran into earlier this morning, while driving to an interview.

While passing a bank, he saw two handcuffed looters (one a hunchback) carrying furniture into a bank. Two soldiers with rifles in their hands were forcing them to return the furniture, which they had been caught looting from the bank. Tod goes over to talk with the soldiers, to find out what was going on.

They tell him that they had just caught the two men as they were looting the bank of its furniture, and that this was the fourth time they had arrested this one individual robbing this same bank. "And here he is back again!" the soldier exclaimed. They said that once a looter is arrested, he was brought to the police station for processing. "But the next thing you know, they are let out again – and they start looting again! So we felt that by humiliating him in front of these people, they wouldn't return." A large crowd of bystanders had gathered across the street from the bank, watching the pathetic comedy unfold.

Tod walks over to the crowd to ask them their opinion of the soldiers' treatment of the looters. A man steps forward from the crowd and says that the soldiers, "Should have punched the looters in the face a few times; then they might not return!"

It is a surprising response but, an obvious one. They hate looters, and would have been more than aware (by word of mouth) that armed looters are breaking into and robbing homes at night, and hijacking vehicles and their occupants by day. The crowd must have got a good laugh at seeing these Americans trying to win the streets back with politeness and Western policing techniques.

The looting of Baghdad is now into the bottom of the ninth inning, with just the dregs left to be stolen. Western law has been, and is, useless here. Handing out tickets for looting is not going to work in Baghdad! The looters must have thought they had died and gone to capitalist heaven on the day the Americans arrived in Baghdad. The liberating force has inadvertently set the stage for the sacking of the city, and the situation is going from bad to worse.

It is easy to second-guess and presume that there should have been some sort of contingency plan initiated to counter the looting. The Americans are just as surprised by the sacking that followed the liberation of Baghdad and the looting fever spreading across the country. In other words, if you accept their explanation, it has caught them completely off guard. Others are of the opinion that it is part of a conspiracy by the Americans to let the Iraqis destroy their own nation, in retaliation for Desert Storm, or for the Americans to justify a long-term occupation.

There are numerous other conspiracy theories which could entertain us into our old age, but hypothetically, it might be said that because of the looting, the job of rebuilding Baghdad and getting the infrastructure up and running, will progress much slower. The actual reality is that Iraq is crumbling more and more, as each day passes.

I am starting to believe that if the Americans lose this war in the long run, and it is far from over yet, it will be largely due to the army of looters, who sucked the country dry before it could get on its feet.

I decide it is time to give the Fanar staff the $100 tip that I have been holding onto. I give the hundred-dollar note to a young man who works as a cashier in the dining room. He is an employee I often chat with and I feel I can trust. I ask him to make sure that the tip is equally divide amongst the 33 hotel staff, or, if they all agree, it can be used to fund a heck of a staff party. Either way, I ask to make sure that everyone gets his or her fair share. Two other staff members are beside me as I hand over the crisp bank note. All three employees thank me graciously with handshakes and kisses on the cheeks.

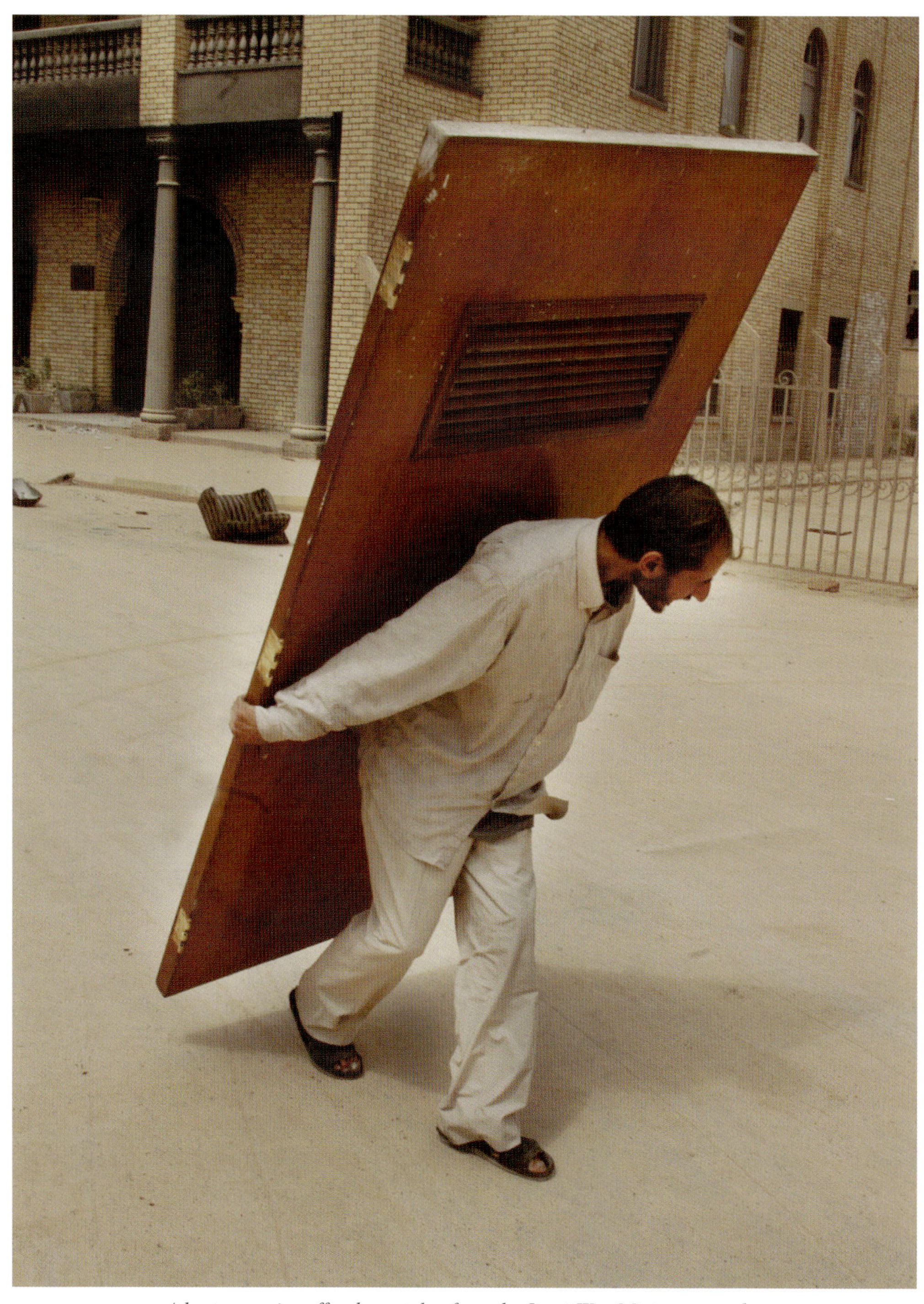

A looter carries off a door stolen from the Iraqi War Ministry complex

I return to the outside patio to talk with Peter and my other *Americares* friends. At the same time I give him a CD copy of the photos I took during the unloading of the relief flight. He has already seen a number of the photos on my laptop, and is very happy to receive the CD.

As we sit there, two young Fanar employees approach me and humbly ask if I have given a tip to the hotel staff. I tell them yes. He apologizes for bothering me, then tells me that the guy I have given the money to, told them he has not received anything from me.

This I can't believe! Keeping a cool head, I walk over to the reception desk and speak with the hotel manager. I tell him the situation, and ask if he can please make sure everyone gets his or her share of the hundred dollars. He is quite upset about what occurred, and after apologizing, he walks right over to the guy in the dining room.

I walk back out to the patio, not wanting to hear any arguing. A few minutes later, the manager comes out to the patio and guarantees that the problem has been resolved. He also tells me that I am a very kind man. I am very relieved by his assurances and want to avoid getting upset by a money squabble; it has been a long day.

I start wondering if the cashier will be given a rough time, now that all the staff knows he tried to rip them off. Ten minutes later, the two employees come out of the hotel and thank me for the gift, and for making sure they received it. They are very happy, and though it may have only been a few bucks to me, I knew it meant a lot to these hard working people, just judging from the thankful expressions on their faces.

A hundred dollars is a lot of money in Iraq, in fact it is a small fortune to most people living in this country, and would be worth more than a year's wages to most. When I arrived in Baghdad, the Iraqi Dinar exchange rate was 3,600 Dinar for one U.S. dollar. But the Dinar has gone up in value over the last three weeks, and now one U.S. dollar is worth 1,400 Dinar. This is inflation Iraqi style.

I leave for supper with the *Americares* gang, and on the way, I see a man walk up to a restaurant patio, grab a plastic chair, then start to walk off with it. The restaurant owner comes out and starts tugging at the chair. The thief pulls the chair out of the owner's hands and walks off down the street with it, while the owner stands cursing and waving his arms in frustration. This is looting at its most rudimentary level – but it is still looting, and this kind of looting is happening everywhere. It is every man for himself. Saddam was the worst looter of all. He skimmed the countries oil profits for himself and lived in fairytale palaces while the population writhed in poverty.

Back at the Fanar, I sit outside talking with Jennifer and drinking coffee. We see some lightning bolts far off to the west. But it is probably heat lightning, and brings no moisture.

It is nearly 1 a.m., when I see three soldiers on foot patrol pass by the front of the hotel. This is the third time in as many minutes that I have seen these same soldiers. They do not appear alarmed; their weapons are lazily slung over their shoulders. Finally, I walk up to one of them and ask if there is something going on in the neighborhood that could present a risk to us sitting outside? They both look at each other, and smile, then one of them points up to the side of the Palestine and says, "That's what's going on. We're just watching the show."

A group of journalists are having a going-away party on the roof of the Palestine, and floodlights have been set-up to light up the top floors of the hotel. Illuminated against the hotel walls are the giant sixty-foot shadows of two people making love, and performing other, more refined acts of love. Their actions are spilled across the upper wall of the hotel like huge, amorous shadow-boxers. I don't know if the performers know they are the cheap entertainment for the nighthawks; maybe they do. A small group of people have gathered on the street corner by a lamppost, watching the show with their heads bent upwards, like sunflowers stretching for the sun.

I chuckle, and head upstairs to pack my bags and get what will be my last night of sleep in Baghdad. It is such a consoling thought, knowing that by tomorrow night at this time, I will be in the luxury and safety of a Jordanian hotel. My bags are mostly packed for the morning drive to Amman. I just have to throw a few last things in before I leave.

While on the balcony recording my diary and having a cigarette before bed, I look down onto the street to see the street kids sleeping under their cardboard sheets, at the same spot under the Palestine bushes. I smile, looking down at this little family of friends sleeping like sardines in a tin. And how they are a family; a family of orphans, though still a family.

But something is askew, something inhumanly ugly. I see a man lying up snug behind the back of one of the young girls – he is screwing her! It is one of the young glue sniffing girls I saw yesterday. She might pass for a nine-year-old, but I doubt it. As the man's hips push in and out, the little girl edges her body away from him, trying to avoid his force. Numb and in shock, I stand frozen for a few seconds (I must be dreaming, I say to myself – but it is no dream). Grabbing my camera, I rush down to the second floor, thinking I can grab a photo of the guy and bring it over to the soldiers. They could use the photo to arrest him and get him off the street (or they could beat the beast to a bleeding pulp in some dark laneway). These children are friends of some of these soldiers.

But by the time I grab my camera and feel my way in the darkness to the second floor (where I am within range for a photograph), the whole group of about seven kids are awake and sauntering down the poorly lit street. As they drag their cardboard beds behind them, I can hear the muffled crying of the children, and look to see the same man, or in this case – the bogeyman – following twenty feet behind the displaced young cast. They disappear into the inky blackness, shuffling towards the dim lights of an army checkpoint outside the Palestine Hotel.

I ask myself why I had to see this rape? Why on my last night in Baghdad, so close to leaving this hellhole, did I have to see this? But it is destiny, I am supposed to see this, it is no fluke! It is part of my lesson, my lesson of war and the barbarity of humanity.

Lonely, nauseated, withdrawn and confused, I lie shaking in my bed, with the visions of this latest horror playing over and over in my head. I think of my family sitting at home, waiting for me to fly into their lives again. And I think about what I will be leaving behind. I am encased in guilt, knowing that there is little I can do for the innocents of Babylon, except to let others read what I have lived, and what they are living. There are no rules here, you just have to survive. That's all that matters.

A machine-gun sounds in the distance, echoed by returned rifle fire. The howling and yelping of the wild dogs smothers away the weapons fire, as the beasts tangle once again for dominance on the dusty plain along the riverfront. It has been a horrendous day of misery and painful self-exploration. I lie in my bed, bound by despair and covered with guilt.

Day 33. Monday, May 12th

*(Up at 4:30 a.m.; feeling like a sitting duck; waiting for the Jimmys; "we're heading out of Baghdad";
I will never forget; trucks filled with foodstuffs; the sandstorm; 'Ships of the Desert'; trucks line up at
Jordanian border; officials confiscate my gifts; given the phone number of the Jordanian CIA; my
passport is stamped; crossing from Iraq into Jordan; a stop in Ar Ruwaysha; inhumanly hot; arriving
in Amman; staying at Le Royal Hotel; lobsters in the hot tub; cappuccino and chocolate truffles;
supper with Kenji; slurping my soup; weighing myself)*

I am up at 4:30 a.m., making sure that all my baggage is in order. In darkness, I leave the Al Fanar Towers for the last time, with all my possessions on my back and in my hands. I start walking to the shuttle office, a block away. It is an unbearable weight to carry and I breathe heavily walking along the dark empty street. Reaching the front of the office (which is closed), I put my baggage down against the building and tuck myself into the dark recess of the doorway, to stay out of sight from night stalkers.

With all my luggage and cash on me, I feel like a lame duck waiting for the hunter. Realizing that I could get robbed blind, I decide to carry all my gear back to the front of the Fanar, where I will be safe.

The Jimmys arrival time is at 5:00 a.m., but they haven't shown up and it's almost 5:30 a.m. Ten minutes later, a Jimmy arrives at the front of the Fanar with Kenji in the front seat. We pack my gear into this vehicle then drive

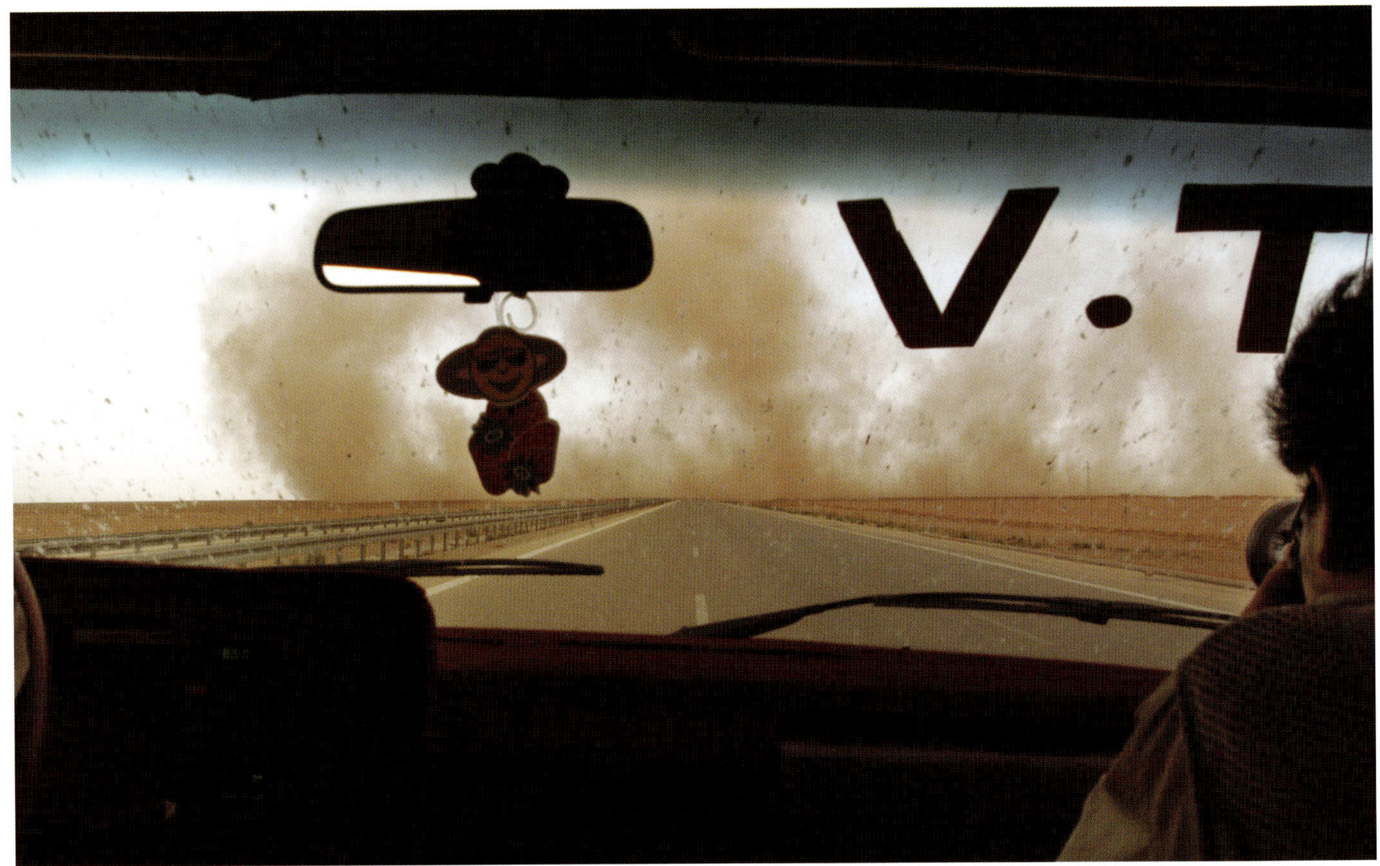

Japanese photographer Kenji Shimizu snaps away as the leading edge of a sandstorm advances across our path on the highway to Jordan

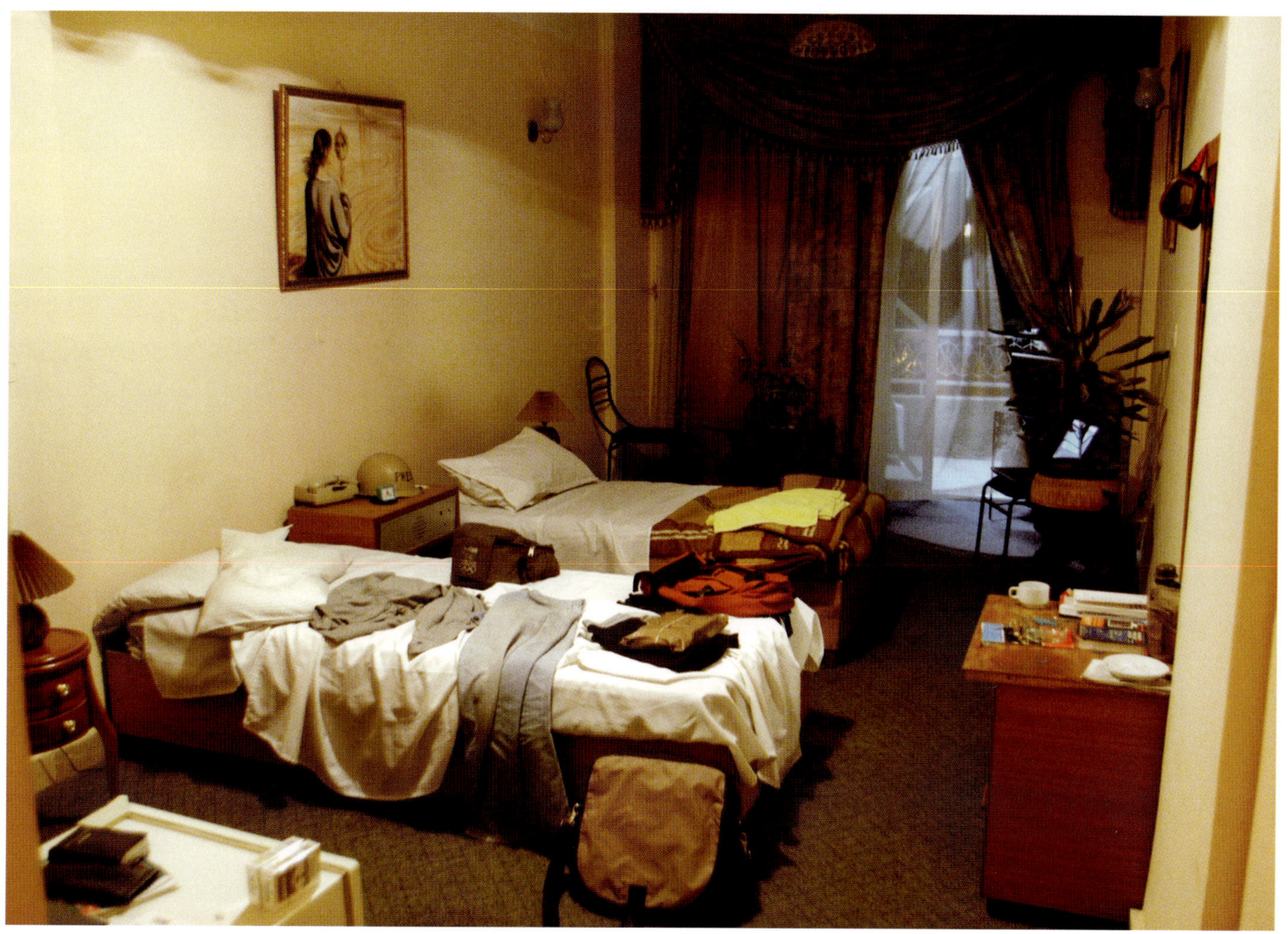

The author's room on the 7th floor of the Al Fanar Towers before his departure for Jordan

over in front of the shuttle office, waiting for the other Jimmys. A short time after, a second Jimmy arrives with two German journalists.

We wait around for another twenty minutes, then I tell Kenji that we have to get going, even if just two vehicles. The two drivers are just hanging out smoking cigarettes and joking; they are in no rush. We walk over and tell the drivers that we want to leave now (we have not paid for the trip yet, so it is time to play hardball and get the drivers moving).

Both of us are very agitated, me in particular (because I hate waiting for people who cannot keep a rendezvous time). The driver explains to us that one of the journalists is in bed and holding up the convoy. I ask him how one man can hold up seven Jimmys. I start to realize that this guy is trying to bullshit me. Speaking clearly and forcefully, I tell him that we either leave now, or we will cancel our trip and return to our hotel. "It's now or never," I tell him. He makes a call on his satellite phone, then turns and tells us, "We're heading out of Baghdad!"

We jump into the vehicles and start driving away from the hotel complex. I slouch back in my seat and take a long, deep breath as Baghdad blurs past my window.

Before long, dawn breaks and we are driving across the endless Iraqi desert, heading west, on the first leg of my journey back to Montreal. An hour out of Baghdad, we pass by three large transport trucks, brimming with sacs of food-stuffs bound for the city. Shepherds herd their flocks of sheep and goats along the fringes of the highway, looking for tufts of vegetation in the yellow-brown vastness.

We watch as a tidal wave of red sand blows across the plain, enveloping our car in a red fog. The driver asks us to make sure the windows are rolled up tight as he turns on the wipers to clear away the thick dust covering the windshield. The storm, a pleasant distraction in this landscape of mirages, blows over us in a few minutes. We stop for a leak on the overpass where the Syrian passenger bus (see April 12th) sits destroyed by an American air strike, near the town of Ar Rutbah.

Continuing on, we pass a large herd of 75 camels being herded along the side of the highway by two Bedouin care-takers. Camels are rarely seen in Iraq, let alone in such large numbers. In all the travelling I have done in Iraq or other desert nations, I have seen very few of these Ships of the Desert. GMC Jimmys and other 4-wheel drive vehicles have rendered the camel largely obsolete.

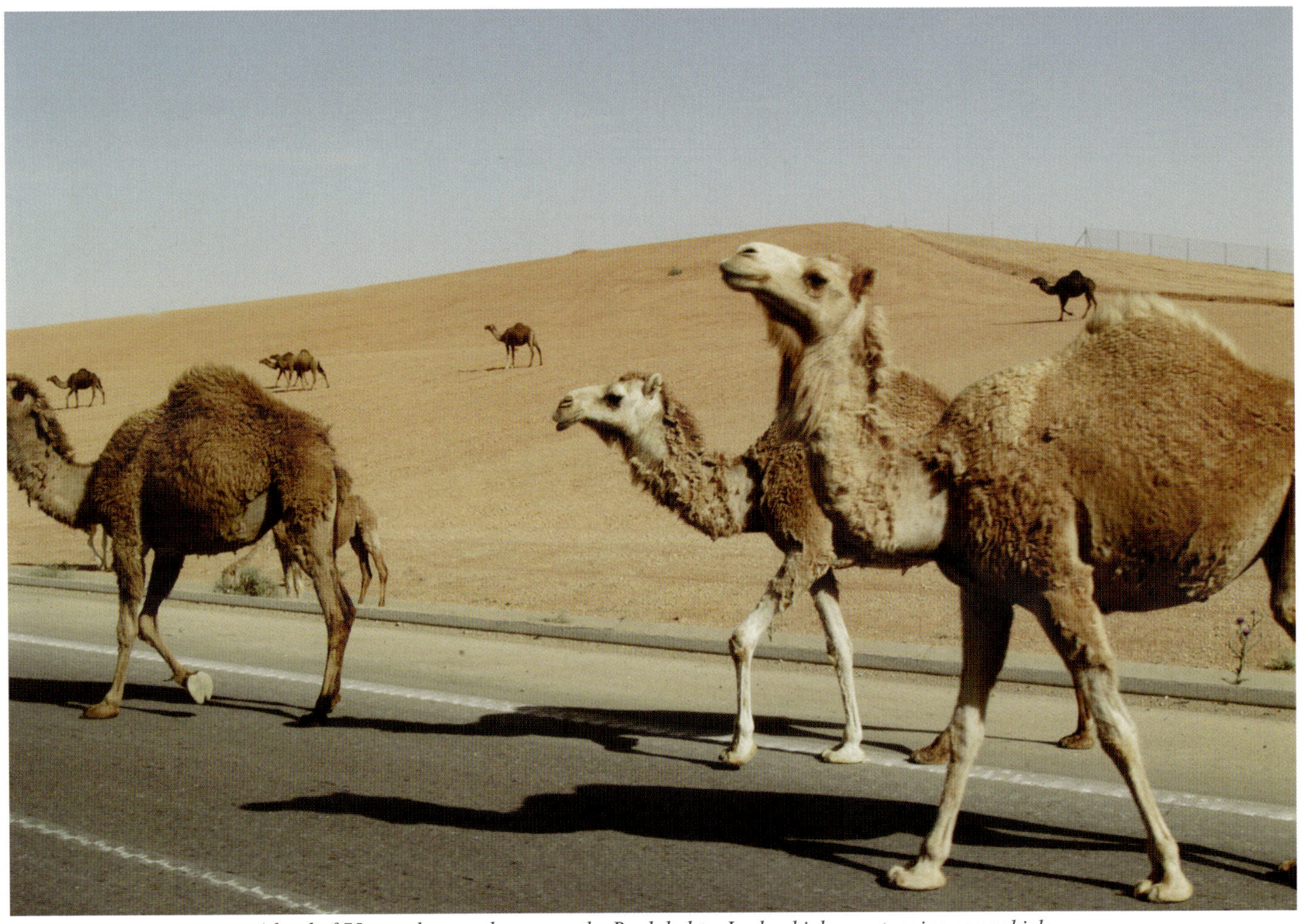

A herd of 75 camels meander across the Baghdad-to-Jordan highway stopping our vehicle

A mile before the Iraq-Jordan border, we see a long chain of large trucks forming a line-up to the border crossing. They are mostly tractor-trailers, lined up two abreast. Using the lane reserved for cars, we pull up to the Jordanian border checkpoint and wait for our turn at the inspection station. There are seven or eight border officials (some dressed in civilian clothes, some in police-style uniforms), opening baggage and questioning journalists from the Washington Post who are just ahead of us. The guards are very thorough, taking their time as they go through the baggage.

We are signalled forward by one of the officials, and our Jimmy pulls up alongside the long plywood inspection tables. I am asked to enter a small office (more like a telephone booth) where an official pats me down, making sure I am not carrying a concealed firearm. The official is very polite, and apologizes for the inconvenience of being searched in this manner. I tell him to do his job, and then thank him for his courtesy. I have a special admiration for the Jordanian people; they are a worldly, friendly people, and if I had to live anywhere in the Mid-East (including with my family), this progressive nation would be my first choice.

Leading me back to the long inspection tables, he asks me to open and dump out the contents of my baggage. Opening up and spilling out my large green pack, he finds my red and gold officers' flashes that Simon had given me. The inspector calls over another man (as I bite my tongue), who now helps him unpack my bag. They pull out the two bayonets, two flags and an empty ammo belt. He asks what I am doing with the items, and where I got them. I tell him the flag and bayonet are from my Marine friend Nino, and the other items I picked up during my travels across Iraq. The inspector, dressed in street clothes, tells me that I am not allowed to carry these objects across the border. I explain that I knew there were restrictions on firearms, but not on knives or flags. But the official says their policy is not to allow any war memorabilia, of any sort, into Jordan.

I try my best to convince the officials of my lack of ill-intent, but they refuse to let the objects pass. I ask if there is a head official with the Customs and Immigration Department with whom I can further my plea. Pulling a pen and paper from his shirt pocket, he jots down a phone number and hands it to me. "This is the phone number of the Jordanian CIA Headquarters in Amman. They are the people in charge of the items now. It is up to them; it's in their hands." I thank him, and then ask for a receipt for the items they are holding onto. I follow him back to the booth and he writes out a receipt, all in Arabic, and hands it to me.

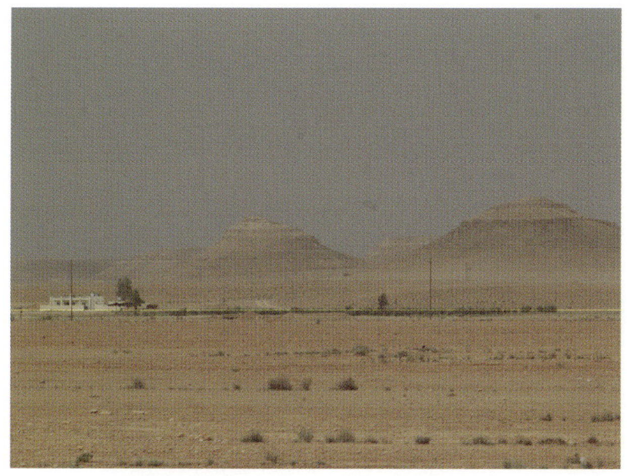

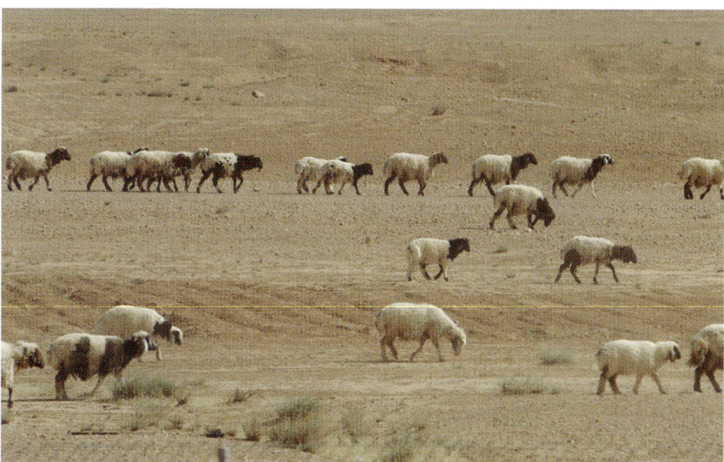

Rocky bluffs rise out of the desert sands

Sheep scrounge a meager existence from the dry plains

The inspector tells me I am free to go into the passport office and get my passport stamped for clearance into Jordan. I get it stamped, and then go into the Duty Free Store to buy some candies and a carton of Marlboro's. Kenji is taking longer getting his papers stamped, but soon joins me outside the Duty Free.

Climbing into the Jimmys, we drive past the border crossing, and then have to stop at a police checkpoint manned by one solitary officer. He takes the items receipt from me, and tells me he will keep it and forward a copy to the CIA in Amman. He smiles and wishes us a fast journey, then waves us on.

I am very disappointed and disheartened by what happened at the border, though I try to put it aside as there is not really much I can do about it right now. The reality is that I am safely in Jordan, and I might still get my gifts back.

We stop for lunch at the Jordanian border town of Ruwaysha. The last couple of hours drive to Amman is incredibly uncomfortable from being stuck in the car so long in the heat. The desert here looks like a Mars landscape – boulder-strewn, inhospitable and useless. It seems as though we will never reach Amman. Kenji and I are totally exhausted, and becoming slightly delirious.

Finally, we reach beautiful Amman, after a torturous twelve-hour journey! The Jimmy drives up to the front doors of the sumptuous Le Royal Hotel (where Kenji's newspaper had already booked him a room). A gaily-dressed doorman steps forward and opens the Jimmy door, then tipping his top hat and smiling, he welcomes us to Le Royal. I go inside to inquire about the room prices at the reception desk. The price is right, and I decide to take a room at $80 a night. The Intercontinental costs $120 a night, but this place is just as classy, if not more.

The hotel is opulently decorated in marble, glass and gold. The rooms are elegant and spacious, with a large TV and a big, deep bathtub. I arrange to meet Kenji at the pool and spa facility of the hotel, and then go to my room to unpack my bags and get some clean clothes on. I am back in civilization, and feel like wearing something nice, and clean.

Down at the spa, Kenji and I sit in the hot tub, boiling away like lobsters at a clambake. Then we splash around in the swimming pool until our skin returns to a normal color.

Just for a laugh, I hop onto the scales near the shower stalls. My jaw drops! It reads 132 pounds! I left Montreal weighing 164 pounds. This means I am losing close to a pound per day. Perhaps I am surviving on adrenaline. I can feel that my body has changed and my bones are starting to protrude (especially around the hips, knees and shoulder blades). I'm running on empty!

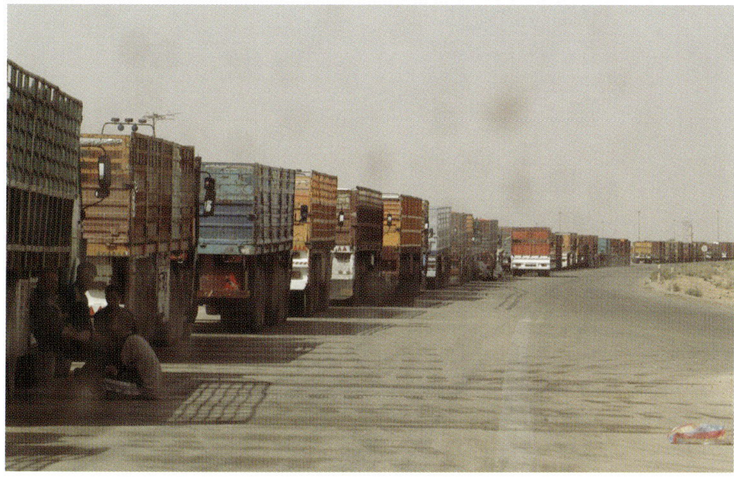

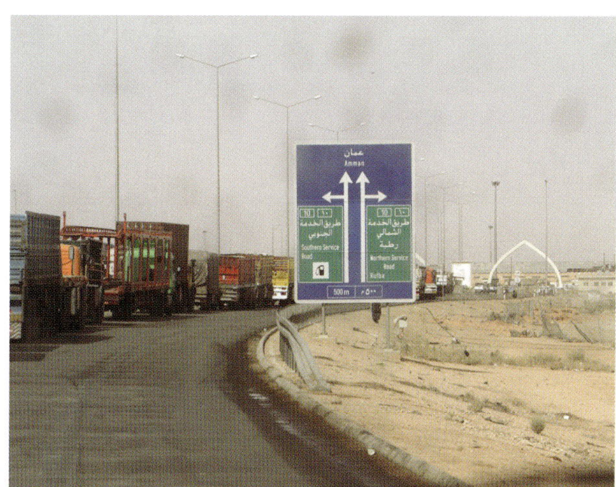

Long line of trucks wait their turn to cross into Jordan from Iraq

Just short of the Iraq-Jordan border

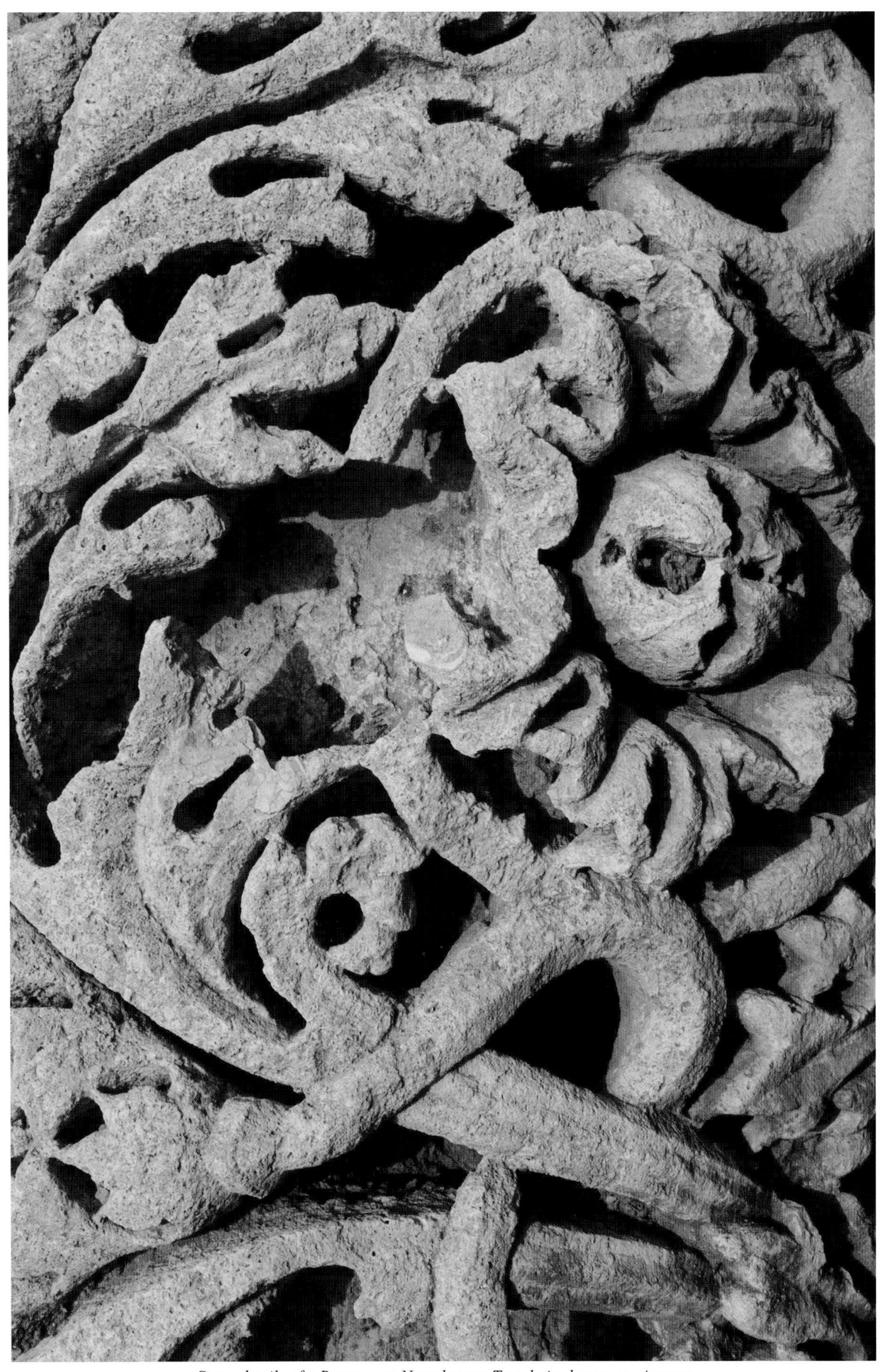

Stone details of a Roman-era Nymphaeum Temple in downtown Amman

After our soak, we get dressed and head 'double-time' to the hotel executive lounge. Stepping into the exclusive chamber, we realize we have left this earth and been re-born as gluttons in a taste bud heaven! Cappuccinos with chocolate sprinkles and shavings, cheesecakes, light pastries, truffles, fresh fruit, dishes filled with cashews, chocolate mousse cake.

It is incredible to eat this kind of food again and feel safe! Kenji and I are slowly emerging from our confining war shells and paranoia, and sucking up the luxuries of the modern, free world. It is an indescribably alien sensation, a re-birth, a new beginning. This completion of success and survival is part of the lure of war journalism, and words cannot do it descriptive justice. It will take a couple of days to climb back out of the pit of Iraq, and into the dimension of this other world. Normality slowly overwhelms you, like someone slowly turning up the lights in a dark room. So I guess you might say, you come in from the darkness of war, to the light of peace.

For supper, we eat at a Japanese restaurant on the second floor of the hotel. Kenji tells me that if you do not slurp when you drink your soup in Japan, it means the soup is not good. So, I start slurping my shrimp noodle soup. The meal is delicious.

Kenji and I are considering postponing our flights home and going for a day or two to the Red Sea or the ancient City of Petra. But first Kenji has to hear from his boss in Japan, to see if they need him back right away. We will find out tomorrow.

I e-mail my family from my room, letting them know I am safely in Jordan. In the message I let my wife know that I would like to have scalloped potatoes, baked ham and steamed mussels for my first meal back home, if she would be so kind. I tuck myself into bed, hoping to get a good night's sleep, but I end up staying up late, watching one of my all-time favorite horror movies; Damien. It suddenly occurs to me that my assignment in Iraq is finished; there is nothing else for me to cover. It is over! I slip off to sleep with a satisfying bellyache, full of rich luxury food, and a mind at ease.

Day 34. Tuesday, May 13th

(Buying gifts for my family; ruins of a Roman-Era Nymphaeum Temple; back to the Rozana Hotel; the Jordanian CIA working in Le Royal Hotel; coffee, cookies and a chat with the Jordan CIA; using calmness and logic; an agreement between Mid-East nations; "these aren't cultural objects"; a new system of security; a century behind; a grave new world)

Kenji and I meet in the executive lounge for a light breakfast, then take a taxi to go shopping for gifts and to get a look at the city. The narrow streets of old Amman are burning hot, and we keep our walking to a minimum. It is a very uncomfortable, enveloping heat, intensified by the asphalt and breezeless stagnation of the alleyways.

We come across the working excavation of a large post-Christian Roman-era ruins, carved into the limestone rock of a downtown hillside and surrounded by the sprawl of the modern city (Amman is built upon a series of limestone ridges and hills). They are the ruins of a Nymphaeum Temple, a temple or sanctuary, complete with bathing pools, for Roman nymphs and divinities. It is a time capsule of beautiful stonework and design that shocks me with its spacious simplic-ity, and hypnotizing geometry. We walk about the site, taking pics and looking at the detailed carvings. I would loved to have spoken with some of the archaeologists, but none can be found.

After shopping, Kenji goes back to Le Royal, while I take a taxi to the Rozana Hotel (where I stayed when I first arrived in Amman on April 10th), to pick up my extra gear left behind before leaving for Iraq.

After picking up the gear and going back to the hotel, Kenji tells me his boss called to say he wants him back in Japan as soon as possible. He is to leave early tomorrow morning, a couple of hours before my scheduled flight. Sadly, we are forced to cancel our vacation plans to the Red Sea and Petra. Now it's time to go home!

Since I will be leaving tomorrow morning, and therefore have little time left, I decide to phone the Jordanian CIA, to see if I can speak to someone about getting my confiscated items back before I leave Jordan.

I approach the Customer Service counter in the hotel lobby and ask the hostess if she could call the phone number that the border official had given me (it is written in Arabic). She dials through the number and reaches the agency recep-tionist, who tells the hostess that she cannot help us until Thursday, as Wednesday (tomorrow) is a holiday, and all the staff left work early today. So it appears there is no way of reaching the agency until Thursday, when I will be in Canada.

I explain to the hotel hostess the problem that I ran into at the border. She seems to be sympathetic, and understands my dilemma. Then, like a bolt of lightning, she nonchalantly pronounces, "We have three CIA agents working in the hotel, why don't I try to reach one of them for you?" I ask her what she means, thinking that perhaps I misheard her. "We have three Jordanian CIA staff working here in the hotel round the clock. Let me call one of them for you," she insists. "Sure," I tell her. "That would be very kind of you."

A few minutes later, a middle-aged man walks up to me at the Customer Service Desk. With a handshake and a smile, he introduces himself as Abon, an agent of the Jordanian CIA. The hostess and the agent and I sit in the hotel discussing my situation, while drinking coffee and eating pistachio biscuits. Soon after, a second CIA agent named Omar, appears at our table and joins us. They both seem like fine gentlemen, and professional.

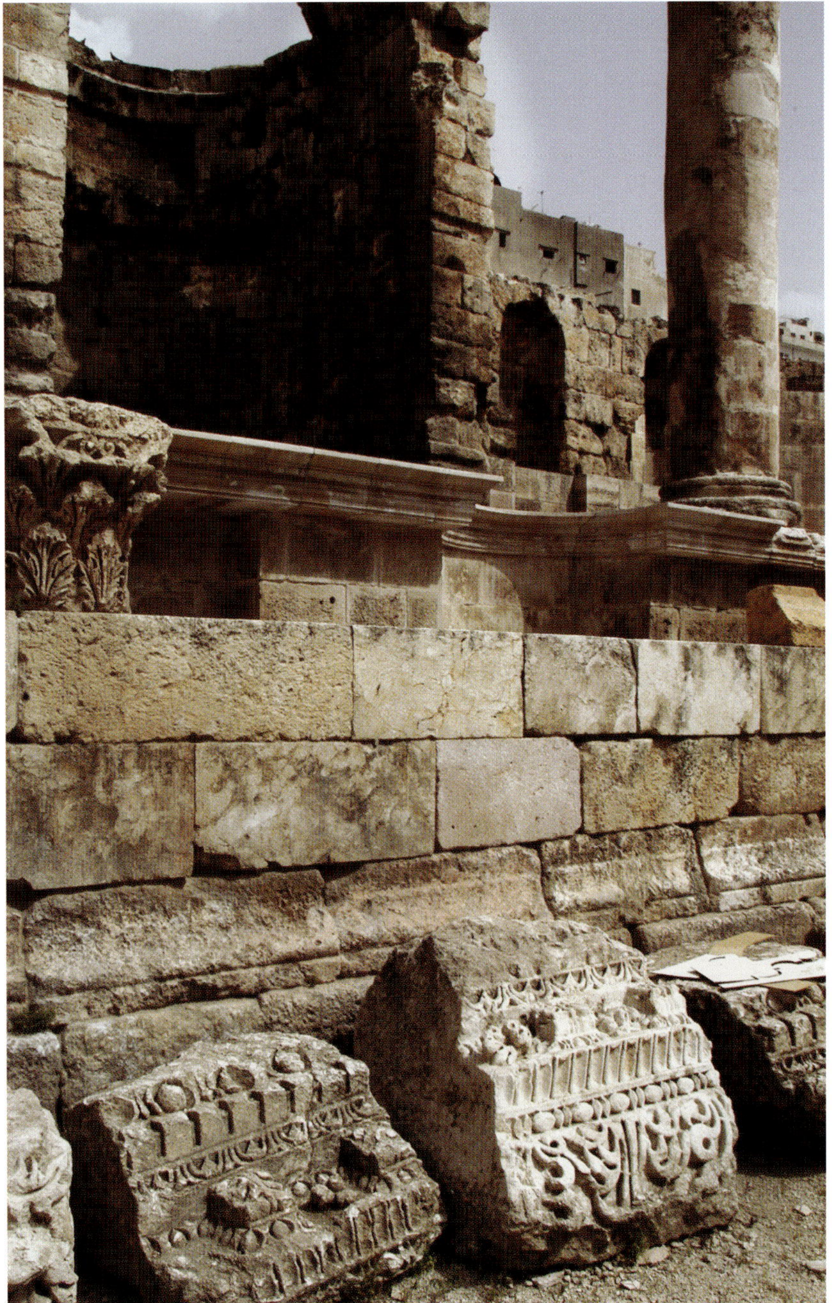

The Nymphaeum Temple was built around 200 A.D. It is presently under excavation

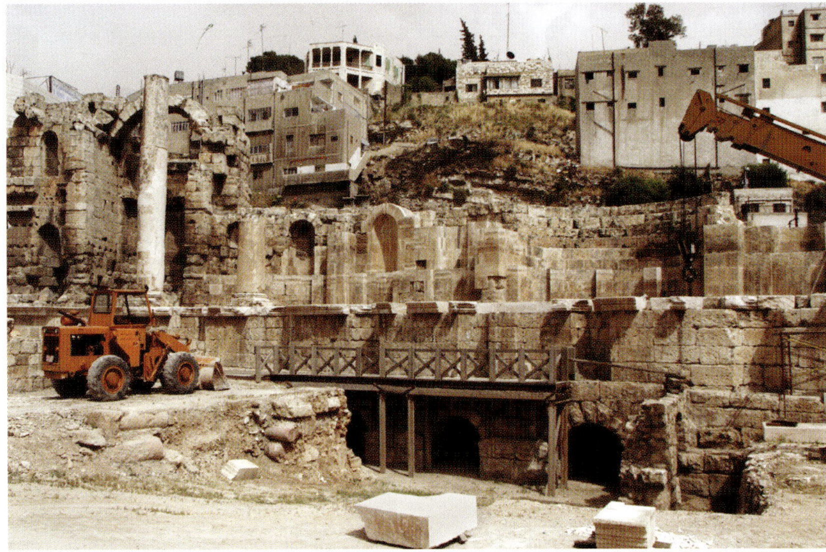

Modern and ancient Amman share the same hillside. Excavation will take 7 years

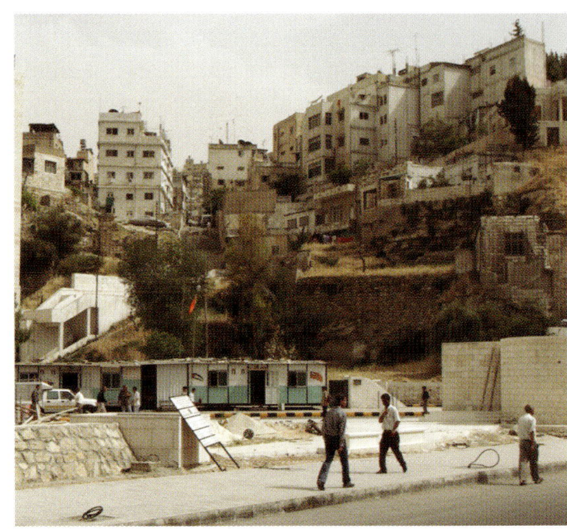

Amman is built on a group of hills

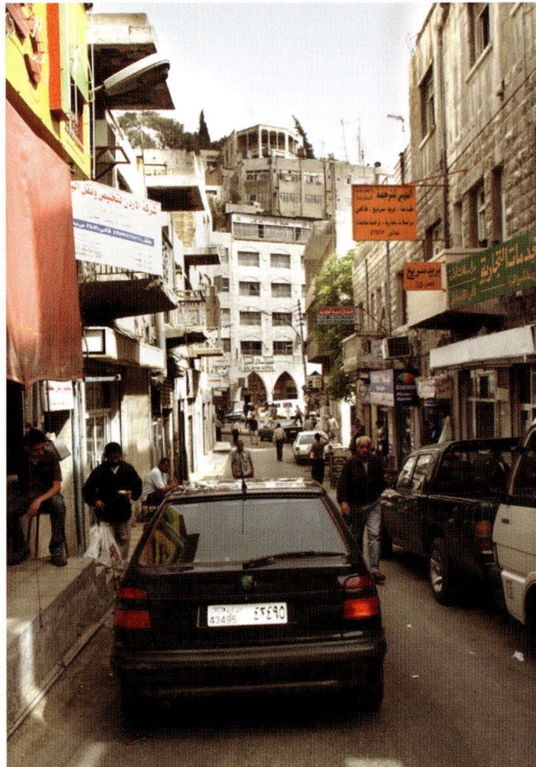

Narrow streets can be traced to the Roman era

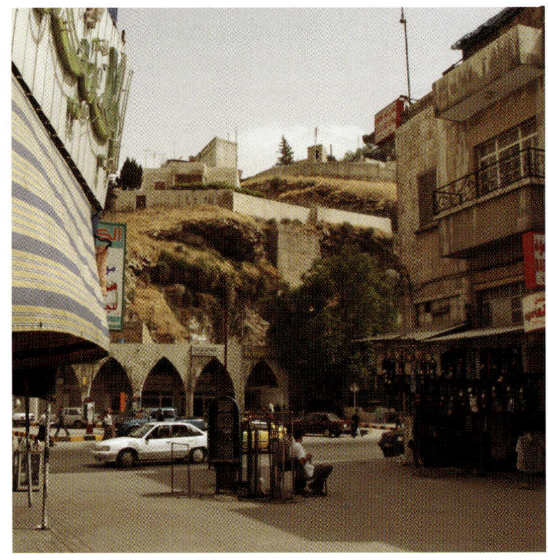

The history of Amman is over 7000 years old

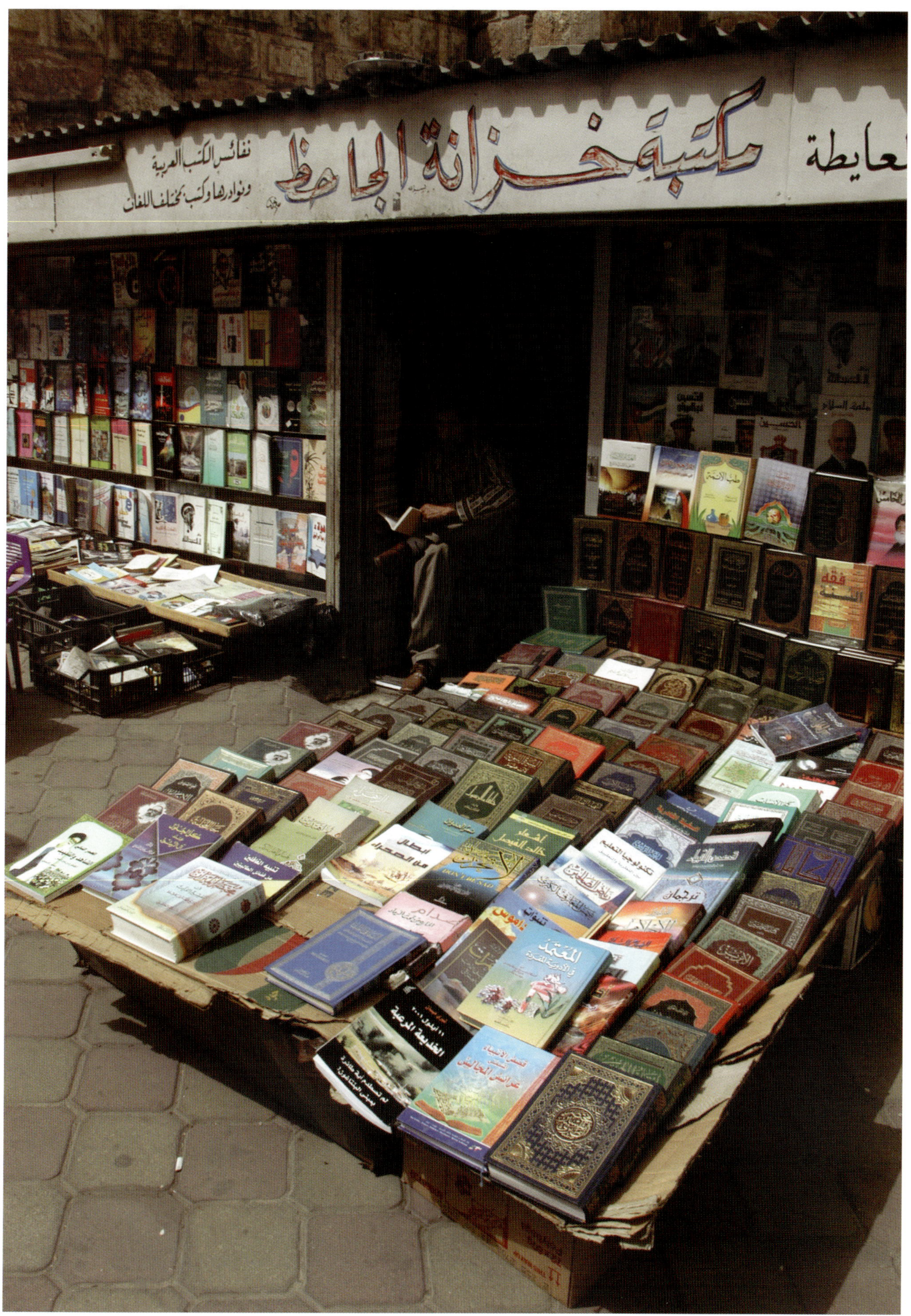

Bookstore in downtown Amman

At first Abon refuses to acknowledge that the CIA has agents working at the border, but he soon admits to the fact (rather than embarrassing himself with an obvious lie). After this, I ask him to treat me with a little respect and dignity, and not to insult my intelligence. I am confident and rested; I have little patience for this sort of game.

Trying to change tactics and the direction of the conversation, I show them my map of Iraq, outlining where I have travelled. They are quite impressed by my extensive travel agenda, and my reasons behind writing the book. Now they should better understand who I am.

Everything goes well; the conversation does not become heated or disrespectful. I use calm and logic to persuade them of my good intentions.

At one point in the discussion, Abon comments that my items may have been looted from a museum in Baghdad. I openly chuckle, telling him that his comment is absolutely ridiculous, and that you can easily find or purchase any of the same objects in Baghdad for a few coins or a couple of packs of Marlboros! These comments make it embarrassingly clear – that neither of these two agents (nor perhaps their government) have any clue as to what is really going on in Iraq, much the same as the Kuwaitis don't. I kind of feel sorry for them; they are good men, but ignorant.

I tell them the confiscated items will be used when I give talks or lectures on my book and travels, to bring the audience closer, and give them something to touch and see from the theatre of war. Holding and smelling a bayonet, pulling it from its hilt, with its sharp pointed blade tip and gun greased handle, is something you cannot describe in words or pictures – it stimulates the mind and brings you closer to the subject – war! It's like finding an Indian arrowhead in the garden; you pick it up and your imagination explodes, hurtling you back in time to when the Indian shot the arrow at the deer in your backyard – three-thousand-years ago. No other method, next to being in the war zone, can stimulate this raw desire to imagine and expand one's resource of book-bound or visual reasoning.

Abon says he is waiting for a call from his boss to decide how to handle my request. He is rather upbeat, and says it should all work out for me. I suggest that the items be brought to the Canadian or British Embassy and put into a diplomatic pouch for transport to Canada.

Finally, after sitting with these people for over an hour-and-a-half, Abon receives his expected call. He turns to me and explains what his boss explained to him. He says there is an agreement between the Mid-East nations and the United Nations, not to allow the transport or possession of any military object across the borders. He says that the items must be returned to Iraq, "They are a part of the cultural heritage of Iraq."

I start laughing while shaking my head, "These items are about as culturally important to Iraq as can of Coke is to a Bedouin!" I tell them. "Not only that, these weapons are mass-produced in Germany, Italy, Russia and France. Sorry, but your argument is illogical." I can read Abon's face like a cheap movie poster. He is totally embarrassed at having to give me; 'the company line,' "We must send them back to Iraq," he says apologetically.

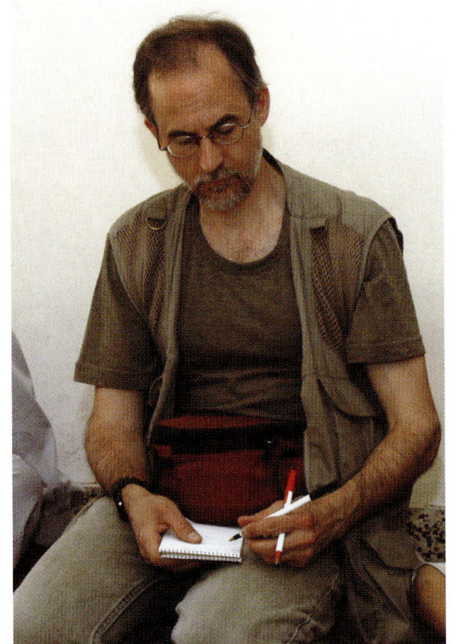

James Rupert of Newsday

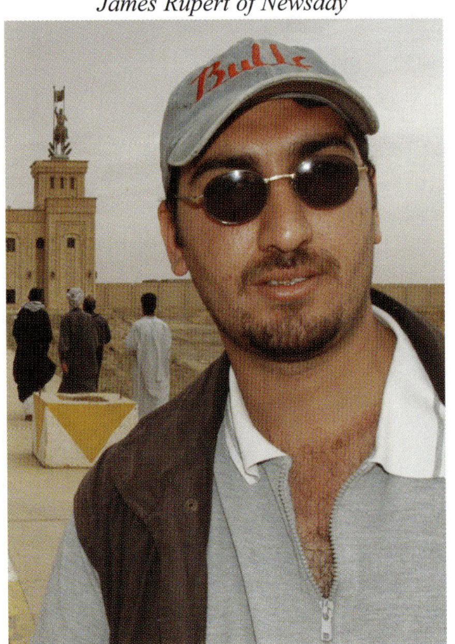

Haider, our interpreter and guide

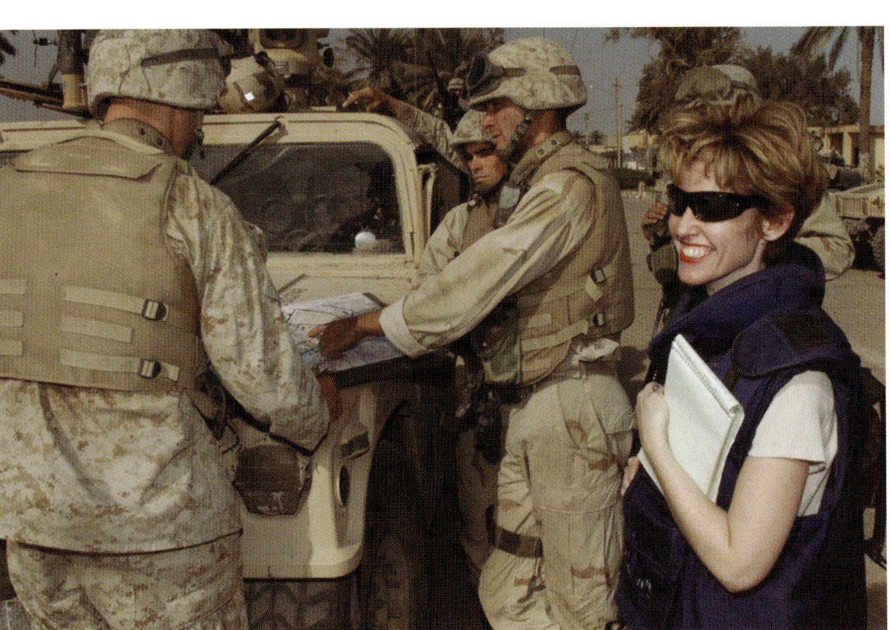

Tish Durkin, a freelance reporter for the New York Observer

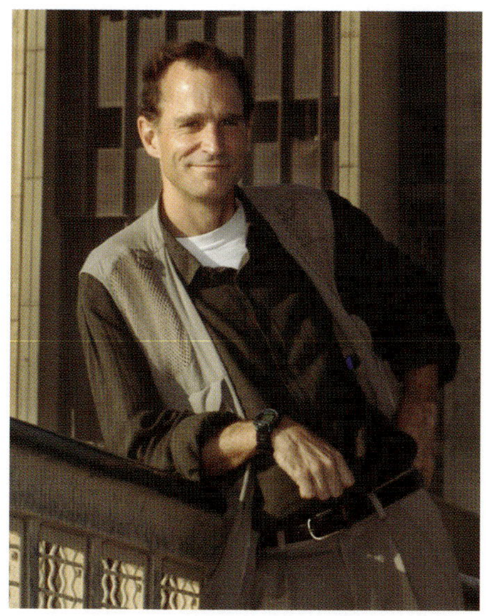

Tod Robberson of the Dallas Morning News

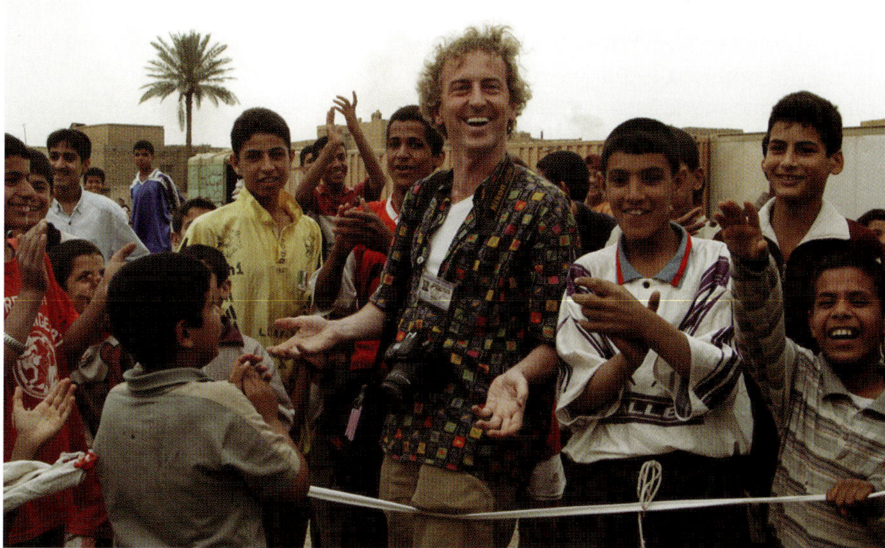

Independent film maker, Sean O'Sullivan has a heart as big as Mount Everest

I am now extremely angry, and tell Abon that I didn't expect such trivial bureaucracy from a modern and apparently progressive nation like Jordan. I am very let down – I admire the people of Jordan. But this meeting has tarnished my image of the Hashimite Kingdom of Jordan. I start having second doubts about my security in this country. Perhaps Jordan is not as modern as it appears, like Kuwait (which is a scary thought). A city or country can have the facade of a modern metropolis, but that's just window dressing if your government security structure and freedom of independent thought is a century behind the modern, progressive real world. Tribalism is still an integral part of society here and influences the workings of the government and every other facet of

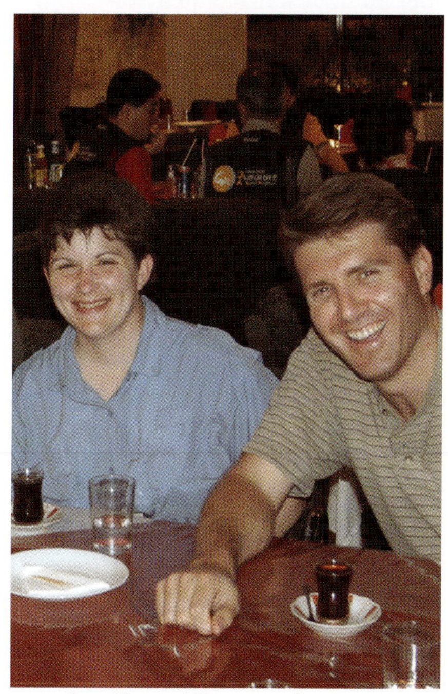

Jennifer and Peter out for supper

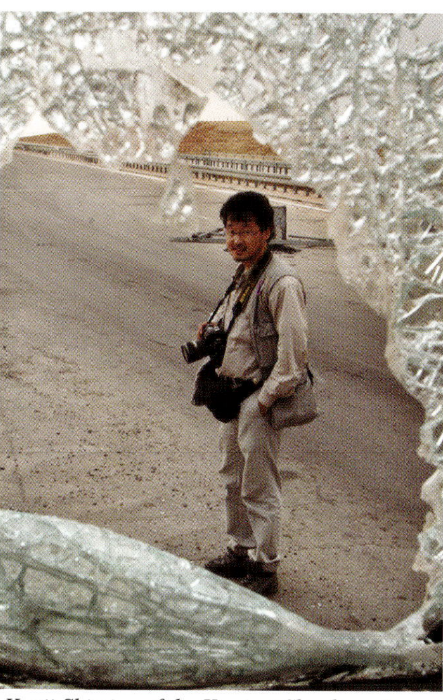

Kenji Shimizu of the Yomiuri Shimbun, Japan

society. This is a stigma that nations such as Jordan have to shed before really taking their place at the world table.

As our meeting breaks up, I find Kenji relaxing and enjoying the culinary goodies of the executive lounge. We decide to go out for supper at an Italian restaurant, away from the hotel. During our meal, Kenji and I delve into the possibility that the Americans, after the 9/11 terrorist attacks, have implemented a new network of security in these nations, helping to align and consolidate their allies throughout the region.

It is a grave new world, and as a result, American intelligence gathering technology has been implemented in Jordan (as well as in other allied nations). It is George W. Bush, who after the terrorist attacks stated that, "You're either with us – or against us!" So what's a country to do when the junkyard dog has you cornered.

But the new security programs are obviously open to abuse, and the monitoring and intimidation of media is a result of the new eavesdropping technology (the monitoring has always been there, only at a less sophisticated level). The nations that have the security do not have the necessary laws implemented to protect journalists and keep up with the electronic abuse (especially freelance journalists, who do not usually have the backing and power of a large news organization). Nations such as Kuwait and Jordan have not kept pace in protecting journalists who fall prey to their web of advancing technical paranoia. Until these nations seriously step forward to protect journalists from abuse, they will never realistically be able to find their place at the world table.

The number one threat from the fallout of this surveillance is a loss of freedom of speech, and the manipulation of the media for political or other sinister ends. But what else is new? In this age of globalization and computers, the freedom of the press is actually becoming more restricted and controlled. The end result is that journalism is being used by influential individuals, lobbyists and nations (who twist the truth into self-serving propaganda) to push their own agendas.

I am not opposed to increased security procedures, nor the Jordanian CIA blueprint, which I feel is a most necessary strategy in the battle against the spread of terrorism, but it should not infringe upon the freedom of the press or be used as a tool to harass and discredit the press. Surely the Government of Jordan would agree with this – if you don't have a free press, you don't have a free country!

After dinner, Kenji and I head back to Le Royal, and drink a coffee before turning in for the evening. I give Kenji (who leaves early tomorrow morning for Japan) a big hug, and tell him that we will meet again some day. I will miss my good friend and never forget him.

Day 35. Wednesday, May 14th

(Morning flight to Paris; airport inspection of my bags; five Iraqi Airlines planes at the side of the runway; I meet Patrick; growing insurgency; not very optimistic; I feel empty and incomplete; "Maybe these people have lost their souls"; my world is so much smaller)

I am up early packing my bags for the flight to Paris, which leaves at 10:30 a.m. this morning. After eating a light breakfast of coffee, fruit and a pastry, I take my bags down to the lobby and pay my bill. The front doorman flags me a taxi and I leave Amman for the airport, about an hour's drive away.

The airport is bustling with passengers getting ready for their flights and others just arriving. I take my bags over to the customs inspection area, and place them onto a long metal table. The solitary inspector, a little round man, goes through my small backpack carrying my camera gear, then my computer gear. He starts inspecting my large rucksack (which took me over an hour to pack). It has so much crammed into it that it might take another hour to re-pack it. The customs official must have been thinking what I was thinking. Realizing it would be a daunting task to go through it all, he checks only the top couple of layers, then motions me over to the immigration stand to have my passport stamped. I pay an exit tax of about $20 before boarding the plane.

As the Air France plane taxis down the runway, I see five Iraq Airlines passenger planes parked at the side of the airstrip. (They were flown out of Iraq before the war started, and grounded by Jordan at the outbreak of hostilities).

Landing in Paris, I board another flight for the last leg of the journey home to Montreal. During the flight across the

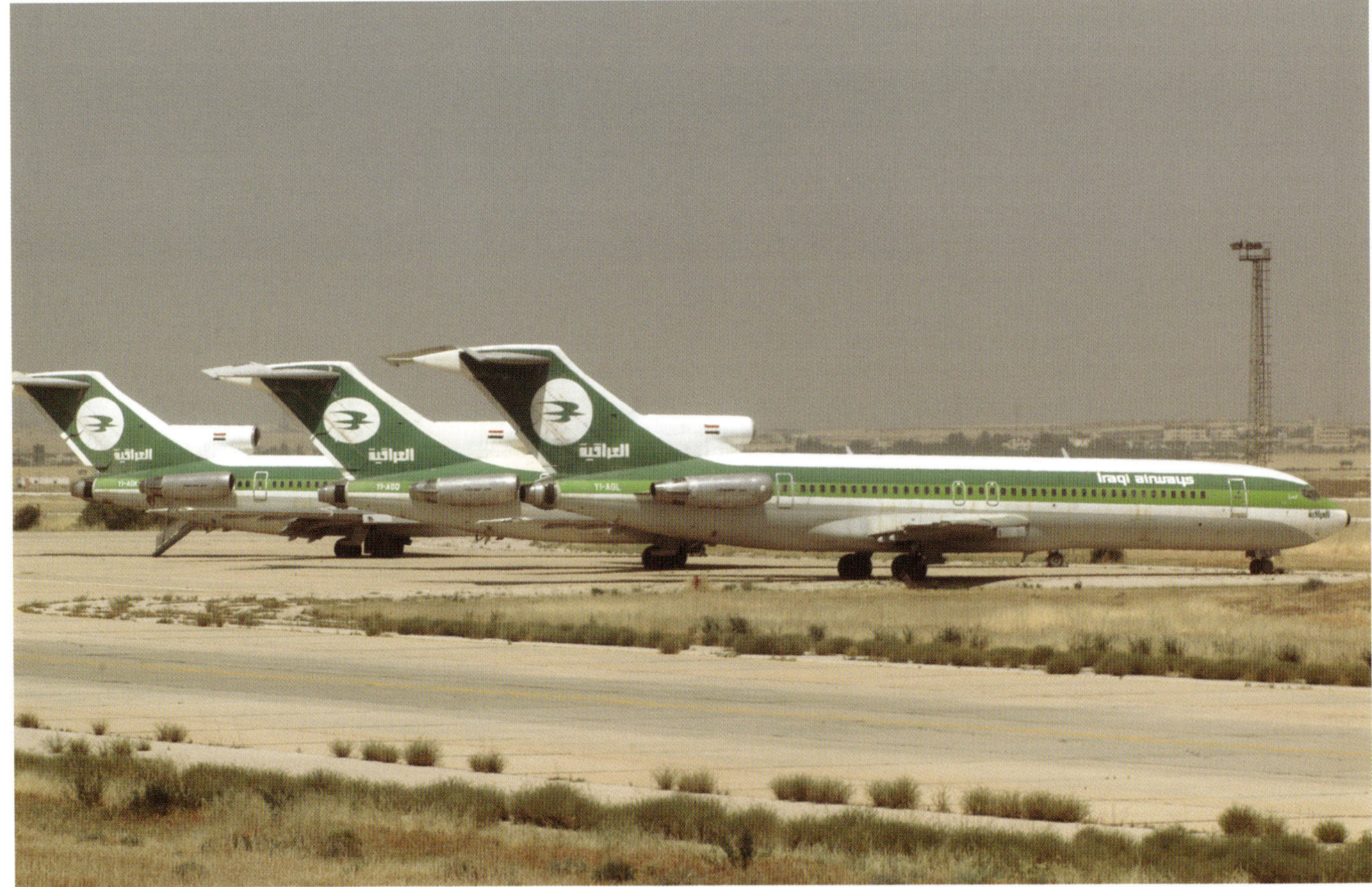

Iraqi Airways passenger planes were flown out of Iraq before the war and parked on a runway at the Jordanian International Airport

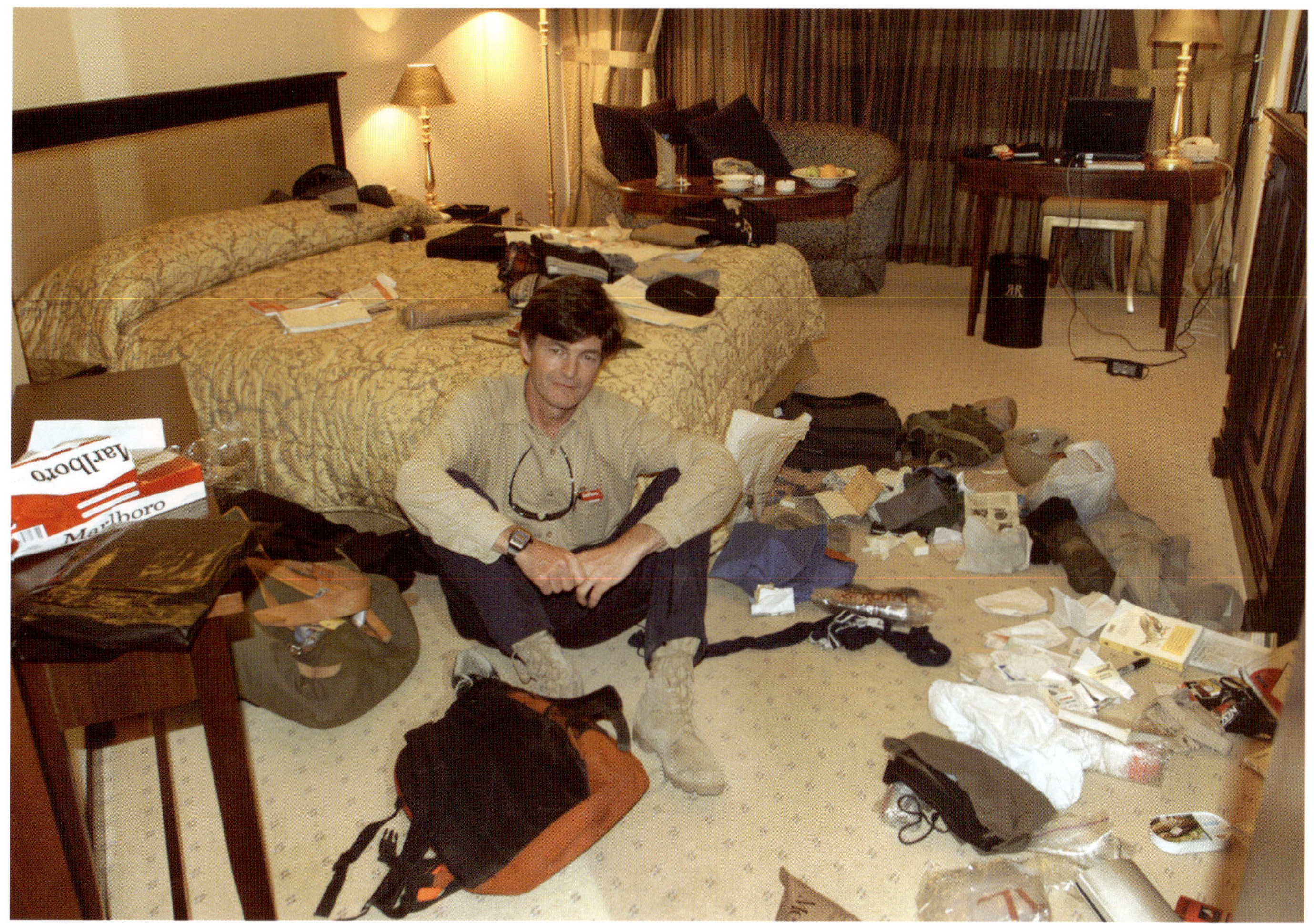

The contemplative author relaxes while packing his gear on eve before flying back to Canada. The trip to Iraq was a staggering success

Atlantic Ocean, I am seated beside a bright young man named Patrick, from the Montreal suburb of Ville St Laurent. He is just returning with his mother from Lebanon, his family's country of origin. Patrick is a computer geek, and very knowledgeable with the cyber language. I bring out my laptop and give him a small viewing of my photos from Iraq.

We talk about world events and the roadblocks to peace in the Middle East. I describe the situation in Baghdad and the rest of Iraq, telling him that I have little hope for the country, which is still being torn apart by looting, and the growing insurgency within. My predictions for a stable Iraq are not very optimistic; in fact, they are closer to being gloomy. I tell him that I believe Iraq's demise was due to a number of combined factors, the most decisive being the Americans' unpreparedness for the anarchy that dominated after the downfall of Baghdad.

In Iraq, I witnessed the darkest side of man. I ask Patrick what he thinks would drive such a large part of the Iraqi population to steal from each other and lose all sense of humanity towards their fellow man. This festering question has followed me right onto the plane, leaving me feeling empty and incomplete. I need to know the answer before my work is truly finished!

Patrick could not have spoken more eloquently or more descriptively, when he addresses my concerns. "Maybe these people have lost their souls, or they have shrunk, and now rest hidden somewhere deep in their bodies. Maybe they have become animals!" he implies. "But they're actually good people! You have to remember what these people have gone through!"

Every cell in my body is tingling – my body is one big goose bump. His words of simple wisdom have lifted the weight of the world from my shoulders, I am free of my pain!

"That is it," I tell Patrick! "This is the answer I so much needed! We are all one! There is hope for humanity! There is hope!"

As the plane lands and taxies down a Montreal runway, I look out the window to see the world I left behind five weeks ago. It looks much smaller now – so much smaller.

Robert J. Galbraith
August 30, 2004